NANCY

The Life of Lady Astor

Nancy about 1914

NANCY

THE LIFE OF LADY ASTOR

Christopher Sykes

'. . . to spend Sunday with a volcano . . .'
G. B. SHAW

COLLINS
ST JAMES'S PLACE LONDON
1972

William Collins Sons & Co Ltd
London · Glasgow · Sydney · Auckland
Toronto · Johannesburg

First published October 1972
Reprinted October 1972
© Christopher Sykes 1972
ISBN 0 00 211485 2
Set in Monotype Bembo
Made and Printed in Great Britain by
William Collins Sons & Co Ltd Glasgow

*To the memory of my
friendship with Bill Astor,
1926–1966*

CONTENTS

ILLUSTRATIONS

PREFACE

AT the end of each chapter of this book, with one exception, I have added a brief summary of the material on which I have drawn. I have hoped that this may tend to the reader's comfort, and that it makes preliminary notice of acknowledgement otiose. I should, however, in this place remember my debt to the litearry executors of Nancy, Lady Astor, namely her son, Mr John Jacob Astor, and her nephew-in-law, Sir Edward Ford. They placed the whole of Lady Astor's considerable archive at my disposal, and have given me great personal help and encouragement. I am also much indebted in the same sense to Lady Ancaster, Mr David Astor and Mr Michael Astor. The essays collected by Michael Astor, and which he has allowed me to use freely, have been invaluable. As mentioned in the text, Michael Astor originally intended to publish these essays under his editorship, in a book having a similar form to that of *T. E. Lawrence by His Friends*. He abandoned this plan and instead produced *Tribal Feeling*, the most interesting study of Lady Astor to appear so far. Even when occasionally disagreeing, I owe much to its insight. I have mentioned several times in the text my debt to Lady Astor's niece Mrs Lancaster, to her sister Mrs Winn, and Reggie Winn. What understanding (if any) I show of Virginia and the background from which Lady Astor came, I owe chiefly to Mrs Gordon Smith, who not only told me of her own memories but introduced me to a great number of people in Virginia. I wish also to express my gratitude to my friend Miss Kay Halle for her help and hospitality while I was in Washington in 1969, and to my friends Ronald and Marietta Tree, who hospitably helped me in my research when I was in New York at the same period.

I am much indebted to Miss Margaret Jones, a former secretary to Lady Astor, who put the bulk of her papers in order, with a catalogue, thus saving me many months of work. As before, I must thank Dorothy Baker for literary advice, and Deirdre Wheatley for producing typescripts. I must also acknowledge the help frequently given to me by the London Library.

CHRISTOPHER SYKES

Chapter 1

ORIGINS

In 1951, six years after she had retired from politics, and a year before the death of her husband, Lady Astor was invited by an American publisher, who was also a friend, to write her autobiography. She was very reluctant to accept the offer. She was not a born writer and she knew it. 'She realises,' wrote Lord Astor to the publisher, 'that she influences people by direct personal verbal contact and not by her written word.' He wrote this in November 1951 in a letter which closed the venture.

Lord Astor's comment was a true one, but in this instance his judgement, like that of the publisher, was completely at fault. Lady Astor was often asked to write her memoirs in the course of her later life, and until 1951 she refused without hesitation. But on this last occasion, perhaps because the publisher was a friend, she accepted in principle, and only abandoned the attempt after a struggle. Being a person with little critical ability as regards writing, she evidently had no notion how remarkably good her attempt was. Unconfident of possessing the needed talent, she listened to her publisher when he thrust on her, as he did frequently and abundantly, criticism and advice, both of which were bad.

She was among the five or six most famous women in the world. Her fame rested on solid foundations. She was the first woman to have taken her seat in the British House of Commons. She had remained a prominent member from 1919 to 1945, and throughout these twenty-six years of convulsion, anxiety and destiny, she had always lived and acted in the forefront of events. She was loved and hated, admired and deplored, as is the fate of most of the famous, both in life and after. It seemed to the promoters of the autobiography that if such a career was to be described at first hand, then it should be described worthily, and by that they meant it should be written in terms that would make the record a monument to an age.

This was the publisher's fatal error, for if there was one thing that Nancy Astor was *not*, it was monumental. The quality was wholly alien to her. In vain, the publisher pointed to the example of Winston Churchill who had brilliantly combined autobiography with a chronicle of his times;[1] in vain, enormous collections of notes, letters and Press-cuttings were put at her disposal by Lord Astor so that she should not lack for material in the erection of the imposing edifice. It was no good. If she was to write, she could not do so in the majestic manner of Winston Churchill, nor following the example of those rightly admired historians who can produce from a vast accumulation of facts a clear, concise and expertly sifted study. She could only write in her own way: impetuously and from the emotion of salient memories. It was not long before discouragement defeated her and she abandoned the whole enterprise. But she left a draft. Unfortunately, the story it tells ends before 1919 and the years of her great fame. It is untidy and contains many inaccuracies and important omissions, for her memory had weakened gravely, but for all its defects it is a document of admirable vividness and candour. It contains by far and away the best record of her early days.

She was born in Danville, Virginia, on the 19th May 1879. Her father was called Chiswell Dabney Langhorne and came of a long established farming family which had enjoyed modest prosperity in his young days and had lost almost everything in the Civil War. By 1879 he had lived through years of the utmost poverty, but was now making his living as an auctioneer. He had a wooden 'frame-house' (now demolished) in Broad Street, the main thoroughfare of Danville which was then a very small town. The site is marked today by a sign on a post in front of the present building. On one side is recorded that here was the birthplace of Irene Gibson, the original 'Gibson Girl'; the other side celebrates the birth of Mrs Gibson's yet more famous sister. A few yards beyond the site is Lady Astor Street, so renamed in 1922.

Nancy was the eighth of Chiswell Langhorne's large family. He had eleven children in all, but three died in infancy. 'As far as I remember,' wrote Nancy in 1951, 'we regarded their deaths with childish callousness.'

She was christened Nancy Witcher after her mother, and, as with

1. The publisher may not have known the remark on *The World Crisis* made by Arthur Balfour and recorded by Mrs Dugdale (Vol. 2, p. 337): 'I am immersed in Winston's brilliant autobiography, disguised as a history of the universe.'

her mother, was always known in the family and among friends as 'Nannie'; indeed, her uncorrupted first name seems never to have been used, except in formalities, in her native country. To this day, in popular speech, Americans refer to her as 'Nannie Astor'.

Her immediate ancestry was interesting and, with her first background, indicates surely enough the origin of many of her characteristics. Her father was born in Lynchburg in 1843, and his early life, spent largely on his grandfather's farm nearby, was a joyous one and typical of the more privileged society of Virginia in the days before the 'War between the States', as the terrible conflict of 1860–1865 is often called by preference in the Southern States. Though modern techniques and invention had greatly increased its wealth, the Virginia of those days had changed little since the eighteenth century and the age of Thomas Jefferson. Predominantly rural and agricultural, it enjoyed a well-balanced economy, and if one forgot the horrible features inseparable from slavery (and on many well-run estates this was not difficult), Virginia was indeed a delectable refuge, a land of hard and rewarding work and abundant simple pleasures. As in the eighteenth century, both in America and Europe, field sports provided the main relaxation. As in Britain there was much shooting and fox-hunting, and with the latter went a cult of the horse, a natural feature of a land where good pasture provides an ideal breeding ground. The pleasures of riding were a very prominent part of Virginian life, and so to some extent they have remained, for even today, when the horse is no longer a necessity, a great part of its cult persists. Early in life, Chiswell Langhorne had become an enthusiastic sportsman and a very good rider.

The dual patriotism of Americans, to the state and to the Union, is too familiar for comment. In those days, in Virginia, it was fierce and uncompromising. It is no surprise to learn that when the Civil War broke out in 1861, Chiswell Langhorne, though not yet seventeen years old, volunteered for service and bore arms throughout the struggle. To the end of his life he remained passionately devoted to the Confederate cause and the State of Virginia. He inclined, though later with the moderation that comes with age, to regard Northern Americans, 'Yankees' as he usually called them, with some hostility.

With the end of the war, the happy life of Virginia seemed to come to an end; to a hopeless and irrevocable end. The ruin of the state seemed complete, and with reason. Giving impressions of his first visit to Virginia, about twenty-five years after the end of the war, Angus McDonnell, who was to become a close friend of the family and Nancy's devoted admirer, wrote as follows: 'Mr Langhorne told me that when he got back to Lynchburg, after the war, there was nothing left of the old life; the countryside was decimated; there was practically no stock of any kind on the farms, neither horses, mules, cattle or sheep; they were using parched corn for coffee, if they could get it, and it was quite a while before the neighbourhood could get together enough money as a joint effort to buy a team and waggon to send to Illinois by road, to buy salt for the community.'

To Angus McDonnell Mr Langhorne described his post-war situation thus: 'I had nothing but a wife, two children, a ragged seat to my pants and a barrel of whisky.' Remembering the aftermath of those days his daughter Nancy wrote in 1951: 'The world as [Mr Langhorne] had known it had come to an end. Home and estates were ruined, property was split up, and the slaves had all gone. An old order had passed. The new one had not begun. The smashers-up and pullers-down were busy, and the builders-up had not yet come on the scene.'

In this wretched time of defeat and demoralisation many people of Chiswell Langhorne's sort in Virginia gave up what seemed an un-equal struggle and fell into degeneracy. He was not so disposed. Un-propertied materially except for his barrel of whisky, and for the help of an aunt who had saved a flour-mill in Lynchburg from the family wreck, he set himself to exploit a remarkable social charm which was conjoined with force of personality. He had the rare and valuable gift of being able to talk men into doing what he wanted, which then usually meant employing him, and even grave misdemeanours in the course of the resultant employment did not seriously impede his progress. For example, when his fortunes were more than usually low he took on the duties of night watchman at a clothing store. One night he rang the fire alarm in the first hours. The alarm was promptly answered by the fire brigade, but no sign of a fire could be detected for the good reason that there was none. When asked to explain his conduct, he said that he had rung the alarm to relieve the monotony of his task and to soothe his wish for companionship.

His high spirits never left him, and to the end of his life, except when conducting family prayers, he was never formal in manner; sometimes, it was said, the opposite to excess. No one who knew him ever seems to have called him 'Chiswell'. If he was not on distant terms, he was invariably addressed as 'Chillie', pronounced 'Shillie', and since no one in Virginia now refers to him except by that nickname it seems convenient and not disrespectful to use it here.

Chillie was a born actor. This was of the greatest help to him in the bitter post-war Virginian world in which to make one's way the most profitable course most often was to live on one's wits. A well-authenticated story is told by his grandson, Mr Langhorne Gibson, of days when he earned his living as a travelling salesman. By ill luck the only opening he could find in this line of business was in selling pianos, and he suffered from the serious handicap of not being able to play a note. But his acting talent was equal to this challenge. His wife had had some musical education and she taught him a few chords which he carefully memorised. On arrival at the customer's house, with the piano on a mule-drawn waggon, he would, after unloading, and after expatiating on the artistic splendour of the instrument, rumble out a chord or two. Then he would say in his most winning manner, 'I'd be only too glad to play more for you, sir (or ma'am), but I recently sprained my wrist and the doctor has absolutely forbidden me to play. But sir (or ma'am), reflect that it is the *tone* of the instrument that counts. You, I am sure, can judge. Just listen to this!' And the chords would be rumbled out again.

He wearied of peddling pianos, especially as (like his daughter Nancy) he had neither taste nor interest in music, and so he soon turned to more congenial employment, closing his adventures with the greatest of musical instruments in a fittingly dramatic manner. It is said, on Mr Gibson's authority, that his last piano-customer was 'unusually hesitant', and so as to conclude the deal and ease the return journey, 'he threw in the mule and waggon as a bonus.'

From pianos he turned to pictures. To quote Mr Gibson again: 'He was offering at bargain rates still-lifes of watermelons, fish; Romeo and Juliet; Stonewall Jackson dying in his tent, as well as the surrender at Appomattox – each one at only seven dollars. A portrait of General Lee could be had for nine dollars. A bargain! He could sell anything.'

The last sentence tells a crucial fact. This happy-go-lucky, hand-to-mouth adventuring life, never without anxiety for a married man and a father, was an impractical one, however inevitable. The wise thing was to harness his acting ability and his salesmanship to some thriving industry with a present and a future. Amid all the wreckage, Virginia had such an industry in its tobacco. Sometime in the mid-seventies

Chillie Langhorne became a tobacco auctioneer, and at length, at about the age of thirty or thereabouts, he found something resembling steady and, in a humble way, remunerative employment.

He is described as the most gifted auctioneer of his time in the United States. It is said that for the sheer entertainment of his performance large crowds gathered at the tobacco market in Danville, with good results on sales. Whether accurately or not, his daughter Nancy said in her unfinished memoir that he used to auction horses. He is said to have invented what is called the 'gobble-gobble' style of auctioneering, an extraordinary and, to those not in the trade, more or less incomprehensible use of rapid jargon patter. It was the comic effect of this new style which drew half the crowd, but besides that it kept the buyers on the alert. Chillie began to be well known, and through being well known he began to make useful acquaintances.

He was achieving success, but very modest success. He could afford to keep his family in safe but mediocre circumstances in Danville, and this was his situation at the time of Nancy's birth. He was not satisfied with his position, for he was an ambitious man.

Nancy's mother came of Irish stock, of a family named Keene who were neighbours of the Langhornes in Lynchburg before the Civil War. Nancy Witcher Keene was four years younger than her husband. They were married in Danville, while he was still serving in the Confederate Army, on the 20th December 1864. She was seventeen years old and he was just twenty-one. Their first months of married life were spent in the Confederate military camp at Danville, where young Mrs Langhorne worked in the hospital tent. They were in Danville when the last Confederate Government met there, about four months after their wedding, and immediately before the final defeat of the South. With peace came the bleak prospect of a new start in life. To quote again their grandson Mr Gibson: 'This couple, and others like them, possessed a courage and a hope so great that it makes us very humble in our admiration of them.'

Nancy Witcher Langhorne is something of an enigma in the story of her daughter. She died early, at the age of fifty-five, so that it follows that there is hardly anybody alive today who can claim to have a memory of her, and none with an intimate memory. There is no contemporary account of her. In contrast with her loud, go-getting husband, she may appear as a pale and ineffectual being. This is certainly wrong.

In her 1951 draft, Nancy told something of the mutual relations of her parents, unconsciously contributing a self-portrait. She said: 'People who knew my mother in those days [about the time of Nancy's birth] said she was very pretty with a beautiful figure, but her great charm was her gaiety and her goodness. I dare say goodness and gaiety were not found together any more often then than they are now. One way and another she must have had quite a time with Father. He adored her, and he never looked at another woman, but he had an ungovernable temper, and the common male weakness of expecting her to make one dollar do the work of two. I don't think he ever gave her quite enough money to run the large family on, even when the days came that he had plenty. He often expected her to do the impossible and was angry when she failed. I think it was this curious attitude of his that turned me into an ardent suffragette. I cared so tremendously for Mother. I did not only love her, I recognised with all my heart her goodness and her wisdom. Very early in life I sensed that she had the stronger character. But Father had the power. He held the purse strings. He was often bad-tempered and unreasonable. I felt if Mother had had independent means she would not have had to stand that. I felt that men put women in this position for this very reason, that it rendered them helpless. They had no kind of independence. It seemed to me wrong then. Over all the years I have not changed this point of view. I think it is wrong still.'

Mrs Langhorne was a devoted and loving wife, but she was not one of those people who cannot love without illusion. She knew Chillie's faults and she could and did express opinions on them. She seems to have had a persistent suspicion of the personal charm on which so much of his success depended. She once said: 'Nothing is so bitter to me as to be told how attractive Mr Langhorne is.' Nancy recalled, in the 1951 draft, a story that reflects a critical attitude which must not be confounded with loss of affection. Here it is in Nancy's words:

'Someone once told Mother, "Oh, Mrs Langhorne, your husband has such lovely eyes." "Don't be taken in by that," said Mother. "He looks just the same at a batter cake." '

A photograph of Nancy and her mother, taken not long before Mrs Langhorne's death, tells much. They are both in profile. The resemblance is striking. Both have the same slightly aquiline nose, both (though the resemblance is obscured by different hair-dressing) have the same strongly prominent forehead, both the strong, almost

Napoleonic chin. The older woman has all the look of one who has valiantly and cheerfully struggled through hard times, the younger the innocent expression of one with experience before her. Their mutual love is not hard to understand. They shared strength and will.

From what little evidence remains, in fact, it is not hard to picture Chillie Langhorne's wife. Yet the enigma cannot be wholly dispelled. In her 1951 draft Nancy wrote this: 'Mother never wanted any children. She had eleven, all unwanted, and not one of us has ever suffered the slightest frustration on that account. I was the seventh unwanted child.'[2]

What does this mean? There is all the evidence needed to prove that there was no lack of maternal instinct in this generous-minded woman. As Nancy herself said in her memoir: 'When Mother died, each one of us felt convinced in our heart that we had been her favourite. Each one of us knew she had loved us best of all.' Yet there is Nancy's plain and forbidding sentence: 'She had eleven [children], all unwanted.' It may be an overstatement, possibly only referring to some repugnance for the sexual act (such as Nancy herself suffered), but if so, the overstatement is extreme and quite untypical of the style and character of the draft.

It is easy to feel some indignation at the way the prospective publisher in 1951 discouraged Nancy by excess of advice, but he has one's sympathy when he asked for an elucidation of this passage. She never gave it, so the enigma remains.

Very soon after the birth of Nancy in 1879 Chillie Langhorne's life began to take a new turn. A man of about his own age called Liggett, who shared his ambition and enterprise, used to attend the tobacco sales, and he was quickly convinced that the spirited auctioneer could use his abilities to advantage in other and more profitable forms of business. He made friends with him and the two men went into partnership in a general trading firm. It was thus, about 1880, that Chillie Langhorne first began to be involved in one of the greatest American industries of the time, the railroads, booming through the post-war reconstruction policies.

The two of them had very little capital (mostly Liggett's, one gathers), and no material for the building of the humblest of railroads.

2. Reliable authorities describe her as the eighth child. As mentioned, the draft shows many lapses of memory.

The industry was a dangerous one for the unequipped aspirant. As Chillie put it himself, he could sell any kind of tobacco, good, bad and indifferent; but 'you can only sell *good* railroading'. Neither of them knew the first thing about how to build a railroad. Neither of them was in the least dismayed. Mr Langhorne Gibson records Chillie's reaction to the situation: 'Why not bid on a contract and "sub" to those young engineers who could get the work done and done well?'

Chillie Langhorne was a gambler, a great and, it seems, ruthless and successful poker-player, but this was not mere gambling. If he knew nothing about railroading he knew a lot about men. He had wonderful skill in getting the best out of his labourers, a difficult feat when emancipated Negroes were often reluctant to work. He did it not by ruthless driving so much as gaining their confidence or, as he put it, by 'kidding them along'. From his army days he knew many engineers, many of them now out of work. These were the men to whom he would 'sub'. He had a flair for detecting ability.

He had another advantage. Being a man of so much infectious gaiety and sociability, he had a wide acquaintance and this included the group of men who were financing two large construction projects: the Atlantic and Danville, and the Virginia Central railroads. He and his partner were awarded, or more probably Chillie talked his friends into offering them, a railroad contract which they duly subcontracted. 'Only Yankees and niggers work.' Chillie used to say, 'I'm not such a damn fool. I get other people to do the work for me.' This was unjust self-parody. In fact, he worked very hard in these days and, as Mr Gibson says, 'he was fast in picking up the technology of engineering in the field'.

This first venture was a success, and Chillie's personal profit from it was $8,000. He devoted a large part of it to buying engineering equipment, thus making the partners more eligible for further contracts, which Chillie obtained. The partners prospered and they began to take on a variety of engineering contracts outside the railroad projects, making profits though none very spectacular. Chillie felt the urging of his restless ambition and began to look farther afield.

By 1885 the partnership dissolved, amicably it seems, and Chillie was easily persuaded to leave provincial little Danville for the greater opportunities of the state capital, Richmond. Here was the centre of the tobacco trade, and four main railroads were spreading out from the growing city. So to Richmond the family migrated and took up quarters in a house on Main Street. For a while things went well, but in this new world of much fiercer competition than that of Danville, surrounded by contractors, moreover, who unlike him had a well-grounded knowledge of railroad and other engineering, Chillie Langhorne's luck failed him, and soon he was back where he had started, a tobacco auctioneer who could always draw crowds by his gobble-gobble, but only make a small living. The family became very poor again, moved from Main Street to a humble part of Third Street. Things looked up again and the family moved to the more pleasing district of Grace Street, and then there came what looked like disaster. All his ventures seemed to fail simultaneously, except his auctioneering. He and his wife reluctantly and bitterly decided that they must acknowledge defeat. They planned that Mrs Langhorne and the children would migrate to Albemarle County in the west of Virginia and lodge, for as much as a year perhaps, with a cousin, Charles Price. Chillie himself would stay in Richmond in cheap lodgings, and try to get work in addition to his auctioneering. They decided they must give notice to all their servants. It was a dismal solution, but none other offered.

Then Chillie Langhorne's luck turned again, this time finally. It is some irony in the story that he at last found a prosperous opening through the benevolent interest of a Northern soldier.

He met a certain Colonel Henry Douglas,[3] formerly of the Union army, whom he had come to know some years earlier, probably in Danville. They had remained friends. Colonel Douglas asked him on this occasion what he was doing. He replied that he wasn't 'doing any too well at the moment', and was, in fact, arranging to remove his family to the country. In turn he asked the Colonel what he was doing, and he told Chillie that he was building railroads. It has been said that something in the way Douglas replied showed that he was having difficulties, and that Chillie rightly guessed that he was at a loss as to how to deal with his Negro labour force. A few questions proved the guess true. Chillie said to him: 'Then I am the man you want because I can manage men and horses.' He added, 'Give me a chance.'

His grandson has said that he could sell anything, but that what he

3. In her 1951 draft Lady Astor calls him 'General Douglas'. I follow Mr Langhorne Gibson who calls him Colonel Douglas, but I follow Lady Astor's memoir in the main. Many versions of the incident are known, but I find hers more moderate and therefore more convincing.

could sell best was himself. He did so on this occasion. It is true that Colonel Douglas knew him and probably something of his career, but it is surprising, nevertheless, to learn that Douglas engaged him on the spot. He offered him a senior managerial post with a large salary. Chillie rushed back to Grace Street where the unhappy family and their tearful servants were involved in the wretched business of packing up the household, a business that was almost completed, so much so, in fact, that two pet billy-goats had actually been crated. He cried out to them all: 'Damn it! Stop everything! I've got a job!'

In the first part of this chapter the main authorities followed are the correspondence between Lord and Lady Astor and the prospective publisher, and the 1951 draft for Lady Astor's memoirs. The sketch of Mrs Nancy Witcher Langhorne (originally Keene) is chiefly based on the 1951 draft, and with reference to a lecture, 'Chiswell Dabney Langhorne 1843–1919', given by Mr Langhorne Gibson to the Albemarle Historical Society in 1955. The details of C. D. Langhorne's varying fortunes are given with precision in the same lecture. To the same source can be attributed most of the sketch of C. D. Langhorne, and also to accounts of him given to me by his grand-daughter, Mrs Nancy Lancaster. Much is owed also to a reminiscent essay by the late Angus McDonnell written for Lady Astor's son, Michael Astor. Mrs Langhorne's remark about her husband, 'Nothing is so bitter to me as to be told how attractive Mr Langhorne is', was told to me, among other interesting details, by Mr Egbert Leigh whom I met in Washington in 1969. He did not know Mr or Mrs Langhorne, but has for long known the family from whom he heard the story. The only published works consulted in this part of the book are *Tribal Feeling*, by Michael Astor (1963), and a biography, *Nancy Astor*, by Maurice Collis (1960).

Chapter 2

FROM RICHMOND
TO MIRADOR

THE first family home of which Nancy was conscious was the house in West Grace Street. This we can know from what she told a lifelong Virginian friend, eleven years her junior, who first met her in the Richmond days. Remembering that Nancy was six in 1885, it seems reasonable, in view of what she told her friend, to suppose that the changes from Main to Third to Grace Street all occurred within a short space of time. Whatever the facts, her first memories were undoubtedly of changing fortunes, ups and downs from modest comfort to grinding poverty before the next 'up'.

The family was never to be poor again, but her memory of poverty was never to be cancelled, and it influenced her behaviour throughout life, both in public and private. Much later she showed her active sympathy with poverty in her political support of numerous reformist measures for the alleviation of hardship, especially as it bore on wives, widows and children, and in princely benefactions which are still remembered; she showed it in sometimes utterly reckless acts of private generosity, occasionally unwise in the world's judgement, though of the kind blessed by the Saviour. Her early memories were probably the cause too, very much later, of absurd fits of panic about money matters. The strength of these childhood impressions must not be exaggerated. They were rarely a dominating influence on her life, but they were always an influence.

It may be as well now, for the reader's convenience, to state just what is meant by 'the family', since it was completed in Richmond where the last of the children was born. The first child of Chiswell and Nancy Langhorne was a boy, born within a year of their marriage. He was called Keene after her family. The next child was a daughter, Elizabeth (always called Lizzie), born a year or so later. There followed another daughter, Irene (always pronounced Ireen), and another son, Harry. The next in order of age was Nancy, that is, of the survivors. The three infants who died were born before her. Next came her sister

Phyllis who was closest to her both in age and affection. Then came the third son, William, always known as Buck, and last of all Nora. The children numbered eight, three boys and five girls, with twenty years between the eldest and youngest.

As with most leading cities of the United States, the Richmond of today is markedly different from what it was in the late nineteenth century when the transformation was still in early stages. Virginians of today will tell you that there is now no trace of the 'gracious living' which marked the city in the old days. To a large and melancholy extent this is true, but the visitor can sometimes recognise charming survival where the native only sees wreckage. There remain whole long streets built in the eighteenth century urban style which in America, and especially Virginia, lingered long into the nineteenth century, and is still widely used today. The area round the Capitol and St Paul's Church, in the city centre, is still impressive, not only because it is well planned but because it retains so much good traditional building, notably in the fine Capitol itself and in St Paul's.

But in the days when Nancy was a little girl the city must have been entrancing. It is well described as it was at a little later date by the friend already referred to, and who is now Mrs Trigg Brown.

'The city was a "gas-light" one in 1890, and telephones were almost a luxury. The streets were unpaved, and in wet weather the crossing of them was made by stepping on the spaced long and wide stones. *People walked*; the after-church Sunday parade up Franklin Street would have vied with New York. People drove and rode horseback through the city. It would seem that everybody knew everybody: at least this was true of the residents of Franklin, Grace, Third Streets and Park Avenue. Street cars as well as a famous car drawn by mules were the more popular modes of transportation . . .'

This was the sort of life that the young Nancy first knew, and of which the Langhornes became privileged and prominent members after Chillie's fateful meeting with Colonel Douglas, for he rapidly proved his worth as a manager of men and horses, and as a contractor. He was not only rescued from poverty: he rapidly began to become a rich man.

Nancy gave a vivid, if disconnected, account of the life of the family in Grace Street. Their butler was a coloured man who was so fearful of the banditry in the city that he would let no one into the house whom he had not seen received there before.

'A friend came to visit one day,' Nancy related, 'and the butler opened the door a crack and said, "Mrs Langhorne she ain't home." Then he slammed the door in the visitor's face.

'Two hours later, thinking Mother might have returned, the visitor tried again, this time to be met with "I done told you once Mrs Langhorne she ain't home!" and the door was slammed in her face again.'

She gave details of the family life as seen through young eyes: 'Lizzie and Irene already growing up seemed to us glamorous figures of romance, leading exciting lives in which we played the part of on-lookers.

'The house in Grace Street had a large yard[1] but we ran wild. One of our greatest delights was to play in the streets. We played baseball and Prisoners' Base. I was always fondest of boys' games, and proud of the fact that I was a very fast runner . . . I am afraid we were rather hooligans for, years after, a famous Richmond pianist told me that he had always been in perfect terror of passing our house because we were apt to throw stones at him.

'Father was good with his daughters. He was strict and often unreasonable, but he encouraged us to be ourselves, to be real persons and take risks . . . I have always been grateful to him for teaching us courage, and for his attitude towards us . . . [He] used to take us all for Sunday walks. This was a great occasion for we did not go out with him much. He would talk to us as if we were grown-ups, which I loved, and we would all make great efforts to shine and please him. The next minute he would spank us and send us to bed for some remark he did not consider suitable, though as often as not we had no idea why.

'I remember one day he took us all down to see a new horse. We stood in the sun by the stable door admiring it, and Father asked us all to help him choose a name. The sire had been Prosper, so the name had to begin with that. I thought I had got something really good. I said, "Why not call him Prostitute?"'

'The result was terrific. "Go to your room!" thundered Father.

' "But why?" I asked tearfully. "Why?"

' "Your mother will explain," was all he would say. So I went to Mother. She, too, was horrified and quite at a loss, and could not explain anything.

1. The English reader should be aware that in American usage 'yard' usually means garden.

'Father was very strict. His word was law. He would have complete obedience. There was no talking back . . . We took it out of Mother. Though we were fond of Father we were always delighted when he went away and we had her to ourselves.'

As one would expect of a family whose head was Chillie Langhorne, its life was tempestuous by nature, and without Mrs Langhorne's calming influence, shouting matches might have been even more frequent and violent than they were.

Nevertheless, there was no lack of mutual affection, and in Nancy's 1951 draft one is conscious of deep love informing the account of each of her brothers and sisters, with one possible exception, and that is to be found in what she wrote of her eldest sister. Towards her, Nancy seems to have felt some resentment which many years had not obliterated. Here is what she wrote: '[Lizzie] always seemed to us – and to Mother also, I think – some years older than Mother herself. She was a fine character, loyal, sincere and very serious minded, but she was terribly bossy. Probably it is difficult for the eldest girl in a large family not to become a bit of a tyrant. I think in her secret heart she considered Mother unsuitably young and gay.

'From Lizzie I had far more spankings than I ever did from Mother or Father.'

The Langhorne sisters first became well known through the beauty of the second daughter, Irene. All memories of her, and there are many, testify to an extraordinary sweetness of nature. Nancy wrote of her in 1951:

'While she was still a schoolgirl there were paragraphs in the papers, which used to annoy Father very much, saying a raving beauty was growing up in Richmond Virginia, who would become the talk of the country. It was not then considered the thing to be talked about in the papers, and I remember when, later, one of them printed Irene's picture, Father threatened to go to New York and shoot the editor.

'Irene wasn't only beautiful. She had wonderful charm. . . . When she came in, it was like the sun streaming into the room. Nor did the praise and adulation she got ever go to her head. She remained entirely unspoiled and this was wonderful. Mostly she laughed at the fuss people made of her, and no doubt her brothers and sisters played their part in keeping her humble. I remember once when she came back from a visit where she had been the belle of every ball and the papers had been full of flattering paragraphs about her, saying she was the

loveliest girl in America and bid fair to become a reigning belle – we
all fell on her. "You may have looked beautiful at the party," we told
her, "but people ought to see the way you look now." Irene took it all
in good part. . . . From the start she was the acknowledged family
beauty, and none of us ever questioned it, and were quite satisfied to
be the beautiful Irene Langhorne's sisters. Father adored her. She could
do no wrong in his eyes, and she was very tactful. She never disagreed
with him.'

The episode of the family assault on the family beauty probably
occurred at the very end of their Richmond days, or early in the next
phase of their lives.

As mentioned already, Phyllis was and remained her favourite sister,
but she says little about her in the section of the draft from which the
foregoing quotations come. She has much to tell of her brothers, but
this belongs to the next chapter. Nora was not yet old enough to come
significantly into her story. 'She was the baby,' wrote Nancy, 'and we
considered Mother spoilt her dreadfully.'

In 1886 or possibly a year later, Nancy went to school for the first
time, to a day-school near Grace Street kept by Miss Julia Lee, a
relation of the Confederate General who was then, and was to remain
throughout her life, one of Nancy's heroes. There she learned to read
and write. 'Miss Julia was gentle and sweet,' she recorded in 1951, 'I
must have been happy there, I remember so little about it.'

In 1888, when Nancy was nine, she went to school in Richmond in a
more serious way. According to Mrs Trigg Brown, who was at the
same school when she herself was one of the youngest pupils and Nancy
was in her last term, it was a very good one. It was known in Richmond as 'Miss Jennie's', and was founded and owned by a certain Miss
Virginia Randolph Ellett who, by all accounts, was an ideal teacher of
children. She had the knack of arousing young curiosity. All her
charges became enthusiasts of her special subjects: history, English
literature and art. In her literary classes she overcame the obstinacy
with which children meet the more difficult subjects by turning
them into a game. For instance, she inveigled them into illustrating
Chaucer's *Canterbury Tales*. Above all she taught the children to love
words.

Mrs Trigg Brown says that 'Nannie became a lover of words, and
for years after she left school she opened her dictionary every night
and learned two new words.' It has occurred to the writer that in her

earliest adventures into the rich and delicate vocabulary of the English language, Nancy may have stumbled on the word 'prostitute', but failed to absorb the precise meaning of a probably euphemistic definition. Nancy left her own vivid impression of Miss Jennie's teaching methods which were then revolutionary. 'She was a brilliant teacher,' she wrote, 'she taught me the greatest lesson a child can learn, and perhaps the only one it really needs: how to learn. She took all the loose ends of all the things I had begun to puzzle over, and the odd scraps of knowledge I had acquired here and there, and tied them together for me. She began with philosophy, and came on to Greece, then took us through Greek history and so to Italy, France and England. As she taught, she took the history and the geography along with it, so that what we got was a length of close-woven tweed, rather than the untidy patchwork so many young minds are left with at the end of an education. She gave me a thirst for knowledge and a real liking for learning. She gave me my passion for reading that has lasted the rest of my life. She was deeply religious. She never preached at us. It was something in the air all about her.'

If further testimony is needed to show the excellence of Miss Jennie as an educationist, then one has only to know the remarkable fact that at the age of seventy, when she was still teaching, she travelled to England in order to attend a course for teachers at Oxford University. She attended as a student.

Her influence on Nancy was strong and enduring, but it would be a mistake nevertheless to picture Nancy as the happy schoolgirl she was in her unthinking earlier years at Miss Julia Lee's little academy. No daughter of Chillie Langhorne was likely to accept school discipline complacently. Nancy thus recalled an incident: 'I was struggling with my seven-times table. Multiplication was always pain and grief to me, and on this particular day Father had said that if I did not master it I was not to go to the drag hunt next morning. I simply had to go to that drag hunt. So I prayed long and earnestly: "O God, please burn down the schoolhouse. Please burn down the schoolhouse entirely. Save Miss Jennie and Miss Jennie's mother, please God, but let the schoolhouse go. Burn down that house!" He didn't.'

Many years after, the school was reorganised and officially named St Catherine's. The schoolhouse which had been the subject of Nancy's petition, and was situated within Richmond, was abandoned for a new site in the suburbs. This caused transport difficulty for Miss Jennie.

Some former pupils who were Nancy Astor's friends wrote to her in England asking for a subscription towards a car for their old teacher. An answer by cable came back from Cliveden: 'Mechanise Miss Jennie. Get her a chauffeur. Send bills to me.' And so it was done.

In researching the childhood story of Nancy Astor, one may peer hard for early signs of political interest or awareness, and the search does not yield much, but is not quite barren of result. The Langhornes were not a very politically minded family in those days, with the exception of one of Chillie's sisters, Aunt Lewis as she was known to the children. Mrs Lewis was the intellectual of the family group, a strong-minded educationist who not only founded the first schools for coloured people in Virginia, but taught in them herself. 'She voted Socialist at eighty,' wrote Nancy in her memoir, 'because she said she was tired of both Republicans and Democrats, and she wanted a change.'

There was only one great political issue which comes out prominently as a family interest, and of Nancy in particular, and that was the general Virginian preoccupation with the Civil War, most lucidly expressed in the words 'Up the Confederacy!'

Mrs Trigg Brown tells of a time when Nancy was about sixteen years old, and she herself, the exact contemporary of Nora, about five.

'Richmonders of all ages were still ardent Confederates and gloried in being called Rebels. A Confederate reunion found the city overrun with veterans, and hundreds of private homes were entertaining their family heroes. The great climax was the parade. Nannie saw the parade standing on the stone wall in front of the Jones' house. Nora and I raced back and forth between that house and ours, joining our families in waving flags and yelling, led by Nannie. Our loudest shouts came when a group of old vets came by carrying a banner that read, "43 DAYS ON ROTTEN CORN MEAL, CATS AND PICKLE." (I wonder where they got the pickle?) Again and again bands went by playing "Dixie", and did we join in! I can see Nannie now, balancing on that stone wall, yelling louder than anyone, and yapping at her friends if they didn't yell and wave: "Great saints, what's the matter with you?" This was a grand signal for us to include ourselves, and we jumped up and down, yelled, fell off the wall, and scrambled back to her shouts of, "Come on, let 'em *hear* us." You might well have thought that the

Right: Mr and Mrs Chillie Langhorne in the grounds of Mirador. *Below:* Angus McDonnell – who probably took the picture above – on the steps of Mirador with Nancy Shaw

Left: The young Mrs Astor dressed for her presentation at Court by the United States Ambassadress. *Right:* Nancy about the time of her marriage to Waldorf

South had won the war! It always had in Nannie's thoughts, and her love for the Confederacy lasted her all of her life.'

Religion was to remain a life-long devotion of Nancy, and her ardent piety had a first origin in her earliest experience of family life. For all his Falstaffian worldliness, Chillie Langhorne was a typical Virginian also in his deep Protestant faith, and the same faith was held by her mother. Bible-reading and family prayer were essentials in the family life. Nancy's first experience of church-going, as she remembered it, was in the Cathedral Church of Richmond, St Paul's. It is a noble building, founded in the early nineteenth century, very reminiscent of the 'Waterloo churches' of London, very English, with the strong difference of such buildings in Virginia. It is easy to recognise how delightfully cool it must be during the hot Virginian summer. It is easy to have the feeling that this is a satisfying place in which to pray. 'I was the greatest church-goer imaginable,' Nancy told Mrs Trigg Brown about those days.

There can be no doubt that religious faith and emotion were a part of Nancy's being from her first conscious days, but the profound religious sense which (much later) made her a proselytiser for Christian Science, a 'Hallelujah Lassie' as she once described herself, came later, after Richmond, in the next phase of her life.

As a manager of horses and men, Chillie Langhorne continued to prove his worth abundantly and before very long he was in a position to branch out into a railway contracting firm of his own. He could now indulge his family in pleasure trips which a few years before would have seemed luxuries beyond reach. The greatest of these was to escape for a while from the heat of the long summer. He used to take them north to White Sulphur Springs in Montana where they would stay in 'a lovely old-fashioned hotel', and there they spent their days fishing, riding and swimming. On their Sulphur Springs holiday of 1890 Nancy experienced an affair of the heart. She described it thus in 1951:

'I fell in love in Sulphur Springs. A boy came to the same hotel. I was eleven. He came with his father, and his mother had just died, but the chief thing I remember about him was his shoes. He wore the most beautiful shoes, and they were always spotlessly clean. I think this was my first love affair, and it is sad that I remember nothing about him. Only his shoes.'

Chillie had never lost his taste for country life and sport; if anything it had increased with his long enforced separation from such delights, so he decided, now that he could afford it, that his best plan would be to buy a house and estate in Virginia not too far from Richmond, but not too near. If he found the right locality he would be spared the trouble of the yearly journey to Montana, and of spending his summer holiday with Yankees. Also he would have a country home to retire to, and he always said that he intended to retire early. 'Only Yankees and Blacks work after they're sixty,' he used to say, 'I want to enjoy my last ten years.'

Through railway business he knew every part of Virginia, but the part to which he felt most attracted was Albemarle County, especially the cooler country west of Charlottesville towards the Blue Ridge Mountains. Here he found what he wanted, a fine Virginian country house with a farming estate. It was called Mirador.

The house is situated about seventeen miles west of Charlottesville, in Greenwood, which even today is so small as hardly to constitute a village. In so far as it is one, it is so widespread that most of its houses are still far apart. In those days it was little more than the name given to a stop on the railroad for a still sparsely inhabited area.

The house itself is typically Virginian in style, red brick with white stucco pillars and pediment in severely classical style which is followed in the wooden framing of the windows. As with St Paul's in Richmond, as with most Virginian architecture, its date could be easily mistaken for an earlier one. As with many buildings throughout America, a major feature is the high front staircase which was here, as in most parts of America, especially in the Southern States, a general meeting-ground of the family and their guests in warm weather. Hundreds, perhaps thousands, of unposed snapshot photographs of the Langhornes and their friends have this staircase as the setting.

The house was built in 1825 and bought by Chillie, probably in 1892.[2] The family moved in either at the end of that year or sometime in the next one when Chillie had added on a wing, rigorously conforming to style, on each side. The migration was not a definitive one. It would seem that Mrs Langhorne moved in with the children, and thereafter remained most of the year at Mirador, except in winter

2. In her memoir of 1951 Lady Astor gives 1891 as the date. Mr Langhorne Gibson gives 1893. The plaque erected outside Mirador gives 1892. It seems to me that 1892 is the correct date but that rebuilding delayed the family's arrival till 1893.

when the whole family lived in Grace Street again. For Christmas, however, they all went back to Mirador where the feast, as one would expect of Chillie, was held with high wassail.

The family house in Richmond was kept till so late as 1902, and Nancy and her sister Phyllis lived there with their father during term-time at Miss Jennie's, with occasional weekends and all the holidays at Mirador. Chillie himself seems to have followed much the same routine. The house in Grace Street took second place and began to be forgotten as the other one captured the imagination of the family. The Grace Street house has long ago been pulled down, and none of the former Langhorne inhabitants ever expressed any regret for its disappearance. So little did her Richmond home mean to Nancy herself that she consistently misspelt the name of its street in her unfulfilled attempt at autobiography. When her thoughts, or those of her brothers and sisters, turned to earlier days, they instinctively turned to the countryside extending east from the foot of the Blue Ridge Mountains and to this Virginian country house.

Mrs Barbara Trigg Brown has supplied valuable material for Lady Astor's Richmond days in a memoir which she wrote for the Astor family shortly after Lady Astor's death in 1964. In shortened form it has appeared in *The Richmond Times Despatch* and various magazines in the U.S.A. Mrs Trigg Brown, whom I met in Richmond, Virginia, in 1969, has given me the full text which I have used. Further details are taken from Mr Langhorne Gibson's lecture to the Albemarle Historical Society. As in Chapter 1, a main source which is indicated throughout is Lady Astor's unfinished autobiography. Mrs Lancaster is the authority for much of this chapter, notably on C. D. Langhorne's views on early retirement. It may seem impossible to misspell so simple a term as 'Grace Street', but in her memoir Lady Astor invariably described it as 'Gracey Street'.

Chapter 3

MIRADOR

BEFORE the migration from Richmond to Albemarle County, the eldest daughter Elizabeth had been married in 1884 to Thomas Moncure Perkins, a member of a Virginian family, long established like the Langhornes, and through their Moncure relatives belonging to one of the ancient settler families of the State. She was the only one of the Langhorne sisters to make her home in Virginia, and of her, Nancy's son Michael Astor has written in his remarkable autobiographical book, *Tribal Feeling*: 'Lizzie never took part in the social life of New York. She married before the Langhorne family had properly found its feet and as a result of this, as her younger sisters grew up, she came to feel that she had been deprived of partaking in the pleasures of a more exciting world than the one that the neighbourhood provided. . . . The parochial life was not one that could properly contain any of Mr Langhorne's daughters, and Lizzie did not like feeling provincial or being reminded of it by her family. But if Lizzie Perkins never succeeded in moving out of the neighbourhood there were compensations to be had in the life that centred round Mirador. . . .'

That life had many ingredients: abundant sport with the Virginian cult of the horse taken to Virginian extremes; long weekends when Chillie would arrive, often without warning, bringing a large number of his business associates, making impossible demands on his wife for their entertainment; fun and fooling in plenty with family theatricals for the neighbours; tempestuous rows which almost literally shook the house to its foundations, leading, so it seemed at the moment, to divisions past healing, till the row in question would suddenly blow over and leave not a rack behind.

The essence of life at Mirador was hospitality, and one may safely guess that Chillie was indulging to the full the sociable tastes that his long years of poverty had forced him to suppress. Those who knew Mirador when he lived there remember how he liked to sit at the end of the lawn where the little road of those times (a broad motorway today) ran past his boundary, and how, whenever he saw a passing traveller, he would hail him and ask him in, whether he knew him or not, and regale him with whisky and mint juleps and, if he took a fancy to him, would force him and his party to stay and dine.

Though he was frequently away on business, Chillie was the undisputed lord of Mirador. Everything was arranged and run as he alone wanted it. Mr Langhorne Gibson says of these days: 'There were big railroad jobs now on the books of Langhorne and Langhorne – along the Big Sandy River in Kentucky, in Gladstone, large masonry projects too. "All over the place", as we describe work of this sort, but no place was so far away but that he was not at home in Mirador much of the time.' In another passage Mr Gibson says: 'These weekends of riding, shooting, poker and juleps must indeed have been affairs of pleasure for all but the housekeeper.'

The cult of the horse at Mirador was considerably bolder than would be likely to be found in a country family given to sport in England. Nancy took a prominent part in it, and later, her passion for horsemanship was one of the things which first took her to England. All the family were taught to ride well, but Nancy and Phyllis were the acknowledged stars. Of the two, Phyllis was, by Nancy's own verdict among others, the most accomplished horsewoman, Nancy herself inclining to exhibition and rashness and thus liable to spoil a horse by driving it too hard. They learned in a tough school. Horses were bought as raw yearlings or two-year-olds, and the difficult and, in unprofessional hands, dangerous task of breaking them in was undertaken by the family. Nancy recalled in 1951: 'I remember seeing my sister Phyllis breaking in a two-year-old, sixteen hands. The horse reared and swayed, but Father just said, "Damn it! Give him his head!" '

They rode to hounds with the dash of people determined to excel not only before the whole 'field' but in each other's eyes. In the summer they made sensational appearances in the show-rings of Charlottesville, and Mrs Trigg Brown remembers a later occasion when Nancy tied with another young woman; they strove for victory through some three or four extra rounds, the final 'jump-off' being over obstacles raised to a height of five feet. To anyone with a shaky nerve on horseback, or with a natural antipathy to the animal itself, Mirador would have been hell on earth; but to Chillie and the young horse-loving Langhornes it was, as Nancy said years after, 'a sort of Paradise'.

Nancy wrote in 1951: 'All the estate hands and servants [at Mirador]
were coloured people. I cannot remember a time when I did not love
some coloured man or woman just as much as anyone in the family.
To me they seemed to be part of the family. Only those who have
lived in the South in the old days will understand this.'

In fact, the situation is not very difficult to understand. The relationship of the white propertied Virginian to his coloured subordinates had
for centuries, since the beginnings of the slave-trade, been a paternalistic
one, and, like all paternalist relationships, it could be the occasion of an
edifying sense of responsibility or of gross abuse. It is safe to suppose
that had Mr Langhorne owned Mirador in the age of slavery, he would
have been one of the 'good' slave-owners, but as it was he continued
their benevolent paternalism, as was the case with many Virginians in
his kind of position. This was not due to some peculiar virtue, but was
a natural consequence of the fact that good slave-owners, certainly in
Virginia, seem to have outnumbered the bad – or else there would
probably not have been a Civil War. One must remember too that
any anciently established relationship, even a bad one, can in the course
of time take on a smooth and graceful character. Even today, when
'Black Power' and other even more extreme racist movements have
further heightened the tension between Negro and white, the inter-
course between the two peoples in Virginia is far more easy and un-
troubled than in other, especially northern parts of America. This is
not a digression: Nancy held firmly and obstinately throughout life
to the opinion that her land of origin alone held the secret of how to
deal with the immense question of black-white reconciliation and
relationship. She saw the benevolent paternalism of her father. She was
impressed by what she saw. In the future she was to make too many
generalisations from what she had seen.

The foregoing paragraph may strike too solemn a note to harmonise
with the continuing jollity (when the tempests were not lowering or
flashing) of life at Mirador. Nancy's interest at that time in the large
coloured population of Mirador was in no way sociological: it was a
matter of affection, comedy, and sometimes (according to her frustrated memoir) of remarkable observation.

Of all the many coloured servants of Mirador, Nancy's favourite
was the nurse who had been with them since her earliest days. She was
called Liza Piatt and known to the children as Aunt Liza. (In Virginia
in those days the coloured upper servants were usually known as Aunt

or Uncle.) In her earlier days Aunt Liza had been a slave. She smoked a pipe and kept her money in the knee of her stocking, and this tempted the children to tease her by trying to pull her stockings down, pretending to rob her. But there was a serious element in the affection of Aunt Liza and the children. According to Nancy, she herself got a great deal of her religious instruction from her nurse. 'She could not read or write,' Nancy told in 1951, 'but she knew the Bible from beginning to end, though occasionally she got the characters a little mixed. She was no admirer of the Virgin Mother, for she just could not bring herself to believe that story, but she was deeply religious, and she would tell us stories of Mr Jesus by the hour.' (The reference to the Virgin may be an unconscious gloss coming from later opinions.)

Nancy is very interesting in what she had to tell about the morality of the coloured people. They were honest, and to have stolen money, clothes, or jewels would have seemed to them as wicked as it seems to law-abiding people anywhere. But to steal food was a different thing. As Nancy put it: 'Food was considered a right. They said God made food for everybody.'

Again, borrowing without permission was not looked on as reprehensible. Nancy told of a servant called Sam who used to wait at table. 'Sam was a sporting character,' wrote Nancy, 'and a particular friend of mine. He used to take Father's gun and go off shooting when Father wasn't around. I knew quite well what he was up to, and many a lie I told for Sam, protecting him.

'One day he appeared at table, and Lizzie suddenly saw he was wearing Father's gold cuff buttons. "Sam!" she said. "Where did you get those?" "Miss Nancy, she loaned them to me to go visiting," said Sam.

'Not for a moment did it enter my head to contradict this flight of fancy. I said yes, I had loaned them to him as Father was away and would not be needing them.'

Her most interesting observation of coloured people in Virginia refers again to their religion. She reported thus: 'Aunt Liza told me how coloured people would "seek", sometimes for two or three weeks, for God, and not find Him. And then all of a sudden He would come to them, and they would shout and dance and cry, "Oh! God came to see me last night!" and they would go round shaking hands, and say, "Mr Jesus he said to me, 'Don't you go for to do any washing this day – you go right to your prayers.'"'

One may easily get the impression, reading about America of the late nineteenth century, that domestic servants, drawn from the coloured population, were so plentiful that there was no such thing as a domestic service problem. This was not altogether so. It is true that the problem compared to that in other lands was a small one, but it existed. The very fact of emancipation, and the enjoyment of a new freedom by the coloured people, meant inevitably that former slaves had a taste for travel and changing employment. At the same time one must remember that, even so late as the nineties, and even later than this, Virginia had by no means recovered from the Civil War. Business throve and broke down; it was an age of sudden fortunes and sudden bankruptcies, attracting employment to all parts of the country, with unexpected outbreaks of unemployment. For a variety of reasons, economic and psychological, both the white and coloured populations had become much more nomadic than they had been in the former time. This helps to explain the extraordinary generosity and the occasional tyranny of Chillie's mastership of his coloured work-people.

He was short of farm-hands at one time when he heard of a coloured labourer, not far from Mirador, called Brown. Chillie went to see him and found that he had a large family, as big as his own, and covering as wide an age-span. He immediately spotted that if he was to break up this family he would thereby increase the risk of losing any of them whom he employed. Instantly he saw the solution and instantly, as was his way, he made the Brown family a proposition. At Mirador he would employ them all! He would house them and feed them well, and pay them two hundred dollars a year. They accepted.

Something more of tyranny appears in his conduct towards his Mirador cook, Aunt Ann. She was a great artist and, like many artists, she suffered from some instability of character, though she was strong-willed. She came from Albemarle County and resolutely refused to accompany the family on their yearly migration to Richmond. She insisted on remaining at Mirador throughout the winter. Chillie saw great danger of her deserting in his absence, but his ingenuity (and ruthlessness) soon found a solution of the problem of Aunt Ann. She had lost many of her teeth and so her master arranged that she should have a fine and expensive set of false ones from the leading dentist of Charlottesville. But this magnificent gift was made on a condition: every year when the family departed for Richmond, Chillie took the teeth with him and only gave them back to Aunt Ann on his return. This unusual arrangement seems to have worked satisfactorily.

In her memoir, Nancy, having praised her father's attitude to his daughters, went on to say: 'He was not so good with his sons. He never let them go. From time to time he would say: "You ought to get out and earn your own living." Delighted at the prospect, off they would go, but before they got very far, Father would call them back again.'

This parental possessiveness was to have tragic results. Michael Astor puts the matter in strong terms: 'Of Mr Langhorne's three sons, Keene and Harry, the eldest, turned out to be intelligent, versatile, idle and wild. They were intimidated by their father, and they both developed an overpowering attachment to the bottle. They married, they made friends, but they made little else of their lives.' They both died of tuberculosis when they were still young men; only the youngest son, Buck, lived to a mature age, though he too died early, at fifty-seven, and, like his brothers, of tuberculosis.

The genesis of Keene's and Harry's 'overpowering attachment to the bottle' appears to be open to a simple explanation. Though Chillie downed more than the average intake of mint juleps and of egg nogs; though he claimed to have one of the finest cellars in Virginia and plied his guests liberally with its contents, he was extraordinarily strict with his sons in the matter of drink. Till the age of twenty they were forbidden all wine and spirits, and after that their drinking was limited by his severe supervision. Or rather he thought it was. Inevitably his sons rebelled and there was much furtive drinking; even young Buck soon had a skeleton key to the whisky cupboard.

Sometimes rebellion flashed out in the open. Keene or Harry would simply disappear on occasion and return days later, oppressed by hangovers. Nancy gave the details of one of these flights. 'Keene was the most like Father,' she wrote. 'He was an amusing and attractive person. For a time he too had a job on the railways. He once managed to spend five thousand dollars in one week in a small town in Virginia that had nothing but a store, a railway station, and one house. Nobody could imagine how he had done it. Later it turned out there had been a travelling circus in the neighbourhood and Keene had entertained it for a week. He had done the thing in style, sending down to Washington for the food. Unfortunately the railway company were not enthusiastic for this lavish hospitality.'

Nancy wrote of Harry that he was 'the best-looking, and probably the most intelligent of the family. Unfortunately he died too young to prove it. . . . Harry was a year older than I, and we were in the nursery together. My chief recollection of him is that he used to black his face and put on a white nightgown and preach to us. He got that idea from the coloured folk who were all deeply religious. I also remember he was very modest. Phyllis and I used to kick up our heels in front of him, just to annoy him.'

She said nothing about his excesses, but there is no reason to doubt Michael Astor's testimony. Sobriety was not a Virginian virtue in those days. An incident told to Mrs Trigg Brown by a Mirador neighbour, Miss Ella Williams (today Mrs Gordon Smith), throws a clear light on the drinking habits of the time: 'Ella was at Mirador for lunch one day as Nora's guest, and she confessed herself slightly bewildered at the rapid pace of the conversation when a message came and was delivered to all. A relation was at Greenwood [station] in a state of intoxication, and would Mr Langhorne send and get him. With a long string of epithets, Mr Langhorne made it known that he would not send for him. The gaiety continued without a ruffle. In due time someone brought the unfortunate young man to the house. A masculine voice was heard shouting from the hall that he was going upstairs to shoot himself. From her place at the table Nannie called to him to go ahead, that it was a good idea. Silence. In the hall after lunch she called up to him again that no shot had been heard. Of course he was asleep, and on awakening he returned to the family group to be received as if nothing unusual had happened.' It was not long before Nancy came to take a less tolerant view of all this drinking.

Amid the high spirits and sport and reckless hospitality of Mirador the deep religious faith to which the husband and wife were devoted persisted as the central part of all their lives. In fact their religion became intensified in Mirador, though the first days augured ill for their relations with the Church.

Chillie quarrelled with the rector of Greenwood. The subject of their quarrel was a spittoon. Chillie's prowess in spitting was so prodigious both for distance and accuracy of aim that it is remembered in Virginia to this day. He declared that the habit was so strong on him that at his age he could not be expected to sit through a whole service without recourse to his spittoon, or cuspidor as it is genteelly described in American usage. The rector resisted the introduction of a cuspidor into his church and maintained moreover that spitting in church was irreverent in itself. The difference between the two men was absolute. War appeared inevitable. Then the rector gave way and the cuspidor was brought to Emmanuel Church across the road every Sunday by one of the Mirador servants. The rector had shown himself to be an astute psychological tactician, for this rebellious parishioner now felt that he owed it to the rector and himself to show that an addict to the habit of spitting could be an example to all Greenwood of what a Christian gentleman should be.

He had a dog to which he was greatly attached, and unhappily the dog took to worrying sheep. It caused havoc among the flock of a neighbour, a certain Mr Johnson who, after vain warnings and entreaty, was at last driven to shoot the dog dead on one of its raids. The fury of the dog's owner may be imagined. A day or two after this tragedy was a Sunday and both Chillie and Mr Johnson were in the congregation. The rector chose for his text a passage in the Lord's Prayer: 'Forgive us our trespasses as we forgive them who trespass against us.' After church the members of the congregation were standing about chatting by the door. Chillie came out and made straight for his neighbour. 'Johnson!' he roared, 'You shot my dog! And – damn you! – I forgive you.'

Later the rector persuaded him to be confirmed and take Communion. The coloured lady who used to clean out Emmanuel Church remarked: 'If Mr Chillie done joined up, then every last sinner may up and join.' But he undertook his confirmation in all seriousness.

There was another religious influence on Mirador stronger than that of the rector, one which made a specially deep impression on Nancy. This came from a remarkable Englishman called Frederick Neve. He was a graduate of Oxford University and had served with much success as a minister in three English parishes. In 1888 he came out to Virginia, at the age of thirty-three, and took up the duties of minister, with the rank of Archdeacon, at St Paul's Church at Ivy, a small town halfway between Greenwood and Charlottesville. He volunteered for this post when he heard that there was a demand for an English minister and that there was a small population of poor hill farmers living off the land in the Blue Ridge Mountains nearby. They were in great need of care. Some of them made a scanty living as timber-workmen, when work offered, and their families lived in the utmost destitution. These forgotten people were a lingering remnant of that darker element of human failure and misery in America's pioneering past, and their lot had worsened since the devastation of the Civil War. They lacked all medical care; except for the crude endeavours of the few semi-literate among them, they had no means of education, and were almost totally ignorant of the Christian faith. Archdeacon Neve went to Albemarle as a missionary. He remained there till his death when he was over ninety years old.

Mr Langhorne Gibson has described him as 'strong and gentle', and 'fierce in his dedication'. In Albemarle he received a stipend of no more than five hundred dollars a year. His only means of transport was a stout horse called 'Old Harry'. Mr Gibson gives this brief sketch of his work in the Blue Ridge Mountains. 'Year after year in all conditions of weather he rode or drove his "Old Harry" over the clay roads often deep in mud, up the lonely wagon trails to the forlorn and poverty-stricken mountaineers where he tended sick mothers, helped the fathers, and baptized the children.' He had to battle with suspicion and to the end some of these people believed he was a disguised revenue officer.

He was quick to detect the religious impulse in Nancy. He showed his skill as a fisher of souls by appealing to her sense of adventure. When she was fourteen he persuaded her father to let her join him as he went his pastoral rounds so that she could see religion in action outside the walls of a church. From this circumstance it is often believed that he used to take her to spend a day with his unhappy mountain parishioners, but Neve's successors say that he never did so. The roads were not safe; many of the mountain people were fierce and lawless. What he did do was to deepen a faith which hitherto had been child-like, and to show her something of the world outside, and what religion could do there.

In her own abrupt way Nancy wrote this of him: 'He was six foot three and he had very large feet. He used to preach to us on Sundays and he was the worst preacher I ever heard. But he was a man of God. . . . From the first I loved and respected him. Father used to say of me I didn't respect anything except goodness, and that is true. I have always liked and admired brilliance, but I loved goodness. The Archdeacon became one of my best friends. I wrote to him every month for forty years.'

Through him she came to know an organisation called 'The Sheltering Arms'. Of the latter Nancy wrote that it was 'a home in Virginia where old people and cripples were taken care of. I began to take an interest in it and to visit the people there. I don't think I had realised before how many poor and unwanted people there are in the world.'

Chillie had an old-fashioned prejudice against missionaries. He thought them – if not exactly fools – people who misdirected their energies and tackled problems the wrong way. He never gave anything to missionaries, but in this case he relented. If Archdeacon Neve (and Nannie) wanted him to – damn it! – he supposed he had to. He became a generous subscriber, though he always thought the mission a mistake.

As the Langhorne sisters grew up and began to become beautiful young women, they began to attract admirers and suitors. The young men from the University of Virginia in Charlottesville (that loveliest assembly of classical buildings in the whole State) would come out to Mirador in increasing numbers. Chillie and Mrs Langhorne looked on complacently for the most part, but with a little more of apprehension in the case of Irene who was by now of marriageable age. The family beauty had the greater share of suitors, as a matter of course.

It has been noted already that Chillie was ambitious, but his ambition was not of the kind that leads to the absurdities of self-importance or pretentiousness. Having acquired wealth he determined to live in future as a Virginian gentleman who possessed a fine estate. From here his ambition naturally extended to questions of social position, but for all that he did not, in the usual spirit of the newly rich, turn his back on his past, or forget that he came of farming stock. He did not waste his means on fashionable display. Irene was asked to all the parties and balls given by the leading hostesses of Virginia and to those given by the fashionable families round about. The other young ladies would arrive and depart in finely turned out equipages, but not Irene. Years after she told Nancy of 'her mortification at the carriage Father kept and would send to fetch her from parties. The beautiful Miss Langhorne, belle of the countryside, would be fetched away in a ramshackle turn-out driven by a funny coloured boy whose hat was all wrong and whose coat did not fit. Father did not consider such things mattered. He had a carriage and that was enough.' But Chillie was nevertheless ambitiously determined that his favourite daughter should marry 'well'.

Soon the multiplicity of her suitors began to cause her parents more serious concern, a concern reflected with less seriousness in the younger generation. Nancy described this part of Irene's story in her memoir: 'We began to spend a lot of time speculating who, of her many beaux, Irene would finally marry. The house was always full of suitors. Young men, old men, foreigners of every kind, literary men, rich bankers, all came along to ask for Irene's hand.

'She had sixty-two proposals.

'I certainly did enjoy Irene's beaux. Many of them were literary men and as Irene had no literary talent whatever they often recited the poetry they had prepared for her, to me. I could appreciate it.

'The funniest of Irene's beaux was a rich banker. He was quite twenty years older than she was when he appeared to pay his addresses. It never occurred to him that this young Southern girl would not jump into his opulent arms.

'Irene had a horror of him and would never go anywhere with him alone. They used to sit in the garden in full view of the house, and the banker would make manful efforts to kiss Irene's hand. One day she borrowed the gloves Algy Craven used when he put liniment on horses' feet, and the next time the banker tried to kiss her hand she stuck one of them out and let him.

'He sent her a diamond watch and a letter in which he said, "If you don't like it, take it to the mill pond and throw it into the deepest part." Another of her beaux sent her a cart to break horses. He too told her if she did not want it, to throw it in the mill pond. We were all thrilled and had our swim suits ready, for it looked as if this might turn out to be a good thing.

'Unfortunately, Father made her send all the presents back.'

She had not long to wait before she met a man who fell passionately in love with her and whom she loved fully in return. He was an artist, as yet little known, called Charles Dana Gibson. He came from New England.

Irene told her father about him and something about their mutual love. She asked Chillie to invite him to Mirador, and reluctantly he agreed to do so.

On the appointed day Dana Gibson arrived with his baggage. He was a tall young man of friendly appearance and manner, and on getting out of his buggy at the door he found himself confronted by the short stocky figure of Chillie looking up into his eyes with no sign of friendliness at all. Gibson greeted him and then turned to pay his driver.

'Hold on there a minute,' said Chillie. 'Let him wait. You won't be able to stay too long; the train leaves for New York early this evening. And besides, I don't want any damn sign-painter from the North coming down here to interfere with my daughter's life.'

Gibson showed no trace of offence. Smiling, he replied: 'So this is what you call Southern hospitality, Mr Langhorne.' He had chosen a vulnerable spot for his thrust.

Instantly Chillie looked on the young man with fresh eyes and, as he told later, he felt a sudden liking for this handsome Northerner. 'Pay him off, young man,' he said, 'and come on in.'

But for all his new feeling for him, Chillie was by no means reconciled to the notion of Dana Gibson becoming his son-in-law. He showed friendliness, it is true, but with intervals of intimidating gruffness which had no effect on the determined lover. Nancy was a witness of the whole episode. 'Once when he was staying with us,' she recalled in 1951, 'Dana had a pain in his stomach. Father gave him a dose of what he thought was salts, but it turned out to be saltpetre.

'It was a long time before Dana could be persuaded Father had not done it on purpose.

' "Are you going to marry this damned charcoal artist?" he would demand angrily.

'Presumably Irene said she was.

' "Do you realise," stormed Father, "that if anything happens to him, you will starve?"

'Then Dana went driving one day and had an accident and broke a bone in his hand. Father brightened. He was full of hope this might put an end to the romance. But it didn't. After she met Dana Gibson, Irene never looked at anyone else.'

The engagement was long, as was the custom in those days, but longer than usual because to win Chillie to the union took time and patience. Dana Gibson's first visit to Mirador was in the summer or early autumn of 1894 and his marriage to Irene did not take place till

November 1895. By that time Chillie and his son-in-law had become firm friends.

Nancy described her part in the wedding ceremony and in so doing added something to her self-portrait: 'Phyllis and I walked together in the bridal procession, and there is a little note in my mother's scrap-book which records that "Nannie Langhorne made her formal bow to society and by the right of every Langhorne immediately became a belle".

'I wasn't concerned with anything like that. My chief memory of that day is my delight at having got Irene married at last. For it had always been an understood thing that when she left home I would have her room! Until then I had always shared a room with Phyllis. Dearly as I loved her, I longed for a place of my own. I moved in that very night.

'Phyllis had a day off school and her first grown-up dress. I remember her walking beside me, looking lovely, with tears running down her face. Phyllis was always the sentimental one and cried easily.'

Concurrently with the wooing and marriage of Irene, Nancy's own love life began. The episode of the boy with the beautiful shoes may be taken as a prelude, more or less unconnected with the main work which opened when Nancy was approaching the age of fifteen. The first scenes belonged to opera-bouffe.

There was a young man of eminent Virginian family who was an undergraduate of the University at Charlottesville. His name was St George Bryan. He fell passionately in love with Nancy and she with him. He proposed, she accepted, and they were engaged (not formally) for more than a year. The course of their love ran very unsmoothly, and what little is remembered of it suggests that Nancy was going through a phase of intense girlish romanticism. 'He was eighteen and very good-looking and I adored him,' wrote Nancy in 1951. 'Our romance con-sisted mainly in our going for rides together. He whistled beautifully and would whistle me the latest tunes.' But the idyll was shattered by an accident to which he failed to respond with courage or show himself the perfect knight of her imagination. One Sunday the usual church parade after service was going forward in Greenwood, and Nancy and St George Bryan, both dressed in their finest, were walking together, when suddenly her petticoat slipped its moorings and fell to the ground.

She requested her lover to pick it up and carry it for her. Deeply embarrassed, he implored her to do this herself, and she saw at that moment his craven dread of appearing ridiculous. They were both hot-tempered people. She burst into the anger of disillusion at this betrayal; he responded with the wrath of rebellion at her tyranny. The 'engagement' was terminated on the spot. But after some time it was nearly renewed. St George Bryan's father was displeased with his son's progress at the university. He put it down, quite rightly, to the influence on his studies of the cult of the horse, and he exacted a promise from the young man that he would give up hunting and steeplechasing until he had obtained his degree. He kept his promise as well as he could, but not very well. He had one outstanding horse which was fancied for a valuable steeplechase to be run at Charlottesville and he could not resist the temptation of riding the race himself. Perhaps he was influenced towards this promise-breaking by his knowledge that Nancy would be there. At all events, he braved the fact that his father would also be there, and disguised himself with a false name and beard. All went well during the parade of the horses in the paddock, the saddling, the mounting, the parade of horses with jockeys up on the course, the canter to the gate, the start, and the first fences and furlongs. Then came disaster. At a large fence right in front of the stand where his father was watching, his horse fell, and in the crash the false beard came off and he was left exposed and unconscious on the ground. Nancy instantly recognised him, rushed to him as he was carried off the course, and made her way to where he was being tended. She knelt by him and laid the head of her stricken lover on her lap whilst his unseeing face was besprinkled by her tears. Then he came to and was sick. That was the end of the romance.

Others quickly followed. In her memoir Nancy mentioned one admirer who 'wrote me poems and letters, but my only feelings were of nausea'. She claimed to have received sixteen proposals before her first marriage, a modest score compared to Irene's sixty-two, but impressive nonetheless. Though the 'letters and poems' from the unnamed admirer may have nauseated her, she was not averse to the supreme evidence of devotion. She mentioned in the memoir (without precise indication of date) that 'at one of the Yale Proms I met Frederick Kernochan. He fell in love with me, but he never proposed. I did not know why, and I was very annoyed when he said one day: "You will be very attractive when you are eighteen or twenty. Someone will fall in love with you then." I thought it peculiar. Why wait so long?'

Though Chillie had come to like his second son-in-law, he decided that the rest of his daughters' marriages must be 'good' ones, and so he made the conventional move in that direction. When Nancy reached the age of seventeen, it was decided that she must go to New York to attend a certain 'finishing school' of the utmost fashionability, known as Miss Brown's Academy for Young Ladies. This meant not only the end of her education by Miss Jennie, but the end of her formal education of any kind. The loss was to be haphazardly repaired, but never made good. Except for visits to friends Nancy had never left home before, and now she had to go far away and live among strangers. She had never left Virginia except in family migrations. Now she had to face the terrors of moving alone into the grown-up world, and becoming grown-up herself.

For a short time, such as seems very long to a child, she had to say goodbye to Mirador, to her lovable, tyrannical, amazing father; to her adored mother and Phyllis; to Keene, Harry, Buck, little Nora and Lizzie Perkins; to Aunt Liza and Aunt Ann and Sam of the cuff buttons; to the multitudinous admirers supplied by the University of Virginia; not least to the horses, the hunting, the dogs; and to the aunts who were aunts by consanguinity, formidable Aunt Lewis, already mentioned, and another less noteworthy aunt, Mrs Hutter, of whom Nancy related that she 'wrote the worst poetry in the world; had an unsatisfactory husband and several unsatisfactory children, and thought them all wonderful.'

She entered onto the next part of her life.

As in the preceding chapters the main source is Lady Astor's 1951 autobiographical draft. Quotation and textual dependence on the draft are indicated throughout. The same is true of Mr Langhorne Gibson's lecture to the Albemarle Historical Society where the source is indicated, with the exception of his account of Dana Gibson's first meeting with C. D. Langhorne, and his description of Frederick Neve which is quoted not from the lecture but from a booklet he wrote on Emmanuel Church. Further information on Archdeacon Neve was given to me by the latter's successor, the Reverend Mr Whittle of St Paul's Church, Ivy, Virginia. Mrs Trigg Brown's memoir also remains a basic document. The episode of Aunt Ann's false teeth I owe

to Mrs Gordon Smith (formerly Miss Ella Williams), with many other details of the
life at Mirador and in Virginia at that time. (She contributed much to Mrs Trigg
Brown's memoir.) In the course of discussions she told me about the affair of the
cuspidor, of C. D. Langhorne's impetuous engagement of the Brown family, his
increasing ambition for his daughters, and his ambivalent attitude towards the work
of Archdeacon Neve. To Mrs Nancy Lancaster I am indebted yet more than in the
second chapter, chiefly for her memories of Mirador in the time of the Langhornes,
and many illustrative anecdotes and family details. The story of Lady Astor's youthful
romance with St George Bryan was given to me by his son, Mr John Bryan III,
whom I met in Richmond in 1969. The only published work I have used in this part
of the book is *Tribal Feeling*.

Chapter 4

EARLY SORROW

NANCY was not happy at Miss Brown's Academy for Young Ladies. The new world into which she was thrown proved to be much newer than she could have guessed, and it was not a world which welcomed a young Virginian. In 1951 she well summed up the contrast between her and her new companions: 'I have never forgotten how [the Academy] horrified me. We had all been brought up in a forthright and natural atmosphere where nobody talked of money or thought a great deal about clothes, and our approach to boys was healthy and unsentimental.[1] Miss Brown's young ladies thought and talked of nothing but their wardrobes, and how much money their fathers made, and there was always a selection of odd and, to me, quite revolting affairs going on between them and young men. I remember my shame and horror when one of my companions winked at a man in the street. At that time I had one tailor-made and two dresses that had been made at home, so I did not rate very high. The girl I roomed with had ten or eleven suits and dresses, and masses of jewelry which was left lying around everywhere.' Miss Brown's Academy seems to have sounded a faint but authentic echo of New York in 'The Gilded Age'.

Thrust among these artificial and disagreeable young ladies, Nancy found herself looked down on as a raw country lass from a remote and therefore insignificant part of the United States, in short as a person of wholly inferior status and contemptibly small means. Hitherto, and for the matter of that ever after, she regarded her Virginian birth as the highest of privileges, and Virginians as people accounted, as a matter of course, among the natural aristocrats of the human species. The attitude of her schoolmates came as a horrible surprise. Faced with this challenge, she did exactly what one would expect; she challenged her schoolmates back, chiefly relying on her immense fund of tomboyish humour. If they thought Virginians were raw and unsophisticated, she

1. Her adventures with Mr St George Bryan suggest that this adjective was un-critically chosen – but one gets the meaning.

would astound them with rawness such as they had never imagined. 'I set out quite deliberately to shock them all,' she wrote of those days. She took to wearing garish tasteless clothes, notably a yellow blouse with a green bow on one side and a pink one on the other. She spoke in an apparently innocent and open way about her family, assuring the young New Yorkers, among much misinformation about her homeland, that her father was a perpetual drunkard and that her mother kept the home together by taking in washing. One may guess with fair certainty that she exaggerated her Virginian accent till that difficult speech was almost incomprehensible. The treatment was successful. 'They came to look on me,' recorded Nancy, 'as an exciting if not very desirable character.'

'There was one nice girl,' she remembered in her memoir, 'I could have made a friend of there, to whom I became quite devoted, but I was never allowed to go to her house.' The friendship was smothered at birth by Chillie as soon as he heard of it. The girl's father was a newspaper man; by a strange irony he was, some time later, to become the owner of that paper whose editor had been threatened by Chillie with shooting.

Her reputation at Miss Brown's Academy for Young Ladies entered a new phase of wonderment when her sister Irene first called to take her to Long Island for a day's riding. Dana Gibson had his studio in New York and had already made and published numerous drawings of Irene: 'The Gibson Girl' had been conceived and born. His work was regularly published in *Life* magazine. His fame, and that of his radiant model, was still in early stages but already they were both celebrities in New York, and celebrities moreover who were highly esteemed by the society to which Miss Brown's young ladies aspired. To the end of Nancy's residence in the Academy the young ladies were perplexed by her claim to sisterhood with this phenomenally beautiful favourite of 'The Four Hundred'. Was she perhaps a waif to whom the brilliant Mrs Gibson was showing charity? Perhaps they remembered Nancy's tall stories, and wondered whether this story of sisterhood was not the tallest of them all? Yet the fact remained that Mrs Gibson called on all holidays and weekend days, whenever she could, in fact, to take the washerwoman's daughter out riding, and certainly the famous young lady of fashion could not have been more familiar and kind to the waif if the latter really had been her sister. The puzzle remained unsolved.

Nancy enjoyed her practical joke, enjoyed acting the leading role in this farce of her own invention, but underneath all her delight in the clowning, and the wild clothes, and the fooling of these spoiled children, she was desperately miserable and longing for home as only a child can. And then suddenly rescue came. Her release from what seemed like life-imprisonment was thus described by her: 'To my intense delight Father and Mother appeared one day to visit me, and seeing how wretched I was, decided Miss Brown's Academy was not the place for me. I can still remember the gratitude and relief that filled me when Father broke the pleasant news to me that I need not stay.' But her indignation at this finishing school and everything it represented remained with her for life. 'I don't remember learning a single useful thing at that school; they did not even teach manners,' she wrote in 1951. But as Miss Brown's Academy for Young Ladies fades from the story one may be liable to a feeling of some regret that Nancy never thought to leave us a description of Miss Brown.

'It was wonderful to be home again after that ghastly finishing school,' she wrote in 1951. 'We were at Mirador, and those were lovely summer days. Father, in common with everyone in Virginia, used to take a nap after lunch, but Father napped in unexpected places, and if you in-advertently came on him and awoke him, it was like rousing Jove. We then had to sit beside him and fan him to keep the flies off until he went to sleep again. I used to do this, and when he was just dropping off, delicately touch the end of his nose with the fan. We had riding, and picnics, and parties in Richmond and Charlottesville.'

Everything was just as it used to be and Nancy was blissfully back in the old life, for a while. When she said that she learned nothing useful at Miss Brown's Academy, this may be taken as literally true, but it would be quite wrong to conclude from it that she learned nothing at all in her exile. Far from it, in the course of paying social calls with her sister she had learned a little, but enough to whet her appetite, about the delights of New York glamour, and she was not unaffected by its seductions. One should remember again Michael Astor's comment that 'the parochial life was not one that could properly contain any of Mr Langhorne's daughters.' She had caught the infection of Chillie's social ambition. She loved Virginia, but that did not for a moment mean that she was indifferent to exclusion from the luxurious cosmo-

politanism of New York, a possibility which the pompous sneers of
her fellow-students at Miss Brown's Academy had brought home to
her.

She felt drawn back to New York by ties of sentiment as well, not
only by her strong affection for Irene, but by a friendship she had
formed with a girl of the same age, whom she had met in New York
but not in the Academy. She was called Alice Babcock and the two
were to remain on the closest terms of affection till Alice's death at the
time of the Second World War. She married Mr Roger Winthrop, a
kinsman of the recent United States Ambassador to Great Britain.

When Nancy told her parents that she wanted to go to stay with
Irene in New York, they raised no objections. She went and thus
innocently walked into disaster which was to disfigure the next years
of her life.

New York in the 1890s was a world of crazy luxury and the intoxication of sudden wealth. The 'Gilded Age' has been described many
times and by able hands, but nowhere better than by Mrs Harry Lehr
who in her young days was very much a part of it. Here is one of her
impressions of the gilded society, at just about this time: 'Evenings
given over to balls, to dinner-parties. Evenings at the Opera where
every woman wore full regalia to outshine her neighbours. Diamond
tiaras, ropes of pearls, enormous sapphires and emeralds, such a pro-
fusion that the problem was to find a novel way of wearing them.
Mrs John Drexel, "Cousin Alice" as Harry Lehr insisted on calling her,
wore her priceless pearls set in a wide band which crossed over her
ample bosom and down her back like a Sam Browne belt. Mrs
Frederick Vanderbilt, having heard that Venetian beauties liked to toy
with a single jewel on the end of a chain, decided that it would be
even more original to have hers hanging before her feet. So she always
progressed to her loge at the Opera kicking a great uncut sapphire or
ruby attached to her waist by a rope of pearls.'[2] There were fancy-dress

2. Mrs Harry Lehr was originally Elizabeth Drexel, one of the richest young
heiresses of New York. Her husband Harry Lehr was a famous New York personality,
known for his wit which caused him to be patronised by the leading New York
hostesses, even the exclusive Mrs William Astor. He was one *arbiter elegantiarum*
among several. (See *Incredible New York*, by Lloyd Morris (N.Y., 1951).) He had small
means and obtained his apartment, clothes, wines, and the food for his dinner-parties
free from the tradesmen for the sake of advertisement. He successfully wooed
Elizabeth Drexel, and informed her on their marriage night that he was a complete
homosexual with a strong physical aversion to women, and that he had married her

balls in rooms decorated in the style of the Hall of Mirrors in Versailles, and equally lavish joke-parties for dogs, monkeys, and other pets; bird-parties where golden cages filled with rare birds hung round the room, and swans swam in a miniature lake in the middle of a vast table; baby-parties with the guests in pinafores and baby bonnets and talking baby language. It was a world riddled with snobbery and consciously mad. If they had ever heard of him, Trimalchio was their model.

Nancy was too young to have judgement in which she had confidence. She was always attracted by high spirits. The gilded age was too alien to her upbringing to allow her to surrender to it, but that does not mean that she resisted its glamour. She was always susceptible to glamour. She was now, at seventeen and a half years of age, entering on to her remarkable womanly beauty, and not surprisingly there occurred here in New York the first serious romance of her life. The story is best told in Nancy's own candid words:

'I went North to stay with my sister Irene. I was described by the papers at this time as "a pretty, dashing and sweet schoolgirl", but I have no very real idea of the kind of person I was. I enjoyed life immensely, and took things as they came.

'One day I was taken to a polo match. There was a rather spectacular young man playing. He rode a one-eyed pony they told me was famous, and took some fearful croppers from which he arose none the worse. Afterwards he came over and talked to us, and was introduced to me as Bob Shaw, son of an old and distinguished family. It seems as soon as he saw me, he made up his mind to marry me.

'I was so young that when rumours began to go round, everyone said there must be some mistake. I wasn't officially "out". I can't remember all the ins and outs of it now. I suppose I was flattered and pleased to have made this spectacular conquest. I liked him, and it was pleasant to be the centre of the picture all of a sudden. But in my own heart I was never sure. The still, small voice that is in most girls' hearts

---

for her money alone. To spare her mother's feelings (and perhaps her own pride), Mrs Lehr did not obtain a divorce or annulment. Lehr died in a state of insanity after an unsuccessful brain operation in 1929. She lived thereafter till 1940 at 52 rue des Saints Pères, Paris, in a majestic hôtel which she restored and which was once owned by the Marquis de Cavoye, the friend and *maréchal des logis* of Louis XIV. She grew markedly eccentric in her later years (when I knew her) and seemed at moments to believe that she was the Marquise de Cavoye, but this did not prevent her writing, with the editorial aid of friends, a remarkable autobiography.

warned me I was not really in love with him, but I did not listen, or if I did, I could not understand the message. The entire family were in favour of the marriage.

'We became engaged – and then I broke it off. We became engaged again. His mother read me a terrible lecture, telling me I was breaking Bob's heart and ruining his life, and that he needed me. Finally I agreed to marry him. I suppose for a little while I persuaded myself I was in love with him, but I know now I was wrong. I wasn't in love with anyone. Only with life.

'One of the things that influenced me was his family. I loved his father and mother, particularly his father who was a very remarkable old man. He collected pictures and had one of the finest collections of Botticellis in America. He taught me all I knew about pictures.

'It is strange, looking back on it, to see how through it all there ran uneasiness, a note of warning. It was not only I who was aware of it; Father was also. Something made him go to Mr Shaw and ask him candidly if there was any reason why Bob should not marry me. He was assured there was none, although both Bob's father and mother knew very well at the time that their son was an alcoholic.'

Here Nancy's memory evidently failed her, and this made her unwittingly unjust to her first parents-in-law. The story was more complicated than she describes. It is the fact that her father became worried by stories which he heard about his future son-in-law and went to Boston to make enquiries from Mr and Mrs Shaw. They replied that he was certainly wild, given to dissipations and youthful follies, but that these were to be considered as no more than any rich young man's wild oats, and that marriage would soon lead him to settle down. The answer did not quieten Chillie's suspicions, and on his return he strongly advised his daughter to abandon the marriage, and in this he was joined by his wife. But Nancy clung to her fancied love. She refused to listen to the advice and insisted on having her way till her parents relented.

Robert Shaw's parents did not know, in all likelihood, that their son could be described as an alcoholic rather than as a fast young man, and no one concerned in the affair had any notion of the real and tragic peril of the match. For, unsuspected, there was the taint of mental illness in Mrs. Shaw's family. Her father was a Swiss scientist called Agassiz who held a post in Harvard University. In his later years he grew liable to nervous breakdown. A more tragic fate overcame his daughter

Mrs. Shaw long after this time when she became hopelessly insane. It is not suggested here that her son Robert Shaw was himself insane, but it is suggested that his excesses, and his crazily irresponsible behaviour which comes out later on in the story, far from being youthful wild oats, indicated some inherited lack of mental balance.

To return to the story. After a long engagement they were married in October 1897 at Mirador. 'Phyllis was my maid of honour,' Nancy told. 'There was an altar with white flowers and silver candlesticks at one end of the big drawing-room.' She confessed, with typical forthrightness, to some pique when the newspapers referred to her, during her engagement and in reporting her marriage, not as 'the lovely Miss Nancy Langhorne', but as 'the beautiful Irene Langhorne's sister'.

The marriage was a complete failure from its first day. Robert Shaw, according to Michael Astor, 'supposed he was marrying a typical Southern belle. He woke up from his reverie with the surprise of a man who has unsuspectingly got into bed with a wild cat.' On the second night of the honeymoon which was spent at Hot Springs, Nancy fled and made her way back to Mirador. 'Mr Langhorne,' according to Michael Astor, 'tried to comfort his daughter, and allowed her to stay a few days, after which he sent her back, telling her she had better go through with it.'

She went back to her husband and the situation only worsened. Nancy told after: 'I felt much as I had done as a child [when I was] marooned on the wrong side of the railway years before, when I prayed and a kindly bagman came and took me home. I was so homesick and miserable that Bob took me back. I was only eighteen and apart from the brief interlude at the Academy for Young Ladies in New York, I had never been right away from all my own people before.'

She seems to have fled from Shaw on another, perhaps on several occasions. Theodore Roosevelt's son-in-law, Nicholas Longworth, once had a curious experience which he told his wife from whom the writer heard the story. One day he was in the large booking office hall of Washington station before travelling somewhere on business, when he saw a disconsolate young woman sitting miserably on one of the public benches. He knew the Langhornes and immediately recognised Nancy. He went over and asked her what she was doing there. She told him that she had had a terrible quarrel with her husband who had told her to get out of the house, and that she had taken him at his word and left without baggage or more money than happened to be in her purse. She had taken the train as far as Washington where her money had run out and she was wondering how she was going to get to Greenwood. Mr Longworth remade his plans for the day and brought her back again to Mirador. When this happened is not remembered: her whole married life with Shaw occupied less than four years crowded with dismal events. This is how Nancy described the end of it.

'It is difficult to bring back any kind of picture of those days. It happened so long ago and in a strange fashion touched me so little. I cannot remember when things began to go wrong. Perhaps they never went right. I discovered Bob was not always truthful with me. He started drinking again, and I was horrified and frightened. I went to stay with him at his own home, and I think it was then I learned drink had been his trouble for a long time. His parents had hoped that marriage would cure him and help him settle down, but it did nothing of the kind. I was too young and inexperienced to handle such a situation. Like many another young girl, I fought for a long time against acknowledging the mistake I had made. I avoided the unpleasant truth. My baby was born. For a little while that took my mind off my unhappiness. But presently there came a time when I could not bear it any longer.

'I went to his father and told him I could not go on. Mr Shaw was very kind and much distressed by the whole affair. I think they had hoped marriage was to put an end to all Bob's difficulties, but it had not done so. "Go back home for six months," he said. "I'll get him right."

'But it did not work out. When the six months was over I went back. Bob was still drinking, and now there was another woman in his life.'

One important detail was missed by Nancy in her 1951 record. Her father did not acquiesce in the breakdown of this marriage which he had tried to prevent, and Mrs Trigg Brown asserts that in spite of disapproving his son-in-law's dissipation, he had much affection for Robert Shaw. Hoping that his daughter's aversion to her husband was probably nothing more than an expression of homesickness, he bought them a beautiful country house very near Mirador. Here they lived together for some months, but this attempted solution also was a complete failure. They separated for good in 1901 and Nancy went back to the old life at Mirador again, for a while.

There ensued a protracted argument about Nancy's future which seems to have lasted for several weeks. She had grounds for divorce, for apart from the 'other woman' her husband in his drunken rages had treated her with physical cruelty, but she refused to take a step which, so she believed, was contrary to her religious faith and which would bring disgrace on her family. She had an alternative: to sign a deed of separation. Many of her friends urged her not to do this, but to face a divorce case, no matter how disagreeable, as otherwise she ran the risk of never being able to marry again. It is interesting to note that among those who counselled her most strongly against formal separation and in favour of divorce was Archdeacon Neve. But she would not listen and duly signed the deed, though not till October of 1902.

In her 1951 draft Nancy told how she once said to her father, 'Your beautiful daughter is back again, unwanted, unsought, and part-widowed for life.' But her mother had other ideas about her: she said to one of Nancy's sisters: 'Somehow I don't think the world has heard the last of Nannie yet.'

Then suddenly, very soon after signing the deed of separation, circumstances wrought a change in her situation, and Nancy found herself more or less forced to take the step that was so abhorrent to her religious conviction.

It came about in this way: her parents-in-law (to whom she remained very attached) came down from Boston to Mirador, some time in the late autumn of 1902. They had grave news. They had come to persuade Nancy, despite the deed of separation, to institute divorce proceedings against their son, for if she did not do so, they explained, Robert Shaw stood in the utmost danger of a criminal prosecution. Their son had told the other woman in the case that he was in fact divorced from Nancy and, either through ignorance of the law or through foolish bravado, had gone through some form of marriage service with her. One day she or her family would find out the truth, in which case the family, if not she, would be likely to take action and Robert Shaw would inevitably be sent to prison for bigamy. Faced with this turn of events, Nancy needed only a little persuasion to agree to do what they wanted. To soften the scandal Mr and Mrs Shaw proposed that she should apply for the divorce on grounds of incompatibility of temperament, but this she refused to do. 'I took a firm stand on the Bible,' she wrote of these events. 'I would only have it on the grounds of adultery, and that was how, in the end, it was.'

Nancy told in her memoir how the divorce went through with 'astonishing little fuss . . . handled by competent lawyers, and put through quickly and quietly'. She told also how 'the Langhorne family were always in the limelight, anything they did was apt to make headlines. I was bothered and unhappy at having brought such a thing on them, but they were all wonderful to me. They backed me up. They knew I had to do it.'

The divorce proceedings were concluded in the absence of the main parties on the 3rd February 1903, in Charlottesville. On the same day Robert Shaw legally married his second wife in New York. The story did not have a conventional moral ending on the husband's side. Robert Shaw's first marriage had been accounted a 'good' one and was welcomed by his family and the society of Boston and New York. His second marriage was accounted as a very 'bad' one indeed, the act of a foolish, irresponsible and quite conscienceless young man. An early break-up and a second divorce were confidently predicted but, in the event, they lived happily ever after.

Nancy was by now emotionally exhausted by what she had been through, and so Chillie and Mrs Langhorne decided that the best thing was to take her away in the hope that foreign travel and new scenes would restore her spirits. Thus it came about that she visited Europe for the first time. She left in February 1903 with her mother and her great friend Alice Babcock, for her parents judged that a girl who shared all Nancy's high spirits and whom she loved would be an ideal companion likely to bring out again the other's gaiety and love of life. The choice was less ideal than they supposed, for Alice Babcock was at that moment recovering from an unhappy love-affair. 'She was,' so Nancy recorded, 'as fed up and disillusioned as I was.' They had fun together all the same, and their bond was strengthened by a decision they took in common: that they hated men. 'We would have nothing to do with them,' Nancy said, 'either on the boat or on the golf links. We played around together, ignoring all friendly advances. I remember some of the men looked at us askance after a time – but in those days I had not the slightest idea why.'

They went first to France and then from Paris Mrs Langhorne and the two girls travelled to England. From the first moment of arrival Nancy was entranced by everything that she saw about her. 'I loved it,'

she wrote in her memoir. 'I had this strange feeling of having come
home, rather than of having gone abroad.' They had many introductions, thanks to Irene, for Dana Gibson's rapidly expanding fame
had taken him and his wife for a brief visit to London where he was
now as well known and esteemed as in New York. Among compatriots
they met Mrs Astor, the wife of John Jacob Astor IV (a cousin of
Nancy's future father-in-law), and she was so delighted by the two
young women that, hearing that the whole party was very shortly
to return to the United States, she asked if they would not all stay with
her for a month. It was arranged in the end that Mrs Langhorne would
return alone to look after Nancy's little son, while the two young ones
would remain with Mrs Astor. They had all the fun of the fair in the
first resplendent winter season of King Edward VII's reign. It would
seem inevitable that while staying as a guest of Mrs Astor she met her
future husband, but in fact there was no such encounter. In the spring
she and Alice returned home, and of this Nancy wrote: 'I was delighted
to be there again. I took up the old life as if I had never been away,
knocking around in a shabby old riding habit most of the time.'

The old life was enlivened for Nancy by a new friendship, or rather a
new love which was reciprocated by Nancy with friendship. Her new
admirer was an Irishman of Ulster, Angus McDonnell, the second son
of the Earl of Antrim. He was at this time twenty-two years old. He
had gone to the United States to work in the railways, and in the winter
of 1902–1903 he was stationed in Texas. His mother and elder brother
were visiting Canada at the time, and he travelled north to meet them
in Ottawa and then accompanied them to New York from where they
were to sail for Europe. In a short memoir (already cited) which he
wrote on Nancy and the Langhornes in 1953, Angus McDonnell told
as follows: 'At lunch, before going on board, someone said to my
mother: "You will have the most delightful travelling companions,
Nannie Shaw: she is going abroad with her mother, Mrs Langhorne,
and a younger sister, for two or three months, to let matters settle
themselves after obtaining a divorce from her husband, Bob Shaw."'[3]
    'I had said goodbye to my mother on board and was waiting on the
dock, feeling very lonely and unhappy to see the last of them and

3. McDonnell, writing long after, evidently confused Lady Astor's first and second
voyages. On the latter she was accompanied by her sister Phyllis.

repeat those painful goodbyes between the ship and shore, when my mother appeared at the ship's side, accompanied by one of the most attractive young women one could wish to see. . . . She was carrying a large bunch of red roses that one of her beaux had sent her to the boat, and was looking gay and excited at the prospect of going to Europe for the first time.

'My mother introduced us, and much to my confusion and the delight of the passengers and those that had come to see them off, Nannie threw her roses to me, saying she would look forward to seeing me on her return to Virginia in the early summer.

'Later in the year, when I got to know her well, I realised that the rose episode was very typical of her: she had always liked being in the centre of the stage, even if it was a small one, and she would not hesitate to make others self-conscious in so being. On this occasion, though I remember feeling miserably shy and foolish, holding a great bunch of red roses, I also remember thinking to myself, I hope she comes home soon.'

By the time she did come back, Angus was no longer stationed in Texas but at Manassas in the north-west of Virginia, eighty miles from Charlottesville. He announced himself and was invited to Mirador for a weekend. He was shy at the longed-for prospect as he knew that Mirador life was 'high-toned' and he only had 'one semi-respectable blue serge suit, unfortunately shiny at the seams and elbows, and by no means free from grease spots'. So great was his shyness that at Charlottesville his courage failed him and he telephoned to Mirador to say he would drive out the next morning.

'Sunday morning came,' he wrote in his essay, 'a beautiful early summer day. I hired a buggy and an old yellow horse to drive out the eighteen miles. At that time there were nothing but dirt roads. . . . They consisted of bottomless mud in winter, and almost bottomless dust in summer, and the farther I went, the more the grease spots on the one and only suit came out of retirement, just as a photographic plate develops. By the time I arrived, I was almost choked with dust, with a tongue as dry as a parrot's and most miserably shy.'

But the enchantment of Mirador and the happy liveliness and gaiety of the family made an instant impression on him and he lost his shyness straight away. 'They were all so natural and welcoming, especially Nannie and her mother, giving me news of the family at home, that by lunch-time I had even forgotten the spots on my suit.'

The whole family liked him as much as he liked them. Chillie, whom he described as 'one of the most lovable characters I have ever met', made it plain from the first that he relished the company of this amusing young Irishman, while Angus himself felt at home here, in part because, as he wrote, 'there was something so like Ireland about it'. But the deepest reason for his attraction to Mirador was Nancy. 'For the next few years of my life,' he wrote, 'my feelings for Nannie influenced me more than anything else.' His first real meeting with her at Mirador confirmed his love-at-first-sight of some four months before. 'As for Nannie,' he wrote, 'just as I thought when I saw her on the boat, she was as pretty and attractive as she could be – gay, laughing blue eyes, generally blonde colouring, the neatest, trimmest figure imaginable; though physically very strong, with lovely feet and ankles; capable rather than pretty hands; her whole make-up the embodiment of youth, vitality and energy.' He was in love with her and he did not forget his love for many years.

As he was saying goodbye to him on Monday morning, Chillie said, 'Glad to have had you here. Come again some time.' Angus replied, 'Yes, sir, I will come again next Sunday.' Chillie was momentarily taken aback. 'Well,' he said, 'I didn't quite mean that, but come anyway if that's the way you feel about it.' He did come the next Sunday, and many after, and before long he was given a room which he shared with Buck, now aged eighteen, and with an old pointer 'Bob'. He used to stay as one of the family whenever he could spare the time from his work in Manassas. But not long after his first meeting with them, a frightful tragedy overcame the family. What happened is best told in Nancy's own words: '. . . There was a big horse show at Lynchburg. I did not particularly want to go, but Father was very anxious I should. He liked to see me jumping. It never bothered him, he was quite without fear of any kind. In the end, to please him, I entered. Father went on ahead. Mother, Keene and I followed by train to join him there. We had lunch in the train, and I can remember to this day exactly what we had. We had beaten biscuit and Virginian ham, and I still think this is the finest lunch in the world.

'Mother seemed perfectly all right, except that she complained presently of a headache. No one thought anything of it. We put it down to the train, and to the fact she was always a little nervous when I was jumping. Often, when she saw the five-foot jumps I took at these shows, she would say, shuddering:

' "One of these days I shall die."

'At dinner that night Mother looked so pretty and lovely that I remember Father looking at her down the long table and saying,

' "You are looking very beautiful tonight, Mrs Langhorne."

'Mother gave him a smile and said she was very glad to hear it. I was in high spirits. I thoroughly enjoyed these shows. I was in a great hurry to be off. Both Keene and I went on ahead. I remember kissing Mother and giving her a sort of playful push and telling her to hurry. Never for an instant dreaming this would be the last time I saw her alive.

'So Keene and I went on. Father and Mother were to have followed us immediately but they did not come. Suddenly I, who was so seldom nervous or given to any sort of foreboding, was full of them and could not say why. I left the show and went home.

'I found the house in darkness and Mother dead.

'She was only fifty-five.'

This was at the end of the summer of 1903.

As before, the main source is Lady Astor's 1951 autobiographical draft, as indicated throughout. The story of Lady Astor's first marriage follows the same source, with some additional material from Mrs Alice Longworth with whom I had two long conversations in Washington in November 1969, a note taken from Mrs Trigg Brown's essay, and other material drawn from my visit to Mrs Gordon Smith in 1969. The episode concerning the late Angus McDonnell is taken from his essay, 'The Langhornes at Mirador', written in 1953 for Michael Astor. The break-up of Lady Astor's first marriage is easily confused as to dates since so many people who have written about her have been unaware that its dissolution proceeded in two unconnected stages, legal separation and divorce. 1901 and 1903 are both given by reliable authorities as divorce dates, whereas the separation was in 1902 and the divorce in 1903. Official copies of the deed of separation and the marriage certificate relating to Robert Shaw's second marriage is in the Astor archive. For the events leading up to the marriage, I am indebted to Lady Astor's niece, Mrs Reginald Winn, whose account agrees with that in Mrs Trigg Brown's essay. Other versions, hostile to the Shaw family, arise from Lady Astor's defective memory and can be discounted. Published works consulted are *Tribal Feeling*, by Michael Astor, and *King Lehr and the Gilded Age*, by Elizabeth Drexel Lehr, London, 1935.

Chapter 5

LOVE AND MARRIAGE

SEVERAL people who first met Nancy in or after 1903 noticed that under her unquenchable vitality and comedy there was a persistent strain of melancholy. Very likely it was always there, as is the case with most very high-spirited people. The sudden death of her mother greatly intensified it and made it noticeable to those she knew well, not only at the time but to the end of her days. There was no exaggeration when she wrote in her memoir: 'That was sorrow such as I had never known or imagined. The light went out of my life. I was ill for months, in a wretched, nameless fashion.' She wrote also in 1951: 'The memory of those days is like a shadow on the heart still.'

She stayed on at Mirador as a matter of course, and as the eldest of the family now she tried to fill her mother's place in running the home; inadequately, she felt, as she was of such different temperament, but she made strenuous efforts. 'I even took to gardening,' she told, 'a thing I thoroughly disliked and had never turned my hand to before. I remember kneeling one day, weeding one of her flower-beds, trying to keep it the way she would have liked it, trying not to think about the days that were no more. William, the coloured gardener, was working nearby, but he left that job and came and knelt on the opposite side of the flower-bed and worked with me. He knew how I was feeling. I was ill with misery and I remember what a comfort it was when I looked up through the tears I could not control to see his kindly black face smiling at me. At that time I had no plans, no dreams, no hopes save that my little son, then at his most enchanting, would grow up sober.'

There was one role that she could not in any way take over from her mother, and that was as the peace-maker of the family; on the contrary, she was a storm centre. On one occasion, for instance, while she was away visiting, her father decided to engage a housekeeper, and on her return she was horrified to note that at lunch this newcomer settled herself in her mother's chair at the head of the table. A crisis of immense violence immediately ensued, Nancy protesting that occupation of her mother's chair was her privilege and, for that matter, so was the housekeeping; the turmoil increased: she rushed upstairs and began to pack her trunks and cases, declaring that she would never inhabit Mirador as the subordinate of this interfering nobody, etc., etc. She won the battle, the poor housekeeper departed, and Nancy was conceded the throne at the cost of frayed nerves all round. The only member of the family who could replace her mother as the peacemaker lived far away in the north. Angus McDonnell, who witnessed many such scenes, wrote: 'Remembering family rows, I can hear Mr Langhorne say, "Well, I will have to send for Irene." '

Angus McDonnell has an interesting note on this period of her life, with some general reflections: 'Nannie kept house rather sporadically for Mr Langhorne for the next two years, but it was not altogether a success. They were both forceful personalities, very much alike in character, except that when Mr Langhorne set himself a goal he was a very good judge of his own capacity, whereas it always seemed to me that Nannie was apt to set herself a target beyond her capacity, and she never seemed satisfied when she got as far as her delightful appearance, great charm, extremely nimble wits, and somewhat limited education would take her. It was during the period that she kept house for Mr Langhorne that I saw most of her, and living quietly in the country she was at her very nicest. Everybody loved her, both black and white, and nobody was more fun. She made no secret, however, of her intention to seek pastures new, farther afield.'

Nevertheless, for a considerable time she made no move towards Europe, partly, one may guess, through the hesitation that often goes with great unhappiness, partly through a sense of duty. If her father had shown signs of wishing to marry again then she might have considered herself free to do as she chose, but she rightly divined that he would now remain single. Then her father made up her mind for her. About a year after Mrs Langhorne's death, he sent for her. Of this crucial interview she wrote: 'I think he had begun to realise it was not right for anyone as young as I was to remain at home, sunk in gloom, prematurely of the opinion that my life was over and done with. Father asked me if I would not like to go over to England for a season to hunt there. I loved the idea and was eager to go, but I did not think it right to leave him. I did not think it was what Mother would have wanted me to do, but Father, who probably knew best, disagreed. He thought it was what she would have wanted me to do. Moreover, he

promised that he would come over for Christmas himself. So off I
went with Bobby and his nurse, and my sister Phyllis and her children
and governess.'

It should be explained that Phyllis was now married to Reginald
Brooks by whom she had two children. The marriage was unhappy
and gradually moved towards estrangement and divorce.

They began their visit by staying at Fleming's Hotel in Half Moon
Street, and the children would play in Green Park nearby. As before,
Irene's introductions gave her a wide acquaintance in fashionable
society where, largely due to King Edward's influence, Americans 'of
the right sort' had become very welcome. All went smoothly for the
two sisters in London, but their course was less easy when they moved
into a different sort of fashionable world at Market Harborough when
the hunting season began in November. They took a hunting box
called Highfield House, outside the town on the Bowden Road. There
in the midst of the finest hunting country in England they followed the
hounds, at first riding hirelings till Chillie presented them with
horses of their own. In this society go-ahead young Americans with
marked American accents were not readily accepted – or only accepted
with questioning.

Confronted by this challenge, Nancy ran true to form. She did not
follow an appeasement policy. She had met the kind of situation
before in Miss Brown's Academy for Young Ladies, and she applied
a tried solution. Again she relied on her acting ability, but this time she
set out not so much to shock as to amaze her critics. Few of her fellow
hunters and huntresses knew Americans except by hearsay, and so she
gave them what she guessed they expected: she played the part of the
forthright, no-nonsense daughter of Uncle Sam, as bold in her speech
and manners as in her horsemanship. With or without provocation
she let fly and fairly drew the limelight on to her. On her very first
day hunting, as hounds were streaking in full cry across country, she
leaped over a high fence under a branch and was thrown into the mud
of a ploughed field. Instantly a rescuer was at her side leading her horse,
offering to get down to help her to remount, when she angrily shouted
at him: 'Do you think I would be such an ass as to come out hunting
if I couldn't mount from the ground?'

By such conduct, consistently maintained, she kept them guessing,
wondering what sort of explosive meteorite had landed in their midst.
Not that she met with solid resentment. It is needless to say that a

brilliantly lovely young divorced woman did not want for admirers among the sportsmen, but they were dismayed to find that for all her flirtatiousness and merriment she was icily virtuous, moreover dangerously so, as her puritanism did not only mean that she went to church regularly and only drank tea and barley water, but that she did not scruple to threaten with exposure and ridicule anyone who even hinted at dishonourable transgression of the very lightest kind. For all that, the women of this society not unnaturally tended to look on her with much suspicion. When she first met Gordon and Mrs Cunard, the latter received her with rude and open hostility. 'I suppose,' she said, 'that you have come over here to get one of our husbands.' Nancy immediately replied: 'If you knew the trouble I've had gettin' rid of mine, you'd know I don't want yours.' Mrs Cunard was an Irishwoman abounding in humour, and this exchange immediately transformed her into a life-long friend. Oddly enough the same proved to be the case with her would-be rescuer on her first day out with the hounds. He was General Holland, and he and his family remained her affectionate admirers.

Nancy made no enemies at Market Harborough; this meant that it was not long before she had numerous suitors of honourable intention. Her surviving private letters contain a remarkably large number asserting undying love, often supported by maternal and sisterly pleas on behalf of the wooers. One of her Market Harborough suitors was a titled person. When news of his failure got around, 'I remember,' she wrote in her memoir, 'one hunting acquaintance, who himself looked longingly at the House of Lords, saying to me reprovingly: "I think you should realise, Mrs Shaw, that it is a very serious matter to refuse a peer." '

During this time of ephemeral love and wooing, two affairs of the heart stand in contrast. One concerns the persistence of an old love, the other the rising of a new and reciprocated one.

Angus McDonnell remained deeply in love with Nancy, and the fact that she only returned it with friendship gradually embittered him. There is an undated letter which was left for her on the boat and belongs to October 1904 when she sailed. A short quotation in which he refers to a proposal of marriage gives its spirit.

'I was a selfish beast even to have asked you, and you will see how selfish I am as this letter is all about myself. Now, Nannie, please do believe me when I tell you that I know you never gave me any encouragement, the only thing is you have been far too good for me. . . . Nannie, please don't bother and think I have got the humps, because I shall be quite all right, and you are doing a great kindness to me in that I can love you better than anything else in the world, and that through it I may one day develop into a man.'

One Angus letter of 1905 is somewhat puzzling. It is dated October 5th, about two months before she left America for a second hunting season in the Shires. It is very cheerful in tone. He was now working in a company of his own, of which Chillie had evidently been a generous backer. The letter glows with the good spirits of success. For some reason it seems to have irritated Nancy, though it is affectionate and in no conceivable way offensive. It may be that she preferred to hear from him the outpourings of unreturned love. On the other hand, he may have unknowingly made a wounding *gaffe*. She minuted the letter, obviously to her father: 'Do destroy this. It's really to show *you* how contented he seems – at least interested. I hope it's not wrong *my* reading it – !' The offending sentence was probably the following: 'Am so glad the hump is getting better, buck up and get something to do and it don't feel half as bad.' This reads as a flippant comment on an emotional wound which Nancy was suffering through a love-affair in England.

The man in the love-affair was Lord Revelstoke, whom Nancy had met in the hunting field during 1904. He was a man of attainments. On succeeding his father in 1897 at the age of thirty-four, he found that the family banking firm of Baring Brothers was in a feeble state, and on becoming a senior partner he set himself to restore its former prosperity and eminence. By prodigies of hard work and a flair for finance he succeeded in a remarkably short time: by the winter of 1904–1905 he was one of the leading bankers of England, indeed of Europe. He was to enjoy a wonderfully successful life except for one failure which he regretted to the end of his life.

He was a spectacular figure, admired in society as an impeccable dandy. When he drove from his house in Carlton House Terrace to Baring's Bank or the House of Lords, the exquisiteness of his brougham and horse and harness and coachman were such that the police instinctively cleared a way for him, as for royalty, regardless of the traffic situation. He was admired as a cultured man but he seems to have been without wit or much sense of humour. His dinner-parties were the subject of awed admiration, and he had one of the best cooks in London, the famous and beautiful Mrs Rosa Lewis. Early in their acquaintance he fell deeply in love with Nancy, and probably for the first time in her life, perhaps indeed for the only time, Nancy fell deeply in love too. She never quite forgot the failure of their mutual passion, though the failure was almost certainly of her doing, not his.

It remains one of the most enigmatical incidents in her life. The whole truth of the matter is probably lost for ever. It was for long the subject of gossip, but the accepted tales are contradicted by what evidence there is. That evidence is contained in Lord Revelstoke's letters to her. They are not always easy to interpret, as he was a man with a typically English incapacity to express himself, but they compose the only contemporary witness of what happened in the course of this strange story.

Her own letters to him have unfortunately been lost.

It is as well, nevertheless, to begin an account of this episode by giving Nancy's own record in outline.

After telling of the rejected lovers of Market Harborough, and the advice of the fervent lord-worshipper mentioned above, with other lightly considered amours, she suddenly announces: 'Then I fell in love, but not with the right man.' She says a little further on: 'I was deliriously happy, the way young people in love are happy.' Her father came to England for Christmas 1904 as he had promised. He met this immensely eligible suitor, and Nancy goes on to say: 'Father disapproved of him at sight. He saw through him. But I thought him an Apollo (although he was bald).'

She concludes the story thus: 'Little by little I came to my senses and discovered that he was an appalling snob. Other things also came to light. I had taken it for granted that he was an unattached bachelor, but he wasn't. He had been having an affair, that had gone on for years, with a married woman years older than he was. She had been away, and when she got back and heard what was in the air between him and me – I think she began to sow doubts in his mind. I don't know. That is what I believe must have happened. Though we had not become officially engaged, we had got as far as discussing our future together, and it was then that he asked me: "Do you really think that you could fill the position that would be required of my wife? You would have to meet kings and queens and entertain ambassadors. Do you think you could do it?"

'That was the death blow to my love for him. That was the end of

it, although he wrote to me for some time after I went back to Virginia.'

This version was not a fabrication. It is founded on facts, but the
letters throw a very different light on them.

The 'married woman years older than he was' is never mentioned
by name, or even referred to anonymously in Lord Revelstoke's
letters, and it is easy to infer that she was not mentioned in Nancy's
letters. She was Lady Desborough. It is undisputed that Lord Revelstoke felt a romantic devotion to her. So did other men, and it is
generally believed by the few people who remember her at that time,
that, in the fashion of the day which was still under the influence of
the Gothic revival, she played the part of a Queen of Beauty surrounded
by troubadourish admirers. It should perhaps be remembered that she
and her husband had been members of the 'Souls'. She had two
'court favourites', Lord Revelstoke and Evan Charteris.

If, in fact, Nancy's worst suspicions were justified, then one can only
say that Lord Revelstoke, as self-portrayed in his clumsily written
letters to her, was in a class of his own for hypocrisy and double-
dealing, and this is the absolute reverse of the impression that the letters
make on one. He emerges as a very naïve man; as a man of well-
educated but uninteresting mind, and completely straightforward. He
also emerges as a man so much in love with Nancy that to her lightest
and most unreasonable rebuke (for instance, she once scolded him for
replying with lack of warmth to a telephone call at 7.30 a.m.); to her
most unjustified tantrum he replied with positively servile apology, and
declared frequently that she was always in the right and that it was his
lasting joy to do her bidding in all things.

The dates are another important factor. The letters show that the
separation was not an abrupt affair caused by one remark which made
the scales fall from Nancy's eyes. After the hunting season Nancy went
on a motoring tour of France with Phyllis in April 1905, and after
returning to England she did not sail for the United States until early
July. This is the period where one would expect to find evidence of
the final breach. It is not there. Evidence does admittedly appear that
Nancy was treated to mischief-making gossip about her admirer, and
there is also some evidence of Nancy's love beginning to cool. For
example, at the time of the motoring tour Lord Revelstoke attended a
banking conference in Paris, from where he planned to go south to
Monte Carlo to meet the sisters; but the day in mid-April when he

was due to arrive in Monte Carlo was after the day when they were due to leave according to their schedule, so the unfortunate lover travelled to Monte Carlo to find that they had left the day before. He does not reproach her but sends her a good-humoured and loving letter in which his disappointment is merely mentioned. There is no sign of this incident being a portent of a breach. When she left for America on the 5th July 1905 he wrote: 'It's quite impossible to write today, Nancy dear. I simply can't. My heart is so full. Yours ever J.'

This letter of the 5th July was not delivered in time to catch her boat. It was followed by another sent on the 7th July, and here at last evidence of the breach begins to appear, though in a typically per-plexing way. In the first part of the letter he acknowledged one sent by her to him from Queenstown, and he describes it as 'a very sad little letter, and I hated knowing how sad you were when you wrote it'. The wording suggests that she sent a letter of sorrow at their parting, but this is quite wrong, for later there is a reference which makes it clear that her sadness was occasioned by a quarrel. The passage begins by mentioning her French maid Emma. Usually Emma appears as a figure of fun and private joking in the correspondence – for example, when she has had a hunting accident he sends a telegram to Market Harborough and signs it 'Emma' – but in this letter she is referred to seriously as a prime mischief-maker. He tells how he went to visit a woman friend of them both (name illegible) and continues: 'I can't tell you how good and understanding she was. She frankly told me she had been urging you to dismiss poor Emma entirely & that connection is I think perhaps in part responsible for the tone of your letter just received.' There had, it is true, been previous references to Emma's malign influence but all facetious, as all the subsequent ones were to be. The indications so far have been of minor tiffs; this letter indicates something serious.

From the 12th July till the 6th August he wrote nine letters to Nancy, and they seem to have led to his final downfall as a suitor. They are the least interesting of the whole collection and can be described as a dreary catalogue in nine sections of his social activities. Then on the 11th August 1905 he writes a letter in answer to what was evidently a bombshell from Nancy written to him on the 31st July from Mirador. In this letter she seems to have declared in definite terms for an end not only to their all but official engagement but to their friendship.

She seems from a remark in his reply to have insisted that they 'cannot go on like this'. Her grounds of complaint, as they dimly emerge, seem to have been two: first that his letters about London high society had been dull reading, and secondly (but not so clearly), that she had been disparaged by a friend of Lord Revelstoke, who had not defended her. Her rage had been thoroughly aroused and she requested him to discontinue writing to her.

His reply was written from Aix-les-Bains where he had gone for his health. The letter is characteristic. After acknowledgement he opens thus: 'I quite appreciate and understand every word you say, Nancy dear. You are very wonderful and golden, and you must know that my every wish must be to do what you tell me. I wrote you all those silly details about London not because I thought them of any interest but only because they concerned life to which you were close during the summer.' He moves on to the disparagement affair which he assures her, convincingly, was a misreport. He ends by imploring her to write again in a more friendly tone.

On the day after writing this letter he received another from Nancy, written, however, a day before the one he had answered, and though her letter of the 31st had come as a bombshell, this one of the 30th July was evidently yet harsher. But having withstood the shock of the first letter to arrive, he replies to this one in a slightly more confident spirit. Though he describes her as 'golden' and her evidently ferocious letter as 'angelic', he does defend himself a little more wholeheartedly. For example, he ends the letter thus: 'What possessed you to say you know I haven't missed you? How *little* you must know me really: I don't understand a great deal but I understand your angelic letter quite quite – Nancy, I'm very helpless here – What do you mean when you say "I don't know what I shall do – that's another story & not nearly such a nice one" – What is this when it's translated? Just fancy if *I* were to refer to *you* of "that is another story & not nearly such a nice one". What would you say of me? For life is simple, I think, as far as the big things are concerned & *I* have no "arrière pensée", or other plans or possibilities. I think from your letter of the 31st that you were sorry you'd written the one of the 30th. I will not write again as you tell me not to. But does that mean that you won't write to me? I did so love telling you all the 1000 poor little things that happen & I meant so well. What a pathetic failure I have been.'

Obedient as always, he refrained from writing to her for over three weeks from the 15th August. Then on the 7th September 1905 he is emboldened to write a long letter to her again, from his banking office in the City at 8 Bishopsgate Within. He has received two letters from her which he describes as a 'joy to receive' and the second as 'very *very* nice', though the internal evidence from his reply suggests that these descriptions were loosely applied. His letter of the 7th September is more revealing than most for now at last he appears to defend himself against the charge of infidelity (though Lady Desborough is never mentioned) and against the 'appalling snobbery' of his remark (dubiously reported by Nancy in 1951) about kings and queens and ambassadors. Here are his words on both subjects:

'You silly, there is no mystery at all – only "the impatience of youth" as you say. There is no "dreadful reason" for all this. If it hadn't been for that horrible summer things would have been very different. Nancy *doesn't* come after Russian loans, or 8 Bish (Within) or Aix. How can you pretend to think so. But you're ever *so* wrong, & got such an entirely false view, in thinking that "Kings and Queens" did, & you never believed what I still think, which is the very very *grave* responsibility of taking a young (quite young Emma)[1] & planting her in the middle of a busy life that *can't* be altered, for those Russian loans & Bish Gt, & everything else, would be there, & cannot be given up, even for Emma & it's all my wish for her to be golden. She *hates* them all I know, & always has: & I don't know how far her attraction and dear self wd enable her to stand them. You silly dear, you have been racking your little dear brain for "mysteries" & "dreadful reasons". I implored you long ago to look at something much more simple and obvious & straightforward. But you never would believe what I said, & stuffed yourself full of wild theories about impossible reasons. I have *told* you all the above, more than 20 times. I have a code to myself. I may be impossible and ridiculous. But my conviction must come, ere I do a thing which is after all so all important, and you may think me silly (but you won't, I know) that I value the question as to the constant and unfailing happiness of the person with me.'

After assurances of his sincerity he refers to an occasion in the spring when a gossip writer in the Press had hinted at their engagement, and he tells her the following: 'A man – an elderly man – said to me in the summer when that thing appeared in the D. Mail – "The only

1. Meaning Nancy of course.

thing I ask myself about you & – Emma – is that (I have not seen her very often) – the thing that principally has struck me about her (under her beauty, he added, with a charming little bow) is her enormous vitality & quickness, & I ask myself whether she could stand *you* & your many business preoccupations for the term of her natural life." It went like a knife into me, as it was a friend and not meant spitefully to me.'

The rest of the letter makes no new point, and assures her again that he deserves her trust. He says at one point: 'Perhaps I'm a silly idiot, but I *know* I'm honest.'

The letter was as far as he went in counter-offensive at any time. Some days before the 13th September he received another 'dear' letter from Nancy which he claims to have read with 'joy', though again the contents do not seem to have been delightful. She had received his letter of the 15th August and complained that it was not written on paper with a printed address (an odd objection considering that she had forbidden him to write at all) and she evidently pursued the matter of 'mysterious reasons' a little more explicitly, not having yet received his long letter of the 7th September. One brief passage from his reply is worth giving as it quotes something of what Nancy said on the major difference between them. 'I wrote you a long letter by the Camparia. I do hope it will disabuse your dear mind as to my "mysterious reasons" etc. My dear, there are none, and as to "my life being complete and there being no room", I wish you could see me now.'

After this letter the major issue, the rift between them, unexpectedly but unmistakably fades from the correspondence. His feelings towards her remained quite unchanged after the storm. What her feelings were towards him remain an unsolved riddle. The main part of the story ends here in the late autumn of 1905, and it may be as well to sum up the situation briefly, at this penultimate stage.

Nancy's 1951 draft makes it quite clear that she believed that Lady Desborough had intrigued against her, sowing doubts in his mind. The quotations given above show no signs of doubt on his side but rather of the agonising persistence of his love. The same is true of the whole of his correspondence, though after her second marriage his expressions of devotion are restrained and 'correct'. If Lady Desborough did try to break the attachment through possessive jealousy and disapproval of Americans (and having known the lady in her later years the writer finds this hard to accept) then she manifestly failed. His defence of his almost certainly misreported remark about 'Kings and Queens and ambassadors' rings true, and, unless the whole of this letter is a lie from beginning to end, is in fact much to his credit. Nancy had probably little notion of how the crushing routine of the social obligations attaching to big business, the wearisome public dinners with long speeches to finish with, the wearisome entertaining, not only of kings and queens but of a host of unsparkling colleagues of all nations, continuing without mitigation for years on end, might have been too much of a burden for her natural high spirits. She only knew the gayer side of his life. He was surely right to warn her of the grimmer side.

He comes out creditably too, to express a personal opinion, in his dismissal of the 'dreadful reasons', assuming that they refer to his relations with Lady Desborough. Such absolute denials, so artlessly expressed, with their frequent pleas to be trusted as his honesty deserved, cannot be made to read like the machinations of a deceiver. It is true that Shakespeare's Iago accomplished his will by insistence on his honesty, but he is renowned not only for polished hypocrisy but for the sharp observation and agility of mind without which hypocrisy cannot assume its necessary disguise. Lord Revelstoke was not a man of agile mind or fine observation.

To look for a moment at the other side. Nancy had been scared by marriage. In 1905 she was twenty-six and she had had excess of experience. As often happens in such a predicament she did not know her own mind. It was in her own mind, not in her lover's, that doubt had been sown. The indications are that she returned to America in July 1905 in a state of extreme emotional bewilderment. All this may be reasonably deduced from the remains of the correspondence. One may go further and say that if the correspondence had ended with the bombshells of the 30th and 31st of July 1905 there would be no enigma. But such was not the case. What, then, do the bombshells mean? The writer's own view is that they indicate the revived influence of her father who had no liking for Revelstoke. She submitted to his influence, but the love, whose reality she did not deny, had struck too deep to be summarily dismissed, as she attempted. Soon she was back with her hesitations. But there is further and more remarkable evidence of how deeply her feelings had been engaged, and that the love she had felt, even though it faded, left a lasting wound. It is certain that for more than twenty years after this she did not forgive Lady Desborough for a probably imagined crime.

As may be imagined, Nancy did not lack for other British suitors, some of whom were attractive to her. Among people whom she had come to know on close terms in London were Mr and Mrs Asquith. Before she left England in July 1905 she appears to have taken the very unusual step of asking Mr Asquith for advice as to which of her suitors she should marry. In early November she grew impatient and wrote to him demanding his considered and long-delayed opinion. He replied on the 12th November:

> 'You must not reproach me, my dear Mrs Shaw;
> It's not like a Redskin selecting a squaw;
> For there's no tougher problem, in logic or law
> Than to find a fit mate for the lady called Shaw.

'At this point my Muse deserted me, and I descended to the dusty highway of prose.

'I was very glad to get your letter yesterday (you see how prompt I am in replying); for I had rather be scolded for imaginary sins than be altogether forgotten.

'You would have adopted a gentler and more patient tone if you had known or guessed – as you ought to have done, for what is a woman worth who is without these finer & subtler intuitions? – what hours of hard but futile thinking, of eager but baffled searching, I have given to the fulfilment of my promise. More than once I have felt sure that I was on the eve of the Great Discovery, and as I was arranging that the gentleman should be photographed, I awoke & found that it was only a dream.

'I have not abandoned the quest, but I am less hopeful than I was. So many qualities are needed; and when it comes to the fruit in any particular case I find that the one thing lacking is the one thing needful. Can it be that I am over-fastidious? or even a little jealous? Impossible!

'Anyhow I hope that you will soon turn your back on the farm, and make tracks across the Atlantic, and give me a few hints that will ease and help my task. Will you?

'Yours very sincerely H.H.A.'

Mr Asquith's letter, addressed to 'Rirados (?), Greenwood, Virginia' (an eloquent comment on Nancy's difficult handwriting), appears to be the only one he ever sent her. At any rate it is the only one to survive, but any silence on the part of the statesman was within the next few years to be compensated by a host of letters from his wife Margot.

The decision for which Nancy had invoked Mr Asquith's help was to be made for her very soon after receiving his letter. She did not leave America for England and a second hunting season till December 1905. This time she was accompanied by her father, and among their fellow-passengers was Mr Waldorf Astor. He was the son of Mr William Waldorf Astor, the major heir to the vast family inheritance. After meeting with political disappointment in his own country, and following a diplomatic career as United States representative in Rome, William Waldorf Astor had decided that he preferred the old to the new world and had settled since 1889 in England. At the time of his appointment to Rome in 1882 his son Waldorf was only three; his childhood was spent on the continent of Europe, after which he and his younger brother John Jacob were given an entirely English education, from a preparatory school to Eton, finishing with New College, Oxford. Waldorf was an Englishman by circumstances, though not technically British until he was twenty, when his father took out naturalisation papers in 1899. Waldorf was at that time an under-graduate at New College.

William Waldorf Astor does not play a very large part in Nancy's life, but it was an interesting one, and the reader should know something about him. He was a conservative of conservatives, and had become a moody recluse after the early death of his wife in 1891, though he never lost his vitality or his strong imagination and deter-mination. He was the author of two historical novels, one called *Valentino* (about Cesare Borgia), published in 1885, the second *Sforza*, published in 1889. Much later in 1889 he published a set of short stories under the title of *Pharaoh's Daughter and Other Stories*. They all, in conformity with the fashion of the day, are disfigured by plentiful tushery, in fact a tale of the Napoleonic wars in his last volume contains the sentence 'Tush fool! Think you to bandy reasons with a Czar?' His books are interesting today mainly as expressions of a deep romantic strain, the same strain as caused him to buy the great and historical house of Cliveden in 1893, and later the ancient castle of Hever; the strain that led him to turn his back on the pushing, modern United States and on his native New York above all.

He was an autocrat in his numerous households, in Lansdowne

House (which he rented for some years), in Cliveden, Hever, in his Italian villa near Sorrento, and in his original London house and office on the Victoria Embankment. His word was law and he demanded rigid obedience from his family, his retinue, his professional staff, and his guests who, according to Michael Astor, did not for that reason much enjoy his hospitality. He held sway over his own in the manner of his hero Napoleon or one of those Italian princes who fascinated him. As happens to most men of autocratic temper, his self-will led him into some failures. In 1892 he became a newspaper proprietor. He bought the *Pall Mall Gazette* and with brilliant flair appointed Henry Cust as his editor, though Cust had at that time no experience of journalism of any kind. Harry Cust rapidly assembled a shining company of contributors, including Kipling, Wells, Barrie, Charles Whibley, George Street and Alice Meynell. Circulation increased and the 'P.M.G.' soon became the leading evening newspaper in the country. But Cust was not a tactful or obedient editor, and from time to time he either disregarded his chief's instructions regarding policy or interpreted them so loosely as amounted to the same thing. Furthermore, he rejected William Waldorf's own contributions as beneath the required literary standards, though he did publish a few in the weekly edition known as the *Pall Mall Budget*. In 1896 William Waldorf Astor requested his resignation. This Cust refused and he was dismissed. The *Pall Mall Gazette* did not recover till fifteen years later when William Waldorf Astor saddled himself with another equally intractable editor.

His sons inherited their father's strong will, with the inevitable result that as they reached manhood they rebelled, his eldest son, according to Michael Astor, going so far that one day he 'turned round and told his parent that he, with his antiquated notions, could go to Hell'. The shock to Mr Astor must have been immense, but Waldorf's unfilial rising did not lead to estrangement. Mr Astor loved his son, but his nature was so essentially inward, uncommunicative, and apparently cold, that he could not give his children the sympathy they needed at the age when sympathy is most precious.

Waldorf Astor had inherited his father's seriousness, some of his obstinacy with his strong will, but not his father's melancholy. From his youth he had felt a deep sense of obligation and the duty of public service of an enlightened kind, such as was not to be traced, or at any rate in any marked degree, in his father. At this time, when he was twenty-six, he was undecided as to his course in life. Already he had met good fortune, success, and what looked like disaster. His early years had been filled with promise. At Eton he had done wonderfully well ending with a high pass mark into Oxford and New College. But serious as he was, Waldorf Astor was not a mere sobersides and he showed that he was not free from temptations towards frivolity. The delights of Oxford retarded his ascent, and the story of his university days is rather one of hunting, riding to the drag (of which he became Master), polo and fencing (in both of which he represented Oxford), and the pleasures of the Bullingdon Club, rather than one of steady application. At Oxford he even began his racing career and as an undergraduate laid the foundations of the bloodstock stud and stable which was to achieve fame. In fact, he did so little work that he only just scraped through the schools with a fourth class degree. But his university career was not regarded as one of failure. He emerged from it with the reputation of a first class sportsman.

Within three years of his leaving Oxford in 1902, he had to abandon all personal part in his sporting recreations. A weakness of the heart had already been detected soon after his schooldays and he had had to give up rowing while at Oxford. An angina condition was now diagnosed and with it a tendency towards tuberculosis. Early in 1905 he had to give up hunting and polo, and indeed all strenuous exercise, including winter sports in Switzerland of which he had become an early enthusiast. His sister Pauline's marriage in 1904 had taken from him his closest companion. When he sailed from America on the same boat as Nancy he was recovering from the strain of accumulated ill fortune such as might have crushed many men. But his sense of purpose, though now more than ever before without direction, remained unweakened. From his young days to his last he had a modest, very quiet manner through which an inner strength of character and will were visible. It was something that was lacking in both Angus McDonnell and Lord Revelstoke. Waldorf Astor could never be abject.

Nancy and he met on the boat, and Nancy recorded this solemn moment in her life with characteristic lack of solemnity. 'I am not a good sailor, and I remember putting Amos Laurence off when he came one day and said young Waldorf Astor was on board and wanted to meet me. I said later on perhaps. So Waldorf wooed Father. He knew what he wanted. It seems he had made up his mind he was going to marry me. A clever man can always find more ways than one of getting what he wants. Waldorf knew all the ways. He was very good-looking and he had, and still has, immense courtesy and very great personal charm. He soon had Father eating out of his hand.'

Characteristically she forgot to mention the most important incident of the voyage, namely the moment when she did meet Waldorf Astor. She was immediately attracted to him. The friendship continued ashore all the more easily as Nancy and her father knew many of his relations. He and Nancy were exactly the same age, having both been born on the same day of 1879.

They saw a great deal of each other though their most natural meeting-place, the hunting field, was now denied to Waldorf. Little is known of the details of their early relationship because so few of their letters of this time have survived, and Nancy's only reference in her memoir is not only very brief but not very clear as to meaning. She said, 'All that winter he was somewhere around, and we got to know each other better. When spring came I said to Father, "I must either marry someone over here, or go home." '

In spite of her new and strong emotional interest the correspondence between her and Lord Revelstoke continued. She was a hard task-mistress, and though the notion of marrying him was now remote from her mind, this did not mean that she granted him his manu-mission. It was not a thing that she granted easily to anyone at any time.

The correspondence showed little change of character. On arrival in England he gave her a dog which he had been keeping for her. A little before the 17th December 1905 he sent and she accepted another gift, a Shetland pony for her little boy. The tone of the letters and these accepted gifts indicate a fully maintained relationship. Then suddenly on the 22nd December he sends her a letter of grief, obscurely expressed as usual, and open to a variety of interpretation, but manifestly written after receiving first news of her new romance. Here is the main text:

'I want so much to thank you for being so golden & understanding: for I think you must have known how much I heard today which I did not know before: and as for me I like to think that you understood the reasons why I have been so unhappy. Much more deeply unhappy than I hope you will ever have any idea of.

'I only trust that you feel I have *some* excuse. I told you all today & I meant from the very bottom of my heart every single word I said. Shall you be able to send me a little line here to tell me you know I did?'

The little line she did send was not purely anodyne to judge by his next letter on Christmas Eve. It would seem that, not having received his pathetic letter of the 22nd, she wrote him a scolding letter to Chatsworth because he was spending Christmas there with the Cavendish family and not in London where he could entertain her. His reply from Chatsworth, which could with reason have been indignant, was even more than usually abject. After some preliminaries about bad posts 'at this festive season', he goes on to say: 'Your dear letter of Friday also reached me: I am grieved at your being [displeased] at my coming here: but you will be fair, I am sure. You always are. Remember I've constantly spent Xmas here for 10 years. I *didn't* last year, & hurt the old D[uke of Devonshire]'s feelings very much. This year he enquired particularly whether I was coming weeks before there was any idea of your coming over. I said I would. It is very probably the last time as he is getting very frail & has been a very old & good friend to me.

'It seems so desperately hard to do what is right. I never seem able to do so, or to please anyone. I am deeply unhappy – that's why I asked you if you realized but surely you do – what this means to me.'

The epilogue to this story is involved; though open to brief and tidy description, the event itself was far from tidy, and it would occupy much space to relate in detail; here only the main facts are given. The difference over the Chatsworth Christmas party was evidently soon resolved, and his New Year letter to her (accompanied by more gifts) shows him as a wooer in competition with Waldorf Astor. He says characteristically: 'I know that whatever you decide will be right.' She was not yet engaged to Waldorf Astor; she had not yet made up her mind, and his hopes though visibly failing were not dead. Through January and the first half of February his letters continue, deeply affectionate, ponderously humorous on occasion, always worshipping, but never very interesting. (A letter of the 11th February 1906 referring to 'Rosie' being in trouble with the police does not refer, as a first reading may excitingly suggest, to Mrs Lewis, but to a horse of that name.)

On the 19th February he wrote her two letters, the second asserting the sincerity of the earlier one which is a significant and moving document. For the first time in the course of the correspondence he makes her a definite proposal of marriage. Judging from his answer of the 22nd to her refusal, she seems to have rejected him in harsh terms. For once he does not describe her letter as golden, dear or understanding. He says: 'I found your letter when I got home last night, written I thought by a different Nancy to that one who talked to me on Monday – and you never telephoned.' The proposal was not renewed, but the correspondence continued. Lord Revelstoke's hopes must now have appeared to him ruined beyond repair, but Nancy had not yet decided on her future. It appears that she may have ultimately made up her mind because of a singular intervention from outside, which should now be considered.

Waldorf Astor had not had a career of gallantry, but he retained a warm attachment to a woman famous for her beauty and vivacity and spectacular position. She was Crown Princess Marie of Rumania, the granddaughter of Queen Victoria through her second son, and the wife of Prince Ferdinand of Hohenzollern-Sigmaringen who had been adopted by his uncle, King Carol I, as heir to the Rumanian throne. In his diplomatic days William Waldorf Astor had become friends with the King of Rumania and Queen 'Carmen Sylva' as she liked to be known, the latter and Mr Astor having literary interests in common. He would take his children with him on visits to Bucharest and these occasions were immensely welcome to the Crown Princess who by her own account suffered perpetual homesickness for England and was not reconciled to the dismal and meretriciously splendid life which she was compelled to follow in her new country. She grew very attached to the three young Astors: Waldorf, his brother John and their sister Pauline, but especially to Waldorf who was near her age, being only four years her junior.

Marie of Rumania has been much mocked by the world, but she deserved its sympathy. She is foremost a tragic figure. Following the iniquitous dynastic customs of her time, she was married in 1893, when she was not yet eighteen years old, to a man whom she hardly knew and who was in love with another woman. She was exiled from then on. She was beautiful, vivacious, clever, of good heart and of a mind that might have been admirable if it had been allowed to develop. Unlike many of the royal sisterhood she was intelligent enough to understand the wrong that had been done to her, and she was not, at this time at any rate, reconciled to the 'gaudy humdrum', or to the deprivation of a wide circle of friends and contemporaries, to which dead political traditions had condemned her. She was threatened by suffocation and her much criticised exhibitionism was a gesture of escape. Her friendship with the young Astors was like a breeze in a

shut prison. It has been said by knowing people that her feelings for
Waldorf were romantic. They probably were. It has been said that
his feelings for her were likewise tinged with romance. They probably
were. When a handsome, interesting young man and a lovely, interesting young woman become friends and no tinge of romance is to be
detected, the only explanation is that they both come under the heading
of cold fish.

Nancy's attraction to Waldorf and his love for her soon began to
be talked about. As mentioned, the unhappy Revelstoke evidently
knew about it as early as December 1905. The news reached the Crown
Princess through Waldorf's letters to her. She knew about his recent
misfortunes and the prospect of his marrying a woman with whom
he was passionately in love gladdened her. It seems that in the second
half of February she was inaccurately informed that Waldorf and Nancy
were definitely engaged, and on the 20th she was moved to write a
long letter to Nancy whom she had never met. It began: 'Dear Mrs
Shaw, I hope it won't seem strange to you getting a letter from me,
but since many years now Pauline and "Mr Anne" as we call Mr Astor
have been such great friends of mine that I cannot but take very great
part in the happiness that has now come to him. It is difficult writing to
someone one does not really know, but Mr Anne has told me so much
about you in his letters that I feel in a way as if I *did* know you. He has
been through hard times because of a good deal of bad luck, ill health
and disappointments, and so it is the greatest joy for his friends to think
that such happiness is now soon in store for him.' She pleads that she
may be accepted as a friend. 'I hope you won't mind my having written,'
the letter ends, 'and my repeating that I'm longing to know you.
Marie.'

For a princess to write thus was no doubt unconventional by the
standards of the time, but on the 27th February she was moved to a
greater breach of custom. News had reached her after sending her letter
that not only were Waldorf and Nancy not engaged but that Nancy
had after all decided against the marriage. She now took it on herself
to write an apologia for her friend, and to plead in passionate terms
with Nancy not to reject his love. The letter is long, about twelve
hundred words, and of considerable interest for what it tells of Waldorf's early life and for its conscious and unconscious autobiographical
touches. One cannot but respect the writer, as one must respect anyone
who is careless of a rebuff in a good cause. The letter ends: 'I hope you

will try and consider me a friend – I know it seems an awfully un-conventional thing to have done but forgive me. Marie.'

Not having received an answer by the 2nd March she sent a tele-gram: 'Hope my letter reached you safely and that it will help you to see that you could rely on having true help for you and your boy and a happy peaceful life. Marie.'

The Crown Princess's next letter, written to Nancy on the 7th March, shows that her intervention had been decisive. 'I so well understand all your hesitations,' she wrote. 'It's a big step to take and one that can't be decided hurriedly when one is not quite sure of one's own feelings. We had almost given up hope, and I could not reasonably hope that my letter would make such a difference, but if it helped ever so little you can imagine how happy it makes me as I would have done anything to try [?] Waldorf's happiness for him.'

To meet Nancy became an obsession with the Crown Princess, as her numerous subsequent letters show again and again, but in the event they did not meet till the summer of 1911. This was Nancy's doing. She was suspicious of a woman who knew Waldorf Astor so well, probably better than any other. When Nancy was not herself generous she tended to be the reverse, for moderation was alien to her. She repaid the Crown Princess's offer of friendship and her reckless generosity not only with suspicion but with calumny, though the worse of these two was probably due to thoughtlessness later in life when her memory was unreliable; but it was a sad, unworthy outcome. Happily Marie of Rumania never knew of these subsidiary results of her wonderfully indiscreet intervention. She only knew of the main result and rejoiced at its success.

On the 8th March 1906 Nancy telegraphed to her father, who was getting anxious about her future, to the effect that he could publish news of her engagement to Waldorf Astor. He informed the Press immediately, and on the 9th March *The Times* announced that 'a telegram through Lattair's agency from Richmond Virginia says: "The engagement is announced of Mrs Nannie Shaw, formerly Miss Langhorne, to Mr Waldorf Astor, son of Mr W. Waldorf Astor of London. . . . The marriage will take place in the spring."' No other or more official announcement was made.

On the day before, on the 8th March, Nancy had written to Lord Revelstoke to tell him of her final decision, and he sent her a suitable and sorrowful reply. She had evidently told him that a meeting would be painful for both, but in his answer, while saying that he understood that 'the strain' might be too much for her, he renewed his plea. 'I should like to see you,' he wrote. 'It is impossible, so impossible to write of anything.' They did meet a week or so later judging from a letter of the 18th March in which he thanks her for returning his handkerchief and promises to send her a second volume of Browning's poems. He ends pathetically: 'I have no plans for now or indeed for any time.'

They continued to meet during the next five weeks. On the 2nd April he wrote to her about his wedding present to her, a diamond bow modelled on a piece in the crown jewels of Louis XV. On the 16th he gave expression to his grief. He sent her a short note telling her that he had received a promised locket enclosing some of her hair, and mentioning the not relevant news that he had recently been to Paris once more, in connection with the Russian loan. In the left-hand top corner of its single page is written: 'This all *awful* to me', and the letter ends, 'I am very low & wretched'. On the 18th April he sent her the diamond bow. On the 2nd May, the day before her marriage, he sent by messenger his last letter to Nancy Shaw.

'My dearest Nancy,

'I met the little boy on the step just now bringing your note. God bless you, always. I shall *never* forget – & shall never be able to tell what I feel, except, *Bless* you, for ever and always. Your J.' And thus, though he continued to write to her at long intervals, that part of her story finally closed. He never married. She never believed in his sincerity, or so she came to think.

On the 3rd May 1906, Nancy married Waldorf Astor. She had had a private interview with the Bishop of London who, after hearing the circumstances of her divorce, issued permission in her favour for the full Anglican marriage ceremony to be celebrated in any church of his diocese. The wedding took place in All Souls Church, Langham Place. William Waldorf Astor was unwell and could not attend, so on their way to Dover by motor the bridal pair called at Hever Castle to see him. For their honeymoon they went to Cortina in the Swiss Tyrol.

A main source of information, indicated throughout, continues to be Lady Astor's 1951 autobiographical draft. The opinion of her hidden melancholy is drawn from conversations with Mrs Alice Longworth, Mrs Gordon Smith and other people who knew her at this period of her life. Mrs Trigg Brown's essay is the authority for the incident of the housekeeper at Mirador. All episodes involving Angus McDonnell are deduced from his aforementioned essay and his letters in the Astor archive. The account of Lady Astor's adventures at Market Harborough are drawn from her 1951 draft, references in her correspondence of the time, but chiefly from an essay by the late Victor Cunard written for Michael Astor and used by him in his book, *Tribal Feeling*. The account of Lady Astor's relationship with Lord Revelstoke is again taken from her memoir but, as indicated, chiefly from the collection of his letters in the Astor archive. From this is also taken the letter from Mr Asquith. Additional information has also been given by personal friends of Lady Desborough and Lord Revelstoke, who prefer to be unnamed. The brief account of William Waldorf Astor is taken from *Tribal Feeling*, *Incredible New York*, by Lloyd Morris (New York, 1951), and *Nancy Astor*, by Maurice Collis. The account of his son, Waldorf Astor (later the 2nd Viscount Astor), is taken from the same authorities, but chiefly from the letters of Crown Princess (later Queen) Marie of Rumania to Lady Astor, the only full contemporary account, so far as I know, of Lady Astor's husband. These letters also belong to the Astor Archive. The reference to Henry, usually known as Harry Cust, is taken from *Tribal Feeling* and *Orientations*, by Ronald Storrs (London, 1937). Details of Queen Marie's marriage are taken from *Queen Mary*, by James Pope Hennessy (London, 1959).

Chapter 6

A NEW LIFE

FROM the day when she married Waldorf Astor, Nancy's legendary life began. Before May 1906 she had made an impression wherever she was, but from this time on the impression had repercussions far beyond her acquaintance, and myths multiplied as rapidly and widely as the remarkable reality made its impact. To distinguish myth from the reality is not always easy.

She was at the very height of good fortune; things had indeed gone well for her. She had married the heir to one of the richest men in the world, and in unusual circumstances. With her idiosyncratic, intensely American character she might never have found happiness in a marriage not with a fellow American, and in her husband she found one who was also an established citizen of the England with which she had fallen in love at first sight. She recorded that on her engagement she was in fear of her intimidating father-in-law who had not disguised an earlier hope that his eldest son would marry the daughter of some noble English house, but in the event her fears were illusory. Mr Astor took to her instantly.

The famous portrait of her as a young married woman, painted by John Sargent in 1908, tells all one needs to know about how she met her new prospects in the world. The picture has been adversely criticised as superficial, but why should the likeness of a radiantly happy young woman plumb the depths of human destiny?

The reality of her happiness in her marriage to Waldorf Astor is not in any doubt. It was not a love match in the usual meaning of the phrase. She did not marry him, as she had nearly married Lord Revelstoke and as she had married Robert Shaw, because she was swept off her feet. It was not a calculated marriage of convenience either: she was not a calculating person. That social ambition and the prospect of great wealth played no part in her choice is, of course, not to be maintained. Both meant much to her, but it is to misinterpret the very essence of Nancy to suppose that she sacrificed her life to such things. To express a personal view which has had acceptance among people who knew Nancy best, it has seemed to the writer that she and her husband were bound together by a deep sense of need. There was so much of emotionalism in her being; self-control came to her with such difficulty and wilfulness so easily, that she might have wasted her talents in exhibitionist absurdity and lost what was finest in herself, without a person of well-disciplined, clear, single-purposed mind as her continual companion and guide.

In Waldorf Astor she had such a companion. But he too stood in danger from his own temperament, and from this Nancy saved him as effectively as he saved her. Like all men of severe and earnest mind he might have developed the repellent features of Puritanism: he could conceivably have become a stiff, unsympathetic kind of man. People who knew them were often surprised that he appeared to enjoy her wild fooling, supposing that, with his own correctness, he must have been made uneasy by her loud defiance of convention. The truth was more or less the opposite of this. None of what has been put forward here is open to proof. It is only claimed that some such psychological balance as indicated above can go some way towards explaining how two people, who were as different as can be imagined, found trust, understanding and happiness in each other.

William Waldorf Astor treated his son and daughter-in-law with lavish generosity. He made an enormous settlement of money on him, and as his principal wedding present he gave them his beloved Cliveden which thereafter became their principal home. They were to have other houses as well, but their names were and remain more closely associated with Cliveden than with any other, and they associated themselves thus too.

It is a house of arresting outward splendour, perfectly sited on its immense terrace which crowns a hill overlooking a graceful curve in the River Thames above Windsor and Maidenhead. The original house, sometimes known as Cliefdon, was built in the 1660s by the second Duke of Buckingham who was followed as owner or tenant by several eminent persons, none of great historical account, but including as a matter of some interest a Governor of Virginia, Lord Orkney, and 'Poor Fred', the Prince of Wales who was father to George III. This first house was destroyed by fire in 1795, not rebuilt till 1824, after which it was yet again burnt down in 1849. Of the original Buckingham house nothing now remains except the terrace. The present house is the work of the greatest of Victorian architects, Charles Barry. He built it in 1850 for the Duke of Sutherland, using the Italian style which he understood more perfectly than any of his British contemporaries. His lordly creation evokes with consummate skill and without mere imitation the baroque magnificence of the Restoration, enhanced by a stately Latin inscription running round the entire top course of the main walls. The inscription celebrates with Roman terseness and Roman numerals the history of the house, and was drafted (one may be surprised to learn) by Mr Gladstone. Modern Cliveden is of gigantic size and imperious character, seeming arrogantly to proclaim a perpetuity of family tenure, but in fact, compared with other great English country houses, it has never been the residence of a single family for very long, and the tenure of the Astors beginning with William Waldorf's purchase from the Duke of Westminster in 1893, to the death of his grandson in 1966, is the only episode in the history of Cliveden during which a single family lived there as the owners in the course of three consecutive generations.

Within, the house remains less to the taste of the present than does the classic exterior. Most people find the great hall too self-consciously impressive to be a happy place; indeed, the portrait of Nancy by Sargent hanging in a corner strikes a jarring note of cheerfulness.

Beyond the hall the main ground floor rooms are more elegant and pleasing. They are decorated extravagantly in the Italian classical style of the late nineteenth century, full of colour, owing much to inlay of the most perfect workmanship, but the visitor does not meet irresistible beauty till he reaches the south-west corner. Here is the dining-room, the masterpiece of the Cliveden interior. It is furnished with materials bought by William Waldorf Astor, French carved panelling and other wall decoration of the eighteenth century, and a main table, chairs and sideboards of the same date, originally made for the hunting lodge at Asnières of Madame de Pompadour whose bust stands on the marble mantelpiece.

To this princely home Waldorf and Nancy Astor added not long after marriage a London house of the eighteenth century, 4 St James's Square, which stands on the east side. Later, in 1911, they built a country house for themselves at Sandwich, and this house, built in the tasteless but cosy style of its period, was used for golfing holidays. They named it Rest Harrow. In time they also bought a sporting property in Scotland, in Glencoe, which they sold later in favour of one on the island of Jura, and in 1909 they bought their famous house in

Plymouth. So much private ownership of houses was in no sense typical of any kind of person then, but it was not so extraordinary or rare then as now. This is a point that must be stressed or one can have a very fallacious idea of the position occupied by Mr and Mrs Astor in society. So much ownership was indeed much criticised, but then it was not generally or instinctively disapproved by ordinary opinion.

Nancy loved Cliveden from her first days as its mistress (she hardly knew it before), and yet strangely enough, with her intense devotion to home, which had already found expression in her love of Mirador, she had a certain insensitiveness to her surroundings. She was, one may perhaps say, too egocentric to pay them the attention that they expect of a lover of houses. Her niece Nancy Lancaster once said to her (long after this time), 'You never blend into a room or an atmosphere, Nannie – you can be like an electric bulb switched on suddenly in a room lit by candles.' It followed that she was not daunted by Cliveden; rather did she meet the challenge of the place with her own aggressive force of character. 'The Astors have no taste' was her typical and uncompromising judgement on the labours of her father-in-law, and she proceeded to undo much of them.

She not only swept contents away but attacked the very edifice itself. From the hall she ordered a mass of stone antiquity to be removed; Roman statues and busts and stupendous wine jars and sarcophagi. 'The keynote of the place when I took over,' so Nancy recorded in 1951, 'was splendid gloom. Tapestries and ancient leather furniture filled most of the rooms. The place looked better when I had put in books and chintz curtains and covers, and flowers.' She had the entire floor of the hall, an Italian mosaic stone design, dug up and replaced by comfortable parquet, and another of her father-in-law's favourite importations removed at the same time: an Italian ceiling in the dining-room, painted under William Waldorf Astor's personal direction, representing an Olympian banquet, the whole executed in imitation of French eighteenth century style. This dubious work of art was replaced by authentic ceiling decoration of the time of Louis XV. Nancy raged through the house like a refining fire, but though she accomplished much and brought the dining-room to perfection, she could not wholly expel the 'splendid gloom' imposed by her predecessor. When he gave Cliveden to her and her husband he told her that he intended never to return to the house which he had owned and loved and refashioned.

The work on the house began very soon after they returned from their honeymoon in Italy and Switzerland. In the middle of the summer of 1906 they left England again, this time for America, for Virginia, the plan being that Waldorf Astor should meet Nancy's relatives and friends and see her native land. He had never been to Virginia before.

Though they were so very different, he and Chillie had become mutual admirers and firm friends, though this does not mean that they necessarily knew each other well. Waldorf had not seen Chillie on his home ground, and he saw him now, as though on a magnified scale, fairly revelling in an occasion for every extreme of Virginian hospitality. When it was known that this famous newly wedded pair were to visit her father, and that the latter was to entertain for her, there was as much pressure for invitations as there was willingness on the host's part to extend them. In the course of their long stay from late summer to early autumn two parties were held in succession to celebrate the visit, one at Mirador and one at the Williams' house, a quarter of a mile or so away on the hill opposite. Each party began in the afternoon and lasted to the next dawn. Each was on a sumptuous scale.

Nancy rushed round Mirador greeting family friends, 'uncles' and 'aunts', horses and dogs, in a happy daze. She took her beloved Aunt Liza aside and showed her photographs of Cliveden, explaining to her that this was her new home, and 'Oh, Miss Nancy!' exclaimed her old nurse, 'you'se sho' done outmarried yo'self!'

Her husband could not but find the occasion a strange one, and it was noticed that he did not disguise some perplexity at the mixture of old world courtesy and wild disregard of convention that marked the celebrations. There had been no harsh scrutiny of guests by Chillie, and those he entertained included at least one highly eccentric figure of American society, a gentleman of fortune who had migrated from Virginia to the North but had later found it politic to return to his native state, having been certified insane by a court of law in New York, a decision not supported by the courts of Virginia. He arrived on this occasion to stay, not at Mirador, but with the Williams family, bringing with his other baggage a 'shoe shine box', filled not with brushes and polish but with cooked peas. He explained to the servants that this was all the food that he would require during his visit and that he did not propose to attend the household meals. He met none of the other guests, not even the bride and bridegroom, but kept to his room, making only one appearance when, on the night of the dance given at the

Williams' house, this Edward Lear figure was seen in the small hours waltzing gracefully and alone round the lawn.

The bride and bridegroom returned to England by the *Cedric* in the second half of September. On the 19th her father wrote one of his few letters to Nancy which has survived:

'My dear Nannie,

'I won't say how I have missed you for fear you may return. (How is this for an Irish bull?) Realy I am almost sory I let you come to Mirador the parting was such a rench for me. We are getting on very well. Nora is trying her best at house keeping & I am keeping buisy. Catherine has just been phoned for to come home as her farther was dieing. To add to our depression its been raining for two days. I read your little note & today also a nice letter from Waldorf which please thank him for. I sent the Ham Pickle & Apples to you at the boat & hope you & Waldorf may enjoy them. Take good care of your self & rest up or you will be old and ugly before your time. Don't let Bobbie forget me & be as nice to Waldorf as he is to you. Good by my dear. I didn't realize how I loved you till you left me. Send me your address & see Irene as soon as you can. Give Waldorf my best love & kiss Bobbie for me.

'Affecty C. D. Langhorne.'

On the sea voyage home Nancy had an illuminating experience. The crossing, she recorded in 1951, 'took eleven days at that time, and it was terribly hot. . . . I did not go down to dinner one night. I went out on deck where it was quiet and cool. Presently, one by one, some of the men came up from below to get some air. They were all ordinary seamen, and I got talking to them. Before I had finished there were eight or ten of them and we argued about this and that and discussed things in general. They told me their troubles and I told them mine. We talked politics too.

'Presently the people came up from the dining saloon, and stood listening. One man, a parson from Brooklyn, leaned on the rail on the upper deck and watched us. He said, "I would give my life to be able to do what that girl is doing down there."

'That was the first time I knew I could do it.'

The discovery was one that she was sure to have made quite soon. It was some time before she acted on it.

Her father's letter to her makes allusion to illness, and consequent need of rest. Such allusions could be multiplied fiftyfold at least.

From her girlhood her health had been the cause of anxiety and she had been treated as a person needing special care. She had, for example, been denied the pleasure or ordeal of a coming-out ball as it was feared that the strain might be too much for her. In all memories of her young Virginian days there are references to puzzling breakdowns: she was liable to sudden nervous reactions which left her in a state of exhaustion, and these were often accompanied by severe headaches. Hopes that her uncertain health was a young weakness which would vanish with maturity were disappointed, and four years after this time, in her thirties, her frequent relapses into invalidism became alarming.

It was thus her fate that she shared ill-health with her husband. It was as though with the abounding good fortune meted out to them, the heartless gods with classic Olympian malice denied them the gift most needed to enable them to enjoy it. This young, ambitious and gifted man found himself confronted with the prospect of leading the pleasing but tame life of an invalid country gentleman, and saying goodbye not only to the sporting recreations in which he excelled but to all the enticing prospects of 'the great career', which but a moment before had seemed to be within his reach. She had the prospect of sharing his retirement.

Nancy never liked a tame life. She was determined, as she owned candidly to Mrs Longworth, that the cruel handicaps suddenly imposed on her husband would somehow be overcome and that he would nevertheless have a public career of the utmost eminence. She showed again (if a former analysis is correct) that she could supply a need, in this instance a recklessly courageous will to conquer. She fairly infused her own passionate determination into her husband, and, according to the account she gave to Mrs Longworth, she did so with ruthless and even threatening aggressiveness. But here one can easily misjudge their mutual situation. Waldorf Astor was not a respectable version of Macbeth: he was not a man who was only galvanised into action by the ambition of his stronger-souled wife. His ambition was as vigorous as hers, and he was as possessed of as stern a will, but a rational will, and he sought for the rational outcome. She had the irrationality of a wilful appetite, and she sought not the reasonable or unreasonable outcome but the one which satisfied it. She had the instinctive wisdom which makes those who have it defy fate, and he was gladly led by it.

They discussed their future and reached an important decision. Regardless of the fact that he was liable to periods of complete physical prostration, Waldorf would enter the House of Commons and aim at a statesman's career. On her initiative, according to her 1951 memoir, they discussed the matter with two friends, Arthur Balfour and Lord Curzon. Of his political convictions at the time Nancy wrote in 1951: 'Like so many people of that day, Waldorf was at heart a Liberal, but he liked the Conservative programme.'

Waldorf's proposal to stand for Parliament was conveyed to Party headquarters with the approbation of the Conservative leader. The result was the immediate offer of a safe Conservative seat, but Waldorf refused it. This was not his way. He had no wish to be numbered among those convenient Party members, more esteemed for their contributions to Party funds than for reasoned political conviction. He knew that he was politically inexperienced and he wished first of all to learn. He was the most methodical of men. As early as his first days after leaving the university, when he had already begun to establish his bloodstock stud, he made a close study (which he never relinquished) of Mendelian theory and for a while apprenticed himself to a veterinary surgeon. So now he decided that after a period of thorough study in the Conservative Central Office, he would face the challenge of contesting a seat where victory was at least uncertain and thus add substantially to his first-hand knowledge of political strife. As a result he did not contest a seat till 1910. It may be that when the Whips found that the new recruit was not as docile as they might wish, they did not bestir themselves to accommodate him in a hurry, and that this accounts for a rather surprisingly long interval between his decision and his entry into the lists. One must not forget, however, the delaying struggle, never successful, to overcome his ill-health.

The first three and a half years of their married life form a period when public affairs played less part in it than any other. As with all other young married couples they were largely occupied with the organisation of their home, in this instance, of course, on the great scale of the Astor fortune. Nancy, as noted already, was not an efficient housekeeper, but with the aid of an experienced professional, Mrs Addison, the great household of Cliveden was soon working smoothly. One of the household staff remembers some minor details of the routine: 'There were four men in livery, the Under Butler and us three Footmen. We wore yellow silk stockings, kneebreeches and buckled shoes every night for dinner, and powdered our hair if there were more than eight for dinner. This was always a troublesome business

Above: Princess Marie of Rumania riding astride (considered fast for women in those days). *Below* in the Royal Palace

Nancy and Waldorf shortly after their marriage

as we had to wash our heads in very soapy water to make a lather and then comb the hair into position and then add the powder and leave it to dry, and it would set quite hard and your head became tight as if in a vice.'

Nancy had her father's impulsive hospitality, and this was one main basis of her social success: Cliveden had been known for nearly fifteen years as the vast scene of William Waldorf Astor's seclusion, and now suddenly it was the opposite, a place of continual merriment and entertainment, a meeting-place of the eminent, the famous, the distinguished, the privileged and titled, all with a touch of American informality and her own eccentricity which gave her parties a spice not always to be found in the strongholds of high society. Not long after marriage the accolade of fashionability was accorded the new master and mistress of Cliveden. A gracious request was conveyed by telephone from Windsor, and on the same rainy summer day King Edward VII drove over with a party of intimates including his long standing favourite Mrs Keppel and his new favourite Mrs Willie James. The rain stopped, the sun came out in a burst of king's weather, and the great royal guest found his visit so 'agreeable' that he would not go till eight o'clock, to everyone's great inconvenience.

But she could not take fashionability as seriously as most young leaders of society. Years later she gave a blunt explanation: 'You can't be a snob if you're a Virginian because we can't imagine anyone being above us.' She made it plain in her memoir that for the sake of fashion she could not endure boredom:

'One night King Edward came to dinner in a house where we were staying. They played cards till 1 a.m., and all that time I had to talk to a dull equerry. Three solid hours of dull talk. It was too much. No one spoke when Royalty was present, until Royalty spoke, so on some occasions there were long and blighted moments.'

What Nancy sought in society was excitement, and excitement of a high kind: to meet and know the leading personalities of her time, to be a part of her own time, to satisfy the curiosity which was first aroused in her by Miss Jennie, and left in some disarray by the early closure of her formal education.

On the 13th August 1907 she gave birth to a son at Cliveden. Within a few days of this event, the ecstasy of the young parents was chilled by a sobering piece of news. From her affectionate and alarming father-in-law there came an affectionate and alarming message. In his joy at the birth of his grandson he forgot his resolution never to revisit Cliveden, and he announced his imminent arrival in order to see the baby and greet his son and daughter-in-law. This was too much for the courage of either. 'Waldorf and I were horror-stricken,' she told. They awaited the visit with quailing hearts, and for once the battle went out of Nancy's spirit. When the dreadful moment arrived she fled to her bedroom after saying to her husband: 'Anyway, you will have to cope with him, I am glad to say. I am in bed, in an interesting and delicate condition. I mustn't be worried.'

Mr Astor was as unpredictable as he was formidable. At seeing the new Cliveden with his Roman senators, funerary urns, wine jars, sarcophagi, suits of armour and his ancient Italian furniture expelled, and his vast mosaic floor torn from the ground, amid much other transformation, he made no harsh comment nor murmured 'Ichabod'. Having looked, he said to his son: 'The first joy of possession is to change everything around and remould it nearer to the heart's desire.'

Alerted that no storm had broken nor was threatening, Nancy received him in her room. 'He came up to see me and the baby,' she told, 'and was very gentle and sweet to us. He gave me a beautiful silver cup to commemorate the child's birth. I said, "If I have seven sons, will you give me a cup for each one of them?" He said he would. But I never got the cups.'

Until the last phase of William Waldorf's life there was no grave disagreement between him and his fiery daughter-in-law, but instead, a warm relationship, and it may be that as she supplied a need to her husband she did the same to his pathologically shy father.[1] She briefly described their relationship in her 1951 memoir, and it is convenient to remark here on a total paradox to which it gave rise. 'He and I always got on immensely well together,' she recalled, 'although we had many passionate arguments. I thought it a terrible thing to have entirely abandoned one's own country, for we had all been brought up as passionate patriots.' But what, the reader may ask in bewilderment, did she think she was doing herself? There is a strong and persistent American opinion that an American who changes nationality to English, even in the case of an American woman marrying an Englishman (especially if the marriage is profitable), is guilty of a renegade act. Questions as to whether English persons adopting American citizenship

1. 'Sir Harold Nicolson, who knew William Waldorf, has described him to me as the shyest man he ever met.' Michael Astor. *Tribal Feeling.*

should be likewise regarded are not pursued in the United States. It is a waste of time to look for logic in any matter involving nationalism, and Nancy was never a model of logic. Though it concerned serious matters, this dispute seems not to have disrupted affection or good humour until ten years later when it took a grave turn, led to a painful breach, and ironically to Nancy's second career and fame. But that belongs to another chapter.

It was suitably at this happy period in their lives, when she had been blessed with a son by her marriage to Waldorf, when she and her husband had defied a cruel fate by their cheerful resolution, and when she was enjoying acclaim, that Sargent painted the great portrait already alluded to.

The attractive and unconventional pose shown in the portrait, though very characteristic of Sargent, seems to have occurred to him fortuitously. According to her own account, Sargent first planned to depict her carrying her little second son pick-a-back, then thought better of it, having lighted on this attitude while trying out poses for her and the child.

She kept most of his letters to her, and from the evidence of this long (almost illegible) correspondence, she seems to have met him fairly early in her English life. The first of his surviving letters to her was written on the 7th December 1907 and suggests that they knew each other pretty well by then. He ended the letter: 'I will clear a space around you, I will remove all that does not breathe to you of that passion which I have not been able to conceal and which by this means I will make you share or die, or know the reason why – Whereas I am so sorry I am engaged on Thursday; now I am catching a train. Yours sincerely John S. Sargent. P.S. I love writing to you – do let me write every day.'

The mock-amorous tone is in almost every letter he wrote to her. It was a frequent response by men she knew to her captivating and bantering ways, so much so, in fact, that if little was known about her life, her letters would indicate to many an extraordinarily loose-living woman. In the case of her relationship with Sargent, the fallacy would be especially gross. Not only was Nancy, by conviction and by pre-ference, as chaste as ice, but John Sargent never provided the least occasion for scandal, his private life, in the words of his friend and fellow-American Logan Pearsall Smith, 'forming one of the greatest vacuums in the Universe.'

To return once more to the picture. It was the result of long labours. Parts of the correspondence, which persisted from 1907 till Sargent's death, are evidently missing, but the indications are that he began work on it in the autumn of 1908. On the 23rd November he writes to tell her that the picture is advanced enough for her to see it. As he was invited to spend Christmas of 1908 at Cliveden, one may assume that the sitter was not displeased.[2] By the 24th March 1909 the picture was still not finished as he had repainted the background and, after further reflection, made her 'bump into a column'. To the end he seems to have felt that the background was unsatisfactory. The picture was hung in the Royal Academy in April.

On the point of realism and that alone the picture incurs criticism: the portrait might as easily be that of a tall, even a very tall woman, whereas Nancy was of diminutive height. It was a great part of her attraction.

Lions roamed round Cliveden, but Sargent seems to have been the only eminent painter hunted or enticed thither at any time. There were no musical lions: Nancy owned to a complete ignorance of their art. Her favourite species were literary and political, and among her early literary friends were two of the most distinguished she was to know, Henry James and Rudyard Kipling. With neither of them did she correspond, to our loss, and she said little about Kipling and nothing about the other in her 1951 memoir, but a majestic phrase from Henry James, delivered doubtless in the course of one of the master's enormous patience-taxing explorations, is remembered, though its context is forgotten.

To this energetic young Virginian, whose 'predicament' was of the kind he had made his special study, he spoke, whether in warning or admiration, of 'the dauntless decency of the English'. She was to remember that phrase.

Nothing comparable is remembered from Rudyard Kipling at the height of his powers. He found himself ill-suited to Nancy and Cliveden though he was quite a frequent visitor. In her memoir Nancy speaks

2. Sargent refused the invitation, and his reason for doing so throws a pleasant light on his character. It was his custom to entertain at a Christmas dinner in his studio some twenty lonely people of his acquaintance. In explaining this to Lady Astor he asked her not to make his reason known to anyone else.

kindly of him and says how much she admired his family devotion, but this seems to have been a conventional tribute written without reflection. She told what she really felt to Maurice Collis: 'I found him dour. He was very poor company. He didn't seem able to take things lightly. And there was something laughable about him, though I know I shouldn't say it. He would sit on the sofa with his wife, an American, and before answering a question ask her opinion. As one couldn't get him away from her, it was impossible to do anything with him.'

As for the political and more public lions, it is only necessary to state that they all came to Cliveden at some time or other in these years, among the most frequent visitors being Waldorf's two political patrons, Arthur Balfour and Lord Curzon, both of whom sound the mock-amorous note in their correspondence. 'Delighted to come July 3rd,' reads a skittish telegram of October 1908, 'the very suggestion makes me think I have a long life before me. Arthur Balfour.' And another of August 1911: 'Perfectly divine Arthur Balfour.' The letters of Lord Curzon (nearly all undated and many delivered by hand) are less restrained, so much so, in fact, that it is difficult at moments to resist a suspicion of dishonourable designs. Then the tone of his letters, addressed to 'My dearest' in most cases, and with sly suggestions of a recurrent desire to kiss her neck, changes abruptly after the 9th December 1916 when he sends her a letter, couched in majestically formal terms, announcing his forthcoming second marriage. Thereafter the letters are few, cold and uninteresting.

Nancy sometimes bullied her guests. She is reported to be one of only two people who had the temerity to rebuke and mock the acquisitiveness of Lord Kitchener. (The other was Harry Cust.) His towering figure was to be seen at one of the Cliveden house parties in 1911. With his well-trained eye for valuable porcelain he had made a fine collection, and he used to express his admiration for other people's porcelain in a way that made it difficult for them to avoid offering a gift – an offer which was always and immediately accepted. When Nancy saw the great man's glaring eye devouring the Astor china she said to him quite simply: 'I am not going to give you anything.'

In one respect the geographical situation of Cliveden was bitterly ironical. The nearest great country house, with adjoining property, was Taplow Court, the home of Lord and Lady Desborough. On the surface the two households lived in polite amity though they rarely met. Guests at Cliveden were expected not to pay a visit to Taplow in the course of their stay, and Lady Desborough's guests dutifully avoided Cliveden while at Taplow. Since many of the same people visited at both houses the arrangement was only maintained with difficulty; nevertheless, it was not till three years after her marriage to Waldorf that Nancy got to know the younger generation next door. Her favourites among them were Lord Desborough's two elder sons, Julian Grenfell, who was nine years her junior, and Gerald, always known as Billy, who was two years younger than Julian. They were both young men of extraordinary brilliance, and Julian Grenfell's 1915 war poem *Into Battle* is still famous. He came down from Oxford in the summer of 1910 and joined the army. A brief and telling description of him in Evelyn Waugh's biography of Grenfell's friend Ronald Knox (from whom Waugh had his information) makes it easy to understand why Nancy and the young heir to Taplow were easily drawn to each other.

'Julian Grenfell,' wrote Evelyn Waugh, 'in an exuberant, impersonal way, disliked everyone he did not know and loved all he knew constantly and tenderly. He was never a scholar like his brother Billy; he read too widely and too erratically for success in the Schools. A fine horseman and shot, a ferocious boxer, exulting in wild and natural things, he overtrained and overtaxed himself; moved by a passion to perfect his magnificent physique, he sometimes fell ill and moody. Born in the heart of the governing aristocracy to a mother who lived in a circle of devotees, he resented her occupations in the fashionable world and the endless, elegant house-parties in Taplow.'

In the first part of November 1910 he sailed with his regiment to India, and a letter dated the 11th, written by him to Nancy during the voyage, is of interest. Here is a short extract.

'Darling Nancy, Thank you awfully for your letter. I put you top easily for good-bye saying, or rather not-saying, which is so much better. You will go to heaven for keeping people cheery.

'Ld D, with his accustomed generosity, gave me "boot and saddle and horse and away", and I left England wanting for nothing. Never has anyone had such a good father. Terrible to say, I've got everything in the world I want, and a great deal that I don't want. It is delightful of you to want to give me a present – but the only thing I want is those three wasted years when you lived at Cliveden and we did not know you, fools that we were and blind.'

Billy had much in common with Julian, a passionate love of games, especially football and tennis for which he obtained a 'blue' at Oxford. He seems to have been a courageous but inept horseman, had a facile and delightful wit, and (as mentioned by Evelyn Waugh) he had great intellectual ability. Like others he adopted the bantering mock-amorous tone towards Nancy, and teased her unmercifully. He told her in a letter of November 1910 that Lady Essex 'told me you had said you were madly in love with Julian, and that *I* was madly in love with you. I told her that on the contrary I was indifferent to your affections which were wholly centred on myself and Waldorf. It serves you right for gossiping; but I fear she didn't quite believe me.' In an undated letter of this time he wrote: 'Of course John would love you – he does already (John Manners I mean not Jonas Maccabaeus alias Lord Revelstoke) but don't give me up for him Nancy! I know he is infinitely nicer but it would break my heart. I conceal such a fiery Nature under an exterior resembling suet.' He seems to have had a great dislike for Lord Revelstoke which perhaps Nancy secretly enjoyed. 'Dear God, what a man!' Billy wrote of him, 'He has the mind of a haberdasher who reads the social column in the Daily Mail every morning before retailing second-hand trowsers and "Modern Society" and Browning on Sunday afternoon.'

His letters show that Billy was concerned to heal the breach between Nancy and his mother. He wrote to Nancy on the 30th December 1910: 'You know that you laughed me to scorn the other day when I told you that Lady D. liked you. However it is *quite* true; she told me last night that she liked you very much and thought you an excellent friend for her children. I am so very glad aren't you? it will make everything a world simpler.' But a later letter (undated) shows that his hopes were false. 'The Lady D. seems to regard you as an ideal friend for her children, but declines the honour herself. I wonder why? It can't be that old stone-cold John.' But it certainly was. One must remember that Nancy's open nature made her indiscreet, and she never kept her feelings about Lord Revelstoke and his supposed misdeeds to herself. Nevertheless, Billy persisted, and according to another undated letter he persuaded his parents to invite Mr and Mrs Astor to dinner, an invitation that was not accepted, probably (and with relief) owing to other engagements. But a visit from Cliveden to Taplow Court was made. Billy wrote in another undated letter which probably belongs to the spring of 1911: 'Is it true that you took your babies to tea at Taplow Court? The scene must have resembled one of those charming sacred pictures by Fra Bartolomeo representing the reunion of the Dove and the cockatrice and their respective families.'

But all these attempts at composing a distressing difference, which was probably based on nothing, failed during Julian's and Billy's lifetimes. This seems to have been a clear case of *idée fixe*, which nothing could remove, not even shared sorrow when Julian Grenfell's career and promise were ended by a fatal head-wound in 1915, and Billy Grenfell was killed leading his men in an attack the same year. One may be moved to remember the words of Carlyle – Beware, my friends, of fixed ideas.

Whenever American acquaintances, especially those of Virginian days, visited England they were not only invited but summoned by Nancy to Cliveden and later to St James's Square. She sometimes took offence if an American, even one hardly known to her, failed to call. There was, however, one old friend of Virginian days who tended to throw something of a shadow over the glitter. This was Angus McDonnell. He was still in love with her. He assured her that he was not, but his protestations do not ring true. He wrote in the course of a letter of the 5th January 1909: 'Now you say you have lots to talk to me about. Now really be honest. You know quite well that when you talk to me now you feel you have got to come down to my level which I don't resent in the least, because I guess the level is down in the basement, and undoubtedly yours has gone up and mine has gone down. However you are the best friend, man or woman, that I have ever had, or anyone could ever have, and I love you and mother more than any one else in the world.'

This is not the language of a heart at peace. The letters continue in much the same strain: assurances of happiness and recovery, unmistakable indications of an unquenchable and torturing love. Some of his letters are apologetic and evidently follow unpleasant quarrelsome scenes. The position created by Angus's love was difficult for Nancy. To refuse her old friend the house would have been odiously cruel, yet to receive him as a guest could hardly do other than keep alive his frustrated yearning for her. Unfortunately she allowed her possessiveness to complicate a painful relationship.

Angus (and it was part of his attractiveness) was somewhat irresponsible, and both his mother, Lady Antrim, and Nancy exacted a promise

from him that he would not marry without first consulting them. In
the event he broke his promise when, in December 1913, he married
the daughter of Henry Arthur Jones the playwright. There was nothing
against her. The obvious and sensible course was for Nancy to forget
and forgive and make friends with Mrs McDonnell, but this she would
not, perhaps could not do. It emerges from his letters that on his
wedding day she sent him an angry and wounding telegram, and when,
in February or March of 1914, she met Angus and his wife, the encounter was very unhappy. There was a certain cruelty in her which
could make her merciless to vulnerable people, such as Angus. The
fact accounts for the bitterness in his essay about her, and some
injustice to her as well.

Her possessiveness, when conjoined with cruelty, could sometimes
utterly distort her judgement. This seems the place to dispose of a
calumny concerning Waldorf and Queen Marie of Rumania, which
has already been referred to, and which has twice been published: in
Maurice Collis's biography and Michael Astor's otherwise very reliable
memoir, *Tribal Feeling*.

In both these books it is related, on Nancy's authority, that, on her
honeymoon, her husband used to receive daily letters from Crown
Princess Marie and that Nancy protested and even threatened to leave
Waldorf if the correspondence continued. There is no word of truth
in this. The story can, in fact, only be true on the understanding that
both the Crown Princess and Waldorf behaved towards her with the
basest imaginable duplicity – a ridiculous and indeed impossible proposition. There were frequent, perhaps tactlessly frequent letters from
the Crown Princess during the honeymoon, but they were all written
not to Waldorf but to Nancy. They all urged her and Waldorf to come
to Rumania before returning to England. There was only one communication between Waldorf and the Princess during this time and
that was a letter he wrote to her, at Nancy's request, explaining that the
proposed journey to Rumania was inadvisable for health reasons. The
letter was answered by the Crown Princess not to Waldorf but to
Nancy. The letters between the two women did not cease, and continued till their ultimate meeting in 1911, and after that to the year of
the Queen's death in 1936. Nancy grew to like her, but the astonishing
slip of memory she made regarding her relations with Waldorf does
seem explicable only on a psychological hypothesis, namely that deep
down in her mind her suspicion remained invincible, and that there

could never be rooted from her memory an egotistical exasperation at the fact that Queen Marie had once been Waldorf's closest woman friend.

There was never a person of more contradiction than Nancy. It is almost true to say that she had in greater or lesser degree the opposite of all her qualities. She could be fanatic, she could be extraordinarily broad-minded; she could be cruel, she could bring comfort as no one else was able to; she could be foolish, she could be remarkably intelligent; she could be tyrannical, she could be humbly self-critical. The jealousy and possessiveness likewise had its reverse in her character. Her papers contain letters which show that in several cases, in which the marriages of people she knew were threatening to founder, it was to her that the persons concerned instinctively turned for advice and help, and that she gave it effectively and, in proved cases, with happy results. It may be cynically objected that such action is consistent with the possessiveness and self-esteem of those who 'have had their reward'. Not so with Nancy. First it should be pointed out that, indiscreet as she very often was, these activities were kept secret by her and remain known to very few people. Secondly, and even more importantly, one should note that such 'marriage guidance' activity was not the expression of a natural taste with her, as it is with many good-natured women. On the contrary, the strong possessive bent in her character frequently caused her to regard the marriages of her friends with irritation. She sometimes childishly resented having to take a second place in the affections of anyone she loved. She knew her fault and she once described it to her brother-in-law Robert Brand[3] in typical forthright fashion. They were at Cliveden in the gardens in springtime. Two pigeons flew overhead. 'You know, Bob,' she said to him, 'I can't even see two mating birds without wanting to separate them.' Her benevolence arose not solely from a good heart, but from self-discipline and sense of duty. If origins for this are to be found, the most likely are her mother and Archdeacon Neve.

Nancy's story, as told here, is now chronologically in some confusion. Some incidents have taken it beyond the end of the pre-war era and one to 1936. It is now time to hold on to a firm date and continue from

3. Robert Henry Brand, later first Lord Brand (1878–1963). He married Lady Astor's sister Phyllis in 1917.

there. The most convenient is late 1909. It was then that Mr and Mr Astor first took up residence in Plymouth where a new scene of activity rapidly developed. Before proceeding to the new chapter, a last, small but not insignificant incident belonging to the part of Nancy's life dealt with in the present one may be remembered.

Nothing can fade so rapidly as the excitement and glamour of high society, and when their time vanishes they usually leave almost nothing behind. It follows (and it is no criticism of their authors to say so) that most of the many letters of 1907–1910 preserved in the Astor archive are of very little interest today. The great names emerge and recur and one's attention is not held, except occasionally – when the name is one that has the power to excite curiosity even over the most trivial detail.

On the 4th July 1907 there was a party at Cliveden which at the last moment Waldorf was unable to attend. Nancy wrote him an account of how the occasion had gone off. The Duchess of Connaught and her daughter, described as 'Pss Patsy',[4] were the star guests it seems. Then towards the end of the letter comes a little sentence that makes one sit up, though it is not arresting either in style or intention: 'Winston Churchill was full of regret at not finding you here – I thought him most interesting to talk to.'

The wording suggests a first meeting. If so it was the beginning of a long, sometimes stormy and always uneasy relationship between two people neither of whom seemed to understand the other, or to have made much effort to do so, and yet who could not resist a measure of mutual attraction.

4. Princess Patricia of Connaught, known after her marriage as Lady Patricia Ramsay.

Lady Astor's autobiographical draft continues as a major source, though less so than in previous chapters as the contemporary documentation and surviving memories become larger, more varied, and accessible. The opinion put forward as to a sense of need between Lady Astor and her husband is primarily based on her letters to him. These are inevitably few for the period under consideration, though rather more than would be expected of a newly wed couple, owing to Lord Astor's enforced absences from his wife for reasons of health. Michael Astor's book has valuable material on Lord Astor's health, and on his character. For the account of Cliveden I am indebted to the help of the Royal Institute of British Architects and to the National Trust Booklet, also to the books by Michael Astor and Maurice Collis who have interesting details regarding Lady Astor's alterations. I have relied also on personal memories of the house which I visited once during Lady Astor's 'reign' and frequently in the time of her son, the third Lord Astor. Opinions on Lady Astor's imperviousness to her surroundings are drawn, with much other matter, from consultation with Mrs Nancy Lancaster. The account of the reception of young Mr and Mrs Astor in Virginia in 1906 is almost entirely drawn from the memories of Mrs Gordon Smith who as a child witnessed the celebrations, together with additional matter from Mr Langhorne Gibson. The few details of the household management, etc. of Cliveden in Lady Astor's early married life are drawn from Maurice Collis's biography, Michael Astor's book, and from an essay written for the latter by Mr Edwin Lee, for many years Lady Astor's butler. The noted remark of Henry James is to be found in Maurice Collis's book, in which (as indicated) is to be found a first-hand description of Rudyard Kipling more pungent than the one in the 1951 draft. The notion that for an American to take British nationality is somehow wicked is very common in the United States, and I have heard it often from people whom one would not otherwise suspect of anglophobia. The account given of the relations between Taplow and Cliveden follows two wholly agreeing and independent accounts given to me by persons who were on close terms with Lady Astor and Lady Desborough and who prefer not to be named. The account of Lady Astor's relations with Angus McDonnell is influenced by information given by his sister-in-law, the Dowager Lady Antrim, and by his nephew, the present Lord Antrim. The account of the relations between the Astors and Queen Marie of Rumania is drawn from the correspondence between Lady Astor and the Queen in the Astor archive. The quoted remark of Lady Astor to her brother-in-law is taken from an essay which the late Lord Brand wrote for Michael Astor who used it in *Tribal Feeling*.

Chapter 7

INTO POLITICS

As related already, Waldorf declined the offer of a safe seat in 1907. He manfully preferred to learn the hard way. In July of 1908 the Conservative Association of Plymouth accepted him as the Party candidate. In the next year, 1909, the Astors bought a house, No. 3 Elliot Terrace, in the southern part of the town on the Hoe. This remained a family property till Nancy's death.

The purchase of the house in Plymouth illustrates that valiant streak of obstinate determination which was a strong characteristic of the man and his wife. The chances of a Conservative victory at Plymouth then were feeble. The candidate and his wife decided there was only one thing to do: to sit it out; by such means Waldorf would be elected in the end even if it took years and years. The purchase illustrates another characteristic as well: the Astors belonged from the beginning to a surprisingly rare type of parliamentarian: one who contrives a 'special relationship' with the constituency concerned. Few of the great figures of parliamentary history belong to this kind; few are associated with an area. Even the most cultivated citizens of Malton in Yorkshire forget that in the good old days of rotten boroughs and lordly patronage their forbears were represented at Westminster by no less a figure than Edmund Burke; the name of Oliver Cromwell does not receive special honours at Cambridge; nor does that of Pitt at Salisbury. The exceptions are few and modern. Lloyd George's association with Caernarvon and James Maxton's with Glasgow are only equalled and perhaps surpassed in fame by the association first of Waldorf and then of Nancy Astor with Plymouth. They made it their own; they adopted it. Nancy's possessiveness, put to good use, may have had something to do with it.

To the last thought one may add another: that both of them may have been consciously or unconsciously influenced by their American traditions. The association in the public mind of a representative and his constituent area is usual in the United States.

In 1951, Nancy wrote of her first visit to Plymouth: 'The moment I got there I had the strangest feeling of having come home. It was not like a new place to me. I felt that here was where I belonged. I remember sitting down and writing to Father to tell him all this. He wrote back saying there was nothing strange about it. One of the Langhornes was Member of Parliament for St Just in 1697, he told me, and a branch of the family had then been settled in Devonshire and Wales.' Elsewhere she said that these ascriptions were dubious.

1910 is for ever memorable in British political history as one in which two general elections were held, the first in January, the second in December. The issues were crucial. The general movement towards democracy, which had gradually persisted since the first Reform Bill, had accelerated rapidly after the electoral triumph of the Liberal Party in 1906 and after the Labour Party had become a parliamentary force to be reckoned with. The major political issue in January 1910 was whether or not to support Mr Asquith's government in its endeavour to abolish the major powers of the House of Lords which had rashly thrown out the 'people's budget' in 1909.[1]

If this had been the sole issue prejudice and emotion would have been formidable enough, but there were many others, especially the growing menace of civil war in Ireland, and not far behind this an increasing alarm at what seemed the committed policy of aggression by Germany, against which the Government was accused of taking feeble measures.

Waldorf proved from the first to be an excellent candidate and his slender chances of success soon turned to hopes of victory. According to a contemporary account, Nancy was at first a shy canvasser, but soon gained confidence. Her own account is revealing.

'It was my first adventuring into politics and I got very keen on local affairs. That has always been the angle that interested me most. I liked the personal part of it, the going about and into the people's homes and getting to know them. I remember people gave us a lot of advice on how to fight an election, a lot of it bad. Someone told Waldorf he ought to buy a yacht, but I did not think much of that. I said no, it was the people I wanted to get to know, not the fishes.' She does not mention her husband's feelings about this yacht proposition, but they are easily guessed. His father's political prospects in

1. Lloyd George, the architect of the Budget in question, is said to have been delighted at the action of the Lords, and to have exclaimed, 'Now we've got them!'

the United States had been irrevocably damaged by the ostentatious wealth of some of his family and the son was not likely to incur the same odium among the bitterly divided electorate of Britain in 1910.

In fighting the January election, Waldorf Astor suffered a disadvantage in his electoral colleague. Those were the days when many constituencies returned two members, and Plymouth was among these.[2]

Waldorf found himself standing with Sir Henry Mortimer Durand as his Conservative partner. Durand's story is a sad one. He was born in 1850 and after a brilliant career in the Indian Political Service, he took to the diplomatic service where he failed. At the age of sixty he went into politics in the hope of recovering his reputation, but he proved too old to learn a new and difficult trade.

His political incapacity seems, according to Nancy's account, to have been exploited with skill and lack of scruple by the Liberal interest: 'When a question was asked, Waldorf would get up to answer, but the people would shout: "Not the young gentleman – we want the old gentleman," because they knew that the old gentleman would probably be unable to answer.'

Nancy claimed to have visited between twenty and thirty thousand houses – surely an exaggeration! But she undoubtedly visited an enormous number of the electors, and she wrote of her canvassing methods:

'I used to say to the lady of the house when she opened the door to me, "I am Mrs Astor. My husband is standing for Parliament. Will you vote for him?" Mostly they were eager to hear what we had to say. Mostly they listened intelligently. Some would say, "But I am a Liberal", and then I would explain how Waldorf was too, at heart, but that he thought the Conservative platform was the best and so was fighting on that. All through my life I have found that if you go out

2. Until the Reform Act of 1885 most constituencies returned two members, i.e. the two who headed the poll, and the electors had two votes which they could not, however, use for one candidate. Under this system it was usual for a constituency to return two members of the same party, but quite common for it to return members of opposing parties. After 1885 one-member constituencies became the norm, and two-member constituencies became an important though diminishing minority. Some remained as late as the general election of 1945. The last of them were abolished by Mr Attlee's first administration. I owe elucidation of this matter to a letter from Lord Blake, Provost of The Queen's College, Oxford.

to people in a friendly spirit, that is how they will receive and listen to you. The trouble with so many English people is they cannot, however hard they try, be quite natural with other people. It is difficult for them not to be just a little patronising. I don't know why that is. Maybe it has something to do with the climate over here. In Virginia it is something we simply do not understand. I suppose it is because there never were the same class distinctions to make artificial barriers between people.'

All hopes for Waldorf Astor's electoral victory were dashed when he was suddenly overtaken by one of his recurrent attacks of ill-health. This time the attack was extremely serious and he had to leave Plymouth and the campaign hurriedly. They could only return for the last three days. Nancy recorded: 'We lost. But from the scenes of enthusiasm that greeted us on every side, anyone might have thought we had won. They took the horses out of our carriage and dragged it back to the house. It was all very touching and very exciting.'

They were sure now that if they sat it out they would win, and they were to be proved right before the end of the year. In the meantime Nancy became involved in a very curious, partly social, partly political correspondence with one of the most famous personalities of the time, the Prime Minister's wife, Margot Asquith, who was Nancy's senior by fifteen years.

As already noted, Nancy seems to have known the Asquiths well from some time before her second marriage, and while St James's Square was being put in order, she and her husband lodged in the Asquiths' house in Cavendish Square. It is likely that Nancy and Margot corresponded long before 1910, but only from May of that year have the papers been preserved and then only those written by Margot. However, as Margot took Nancy up on almost every point she seems to have made, the content of the missing letters is not hard to guess.

The two ladies were very dissimilar but they had characteristics in common, notably unquenchable vitality, abounding courage, and the desire and capacity to shine not only in fashionable society but wherever they happened to be. Both were histrionic. When Margot found herself in a railway carriage full of strangers (and she often travelled 3rd class for the purpose) she had a disconcerting way of addressing the company (especially if any of them were so disrespectful as to read in her presence) by announcing her identity and delivering a lecture. 'Now, I am

Mrs Asquith,' she would say, 'and I expect you would like me to tell you something about my husband.' The audience willingly or otherwise was held captive by conditions of travel, though there was one occasion when a woman rebelled and, suspecting that a joker was at work, gave Margot a painful barge in the ribs, exclaiming: 'Oh, get along with you!' But this reaction appears to have been unique. No such scenes are related of Nancy's railway journeys, but if they were they would not strain credulity. The very moving account given in Margot's memoirs of how she got into an argument with General Booth during one of her journeys and, in response to his challenge, prayed with him on her knees in the railway carriage, can bring Nancy to mind.

They both enjoyed a reputation for wit that was in both cases largely undeserved. Both had the gift of quick, uninhibited, often boisterous repartee, a different thing, and to both are attributed some remarks which can stand the test of time. Margot's self-description: 'I haven't got a face – I have two profiles' is admirable, and her rejoinder to someone who asked her what she thought about ghosts: 'Their appearances are against them' is worthy of Voltaire. But such strokes are rare in both cases. The fact is that they were both so talkative and said so much on so many subjects that they could hardly avoid saying something good sometimes about something. To express a personal opinion from experience, Nancy was by far the more rewarding to talk to. She had the art of conversation. Margot was without it. In the ordinary commerce of life, Margot simply upturned the contents of her mind on whomever she was with, and while these contents could be very interesting, they sometimes consisted of a wearisome name-dropping gabble such as she too faithfully reflected in the lesser pages of her famous autobiography. There was always give-and-take with Nancy.

But if the two of them had things in common the differences were essential. Margot was a much harder person, and the kindliness which illuminated and often redeemed Nancy's character was very little and very rarely to be found in the other. Though she made some mistakes about her own personality, Nancy had better self-knowledge than Margot. Self-criticism, which came naturally to Nancy, seems to have been quite alien to Margot, and self-conceit irrepressible. Nancy, superficially the less clever, undoubtedly enjoyed some great parliamentary successes. One cannot imagine Margot following a career as a Member of Parliament that would not have been disastrous through-

out. Let Margot not be blamed for what she never attempted – but it
is apposite to remember that she looked on herself as a percipient critic
of politics whereas, in fact, she was almost devoid of political judgement. For all their differences they had one great thing in common: in
their very different ways both of these famous ladies amazed and en-
riched the England of their time. Both were much resented and much
loved.

In 1910 Margot's letters (full of allusions quite obscure today)
breathe a delicate affection indicating, like Mr Asquith's sole surviving
communication, an established and happy relationship. There is one
little irony about the letters worth remarking: Margot, in common
with many of Nancy's correspondents, complains frequently about the
illegibility of the other's script which was indeed, at its worst, so
extreme that one may wonder whether some of her letters have ever
been read by anyone except the author at the moment of composition,
Nancy herself having often been unable to help in the matter later.
But though Margot's script offers few problems on its own she had a
maddening habit, common at the time, of economising on notepaper
by writing vertically across what she had already written horizontally,
the results only being decipherable today with a magnifying glass and,
one may guess, gravely perplexing even to a contemporary reader
when the ink had not yet faded. A biographer may at moments be
lazily grateful that only one side of the correspondence has survived.

The first letters show great affection for Nancy, but always with a
demanding note, for Margot, like Nancy, was a possessive friend.
Later letters make the character of their relationship yet clearer. As the
older and more experienced woman, and one whose husband was a
successful politician, Margot treated Nancy as a protégée, and the
evidence is that Nancy was an eager and docile pupil. It is greatly to
Margot's credit, and typical of her, that the fact of Waldorf having
settled for 'the wrong party', in spite of his Liberal inclination, never
occasioned the least reproach from her. There can be no doubt that
the Asquiths brought an element of civilised inter-party relationship
to an era of bitter faction, in some ways worse than our own, and this
close friendship with the Astors was one of many examples which
could be cited. But in this particular instance, circumstances developed
which disturbed the initial harmony.

In the December General Election of 1910 Waldorf Astor was
elected to Parliament, taking his (new) Conservative colleague, Shirley

Benn, with him. 'I shall never forget the excitement of election night –
my first successful one – ' wrote Nancy in 1951, 'or the suspense as we
waited for the votes to be counted. There was a torchlight procession
afterwards all through the town. It was a wonderful time of triumph
for us, for at last we had achieved what we set out to do.' This success
was not likely to make the smallest difference to the Astors' pleasant
relations with Margot, as indicated already. But it was followed by
another success which made Waldorf Astor more than a promising
back-bencher, but someone of weight in Conservative councils. This
did make a difference.

The *Pall Mall Gazette* had never recovered the splendid position it
had enjoyed under the editorship of Harry Cust. William Waldorf
Astor, encouraged by his eldest son, had for long sought for someone
of equal ability to restore the glories. Towards the end of 1910 they
found their man in James Louis Garvin, at that time editor of the
Observer and in a state of conflict with his chief Lord Northcliffe. An
involved negotiation began and Waldorf acted throughout for
his father who was spending the winter in Sorrento. The outcome was
worthy of the princely Astor way: to obtain J. L. Garvin for the *Pall
Mall Gazette* the only safe procedure was to buy the *Observer* from Lord
Northcliffe and employ Garvin as editor of both. This William Waldorf
Astor did on his son's advice in April 1911. It was a sound investment.
In 1908, when Garvin had taken over the editorship of the *Observer*, it
was a failing paper and likely to disappear soon. He restored it to
prosperity and influence in the course of three years hard work. The
revival was the admiration of Fleet Street. But Garvin was as stubborn
as his chief Lord Northcliffe, and the result was the early dissolution of
their successful partnership. He was always a difficult man to work
with, though it should be noted that those with whom he disagreed,
including Northcliffe, did not lose affection for him. The long later
association of Garvin with Waldorf Astor was a tense one throughout,
but affectionate at the same time. There is a letter written in late 1912
by Waldorf to Garvin in which the former describes not only his purpose as acting chairman but his aim in undertaking a political career.
Here is the central passage:

'My own personal object and hope in life (including politics) is to
be able to get certain things done, with, through or under the right
people. I don't wish to spend time hunting for or shaping a career –
my time and energy had much better be spent in getting things done.

. . . If the career follows and accompanies, by all means let it do so, but it would be a useless end to aim for if it had to come first! Therefore don't let's worry too much about an official career.'

This interesting self-analysis gave Garvin a reliable forecast of the type of career which lay before Waldorf Astor, a man who preferred to achieve by influence rather than by assuming a position of command. A few years after this time his attitude changed to some extent and he developed more conventional political ambitions, but circumstances prevented their realisation and his political future was much as he described it in this letter of 1912.

In the new Parliament (which was to last till 1918) Waldorf Astor was quick to make his mark. This was in large part due to his activity in a now forgotten piece of parliamentary history which should be briefly recalled. It is pertinent to this biography as (at some risk of over-subtle interpretation) the episode can be seen as a divisive factor between Nancy and Margot.

The defeats of 1906 and 1910 had had the foreseeable effect of in-creasing faction in the Conservative Party, and though the latter did not split it came into danger of such a thing. The 'last-ditchers', the anti-Home Rulers, the defenders of the Lords, became more extreme and thus more in opposition to the 'progressives', while these replied by forming themselves into a parliamentary group described as the Unionist Social Reform Committee. They found a leader in the rising hope of the party, F. E. Smith, later Lord Birkenhead. The Committee appears in retrospect to have been an attempted revival of Lord Randolph Churchill's Tory Democracy. It took a modern form in pursuing its aims through fact-finding sub-committees which went far beyond the parliamentary world in the search for information and remedies. They might almost be described as an unofficial and self-constituted Royal Commission. The Committee might have grown into an important element of the House of Commons if the Ulster dispute had not come to divide its members. It was never a closely-knit body, but it was sufficiently coherent to cause the utmost alarm to the extreme right-wing diehards, notably Walter Long and Frederick Banbury in the House of Commons who, wrote Waldorf Astor in 1951, 'would have strangled us if it had not been for F.E.'s protection'. The Committee members were mostly young men of short parlia-mentary experience. Many of them such as Leslie Scott (later a Solicitor-General), Edward Wood (later Lord Halifax), George Lloyd (later

Lord Lloyd), William Ormsby Gore, Mark Sykes, Samuel Hoare, and a little-noticed member called Stanley Baldwin, had considerable careers ahead of them.[3] The two most radically minded members of the group were Waldorf Astor and Lord Henry Cavendish Bentinck.[4] In December 1911 when Lloyd George's Health and Unemployment Insurance Bill passed its third reading, these two became the cause of scandal. They voted with the Government against their party. Lloyd George's great measure was in complete accord with what Waldorf had come to believe as a result of his study of social conditions in Plymouth, and he felt himself obliged to act on a matter of principle. It may have been this incident which established the friendship of the Astors with Lloyd George. Certainly it was about this time that he was first their guest at Cliveden. Later Waldorf accepted Lloyd George's invitation to be chairman of the State Medical Research Committee.

Nancy's social career had persisted and grown; as the wife of a noted and controversial Member of Parliament, and of the *de facto* proprietor of a newspaper which was among the most esteemed in the country and edited by the most talented man in his profession, she rapidly moved into the position of a leading political hostess. She became a young and modern rival to the Queen of Toryism, Lady Londonderry, but with yet more of difference than one might expect. She still had all her taste for adventure. She did not confine her political hospitality to the established or manifestly promising. Outside the world of professional politics she and her husband had begun to make friends with a group of Oxford men, little known then in England, who were to become of political importance in the future. They are best known under their collective nickname 'Milner's Kindergarten'. Lord Milner himself had left South Africa in April 1905. The young men whom he had trained in administration and, in many cases, fired with his ideals, began to return to England in 1909 and 1910, one of the first of them

3. The other members of the Committee were J. W. Hills (later Financial Secretary to the Treasury), Arthur Griffith Boscawen, C.A., Montague Barlow (later Minister of Labour), J. G. D. Campbell, Lord Wolmer (heir to Lord Selborne), Charles Bathurst (later Lord Bledisloe and Governor-General of New Zealand), S. Goldman, Henry Percy Harris (formerly a chairman of the L.C.C.), and Lord Alexander Thynne. The secretary of the group was Maurice Woods and alone of them not a Member of Parliament.

4. He lived from 1863 to 1931 and was the younger brother of the 6th Duke of Portland. (Burke.)

to meet Nancy, late in 1909, being her future brother-in-law Robert
Brand who had been friends with Waldorf as an undergraduate. At
about the same time she met Lionel Curtis and one who was to become
one of the closest friends of her whole life, Philip Kerr, better remembered today as Lord Lothian. A year or perhaps two years later, she
made friends with Geoffrey Dawson[5] who was to acquire a much
criticised fame as editor of *The Times*.

The Milner Kindergarten were not people of any party allegiance,
but they could all be described as liberal in the unspecialised sense of
the term, and they were temperamentally attracted to the liberalist
conservatism of Waldorf Astor. This and similar turns of events seem
to have caused irritation to Margot. The grotesque form that her
irritation took in a long letter of the 12th August seems to indicate
that this was jealous annoyance at the Disraelist liberalism of the Astors.
One has the impression of uncontrolled emotion finding expression
in nonsense. The letter was written from the Asquiths' country home
near Abingdon. The occasion seems to have been an invitation to
Cliveden. It is more or less devoid of central subject, apart from self-
portraiture. It contains perception and absurdity in kaleidoscopic
mixture, but the self-portraiture is valuable. This is Margot to the life,
and anyone who met her will hear an echo of her voice, especially if
he reads the letter quickly without pauses.

'Dearest Nancy Yr letter made me feel *nearer* to you. You and I have
much in common – joie de vivre and I think love of our fellow
creatures it seems a pity never to meet. I can't leave here as I write &
read and am resting. However full my cottage is (it holds 8) I live a
life apart (as if I were a great author a sort of George Meredith!) I hear
nothing of what is happening there I stay in my beautiful Barn bed
room, wide corn granary windows looking immediately below me
on to a green currentless tributary of the Thames ("liquid 'istory" as
John Burns called it – so brilliant I think this description!) & I write
my political diary & separate my political letters from the Kings
letters to Henry & notes of all the cabinet secrets etc. how can I do
this if I go visiting? I've bought this ideal hovel for the purpose of not
spending the end of my youth giving all I've got in useless conversation
to moderate people.

5. At this time he was known as Geoffrey Robinson. He changed his name to
Dawson by royal licence in 1917 on inheriting a Dawson estate in Yorkshire through
his mother's family. D.N.B.

'Thank you darling all the same. I wd like to have seen you and Waldorff but why didn't you ask Henry and me to see you once the whole year? Politics? I will say *one* thing to you (as a much older & far wider-ranged woman than you by education & inclination can ever be.) You will never be a leader in any society or have authority influence or first-rate society if you xclude yr political opponents or have not the intellectual temper or social grandeur to be able to argue on big political points – You may have a rollicking picnicing life full of the best of the West end – full of Newmarket fashionable society – full of every kind of splendid Tory from George Curzon to Ld Marr and Kellie – you may have delightful worldly women round you from Adele and Ada to Frances Horner & Mary Drew: possibly a few non-party professors who will sample you and yr outlook on life, be inveighled into dining a lot with you & gradually grow socially dim & retire to their Oxford sphere – you will have this & *a lot more* but what you will NEVER have & no woman xcept myself HAS ~~ever had~~ got [sic] (~~xcept praps Dss of Devonshire~~) [sic] is the companionship of fine free talk – & brilliant arguings – from EVERY political point of view – of yr present not only famous but agreable witty political opponents & yr own party friends! All my life I've met both sides. Arthur Balfour said that he and I who were the life and creators of "The Souls" brought this mixture of the very *best* and cream of both sides into Vogue & that society was never so amusing as it was then as there are no wonderful young men & women coming on – (men who have all governed the World even the densest of them Minto was Viceroy!) You say like a child: "I know yr feelings about politics I hope you will *never* know mine!" You don't know my feelings nor do I know yours. You have never made a study of any political topic – never read a bill – never followed a debate closely – that you cd write down the shades of various opinions between men of yr own side B Law we will say & A.J.B. or of our shades of opinion Henry we will say & any other member of our cabinet (every man has his own colour none are divided into black & red). You are too young & crude to go into all this & why shd you?! Instead of bothering to learn – take my advice don't think all that F. E. Smith & Ld Winterton say is the sermon on the mount.

'You add "Don't let's ever talk politics". My dear I *never* talk politics with my own sex for I've never met one now a days with the smallest political knowledge. In old days I had wonderful talks with older women than myself strong Tories & I *loved it*, now the females are divided into butterflies & suffragettes. I can only talk to Lady Frances Balfour.

'I *cannot* quarrel & am delighted to hear yr views – As you know I can talk to Waldorff with ease – all big-minded men can discuss points of disagreements. Every Monday H. dines at Grillons & has the finest possible talk on political & other subjects with the best living talkers Morley, Arthur, Birrell, Lang, Elliot & masses of others. Don't talk about "bitterness about H. Rule" but study what you say really interests you Capital and Labour & when L. George starts a grand thing like the Insurance, help with Waldorff to make it understood by the common people – Fix yr mind onto a few things & know them. You say very sweetly "if you cd give the P.M. yr great heart". My poor darling what have you ever got out of my P.M. who is *particularly* fond of you and Waldorff beyond a little chaff – you've never tried to learn anything from him. Do you suppose when I used to talk to Ld Salisbury or when I talk to Arthur I merely trip them up with a meta-phorical toe or a pillow fight after meals? Do you get the best out of the biggest men we have got by just d - - g them or praising them according to whether they take yr view or theirs on any subject? I know you and Waldorff are fond of us & if you are not fond *enough* of us to risk us meeting yr political gods (I know the best of them & see them all but *wish* I saw more of George) then dearest we must part & care for each other theoretically wh to me means *nothing*. I only care for a vibrating real Love. I miss Ann more than anyone in London & *long* for her. Am sorry you go to Virginia so soon – I stay here till 4th Sept when H. goes to the King. If you wd tell me when you cd spend one or 2 nights here we wd love it. Why not this Friday & back to Cliveden Sat 17th for yr party-loving Margot.'[6]

6. Apart from those of such famous men as Bonar Law, F. E. Smith, Lloyd George, John Morley, and Queen Victoria's last Prime Minister Lord Salisbury, certain names in the letter may be obscure to many readers today. ('Arthur' invariably refers to A. J. Balfour, 'George' to Lord Curzon, and 'Henry' and 'H.' to Mr Asquith.) John Burns (1858–1943) was elected one of the first three Labour Members of Parliament in 1892. Though not a member of the Liberal Party till 1910, Burns served as President of the Local Government Board from December 1905 to 1914. Lord Mar and Kellie (1865–1955) was a Representative Peer for Scotland from 1892 till his death. 'Adele' refers to the American Lady Essex; 'Ada' probably to Mrs Ada Leverson the novelist and valiant friend of Oscar Wilde. Frances Horner was the wife of Sir John Horner of Mells in Somerset. Mary Drew was a daughter of Mr Gladstone. She married the

What does the recipient of such a letter do by way of response? The first impulse surely is to answer back to this torrent of arrogance, insulting patronage, and sheer misrepresentation, all implied under a show of affection, with an answer of straight and fierce and rude defiance, and, unless the writer has utterly miscalculated Nancy's character, such must have been her first impulse. But there were others which weighed more. It would do no good to her husband's political career, committed as he was to liberalist political beliefs, to be on particularly bad private terms with the household of the Liberal Prime Minister. But perhaps a deciding factor was that the parade of affection in Margot's letter was not false, for all the grotesque character of this reply to an invitation (let that paradox not be overlooked).

For whatever reasons Nancy took the masterly course. She did not answer and Margot was stirred to some degree of regret. She wrote again on the 25th August:

'Darling Nancy, I hope I wrote nothing in my long scrawl that hurt you – I was not the least vexed only keen. You *never* offend me but as you've not written I feared I might have vexed you.'

That was as far as Margot went in retraction. The rest of the letter is devoted to further denunciations, not of Nancy now, but of the Press for their maltreatment of 'my P.M.' and concludes 'all I want to know is that you are not vexed with yr loving Margot'.

Since the correspondence continued spasmodically but voluminously for many years to come, and the Astors dined at 10 Downing Street that autumn, Nancy evidently showed a forbearing spirit and the

rector of Hawarden, later Canon of St Asaph. She published diaries and letters in 1930.

The allegedly 'dense' 4th Earl of Minto (1845–1914) succeeded Lord Curzon as Viceroy in 1905 and held office with memorable success till 1910. The 6th Earl Winterton (1883–1969) was a notable Conservative member of the House of Commons from 1904–1951. Lady Frances Balfour, a daughter of the 8th Duke of Argyll, was the wife of A. J. Balfour's brother Eustace. Augustine Birrell (1850–1933), a Liberal statesman and author, is mainly remembered as Chief Secretary for Ireland from 1907 to 1916. Lang is Cosmo Gordon Lang, Archbishop of York, later of Canterbury. Arthur Elliot (1846–1923) was the younger brother of the Viceroy Lord Minto. He was a gifted politician and journalist. The laments for 'Ann' [Lady Islington]'s absence are explained by the fact that in 1912 Lord Islington, who from 1910 had been Governor-General of New Zealand, was appointed Chairman of the Royal Commission on the Public Services in India.

friendship was not broken. One does not readily associate Nancy with the virtue of patience, but she certainly showed it in her dealings with Margot. Apart from her instinctive good nature, she may have been helped to do so by her knowledge of the high regard in which Mr Asquith held her husband.[7]

The debate persisted but for some eighteen months there was no aggression by Margot comparable to the attack of August 1912, instead frequent and convincing assertions of her deep affection. Then in the summer of 1914 battle was joined again. Margot was roused to fire another thunderous broadside, with the political accusations once more in the ammunition and some anti-Americanism thrown in. Nancy had offended by inviting Margot's daughter Elizabeth[8] to a party, perhaps a young weekend at Cliveden, without the rest of the family. This may not strike the modern reader as a shocking thing to do, or even a slight neglect of convention, but it shocked Margot into writing a letter which was extraordinary even by her standards.

'Dearest Nancy,

'You said you wd tell which I quite understood & I'm sure it was very dear & kind of you to let Elizabeth have fun & to ask me to dinner (wh you didn't do at first [illegible word]!) but of course to you I can't not be frank. There is a kind of cruelty in trying to boycott old and real friends because they belong to one of the 2 great parties in the state. We must have Tories & Radicals & out of this clash *much* better things come than under Bureaucracy (India) or Kaisers or Presidents. I've never been rude or narrow tho I've been keen & xcited. I've always been myself & am sure wd willingly change but I'm the sort of person that is difficult to modify. I understand Love & Friendship. London Society does *not*: it understands doing what the others do. If you & Waldorf[9] had been giving entertainments this year & had not asked Henry & us I shd have been amazed but then I know Waldorf has no snobbishness in him. He wd never have joined in the cry "Give us Barabbas!" (a text I shall preach on one day). Half of the crowd that

7. Asquith described Waldorf Astor at a private political dinner as 'one of their best men – fine manners, good brains and, rarest of all, high and honourable ideals'. Mrs Asquith to Mrs Astor, 2.12.12.

8. Later Princess Antoine Bibesco (1897-1945).

9. For the first time in the correspondence Margot spells the name correctly, but with a visible erasion.

yelled that did it because the others did. They had no dislike for Christ at all xcept a very few. It's so easy to forgive one's enemies but difficult to forgive one's friends. I suppose separating me from Elizabeth when she is 17 and the love of my heart or trying to hurt me by not asking her at all I naturally feel deeply & if I died lots of you wd say you had loved me & been one of my dearest friends & that I was remarkable. As for Henry he is so different to other people that people shd all flock to see more of him before he dies of overwork. This is a letter of love & not of scolding.

'Yr affec Margot'

This letter, with its implied accusation of the most horrible mischief-making and denial of friendship, and its suggestion that Nancy (unlike Waldorf) might have been numbered in the mob which screamed for Barabbas, is a most surprising document, especially occurring in a correspondence in which invitations were frequent on both sides. This time Nancy may have taken offence. No other letter from Margot is preserved for nearly a year, but since the resumed correspondence shows no sign of a preceding break, the gap may be due to nothing more dramatic than the loss of papers.

The political life of the Astors outside Parliament was largely concerned with their increasing involvement in the activities of Milner's Kindergarten,[10] and these activities mainly revolved about their quarterly magazine whose first number came out in November 1910. It was called *The Round Table*. Once again Nancy met the lingering Gothic revival but this time in a form that she welcomed.

The Kindergarten was a unique phenomenon in British history. Beyond those named already, the group was composed of John Dove, Patrick Duncan, Richard Feetham, Lionel Hichens, Dougal Malcolm, Peter Perry and Hugh Wyndham (later Lord Leconfield). Membership was very exclusive and even L. S. Amery, who collaborated closely though not uncritically with them, both in Africa and Great Britain, was not unanimously admitted by them as an authentic 'Kind'. Their

10. The origins of the famous nickname are obscure. It may have started as a gibe against 'Milner's young men' by Milner's political enemies, or as a term of facetious endearment used by Milner himself. It was first publicly used in a hostile sense but thereafter adopted by friends and by members of the Kindergarten themselves.

ideas derived from Cecil Rhodes by way of Lord Milner who had given
to Rhodes's Imperial vision a needed touch of sobriety.

As persons critical of the parliamentary system they shared an extraordinarily exaggerated belief in the value of exerting influence on men
of position, and underestimated and were even repelled by any direct
appeal to men in the mass. Their ideal was the British Empire, and
under the influence of Milner's teaching they were alarmed for its
future. They saw the existing loose association as leading to dissolution.
Their main purpose was to weld the Empire into an organic whole and
give it a central direction. To prepare for this they took to travelling
to all the British Dominions and forming contacts with a few chosen
men. The chief of these energetic travelling salesmen were Philip Kerr
and Lionel Curtis, the latter being the more active. Kerr became
sceptical of the centralisation plan and abandoned it before long. They
were all agreed, however, that their main instrument for the propaga-
tion of their ideas should be their quarterly magazine whose circulation
was typically restricted to small numbers. Remembering King Arthur,
these revivalists called it *The Round Table*. They described their
monthly meetings as 'Moots'. They were young and high spirited and
by no means without sense of humour. They laughed at their own
absurdities while taking their dedication with pious gravity.

Their liberalism which attracted them to the Astors was of a kind
hardly recognisable today under that name. In their South African
work they showed little concern for the aboriginal population, and
when they talked, as they often did, about racial problems, they
referred, except in very rare cases, to the tensions between the British
and the Boers. They were unashamed Imperialists with a tendency to
British nationalism, their great object, in which they failed, being to
stimulate so enormous a British immigration into the Union of South
Africa that the Dutch Afrikaaners would be reduced to an uninfluential minority. Such policy sounds like reactionism of the darkest
Conservative hue today, but in the years leading to the First World
War these things looked quite different and were so in intention.
Their nationalism was based on a sincere belief that Britain, alone of
the nations of the earth, had discovered the secret and art of enduring
civilised rule. They found sympathisers in the Unionist Social Reform
Committee. Waldorf Astor (though not eligible to be numbered
among the 'Kinder') attended several moots, and Nancy found in the
central simple idea which animated the Kindergarten, namely the

unity of the English-speaking world, one which was already her own and to which she held throughout her life.

Some of the moots were held at Cliveden and those members of the Kindergarten who had returned to make Britain, and not South Africa, their permanent home and the scene of their careers, all became her close friends. These were Robert Brand, Lionel Curtis, Lionel Hichens, Philip Kerr, and later Geoffrey Dawson.

Without exception the returning Kinder surrendered to the dazzling charm of young Mrs Astor. Her impact on them is perfectly described by Robert Brand in the essay which he wrote in 1959 for Michael Astor:

'She wanted to get in touch with young people, who seemed to her interested in serious affairs, and soon got hold of Philip Kerr and Lionel Curtis. For some reason I did not get to know her so soon. However, after a while she asked me to Cliveden and then to a week-end alone with her at Rest Harrow, Sandwich. I remember her saying to me at that visit: "Are you an Honourable? I see a letter addressed to you like that." I said, "Yes." She replied: "I am astounded. I thought you were absolutely middle class."[11] It was at the same week-end that, as she was writing a letter, she said to me suddenly: "Would you read this letter I am writing and tell me what you think of it? It is to my sister Lizzie." Lizzie Perkins was her eldest sister, whom I never had the good fortune to meet, as she died not long after. In this letter Nancy was "lambasting" her sister, who was not well off, for spending so much of the money she was giving her on hats. I said to her: "I don't know your sister, but if you ever want her to speak to you again, I wouldn't send it." I have no doubt the letter went. This was an instance of Nancy's surprising frankness to comparative strangers, as I was at that time.

'She certainly had a profound effect on the "Kindergarten". . . . We did not know it at once, but there was also an innate and irresistible force inside her, a sort of "power" engine, something that enabled her and indeed forced her to cut her way through life, something that compelled her to try to reform the world, and even to make the universe do what she wanted. She had many weapons available for the task, beauty, wit, an uncanny instinct both to hit upon one's weak or sore spot and sometimes to rub it hard and also to divine in a flash what one's inmost thoughts were. She had incomparable courage,

11. Brand was the second son of Lord Hampden.

great wealth at her command, which she used and which Waldorf was delighted she should use, and great generosity. She had money of her own, but as she used to say: "I didn't marry an Astor to spend my own money." Her reflective power was not so strong as her instinct. Reason was not a weapon she cared to use much, if at all, but she certainly had a very powerful intuition, which worked like a flash. Her charm was such that we all fell easy victims. She liked our society because she was full of desire to do things in the world.'

The Kindergarten men were all prone to fall in love with Nancy, and one of them, Philip Kerr, did so, but not till some time after they had come into close acquaintance. Robert Brand seems to have come near to doing so, how near or how far is not easy to judge from the equivocal account in his essay. At all events, in 1913 Brand went to the United States on business for Lazards Bank, and through the Astors he met Dana and Irene Gibson. At their house in New York he met Irene and Nancy's younger sister Phyllis. She took him to visit her father at Mirador. To quote Michael Astor: 'After a few days he discovered that he was falling in love again. He loved my Aunt Phyllis for the rest of her life.'

Nancy was becoming more and more preoccupied by the political world, and her correspondence with Lionel Curtis shows how her new friendships with the Kindergarten tended to draw her towards the numerous critics of the rising star Winston Churchill. After a political weekend at Cliveden in the summer of 1912 he wrote to her in the course of a long letter typical of others:

'Last time we met Winston Churchill at Cliveden I came out in the evening on the Terrace to look for Bob & saw him walking with Winston on the lawn. On joining them I found them engaged in a lively discussion of devolution.[12] Bob was arguing the impossibility of effecting social reform in England in the present congested condition of the executive & Parliament & was arguing that a devolution of certain executive & legislative powers on provincial administrations & legislatives was an essential preliminary. Winston was combatting the idea & indeed ridiculing it until I lost patience (you know my patience is as long as a hot summer night) & burst out "But what Brand is advocating & you are ridiculing is not his policy but yours – the official policy of your liberal government to which you have again &

12. "Devolution" was then understood as a term indicating a gradualist solution of the Irish Home Rule question.

again declared that Home rule was only the first step." He laughed shrugged his shoulders & said something cynical which I forget, & then with curious facility drifted into seeing what could be said for such a policy & what use could be made of it for platform purposes at an election. You know how in private conversation he tries on speeches like a man trying on ties in his bed room to see how he would look in them.'

To this time belongs a well-known story of Winston Churchill and Nancy. It sounds like an invention but is well authenticated. He and the Astors were staying with Churchill's cousin, the Duke of Marlborough, at Blenheim Palace. Nancy and Churchill argued ferociously throughout the weekend. At breakfast one morning Nancy said to him: 'Winston, if I was married to you I'd put poison in your coffee.' Winston Churchill replied: 'Nancy, if I was married to you, I'd drink it.'

Bob Brand's essay mentions that his years of overwork in South Africa adversely affected his health. This was also true of Philip Kerr who seemed, indeed, to have suffered permanent injury. He became increasingly liable to attacks of nervous prostration, accompanied by minor physical disorders, which for the moment affected his mind. Since his return in 1909 he had, despite such breakdowns, travelled on an exploratory mission for the Round Table to Canada in the autumn of the same year, and from Canada had undertaken a research journey to the United States to find out something about the Negro problem. (Kerr was one of the very few politicians and administrators of South Africa who seriously concerned himself with black-white relations.) In addition he had edited the *Round Table* and contributed to it long and intricate articles on Imperial and world-political matters. Part of his trouble seems to have been that he enjoyed the distressful blessing of an active imagination which would not leave him alone, and which he could not firmly control. It made him extraordinarily restless. Lionel Curtis wrote about him in a letter to Brand: 'This constant craving for movement is a moral defect which he should realise. Let us face the facts, Bob, quite brutally that this craving for the excitement of change is Philip's great danger. . . . My heart yearns over Philip. . . . He has so nearly all the qualities needed for the fulfilment of a great purpose and I am wondering whether he will develop the stability of character necessary unless all his other gifts are to be thrown away.'

There were reasons other than overwork to add to Kerr's emotional and nervous strain. He was an intensely religious man and remained so to the end of his life. His father's family, and that of his mother who was a sister of the Duke of Norfolk, were devout Roman Catholics. In the first part of his life Philip Kerr partook fully of their pious devotion, and when he was an undergraduate at Oxford he contemplated taking holy orders. At Oxford, however, he lost his youthful sense of certainty mainly (according to Brand) through reading Bernard Shaw, though he still retained his loyalty to 'the old Faith'. This was the cause of deep unhappiness to him as, soon after his return from Africa, he had fallen in love with the daughter of one of those intensely Anglican aristocratic English families, rich with monastic spoils, to whom marriage with a Roman Catholic could only be viewed as a calamity of a sacrilegious kind. He knew that by renouncing his faith he could obtain his happiness, but he refused such an act of interested apostasy.

In his distress he turned for counsel and consolation to his new friend Nancy Astor. It seems that he had first met the Astors at Hatfield in 1909, but his first letters to her which have been kept date from December 1911. They show clearly enough that the relationship was by now close and affectionate, and the first ones are concerned with this distressing love-affair about which he urges her to show discretion. He expresses his gratitude for her sympathy and active kindness on his behalf. 'I shall never forget what you did for me,' he wrote in the first of the surviving letters. 'I shall not be demonstrative about it, but if you ever want me to help you or do things for you, I rely upon you to tell me.'

He wrote her five more letters in the course of a hard-working journey which took him to Turkey, Egypt, the Sudan, India, Burma, the Malay States, China, Japan, Canada and the United States. After the first of these five letters he did not again raise the subject of his love affair. He returned to England in August 1912. During the succeeding autumn the romance came to an end, chiefly, it may be deduced, from a letter to Nancy of the 3rd December 1912, owing to the religious difficulty, but also because the lady's feelings for him seem to have cooled. His distress caused another breakdown in health. Sir Bertrand Dawson was consulted and he advised an extended period of

The Sargent portrait

Above: Nancy as an invalid. *Below* as a young mother, Bobbie Shaw on her left and Bill as a baby in her arms

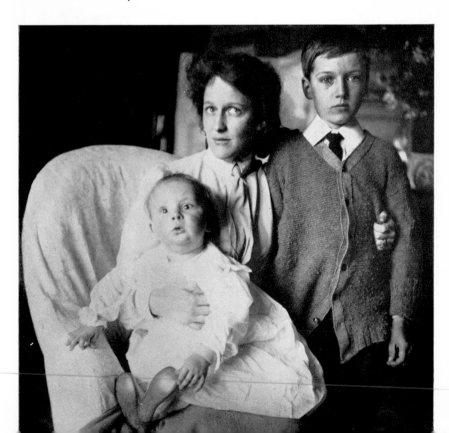

rest at St Moritz. Nancy was also suffering at the same time from one of her increasingly alarming spells of nervous and physical prostration. She and Waldorf went to St Moritz in January 1913 and they invited Philip Kerr to come with them and stay at the same hotel.

It was now that Kerr's friendship with Nancy deepened into a profound attachment that lasted till the end of his life, a passionate and platonic mutual devotion. From now on they saw each other frequently, and when they were parted, as they often were when Philip Kerr was on his journeys, they wrote to each other. In November of 1913, after he had suffered another bout of ill-health and had been advised to escape the English winter, he went to India.

Kerr's letters to Nancy during this journey are very interesting because they indicate a new element in their relationship which before long was to be a dominating one. Gradually, almost imperceptibly, he moves into the position of a spiritual counsellor. This graver aspect of their friendship, which clearly antedated his journey to India, is first found in three letters of December 1913, which were posted together on the 23rd. The more serious note is introduced in what might seem to modern readers an unpromising context, a reference to Hugh Walpole's recently published novel *Fortitude*.

'I like "Fortitude". It's as you told me, quite one of the best of modern novels. It's so much stronger and cleaner than Wells & Compton Mackenzie & there's freer poise about it & inspiration, & it shows life as it really is – an endless struggle against the lower forces in ourselves and round about art. I like two phrases in it too. One I wrote you before "It isn't life which matters, but the courage one brings to it", & the other "Art is listening – listening for the voice of God". That's quite true. . . .' After *Fortitude* he began to read *The Brothers Karamazov* in a copy which Nancy had read, marking passages which struck her. The reader may be relieved to know that Kerr was instantly and overwhelmingly impressed by the superiority of Dostoyevsky over Hugh Walpole. It seems from Kerr's letter that Nancy had marked those illuminating passages in the novel which treat of sacred love. One reads: 'In so far as you advance in love you will grow surer of the reality of God & of the immortality of the soul. If you attain to perfect self-forgetfulness in the love of your neighbour, then you will believe without doubt and no doubt can possibly enter your soul.'

His faith, for which he had made a great sacrifice, was continually weakening. Before he went to India he had decided to go into retreat in a Roman Catholic religious house, in the hope of recapturing and confirming his belief. 'He did so,' wrote Brand in his essay, 'and came out three weeks later, saying that he was again an unbeliever and an agnostic. But that did not settle the matter. He had to have some guiding faith.' He sought it in the East.

'Philip went to India,' wrote Brand, 'partly to see if he couldn't find the truth he was looking for in Buddhism or from Gandhi, whom he went to see, but not much came of this search, though Gandhism always had a fascination for him.' Then suddenly he found what he took to be the truth at the same time as Nancy did, in the first half of 1914.

In the foregoing chapter, for the first time in this record, Lady Astor's 1951 draft becomes a minor source of information. Apart from her accounts of the two general elections of 1910, she tells little about this part of her life. Political sources used are Sir William Munday's essay written for Michael Astor, two short political memoirs written by Lord Astor in 1951 to help Lady Astor in her autobiography, and an anonymous aide-memoire, also of 1951, probably dictated by Lord Astor for the same purpose, dealing in greater detail with the Unionist Social Reform Committee. I know of no other account of this group. The reference to Sir Mortimer Durand is taken from the Dictionary of National Biography. For guidance in the general history of the time, I have leaned chiefly on Volume VI (1905–1914) of Elie Halévy's *History of the English People in the Nineteenth Century*. The account of the Astor acquisition of the *Pall Mall Gazette* and *The Observer* is taken from *Life and Death of a Newspaper*, by J. W. Robertson-Scott (Methuen, 1952), and *J. L. Garvin and The Observer*, by Alfred M. Gollin (London, 1960). The letters from Margot, Lady Oxford and Asquith to Lady Astor are in the Astor archive. The account given of the late Lady Oxford is based on a slight personal acquaintance and discussion over the years with many people who knew her well. I am also indebted to Mr Mark Bonham Carter's introductory essay to the shortened version of her autobiography which he edited. I heard the story of the 'railway carriage rebellion' personally from the late Lady Oxford, and my sister Lady Elwes was once one of her railway victims. It is a curious fact that there is no mention at all of Lady Astor in Lady Oxford's memoirs, and only one brief reference to Margot in Lady Astor's 1951 draft. Yet they corresponded till Lady Oxford's death in 1945. The poisoned coffee story is related in the autobiography of Consuelo, Duchess of Marlborough. She was present when the incident occurred.

Apart from the letters of Philip Kerr (Lord Lothian) to Lady Astor, all of which are in the Astor archive and of which a few were used by Sir James Butler in his *Life of Lord Lothian* (London, 1960), the account of him here is drawn from Sir James Butler's biography, Lord Brand's essay and his article in the D.N.B., and the admirable account of the 'Kindergarten' given by Professor Walter Nimocks in *Milner's Young Men* (U.S.A., 1968; London, 1970), which is the only definitive record of this famous fraternity, otherwise vaguely and often inaccurately referred to in memoirs of the period. I have had recourse to Michael Astor's *Tribal Feeling*, and to Maurice Collis's *Nancy Astor*.

Chapter 8

RELIGION

As all memories of her, and her draft autobiography make plain, Nancy was not a person who suddenly awoke to religion. She was religious from her early childhood. She was not one who suddenly 'saw the Light', but she was one who was apt suddenly to see tones in the spectrum hitherto unsuspected by her. The evidence is that in her pre-war English days she was in a state of spiritual dissatisfaction. She was a conforming Anglican but, as Philip Kerr's letters indicate, she, in common with him, sought for a convincing belief outside (if not in conflict with) the communion to which she belonged. She was ready to be converted, and conversion came in the first part of 1914.

The subject may be best understood by approaching it from some distance, and then the paradox and the dramatic character of the event become more visible. It is also thus easier to emphasise how the event, like all events in Nancy's life, was influenced by personalities.

She was not a disciplined reader but at this time she was still an avid reader. One cannot go through *The Brothers Karamazov* marking passages unless one is that. She was, as mentioned in a previous chapter, drawn to the company of literary men, but unlike some other lion-hunters she was drawn to them because she was interested in what they wrote, and she was never awed by their fame into indiscriminate respect. The description of Kipling which she gave to Maurice Collis shows scanty veneration for the bard of the Empire, and her remarks to Collis about another famous literary visitor to Cliveden, James Barrie, show that the latter's famous spell was ineffective with her. 'He got spoiled,' she said, 'and lost all his homely Scotch ways after being taken up by the nobs. His cottage charm went and he became ridiculous.' But she remained capable of a high degree of literary hero-worship as other of her friendships, notably that with Bernard Shaw much later, clearly show.

It comes as a surprise to the student of Nancy's life to find that in the last four years before the First World War her closest friendship with a writer was with Hilaire Belloc. How the friendship began is not known but they probably met through a friend of both: Lord Revelstoke's younger brother, Maurice Baring. The first letter from Belloc to Nancy to be preserved is of the 31st December 1911, and it is not the letter of a comparative stranger. He was in Belgium at the time researching for his book on the Battle of Waterloo, published in 1912. 'It was about half way between Wavre and Plancenoit, two villages of some fame, that I would have written to say that I should be delighted to come on that Wednesday to lunch, had I had pen, ink or paper; or had it been fine. But I was under worse conditions than Blücher and I just put it off. True I had (a) no army to conduct, (b) no bruises from falling off a horse, and (c) no old age – a vile disease. But on the other hand I was aleph [written in Hebrew] in the rain, Beth [Hebrew] cold, and Gimel [Hebrew] worried by mud. I put it off past Ligny and Quatre Bras. Then I did the lazy thing and telephoned.'

What did these two very different people have in common? The answer is they had much. For one thing, Belloc knew America, had American relations and was married to an American. Although his opinions on the United States were idiosyncratic to a degree, often wilful and sometimes crazy, they were informed by insight and sympathy, and affection for the kind of America from which Nancy came. Like Nancy he was not a born Englishman but an enthusiastically naturalised foreigner. (Like her, he did not speak with an English accent.) Throughout life he was a wonderful conversationalist, rather in the style of Doctor Johnson. They had a bond in a common delight in humour, in roaring, farcical humour. Quite early in their acquaintance Belloc was the victim of one of Nancy's practical jokes. She recorded it thus in 1951: 'Every Tuesday I had a literary lunch at St James's Square. All my literary friends came. Every Tuesday Waldorf had a committee at the House of Commons, so he was never there and for a long time Belloc never met him. So one day I persuaded Dr Jameson[1] to pretend he was Waldorf and stone deaf. This he did most successfully. Belloc was touchingly polite to him, and quite horrified when I kept making rude remarks about him, saying, "Don't bother about him. The old boy is deaf as a post." '

1. Sir Leander Starr Jameson (1853–1917), famous as the leader of the notorious 'Jameson Raid' of 1895. He retired from South Africa in April 1912, after which he lived mainly in England. D.N.B.

This cruel prank is not likely to have inflicted a wound on the author of *The Bad Child's Book of Beasts*, *The Modern Traveller*, and the brutally comic *Cautionary Tales for Children*. It is likely to have increased a friendship in which, as with that of Nancy with the Grenfell brothers, jesting and farce played a prominent part. His letters to her are a perfect monument (if such were needed) to his comic muse. The humour is always of the broadest, disregards the demands of good taste, is riddled with his obsessions, and is often of the wildest clowning. In May 1912 the Astors went to Paris and Belloc gave her an introduction to Philippe de Nolhac, the leading authority on Versailles at that time. He wrote on the 11th: 'My dear Mrs Astor, what a pity! Nolhac doesn't speak English. He can't talk to you. What a world. He knows *all* a man can of Versailles and is so very grippy or strong-handed in his learning. Go and see him. Point to your mouth and say "Wa! Wa!" like the savages and say "Machin! Chose! Belloc! Wa! Wa!" – and be shown things. I was born in that pavage. $3\frac{1}{2}$ miles off. I wish and vow – no man should ever leave his native field. I note that you return in some days and I shall eat gently and cleanlily. What is the Hotel Crillon? Rothschild's neighbour? Very sincerely yours H. Belloc.

'P.S. Go and see Carnavalet in Paris. Go and see it. The Keeper is a rich and highly crapulous Jew called Cain. You remember Cain? He killed Abel. He is a friend of Sassoons. Eugh. Also Ough! Pugh – his father was the sculptor.'

Belloc's mania about the Jews is found in a regrettably high proportion of the letters, and though one can hardly help laughing at the way he expresses it, one cannot fail to regret this 'infirmity of a noble mind', to put it very mildly, especially in the case of this friendship where it seems to have done mischief.

Judging from a Belloc letter of the 24th May 1913, Nancy appears to have resisted the anti-semitic poison for a while: 'You tell me Rufus Isaacs is a changed man. Well he can only change one way.'

The reference is to the Marconi scandal in which Rufus Isaacs, then Attorney-General, Lloyd George, and the Master of Elibank, the Liberal Whip, were implicated, none of them wholly honourably. Belloc, of course, as a disciple of the French anti-Semite leader, the odious Edouard Drumont, saw the scandal as part of a huge conspiracy conducted by 'these Asiatics'. He wrote her a letter on the 18th June 1913 in which he described the trial of his friend Cecil Chesterton (G. K. Chesterton's brother) for libelling Isaacs in his paper *The New*

Witness. It was a spectacular case in which F. E. Smith and Edward Carson appeared for Isaacs, and Ernest Wild for Chesterton, before Mr Justice Phillimore at the Old Bailey.

'I was in court all the time after I got back,' he wrote. 'You would have laughed! Carson's brogue, Isaacs' Green Face, and Phillimore's atrocious bad acting and voice like the wife of a rural dean, Cecil reading Huxley's essays surreptitiously under the edge of the dock to pass the time – the whole thing was quite out of nature! – and then the collapse at the end! With Phillimore having in one breath to say that criticising our great English families was the Sin against the wholly Ghost *and* that the powers that be daren't risk imprisonment. (I mean *Holy, Holy Ghost*. By great English families I mean [and he meant] Samuels, the head of which is Lord Swaythling.) Even the policemen at the Old Bailey were laughing.'

When he was an older man Belloc adopted civilised (though always utterly unrealistic) ideas about the Jews, but by then his friendship with Nancy was more a memory than a reality. No pleading and no casuistry can clear him of the charge of hysterical anti-Semitism at the time when this friendship was at its height, and an admirer of Belloc may justly have an uneasy feeling that he it was who implanted a suspicion of Jews in her mind. She was rarely suspicious by nature, but could be made so by influence, if skilfully exerted.

The friendship, however, lay on deeper foundations than shared prejudice and shared laughter. There was something graver. For him, as for her, religion was the most important thing in the world. He made little mention of religion in his letters but what there is may be taken as showing by its freedom that religion was something they often discussed. In the July of 1912 Nancy's son Bill, then five years old, was taken seriously ill and it seems that his life was despaired of. She wrote to her friend in her distress and on the 14th Belloc answered Nancy as follows:

'Dear Mrs Astor. The depth of the country from which I write leaves very few moments between the coming in of a post and the only opportunity I have for reply. . . . Hence I can write but a word – and by all my experience and by my own nature that word can be of little use. The profound truth in all these things sounds like platitude or folly today because there is no common Faith in England. It is this: that all human life is subject to conditions of peril and sorrow which are intolerable unless, unless we get some hold upon why we are here and what we are doing. God made us: and the same force which created these awful necessities is the origin without which the love of children itself could not be. The strongest and most terrible thing on earth, though the children never know it, is the love of children. Meanwhile out of such perils the greatest good and happiness comes when by some providence they are averted, and you must not think it is a folly in me if I tell you that they are to be prayed down. In this family of mine the many and increasing perils have never had added to them such a trial as yours: therefore I will have all my little children pray for yours and that to Our Blessed Lady who never fails us unhappy children of hers – at least so I have found it, always.

'I should not write either with so much confidence or with so much crudeness were it not a Faith that possesses me altogether. I also [illegible passage] will pray for your son and for the whole family [? illegible].

'I cannot write otherwise; it is all I know of succour in this place of mortal combat little and great, in which we so hardly save ourselves and those intense affections without which we could not be ourselves.

'Very sincerely yours H. Belloc.

'If I had put it better I should have put it less truly.'

The malady was protracted and Bill was not out of danger for more than ten days when, according to a letter of the 28th July, Belloc heard the good news from his contemporary and Oxford friend Basil Blackwood[2] and from a letter which arrived on the same day from Nancy to her friend.

What is most interesting in the last-quoted letter is not only the expression in it of a faith, accepted with complete trust and unquestion, of religion in its most traditional form, but of the fact that such expression was accepted by Nancy with respect. The kind of religious devotion it represented was remote from her own Protestantism, but at this moment she was engaged in religious search and she was thus not easily alienated from any sincerely held conviction.

The correspondence with Belloc is so extraordinarily curious and entertaining that Nancy's biographer is easily tempted into devoting much space to it, but in the present chapter this would be a digression. What needs to be emphasised here is that in Belloc she had a friend of

2. Lord Basil Temple-Blackwood (1870–1917) was the third son of the Viceroy Lord Dufferin and Ava. He was the 'B.T.B.' whose illustrations to Belloc's comic verse give him enduring fame.

brilliant if erratic intellect who, though inclined to absurd narrowness in his religious opinions, had abounding sympathy with anyone preoccupied with religious search, for it must not be forgotten that in his own young days at Oxford he had come near to losing his faith and had rediscovered it largely through the influence (before their marriage) of his wife Elodie. In a sense he was a convert, a fact which goes some way to explain the aggressive Catholicism in his writing. Though impossible to prove, it is hard to resist an impression that at this time he had indirect influence on Nancy.

Belloc's own religion was, however, not congenial to nor understood by her, and she remained a perplexed searcher. There was at that time an odd quasi-religious movement in the United States called 'New Thought', and on one of her visits to America Nancy had become interested in it, and in turn interested Philip Kerr. Bob Brand watched this development with some dismay because many years before he had met the movement and regarded it with contemptuous scepticism. He wrote in his essay: 'The idea behind New Thought was that if you only thought about something hard enough, health or whatever it might be, you got it. I remember buying a New Thought pamphlet entitled "Dollars want Me". The argument was that if you only thought about dollars hard enough they came rolling in from every direction.' He may not have given a wholly dispassionate account of New Thought, but however that may be this now vanished movement plays only a fleeting part in Nancy's story. 'Whatever there was in this idea,' he wrote with an almost audible sigh of relief, 'it was not sufficient for either Philip or Nancy. They wanted something more satisfying.'

This they both found, but by gradual and roundabout stages. On a visit to the United States, in the later part of 1913, Nancy came into contact with another new religion, founded less than forty years before and which was rapidly expanding. It was more worthy of serious interest, and was known as Christian Science. Nancy was encouraged to study it by her sister Phyllis. She looked at the foundation document of the movement, Mrs Mary Baker Eddy's famous book *Science and Health*, and she sent a copy of it to Philip Kerr which he read on his return journey from India. What is curious in this episode is that at this time Nancy gave the book only superficial attention and, judging by his letters, Philip Kerr did the same. Phyllis was never converted to the new religion.

His pre-1914 letters show that there were some strands in Philip Kerr's thinking which were not antipathetic to the basic teaching of Christian Science, namely, that a believing intellect resulted in perfect health not only of the mind but of the body, that *mens sana in corpore sano* was an essential article of the Christian faith as it was taught by Jesus Christ and his immediate disciples, and illustrated by their miracles which were in fact natural phenomena resulting from Truth entering life. But he was still far, and Nancy was too, from full acceptance of Christian Science.

In February 1914 Nancy became very seriously and very painfully ill. An internal abscess was diagnosed. Her doctor, Sir Bertrand Dawson, insisted on an operation. After it was performed, he warned her that a second one would be necessary. She wrote to tell all this to Philip Kerr. He answered her from his home-coming boat on the 12th March, adding a postscript two days later. The postscript shows some revival of his orthodox Catholicism, and no trace whatsoever of Christian Science influence. 'P.S. March 14th. I've just finished Vincent de Paul. An amazing man, wasn't he? It's wonderful what absolutely unselfish goodness can do isn't it. If ever there was a saint he was one & so I think were most of his "Sisters of Charity". Do you grudge him his posthumous title? If he had met you after your torture he'd have only congratulated you on the opportunity that suffering gave you of perfecting your virtue and your prayer. It's a difficult view to accept but I'm sure it's the right one. I don't regret any suffering I've ever had. Do you? They each helped to make me more of a man. But anyway I hope you've not had to go through that pain again. . . .'

The next of his letters to be preserved belongs to the 13th April 1914 and is quite different in spirit. But by that time much had happened.

After the first operation Nancy fell into a state of mind which she thus described in 1951: 'I don't think in all my life I have ever been so miserable as I was then. I suffered agonies. Presently when I was well enough to be moved, I went down to my sea-side cottage at Sandwich to recuperate. I had a nurse to look after me, and I lay in the sunshine on the balcony that looks out over the sea. The world was so lovely and so peaceful, and I began to argue with myself as I lay there. This I thought, is not what God wants. It is not what he meant to happen. It couldn't be that God made sickness. It turned people into useless self-centred people who became a burden to themselves and everyone else.

I lay for hours there, puzzling it out with myself. I felt there was an answer to this riddle but I had no idea what the answer was.

'Then a wonderful thing happened. Whenever a soul is ready for enlightenment, and awaits it humbly, I believe that the answer is somewhere to hand; the teacher comes.'

Her sister Phyllis arrived from the United States to see Nancy and console her in her wretchedness, and Nancy confided her thoughts about pain and illness to her. Phyllis reminded her of her former interest in Christian Science and awoke a zealous curiosity. 'She told me,' wrote Nancy in 1951, '. . . there were people in America who believed as I did, that God never meant there to be sickness and suffering, and who could be cured by prayer. I was deeply impressed and in a way comforted, for it was a confirmation of something I had felt instinctively must be.'

It so happened that there was in England an American Christian Science 'practitioner' (as those qualified to deal with illness according to Christian Science are called) who was well known to Phyllis. She was called Maud Bull. She knew Alice Longworth and other of Nancy's friends in the United States, but had never met her. After Nancy had returned to Cliveden, Phyllis arranged for Mrs Bull to call on her. Here is Nancy's description of what happened:

'I have never forgotten the things she told me and the message she brought. We talked for a long time. I told her how much I wanted to be well, but I said if it was going to separate me in any way from my religion or shake my Faith, I would not touch it.

' "It will not harm your faith," she said. "It will give you a greater understanding."

'I asked her what I had to do.

' "Read this book," she said, "and I will pray for you."

'The book was Science and Health with a Key to the Scriptures, by Mary Baker Eddy. I read the first chapter on Prayer. It was just like the conversion of St Paul. Here I found the answer to all my questions, and all I had been looking for. If I was spiritual I would not have to suffer in the flesh, I learned. It was like a new beginning for me. My life really was made over. Fear went out of it. I was no longer frightened of anything.'

Mrs Bull left Cliveden the same day. The second operation was performed soon after. So great was Nancy's faith in Christian Science that she wanted the operation abandoned so that she might 'try the new treatment'. But Waldorf was firm. Her recovery, however, with her new confidence, was swift and relatively painless. She told the surgeon 'that this time, except when he prodded me, I had felt absolutely no pain. And it was true. From then on I had done with doctors.'

There is nothing very surprising about Nancy's instant conversion after reading the first chapter of *Science and Health*. Except for a deplorable revision of the Lord's Prayer at the end, it remains one of the finest pieces of modern writing on prayer, and is worthy to stand comparison with some of the great classics of the past. No one with any religious sense whatsoever can read it with indifference or without respect. Most of the rest of the book (to express a personal view) is for believers only, but it seems reasonable to suppose that in the great majority of cases their belief first sprang from this inspired opening. Her faith never wavered for the rest of her life, though it became moderated by later experience. From then on her frequent breakdowns and chronic delicacy became only an evil memory, and she remained convinced to the end of her life that 'her faith had made her whole'.

All this happened in March 1914.

In common with most people who have experienced a spiritual revelation, Nancy hastened to tell the glad news to her friends. She wrote to her early religious mentor, Archdeacon Neve, who did not approve of her step and, in Nancy's words, 'nearly had a fit'. But their spiritual correspondence continued with their uninterrupted affection, though in her letters to him after this time Nancy was careful to avoid the subject of Christian Science.

She also wrote to her friend Hilaire Belloc who had fallen on evil days and was passing through the bitterest ordeal of his life.

Before Nancy's conversion, and after an illness of nearly six weeks, his beloved wife Elodie had died on the 2nd February 1914. The shock and grief were terrible, and his grief remained with Belloc for the rest of his long life. Ill as she was, and in great pain, Nancy had roused herself to do what she could for his consolation. She rightly guessed that what little alleviation was possible could be found in a change of scene and she invited him to come to Cliveden with his children for as long as he chose. He seems to have spent a week there, leaving on the 12th February. He wrote to her on that day from his home in Sussex:

'Glad indeed was I, and glad were the daughters who burst into Paeans of Praise of you when they were at the door – which shows that goodness is a fruitful thing: and pretty well all there is that bears fruit – except evil. Be soon well of your pain, to go on fulfilling such goodness.

'As we went out of the automatic-self-moving-gates your children came in in a little cart and my children waved spontaneously, to their marvel!'

Soon after, he went to Rome, and on his way back, while in France, Belloc received the letter from her which told him of her conversion. He answered her on the 19th March, a week after her letter was sent, for it had followed him to Rome. His letter is an odd one. He had evidently misunderstood the purport of what she had written, for he replies in a strain of the utmost farce. At first glance it appears that the letter is full of Hebrew words, but the writer is assured by a Jewish friend that with one exception the symbols, though resembling Hebrew writing, are in fact gibberish.

'So you have found a new religion!' he began. 'What a pity! Just as I have found – ' and then the 'Hebrew' begins. He said he wanted to convert her to Judaism with him.

The letter ends with a characteristic parade of hobby-horses.

'How are the v. rich in England! How is Joel? – & the Isaacs? Tell me all about them, the dear cosy people – & Sassoon, is he still the bright daring creature he was? & the Leiter-Curzons & all of them – I know so few of them! Here is little news. A draggletail slut, the temporary wife of a mangy politician, has shot a quill-driver – but that will soon blow over. They say here that the Germans (who refused to fight in 1911) want to fight after March this year. I don't believe it.

'Yours in Salaam H. Belloc.'[3]

Most people, on receiving so frivolous a reply to a letter on a very grave subject, would be much offended, but there is no sign that Nancy was. The correspondence continued merrily, and as soon as he was back in England he went to see her. Few of her friends appealed to her sense of humour in vain, even when it concerned her cherished beliefs. This appears later when Nancy came to know Belloc's antagonist (and friend) Bernard Shaw. But for the moment one should attach more

3. Lord Curzon's first wife (d. 1906) was the daughter of Levi Zeigler Leiter of Washington, U.S.A. The penultimate reference is to Madame Caillaux, the wife of the then French Minister of Finance who shot Calmette, the editor of the *Figaro*, after he had published intimate letters exchanged between Caillaux and his wife before their marriage.

importance to the fact that she knew that, for all his parade of gaiety, Belloc was overcome by grief at the death of his wife. His friend Lady Juliet Duff said to him about this time: 'But your religion must be a comfort to you,' and Belloc replied: 'Comfort? No such thing. The Faith is not a drug.'

Towards the end of March Philip Kerr returned to England. He seemed in much worse health than when he had set out. In the first part of April he went to stay with the Astors at Rest Harrow. During the visit he was taken suddenly and violently ill with excruciating internal pain. Doctors were immediately called and they found that he was suffering from peritonitis following a burst appendix. He needed to be operated on with the least delay. The Astors made arrangements with the hospital in Sandwich. The surviving papers show that the surgeon was Dr Crisp English who had performed the operation on Nancy. It is probable that Sir Bertrand Dawson took general charge of the case. Appendix operations were still a fairly recent invention and in those days the danger of death in a peritonitis case was very high. The operation passed off successfully, and Philip Kerr remained at Rest Harrow for his convalescence. When the Astors left Sandwich, about the 12th April, his mother and father came to him.

The experience had opened a new world to Philip Kerr. His spiritual search was at an end. He recapitulated his thoughts in his first letter from his sick bed, dated the 13th April: 'Dear Nancy, I'm going on flourishing. Only it makes the day much longer not having you to talk to and see. I'm only just beginning to realise how much you've helped me – that morning before the operation and every hour since. My faith will grow all right, yours is so infectious. I've been reading S & H [*Science and Health*] and understand it better each time. I've got mother to begin reading it too. She's said nothing about it yet. I told her it had helped me to understand Our Lord's life and work like nothing else ever had. I don't miss you – only as I should miss a great pleasure – no aching or real loneliness – that's the wonder of it. We shall never be alone again. Love to everybody from Philip.'

Nancy had converted him, and the conversion was complete. His Christian Science faith remained with him till the end of his life. A passage from a letter to Nancy written on the 24th April shows that solitude and thought had increased his conviction, and that he closely associated it with his love of her:

'For a year now I've been beginning almost unconsciously to think

what you come out plump with. But you make it all so much easier
and showing how natural and easy it will be.' He regretted that he
could not dispense with all medical aid. His doctors were astonished
at his progress. 'Only I wish,' he wrote, 'they would not dope me all
day with foods and drinks. It makes me depend on material remedies
& it's so difficult not to. I shall get on much quicker when they are all
gone. Still they are very nice and kind.'

His conversion caused him to feel some irritation at his mother's
unchanging and unchangeable Catholicism. 'I sometimes think,' he
wrote in this same letter, 'that my mother is the most simple and
honest-minded bigot I have ever met. She'll believe *anything* if it fits
in with her preconcieted [sic] world and suspects *everything* which
doesn't. What a revelation it will be for her when it comes. And how
much happier and friendlier she'll be. Dear Nancy, I feel better just
writing to you.'

The next day he wrote again, and this letter deserves lengthy quotation as it epitomises the contents of the many letters he wrote during
his two months' convalescence at Sandwich. It shows the development
of certain themes which were to become an important part of their
mutual affection: total surrender to Christian Science as the fulfilment
of Christianity; increasing conviction of the error of all other beliefs;
on his side increasing impatience with traditional religion, especially
that of his parents; distrust and contempt of doctors of whom he wrote
in a later letter that they 'invent disease'. Here is the main text of his
letter of the 25th April:

'You are quite right. It does make a difference being surrounded by
Doctors and Nurses & RCs. It's almost if not actually impossible to
practice C.S. [Christian Science] about your own body. You have a
nurse in the room all day long watching your wretched body, and all
night too, & a doctor comes twice a day & crows excitedly over the
way it's behaving, & all one's relatives come in all day long & tell
one to be careful & not do too much but remember what I've been
through Etc. etc. I only feel really well after reading C.S. for a bit and
your daily letter. But I'm getting on fine tho' it's impossible for me to
forget pain & discomfort entirely in these surroundings. Dr English
comes Monday and then the tube comes out. It's put in to stop the
wound healing too quick! Dr Moon[4] says "That's splendid" every
time he looks at it. The consequence of it all is that I'm going to be a

4. The local doctor.

coward about my eyes for a little longer. In this atmosphere it's very difficult to drive away all fear about pain & all belief in material remedies, & my mother is sure to tell me I'm a fool if I leave off my glasses. So I will stick to them a bit longer. Help my cowardice. I read a good bit in C.S. today. Sin and pain are like lies, they cease to affect you directly you know they are lies. Only it's difficult to be *sure* in my heart at first that they are lies. But I'm getting nearer to it every day. I've had such a demonstration[5] these last few days. D'you know old Moon says that the shock of the bursting of the appendix on Monday morning was the worst it is possible for anyone to have, that I was absolutely unfit for an operation in the morning & that I was probably half off my head. D'you think so? I seldom – no never – had a happier morning. Perfect love certainly casteth out pain as well as fear. . . .'

His joy in his new-found religion made a permanent impression on Nancy's mind. This is not surprising. Nancy believed that she had been the subject of a miracle in faith-healing, and that shortly after this wonderful experience she had been the agent through whom a second miracle occurred. These were not ridiculous fancies: in both cases of illness (even when allowance is made for the often-resented Christian Science ingratitude to the doctors and surgeons concerned) astonishing recoveries had been made, largely through a liberation of the spirit brought about by the influence of the new teaching. Unfortunately these spiritual experiences had some negative as well as positive consequences. Philip Kerr conceived a sudden hatred for his former religion.

The Edwardian age, which can be reckoned to have lasted from the mid-eighties to 1914, was among other things an aggressive age, and much historical opinion accepts the idea that this was the deep basic reason why it foundered in a world war. Every department of life was liable to be influenced by respect for pugnacious character: politics, sociology, philosophy, and of course religion. In the reign of Pius X Catholics were expected to hate Protestants and other non-Catholics; in France and Germany it was the mark of the patriotic Christian, of *le vrai Français* and *der echter deutscher* to look with suspicious contempt on Jews and Freemasons; Protestants, including the compromising Anglicans, were expected to look with the same mixture of dread, hatred and scorn on Catholics. To do otherwise was

5. In Christian Science usage 'demonstration' is equivalent to 'manifestation' in the theological vocabulary of other Christian Churches.

to be a 'modernist', a milk-and-water doubter, to be a pale pacifist and a betrayer of the faith of our fathers. Such was a typical outlook, such was an ever-present appeal to prejudice of those times in all Europe. Nancy heard that appeal from two of her most intelligent friends, and unfortunately (so far as appears) she heeded it.

In the upper classes in England anti-Semitism was very common. It usually took a facetious form. It was not the fierce, merciless passion to be found in central Europe, Germany and France, but it was a good introduction to it. Nancy, doubtless already familiar with the mild and unpleasant prejudice in the English upper classes, learned real anti-Semitism from her friendship with Belloc. It appears quite certain that she had none of this feeling in her early days. As a Virginian gentleman neatly put the matter to the writer: 'Why, in Virginia Nannie just wouldn't have found enough Jews to be an-tye.' However, anti-Semitism was never a serious item in her mental furniture, possibly due to the relatively early end to the friendship from which it came and due to the charm of Dr Weizmann whom she came to know. It was otherwise with her new and growing prejudice against Catholicism which came from a friendship which was never broken.

As with the anti-Semitism this was not something derived from her young days, for all the strict Protestantism of Virginia. The Catholic community there was too small and uninfluential to arouse serious antagonism. An interesting little detail in her 1951 draft may indicate how unaware of Catholicism she was in her youth. She had much to say of her devotion to the lovely church of St Paul's in Richmond where her family worshipped. She made no mention in her memoir, or in any conversation that is remembered, of the arresting fact that almost opposite to St Paul's stands the Catholic church of St Joseph, a humbler edifice built in a similar style. One cannot but feel that if in her girlhood and young womanhood she had had but a particle of the prejudice of her later years she could not have forgotten the juxtaposition of St Paul's and St Joseph's, nor have resisted unfavourable comparisons when recalling the memories of her first years.

It is quite clear from Philip Kerr's letters that when his Catholic allegiance was preventing his marrying, Nancy strove on his behalf energetically, and there is not the slightest shadow of evidence that she wished him to change his religion. Ten years later her attitude would have been very different. The prejudice grew slowly. Not only did the friendship with Belloc continue undismayed for several years yet, but the Catholic-minded G. K. Chesterton remained among her literary lions. But the prejudice grew nevertheless, drawing confidence from Philip Kerr's abandonment of his Catholic inheritance. As often happens with prejudice, she made little attempt to discover the facts of the case; as little attempt as Belloc made, till much later, to find out whether there really was or was not a great Jewish plot against civilisation. Heaven knows that there was and is a case against the Papacy, the Vatican, and much Catholic practice, and the case was strong while the Church was ruled by Pius X; but Nancy never seems to have discovered what the case was. She remained content then and after to base her dislike on old wives' tales, as foolish as those which Belloc took on trust and believed about the Sassoons. There is a bitter irony in her turning so extremely against the Church which Belloc so loved, for he had heightened any tendency she had towards prejudice. Michael Astor has said in his book: 'Her antipathy was innate but her easoning was formed by Philip [Kerr].' Temerariously to express a view different from her son's, the writer has wondered whether the antipathy really was innate, and whether Hilaire Belloc and Philip Kerr were not both guilty, unconsciously no doubt, of closing an open mind.

Whatever the universal truth of Christian Science, it proved true in Nancy's case. From then on she hardly knew illness at all, and she was never critically ill again until the last breakdown preceding her death fifty years after. Her footman (and later butler) Edwin Lee described the change in her way of life to Maurice Collis: 'She told her doctors she did not want to see them any more. And sure enough she recovered and it was not long before she was her active self again. She got colds, of course. If she caught a cold she would stay in that day and do her Christian Science reading, and next day, even if she had a real running cold, she would be all right.'

Like many converts she became an ardent proselytiser, and Billy Grenfell was one among many friends to whom she sent a copy of *Science and Health*. She was disappointed by the response in her own family. Bob Brand related in his essay: 'Waldorf held out stoutly for a good long time. . . . Then later he suffered badly from rheumatism [in addition to his strained heart], and I remember him coming back from a holiday with Nancy in Algiers [in 1924] and having to be carried into St James's Square. It was then that he too was converted. He became a most sincere and convinced believer and remained so. This was fortunate, because it made his domestic life much easier and happier. Nancy tried very hard to make Phyllis join her religion and made a practise of calling me "Anti-Christ" because of what she regarded as my pernicious influence over her sister. But Phyllis looked at the world differently. She had a deep feeling of the sorrow and sadness of the world. She thought Christian Science made people unsympathetic. Anyhow, she had a true and deep religion of her own which she was not prepared to abandon.'

Phyllis and Nancy loved each other as fervently as two sisters can, but Phyllis was always Nancy's severest critic.

In dealing with Nancy's spiritual life, her everyday private life may seem to have been neglected to some extent. Let any such omissions be remedied in a brief epilogue to this chapter. By 1914 she was the mother of four children. In March 1909 she had a daughter who was christened Nancy Phyllis Louise, thereafter officially known as Phyllis and in practice as Wissie or Wiss. In March 1912 she gave birth to the second son of her Astor marriage, Francis David Langhorne, always known as David. Her eldest son, Bobbie Shaw, was sixteen in 1914, was still at Shrewsbury School and was destined for Sandhurst and the army. Letters from tutors show that he was not a tractable pupil. Bill was now seven years old.

In 1912 the family had suffered a grave and famous bereavement. William Waldorf Astor's cousin, John Jacob Astor, was a passenger on the *Titanic* and perished in the disaster. It is said that after the ship had struck the iceberg and its doom was certain, he and his valet changed into full evening dress so that they might 'die as gentlemen'. Among those who wrote letters of condolence to Nancy was a German who was well known in London, Baron von Cramm. He comes into Nancy's story again later.

Her sumptuous life of fashionable entertainment, which Margot so severely criticised for its inadequacy, persisted up to the outbreak of the war, and its scale, staggering to modern notions, is well indicated by Edwin Lee. 'We would probably be at Cliveden for the week-end and on the Monday go to London, 4 St James's Square, or to Rest Harrow, Sandwich, or to 3 Elliot Terrace, Plymouth. We also had a house in Scotland where the family used to go in August and September, but after a week-end at Cliveden we would generally return to

London where Mr and Mrs Astor used to entertain on a very large scale. Dinners between 50 and 60 were very frequent and probably two or three balls for anything up to 500 or 600 would be given during the season and of course receptions were also held. I think the largest one I remember was for 1000 guests. A fairly large staff was kept in both London and Cliveden but most of us used to travel between London and Cliveden. At that particular time we had a very fine French chef who was considered one of the best in the country and a very nice man to work with. He had five girls working with him. We also had a stillroom where all the bread and cakes were made. Baking was done at Cliveden twice a week. The Head Stillroom Maid used to travel always between London and Cliveden. One Under Stillroom maid was kept in either place. There was a very large staff of gardeners and stablemen kept at Cliveden, between 40 and 50 gardeners and about 10 or 12 stablemen. All the lawns on the pleasure grounds were mowed by horses with leather boots strapped over their iron shoes. In the house at Cliveden there was a housekeeper, 6 housemaids, 6 laundry maids and always one or two left in the kitchen apart from the travelling staff, also an Odd Man who used to look after the boilers, carry coal, answer the telephone – a most useful man in every way.'

With her wonderfully restored health Nancy took up her favourite games with renewed zest, tennis and especially golf which was then not often played by women. Her correspondence with Billy Grenfell and her own remark that she 'hunted between babies' show that she still enjoyed the sport which first brought her to England. But the intense 'horsiness' of her early days was left behind, and this is a somewhat curious fact when one remembers that her husband was the owner of one of the finest racing stables in the country. She took little interest in it and rarely attended race meetings. They bored her. On one occasion, so she related in 1951, when she found that there was no escaping some meeting, she took a bible with her to distract her mind.

In 1911 she at last met Crown Princess Marie of Rumania on her visit to London for the coronation of George V. At short notice the Astors gave a party for her at which Pavlova danced. Later the Princess stayed at Cliveden for the first time. Nancy got on well with her but her account in 1951 has unmistakably some ambivalent feeling. 'Princess Marie had immense charm,' she wrote. 'She was another of those rare people who, entering a room, seem to bring the sunshine in with them. . . . I came to love her very much. She held the honest belief that God made Royalty different from other people. She believed with all her heart and soul in the Divine Right of Kings.' It may be that in addition to the possessive jealousy which Nancy felt towards the Princess, her invincible Americanism was somewhat outraged at the Ruritanian servility with which the great lady surrounded herself, even on an informal visit. Edwin Lee told Maurice Collis: 'When she came to Cliveden she was always accompanied by an equerry who had the rank of Baron and was a very tall man. In the morning he used to station himself in full uniform at the foot of the staircase leading down to the hall and wait for her to descend, standing stiffly to attention sometimes for as much as an hour. As soon as he saw her on the stairs, he bowed very low and, as her feet touched the floor, advanced and ceremoniously kissed her hand.'

Nancy tells a surprising thing about herself in connection with the party in St James's Square for the Crown Princess. Billy Grenfell greeted her by exclaiming, 'Oh Nancy! Tonight of all nights! Your hair!' – 'I went to see what was wrong. It resembled a bird's-nest.' In one of his letters Billy says how he looks forward to seeing her 'beautiful untidy face'. She dressed always with care and neatness and in the height of fashion; but all the same she had not the patience carefully to compose or sit through the careful composition of the elaborate coiffures then in fashion. They were not designed for restless people.

Her life in Plymouth as 'the member's wife' was as full of surprises and paradox as was to be expected. 'I took the Primrose League in hand,' she wrote in 1951. 'It was, I found, a great deal too select for me, as then constituted. All the local ladies foregathered from time to time in an orgy of tea parties. I did the whole thing over and made it live again, mixing the women up. Plymouth was a working man's constituency and I soon got the working wives to realise this, and to come in and help.' A leading light of the Conservative Association was a prosperous gin-manufacturer, but he became Nancy's devoted admirer and gave all his energy to maintaining the Astor interest. Referring to this improbable relationship, Nancy said in 1951: 'Of all good men he was one of the best, and devoted to his country. The fact that I was a temperance reformer never came in any way between us.' She was never hampered by the need for consistency.

Every year she and Waldorf went to Virginia and most years Chillie came on a visit to England. He had changed his way of life in some respects. Finding the labour of running Mirador irksome, he made it

over to his daughter Phyllis in 1910, living himself in a smaller house
which he built nearby and aptly named 'Misfit'. From here he would
often survey Mirador through a telescope and create angry scenes if
Phyllis made any alterations of which he did not approve, which meant
all of them. His domineering character had in no way changed. Edwin
Lee remembers him at Cliveden: 'Mrs Astor's father was a great old
character, real tough American, used to chew plug tobacco and was
very fond of a drink. He loved to make Egg Nog and Rum Punch and
got most of the guests tight, much to the disgust of Mrs Astor whose
views were very much against drink of any kind, although it was
always served at lunch and dinner.' In his later years he still maintained
his prowess at spitting and he caused 'quite a thrill in Society' when he
was one day found teaching this difficult art to the Duchess of Devonshire.

'They were gay and happy days,' wrote Nancy of 1914, 'but all the
time the shadow was there, even for those who could not see it. In
Scotland one day I sat with old Lord Wemyss (pronounced Weems).
We watched a glorious sunset over the North Sea. It was a lovely
evening, very bright and clear. Lord Wemyss said sadly: "The Germans are coming, Virginia. They are coming over this very sea that
looks so peaceful and harmless tonight. And nothing will make people
realise it." I thought it the vapourings of an old man. I myself was
one of the people he could not make realise it.

'I remember one of Margot Asquith's parties, and seeing the Russian
and German ambassadors standing side by side, one licking his lips,
the other fingering his monocle. Margot said *sotto voce*:

' "Only those two old fools between us and European war." '

Once more Lady Astor's 1951 autobiographical draft remains a major source of
information, but, strangely enough, she made no mention therein of Philip Kerr's
conversion under her influence. This is easily followed in detail from his letters in the
Astor archive. There is some conflict of evidence as regards the origin of Lady Astor's
interest in Christian Science, between the 1951 draft, Lord Brand's essay and Sir
James Butler's biography of Lord Lothian. I have followed the last work as being the
most reliable as regards the fact that the episode proceeded in two distinct stages.
(Lord Brand warned his readers that his memory for dates was erratic.) As indicated,
the account of Lady Astor's friendship with Belloc follows the latter's letters preserved
in the Astor archive, and I am also indebted to *The Life of Hilaire Belloc*, by Robert
Speaight (London, 1957). I had some acquaintance with him also. For elucidation of

the mock Hebrew in Belloc's letter of the 19th March 1914, I am indebted to Professor Elie Kedourie. I have, as indicated, had frequent recourse to Michael Astor's *Tribal Feeling* and Maurice Collis's *Nancy Astor*, also to Edwin Lee's essay written for Michael Astor. The story of Mr Langhorne teaching the Duchess of Devonshire how to spit was told to me by Mrs Nancy Lancaster to whom I remain indebted throughout for general impressions. The brief account of Mr Langhorne at Misfit is taken from Lord Brand's essay, and from what I was told by Mrs Gordon Smith.

Chapter 9

THE GREAT WAR

'LOOKING back on it,' wrote Nancy in her 1951 memoir, 'it was a very quiet sort of war.' This surprising remark may suggest that she spent her time between August 1914 and November 1918 comfortably knitting socks for sailors and suchlike amid the pleasant surroundings of Cliveden. As hardly needs saying, nothing could be remoter from the truth. The remark was prompted by remembrance of the air-raids of the Second World War.

Nancy wrote that she heard of the declaration of war while playing tennis. She probably meant that she heard of the invasion of Belgium in these circumstances unless, as is not impossible, she was playing tennis late at night in the covered tennis court at Cliveden. If so the locality was suitable. The covered tennis court was to play a great and leading part in Nancy's life in the war.

The Astors' first move was to go down to Plymouth. Of their activities there Nancy related: 'Waldorf discovered the awful tents that were being used by the Y.M.C.A. as canteens, and he built the first Y.M.C.A. hut at Crown Hill Barracks, as an experiment. It was a great success, and he built them six more. They cost about a thousand pounds each.'

Waldorf and Nancy, like many others, immediately occupied themselves with hospital work. 'When the wounded began to come from Mons into Plymouth,' wrote Nancy, 'we were horrified at the places they were put into. Schoolhouses – office buildings – all sorts of improvised places. Some of the conditions were appalling. Waldorf begged the War Office to take Cliveden and use it, but his offer was, for some strange reason, not accepted. We were told it was not needed. The men were so wonderful. That is a thing I have never forgotten and never shall forget. Some of them were still quite dazed, but they had this wonderful spirit. I remember one saying to me:

' "One of us can beat four of these old Germans. We haven't got going as yet, but you just wait!"

'I worked in the Plymouth hospitals when we were down there.

started the men embroidering and knitting – something that has since become a recognised part of the treatment of Occupational Therapy. At that time it had not been thought of.'

(In justice it should be said that it had 'been thought of' but was little known, and Nancy was one of the few who knew about it.)

She wrote of one typical memory of that time: 'I went to my first military funeral. It was a man from Watford. His little wife came, and stood stunned and sorrowful by the graveside. I heard for the first time bugles play the Last Post. I think of that woman still.'

Waldorfs political life continued without much change. The Unionist C'ommittee for Social Reform was still in existence after apparent disintegration through different ideas about Ireland and some enforced dispersal by the needs of war. In some ways, as a smaller group of which Waldorf and Bentinck were the principals, it was more forceful than before, with a clearer sense of objective. The Committee had lost its leader and this did not discommode Nancy on the personal side, as she had taken as strong a dislike to F. E. Smith as he had to her. Early in the war Waldorf became treasurer of the State Medical Research Committee, a body that continued until the establishment of the Ministry of Health.

He was deeply dissatisfied. Nancy explained why in her 1951 memoir: 'It was a terrible grief to my husband that he could not join up and go and fight. He was a young man, tall and handsome, to all outward appearances fit as a fiddle, for his heart condition gave him a high colour.

'He went to Sir John Cowans[1] and asked for the most disagreeable job that was going. They made him a major and gave him the job of trying to check army waste. In a brand new uniform he went into a cookhouse, to learn the job. Then he went round the various units, making checks on the waste. I have often wondered whether people realised the courage it took to do this. There must have been many who resented what they probably called interference by this upstanding and apparently fit young man of military age. It was an almost unbearable position for him.'

In November 1914 Waldorf renewed the offer of Cliveden as a hospital, but this time making it to the Canadian Army. The chief

1. General Sir John Cowans (1862–1921), Quartermaster-General from 1912 to 1919, is generally acknowledged as one of the greatest administrators in the history of the British Army.

commissioner of the Canadian Red Cross came with some medical officers on a visit of inspection. They decided, as the War Office had done, that the great house was ill-designed for conversion to hospital use, but when examining the grounds with the Astors they were impressed by the adaptability of the big covered tennis court and bowling alley. This was a mile from the house, and next door to Taplow Lodge, sometimes known as the Dower House. Here, they said, they could make a hospital, and the Astors enthusiastically fell in with the suggestion: the tennis court was to be the hospital with the staff accommodated in Taplow Lodge. The Canadian medical authorities were told to ask for whatever they needed to make this a model place of its kind; work started immediately and went fast, so much so that the hospital, complete with operating theatres, could be officially opened about the 20th February 1915. At that time the Governor-General of Canada was the Duke of Connaught, so the hospital, flying the Red Cross and the Canadian flags, was named after his wife as the Duchess of Connaught's Canadian Red Cross Hospital. In February 1915 it could hold about a hundred and ten patients. It was continuously enlarged so that by the end of the war it could hold over six hundred. According to Nancy twenty-four thousand men were tended there.

The big house, used partially as a convalescent home, was run on a diminished scale. Except for a few ancients, all the male staff left the house, gardens and stables; Cliveden was run on a war-time economy, with potatoes and cabbages in the place of flowers, by housekeepers, maids and members of the Women's Land Army. Edwin Lee says of those who went: 'Many of our men who joined in 1914, like so many others, never returned, including three of the footmen, the London odd man, and several of the gardeners, stablemen, electricians and night watchmen. I was one of the fortunate ones to return.' Of himself, Mr Lee has written: 'I became a soldier in November 1914 and saw service in many parts of France. I was C.S.M. for a time but my permanent rank was sergeant. I was invalided out in 1919.'

One of the footmen obtained an officer's commission. Of him Nancy wrote: 'He came to see me, and told me that living with us had been a great help to him in his military career. "I know good manners" he said. I felt very guilty, remembering my own table manners which were never of the best, for I pick up and chew my chicken bones in the good old Virginian style. I had horrid visions of poor Henry being slung out of some officers mess, all thanks to me.' Her fears proved groundless.

The sudden crash of war on to the long-established peace of Western Europe is rarely documented in private correspondence in such terms of shock as we would expect. Hilaire Belloc assured her that 'the French will win in this fight of months. But it is going to be very hard.'

A letter, written evidently in the first weeks and from the storm centre, conveys this generally accepted idea that the whole business would be 'over by Christmas'. It was from Paris: 'My dear Mrs Astor, How worried I am!! I was in a small German watering place taking a cure when the war surprised us! We had just time to return to Paris – Being taken by surprise as the rest of us, I am *without any money* and *no buseness transaction is possible*! I am very embarassed. Would it be possible to you, to advance me kindly, a loan of 250 L. which *I shall return* as soon as this terrible war is over. Oh dear Mrs Astor *don't let me wait* your *good answer*. I am waiting so anxiously!!! All my friends here are out, gone to the war, or to their country places, and poor Yvette here with an empty pocket book! God bless you! Yvette Guilbert.' The letter is minuted by Nancy: 'How can I answer this? It's absurd of her to expect me to send it.' She had known Yvette Guilbert for several years. Though no later letter from the great artist to Nancy has survived, one feels that the 250 L reached her.

On the 21st November she had a letter from the front line, from Julian Grenfell. Only in a limited sense is this testimony more realistic than the wishful thinking of those outside the range of the guns. The letter suggests in its last paragraph that she had been urging the teachings of Christian Science on him: 'My darling Nancy, Thank you awfully for your letter. How are you? I suppose you are frightfully busy now, working at hospitals and things? How is Waldorf? I have not seen John out here yet, but he is within five miles of us now. We have had the heck of a time for the last 3 weeks, doing infantry work in the trenches – with our poor horses standing in fields, saddled up, with one man looking after about 10, and shells landing among them and killing a few every now & then. We have given these Huns a great walloping, when they apparently outnumbered us (at one time) by about 5-1. I have enjoyed it all tremendously – every minute of it: but it has been damnably cold. The worst trenches are the ones under heavy shell fire – most of them are. Then you simply crouch in the wet clay for 48 hours, and wait for the shells coming. You can hear them coming, and bet on whether they are going to land in the trench or outside it. The noise is the worst thing – it makes your head simply buzz by the end of the day. Their guns are horribly good.

'The other kind of trench is the one that is so close (30–60 yds) to the German trenches that they cannot shell you. That is the best fun. You snipe away at each other all day. Then they attack, quite slowly, in mass formation, and you just mow them down.

'But I wish we could get some cavalry work, and get in at the brutes with our swords and horses. I believe that will come.

'How is your lover Bill? Please give him my best love, and tell him to come out here with a fur-lined coat, regardless of price. It is bloody cold – black frost and an inch of snow. Our poor horses stay out all night, with only one thin blanket; I can't make out why they are not dead. Just think of it.

'Nancy, you can't think of the soul in this war. It is absolutely at a discount. It is much better for us to leave it out altogether, if one can – and all sentiment too. Bless you Julian. P.S. We get 48 hours on and 48 off, in a farm with the men in a barn. This is our 48 off.'[2]

Nancy's 'lover Bill', Julian's brother, was in the situation of many young men, trying to get into the war. 'I am still here,' he wrote to Nancy in September from a lodging house in Smithfield, 'anxiously awaiting a commission in Lord K's scallywags. They say there are 40,000 applications for commissions, which makes one officer for $2\frac{1}{2}$ men, a somewhat too generous allowance.' Before very long he succeeded in getting drafted as a subaltern to the 8th Rifle Brigade.

Nancy continued her visits to Plymouth and her hospital work there throughout the war, but Cliveden and Taplow Lodge soon became her headquarters. Early in its career the hospital became famous. The first ministerial visit was paid on the 3rd May 1915 by the First Lord of the Admiralty, Winston Churchill. On the 18th July the Prime Minister of Canada, Sir Robert Borden, came to see the hospital, and a day or two later the King and Queen. But between early May and the second half of July there had been interesting developments in the hospital which are best related in Nancy's own words.

'A Yorkshire Canadian, Colonel Newbourne, was sent us. That was

2. 'John' in this letter refers to Waldorf Astor's younger brother who was serving in the 1st Life Guards. He was severely wounded, suffering the loss of a leg, in September 1918.

a very fortunate day for the Hospital, for he was a wonderful Surgeon and a very great gentleman. He was fearless, and unconventional and had a great sense of humour. He also had what is not always the professional Surgeon's trademark, – immense kindliness. He and I worked together for many years. (It was a love at first sight.) We made the hospital not only the best in the kingdom, but also the happiest. I knew that every man in the place would get as good treatment as the Prince of Wales himself could have got. When there was a serious case, Colonel Newbourne would visit the man himself two or three times every night. He was a consecrated surgeon, – whose whole heart was in his work.

'Our honeymoon was broken when his wife came over. She wasn't in the least interested in either the Hospital or the men, or anything very much outside a woman's rather limited orbit. Once when we had Sir Walter Raleigh staying there, and something most interesting was being discussed between him and her husband, to which I was listening wrapt, she interrupted suddenly saying to me:

' "Mrs Astor, I know where you can get the prettiest petticoats for two pounds ten."

'Colonel Newbourne gave her a look that cried for mercy.

'Another time when he was busy in the operating theatre, an orderly came along to say his wife wished to speak to him on the telephone. He went along, picked up the receiver, and said "Is that you, Louise? Go to Hell!"

'Colonel Newbourne is the only living man for whom I ever made mint juleps. I used to take him out, when he was completely exhausted, – and sit him down on the terrace at Cliveden, and make him a mint julep like Father used to make in Virginia, long ago. . . .

'Every week we got people down to talk to the men in the Hospital. One of the great difficulties with men who are becoming convalescent, is to keep them amused. In those days there was no wireless to be turned on.

'It was noticeable that whenever we had someone who really knew their subject and could talk, the men would listen eagerly, whereas they were candidly bored by those frustrated ladies who in any War band themselves together into pseudo concert and entertainment parties, – entertaining, alas, better than they know! The best entertainer we ever had was a barrow boy from Notting Hill. We called him Strawberry. He could keep a ward going for hours.

'Rudyard Kipling came down to us one day and made a wonderful extemporary speech. This was so much appreciated, that he promised to come again, and did so. The second speech wasn't so good, because it was all about an Australian who shot a fox. The men at that time were all Canadians, and they could not see any reason why the Australian should not shoot the fox. So the whole point of the story was lost, because nobody understood it.

'We organised each ward at Cliveden in charge of one of the local ladies, who were responsible for books and flowers, and taking the convalescent patients out for drives and to tea parties. (In the next War there were no local ladies, and no tea parties.)

'The men had great delicacy. They were never familiar. Once George Robey came down and told some pretty vulgar jokes. The men did not like it. It made them uncomfortable. There is always, not very far off, this innate refinement, I learned.

'Presently we had German prisoners sent us. There was a certain amount of resentment and bitterness. I remember one day going upstairs with a bunch of grapes. One of the patients called to me and asked where I was taking them. "To Fritz," I said.

'There were quite a few grumbles and black looks, at this pampering of the enemy. Yet when Christmas came, no one got more presents and Christmas cards than the German prisoners. Everyone in the ward gave them something. "Poor blighters, spending Christmas away from home!" was the general feeling.

'Most of the Germans who came to us were very young, and they had no idea whatever how it had all happened. They were pathetic creatures, some of whom had been snatched from school and had not the slightest idea why, or what it was all about. They had all been told it was a War the English had planned and wanted. I used to go up and talk to them and tell them the truth. One of them wrote me, after he got home. He said he had found that what I had told them was perfectly right.

'The gas cases were the worst and most distressing. At times I felt I could bear it no more, and I remember one day saying "When this war is over, I am going to have nothing more to do with this man-made world. I am going into an old ladies home, and I shall just sit and knit."

'Years later, when I became a Member of Parliament, one of these men wrote me saying:

' "Is this the old ladies home you said you were going to retire into?" ...

'When Robert Borden came to visit England, he came down to Cliveden and asked if there was anything he could do for us. I told him there certainly was.

' "Never take Colonel Newbourne away from us," I said.

'He promised this, and he kept his promise, in spite of all the intrigues and difficulties that always arise at times like this. Colonel Newbourne remained where he was, and was the corner stone on which we all built.'

There survives a heartrending letter, dated the 2nd June 1915, from Billy Grenfell: 'Darling Nance, A million thanks for your letter and for all your love. How could a man end this life better than in the full tide of strength and glory – Julian has outsoared the darkness of our night, & passed on to a wider life. I feel no shadow of grief for him, only thankfulness for his bright and brave example. We are just off to the trenches, looking like Iron Pirates, so no more now except all my love. Yours ever Billy.'

The letters of the two brothers testify, as does Julian Grenfell's poem *Into Battle*, to that astounding gaiety of spirit with which the British armies in the first part of the war faced the ordeal of the first full-scale international struggle in the industrial age, a spirit not easily understood (and therefore sometimes denigrated) when met by the disillusion of later generations.

It seems that after the death of Julian Grenfell, friends of the family tried to get his younger brother posted to a staff appointment, and the fact that Billy wrote to Nancy on the subject strongly suggests that she was active in this endeavour. The common mistake seems to have been made of offering him such an appointment, not issuing an order for his transfer. Here is Billy's undated letter on the subject to Nancy: 'It is too angelic of —— to even suggest taking me on his Staff, but I don't really entertain the idea for a minute. The extra A.D.C. is regarded with such deserved loathing and contempt here. All the Tufts Own Toadies, like —— and —— as they come ambling past our clay-stained columns on ladies' hacks or in limousines; besides what earthly good would I be to ——, beyond washing his bottles, and relieving him of the press of business by losing his more important papers? Nor *could* I really leave the battalion which is already five officers short.

'The men are glorious here. All the boring platitudes about them are thrice true, and we have such good jokes; about the food mostly, as at Summerfields, or what we will do with the "Keyser".

'Noise is becoming perplexing, as our guns are popping off in support of the big attack on our left, so will stop now. Billy.'

(The names are deleted in the original.)

He sent her two short letters on the 14th July. The following is an extract from one of them: 'Such a Chamber of Horrors we have past through, shells thicker than flies, and flies thicker than air, & our nearest and dearest neighbours 37 English & 22 German corpses of varying age & savour – However, that sad strain of Negro-hunnism in my character made me really enjoy it – There is fine Bosch stalking and shooting for them as likes it. It is v. boring behind the line; I shd like a week in Paris.'

He wrote to her again on the 28th July 1915. The last part of the letter runs as follows: 'The best thing at home must be your Cliveden hospital which we all long to visit – Take care of yourself, my pretty, do your hair nicely, & do not overload yourself with charitable works in this ungrateful world. Toujours à toi Billy.'

Two days later on the 30th July he led the right wing of his platoon in an attack. They ran into machine-gun fire and he was killed instantly.

At one point in her memoir Nancy wrote: 'After two years in that first war, we did not look at the casualty lists any more. There was nothing to look for. All our friends had gone.'

The reader may wonder how Nancy combined her strenuous hospital work with her equally strenuous profession of Christian Science. There are two likely answers to the question. One is that she was not an orthodox follower of her faith; she was not temperamentally capable of orthodoxy in any department of life, as the Conservative Party in Plymouth were beginning to find out, and as the party in the House of Commons were to do in the next decade.

This is one answer, confined to personal terms. A second one can be found in Christian Science teaching at the time of the First World War. It was in disarray and found a solution to the immense problems posed by the war in stressing the value of strictly private conviction. Since

April 1914 Nancy and Philip Kerr had reversed roles. In the course of 1915 he wrote over eighty letters to her and every one of them, even the briefest and most trivial, contains expression of his ideas about Christian Science. He became in effect, even if he was not willing to admit it, her spiritual director. His own spiritual director (in so far as such a thing is recognised in Christian Science) was a certain Braithwaite, and after a discussion with the latter in June 1915 Kerr wrote an interesting letter to Nancy: 'We got talking about the war. I told him I was thinking of taking a commission and he seemed doubtful. He is quite neutral himself. He said that the question for him was whether the time had come to take the sword as the best way of combating evil. He admitted that the time might come, but he doubted whether it had come yet. I couldn't quite make out what he meant. He was rather beyond me. Anyhow C.S.ites are evidently all at sixes and sevens about the war. It's a great thing that they all trust to individual judgement, & don't judge others. The general conclusion, I gather, is that if one has enough understanding of the truth one won't go, if one hasn't one will. Do you understand that?'

The 'general conclusion' is easy to disagree with, but not difficult to understand. (All forms of Christianity find themselves perplexed before the evil of war.) At all events, the freedom of action allowed by wartime Christian Science accorded with Nancy's inclinations, and in the running of the hospital she used her faith in the way least open to dispute. She told the story herself perfectly:

'I learned the astonishing power of the mind. The Duke of Connaught was coming to visit the Hospital, and everyone was making some sort of effort to get the place ready for him. There were two sailors who had come into Plymouth after the battle of Jutland. They were so badly wounded that they had turned their faces to the wall and given up. They were not expected to live.

' "They don't want to," the Doctor told me. "No one can do anything with them."

'I went along to see them. I asked where they came from.

' "Yorkshire," said one of them.

'I said "No wonder you don't want to live, if you come from Yorkshire!"

'One of the men raised himself on an elbow.

' "Repeat that!" he said. Yorkshire, he pointed out, was the finest place in the world and if I said otherwise it meant I knew nothing about it. To hell with the battle of Jutland, he said. He was going back to Yorkshire – and he did!

'From time to time Colonel Newbourne would come to me and say "Here is someone I can do nothing with. You take him on."

'Then I would pray and keep my ammunition dry! I would take over. I remember a young Canadian who couldn't take it. He too had given up.

' "I'm going to die," he said.

'I said "Yes, Saunders, you're going to die. You're going to die because you have no guts. If you were a Cockney, or a Scot, or a Yank, you'd live. But you're just a Canadian, so you'll lie down and die! I'll have them send you up a good supper for your last meal and I bet you this wrist watch you'll be dead this time tomorrow. You can keep it till then," I said. "I'll get it back when you're gone."

'He ate the supper I sent him, and he still has the watch. Later when he got back home he wrote me from the Middle West. "They're making a lot of me here" he said. "They think I'm a hero. Gee, Mrs Astor, they don't know how you had to kick me around to make me live!" '

In Plymouth, in a naval hospital reserved for serious cases, Nancy had a strange experience. She stopped at the bed of one man who had been blinded, and said 'Hallo.' She told that 'then he turned his face to me and said "Go right on talking". Then he said: "It's you. I recognised your voice at once. I've often hoped I'd meet you again." '

He was a seaman of the Merchant Navy. Ten years or so before he had been one of the men to whom Nancy had talked on the transatlantic liner, when she first discovered that she 'had this power to talk to people easily and make them talk to me'.

Though Christian Science had had the miraculous effect of rescuing Nancy from a state of near-chronic invalidism, it never gave her nervous stability, and as the war went on she showed signs of nervous strain, not, as before, in periods of prostration, but in sudden temperamental outbreaks. Her correspondence with Hilaire Belloc persisted with all the accustomed gusto, when suddenly in the middle of April 1915 there was a breach. Belloc had written her a letter which seriously angered her. He addressed her as 'My dear friend'. The tone is very affectionate. Here is the offending paragraph: 'Do you notice all around the really interesting signs of weakening towards this strain of the war? I don't think that's a fair way of putting it. It's rather symptoms all round of trying to persuade public opinion to a climb down. It is in the very texture of half the press – I think Harmsworth is working that way. It is most interesting to watch – but lamentable: if anything were left on earth worth caring for. For if the big monied interests compell England to give way it means a coalition against her in a very short time – and no one to fight for her in the future. People used to say when the fight was on against the swindlers and fools of Parliament that it didn't matter what the politicians stole or what bribes they took or how they lied, because the nation worried along the all same. They cared a little for the way our politics were becoming a bye-word in Europe, but for the effect at home they didn't care at all. Now I think it is beginning to come home.'

She had received dozens of letters from him in this vein but now she was enraged. She remembered she was the wife of a politician and a newspaper proprietor. It was at just about this time that William Waldorf Astor, largely at Nancy's insistence, had made over the ownership of the *Observer* to his son. No family was more representative of the 'monied interests' in the country than the Astors. The letter was well calculated to offend and she clearly told Belloc that their friendship was at an end.

He replied with grave formality on the 22nd April 1915:

'My dear Mrs Astor, No I did not mean and could not conceivably have meant that just criticism to apply to you. I have never written discourteously to a woman in my life. Do you think I would now so write to you who have shown me so much kindness in the past? . . .'

There is a short gap in Belloc's letters to Nancy till the 4th May, but this was due on his part to an attack of influenza. After that his letters pour forth again thick and fast, with no sign of penitence, with no reining in of the hobby horses or quelling of the numerous bees infesting his bonnet. She answered his letters affectionately, met him in London, took his children to the theatre, gave them presents, had him to stay at Cliveden for a while in June, and the friendship was affirmed anew. The tempest had passed quickly, as was usual with her, even when she was the injured party as in this case. But tempests were becoming more and more a recurrent phenomenon of her life.

Among the friends she made in the war was the wife of Waldorf's Oxford contemporary, John Buchan. Mrs Buchan (or Lady Tweedsmuir as she became later) loved Nancy but never uncritically. In an essay which she wrote for Michael Astor many years later, she told how Waldorf offered her a cottage on the estate where she spent some weeks with her children, and did some work in the hospital. She left a closely observed account of one of Nancy's passing squalls.

'Nancy I saw at intervals. She did a very good job in cheering up the men in hospital. Her presence in a ward recharged its atmosphere and revivified it. The first week when we lived in the Taplow Cottage we went to tea with Nancy taking a friend, George Drummond, with us. Nancy was welcoming to us, but she was in one of her more enragée moods. She said across the tea table, "I've got no friends, no friends at all, smart or otherwise. I would welcome the butcher's boy from Maidenhead to tea." It made us laugh, so the butcher's boy from Maidenhead has become a family saying with us through the years. George, a more conventional character than ourselves, was horrified by Nancy's conversation. She got on in her talk, to a sort of knife edge of vulgarity and mentioned several people he knew – No, it was not a success taking him to tea there.'

One could illustrate Nancy's tendency to short temper under the stress of terrible years by many other touches, but the point must not be over-emphasised. One must not forget her contradictory character and that one can unsay almost everything that one can say about her. If she faced some of the exasperation of the time with tantrums, she faced most of it with pertinacity.

As suggested earlier, the correspondence with Margot Asquith may have been suspended, as a result of Nancy's indignation at Margot's insufferable letter of July 1914. The Astor archive suggests that relations were not resumed till June 1915. On the 9th Margot wrote to Nancy inviting her and Waldorf to dinner, making it plain nonetheless by the style of this peace overture that Nancy's former affront of inviting her daughter without her was neither forgotten nor forgiven. 'Dear Nancy,' she wrote, 'Will you & Waldorf dine here 8.30 Thursday 17th. It's jolly to think how fashionable we are now!³ We meet thrilling people who don't mind me going out with Elizabeth! I sit next to Horace Farquhar one night Ld Essex another: Mr Bonar Law, Walter Long, &

3. Referring to the formation of the Coalition Government at the end of May 915.

Austen Chamberlain – cause quite a flutter as I meet them going into the Cabinets – I long to see you & Waldorf again & have a nice talk. Such a lot of terrible things have happened since we've met – Henry had such an interesting time abroad.[4] I wd like to tell you about it. Your affec Margot. P.S. Don't fail to come next Thursday or I shall think we are still "suspecte". Do you still take in the Daily Mail & Geoffrey Robinson?[5] My love to Waldorf & tell him we think & always have thought him one in a thousand.'

Nancy kept a copy of her reply: 'My dear Margot, It's awfully kind of you to ask us, but Waldorf is never in one place two nights a week & seldom in London – I am going to Plymouth on Monday to see about our YWCA huts there & make a recruiting speech – alongside Mrs Pankhurst (who I wish was in the Cabinet!).

['Anyhow you would find this disagreeable company these days. The Wait and See Policy has changed me into a fighting woman –]

'Yes I've given up The Daily Mail & Geoffrey Robinson & am taking in the Daily News & Sir Edgar Speyer.'

The passage in brackets above is crossed out in pencil scribblings in the copy, and this may mean that it was suppressed as too rude to send.

Margot replied on the 11th: 'Dearest Nancy. Your letter reads as if you thought Sir E. Speyer a great friend of mine but I daresay it's only your fun! (I am as a matter of fact fond of Sir Edgar but I found her a tiring noisy woman – perhaps not noisy in voice but in mind.) . . . I had a long talk to K about the war Wednesday (he Winston and LL George) & we all felt very depressed. I got an ample apology & £100 (for Red Cross) out of a vile rag London Mail[6] (a sort of inferior Daily Mail) for telling lies about me yesterday – wasn't it dashing of me!'

The references to Sir Edgar Speyer point to a piece of folly which was much practised in the First World War. Speyer, a privy counsellor of German Jewish parentage, was looked on as a spy, and his acquaintance with Mr Asquith used against the Government. The Liberal paper, the *Daily News*, defended Asquith and Speyer. Unfortunately for the

4. The Prime Minister had just returned from a visit to the British Army in France.
5. Both the *Daily Mail* and *The Times*, under Geoffrey Robinson's editorship, were owned by Alfred Harmsworth, Lord Northcliffe.
6. In her autobiography the late Lady Oxford said that she obtained £1,000 from *The Globe*. The error has been repeated.

defence it was later proved that after Sir Edgar had migrated in disgust to the United States he did in fact trade to Germany's advantage through neutral countries.[7]

With doubtful loyalty, but with the excuse of intolerable provocation by this raking up of an old and meaningless quarrel, Nancy sent the correspondence (which is why there is a copy of her reply) to Geoffrey Robinson. He replied in a letter of facetious flattery, written with a ponderous disapproval of Margot which show his radical lack of humour.

This squall passed like the others, though there is again a very long gap in the Nancy-Margot correspondence till April 1916, shortly before the birth of Michael Astor on the 10th. This letter makes it clear that they had met occasionally on friendly terms in the interval. The general impression remains consistent throughout: that they agreed on very little, that there was a mutual attraction, and a mutual irritation. For a while the latter sentiment was held in check by Margot. It may be that now that Waldorf was in the fullest sense of the term the owner-director of one of the most influential papers in the country, the Prime Minister had warned his wife that it was mere silliness to antagonise Waldorf's wife. On the other hand, it may have been a simpler matter: that Margot's affection, which she several times expressed by telling Nancy how much she wanted to see her 'dear little face' again, was not only sincere but the strongest of her emotions regarding her.

Throughout the war, the most important and the least troubled correspondence in which Nancy engaged was that with Philip Kerr. Though they were very different in mind and temperament only the faintest hint of disagreement appears at any time. Nancy was an emotional being in continual danger of being ruled by feeling. Philip Kerr appeared to be the opposite to an extent which repelled some people. It is likely, however, that what appeared as a cold lack of emotion was in fact the consequence of intense self-discipline. In a letter of March 1915 Philip Kerr wrote to Nancy: 'To be always helping others in the right way is the *only* way to love them. To yearn

---

7. See Speyer, Sir Edgar, in D.N.B. 1931–1950. The pages of *Punch* 1914–1918 often illustrate how anti-Germanism became confused with anti-Semitism in popular opinion. The facts of the case regarding international Jewish big business influence on Anglo-German affairs are lucidly stated by Elie Halévy in *The History of the English People in the Nineteenth Century*. Epilogue Book II, pp. 407–408.

about them is just wash. On the other hand lots of people fall into the opposite mistake & think that it helps others to give to others or do to them, what they ask or want. That's like giving into all his whims and requests for chocolate by children. You have to do that to young children, but one has to be on one's guard against doing it too much to grown ups who can think for themselves, for it cuts at the root of all health & happiness by strengthening habits of weakness & dependence. "Sympathy" in the literal sense is a snare. It means "feeling with" another. That doesn't help one scrap. What does help is understanding what the root of the trouble is & pointing out how it can be cured.'

In this governessy statement one may justly discern an endeavour by Kerr to appear as more narrowly single-minded than he was. Though his Christian Science faith was undeviating, his accustomed indecision and tendency to doubt became visible at moments, and with them some self-deception. He wrote to Nancy in a letter of September 1915 in which he criticised his fellow Christian Scientists:

'They are all very down on the poor R.Cs. I always find it difficult to understand exactly why – you don't.'

She did not because she had followed his frequent exhortations to see in Roman Catholicism a sinister and stupid mass of superstition and religiosity. Soon he returned to his usual attitude. 'I'm beginning,' he wrote to her, not very long after the last-quoted letter, 'to understand now the power of truth and love. RCism is just nothing, that is the truth. And the great error people make is to be afraid of it, thus making it real.' Such passages are frequent. They may sometimes have been written to quieten his mind, for it does appear that at moments he found it difficult to face the fact that he was in a position that many people would find objectionable. He was still highly esteemed in Roman Catholic circles, where nothing was known of his Christian Science. In 1915 he was invited by the headmaster of Ampleforth to stay in the monastery for Holy Week and address the senior boys. He accepted the invitation and was fêted as a shining light of the British Catholic community, while all the time he was a secret enemy. It was not a comfortable situation for a man of honour.

It was much aggravated by family circumstances induced by his natural aptitude to hesitation. Until November 1915, he had not told his parents or his sisters of his change of faith. Nancy was his confidante in this, and perhaps the only one he had. He procrastinated during the spring and summer of 1914, and then he procrastinated yet more when the family was overcome by tragedy. Philip Kerr had a younger brother, David, who was twelve years his junior. He was twenty-one in 1914. He joined up on the declaration of war, was sent to France and was killed in his first action, in October. Philip Kerr felt that he could not add to the grief of his family by telling them of a step which they could only regard as betrayal and apostasy. His delay is one with which one can easily sympathise. (But did he have to accept the invitation to Ampleforth where he was accompanied by his unsuspecting mother, and from where he wrote caustic comments to Nancy on the limitations of the religious outlook prevailing among Benedictines?) In late November of 1915, while staying with his parents in Scotland, he finally broke the news, and reported the scene to Nancy on the 28th. His mother, he told her, 'said it was worse than David's death. . . .'

The conclusion of this episode is surprising and edifying on the part of the women involved. His mother and his two sisters never reconciled themselves to his change of faith, and it is said that his mother prayed daily at mass for her son's reconversion, from that day in November 1915 until her death in 1931. What is not so readily expected, and provides an illustration of Christian religion at its finest, is that his mother, like his sisters who acted under her influence, never attached the smallest blame to Nancy, respected her sincerity and never contemplated withdrawing friendship. There were close friends of Nancy, people who were not Catholics but who deplored the slowly increasing fanaticism of her anti-Catholicism, and who urged her to set her prejudice aside before so saintly an example. Nancy always acknowledged that she felt humble before the piety and charity of Lady Anne Kerr, but her prejudice would not die because it was kept alive by Philip Kerr. It was in vain that a learned Anglican of the High Church, Lord Eustace Percy, argued with noble eloquence the merits of tolerance and respect for the whole Christian Church; in vain that Maurice Baring wrote her a moving apologia describing how he, as a Catholic convert, saw the Catholic Church, and impressed on her the need of study before condemnation. All attempt at persuasion was in vain. Philip Kerr was her chosen spiritual director and she would listen to no other voice. His attitude had grown into one of absolute and immovable contempt for 'R.C.-ism' and he conveyed this to

Nancy in whose fighting spirit the contempt was slowly transformed into passionate unthinking hatred. But, as must not be forgotten, the process was very gradual.

The year 1916 opened with a shock for Waldorf and Nancy. In the New Year honours list his father William Waldorf Astor was made a baron. In her memoir Nancy told the story as she remembered it: 'My Father-in-law suddenly found himself with the routine of years shattered and broken, and himself all at a loose end. He could not go to Vichy where he took a cure every year – he could not go to Sorrento where he had a villa he loved. It was then that Lord Farquhar[8] suggested he take a peerage and go to the House of Lords. It would occupy him and give him a chance to be of some use to England.

'We were never consulted or told. I was furious and so was Waldorf. The first we knew of it was when someone rang Waldorf up and asked him what he was going to call himself now.

'Waldorf wrote to his father, bitterly opposing the whole thing. His father who had I think never before had anyone openly disagree with him, was very angry. He asked me did I agree with Waldorf and I said I did. So he wrote a codicil to his will, cutting Waldorf off. All the money that should have come to my husband, went to his sons when they came of age.'

(In fact, though the purpose was to punish Waldorf, under modern taxation this was the most beneficial arrangement he could have made for the family.)

Nancy's exasperation at her father-in-law's ennoblement seems to have been less prompted by political considerations than by that queer and illogical American idea that there is something unpatriotic in a born American accepting such British honours. She was also shocked because it meant that Mr Astor had broken a promise. She described in her memoir how some years before, when rallying him on his abandonment of New York, 'I remember telling him, laughingly, only one thing could make what he had done worse, that was if his blood became blue, and he suddenly turned into a Peer. "Never you do that" I said. At that time he had no intention of such a thing, and

8. Horace, Earl Farquhar, had been Master of the royal household during the reign of Edward VII.

he vowed he never would.' Now he had. The blow to Waldorf's political ambitions was severe. As Nancy put it: 'A peerage was not in his scheme of things at all.'

The quarrel was never fully made up, but amid the fearful events of 1916 it inevitably receded into the background of their lives and thoughts. The first phase of the war with the gay spirit and chivalry which survived amid all its bestiality, and was well represented by the Grenfells and the poems of Rupert Brooke, was slowly giving way to a grimmer and more realistic spirit best represented by the poems of Siegfried Sassoon and Wilfred Owen, and in Germany by the savage satire of the artists assembled around the often-prosecuted and famous Munich weekly *Simplicissimus*. On the Allied side victory now seemed remote, disaster the daily companion, and the certainties of 1914 and 1915 began to be eroded by a sense of doubt.

In this glum year Nancy's private correspondence dwindled, as presumably did that of most people. Even the faithful Philip Kerr's letters to her dropped to an output of nineteen. Belloc only wrote three letters. (They were as gay, as affectionate and as wrong-headed as ever.) There was one letter written on the 26th December from a formerly frequent correspondent, which reached her on the 31st January 1917. It was from Queen Marie of Rumania and was in answer to a letter of condolence from Waldorf and Nancy. The King and Government of Rumania had declared war on the Central Powers, on the 27th August 1916. This rash and heroic act proved disastrous. A German counter-offensive routed the national armies, and Bucharest was occupied on the 6th December 1916. King Ferdinand and Queen Marie had left with the Government for Jassy in the north where, in circumstances of the utmost privation, they were joined by the remnant of the army. Before this, Queen Marie's youngest son, Mircea, who was a little under four years old, died on the 2nd November. This was the occasion of Waldorf and Nancy's letter. The Queen's reply is worthy of being remembered:

'Thank you and Waldorf for your kind words of sympathy. Our trials at this moment are so beyond words that there is nothing to say. One can hardly believe that one is the same human creature as a few months ago. I have had to leave with many others house and home. The Germans are fattening upon all that once was ours, even the little bit of country that still belongs to us may be torn from us soon, then we will be exiles. All these misfortunes are so fantastic that they hardly

seem real. But nothing matters much after the death of my child. To
have sat by his side for three mortal weeks fighting for his precious life
and not being able to save him, that immense and unbearable sorrow
has hardened me against other griefs. Tomorrow we shall perhaps
have also to leave Jassy and then we can call nothing more our own.
I am trying to teach heart and brain to accept the thought but it is
such a preposterous one that it cannot be accomplished all at once.
Certainly the Germans had their revenge against a king who tried
nobly to do his duty towards his country. I am so pleased you are
doing such splendid work, Love to Waldorf. Marie.'

In the first week of December 1916, the first war-time Coalition
broke down; Mr Asquith resigned the Premiership which was filled
by David Lloyd George. Nancy wrote to Margot commiserating with
her on this blow, and in the course of the letter she evidently, as a
Christian Scientist, exhorted her to rely on her inner spiritual strength.
Margot did not reply till the 17th. One may note that, in the way that
became common in Asquith's family, this national event was seen in
very personal terms.

'Dearest Nancy, Thank you for a very dear letter. You say in your
letter you want to see me – *but you never do see me*. Neither Bob Cecil,
Curzon, Austen, Walter or Bonar Law trusted Ll. George but they
are *all serving under him*. Mr Balfour had a horror of the 1st Lord of the
Admiralty Carson so did Bob Cecil (he is Ll. G's right hand man) but
he persuaded Bob, Austen & Walter to back up Ll.G & Carson – I cd
give a longer list than this of the moral shocks I have had in the last 10
days but it wd bore you & you *wd not believe them*.

'The logical conclusion of Xtian Science is that you can fall out of
the window 200 feet & it is only fancy that you are killed – It takes a
Xtian Scientist to believe what you write i.e. that nothing can hurt
"our inner lives". The "God that is within us" wh I have believed in –
in spite of what the clergy say – has become a very shadowy conception
to me in these days. It may be that I believed too much in honour &
loyalty or too little in God. I am tired with packing, & bored with the
thought of finding lodgings, & have been sad at Henry's flue but he
is well & in *great form*! It seems amazing to see such a man! His physical
strength, & persistent vitality, & *fearlessness* – his sweetness & dignity
make even the Prime Minister look small beside him. What I dread
most is that the new Gvt will make Peace then Raymond,[9] Billy,

9. Raymond Asquith had been killed in action in September 1916.

Julian & *all* our loved will have died in vain & Germany will fight again in a few years. This makes me sweat tears of blood & *anguish*. (Will you see me??) Margot.'[10]

Nearly three weeks later Margot was oppressed by second thoughts on this letter, and she wrote again on the 5th January 1917.

'Dearest Nancy, I told [name illegible] I had written you a hasty & biting [?] letter – as I never re-read a letter – (or wd never send one!) I don't remember what I said & if you've got it show it to [same name illegible] & she'll tell me – I only send you a line of love to say I am sorry if I seemed hard but you know being cheated leaves one with an odd sensation round one's heart. I was in bed Xmas week & have been very seedy ever since but Henry is in great form again full of his books & arranging things & answering deluge & floods of letters of a most curious type. It may be that Henry will never be P.M. again but this lot will not last because it is a hopeless machinery I think, & the quarrels wh we were so intimate with I fear will rebegin. Calm & common sense are needed & above all neither Bustle nor heat nor haste, & the reverence wh is the rarest of all things . . .'

Asquith's dignified and cheerful fortitude in the face of disaster (of which these two letters are among many pieces of evidence) disguise the fact that he suffered as bitterly as a man can in such a dire situation. He was physically affected so violently that for some hours it appeared that he had succumbed to a paralytic stroke. Desmond MacCarthy gave a telling detail in his fine literary portrait: 'Some time afterwards – I noted it, because it was a rare gleam of self-disclosure – he said, in dating an event: "Ah, that was while I was recovering from my wound."'

The new course brought new opportunity to Waldorf Astor. At long last his manfully endured spell of duty as an inspector, the last part of which he had spent in ordnance factories, came to an end when Lloyd George appointed him his Parliamentary private secretary. This new duty (which he shared for six months with David Davies), and also

10. The extraordinary extent to which the Prime Minister's wife was uninformed, while believing herself to be the opposite, appears in the last part of this letter. According to Lord Crewe the main reason for the break-up of the coalition in 1916 was the fact that in November Asquith invited Lord Lansdowne to write a memorandum on the possibility of a 'peace of accommodation', and that Asquith expressed his 'complete concurrence'. (Mentioned in Lord Oxford's *Memories and Reflections*, 1928.) Asquith, unlike Lloyd George, came thus under the suspicion of seeking peace.

the committee work already mentioned, which he continued, left him little time for duties outside Parliament. As appears later, his nagging sense of guilt at living in comfort remained unassuaged. He was too modest to recognise that he was the right man in the right place. No giant of British history, with the possible exception of Winston Churchill, depended more on his subordinates than Lloyd George. The man whom his private secretary, Albert Sylvester, recorded as saying, 'Don't notice what I write – notice what I say', was in need of juniors who would save him from impulsiveness. Waldorf Astor was an ideal choice.

In his new post Waldorf became a member of the Cabinet Intelligence Branch which was established by Lloyd George, and popularly known as 'The Garden Suburb' from the fact that this co-ordination office worked in hutments erected in the garden of 10 Downing Street. The original suburb members included three other Members of Parliament besides Waldorf: the radical David Davies, and two Conservatives, Leopold Amery and Sir Mark Sykes. The other members were Professor W. G. Adams of Oxford (chief secretary to the Group), J. T. Davies (Lloyd George's private secretary) and Philip Kerr. The membership changed frequently, expanding and contracting kaleidoscopically as reorganisations followed the fortunes of war or the whims of Lloyd George, and the only suburbanites to remain in the group from first to last were Waldorf, Adams, J. T. Davies and Philip Kerr. In a sense the garden suburb represented the high point of Kindergarten achievement. Their original dream was temporarily realised when the Dominion Prime Ministers and an Indian representative were included in the Imperial War Cabinet. Milner's most lasting achievement in his later years was the establishment of the Ministry of Health, in which the 'honorary Kind' Waldorf was an active and important participant throughout.

In this connection the Unionist Committee for Social Reform made one of its last great public appearances in 1917. Waldorf was now the chairman of the group and in April they produced a penny pamphlet under the title *The Health of the People*. This had the effect of bringing the conception of a Ministry of Health into newspaper discussion, and so helping the cause forward. The pamphlet was well received.

A result of the great enlargement of Waldorf's parliamentary duties and responsibilities was a corresponding enlargement of Nancy's burden of work in the political area. Nancy was more and more required to represent him at public meetings. The experience greatly increased her confidence in her 'power to talk to people easily'. Audiences who assembled in some Plymouth hall or theatre with the expectation of the usual pomposities of such occasions, found themselves in fits of laughter at Nancy's Virginian humour. In May 1917 the new President of the Board of Education, H. A. L. Fisher, came on a visit of inspection to Plymouth, and the great historian (who had taught Waldorf at New College) appeared under Nancy's chairmanship. She sized up the comedy of the situation.

She began by telling the audience that Mr Fisher was by no means popular with his fellow members in the House of Commons because of his two and a half hours' maiden speech introducing the Education estimates. 'He began,' Nancy quoted a friend as saying, 'by doing what I have failed to do after twenty years' practice.' She said that she was particularly well fitted to chair the meeting as education was primarily intended for the alleviation of ignorance. 'I am very keen about education,' she concluded, 'because I suffer from a lack of it, and if you want an ignorant woman to take the chair at an educational meeting, you could not have found a better if you had searched Europe.'

The meeting, after this breezy opening, could hardly fail of success, for Fisher now had his audience with him and he was an excellent and amusing speaker. There were other meetings during Fisher's visit, notably on the 7th May when the Minister formally opened the Astor Playing Fields. On this occasion he capped Nancy's sallies by insisting that the major credit belonged not to the Astors but to himself, because, he argued, without his history lectures at New College, Waldorf would not have been moved to donate the playing fields out of respect for the ancient ideal of education as the equal development of mind and body.

Fisher could have become one of Nancy's closest literary friends, but any chance of that vanished twelve years later. The episode belongs to a later chapter.

1917 was the grimmest of the war years, grimmer than the terrible 1916, and as befitted the time, Nancy's private correspondence dwindled yet further. There is no letter from Belloc of this year; none from Lionel Curtis; only one from Geoffrey Robinson who can henceforth be described by his more familiar name of Geoffrey Dawson. There are only two from Philip Kerr, but this is probably explained by the fact that since he and Waldorf were now colleagues, Nancy and he met more frequently than before. What noteworthy letters have survived are of particular interest, however. She had by now made a new literary friend, Sir Walter Raleigh, the first holder of the chair of English Literature at Oxford. This tall lovable man (most widely remembered today for his quatrain on the human race) had four sons on active service, all of whom survived by some miracle.

On the 23rd April 1917 he wrote a letter of advice to her. Inevitably men had died in the hospital at Cliveden and Nancy was at work organising a worthy cemetery for them. He recommended the following quotation adapted from The Wisdom of Solomon: 'But the souls of the righteous are in the hand of God, and there shall no torment touch them. In the sight of the unwise they seemed to die; and their departure is taken for misery, and their going from us to be utter destruction: but they are in peace. And having been a little chastised, they shall be greatly rewarded: for God proved them and found them worthy for himself.' The last words only were used in the inscription which may be read today: 'They are at peace. God proved them and found them worthy for Himself.'

He used to lecture to the patients in the hospital from time to time, and would consult with Nancy on suitable subjects. 'I haven't a lecture, not yet,' he wrote to her in October, 'You had better wait till one grows. Indeed I promised the other day to write a long article on Hobbes, which article I cannot recommend for the wounded. He lived to 90 and never had his skin scratched.'

The year drew to an end amid disasters and, in spite of a peripheral British victory in the Near East and the participation of the United States (not yet militarily effective), with sombre propositions for a compromise peace in the political world. No household, not even the hopeful one of the Astors, could feel happy in a world that at times seemed doomed to an everlasting nightmare.

Nothing, not even the drug of hard work, could conjure away Waldorf's distress and sense of guilt at being out of danger, and at being envied for his safety. Though he knew he would never be accepted for front-line service, he wanted to get some posting to France so that he might at least share the risks of the troops even in a slight degree. Her correspondence shows that Nancy, well placed for political intrigue, did not become involved in it except in innocuous form. This happened once at the end of 1915[11] and again in November 1917. In that month she wrote to Lord Milner, evidently asking him if he could not arrange for Waldorf's appointment to a Headquarters in France. His answer is interesting as a testament to Waldorf's character, and a comment on life under Lloyd George.

'Dear Mrs Astor, Many thanks for your letter. Waldorf is a great deal more use than he thinks. He would be a great loss if removed from the centre. In that poisonous atmosphere, & with all these hustlers, it really does make a difference to have a man of his character disinfecting the place.

'Nevertheless he ought to have a better job. He ought to have had the L.G.B.,[12] & *very nearly got it*, but for rotten *tactical* considerations (party "claims", balance of this, that & the other & all the rest of it). Better luck next time. One never knows with our flibbertigibbet of a Premier, what he will do with any appointment. If only I could make a Ministry, & then disappear into Erebus the very next minute, how very much better we should get on!!

'I will take an opportunity of talking to Waldorf, without betraying you. Yours very sincerely M.'

Whether or not Waldorf was soothed by Lord Milner does not appear, but there was no transfer and he remained the prisoner of Parliament, his Committees and the Garden Suburb.

There was a third involvement of Nancy in political intrigue during the war, this time on her own initiative, but it was of so mild a kind that it hardly deserves the name. That valiant operator in the promotion of Empire, Commonwealth, and general English-speaking unity, Sir Harry Brittain, was as yet only bemedalled and not conspicuously honoured for his works, and in February 1918 Nancy wrote to Philip Kerr to rectify the oversight. She said at the close of a hilarious letter: 'He is associated in a special degree (see "Who's Who") with our friendship for that great Republic whose perfect, but unassuming, organization for war offers so glaring a contrast to our own inefficiency. I do hope that in any forthcoming eruption of the "fountain of honours" you will contrive to redress this manifest injustice. Yours ever, Nancy.'

11. In December 1915 W. C. Bridgeman wrote to Nancy asking her to use her influence on Geoffrey Robinson in the conduct of *The Times* regarding the Derby Recruiting Scheme. There is no evidence that she did so.

12. Local Government Board. The reference is to the reshuffle of the Government in July 1917.

Whether as a result of this representation or not, Sir Harry was knighted at the next eruption of the fountain on the King's birthday. Nancy's correspondence with Philip Kerr rose to ten letters on his side during 1918, an increase manifestly due to his frequent absence. He had by now become indispensable to Lloyd George and accompanied him on most of his journeys within the country and abroad. When the Prime Minister needed a rest for a day or two Nancy would lend him the house at Sandwich, and Philip Kerr would go there with him. An ideal junior, Philip Kerr was very discreet. His letters give no hint at any time that he was involved in great and crucial events. When on his way to Switzerland in January 1918 for the last tragically fruitless meeting with Austrian representatives in the hope of arranging a separate peace, he wrote to Nancy from Paris but told her nothing beyond his inability to buy chocolates for her at her favourite sweet-shop, and how, in refreshing contrast with his conduct on former Parisian outings, he spent most of his time in the Christian Science Reading Room.

There is only one letter from Belloc in 1918. He visited the American army in France (probably as a lecturer) in April, and there he met a certain Major McCabe who was friends with the Langhornes. The letter is dated 'le 28 Pluvoise, L'An 126 de la Liberté'. He addresses her as 'Citoyenne'. It was written in French which she did not understand, but by this time she was used to his eccentricities and enjoyed them, for otherwise friendship with Belloc was hardly possible. The strange fact remains that after the 28 Pluvoise, A.L. 126, there are no more letters between Belloc and Nancy until 1941. What was the reason for this sudden break?

In her later years she told Maurice Collis: 'He had two manias: against the Jews and against the rich. I had to give him up in the end.'

There was truth in this but only half truth. The ill-effect on the friendship of the mania against the rich has been illustrated. The mania against the Jews was a different matter. As said already, anti-Jewish prejudice was never a serious thing with Nancy. It was otherwise with her anti-Catholicism which was the real cause of the breach. One day in the summer of 1918 Belloc went to lunch with the Astors, taking his daughters, Eleanor and Elizabeth, aged nineteen and eighteen. After lunch Belloc lingered some time with Waldorf, until the latter went off to his affairs and Belloc went up to the drawing-room to fetch the girls. He found all three in animated conversation, the daughters enjoying it hugely. He stood by for a few minutes, found that they were talking about theology and presently realised that Nancy was endeavouring to convert the two girls from their Roman Catholic faith to Christian Science. He was shocked to the very soul. He took the girls away and insisted that they must never meet that 'dangerous woman' again. They never did. They were puzzled. They loved Nancy and never lost their love for her, and only understood later the reason for their father's sense of outrage. At the time, when they asked him he would only shake his head and say that she was 'a verry dangerrous woman'.

The Margot-Nancy correspondence persisted lustily, with all the familiar mixture of hostility and attraction, with savage denunciation of Northcliffe and Bonar Law, with much criticism of Geoffrey Dawson (though she denied having described him as 'a slug' albeit she thought he should join the army rather than serve under Northcliffe), and with occasional but qualified admiration of Lloyd George. The correspondence continued till the 10th May 1918, and then (unless papers have been lost) ceased until October 1919 for no apparent reason. After 1919 the friendship with the Asquith family became tenuous. Perhaps one should remember the suffragettes.

Nancy was still preoccupied with her pious intention of forming a worthy cemetery in Cliveden. In February of 1917 the Australian sculptor Bertram MacKennal had done a head of Nancy. This had pleased her and in September she proposed that he should design and execute a symbolical figure representing Canada to stand in the cemetery at Cliveden as its dominant ornament.

He agreed, and in the course of discussion he persuaded her to sit to him for the head. She agreed, on the understanding that this was not to be a recognisable portrait.[13] So it was concluded and the statue of a female figure with outstretched arms was completed at the end of the summer of 1918, and after the war a replica was presented and sent

13. 'There is not much outward resemblance to you except your inspiration and all that is good in the work comes from that. It is your eyes alone which I think still remain.' MacKennal to Mrs Astor, 8th June 1918. Sir Bertram MacKennal was the first Australian to be elected R.A. His most familiar work is the sculpture on the Edward VII memorial in St George's Chapel, Windsor, and the equestrian statue of Edward VII in Waterloo Place, London. D.N.B.

by Nancy to Canada. If one knows that Nancy modelled for the head, the likeness is obvious, but not otherwise, as the resemblance is effectively lessened by the long flowing hair. The cemetery, situated in a hollow in the woods on the west side of the house, is a place of haunting beauty. At the end of the Great War it contained the graves of forty Canadian soldiers and two nursing sisters.

No hospital, not even such a model institution as the Duchess of Connaught's Canadian Red Cross Hospital, can proceed without friction, rows, umbrage and the rest. Throughout the years of strain nothing very terrible occurred until near the end. The moment came in the last summer of the war when Nancy was pregnant. 'The corner stone' of the hospital, Colonel Newbourne, went away temporarily, either on leave or to some duty elsewhere. What then happened was thus related by Nancy.

'Another Colonel was sent to us, in charge for a time. Everyone absolutely hated him. I was going to London, to have my last baby, and the Matron, herself a most charming and delightful and cultured woman, came to see me. She was almost in tears. She said she simply could not see how she was going to carry on working with the Colonel, without me as a sort of buffer state between them.

'There was nothing I could do about it except hope for the best. When I got back, I at once made anxious enquiries as to how things had gone.

' "Go slow!" someone said. "Matron has fallen in love with the Colonel!"

'I was quite dumbfounded. He wasn't her class, and into the bargain he was dishonest. Mercifully nothing came of it, for he finally got himself into a mess from which there was only one way out. He took it and shot himself, which saved everybody a great deal of trouble and unpleasantness.

'I always think of him bracketed in my mind with Caliban.'

Nancy's youngest son and last child was born on the 29th August 1918. He was christened after many of his forbears and his grandfather's cousin, John Jacob. Since early 1917, her eldest son Bobbie Shaw had been in France as a subaltern in the Royal Horse Guards. He saw action and survived unwounded. Her correspondence shows that she kept her anxieties to herself, and several of her friends were unaware that she had a son serving at the front. In October the main part of 4 St James's Square was lent to the Y.M.C.A. as a rest hostel for officers of the

American forces, and remained thus till June 1919. The hostel was officially styled 'Washington Inn', but popularly known as 'The Waldorf-Astoria'. It was estimated that in those eight months more than five thousand American officers enjoyed a bed in the ballroom which was transformed into a dormitory.

According to her own inexact account, Nancy may have first heard news of the outbreak of the Great War in the covered tennis court at Cliveden. It is very likely that she heard of the Armistice of the 11th November 1918 in the same place.

Lady Astor's 1951 draft for an autobiography remains a principal authority, but unfortunately for the last time. In so far as this hastily improvised piece of writing contains a formal chronology it ends with an account of her hospital at Cliveden in 1918. The biographer says goodbye to this source with heartfelt regret. All the letters quoted are in the Astor archive. The account of the Unionist Committee for Social Reform in its later stages, when Waldorf Astor was its chairman, is partly drawn from a letter of 1914 from Lord Henry Cavendish Bentinck and numerous references in the Press of April 1917 where the U.C.S.R. pamphlet, *Health and the People*, was widely reviewed. The account of the establishment of the Canadian Red Cross Hospital, of the membership of the 'Garden Suburb' (frequently the subject of Parliamentary questions), and of the official visit to Plymouth by H. A. L. Fisher, are also drawn from contemporary Press records. The reference to Lady Astor's personal initiative in the transfer of the ownership of *The Observer* follows family traditions but appears to be undocumented. Mr Edwin Lee's essay written for Michael Astor has again been drawn on, as indicated. The writer has occasionally drawn on Michael Astor's *Tribal Feeling* and Maurice Collis's *Nancy Astor*, though neither book contains an account of Lady Astor's activity in the First World War. References to Philip Kerr (outside his correspondence) are drawn from Sir James Butler's biography. The account of Lady Anne Kerr's attitude to Lady Astor, and that of Philip Kerr's sisters, follows an account given to me by Mrs Nancy Lancaster, to whom I remain indebted for general impressions. The account of the breach in the friendship between Lady Astor and Hilaire Belloc follows one given to me by Belloc's daughter, Mrs Eleanor Jebb. The account of the use of 4 St James's Square in the later part of the war follows information taken from a letter of thanks from the General Secretary of the Y.M.C.A. with the American Expeditionary Forces on the termination of the hostel in June 1919. The writer has had recourse to the *Dictionary of National Biography* and to the new volumes of the *Encyclopaedia Britannica* covering the 1914–1919 war years, published in 1926.

Chapter 10

M.P.

BY 1918 the militant activities and atrocities of the Suffragettes were a mere memory, and in a world of change, one in which women had taken on almost every male task except front-line action in battle and parliamentary duties, the notion that they should be denied the vote began to appear grotesque. Contemporary Press evidence suggests that in this respect the fortitude and death of Edith Cavell had a decisive influence on opinion. When a parliamentary bill proposing women's suffrage was introduced into the House of Commons in March 1917, it met surprisingly little opposition and became law in February 1918. From this point the logical step was clear: to admit women members into Parliament. This was not so readily agreed, even when historians tried to soothe troubled minds by pointing to ancient precedent, since abbesses had occasionally attended the Saxon Witenagemot. The step was taken very late in the war, when victory and a general election in the immediate future were certain. On the 23rd October 1918 Sir Herbert Samuel moved 'that in the opinion of this House, it is desirable that a bill be passed forthwith making women eligible as Members of Parliament'. The motion was carried by 275 against 25. Thereafter things moved fast by parliamentary standards. On the 31st October Lord Robert Cecil presented the Parliament (Qualification of Women) Bill. It was read the second time on the 4th November, and on the 21st November, after being reported and read a third time, and having been accepted by the House of Lords, it received the Royal Assent. There was a hasty scramble among political women for candidature and for the distinction of being the first woman member, for only twenty-three days remained before polling day on the 14th December.

The results were disappointing to the women and their sympathisers. Only seventeen women candidates stood, but a few of them, notably Christabel Pankhurst, were regarded as certain winners. In the event they were all defeated except the beautiful and reckless Irish nationalist, Countess Markievicz, who appears to have stood for election as a joke and was unable by circumstances to enjoy personal contact with the

Dublin electorate, since at the time she was serving one of her numerous
sentences in Holloway Prison. She was the first woman to be elected
to the British House of Commons. She was appalled by her success.
Gay in temperament, she looked with dread at the long hours of
debate and boredom to which she had condemned herself, till she
found a happy and heroic way out. The seventy-three Sinn Fein
members, of whom she was one, refused to take the oath of loyalty
to the King and thus invalidated their elections. She followed their
example, and thus disqualified herself from an intolerable honour.
There were no women, therefore, in the first post-war Parliament
when it assembled.

But there were bound to be women in the House of Commons
soon. That was obvious. Feminism was a world-wide movement which
was especially strong in the English-speaking world. Countess Markievicz is usually described as the first woman to be elected to Parliament,
but in fact she was the second. Canada passed its first female suffrage
legislation before the mother country, in 1916, and was quicker with
the logical next phase. The first woman to be elected a Member of
Parliament was Miss Agnes MacPhail, who took her seat in the
Canadian House of Commons in March 1918.

Waldorf's constituency had undergone drastic constitutional changes
since his election in December 1910. Plymouth was no longer a single
constituency but, in 1917, following a redrawing of parliamentary
boundaries throughout the country, the whole area had been divided
into three, each returning one member only. With gloomy indifference
to local sentiment, the three constituencies had been named West,
Central and East Plymouth. Local sentiment, backed in Parliament by
Waldorf and his fellow member for Plymouth, Shirley Benn, demanded something better, and the three constituencies were finally
named Devonport, Drake and Sutton. Waldorf was allotted the Eastern
constituency, the Sutton division of Plymouth.

The General Election of 1918 is known as the 'Coupon Election', a
term coined by Asquith in the course of electioneering, from the fact
that Coalition candidates approved by the Whips received letters of
commendation from the Prime Minister or Bonar Law. This very
ordinary and (in by-elections) usual procedure has since been judged
iniquitous, but few people regarded it as such at the time. Needless to
say, Waldorf Astor received the commendation of his chief. He was
opposed by an Asquithian Liberal called Colonel Ransome, and a

Labour candidate of some prominence in the Co-operative Movement, called William Gay. The election resulted in a huge majority for Waldorf in the Sutton division. He polled 17,091 votes with a majority of 11,756 over his Labour runner-up.

Waldorf's political career was one of steady advancement, and he believed he could hope to be a leading figure before very long. He had remained Lloyd George's parliamentary private secretary till the Prime Minister's departure for Paris at the end of October 1918, as the fighting in France drew to a close. He was then appointed parliamentary secretary to the Ministry of Food, a post he was holding at the time of the General Election. In the new Parliament he was transferred to the parliamentary secretaryship of the Local Government Board, from where he saw the long labours of Milner and the now defunct Unionist Committee for Social Reform crowned by the establishment of the Ministry of Health in July 1919. He was transferred again and became parliamentary secretary to the new ministry under its first chief, Christopher Addison, a post he retained till Addison's enforced retirement in 1921, by which time many strange things had happened.

There is no evidence that, at the great 1918 moment of feminist hope, Nancy, a feminist from her youth, showed any inclination to join seriously in the fun. She canvassed for Waldorf with her usual boisterous energy and her usual American jollity. She adjured the new female electorate in Sutton to show their womanly wisdom by voting the right way, but of any political ambition at this time no trace appears. The biographical interest still centres on her private life, and in a busy year of humdrum work while the Cliveden hospital and the 'Waldorf-Astoria' were wound up, her private life still largely centred on her friends.

One of her most emotional friendships at this time was with Lionel Curtis, and in 1919 she played a decisive role in his life. In 1915 he had fallen in love with his secretary, Miss Scott, but both he and the young woman were inhibited by an almost morbid correctitude. 'She's a nice girl,' wrote Philip Kerr to Nancy in May 1919, 'and might marry L. if you can cure him of his conscience.'

Nancy did cure him of his conscience. She acted to Lionel Curtis as a persuasive duenna, as Marie of Rumania had done towards herself thirteen years before.

Lionel Curtis and Miss Scott were married, with great subsequent happiness, in 1920, and without Nancy's intervention they might well have been forced apart by their own natures.

Philip Kerr wrote Nancy sixteen letters in 1919. They met infrequently during this time since he spent most of it in Paris on duty as the head of Lloyd George's personal staff, and then in a similar appointment to Balfour. This was a moment of high achievement in his career, when his great abilities and unflagging mental energy first came into public notice.

To make a bold generalisation, British policy centred round the continual battle between the degenerating Northcliffe and the impressionable Lloyd George. If more men in Northcliffe's employment had had the moral courage of Geoffrey Dawson and resigned his service, then Northcliffe's power would have declined and his terrible influence on British policy would surely have been reduced to modest proportions. But the opposite happened. In spite of a magnificent parliamentary success at Northcliffe's expense during the Peace Conference, Lloyd George remained oversensitively aware of public opinion, and he came to believe that he was forced to take more extremist decisions on the peace treaty, especially regarding Germany, than either his judgement or caprice could approve. He felt forced by pressures, of which Northcliffe's was the greatest, to act against his beliefs.

In the course of the ferocious battle Northcliffe said with commendable wit that though Lloyd George knew how to read and write, he practised neither craft. There was truth in this. He had no love of either. Philip Kerr as his intimate and the chief of his personal staff did most of the necessary drafting for him, and without exceeding his functions in any way he was thus able to exert some influence on Lloyd George because his influence was welcome. By his tact and his manifest ability he soon began to exert influence on the Conference in general. Lloyd George told later that he came to be looked on as an assistant delegate rather than as a secretary. It was largely due to Kerr's initiative that the plans for large-scale Allied intervention in the civil war in Russia were scotched as soon as they were.

In view of his later history, Kerr's attitude to defeated Germany is of special interest. He and the Prime Minister were agreed on the folly of demanding unpayable reparations from Germany, but Northcliffe disastrously won that part of the battle. But on another question Lloyd George and Philip Kerr were in the completest agreement with Northcliffe, namely the exclusive guilt of Germany for the outbreak of a world war in 1914. It was Philip Kerr who drafted Article 231 of the Treaty, earning thereby the esteem of President Wilson and Clemenceau. It ran as follows:

'The Allied and Associated Governments affirm, and Germany accepts, the responsibility of Germany and her allies for causing all the loss and damage to which the Allied and Associated Governments and their nationals have been subjected, as a consequence of the war imposed upon them by the aggression of Germany and her allies.'

The head of the German delegation was Count zu Brockdorff-Rantzau. He was a man of spirit but also, as was common with his German class and time, he took a dismal pride in making more enemies than he needed to do. At a special session he rebutted the charge of German war-guilt in haughty language, and further angered the Allied leaders by reading the rebuttal seated in his chair. The reply to Brockdorff-Rantzau from the Allies was drafted by Philip Kerr. The central passage reads as follows:

'Throughout the war, as before the war, the German people and their representatives supported the war, voted the credits, subscribed to the war loans, obeyed every order, however savage, of their Government. They shared the responsibility for the policy of their Government, for at any moment, had they willed it, they could have reversed it. Had that policy succeeded, they would have acclaimed it with the same enthusiasm with which they welcomed the outbreak of the war. They cannot now pretend, having changed their rulers after the war was lost, that it is justice that they should now escape the consequences of their deeds.'

His letters to Nancy do not suggest that when he wrote this or drafted Article 231 he acted against the grain. He refers to the Germans as 'the Hun', and thus described the confrontation of the enemy delegation with the Allied leaders: 'I managed to get into the meeting with the Germans. It was most interesting. Clemenceau was extraordinarily good, and Rantzau very clumsy. He certainly did not improve the Hun's chances of moderate terms. The descriptions in the papers are quite accurate.' The final scene on the 28th June 1919 did not prompt his compassion. 'The signing,' he wrote to Nancy on that day, 'was interesting but not very impressive. Too many people and not a good shaped hall. The Germans were the most awful worms to look at.'

One may conclude, in fact, that Philip Kerr's emotional reactions to the events of the time were the usual ones, but one cannot be absolutely sure from the evidence of his letters to Nancy, as he says so little about those events, even though he was in the thick of them and playing a brilliant part. This particular group of letters is likely, if published, to be much esteemed by his co-religionists, but to come as a great disappointment to any reader who wishes to obtain an impression of that time. He seems to have spent what little leisure Lloyd George allowed him in the Christian Science Reading Room.

On the 18th October 1919, Waldorf's father died at the age of seventy-one. The quarrel with his eldest son had not been composed, and the obstinate old man had added to his offence by accepting promotion to a viscountcy in 1917.

Waldorf had hopes either of succeeding Christopher Addison as Minister of Health, or of obtaining some other ministerial appointment to which he was particularly suited. He was well qualified to be a Home Secretary. But all such hopes (which in view of his chronic ill-health may have been illusory) became more remote as soon as he was a member of the House of Lords. He sought legal advice as to whether the heir to a title of nobility was at liberty to resign it. He was assured that an heir could enjoy no such liberty without new legislation, and Waldorf was no longer a member of the House of Commons where such legislation would normally be initiated. His only hope was to initiate it himself in the House of Lords, or find a friend who would do this in the Commons. In the meantime he could do nothing at all to disentangle himself from unwanted honours.

On the same day as William Waldorf Astor died, a report appeared in the *Evening Standard* that, according to rumour, the Conservative candidate in the forthcoming by-election necessitated by Lord Astor's death would probably be the new Viscountess. This was undoubtedly a lucky guess, no more. Lord Astor had died very suddenly, so much so that since the General Election neither the Conservatives nor the Asquith Liberals had chosen prospective candidates to stand in the event of just such an emergency as this one. (William Gay was still prospective candidate for the Labour Party.) Whether or not Nancy and Waldorf had plans for her to stand when her father-in-law died cannot now be known. There is no documentary evidence of their existence. Whatever the fact, suddenly Nancy and her husband were faced with the need for a swift and crucial decision, and for a week they wrestled with it alone and privately.

The Press, of course, wrestled with it publicly, and the item in the *Evening Standard* acted as a match to gunpowder or the strategically timed sneeze which results in an avalanche. Most of the Press, and especially the provincial Press of the West Country, gave themselves over to speculation. Will she? Won't she? Most opinion began with the belief that she would, but after a few days the prevalent forecast was that she would not. The circumstances were without precedent, the closest, as the *Pall Mall Gazette* pointed out, being the occasion when, after the death of Waldorf's former colleague Sir Mark Sykes in February 1919, his widow was invited to stand for Central Hull but, though tempted, finally refused the offer as personally embarrassing. Would Nancy feel the same about standing for her husband's seat in less tragic conditions? The *Pall Mall Gazette* felt she would, and as this was an Astor paper their view was widely followed as the best informed. Most of the Press began to forecast that Waldorf's younger brother John would stand. For a few days interest turned from the Astors to the Liberal Party, for it became known that the non-coalition Liberal leaders of Plymouth had informally approached Mr Asquith with an invitation to stand. (The former Prime Minister had been defeated in 1918.) A journalist's dream began to form: a by-election featuring a former Prime Minister, a reluctant peer, Margot, and Nancy who was sure to canvass even if she did not stand! But the dream dissolved with Mr Asquith's refusal. Then on Friday the 24th October the Conservative Association of the Sutton Division of Plymouth formally asked Nancy to stand in the Conservative interest, and they made the invitation public. The eyes of the Press turned back to Cliveden. To telephone call after telephone call Waldorf replied that the decision lay with his wife alone. She told one reporter who tracked her down that she could say nothing to the Press till she had given her answer to the Association. On Sunday the 26th October she accepted by telegram.

Most of the Press gave the news in headlines. The *Daily Herald* of the 27th announced to its readership: 'Peer's Wife Enters', with a subtitle: 'To Fight Against Workers At Plymouth'. The article below this announcement, however, was mild and polite, and principally devoted to the virtues of William Gay. The other extreme of opinion was no better pleased with the prospect. The *Morning Post* of the 28th gave a long elegantly-worded growl of a leading article under a consciously cryptic and learned headline, 'Dux Femina Fecit'. The Conservative shift over the years from an anti-Feminist position was sarcastically rebuked, and that an American should stand was deplored. One paper, G. K. Chesterton's *New Witness*, was rather complimentary on this subject: there were so many Jews in Parliament, it was stated, that one more foreign member, this time not Jewish, ought not to be the subject of complaint!

That the *Morning Post* had spoken for a section of the Conservative electorate became clear on the 30th when Alderman Lionel Jacobs of Plymouth announced that he was putting himself forward as an Independent Unionist candidate. If he stood he would undoubtedly split the Conservative vote. On the same day the Asquithian Liberals invited a highly esteemed lawyer of Plymouth, Mr Isaac Foot, to stand in their interest, and on that same day too Nancy arrived in Plymouth. Her chances were obviously high, but the election would not be a walkover.

Apart from anti-Feminism, a growing Labour vote, Mr Jacobs's threat, and the prestige of Mr Foot, Nancy had another difficulty to contend with. 1919 was the year when the United States declared for prohibition of all alcoholic liquor. Nancy had never disguised her abolitionist convictions and pub-frequenters of all parties looked with distaste on the prospect of prohibition in Great Britain. Here was possibly the greatest menace to her success. If she stood as a pro-hibitionist, a 'pussyfoot' as such people were called then, she would very probably lose. Fortunately for her Waldorf, during the war, had spoken strongly against the dangers of prohibitionist legislation to audiences in Plymouth. Wisely Nancy declared herself to be no pussy-foot, but an enemy of drunkenness. Hardly had she done so than Philip Kerr wrote some advice to her on the 30th October on how to run the campaign. He urged her to stand for unadulterated prohibition.

There is a letter from Philip Kerr to Nancy of the 5th November indicating that she replied in a friendly way, but a letter sent by him two days later shows that on second thoughts she had found this high-minded advice which, if followed, could only lead to her defeat, irritating. Her political private secretary at that time was Miss Benningfield, always known as 'Bunny'. She was a fellow Christian Scientist who, like Nancy, did not find that her faith inhibited an abounding sense of humour. She and Nancy were on terms of much affection. It is most likely that she persuaded Nancy not to be influenced by Kerr's extremism. At all events Miss Benningfield wrote to Kerr and he wrote to Nancy on the 7th November.

'Miss Benningfield rebukes me,' he said, 'quite rightly, for my last letter. She says it was impersonal and unhelpful and full of opposition. I'm afraid it must have been, and if so, I'm very sorry for it. . . . Anyhow I'm grateful to Miss Benningfield for telling me off, and I've told her by way of retaliation that she's just got to heal me of the wall or whatever it is you all complain of. . . .' It is a long letter of excusings. This incident did not cause any even temporary breach in their friendship, but after hearing from Miss Benningfield his advice became markedly less definitive. He made no more suggestions for a prohibitionist programme.

The writ for the election was issued on the 3rd November, and on the same day Nancy and Waldorf attended the meeting of the Party Association at which she was to be formally adopted. On the day before, Mr Jacobs had withdrawn, so prospects of victory had advanced. The first of the principal speeches was that of the retiring member proposing his wife as the new candidate. Remembering Nancy's smartness in repartee, he began by assuring the Association: 'I want to tell you straight away, if anybody thinks she is going into this contest in any light-hearted spirit, not realising the responsibilities which will be hers, that person is mistaken.'

One is apt to think that so sincere a moralist as Waldorf would be a restrained speaker erring on the side of tameness. This was not the case with him at all. He was a forceful and emotional speaker with no qualms about hard hitting. Indeed, he had been criticised in the war for what was held to be excessive incitement to hatred of the enemy in a speech given at Plymouth in 1917. He was a tough fighter in party warfare. Personal friendship with Mr Asquith and Isaac Foot did not restrain his attack on the non-coalition Liberals. 'I see in the papers,' he said, 'that Mr Asquith wants to return to Parliament. He thought of Plymouth, but that was not good enough. He was afraid he would get beaten, so they selected a candidate who is accustomed to getting beaten. [Isaac Foot had been defeated in three previous contests.] I do not believe the people of Plymouth want the policy of "Wait and

See". The policy of "Wait and See" nearly wrecked the country during the war, and it has absolutely shattered the old Liberal Party.' He turned with contempt on the Labour candidate William Gay. 'There is a young man who, I am told, has not been a great success as a manager in the Co-op. He is a well meaning sort of extremist belonging to the Bolshevist wing of the Labour Party. If he and his friends had had their way we should have lost the war. [Gay was a pacifist.] I notice, reading his speeches, that he is full of phrases: socialisation, nationalisation, collectivism, syndicalism. We want deeds not words.' Gay threatened a libel action on account of the allegation of failure as a manager, and Waldorf was obliged to withdraw publicly a little later.

After Waldorf had formally introduced her, Nancy made her opening speech of the campaign. It was something new, unexpected and unconventional, as all her speeches were. She was not a good speaker in the ordinary meaning of the term, chiefly because she too easily lost the thread of her argument; she inclined to pack in so many asides that they squeezed out the main theme. But in these speeches as a candidate she showed at her best. She was master of her subject which she expressed thus in her speech: 'I have heard it said that a woman who has got children shouldn't go into the House of Commons. She ought to be home looking after her children. That is true, but I feel someone ought to be looking after the more unfortunate children. My children are among the fortunate ones, and it is that that steels me to go to the House of Commons to fight the fight, not only of the men but of the women and children of England.' To that aim she was true, and her conviction contained profound truth. There was a whole area of needed legislation, which was not only inadequately represented, and inadequately provided for when translated into law, but which could not be otherwise until there were women members of Parliament. But her political intentions in this respect were qualified, for all their intensity. She said: 'I am not standing before you as a sex candidate.' To this ideal she tried but failed to be true.

To go forward again for a moment. When the contest was over Nancy admitted to a feeling of guilt that the first woman to sit in the British Parliament should have been herself, who had never suffered anything at all physically, and nothing unbearable in her mind for the feminist cause. The first woman member, she said, should have been such a person as Millicent Fawcett or Christabel Pankhurst. Her feelings were understandable and do her much credit. But as her friend Mary

Stocks pointed out many years later, it was a great thing for the rights
of women that these should have been first and decisively represented
by a woman whose feminist belief was not identifiable with a feminist
party. It put the whole matter on a general basis. It has been pointed
out by others also, including Lady Stocks, that it was no small benefit
to the feminist cause that the triumphant Nancy Astor was not the
dreaded unsexed ogress of popular and not always misled imagination,
but a woman of extraordinary beauty, nothing if not feminine in the
accepted sense.

This is to anticipate the triumph. Back to the first week of November
1919.

Other items of the speech Nancy made at the adoption meeting on
the 3rd should be remembered because, for the most part, the rest of
her campaigning speeches were not more than variations on the theme
of this one. Nancy had personal charm, and she knew it, and she knew
also that thanks to her ineradicably Virginian character it was of a kind
to please popular audiences everywhere except in a ferociously hostile
camp. She proceeded to give a self-portrait in arresting terms. She said
that years of work for and with the wounded had made her rather like
a soldier herself. 'So if my manners are slightly like a sergeant-major's
you will know the reason why.' She also said: 'Although I am one of
the most serious-minded women in England today I have got the sort
of mirth of the British Tommy. I can laugh when I am going over
the top.'

She concluded with high spirit. 'If you want an M.P. who will be
a repetition of the 600 other M.P.s don't vote for me. If you want a
lawyer or if you want a pacifist don't elect me. If you can't get a
fighting man, take a fighting woman. If you want a Bolshevist or a
follower of Mr Asquith, don't elect me. If you want a party hack don't
elect me. Surely we have outgrown party ties. I have. The war has
taught us that there is a greater thing than parties, and that is the State.'
She was high in praise of the Prime Minister: 'I got to know a good
deal about Mr Lloyd George because I spent a fortnight in Brittany
with him. His heart is as sound as a dollar and he has got courage – Oh –
and he has the welfare of the whole country at heart. I am going to
back him but only in so far as I think he is right.'

She was adopted unanimously.

She was furnished with a letter of warm recommendation, a 'coupon'
from Lloyd George, which had been drafted by Philip Kerr. She also

had letters intended for publication from Bonar Law, Christopher Addison, H. A. L. Fisher, Arthur Balfour and Lord Robert Cecil. The next official step in the election was the formal nomination of candidates, billed to be held on Friday the 7th November, but the campaign was in full fury before that. On the day after her adoption she addressed a meeting of women. 'You have not got much of a choice if you don't elect me,' she said, 'Mr Foot is pledged to Mr Asquith. I like Foot much better than his leader, but as for Mr Gay, my other opponent, he belongs to the most poisonous section of the Labour Party that ever existed on earth,' at which there was laughter and cheering.

From the beginning of electioneering history (it may be assumed) some of the art of a successful candidate has lain in the evasion of awkward questions. Nowadays the usual manoeuvre is to reword what is asked – 'What you are really saying, etc.' – followed by recourse to long-worded jargon and unfollowable statistics. In 1919 most of the electorate were grossly ill-educated, and so less subtle methods were still effective. The candidate and his speakers were usually safe with a quick comic turning of the tables on the adversary, without reference to the subject raised. Nancy used this not wholly admirable tactic with great skill. When question time came at this same women's meeting one of her audience got up to ask a question about pensions for the elderly. She owned to the age of sixty-six. In a flash, and amid loud laughter, Nancy told her she was much too young and pretty to trouble her head about such things.

Another woman asked her about the arbitrary powers given to the police to arrest women walking in any street alone, on suspicion of 'soliciting'. Nancy slid out of answering by a genuine display of wit which remained famous for many years. To follow a contemporary reporter's account of what she said:

'Let me tell you something awfully funny that happened to me. I saw a young American sailor looking at the outside of the House of Commons. I said to him: "Would you like to go in?" He answered: "You are the sort of woman my mother told me to avoid."'

One of her best evasions was on an occasion that called for it. A woman heckler made an obvious and offensive allusion to her divorce and asked her if it was true that she intended to introduce the laxer code of American divorce law into Great Britain. Speaking with a very pronounced American accent, she replied: 'What? Are you in trouble too, old sister?'

Nomination day was full of fresh drama and comedy. It so happened that Nancy and Isaac Foot arrived at the same moment at the Town Clerk's office, with their nomination papers and their cheques for the deposit which a candidate forfeits if he polls less than one eighth of the votes. The coincidence of their appearance together offered a temptation to Nancy which she was quite unable to resist. As Isaac Foot handed over his cheque to the Town Clerk she loudly exclaimed: 'You're the father of seven children! I don't think it right in your position to throw your money away like that!' Isaac Foot took the assault, as he took all Nancy's assaults, with unshakable good humour, and smilingly escorted her towards her car. But before she left, there was another incident, one which illustrates a striking difference between the British customs of that time and our own. Turning on the assembled reporters and photographers, she denounced the behaviour of the Press. 'I have nothing to say against the reporters,' she said, 'I believe they are acting decently. It is the editors who are responsible, and when I get to the House of Commons, as I intend to do, I will expose them all. They should publish facts and treat this election seriously. They forget that I have principles and ideals. They are making my candi-dature funny, but they would make fun of the dead and would do anything for fivepence.'

In our day, when the lightest criticism of the Press is apt to be described as an attempt to suppress liberty, such an outburst might mean political suicide, but in 1919, when the Press was more influ-ential and far more varied than it is today, Nancy's denunciation was printed without comment. One cannot entirely blame editors for their alleged offence in this case and their quotations of 'Astorisms'.

As she and Foot reached her car, she turned to him and asked him if he would not like to make a speech about the need of women in parliament, since there was an audience ready made in the assembled crowd. He said he would make the speech elsewhere and handed her in.[1] That evening, as though to stress the point she had made to the reporters, she made a thoughtful speech in support of the League of Nations.

Elections were more picturesque and colourful in those days. In

1. There was further drama in the course of Nomination Day. William Gay's papers were found to be invalid owing to a technical irregularity, but the objection to his candidature was withdrawn on representations made by the Conservative and Liberal agents.

conformity with custom, Nancy, with Waldorf at her side, often did her tours of the constituency in a landau carriage drawn by two smartly harnessed horses and driven by an enormous liveried top-hatted coachman whose name was Churchward. The carriage, the horses' bridles, the coachman, the candidate, her husband and her party were all gaily decorated with red, white and blue rosettes. Nancy did not make the common mistake of trying to curry favour by adopting a disguise of dowdiness. Contemporary photographs show that she was always dressed in her fashionable best and wore her pearls wherever she went in Plymouth.

Thus the party trotted round the Sutton Division, and whenever they came on a knot of people Nancy stopped the carriage, stood up in it, and began to speak. Sometimes she got out if there was a soapbox or something of the kind to hand, and spoke from the street corner. It was always in backchat that she excelled. An angry female heckler came up at one of these improvised meetings and cried at her: 'Why did you call me a virago at the hall the other night?' 'Did I?' answered Nancy, 'well if I did I go on my knees and apologise.' 'Well you did!' shouted the virago. 'Then let's forgive each other,' said Nancy. 'You forgive me my sins and I'll forgive you yours.' 'I haven't got any!' shouted the virago. 'You lucky devil,' answered Nancy.

Her skill in getting potentially hostile audiences on her side was extraordinary. A coal heaver yelled at her once: 'What has your husband ever done for us?' By a stroke of luck she knew him. 'Charlie, you old liar,' she shouted back, 'you know quite well what he has done,' and seeing photographers around she insisted on being photographed with him. This American extension of the bonhomie pose into which all candidates are forced may not have had much influence, but the frankness and courage with which she tackled her problem as a millionairess preaching social reform was hard to resist. At one meeting she said in the course of an assault on the Independent Labour Party: 'Mr Gay belongs to the unpatriotic section of the Labour Party and poses as a conscientious objector. I have more, far more than I ought to have, but if some members of the I.L.P. possessed what I do, they would not be asking for your votes today.'

It was not a fair assault, but when was there an election that was wholly and perfectly free of the Eatanswill spirit? The sally is reported to have been received with laughter and cheers. It was at this meeting that Nancy coined a phrase (not her best one) which legend wrongly attributes to Mrs Baldwin. 'Mr Gay, the Labour candidate, represents the shirking classes, but I represent the working classes.' It went down well. Once she converted a hostile street-corner meeting into one that was at least prepared to hear her by intervening on the audience's side while it was shouting her down! Churchward became alarmed for her safety and dismounting from the box of the landau waded in with cautionary growls to 'behave yourself', but Nancy turned on him. 'Shut up, Churchward!' she shouted, 'I'm making this speech, not you.' The little crowd may not have voted her way, but they listened to her after that.

One piece of backchat deserves a better name and qualified as real wit. At one of these street meetings a man began to hurl obscene abuse at her. She turned away from him to where some women were standing and said: 'I want every woman in this street to see that that man does not vote for me. I don't want the vote of a man who uses language like that to a woman when he is sober.'

It must not be thought that Nancy had it all her own way. Far from it. Of one meeting the admittedly biased *Daily Herald* reported: 'There was in the audience one of those learned men of a statistical turn of mind and an insinuating politeness, who launched one question after another on income taxes and super taxes and suchlike awkward things. Amid the din the prompter was apparently unintelligible and Lady Astor confessed she knew not the subject. There was a roar of derision. Then came one of her characteristic declarations. 'I am not a paid politician,' she cried, 'therefore I can afford to speak the truth and declare straightforwardly I don't know.'

It was a good retreat in awkward circumstances, but no victory.

The election was covered by the Press with the thoroughness usually given only to general elections, and simultaneous contests at Thanet, Croydon and Chester-le-Street paled into insignificance. Eminent persons in politics and public life came down to Plymouth, and among speakers who added their prestige to Nancy's cause were Mrs Lloyd George, General Sir John Cowans, and a recently elected and highly esteemed young Conservative member, Mr Oswald Mosley.

To the end she encouraged the hecklers, knowing that they were the instrument on which she played best. 'Come along,' she would cry, 'who'll take me on? I'm ready for you!' and she nearly always scored. 'Go back to America' was an occasional cry against her. 'Go back to Lancashire' she shouted back at one man. 'I'm an Irishman,' he replied.

'I knew it, an imported interrupter!' she shouted again. 'If I'd imported you,' roared the Irishman, 'I'd drown myself in the sea.' 'More likely in drink,' she shouted back. 'I'm a teetotaller!' he cried triumphantly to the alleged pussyfoot. 'Well go and have a drink today,' she shouted at him. 'It might sweeten you!'

By polling day, the 15th November, the majority of Press opinion was that Nancy would win, with William Gay as a close runner-up. No one prognosticated victory for the amiable Isaac Foot. His amiability must not cause the impression that he was a weak fighter, but the difficulty of his position was beyond the capacity of any candidate. Lloyd George was still enjoying a popularity with the public at large not to be equalled till the premiership of Winston Churchill, and his unseated chief Asquith was among the most unpopular men in the country. A spirited Press correspondence between Foot and Lloyd George in which the former solemnly recalled the latter to his Liberal allegiance, probably did Foot much more harm than good in the last phase of the election.

Waldorf had kept in the background, but emerged in the last phase after Gay had put forward a ludicrous misrepresentation of a speech he had made in the House of Commons, endeavouring to prove that in fact Nancy's husband had voted against women's suffrage in 1917. Waldorf enjoyed an easy win.

Polling day came, and with it the usual ostentatious benevolence shown by the vote-hungry candidates. Nancy gave her own extravaganza to the custom when she held a woman voter's baby while the mother went into the voting station. During the wait she let the little darling play with her pearls. 'Always give babies your pearls to play with,' she remarked with charming insolence to some reporters standing by. By luck there was a photographer at hand too.

On the 16th she went to Cliveden to rest. The declaration was not to be made till the 28th November, owing to the delay caused by the collection of service men's votes abroad. On the 19th she received a letter from a supreme representative of High Toryism of the ancient and classic school.

'My dear Lady Astor, I must write you a line about your contest else you will think all sorts of things, or more likely you will not think about it at all – still you might.

'I am as usual lost in admiration of your energy and public spirit. Of course it is a new idea to me and I know I am a hopeless mass of prejudice. I am torn by conflicting emotions – on the one side friend-ship and on the other side purblind fossilized Toryism!

'I should have imagined that you would be exhausted but Alice[2] tells me not – on the contrary. This is a subject of unalloyed satisfaction. (How priggish!!)

'Yours most sincerely Salisbury.'

During this brief 'recess', between the 15th and the 28th November, Waldorf put his political future to the hazard. In the last year of the war he and Nancy had become close friends with a Labour leader, J. H. Thomas, who, before his sudden decay, was one of the ablest men produced by the politics of Trades Unionism. Waldorf, perhaps to stress the democratic character of his intent, persuaded his new friend to introduce a motion in the House of Commons 'that leave be given to bring in a Bill to empower His Majesty to accept a surrender of any Peerage'.

Thomas put the motion with his usual skill, and with a parade of learning which, it may be assumed, was that of Waldorf. He stressed the little known fact that surrender of peerages had once been quite a common custom, and in the eye of the law now depended on a test case brought in the seventeenth century, the judgement on which (disallowing the custom) had been challenged and upheld so recently as 1907 in the Appeal Court.

The motion was opposed by Waldorf's contemporary, Edward Wood (the future Lord Halifax). He said that he spoke 'with consider-able reluctance', mainly because 'the particular individual whose case is the parent of this Bill is one of my warm personal friends'. He gave a variety of reasons for his opposition, but the argument likely to have had most influence was one used more than forty years later on the same question by Mr Enoch Powell, namely that by legalising sur-renders the House of Lords would inevitably be deprived of its best political talent. Neither the Labour nor the Conservative Party wanted to tamper with the House of Lords, the tamest of all Upper Chambers. Thomas's motion was defeated by 189 votes to 56.

The late autumn of 1919 was unusually cold and when Nancy and Waldorf were back in Plymouth for the declaration on Friday the 28th November, the day was one of clouds, ice and snow-flurries. With them they took their son Bill, now aged twelve. In the Guildhall the count was going forward. By midday the candidates had all arrived.

2. Lady Salisbury.

Nancy could not keep still and paced round the room. Whatever her
feelings she disguised them with her usual banter. If she had not always
been true to her avowed principle of not standing as a 'sex candidate',
she was determined not to receive the result with feminine grace or
archness. When she was told that the incomplete results showed
clearly that she was in, she merely replied: 'I knew I'd win. I knew it
before it began.' Someone asked her how she felt. 'As if I'd been over
the top,' she answered, 'and found it wasn't so bad when I got there.'
Some Labour Party officials congratulated her. She thanked them but
added: 'That's what the working class want – honesty. Let the politicians take a lesson and say what they are and what they stand for.'
To another Labour man she was more gracious. He said his party was
glad to see a woman in Parliament but that did not mean she would
be immune from their criticism. 'That's right,' she said, 'we'll differ,
but we won't quarrel.' An angry woman opponent accused her of
having called her little boy a scoundrel. 'Quite true,' she answered,
'he threw a turnip at me.' When the count was nearly finished, and
she heard that her majority would be around 5,000, she said: 'Is that
all? I'd hoped for 8,000, but then you see I'm greedy.'

At length by about three in the afternoon the count was done. An
enormous crowd had gathered in the square, barriers were thrown up
around the Victorian Gothic doorway, and a cordon of police took
post to protect the principals from being overwhelmed. After a long
wait the Town Clerk, Mr Fittall, who was acting as Recording Officer,
emerged with the three candidates, Waldorf, and a few privileged
persons, and led them down the steps to the barrier. Mr Fittall called
for silence and then announced the result: Lady Astor 14,495 votes;
Mr Gay 9,292 votes; Mr Foot 4,139 votes. After the name of Lady
Astor had been called the cheering broke out so loudly that the rest
of the details were only heard by the few who were nearest. Silence for
speeches was obtained with difficulty, only after both the defeated
candidates had added their pleas. At this moment Nancy was, for once,
too overcome by emotion for boisterousness or humour. She merely
declared that she wanted to thank the electors for their confidence in
her; 'I will try to the best of my ability to serve you,' she said, and
resounding cheers and cries of 'Good old Nancy' and 'That's the stuff
to give 'em' answered her.

William Gay congratulated the victor and then announced to his
supporters that he found the result 'magnificent' from the Labour point

of view, his poll having gone up by nearly 4,000 votes. Isaac Foot congratulated Nancy in turn, and described the result as a well-earned tribute to her personal courage and sincerity. He did not refer to the increase in the Independent Liberal vote. He concluded: 'The tide has been running against our party, but our flag is still flying and tides have a way of turning.' Hardly a word of Gay's and Foot's speeches was heard (the reported text seems to be a mixture of afterthoughts and guesswork).

Nancy then called for three cheers for the defeated candidates, after which Isaac Foot called for three cheers for her. With difficulty she and Waldorf made their way to the landau which the Old Comrades triumphantly drew on foot by a circuitous route to the Conservative Club where they were welcomed by the members and Bill.

The crowd had by now moved to the space outside the club building (which was just behind the Guildhall) and there were mass-calls for her. She appeared on the balcony with Bill and her husband and waved greetings. In the big hall of the club she was asked for another speech. By this time she had mastered her emotion and she gave them what they expected. She said that she regarded the result as a vote of confidence in her husband, and showed that his independence of mind and action had won admirers in all parties. It was also, she said, a vote of confidence in the Government and in Mr Lloyd George 'who, with all his faults, is the best we've got yet'. There was laughter and she concluded with the last Astorism of the election. 'I ought,' she said, 'to feel sorry for Mr Foot and Mr Gay, but I don't. The only person I feel sorry for is the poor old Viscount here.'

In those days it was still the custom to use candidates' children as propaganda instruments to win the hearts of electors and constituents. (The writer has an unwelcome memory of driving in a carriage holding a little blue flag with 'Vote for Papa' painted on it in white.) Today the custom might lead to infanticide, but it was otherwise then. After Lord Astor had made a graceful speech in which he announced that his wife would take her seat on the following Monday, Bill was called on to speak. Raising his voice high he said: 'I have seen you elect Daddy, and now I have seen you elect Mother. I thank you very much for it.' He was received with cheers, and doubtless a tear or two from the matrons present.

The next day, Saturday the 29th, the Astors left for London and Cliveden. They kept the hour of their departure and arrival secret, but for all that there was a crowd to meet them at Paddington station. It was mostly composed of women; old suffragettes and their young admirers. The Press was there too in plenty with photographers who persuaded her to pose for a moment. 'Watch what you're doing,' she cried, 'every photograph makes me look a bit uglier.' Many of the women wanted to shake her by the hand, and in the turmoil a burly man at the back roared at her, 'I didn't vote for you,' and 'Thank Heavens for that,' said Nancy loud enough for the Press to hear. Bill was packed off back to school, and Waldorf and Nancy continued their journey. At Cliveden they were met by bonfires, obliged to get out of their car at the park gates, and conveyed to the house in an old Victoria carriage of William Waldorf drawn by cheering estate workers. Then they had one day's rest.

She had achieved much, and if she had been prone to complacent self-congratulation she had reason for it now. Who could have supposed that the career in England haphazardly begun when her father suggested that foreign travel might revive her spirits after her mother's death – who could have imagined that it would end with 'Nannie' as a Member of Parliament? One can only guess at what rum comment Chillie would have made. He did not live long enough to witness his daughter's great fame. His health had broken down, and in 1918 he abandoned his country house, Misfit, and went to live in an apartment in Richmond. There he died, at the age of seventy-six, on the 14th February 1919.

It had been arranged that if Nancy was successful at Plymouth she, as the first elected woman candidate to take her seat, would be introduced into Parliament by Lloyd George and Arthur Balfour, the only two members who had attained Prime Ministerial rank. The ceremony was to take place after Question Time, at or after about half-past three. In the morning of the 1st December she went with Waldorf to inspect the empty chamber and to decide where she would sit. She chose a seat and the Sergeant-at-Arms said he would make a request for it to be kept free for her. It was in a part of the House on the Opposition side where the overflow from the Government supporters used to sit, mostly younger members, and it was where the members of the Unionist Committee for Social Reform used to sit together in the previous Parliament. The place she chose was one usually taken by

Mr William Joynson Hicks who at the time was in India. Waldorf, one may suppose, then coached her thoroughly for the coming ordeal.

She told Maurice Collis that it was now that she remembered Henry James's remark to her about 'the dauntless decency of the English'. She was in great need of it. She knew that many people, including some political friends, regretted the election. Winston Churchill and Lord Chancellor Birkenhead, formerly F. E. Smith, were both appalled at the Plymouth result. Arthur Balfour's cousins, the Cecil family, with all of whom Nancy was friends, showed extremes of opposite opinion: outside the House of Commons the head of the family, Lord Salisbury, had expressed disapproval of feminine membership qualified by personal affection, as noted, while his sister Lady Selborne was looked on as a dangerous agitator for the feminist cause. Within the house one of Lord Salisbury's younger brothers, Lord Robert Cecil, was an active feminist, as has appeared already, while the other, Lord Hugh Cecil, saw the admission of women members as 'a great breach with tradition' which he deplored, and on which he wrote a brilliant and learned article for the *Pall Mall Gazette*, published on the 5th December. It was full of dire prophecies none of which happily has been fulfilled. There were few Labour or Liberal men who felt as strongly as Lord Hugh on the subject, but there were more than a few Conservatives who felt very much more strongly, notably Sir Frederick Banbury, the darling of the diehards.

The moment drew near. The Chamber was crammed that afternoon, and every seat in every gallery was occupied, after prayers. The Speaker, William Lowther, was in the chair. Waldorf was in the Distinguished Strangers Gallery, sitting next to the American ambassador. Her sisters Phyllis and Nora and her three elder children were there too. Questions and answers with supplementaries, on such subjects as coal, gas, tobacco prices, railway rates, old age pensions, the date of the parliamentary recess, housing, supplies to Rumania, continued for more than an hour. At 3.35 Nancy entered the Chamber, but not the House; that is to say, she sat under the gallery at the far end, but below 'the Bar' which is represented by a white line showing the limits of the privileged area. Between the line and the door there is this limbo region, used as part of the Chamber when it is crowded, but not technically of it, and thus allowed to people in her position. She was accompanied by two Conservative friends, Commander Eyres Monsell and Waldorf's brother-in-law Colonel Spender Clay.

The questions and answers seemed to go on for ever, and the hubbub in the House made both difficult to hear. Several members came up to talk to her, and a reporter noted that Sir Frederick Banbury, 'the picture of misery, threw sly glances across at the intruder'. At about a quarter to four Mr Lloyd George and Mr Balfour, both wearing frock coats, appeared in the throng behind the Bar, Balfour peering anxiously in the crowd for the new member. Both of them, according to nearly all reporters of the scene, appeared to be somewhat nervous, and the usually placid Balfour was fidgety. Neither of them had performed this duty for many years, not since their young parliamentary days and there had been no time for a rehearsal. They had seen the ceremony hundreds of times and they were now faced with the difference between being an audience and an actor.

They took up their positions. Balfour's tall figure towered over her on her right. On her left was the diminutive figure of the Prime Minister who was only a little taller than Nancy. She was wearing a beautifully cut, simple black coat and skirt with a white blouse open at the collar, and a neat brimless black hat, sometimes described as 'Tudor' and sometimes as 'three-cornered'. (Speaker Lowther had wisely ruled that all the complicated parliamentary hat-protocol was to be waived for women members, but seeing a behatted member taking the oath must have been torture for Sir Frederick.) She carried no handbag but only a slip of blue paper, her election writ. Question time came to an end – at last. There was a pause, momentary silence, and Speaker Lowther's resonant voice was heard proclaiming the traditional words: 'Members desirous of taking their seats will come to the table.'

The great and monumental moment in the history of Parliament had arrived! But there was an instant anticlimax.

Though the British Parliament may be described as the centre of the drama of Britain, in its normal routine it has a positive genius, except when the Sovereign appears in all the pomp of State at the openings, for being undramatic. Many of the onlookers in the galleries, perhaps many members too, were pained and bewildered when, in answer to Speaker Lowther's words, three men advanced to the Clerk's table, with the accustomed three bows to the Chair. The central figure was unfamiliar to almost everyone present. The sponsors were two of the Conservative Whips. When more than one member takes his seat the order is inalienably determined by the time when the official report is received. Sir Allen Smith's victory at Croydon had been officially reported before that of Nancy, so he came first. He might have fared worse if he had come second. One cannot but feel sorry for him on this day. The ceremony is very brief. It rarely takes more than three minutes. It was soon Nancy's turn.

Here then *was* the great moment, the first time that a woman had taken her seat in the House of Commons of the Parliament of Great Britain. This, whether one approved it or not, was a monumental moment. But the central character of this drama was Nancy, and as has been remarked earlier in this book, she was not monumental. Not by monumentality had she won the election in Plymouth, and not by the monumental was she to mark a step in human progress, her entry into the House of Commons. She was dignified on this noble occasion, but she was also true to herself, to the tomboy of Mirador, to the backchatting canvasser, and the joker at the street-corner meetings. Yet she might have acted more in accordance with the sentimental historian's ideal if there had been a chance for one minute's rehearsal. As it was, when Speaker Lowther made his sign, two of the main actors walked on to the stage unprepared.

Either Balfour or Lloyd George (reports differ) stepped out in front of the others, then hastily withdrew amid a burst of laughter. Then together they advanced a step and made their first bow. The thruster was probably Lloyd George, as sometime in the brief ceremony the Labour member, Will Thorne, called out, 'You'll lose your job, George,' amid more laughter. They advanced to the table, the two sponsors walking a little faster than Nancy who at one point stretched out both hands to hold them in. She was distinctly heard to whisper 'Bow now', which they did but not together. Most reports agree that the third and last bow was made roughly in unison. Lloyd George and Balfour then retired to the Front Bench while Nancy surrendered her writ to the Clerk of the House, Sir Courtney Ilbert, a venerable figure whose long white beard and curled eighteenth century wig (as shown in pictures of the time) can put one in mind of Parson Adams. She then took the oath, holding the Bible in her right hand, and a printed form with the accepted text in the other. She read out her declaration, according to all reports, distinctly and in a voice which was not loud but carried. This part of the business being over, Sir Courtney told her that as a now sworn member she must sign the roll. Sir Courtney was seventy-eight and he took a little longer to find the page and place and pen than a younger man would have done. At all events the pause was such that Nancy could not resist turning round and exchanging a few words with the numerous acquaintances she found sitting just behind her on the Front Bench – an enormous breach of custom, but nothing in the rules against it, so far as anyone knew. Sir Austen Chamberlain, the Chancellor of the Exchequer, was especially embarrassed. He was one of the few members to keep to the custom of wearing a top hat throughout sittings. Normally, of course, he did not take it off to fellow members, least of all when they were going against the usages of the House. Should he to Nancy? He did. It looked, according to some reporters, as though she was going to go down the whole Governmental bench and chat to them one by one as though this was St James's Square. But the venerable Clerk intervened. Here was the book, the page, the pen. She signed and was then conducted by Sir Courtney to the Speaker. There had been speculation as to whether the Speaker should rise to shake hands with a lady. Lowther knew Nancy and was in sympathy with the feminist cause. He had great sense of humour[3], and probably enjoyed in secret the momentary alarm she had caused on the Treasury Bench. When she came to the chair he stretched out his arm full length, drew her near, and whispered some words to her. She went towards the door behind the chair and there she met Lord Robert Cecil who seized her by the arm and smiled joyfully, but said nothing. Then she left the Chamber.

Nancy gave her friends many descriptions of that great moment in her life, but she said little in public about it. However, twenty-four years later, in October 1943, she gave a brief and telling account with a flash of real wit, in the course of a talk in the BBC series 'The Week in Westminster'. She said: 'I was introduced by Mr Balfour and Mr Lloyd George, men who had always been in favour of votes for women. But when I walked up the aisle of the House of Commons I felt that they were more nervous than I was, for I was deeply conscious of representing a Cause, whereas I think they were a little nervous of

3. (James) William Lowther (1855–1949), first Viscount Ullswater, Speaker of the House of Commons, 1905–1921. He is generally acknowledged as one of the ablest Speakers of modern times. He made a celebrated aside often attributed to others. A wearisome member said in the course of a speech, 'I ask myself,' and Lowther was heard to mutter, 'And a damned silly answer you'll get.' *Times* Obituary, 1949.

having let down the House of Commons by escorting the Cause
into it.'

Nancy's first day in the House may be followed to its close before
ending this chapter. Under Speaker Lowther's direction special arrangements had been made for her accommodation in the Palace of Westminster.

Major-General Seely, the Under Secretary for Air, had recently
quarrelled with the Prime Minister on the latter's refusal to appoint a
Secretary of State for his department. He had resigned and his room
had not yet been apportioned, so it was now converted into a boudoir
for women members. A lavatory for women members had also been
installed. For nearly two years Nancy enjoyed these privileges alone.
She shared the rest of the appointments of the House with her male
colleagues; in the general cloakroom she had her name over her own
hook like any other member, though whether she was supplied with
tape to serve as a sword hanger should she arrive armed, seems to be
unrecorded. (There was a hook also for Countess Markievicz.)[4]

To the loneliness of her boudoir she repaired, and then soon re-
entered the Chamber to attend her first debate.

Her seat was directly behind the principal speaker who was one of
the most famous members of his day, by name Horatio Bottomley.
He was orating in favour of a scheme described as a proposal for
'Premium Bonds' which the Treasury looked on with suspicion and
disapproval as an incentive to financial gambling. Bottomley was
answered by an onslaught on the scheme by the Chancellor of the
Exchequer, Austen Chamberlain. The Chancellor's speech was well
received and as he made one point Nancy clapped her hands. Her next-
door neighbour hastened to stop her, and hurriedly explained that the
only form of applause permitted in the House was vocal. The Speaker
had not noticed, or had ignored this breach of protocol, but Mr
Bottomley noticed it, and he noticed her first parliamentary utterance
'Hear! Hear!' when Mr Bonar Law later added his own denunciations
to those of Austen Chamberlain. On the Premium Bond issue Nancy
recorded her first parliamentary vote and Horatio Bottomley noticed
that she went with the majority against him (on a free vote) and that

4. She is said to have gone to Westminster in disguise with a member friend in
order to see her coat hook. Pamela Brookes, *Women in Westminster* (London, 1967).

this brought him some bad publicity in the Press next day. Like most men of a criminal turn he was vain.

That evening she and Waldorf gave a dinner-party in the House to some of their friends, including her two sponsors. After dinner there was a division on the Scottish Land Settlement Bill, and Nancy duly recorded an obedient vote for the Government. She then came back into the Chamber for a moment before going home. On her way out, before reaching the sacred Bar, she saw a friend, Sir John Rees, and she stopped for a chat with him, to the latter's great confusion. Lowther's voice was heard calling 'Order! Order!' Nancy looked round to see what the excitement was, and seeing nothing continued her chat. Again the Speaker called for order, and Sir John hastily explained to her that to stop on the floor of the House and converse on the sanctified side of the Bar during a session was a grave offence. A report of the time describes Nancy as 'skipping' over the Bar and then through the doors and out.

So ended her first day in Parliament on Monday the 1st December 1919.

The material for the preceding chapter is principally drawn from private letters in the Astor archive, as indicated, and from the large mass of Press cuttings contained therein, covering the years 1918 and 1919. Mr Maurice Collis in his *Nancy Astor* evidently examined the same collection of Press cuttings, and I have found his selection from this material very helpful and suggestive in my own studies. We inevitably repeat each other occasionally. I have varied Mr Collis's quotation of Lady Astor's reply to a heckler on a divorce question. The Press gave her words as he gives them, but I have followed an account which Mrs Nancy Lancaster gave me, as she remembered hearing it from Lady Astor. I feel little compunction in selecting in this way as the Press reports both of the election and of Lady Astor taking her seat vary greatly and sometimes radically contradict each other. The best continuous reporting of the election was published in the *Evening Standard*, and the best, by far, of the reports of her taking her seat appeared in *The Glasgow Herald*. The description of the conduct of Lady Astor while the fateful count of votes was being made is based on a minutely detailed report which appeared in *The Illustrated Weekly News* of 6th December 1919, and which seems to be unique. For the feminist background to the General Election of 1918 and the Plymouth by-election of November 1919, I am indebted to Pamela Brookes's *Women in Westminster* (London, 1967) which is an invaluable guide to its neglected subject. As indicated, I am indebted to Lloyd George's *The Truth about the Peace Treaties* (1938) and Mr Frank Owen's *Tempestuous Journey* (1954), and remain in debt to Sir James Butler's biography of Lord Lothian for the account of Philip Kerr's career at the Peace Conference, 1918-1919. The record of the brief debate in the

House of Commons which terminated Lord Astor's hopes of surrendering his title, is to be found in Hansard, House of Commons, 1919, Volume X. Though Lord Astor's intention to renounce his title, if legally possible, was frequently mentioned by him in the election and reported in the Press, the dramatic episode in the House of Commons by which his hopes were dashed by the brilliant conservative advocacy of his friend, went almost unnoticed either by Parliamentary reporters or editors. I have become convinced that Lady Astor's decision to stand for Parliament was reached privately and in consultation only with her husband, through remarkable negative evidence. In the Astor archive which contains a great deal of material for 1918 and 1919, there is not one single item indicating discussion of this momentous step. The clothes worn by Lady Astor on her introduction to Parliament are now in the Museum of Costume at Bath.

Chapter 11

GRANDEURS ET MISÈRES
D'UNE VICTOIRE

THE autumn sitting of Parliament was nearly at an end when Nancy took her seat, and though the dauntless decency stood her in good stead, she had been a member long enough by the Christmas recess to be aware of danger.

Lord Hugh Cecil remained her faithful friend, although he made no secret of the fact that he believed that Nancy had delivered a destructive blow not only against the Constitution but against parliamentary oratory: the eloquence of Pitt, Sheridan, Burke, Gladstone and Disraeli was not intended for women. The Secretary of State for War, Winston Churchill, was openly hostile. One day she stopped him and asked him straight out why he behaved to her with such rudeness. He replied: 'Because I find a woman's intrusion into the House of Commons as embarrassing as if she burst into my bathroom when I had nothing with which to defend myself, not even a sponge.' Nancy answered: 'Winston, you're not handsome enough to have worries o' that kind.'

Members soon became impressed by her tact, not her most frequently visible virtue. For a long time she never went into the members' smoking-room because she regarded it as a male club, and she only occasionally used the dining-room, for the same reason. She enjoyed a friendly Press for the most part, but with exceptions.

Horatio Bottomley had decided to make an enemy of Nancy. He had reason to resent her. Apart from the fact that she had stolen the show from him on the 1st December 1919, she had dared to enter into rivalry with him before this, for Nancy's election success in Plymouth had owed not a little to her substantial claim to have been a good friend to the soldiers in the war, and it was a self-evident truth to Bottomley and his devoted followers that 'the Soldier's Friend' was to be exclusively identified with the short, porcine, rarely quite sober figure of the member for South Hackney. He opened the campaign on the 20th December in an article which was one of a series called

'In the Barber's Chair', appearing in Bottomley's weekly paper *John Bull*.

It was silly abusive rubbish, unlikely to do any harm, but Bottomley was a dangerous enemy. Though his fraudulency was widely suspected it seemed impossible to prove, and his long career of litigation in which he usually appeared as his own counsel had been remarkably successful and the envy of many professional lawyers. His pose as the soldier's friend had been skilfully manipulated. For a while he had to be content with empty abuse of his new chosen antagonist. Then a week later he found what he wanted, though he did not use it immediately.

Parliament was prorogued on the 23rd December, Lord Chancellor Birkenhead, in reading the King's speech, using for the first time the phrase 'My Lords and *Members* of the House of Commons', in deference to Nancy's presence. Four days later, on the 27th, *The Saturday Review* came out with a paragraph aimed at causing Nancy embarrassment. It ran as follows:

'That astonishing book *Who's Who* for 1920 has reached us. . . . We, however, have not got beyond the first letter of the alphabet as yet: for need we say we were arrested by the biography of Plymouth's heroine, the dashing, peerless peeress, Nancy Witcher, who is described as "the widow" of Mr Robert Gould Shaw at the time of her marriage with Mr Astor. We are loth to think that Nancy fibs: but is this a correct statement?'

Bottomley took note of the information, and began researches into Nancy's past.

The recess was spent by Nancy not only with her family, and in her social routine in the world of fashion, gayer over that Christmas than since before the war, at a time when the irremediable disaster to European civilisation was not yet generally appreciated, but she spent it also in a busy round of speech-making. She seems to have accepted as many invitations as she could.

It became known that she intended to make her maiden speech during the next sitting of Parliament. A Press rumour that she would second a proposed bill to prohibit the use of birds' feathers in women's hats was widely believed, as Nancy was known to be in sympathy. The rumour was false and was followed by another which was still persisting on February 11th, the day when the King opened Parliament, to the effect that Nancy would second the Address to the Throne in the House of Commons. Since custom still ruled that the proposer and

seconder should wear court dress or uniform on these occasions, there
was speculation as to whether she would deliver her maiden speech
in all the glamour of a ball dress with a train, and ostrich feathers, in
spite of her likely association with a Plumage Bill. But the rumour was
false and so this interesting point was not put to the test. In the event
she made her maiden speech in the evening of the 24th February 1920,
on an entirely different subject.

The occasion was a motion by that same Sir John Rees in connection
with whom Nancy had been called to order for the first time on the
evening of her first day in the House of Commons. He moved 'That
this House, while not desiring to return to the pre-war hours of
opening licensed premises, is of opinion that all vexatious and unnecessary restraints and restrictions upon the liberty of the subject in
respect of the strength, supply and consumption of alcoholic liquors
should be abolished.' His seconder was Colonel Ashley. The motion
was opposed by the Government, the first speakers from their side
being Nancy and the member for Carlisle.

Drink law at that time centred on the Defence of the Realm Act of
1914, known popularly as Dora and represented by cartoonists as a
black-clothed middle-class hag wearing Victorian ringlets and elastic-
sided boots. The aim of the act was economic restriction for war
purposes. From Dora was born 'The Liquor Control Board', and from
this body came restricted hours for the sale of intoxicants, the forbidding of alcoholic content above certain defined percentages in
beverages, and other legislation which in principle remains to this day.
This reform impetus was widely resented and widely applauded and,
after the establishment of Prohibition in the United States in 1919,
widely feared. Much of Dora vanished with the victory of 1918, but
the Liquor Control Board was still in existence in 1920 and had another
year of life. One of its innovations, then uppermost in the minds of
those concerned with drink regulation, was known as 'the Carlisle
experiment'. It had been initiated in Carlisle and nearby Gretna in 1916,
with a view to later nationwide application in the light of experience.
The aim was state purchase and state supply of all alcoholic beverages:
a socialist solution of the drink question by state supervision. The
Carlisle experiment was the most strenuous attempt yet made to
introduce a radical measure of prohibition, leading, as many of its
supporters hoped, to total prohibition in Great Britain at a not distant
date.

For her maiden speech Nancy could hardly have chosen a more unpopular cause among the issues of the time than the defence of the Carlisle experiment, and the type of legislation which it personified. Political friends, remembering accusations of pussyfooting, advised her to avoid this debate, but she did not heed them. She had, in fact, little alternative in the matter. Her enthusiasm for reform of the drink laws was known to every reader of the newspapers, and after all the fanfare and fireworks of the Plymouth election, to have sat silent during a debate on the subject would have been unthinkable.

Sir John Rees opened the debate by one of those displays of rollicking facetiousness with which discussions about drink are often conducted. His oratory was to the taste of the time and Press reports refer to him as 'the supreme jester of the House' and speak of his 'dry' and 'mordant wit'. He dwelt on the fanatic character of teetotallers and, referring to Lenin's brief experiment in prohibition, associated teetotalism with Bolshevism. He ended up with much archness. Looking at Nancy, 'I do not doubt,' he said, 'that a rod is in pickle for me when I sit down, but I will accept the chastisement with resignation and am indeed ready to kiss the rod.'

When Colonel Ashley had made a more routine speech in support, Nancy rose. The House was as packed as it had been on the 1st December 1919.

'I shall not begin,' she said, 'by craving the indulgence of the House. I know that it was very difficult for some honourable members to receive the first lady M.P. into the House. [Hon. Members: "Not at all!"] It was almost as difficult for some of them as it was for the lady M.P. herself to come in.' Several reporters mention that when she began Nancy gave some evidence of nervousness in the hoarseness of her voice, but that gradually her tone became relaxed. She showed a nice sense of how to get the ear of the House not only by undeniable sincerity and controlled emotion, but by sticking to facts rather than opinions wherever she could. Early on she returned Sir John Rees's last witticism. She said: 'The honourable member (Sir John Rees) is more than polite. In fact, I should say that he goes almost a bit too far. However, I will consider his proposal if I can convert him.

'The issue raised by the honourable member is really quite clear,' she went on. 'I admit that he did not make it as clear as I would have liked him to do, but it is really quite clear: do we want the welfare of the community, or the prosperity of the Trade?' She made play with the fact that Sir John Rees's motion described the restrictions as 'vexatious'. She asserted that all laws were vexatious. She went on to show by means of official statistics that convictions for drunkenness and cases of delirium tremens had diminished while the war-time restrictions were in force and had more than tripled since 1918. She then came to the most emotional passage of her speech: 'I have as good a sense of humour as any other honourable member, but when I think of the ruin and desolation and the misery which drink brings into the houses of the working men and women as well as of the well-to-do I find it a little difficult to be humorous. It was only the other day – I had been down to my constituency – that I was coming back from what they call the poorer parts of the town, and I stopped outside a public house where I saw a child about five years old waiting for its mother. Presently she reeled out. The child went forward to her, but it soon retreated, and the oaths and curses of that poor woman and the shrieks of that child as it fled from her – that is not an easy thing to forget, and that is what goes on when you have increased drunkenness among women.'

The next ten minutes or so were spent by her dealing, very competently, with the arguments in favour of state ownership of the liquor industry and in giving a one-sided picture favourable to the Carlisle experiment. Presently she turned on her opponent in personal fashion, and in so doing she scored a telling point: 'The honourable Baronet talks about pacifists and temperance men not being fighting men, but I notice that he is a little frightened of revolutions. What makes revolutions? Reactionaries make revolutions.'

Among Nancy's political virtues, respect for the rules of parliamentary debate was markedly absent. It was characteristic of her that in the penultimate stage of her maiden speech she omitted to address the Chair and started to argue direct with Sir John Rees. However, as this was a maiden speech, the Deputy Speaker did not intervene.

One can say that it was symptomatic of the future that though her words were received by the House with respect and admiration there were a few impatient interruptions at the end, a rare thing with maiden speeches. Having made her points she was carried away into over-emphasis with inevitable repetition. She closed on an emotional note, not without humour, and with dignity.

'I do not want you to look on your lady member as a fanatic or a lunatic. I am simply trying to speak for hundreds of women and children throughout the country who cannot speak for themselves. I want to tell you that I do know the working man, and I know that, if you tell him the truth about drink, he would be as willing as anybody else to put up with these vexatious restrictions.'

She was followed by Mr Carr, the member for Carlisle, who gave a carefully reasoned speech in favour of the experiment, though it must be said that in his descriptive passages concerning its effects he portrayed the great city as a quite joyless place. In her first parliamentary days Nancy seemed destined to rob other novices of their deserved and fleeting moments of fame. She had already done this to Sir Allan Smith, and she now did it to her seconder. Mr Carr's speech was also a maiden one, but the editors of newspapers, faced by the newsworthy phenomenon of Nancy's speech, gave it very little space. Even in the House Nancy smothered Mr Carr's glory. The succeeding speakers all praised her with such vehemence that they had little breath left for the other, and the speaker for the Government, H. A. L. Fisher, while praising Nancy enthusiastically, forgot to mention poor Mr Carr at all. In the end Sir John Rees's motion was 'talked out'.

Nancy had now a truly impressive achievement to her credit. She had followed up her electioneering victory by the more difficult and testing feat of a widely applauded speech in the House. She had worked hard for this victory. Philip Kerr's letters to her from Paris indicate that she was seeking his help for her speech as early as mid-January, though apart from some suggested quotations from Mrs Eddy, he seems to have been too busy to respond to her need.

The interior evidence, especially from the excellent balance of her early House of Commons speeches, and the only occasional appearance of blemishes typical of her, indicates Waldorf's strong directing hand. He seems to have given coherent and telling shape to her ideas, but the ideas were hers, mostly fully shared with him. At no time was she his or anyone else's mouthpiece.

There is a pleasant cartoon by Max Beerbohm in which Lord Birkenhead is shown assuring Alfred Duff Cooper that a successful maiden speech is not necessarily fatal to a political career. The danger is a real one and the records of Parliament are well stocked with triumphant openings leading to nothing much after. Nancy was fortunate in finding an opportunity to follow up her success of the 24th February by a short, witty and improvised speech four days later on the 28th. The occasion was the Second Reading of the Representation of the People Bill of 1920. Its purpose was to amend the Act of

1918, which granted the franchise to women at the age of 30, by giving men and women electors equal status with a vote at the age of 21. The Bill originated with the Labour Party and was open to a free vote. It was opposed by Mr George Murray who put forward a partially and wholly unacceptable disenfranchising proposition, namely that the male voting age should be raised to 25, after which the vote should be allowed equally to people of both sexes.

The sense of the House was in favour of the Bill, but the diehards were not silent and one of them, Mr Leng-Sturrock, referred to the Conservative belief that, unless held in check, women would introduce an element of undignified frivolity into political life. 'I take,' he said, 'a high and serious view of the responsibilities of public life. The Plymouth bye-election at which Lady Astor was returned was not marked by that dignity which many desired to see: in fact, it seems to me, from the descriptions I read in the Press, to have been more like a circus than an election.' It was probably this remark that decided her to speak. Mr Leng-Sturrock was followed by five speakers, only one of whom joined him in opposing the Bill, and that only in a qualified way, when Nancy caught the Speaker's eye.

She was received with applause and began by saying that she had not intended to speak, but that she now felt, after hearing the debate, that someone really ought to say something on behalf of the men since there had been so many gallant defenders of the female sex. When the laughter subsided she congratulated Mr Murray on his speech: 'He only said what a lot of members think but have not the courage to say.' She claimed that women brought a greater element of idealism into affairs (which may be open to doubt) but then went on to make the wholly valid point in favour of the Bill that it was a fact of practical observation that women matured earlier than men. In the second half of her speech she referred to Mr Leng-Sturrock's remarks which concerned her personally: 'One honourable member referred to the Plymouth election as a sort of circus. I can tell him that the lady who was elected was not the clown [Loud laughter]. I was not afraid to bring religion into the election. That wasn't very much like a circus [Hear Hear].' She insisted that if more women had the vote the reform impetus would be increased. She concluded by wandering from the subject, her chronic weakness as a speaker, but only briefly and without being called to order.

It was a minor but successful performance and Nancy in her second speech had a little but distinctly added to her reputation. She had proved that she was not a one-speech member and could speak well without preparation. But it was a personal and not a political success. The Bill did not pass into law. Nancy was angered by this renewed assertion of the belief that every man was superior to every woman and she expressed her feelings in her usual way, by sarcastic humour. Her best effort in this direction was not parliamentary but took the form of a story which she told to her guests one day in St James's Square, and which she repeated much later to Maurice Collis. Here are her words as he reported them:

'I was canvassing once for signatures to a petition about a certain Viceroy of India, when I called on Mr Boggs, a grocer. He read the petition carefully and then said, "Who is this 'ere man?" "Our Indian Viceroy," said I. "What's a Viceroy?" asked Mr Boggs. I explained as best I could. Mr Boggs, satisfied, dipped his pen in the ink, and then looked up anxiously. "You're not letting the women sign this?" he asked. "No, indeed," said I, anxious for him to get on. "That's right," said he, slowly tracing his signature, "that's right, ma'am. Women don't know anything about these things."'

Though Nancy enjoyed her new success and fame, she fell into a state of depression during the first months of 1920. She seems to have confided this to Philip Kerr alone, and he responded by further appeals to the faith they shared, recalling her to reliance on the 'Father-Mother God' as Mrs Eddy described the Omnipotent Being. She did not readily admit to anxiety, and in this case the only evidence of it is in Kerr's letters. She had cause. A minor one was the appearance of a new enemy on the horizon in the shape of Sir William Joynson Hicks. This able, ambitious and humourless man had been distressed to learn, while journeying in India and the Sudan, that the first lady to sit in Parliament had, in his absence, been given his accustomed seat below the gangway on the Speaker's left hand. Though the reservation of seats, except on the Government and Opposition front benches, is not recognised in the House of Commons, certain seats are customarily accorded to certain prominent members as a matter of courtesy. Nancy would have been wise to have written to him, and if Sir William had written a soothing letter to her, she might conceivably have surrendered her coveted place. In the event, he wrote to Waldorf. This was wrongly interpreted by her as a slight on a mere woman member. (In fact, 'Jix' was something of a feminist.)

This was a small matter, however. There was a greater one in the offing. The findings of a Royal Commission on the subject of divorce had been lately published and a Bill for divorce reform introduced into the House of Lords by the former Lord Chancellor, Lord Buckmaster. It passed its Second Reading in the Lords in April 1920. On that occasion, in his summing-up of the arguments for and against the proposed measure, Lord Chancellor Birkenhead had given the weight of his legal judgement in its favour, in the course of what his son and biographer justly described as the greatest speech of his career. The Bill, by constitutional practice, after passing in the Lords, had then to be introduced for its Second Reading into the House of Commons.

Here was a dilemma far more painful for Nancy than that posed by the unpopular subject of her maiden speech. As the only woman in the House, Nancy had no alternative but to speak.

Her depression probably came from anticipatory dread of the ordeal before her. Such is implied in Kerr's letters. She never admitted to fear except to one or two friends, and her husband; and many people supposed that she was unafraid through insensitivity. This was a misreading of her character, as those closest to her have testified. What sometimes appeared as lack of sensitivity was the result of the over-discipline she exerted to quell fear. Later, when she was no longer alone in her position, she admitted first privately then publicly that her first two years in the House were a time of almost continual and unbearable strain.

The debate took place on the 14th April 1920. The main recommendations of the proposed measure were that, apart from adultery, grounds for divorce should be conceded for desertion after three years, cruelty, habitual drunkenness, incurable insanity and imprisonment for life. No mention was made of the real reason for most divorces, incompatibility of temperament. The resolution was opposed by an Amendment put forward by the most formidable and able of the diehard Tories, Ronald McNeill, a brilliant lawyer, an Ulsterman of enormous height, a dedicated opponent of Irish Home Rule and of most reform.[1] During his long and eloquent speech Nancy made an

1. Ronald John McNeill (1861–1934), later Lord Cushendun, enjoyed notoriety for an enormous breach of order in the House of Commons when, in November 1912, during a debate on Irish Home Rule, he hurled a book at the head of Winston Churchill and struck his target. Nevertheless, in 1925, when Winston Churchill was

interruption which reads oddly. 'Constancy,' he said, 'was a virtue less characteristic of men than of women, but the attributes that attracted the opposite sex withered more readily in the female than in the male. [Viscountess Astor: Hear! Hear!]'

Nancy was the fifth to speak after McNeill. She astonished the House by supporting him and opposing the resolution. She based her argument on religious and historical grounds. Here is the key passage: 'In the Christian world it is the spiritual aspect of marriage that the law attempts to protect, and it is the spiritual element that makes marriages happy. Most honourable members have said that. They all know it, and we women particularly know it. The spiritual idea of marriage, though started in the East, has been more highly developed in the West, and it is that that has elevated the Western women a little above their Eastern sisters. That is the difference between the East and the West. We must do nothing which will weaken it. Therefore I shall support the Amendment. I am not convinced that making divorce very easy really makes marriages more happy or makes happy marriages more possible.'

She admitted that the law on divorce as it stood was in need of reform but on different lines (which she did not indicate) than those proposed by the Royal Commission. She made the point that at the time, less than eighteen months after the end of the war, society was in an unsettled state and that such a reform should not be considered until normal conditions had been restored. She suggested later that the postponement should be from five to ten years. She laid special stress on a point often neglected in discussion on divorce, the effect on the children.

She returned to the point made by McNeill when this beautiful woman had applauded him when he remarked on the swift decay of female beauty. Strangely enough, at this juncture, she indicated an argument which had been elaborated with striking effect by Lord Birkenhead when summing up in favour of Buckmaster's Bill. She said: 'The honourable member for Canterbury [McNeill] has spoken of our fading charms. He is quite right. Women do fade quickly, but the thing that really holds men to women is not the physical charm. It attracts them, but it does not keep them.'

Chancellor of the Exchequer, McNeill served under him, amicably, as Financial Secretary to the Treasury.

It was an able performance, her fourth in the House of Commons.[2] The Press of the time, how correctly it would be hard to say, widely gave the opinion that Nancy's speech was primarily responsible for the defeat of Lord Buckmaster's Bill, in spite of the previous advocacy of Birkenhead, on its Second Reading in the House of Commons. If that is so, she was in great measure responsible for the postponement of radical divorce law reform until the irruption of A. P. Herbert into Parliament fifteen years later.

In laying stress, as too few other pronouncements on divorce have done, on the fact that the primary concern of divorce legislation should be the children, Nancy was undoubtedly in the right; but her general opposition to the 1920 Bill can hardly appear other than wrong-headed at the distance of the present.

Nancy's speech on the 14th April, though well received by the House, irritated a large section of the educated public outside, which saw in it gross reaction. Though she had her supporters, she had a bad Press on the whole. Sir Arthur Conan Doyle, the president of the Divorce Law Reform Union, was interviewed and declared: 'I have read Lady Astor's speech and I am shocked by it.' His comment was in line with a great many others. For the first time since her entry into Parliament, Nancy found herself more unpopular than the opposite. In these circumstances, and through her own fault, she became involved in a ludicrous episode on the 15th April, the day after the Divorce Bill debate.

Sir William Joynson Hicks had by now returned from India, and before resuming his parliamentary duties, he let it be known in the Press that he intended to sit in his accustomed corner seat below the gangway on the Speaker's left. Nancy had already decided that that was where she would sit, as she had done hitherto. She went down to the House early on the 15th, soon after the doors of the Chamber had been opened at eight o'clock – but not so early as Sir William. He had already visited the Chamber, at five minutes past eight, and there he had found the Speaker's clerk and the member for South Hackney, the aforementioned Horatio Bottomley. He asked them both to remember seeing him there. They both agreed to do so. A few minutes made all the difference. When Nancy arrived she found Sir William's card in the slot at the back of the seat. Ancient parliamentary custom allowed

2. On the 26th of March, 1920, Lady Astor spoke on the Temperance (Wales) Bill.

seats to be reserved only by leaving a hat on it, but modern usage had extended the custom to cards for which these slots were designed. Sir William had literally stolen a march on Nancy and she would have been wise to have retired from the fray. But to admit defeat was something she was temperamentally unable to do without at least some sort of a fray first. Ignoring Sir William's card she deposited a pink card with her name on it in the same slot. It was a card for a Committee on Women Police. Whether or not she intended to confront Sir William in the House later in the day and was dissuaded by Waldorf (as seems possible) cannot be known, but the fact remains that though she spent much of that day in the Palace of Westminster, she did not return to the Chamber. But she had placed her time-bomb there, and in the afternoon, after question time, the explosion shook the House.

Sir William rose 'on a point of order' to request the guidance of the Speaker. He opened somewhat unfortunately. 'I arrived in the House,' he said, 'at five minutes past eight this morning and left a card in this seat.' The remark was greeted with ribald laughter which may have perplexed him. He then went on to describe the events of the morning, mentioning his witnesses. He admitted the informality of the custom. The 'Father of the House', by which title the member of longest service is known and revered filially even though his distinction may be dubious, was at that time the Irish author and journalist T. P. O'Connor, and he spoke next to urge some chivalrous relaxation of custom in the case of the first lady admitted to Parliament – but he was shouted down and the point stressed, by the next speaker, that if women in Parliament demanded chivalrous privilege, this made nonsense of the whole theory of sex-equality on which feminism rested. After he sat down numerous other members rose to catch the Speaker's eye, but Lowther terminated the proceeding with characteristic severity and good humour and with a touch of sarcasm. 'I really do not think it is necessary,' he said, 'to continue the "debate". The honourable member who initiated it has stated quite correctly what the rule is. It must be left to every honourable member to decide himself whether he will yield the place he is entitled to take on coming here at eight o'clock to anyone else. If he chooses he can do so; if he prefers to retain his seat, he is entitled to retain his seat.'

Sir William rose to say that he was prepared to make a personal statement and to lay papers before the House (presumably his correspondence with Waldorf), but added that he did not think this necessary. His last remark was greeted by 'Cheers'. This may indicate murmurs of approval or the opposite, and probably not a few muttered remarks of 'Thank goodness for that'. On sitting down, Sir William picked up Nancy's Committee ticket, tore it up, and threw the pieces on the floor.

On leaving Westminster both Nancy and Sir William were ambushed by Press reporters. Nancy communicated to them a declaration of war. 'I shall give Sir William a good run for his money,' she said, 'and he will have to get up early in the morning to beat me.' She also said: 'I realise I made a mistake about the pink ticket – I was in a hurry to attend the Committee on policewomen. But Sir William will have to go to some trouble to keep the seat.' Joynson Hicks met the ambush in a graver spirit. He enlarged on the customs of the House: 'There are seven seats,' he explained, 'which by courtesy are never used except by certain members. These are Sir Edward Carson, Mr Houston, Mr Bottomley, Lord Robert Cecil, Sir Henry Dalziel, Mr T. P. O'Connor, and myself.'

In the event battle was not joined. Nancy, again probably under Waldorf's influence, withdrew from the incident and made no further claim on the coveted seat. To Will Thorne, however, the age of chivalry was not dead, and he gave Nancy his own corner seat, above the gangway, a seat exactly parallel with Sir William's. There she sat regularly for the rest of that Parliament.

The reader may be surprised (and will shortly be surprised again) at the respect apparently so frequently accorded to Bottomley, and never was this odder than at this juncture, considering what the mutual relations of him and Joynson Hicks were shortly to be. The fact was that public men were afraid of him.

After the Divorce Bill debate, and probably noting that Nancy had further weakened her position by her unsuccessful challenge of Joynson Hicks, Bottomley decided that the moment had come to strike against her. He had prepared his case with some care.

His first move was to make sure that the number of *John Bull* in which he printed his attack would enjoy a bumper sale. This he contrived by a vigorous poster campaign for a few days before publication on the 8th May. Instead of the usual one carrying a prayerful portrait of Horatio Bottomley, there was a striking announcement: 'Lady Astor's Divorce'.

Of course the average member of the public, ignorant of Nancy's past, assumed from these three words that she, the puritan opponent of divorce reform, was about to divorce Lord Astor or be divorced by him. The effect of this on the readership was 'healthy', as they say in Fleet Street. Bottomley's readers may have been a little disappointed when confronted with the subject matter, Nancy's divorce from Robert Shaw, but no pains were spared to make the material as spicy as possible. Bottomley's object was manifestly to taunt and goad the Astors into prosecuting him, and he expressed himself in terms which might have been thought certain to achieve his aim. The headline of his main article repeated the poster legend 'Lady Astor's Divorce', and the subtitle ran 'A Hypocrite of the First Water – The Poor and The Rich'.

Horatio Bottomley was a master of that style which artfully combines unctuous moralising with offensive bluntness and implies in every other sentence a heart of gold beneath a rugged exterior. 'I hate,' wrote Bottomley, 'I hate being rude to a woman, but my public duty compels me to denounce Lady Astor as a hypocrite of the first water.' Then, before coming to his main purpose, he denounced her attitude on the drink question. He compared things that she had said during the Plymouth election opposing the introduction of prohibition with later remarks that she had made on the same subject after her election, especially in the House of Commons. From this he cleverly built up the picture of an unscrupulous political manipulator who, having lied her way to a position of influence, was throwing off the mask that had fooled her supporters and was now proceeding ruthlessly to her goal.

The article then moved to Nancy's performance in Parliament on the recently debated Divorce Reform Bill and the subject of her own divorce in 1903.

The main objection raised to the proposed Buckmaster reform had been that it offered openings to collusion, and it was Bottomley's aim to show that Nancy had not only availed herself of a provision in American divorce law which was similar to the proposed provision in the Buckmaster Bill regarding desertion, but that she and her first husband had acted in illegal collusion. As mentioned already, he had done his research with some care. Having established from her marriage certificate of 1906, from which he quoted, that she had married Waldorf Astor as a divorced woman, he went on to give a citation from a damaging article of February 1903 printed in the *New York*

Herald. The main theme of the article was a complaint that her divorce proceedings in Charlottesville had been conducted with what the paper considered a highly suspicious degree of secrecy; the only persons present were the court officials and Mrs Shaw's (i.e. Nancy's) legal representative, Shaw's representative being absent.

To do Bottomley justice, he could not possibly have known the private circumstances behind Nancy's divorce in 1903, and the facts as they stood were certainly open to damaging interpretation if one only followed the account in the *New York Herald.* In fact, as will appear later, the terms of the decree rule out the possibility of collusion, and it was at collusion that he broadly hinted, as the *New York Herald* had done in 1903. Bottomley then returned to the theme of Nancy's insincerity, implying with all his old skill that she had much – perhaps more than anyone could know – to hide. It was now that he made use of the information published by the *Saturday Review* in December 1919. He invited his readers to draw their own conclusions from the fact that in *Who's Who,* and also in Burke's *Peerage* and other works of reference, Waldorf Astor described himself as having married in 1906 'Nancy Witcher, the widow of the late Robert Gould Shaw'. Bottomley revealed that Robert Gould Shaw, so far from being 'late', was a well-known member of Brook's Club in New York. Why should this false entry have been made if there was not something to hide in the divorce?

Such was Bottomley's attack. The charges could all be refuted, if the argument was taken up in a libel action, except the last and least grave one. The allegation of a false entry in *Who's Who* and the rest was unhappily true. This made legal retaliation virtually impossible; not that the case would depend on it, but to have to admit to a silly piece of misrepresentation, undertaken, one may confidently guess, in the interests of Waldorf's political career, would damage the reputations, the 'public image' as people might say today, of Nancy and Waldorf, out of all proportion to the facts of the case. Quite apart from that, to fight back would mean dragging up, and being publicly examined and cross-examined about the most calamitous event of Nancy's life; and what was to prevent Bottomley calling Robert Shaw as a witness? The former could be relied on to make the case as sordid as possible, and apart from the pain that it was likely to cause Nancy, she had to think of the pain it would also cause her eldest son. The only thing to do was to do nothing, to treat Bottomley's outpourings as beneath notice, and to maintain complete silence on the subject. But such a line went sorely against the grain with Nancy. She was unlikely to stick to it.

The House showed its sympathies at the earliest opportunity. On Nancy's entering the Chamber the first time after the 8th May she was received with applause, and Bottomley with angry looks and a few hostile cries. This was widely reported in the Press, though Horatio Bottomley, writing for *John Bull* (and possibly biased in the matter), assured his readers that such demonstrations had been imagined by parliamentary correspondents.

The Press made relatively little comment on the incident, and the only paper which gave a leader to it was the Catholic weekly *The Universe*. On the 14th May it published a long and somewhat confused article defending Nancy personally while condemning her position as a divorced woman. It also took the opportunity to condemn the laxity of American divorce law. In the defensive passages it poured ridicule on Bottomley's accusation that Nancy had spoken insincerely: 'What was really amazing,' ran the article in a central passage, 'and what afterwards made the House of Commons angry, was that Mr Bottomley actually charged the lady with "fooling" that House – as if the facts were not common knowledge. . . . It was just this that made Lady Astor's speech – unhappily in the deeper aspects – so impressive. Well aware of the sword hanging over her head, she yet had the courage to get up and say what she believed to be right, whatever the consequences.'

Here again, in this orthodoxly narrow yet generous-minded article, one may find evidence of that respect in which Bottomley was not held, but with which he was timidly treated. 'While we lament the mistaken course of Mr Horatio Bottomley,' ran one passage, 'we may admit the excellence of his motives.' And in another we read of 'his remarkable qualities which we would be the last to depreciate'.

As was to be expected, Nancy bore herself as if she cared not a fig for the slanders and libels of this man, but in fact she had been hurt deeply. It is surely significant that in her Press-cutting books which contain great quantities of hostile and sometimes very scurrilous matter against her, the place in the entries for May 1920 where the Bottomley article of the 8th was once pasted in by a secretary, has been scrubbed clean and a blank sheet stuck over where it was. Direct evidence continues to appear in Kerr's letters counselling her to master her tendency to melancholy and depression by ever-increasing reliance on her religion. He wrote the letters while out of England while preparing and attending the Spa Conference.[3]

During the summer of 1920 Nancy was almost more in the public eye than usual. Her unpopularity had passed swiftly and she was the centre of both wise and foolish admiration. But within there was always the nagging injury of Bottomley's insult, as Kerr's letters show. She found it impossible to continue to keep silence and at length she spoke out with characteristic courage.

The occasion was the annual meeting of the Unionist Association of her constituency on the 9th July. When the time came for her speech she announced that she wished to make a statement in answer to charges which had recently appeared 'in a certain paper'. For a short while she had difficulty in obtaining a hearing against cries of sympathetic protest. 'Tear it up!' cried some, 'We don't want to hear it!' cried others. When silence was at length obtained and she spoke, she mastered her emotion with some difficulty, a rare thing with her. To follow a contemporary report, she said: 'I have waited for this meeting to deal with charges which, if true, would affect my position as your representative. You would have been entitled to ask whether the charges were true. I assume that you have not done so because you trusted me and may have guessed the motive behind them. If you assumed that there was no justification for the attack, you were right. But however unpleasant it is to deal with the period of great unhappiness I went through seventeen years ago, I prefer to tell you all about it.'

She referred to Bottomley's pre-publication poster campaign 'as an example of the type of method employed in the attack on me'. She outlined Bottomley's charges and then gave her audience a brief account of the circumstances in which she had sought a divorce from Robert Shaw. The speech was bold and direct, but it contained a serious flaw: Nancy was no lawyer and when she came to the legal situation under which she had obtained her divorce her account was difficult to follow, either because the intricacies of the case perplexed her, and led her into confused expression, or because she ignored her notes, as she often did when speaking, and extemporised on a complicated subject. In Plymouth all this made little difference and she received a unanimous vote of confidence. But Bottomley saw his advantage.

3. The Spa Conference, 5th–16th July, 1920, was the first occasion when German and Allied representatives met on a (theoretical) footing of equality since the war.

He was on the warpath again in *John Bull* on the 17th July, asserting that Nancy's reply had been so long deferred because she knew her case was weak, repeating his accusations of double-dealing in the matter of prohibition, pointing out what he considered the suspicious confusion of the legal passage, and returning again to the one point on which the Astors were completely vulnerable, the false entry in the books of reference to which Nancy had not alluded. The contest was over for the time being nevertheless. Bottomley had had bad luck in his timing of the original attack, as shortly after, what interest had been aroused by the case was turned away and absorbed by Austen Chamberlain's controversial 1920 budget. By July the affair seemed to vanish into final oblivion.

Philip Kerr wrote to her from the Spa Conference on the 11th July: 'Well your speech seems to have gone off very well, judging by *The Times*. I'm sure you've done the right thing, though it can't have been pleasant. Don't refer to the subject again! I don't suppose you will want to.' She never did refer to the subject again in public, although it was to be unworthily raised by political enemies three years later. Before then Bottomley's career was over. He continued to print the occasional sneer against the Astors, but after Nancy's courageous action in July 1920, these lost their verve and venom. He slowly vanishes from the story. One of the last *John Bull* attacks appeared during the 1922 General Election and was headed 'Nancy Go Home'. It was not written by Bottomley but by one of his successors who manfully kept the paper alive for a time before it went to other ownership. Bottomley's fraudulency had been proved at last in the summer of that year, and he had been condemned to seven years' penal servitude. Something can be forgiven to the man for his well-known remark to a prison visitor. The latter found him at work on a mailbag and said: 'Ah Bottomley – sewing I see.' 'Reaping,' replied Bottomley.

In the period from Nancy's election in December 1919 to the General Election of 1922, the character of her parliamentary role gradually took shape. The first impression which the record of this part of her life makes on anyone who studies it is of a hardly credible abundance of energy. Her zest for life increased with the enlargement of her activities. Her social life remained as full as it had been in her more frivolous days as a young married woman before the war, in fact, if one takes into account the great number of political receptions she attended, both of the sought-after and the opposite kind, it was very much fuller, and yet at no time could it ever be said of her that she sacrificed for the sake of her delight in society the smallest fraction of her political and parliamentary duties. She was among the most frequent attendants at the House, spoke more often than most recently elected members (her special position, of course, made it easier than for most to catch the Speaker's eye), and she accepted every invitation that she could to make a political speech outside Parliament. Shortly after the events last recorded she made what is best described as 'a progress through Yorkshire', speaking at Sheffield, Bradford, Leeds, York and Hull, and this was followed at intervals by other 'progresses'. She was never long away from Plymouth, where her popularity increased as a self-appointed spokesman for the needs of the Royal Navy, not only regarding reform in her chosen field of improved conditions for the wives and children of officers and men, better education facilities especially for the lower deck, the right of retired seamen to be accepted by Trades Unions as members, but also regarding major naval policy in such matters as the maintenance of naval and merchant naval docks in her constituency and elsewhere. She was largely responsible for some alleviation of unemployment in Plymouth when ship-breaking work was located there in 1921. She said in a typical remark to a Plymouth audience: 'I don't know whether I have become a force in the House of Commons as much as a nuisance.' The answer is that she was a force because she never objected to making herself a nuisance. If she had a cause at heart she would hammer on at it in debate, in Committee, or at question time, to the exasperation often of the minister concerned, until she had either got her way, or some of it, or until defeat was absolutely irrevocable, and in the last case she rarely abandoned the subject for ever. She was only once an initiator of legislation in the full sense, but she was a continual influence, a point stressed in an essay by Lady Stocks. This comes out very strikingly in a case which has already been mentioned.

It will be remembered that on the occasion of her unsuccessful duel with Joynson Hicks, the pink ticket which played so strongly on his feelings was for a parliamentary committee on the subject of women police. This subject occupied her for several years, and it is probably not going beyond the facts to say that without Nancy's ceaseless agitation in Parliament such a body would not have survived the retrenchment recommended by the committee of which Sir Eric Geddes was chairman, the 'Geddes Axe' as it was called. She first raised the subject in Parliament on the 9th March 1921, but she had given the question publicity in the Press in the year before. By March 1921 the force had been reduced in numbers so far as to be a mere token, a shadow of what it had been when manpower shortage in the war made it a necessity. The Government, following Geddes's recommendations, made no secret of their intention to disband the women's police force entirely, and it was only protest, notably by Commandant Mary Allen of the London branch, which kept the body surviving so late as two years after November 1918. Nancy gave this protest renewed energy by parliamentary adoption of the cause. She countered the manoeuvrings of the Government with the tenacity and quick manoeuvre of a first class prize-fighter.

She came near to defeat in this matter, but in the end, by sheer persistence, and thanks to good support in the House, she won. The verdict of history is surely that she won in a right cause. She could have taken for her motto a chapter-heading in Trollope's *Last Chronicle o Barset*: 'It's Dogged As Does It'.

If she lost more causes than she won, she rarely lost without leaving some influence on future legislation. Harder to assess, and more baffling for her at the time, were apparent successes which in fact led to nothing, or were realised in reforms undertaken so long after that her influence is in doubt. Early in her parliamentary career she supported the cause of women in the Civil Service, their right to equal opportunity with men and to equal pay. Her first speech on the subject was made on the 19th May 1920 and she never missed a chance to raise the question again and again throughout her first Parliament and afterwards. In this advocacy she met the frustrating experience of striking at an ever-yielding opponent. The original motion which she supported in 1920 was agreed without a division, but its results were not seen until thirty-five years later, in the Second World War, following the need to fill Embassy posts without delay at a time of manpower shortage and difficult travel. Among the first moves was the appointment by Sir Reader Bullard of the eminent Orientalist, Miss Lambton,[4] to be Press attaché in Tehran in 1939. This appointment went through without a ripple of controversy, and part of the reason may be that Nancy pre-

4. Now Professor A. K. S. Lambton, Professor of Persian in the University of London since 1953.

pared the public for changes which, a little before, had seemed revolutionary in the worst sense.

There was hardly a feature of the variegated modern thinking about
the rights of women and the sustenance of the young which Nancy did
not bring to the notice of the House. The legal conditions governing
Guardianship, the supply of milk to the needy, the protection of the
young from indecent assault, the suppression of prostitution and
brothel-keeping, the elimination of venereal disease, the need for more
appointments of women in prison inspection and public boards of
enquiry; all these causes and many others brought Nancy to her feet,
and those deluded souls who thought that a woman in the House
would be something of a lark or an occasion for flirtatious patronising
soon discovered the immensity of their mistake. Nor did Nancy make
repentance easy. Tact was a minor virtue which she rarely exercised in
Parliament or outside. To no subject did this more forcibly apply than
in regard to her main reforming ambition, to introduce the prohibition
of intoxicating drink.

When she said, as she often did, that she was decidedly not a prohibitionist, she meant that she did not wish tyrannically to impose
prohibition on her adopted country, but she never disguised her hope
that prohibition would ultimately be achieved in Great Britain. Nor
did she disguise her conviction that by the great amendment, the United
States had taken a step towards the Kingdom of Heaven on earth for
which Great Britain was not 'ripe' as she frequently said. The implication that Britain represented a rude, coarse, backward polity compared to her native country exasperated many people.

She often made enemies unwittingly by her tactlessness, but she had
a few enmities which she consciously maintained. One has been
mentioned already, with Lady Desborough. Another arose from her
House of Commons experiences, and the present writer, at any rate,
applauds her taste in this respect. The enemy has appeared already as
the darling of the diehards, Sir Frederick Banbury. This eminent stock-
broker was seventy in 1920 but his manner of life and his opinions
suggested that he had been born well over a century before. He was
admired for his dress which was certainly impressive and becoming:
he never appeared in the House apparelled other than in a frock coat
and a top hat wearing a buttonhole of the utmost beauty and expense.
He was also admired for his wit which, as preserved in Hansard and

Press cuttings, seems to have been of a wholly contemptible kind. It may be that like Charles Sibthorp before him he caught the ear of the House by the utter preposterousness of his ultra-conservatism, though unlike Sibthorp he seems to have provoked laughter which was mostly on his side and not directed at him. He was famed, and admired, for his verbosity and his consequent ability to talk out bills. He represented the City of London. He had a rooted dislike of every sort of reform, especially if it was calculated to relieve the lot of what he regarded as the classes beneath him, and doubly so if it was likely to add to the comfort, to 'pamper' as he would say, women in humble circumstances. Such innovations were the nightmare of this rich, popular and influential man.

It was not till June 1920 that he and Nancy first came into parliamentary conflict. A private member's bill to reduce shop hours was passing through its Second Reading. Nancy had expressed support because she had in mind the women assistants, some of whom were married and lived far off. Sir Frederick very much despised all private members' bills, and would like to have seen the right to introduce them abolished. This bill struck him as particularly obnoxious so he set himself to defeat it in the way he understood better than anyone else. With his limitless resources of clubman anecdote, facetious autobiography and sophistry he talked the bill out. She had seen this odd procedure for the first time at the debate when she made her maiden speech, but then it had had what she estimated as a constructive purpose. Here it had none. She was deeply shocked. She rose and tried to move the closure, but by the rules of the House, of which Sir Frederick had the most perfect knowledge, the Speaker could not allow this. So the bill came to nothing and shop assistants had to wait.

In November 1920 she clashed with him again in a debate in which she was a speaker in favour of a government bill to introduce juvenile courts (or Children's Courts as they were then known) into British legal administration. The system had been proved during a long period since its beginning in the mid-nineteenth century and was already established in Canada and Australia. To Sir Frederick Banbury it was a monstrous measure: it was American in origin, it pampered lower class youths and children, and worst of all the bill provided that in court a woman would invariably be among those sitting on the bench. When Nancy rose to speak he decided to put her off by interruptions, a manoeuvre which she herself often practised. He succeeded. She ended her speech by saying: 'I do beg honourable members, in voting, to consider the type of mind that is opposing this bill.'

Sir Frederick took pride in his type of mind, and so did many of his fellow-members.

There was no great pitched battle between him and Nancy in this Parliament, but the skirmishes were conducted with sharp-edged weapons and both of them showed that they disliked and despised what the other stood for. The rancour became personal. At one moment Nancy had reason to fear him. In the summer of 1921 William Lowther resigned as Speaker. His deputy, the Asquith Liberal John Henry Whitley, was strongly favoured as his successor, but a large Conservative group resented the implication that deputy speakership should automatically serve as a stepping-stone to the Chair, and wished for a more imaginative choice. Their candidate was Sir Frederick Banbury. Happily the prospect proved too much for the majority of members, and the selection of Banbury only improved the chances of Whitley who was elected. He remained Speaker till 1928.

On the 23rd September 1921 Nancy's long ordeal as the only woman member came to an end with the election of Mrs Wintringham as the member for Louth. Like Nancy she became the representative of a parliamentary seat formerly occupied by her husband. In the summer Mr Wintringham, an Asquith Liberal, had died of a sudden heart-attack in the library of the House of Commons, and his widow now stood in his place for his party. She headed the poll by a modest majority of 791 over her Conservative opponent, and had no overall majority. Against all protocol, and contradicting her resolve (which proved impossible in practice) not to be a 'sex-candidate', Nancy sent Mrs Wintringham a telegram of congratulation on this Conservative defeat, and it was published in the Press. Nancy was a prima donna, if ever there was one, but she was never this in the familiar sense of envying others a share of the limelight. She always welcomed new women members regardless of party, and to the end of her political career regretted that there were not more of them.

Like Nancy, Mrs Wintringham was introduced into the House by a leader of her party who was also a former Prime Minister. Nancy suggested that she should be one of her sponsors, but after a brief correspondence, and at Mrs Wintringham's suggestion, she thought better of it, so on the 18th October, into a crowded Chamber, the first British-born woman member was escorted (without mishap) by Mr Asquith and Sir Donald Maclean. Nancy watched the scene with excitement. The two women became close friends.

The terminal note on the sources from which this chapter is drawn is included in that following Chapter 12.

RIDING IN TRIUMPH

THE most spectacular *grandeur d'une victoire* was enacted outside Westminster and outside England. In 1922 Nancy was seized with a great longing to visit the United States which she had not seen since before the war. She felt she owed the visit on grounds of sentiment, gratitude and policy: sentiment for obvious reasons of patriotism; gratitude because the American Press had followed the Plymouth election with almost as much interest as the British Press and had expressed a wide and authentic pride in this achievement of an American woman; policy because anti-American feeling in Britain was strong in indignation at the American refusal to join the League of Nations and, as usually happens, the hostile feeling was rapidly reciprocated. There was an additional reason on political grounds. The irrepressible Margot had been invited in early 1922 to go on a lecture tour of the United States. With courage and tactlessness (in which she resembled Nancy) she took the opportunity to tell the Americans just what she and a large part of the British public thought of them for rejecting the American-founded League. Her outspokenness might have been effective if in the course of her tour she had not shown an ignorance of North America as a whole that was positively phenomenal and drew mockery besides anger upon her. Addressing a Canadian audience in Canada, for example, she referred to 'your Abraham Lincoln'. In so far as one speaker can sway a continent, Margot's visit had heightened the strong anti-British feeling in the United States. Nancy wanted to counteract this.

She took leave of absence from Parliament for approximately seven weeks from the 13th April when she sailed for New York on the *Olympic*, till the 30th May when she landed back again at Southampton. She had been invited to attend a Women's Pan-American Conference to be held in Baltimore in April, and though she did not attend as an official observer for the British Government but on her own initiative, this conference provided a reason for the journey. Her political chiefs encouraged her to go.

She and Waldorf arrived at New York during the night of the 18th
April, but the fun had already begun on the boat. One New York
paper had sent over a woman reporter, described by Waldorf as
'intelligent and apologetically business-like', to interview Nancy on
the voyage. The reporter filed her messages by radio and on publication
they soon excited the rest of the New York Press to competition. Soon
requests for interviews and engagements came to the ship by radio in
increasing volume, and Nancy was touched when one came from her
birthplace, Danville in Virginia. It was clear from the beginning that
this was going to be no ordinary excursion, and Waldorf was from the
first conscious of danger and responsibility. He took charge. 'I feel,'
he wrote in a diary he kept during the visit, 'like the agent, secretary,
manager, booster and adviser of a prima donna, cabinet minister and
circus all in one. The Press are trying to make us into a circus, while
just at this moment one realises the importance and effect of anything
N. may say as an M.P. – the supposed confidant of the Prime Minister –
and absolutely in the public eye.'

Disembarkation began on the morning of the 19th.

From that moment the pace never diminished till the end of the tour,
and was often accelerated. Reading Waldorf's account one marvels how
any human being could have physically survived so much welcome.
On the evening of the 20th she attended a banquet given to nearly a
thousand guests by Ambassador Norman Davis, and in her speech she
found herself obliged to allude to the embarrassing question of the
League of Nations. Although Waldorf 'did not think N. in quite such
good form as on the preceding day', the speech had a good Press. She
had started on the right foot, and from now on, with only one serious
mishap, Nancy had an overwhelming public opinion in the United
States on her side.

On the 22nd April they went to Baltimore accompanied by the
British Ambassador, Sir Auckland Geddes, who seems to have supplied
them with optimistic misinformation. All the time the pace was
steadily mounting. Waldorf recorded of the 23rd April in Baltimore:

'One can only say that the Southern papers are even more enthusiastic
than the Northern ones.

'I sigh daily for – nay, hourly, for our Secretariat from St James's
Square, who know my ways. What with helping with speeches,
dealing with the Press, watching the papers, tackling endless corres-

pondence, answering cable invitations from every part of the States
and Canada, altering dates of meetings, telephoning, fixing cross-
country journeys, etc. etc. it's like being in a maelstrom and in a
monsoon in a thunderstorm.

'Yesterday I asked Geddes how the relations between the U.S.A.
and the U.K. were. He said that almost for the first time in their history
there was no centre of trouble. He was wrong. The more we travel
and meet people and talk to reporters, the more do we realise the
amount of bad feeling which Mrs Asquith has created. She apparently
indulged in crude criticisms, and they also feel that she insulted their
intelligence by the stuff she talked.'

A friend offered them the use of his private railroad car whenever
they needed it during the trip. They accepted, and this enabled them
one day to travel to New York for a Press Lunch, return the same
evening (changing into evening dress in the railroad car) for a Baltimore banquet with speeches, followed by a Presbyterian reception with
more speeches. 'Of course I can feel my hairs turning white,' wrote
Waldorf. He drafted most of Nancy's speeches, but this undertaking
produced its special difficulties. 'Unfortunately on most occasions,
particularly when we are rushed, N. insists on trying each different
method of preparation, of changing her system of notes and of swap-
ping her train of thoughts. The task of helping her on these occasions would turn a nigger's curly locks into the straight wisps of an
albino.'

On the 28th April, having enjoyed less than one day's rest from
receptions, banquets and speeches, they travelled to Washington to
attend further receptions, banquets and speeches. On the day of their
arrival in the capital, Nancy spoke to the Press Club, 'in good vein',
and that evening she and Waldorf attended a Pan-American meeting
which was held in a theatre and addressed by Secretary of State
Charles E. Hughes and Auckland Geddes. Nancy was not billed to
speak and had nothing prepared, but the audience called for her, so
she went on to the stage and 'was really inspired'. Waldorf described
the episode next day:

'I really think last night's performance was N's best. . . . N. had two
minutes of silent prayer and then went down from her box and to the
front of the platform. When she sat down the audience gave a huge
ovation and called her back to bow. She was witty, gently sarcastic,
spiritual, intelligent and eloquent in her speech.'

They met President Harding and were received in the Senate, and as before and throughout reception followed reception. The record in any detail would soon weary the stoutest reader, and it is enough to say that there was no one of eminence whom they did not meet in Washington. Nancy's popularity soared, and the physical stamina of both during days which might have daunted even royalty, never appeared to flag. And yet all this was little compared to what was coming. On the night of the 1st May they left their private railroad car and travelled by special train to Richmond Virginia. They were now joined by Nancy's sister Irene.

Here is the beginning of Waldorf's diary for the 2nd:

'How can I describe events here!

'At 7.10 we rolled into the station. N. had had a theory she could lie in bed till 8. Luckily I was up. The whole of the family and heads of the town were on the platform with photographers and reporters. Out I tumbled unshaved, dirty, barely washed, without even a cup of tea inside me. A brisk reporter stepped up and asked me my first impressions of Richmond, while a row of photographers clicked their instruments! Luckily I was able to beat a hasty retreat into the embraces of the family.

'We bustled N. up while we stood around gazing at each other as if we had all broken our fast and bathed and as if it wasn't 7.10 a.m.

'At last out popped N. Then the fun began. With her usual gift N. turned to a grimy sooty engine-driver and shouted, "I feel as you look." We all felt happy and cheerful after that.

'And then!

'There is a big station at Richmond – a large white marble approach and hall.

'Nancy was ushered into this by stalwart policemen – there was a long alley of children fully 200 yards long with elders lined up behind. As N. appeared a uniformed band struck up "Dixie" and then "Back to Old Virginia", the schoolchildren cheered and as she walked down the centre they threw flowers at her feet and over her. I almost wept. It was a most moving and touching sight, and the sentiment so genuine. People cheering, sobbing, etc.

'I have seen the instructions and apparently every school and every club and every society was allocated a definite quota of places. Civic

Municipal Government appears to have concentrated on nothing but N's homecoming for the past few days.'

They were given hardly any time for any intimate meetings, such as Nancy's with her old teacher Miss Jennie, for when they were not attending receptions (at one of which they stood shaking the hands of the guests for two hours) they were being interrogated by Press reporters. On the 5th May they travelled by special train to Nancy's birthplace, but the journey from Richmond to Danville was in effect another long-drawn-out reception. As Waldorf described it: '. . . not even with a stateroom can we get privacy – particularly with a honey-pot butterfly like N. who flits from rosebud to rosebud (poetic description of fellow passengers) or alternatively as a honeyed rose attracting all sorts of bees, butterflies, etc. Today we had a stateroom but no privacy. Our fellow travellers are kindness itself but don't realise one needs quiet at times. I woke up from a doze to find 2 men expounding to me their views on life.'

At every halt on the way there was a crowd to see her and cheer her and ask for a speech. She found an old lady at one stop who years ago had been visited by young Nancy in 'The Sheltering Arms' with the good Archdeacon Neve. At one of the last stops, a place called South Boston, an odd thing happened. Nancy was asked to make a speech and, always averse to playing what her old friend Henry James used to call 'the terribly pleasant', she launched into a violent attack on the new feminine fashion of wearing very short skirts, denouncing the husbands present for allowing their wives to wear 'those things'. The speech went down well and at the end of it a young reporter asked if he might travel the rest of the way in the special train. She asked him who he was. He said that he was an Englishman, by name Gerard Tetley, and that he was reporting for the two newspapers of her native town, the *Danville Register* and *The Bee*. Nancy had a word aside with her sister and then asked Mr Tetley if he knew much about her family. He replied that he had briefed himself as thoroughly as he could on the subject so as to cover this event efficiently. Nancy told him that he and no other reporter might travel in their stateroom.

When the train started he had a great surprise. He had his pencils sharpened and his pad ready, but the two ladies quickly turned the tables on him. Closeted alone with them (with Waldorf as a watchdog outside perhaps), he found that instead of being encouraged to grill the ladies, they were intent on grilling him. Nancy put him on his honour not to betray their secret, namely that she had no memory at all of her childhood in Danville, while Irene had only a very hazy one. Who, they asked, who were the people they used to know there? Who would expect to be mentioned by them? Were there any stories about them? Mr Tetley briefed them thoroughly, told them the names of all their surviving playmates, and the rest. He kept his word and the incident was only divulged forty-two years later, after Nancy's death.

They arrived at Danville at a quarter to ten in the evening. 'Throngs,' wrote Waldorf. 'Motored to the hotel where we had decided to stay as all N's relations were quarrelling as to who should put us up. We never made a wiser decision. N. estimated before reaching Danville that she had 60 cousins in Danville. She may have had that number a year ago but like rabbits they have since then bred much and often. Litters of them invaded our room at the hotel – all talked at once – all wanted us to modify our itinerary and programme in some different way.'

Friday the 5th May was the great day. According to Waldorf's account it started early. 'This morning I poked my nose out of my room before breakfast – there were rows of cousins sitting rocking and spitting and gossiping so I bolted back and henceforth had to communicate with the outside world through my servant.

'I knew the cousins were rabbits – what's more they've all had several fresh litters during the night. However in spite of their numerical increase they really were kinder and more considerate to-day. But never have I been to so noisy a spot as Danville. It's like being in a merry-go-round with the orchestrelle blasting away and a thunderstorm raging simultaneously.'

The ceremonies began at eleven o'clock and went on till one. The first took place in the Town Council Chamber where Nancy and Irene were made honorary councillors and presented with golden keys. 'The Mayor,' wrote Waldorf, 'an old gentleman with a long goatee, delivered a flowery oration that put the Psalmist, Demosthenes and Gladstone to shame.'

Then the notables moved to the site of the house where Nancy was born. Bands, choirs, joyfully massed schoolchildren formed the main features of this festival with more speeches in that elaborate American style that was still flourishing. If the Mayor had gone to great lengths, he could hardly have outdone Mr Harry C. Ficklen when he presented a silver loving-cup to Nancy on behalf of the citizenry. 'We are here,' he said, 'to greet our baby that went away to stand before Kings and has come back to see us as "just folks" – Bless her heart!'

His conclusion rose to heights rarely attempted. 'I now present to you, Citizens of Danville, your own Daughter, whom we, first of all can claim as "Our Nancy" – gift of little Danville to big old London – gift of the corner of Broad and Main to stately Cliveden on the Thames – gift of Chillie Langhorne and Nancy Witcher Keene, bone of our bone and flesh of our flesh, to Waldorf Astor – "the man's the gold for a' that" – to Lloyd George and Mr Balfour – child of Romance, whose story rivals an Arabian Nights Tale,' etc. etc. With allusions to Nancy as a 'dove of war and an eagle of peace', and others to her un-dying devotion to 'the sacred soil of Virginia', this was the stuff to give them, and the ceremonies concluded with wild cheering. Later the painted board, mentioned at the beginning of this book, was set up in the street in front of where Chillie's house had been.

When the festival was over, Waldorf was approached by one of the reporters who paid him 'quite a compliment'. As he noted in his diary: 'He pulled me aside and said, "Lord Astor, I've seen you called upon several times to speak and I want to tell you I think you ought to think seriously about going into public life also!" '

After a family breakfast-party they left the next morning by their special train and continued their triumphal tour through Virginia, as before with frequent stops at which the now familiar scenes were repeated. To quote Waldorf: 'Crowds – guard of honour in uniforms – flags – officers – swords – schoolgirls – song "Nancy Astor you are some girl" – Flowers – Speech – Train moves on – Cheers.' The Romans wisely believed that the hero of the day needed a check to pride during his triumph. Waldorf and Nancy received this correction soon after Danville as appears from the diary:

'I heard two old hayseeds standing by me in the train discussing N. Their conversation was something as follows:

' " 'S that Laidy Astor?"
' "Reckon so – or perhaps it's her sister?"
' "Why's she called laidy?"
' "She married some furriner."
' "Is that her husband standing by her?" (Looking at an unshaved old boy.)
' "Reckon 'tis."

' "Pity he's so old."

' "I don't think she's that pretty."

' "No, nor more do I."

'And they moved on.'

They continued by Lynchburg and the western part of the State till on the 9th May they reached Greenwood and Nancy's home Mirador. Here she met again her old friend Archdeacon Neve, but again there was little time for any intimate meetings, either with the Archdeacon or the surviving neighbours or 'Uncles' and 'Aunts' who remembered her. The flags, officers, schoolchildren and so on took up almost all their time and energies. On the 12th May Nancy addressed with great success an audience of four thousand in the University of Virginia at Charlottesville. The next day they left Greenwood for Washington, where they found the private railroad car again. They travelled from Washington to Chicago.

As before, Waldorf played a protecting role and cut down the programme proposed by the reception committee of Chicago by half. He had for long been struggling with the Toronto authorities whose plans for the penultimate part of the whole journey in Canada were even fiercer than those they had encountered in the United States. 'It's the Minister of Agriculture,' he wrote in his diary, 'who has the programme in hand. He seems to think N. is a bullock.'

Her return to the North and her reception in Chicago may have been a cause for some anxiety to Waldorf, following an indiscretion in one of her speeches. In general Nancy had been careful in her public expression of opinion, had relied heavily on Waldorf's judgement, and had only spoken extempore when there was no way out. But sometimes she made impromptu remarks that were resented, and no one, unless ignorant of the persistence and unscrupulousness of the American reporting of those days, would blame her. She annoyed American Catholics by the wildly unhistorical statement (very unsuited to Maryland and Canada if nowhere else) that America 'had been founded by Protestants in the Protestant faith'. But she was expressing a common fallacy and her remark made no great stir. Great, however, was her indiscretion when she was manoeuvred into making a statement on American domestic policy.

One of the questions of the hour was that of bonuses to be paid to men who had served with the American services in the war. Surprisingly she took the unpopular side. 'I think the bonus would be a dangerous thing,' she said. 'Look how it worked after the Civil War. A great rich country like the U.S. cannot do too much for the disabled soldier, but for the fit and strong, give them work, not charity.' Great was the rage of William Randolph Hearst, the dedicated enemy of Great Britain, another 'soldier's friend', who was running at that time for the Governorship of New York. 'A patriotic American,' he thundered in his newspaper, 'might properly find a few things to complain about his own statesmen. The subservience of his Government to those international bankers who are the fiscal agents of England; in the snobbish humility of his own representatives in office; in the lack of wisdom and foresight of his diplomatic agents and in the domineering, dictatorial, ungracious, ungrateful attitude of England we so lately saved from destruction.' So it went on, with a declaration that the Hearst Press was not 'unfriendly to England'. It was all very like *John Bull* and, though indirectly expressed, manifestly aimed at the Astors. The article was repeated in other papers both in America and England.

Nancy made no reply and in this she may have been following Philip Kerr's advice who at the time was in Boston undergoing an intense course (known as 'class') in Christian Science. (He had left Lloyd George's office early in 1922.) He wrote to her 'don't attack Hearst or Hylan as persons. It is the impersonal evil, hatred, animosity, greed, political manipulation, which is handling them and from which someday, they, like everybody else will wake up, that you want to rebuke and destroy, with good.'

In the event Hearst's Press attack made no difference to Chicago's welcome which lasted from their arrival on the afternoon of the 14th May, and swirled about the usual receptions and banquets and club meetings and speeches (and an endeavour to photograph Waldorf in the stockyards for advertising purposes), till their departure by train for Canada in the evening of the 16th.

The emotion of their visit to Canada was heightened by memories of the hospital at Cliveden. 'Many a wet eye,' wrote Waldorf in his diary, 'both of men and of women I have seen.' From Toronto they went to Ottawa, where Nancy had a happy meeting with Miss Agnes MacPhail. From there they went to Montreal where women still had not got the vote. On this last point Nancy was asked a great many questions, and she somehow contrived to answer them without offence. She and Waldorf left on the evening of the 19th and were in New York on the morning of the 20th May. It was a Saturday and

they went to Long Island to stay with her old friend Alice Winthrop
and her husband. They came back on Monday the 22nd for her last
public appearance, a banquet to eighteen hundred people given by
The League for Political Education. Another guest was Miss Alice
Robertson, the only woman member of the House of Representatives.
'There were rather too many speeches,' recorded Waldorf in an entry
which quietly conveys a frightening impression of ceremonial en-
durance, and Nancy had to wait till eleven before rising. With typical
courage she chose the League of Nations as the theme for her final
speech of the tour. From the beginning she had been warned to avoid
this topic, and from the beginning she had seen that the topic could
only be avoided by escapist evasion. Her reaction was always the same
when confronted by any choice between diplomatic nicety and outspoken conviction, if the former could possibly be interpreted as an
act of fear. On the occasion of this historic visit she made her decision
early, and regardless of the anxieties she may have occasioned Sir
Auckland Geddes, she spoke out boldly in favour of the United States
going back on their isolationist decision and joining the League.

She guessed rightly that there was an enormous public in the United
States which looked with shame on the new isolationism, and she gave
voice to this sentiment while avoiding, with an intuition which did
not fail her, the kind of phrase likely to provoke hostility. The wisdom
of her belief and her ardent sincerity made her most downright statements acceptable. A remark which she made more than once in the
course of the tour, attacking nationalist prejudice against the name of
the League, was long remembered and was probably repeated by her
at this dinner. 'You need not call it the League of Nations,' she said.
'You can call it anything you like. You can give it a new name every
week. But for God's sake give it a chance.'

Shortly before, there had been disorders in China in which the League
became involved. Nancy used this cleverly to strengthen her arguments.
She told her audience that the United States Government had called on
Great Britain, through the League, to protect American oil interests
in Iraq, but had recently refused to join the League committee of
enquiry into the atrocities against Christian populations as a result of
the disorders in the Far East. 'Now I ask you,' she said, 'which is the
more important in the end – oil concessions or bleeding humanity?'
It was a bold thing to say and it was received with 'prolonged applause'. It made a fitting end to her triumphant enterprise.

It was not quite the end. She left the banquet 'in a blaze of glory', but before going home she broadcast a farewell message on a local radio station of New York. She was staying with her niece Nancy Tree, a daughter of Nancy's eldest sister, and she and Waldorf returned after midnight to the house of Ronald and Nancy Tree to find a supper-party assembled to meet them.

On the 23rd May they were due to sail in the *Aquitania*. Waldorf's diary has this brief last entry:

'Final visits of friends.

'Final words with reporters.

'Final press photos.

'Ship sailed at 12 noon.

'After lunch I slept till dinner.

'After dinner I slept till breakfast next day.'

By an odd coincidence, Mr William Randolph Hearst and his three sons were fellow passengers. Odder still, no encounter between Mr Hearst and the Astors is remembered.

They had a week of rest. Nancy was again at work as soon as they reached London from Southampton on the 30th. She came back to a House of Commons growing restless as the Coalition under Lloyd George showed increasing signs of refusing his leadership and splitting into separate parties. The prospects of a General Election in 1922 became apparent.

The main authority for the first part of Chapter 11 is the contemporary Press and Hansard. To the latter Miss Pamela Brookes's *Women in Westminster* provides an invaluable guide. The relations of Lady Astor and Lord Hugh Cecil may be deduced from his letters to her of a later date and an essay he wrote for Michael Astor. They disagreed politically but shared some religious ideas. The story of her encounter with Winston Churchill in the precincts of the House of Commons is given by Maurice Collis in *Nancy Astor* and has been published elsewhere in articles on both of them. The account of Horatio Bottomley is based largely on Mr Julian Symon's admirable biography (London, 1955) and a study of *John Bull*. Unexpectedly, Mr Symons does not mention Bottomley's campaign against Lady Astor. The account of Sir Frederick (later Lord) Banbury is chiefly taken from the contemporary Press and the very laudatory article on him in the *Dictionary of National Biography*. From the D.N.B. article on John Henry Whitley (1866–1935) is taken the account of Banbury's candidature for the Speakership. As regards Chapter 12, Lady Astor's 1922 visit to the U.S.A. is voluminously reported in the American Press of the time and less fully in the British Press which, at a time of unusual Anglo-American tension, often took an unfriendly or satirical line. Both for the sake of brevity and because it is far the best and most lucid account, the writer has mainly relied on Lord Astor's diary which is remarkably full considering the pressure under which it was written or dictated. Philip Kerr's letter to Lady Astor in connection with Hearst's press attack is dated the 22nd April. For the sake of brevity, chronology has not been strictly followed in regard to this episode. It should be mentioned that Philip Kerr was in the United States throughout the period of Lady Astor's visit, but they met little. His letters to her of this time are, with the exception of that quoted, of minor interest.

Chapter 13

NEW DRAGONS, NEW VICTORIES

BEFORE being given an account of her next political adventures, the reader may wish to know something of what went on behind the scenes, since in recording the tumultuous events in which Nancy was involved between 1919 and 1922 little attention has been paid to her private life.

It was centred as before on Cliveden, St James's Square, Plymouth and Sandwich. In April of 1920 Waldorf had bought the sporting estate, already referred to, on the island of Jura, and there she used to go from time to time for periods of rest in the summer, but one learns with some surprise from Philip Kerr's letters that she found Jura, that loveliest island of the Inner Hebrides, a boring place, and her visits seem to have been made in a strict spirit of wifely and parental duty, and in regard for her health.

As before, Cliveden was the major centre. There exists a record of Nancy's Cliveden life at this time, as observed from the point of view of one of her favourite guests. He was Walter Elliot, then in his early thirties, a parliamentary colleague and fellow-member of the Conservative Party. In 1955 he wrote a memoir describing his friendship and the life of Cliveden, from which these extracts are taken:

'It is the nature of good country-house life to be self-complete. Nancy Astor was able to appreciate this better than most. For she was a Virginian; the child of a culture which was born and bred among great country-houses as surely as ever Brer Rabbit was born and bred in a briar patch. Cliveden was never more itself than in the dusk, on the high paved terrace outside its drawing-room windows. But one always looked for the fireflies, and listened for the grasshoppers – and the mosquitoes. This was the transposition of an old theme into a new key. It added, by that much, piquancy to the whole.

'Imagine, then, a young alien from Glasgow University catapulted into Parliament by one of the chances which arise after a great war, and made free of all this come-and-go, by the endless hospitality and interest of its owners.

'I do not know which was more pleasant; to appear at tea-time in winter when the tea was set in the centre hall before the big fire, or in summer, when it was laid out with infinite detail, under a pavilion roof at the end of the broad terrace. Tea, did I say? It was more like a Bedouin encampment. There was a table for tea, a table for cakes, a table for children, a table for grown-ups, a table for more grown-ups, and generally a nomadic group coming and going somewhere in the neighbourhood of Nancy herself. Cushions, papers, people, were mixed in a noble disarray. Nancy presided over the whole affair like a blend between Juno at the siege of Troy, and one of the leading Valkyries caracoling over an appropriate battlefield.

'Somehow or other the party evolved, arranged itself, separated, and came together again, re-arrayed for dinner. It might contain anybody – Henry Ford, the Queen of Rumania, Mr Charles Mellon, Jim Thomas, Philip Lothian, Bernard Shaw, Tom Jones, Dame Edith Lyttelton, Arthur Balfour, a general, a scientist, a Christian Scientist, relations, protégés, American Senators, whether sober or not (this was the only category to which such licence was extended), people of High Society, people of no society, and, if you were lucky indeed, one or more of the other Langhorne sisters, the only beings on earth whom Nancy really regarded as equals. Phyllis Brand (with her entrancing baby black-eyed daughter Virginia) would appear, sometimes with, sometimes without her husband, Bob Brand of Lazard Brothers, whom Nancy always greeted as a Jew, actual or honorary. Nora, the youngest sister, although married and with a family, was considered by both the others as not having yet grown up, and so was allowed to sing songs, to the accompaniment of her guitar, which would not have been permitted to really responsible people; such songs as the plaintive invocation to Sal

"*has anybody seen my Sal?*
She's so tall and shy and stately"

with its most astonishing denouement –

"*If you see her passing by*
Tell her I'm the same old pal . . .
Although she drinks an awful lot with other men,
She's a darned fine gal."

'Above and beyond the others was Irene, Mrs Dana Gibson, prototype of the Gibson girls; from whom her husband drew the Queen of Ruritania in his illustrations to the romances of Anthony Hope, the first and still the best of the histories of that fabulous land. Irene Gibson received the automatic deference which is extended, amongst women, to the Eldest Sister by all the others, should they live to be a hundred; when she said it was so, it was so; when she frowned, the others quaked; when she applauded, they beamed; when she went away, they were a little relieved. It was a wonderful thing to see this reaction in Nancy, so independent; for though it would not have been true to say that she feared not God neither regarded man, since she was a devout Christian, yet even there she was a Christian Scientist, whose votaries somehow manage to convey the impression that they received founders' shares at a recent re-flotation of the company, and are on intimate terms with the management.

'But we have only got as far as dinner. Nancy, teetotal to the core, never, for all that, attempted to impose her beliefs on her friends. The long table was laden with good food and drink. Twenty people were a small gathering; forty was not unknown. Conversation was general – again, did I say, conversation? – it was a debate, it was a riot, it was a tidal wave, in the midst of which small islets might be seen holding out determinedly in private talk till they too were borne away by the ever-rolling flood. After dinner, in the drawing-room, there were always two fires; a thing I have ever since regarded as indispensable if any large-scale hospitality is to be successful anywhere. If conversation at both, then conversation. If Nancy were in one of her wilder moods, then, at one, acting, games, impersonations of everything in or out of the world, while round the other fire grave and reverend seigniors would be exchanging views upon the Gold Standard or upon the part that technical education would have to play in the century after next.

'After that there is Saturday, when Nancy would gird herself for exercise – tennis or golf – and sally forth, after some high-pitched ob-jurgations against those who remained clustered around the big hall fire, or reading in one of the rooms. "Why don't you all go out, what you want to sit around here for? Go out! Go Out!! Look at the lovely day. Or at any rate go into some of my nice rooms, where I have the flowers. Sitting around here in the dark, all day long."

'Then she would go, hurrying like a deer – *vera incessu patuit dea* – a figure of physical beauty to take the breath from your throat; recalling so sharply her New World ancestry, and marked off so decidedly from the willowy lovelies who flower in the gentler, more temperate landscapes of the Home Counties. She carried, in every fibre, the crisp chic of the highly-bred American woman. She also had their unusual blend of femininity and sexlessness. She attracted men as Diana attracted Actaeon. Sometimes they shared his fate. Indeed she incarnated that ruthless goddess in more ways than one; there was an occasion when the death of one of her enemies, a fellow-Member, was reported to her in the Lobby of the House. "I'm glad," she said shortly. When remonstrative murmurs arose from her companions, she fell into an older speech. "Ah' don' care," she said. "I'm a Virginian; I shoot to kill." '

Walter Elliot was, like Nancy, a religious person, though, to judge from his conversation, no more rigidly orthodox than she was.[1] He rejected, not without sympathy, the claims of Christian Science. Her 'uncompromising Protestantism', he said in the same memoir, 'was familiar and, in my own case, congenial. Then, through the middle of it, tenuous but quite unyielding, like a strand of barbed wire in a hedge, came this unfamiliar streak. One bowed and passed on.'

If he had had the temerity (as he may have done) to say to her what he wrote about Christian Science on this occasion, it would not have been the end of their relationship. Among the contradictions of Nancy were an intolerant faith side by side with good humour in argument with those who looked on it as a delusion. Sometime in the twenties her old friend Mrs Longworth came to stay at Cliveden, and Nancy made a vigorous attempt to convert her to 'Science'. Mrs Longworth resisted stubbornly and Nancy demanded to know why she would not at least experimentally try the new religion. 'Because,' said Mrs Longworth, 'if we are to have Mariolatry, I for one prefer the Blessed Virgin to Mrs Eddy.' Nancy was momentarily aghast, frowned angrily, and then suddenly laughed. Though not usually graced by wit such as Mrs Longworth's, incidents of the kind were frequent.

As is hardly necessary to say, these passing moods of tolerance did not extend to Roman Catholicism in principle. By now she had become a fanatic on the subject. Yet this did not mean that, apart from Philip Kerr's relations, she was without Catholic friends. She had many of

1. In conversation with the writer he once expressed his attitude to spiritual matters as follows: 'If ye loook at the Universe it appears to be rational, but if ye loook a bit closer there's something phoney about it.'

them and Lord Colum Crichton Stuart was one of the most constantly invited guests. As a conscientious hostess she would accord Catholic friends staying at Cliveden facilities to go to mass on Sunday mornings, but she did not let them go without some anti-Popery agitation. 'How you can stand all that mumbo-jumbo!' she would mutter at them as they left the house.

Her anti-Catholicism could however go farther, into personalities, and interfere with the continuation of a friendship. A very extraordinary example of this was in the case of Victor Cunard, especially as he was not himself a Catholic. Since the days when he first met her at Market Harborough in 1904 he had remained devoted to Nancy. In 1922 he went into journalism and was a *Times* foreign correspondent from then until 1937, serving first in Rome and then in Paris. This honourable and, as many would think, distinguished choice of career brought him into Nancy's disfavour, as involving excessive Roman Catholic acquaintance.

There was, however, another reason for this temporary failure to maintain happy relations. In 1922, when the weakening of the bond (estrangement is too hard a term) first became noticeable, Victor Cunard was a young man of twenty-three. That was an uncomfortable age at which to know Nancy, whether as a new or a lifelong acquaintance. As Victor Cunard said: 'She felt it her bounden duty to chastise those weaknesses and uncertainties that beset young men and women. It is not surprising, therefore, that in the hope of avoiding galling though often pertinent criticisms, even those who loved her dearly should, at about the age of eighteen, have sought her company less assiduously.'

No one who knew her has (or could have) better described, than her third son Michael, the contrast between her perfect management of very young children and her frequently bad relations (and here again there were extraordinary exceptions) with people beginning to grow up. He wrote this in *Tribal Feeling*: 'My mother's gaiety acted like magic with small children, her own or anyone else's. It was thrilling and contagious. She enjoyed the whole game of turning everything into a farce, of making fun of the awe-inspiring things of life which was what every child prayed for. And it was not just fun, it was a riot. With children she was in her element. From her they met with something quite different from the usual set of instructions passed on to them by parents and nannies. The average grown-up, when faced with a child – his own or someone else's – will, in self-defence, remember the cardinal rule which is: "Don't get it over-excited." My mother's approach was a more positive one. Her idea was to make it laugh. She scored success after success. Children in slums, children in prams, children with weeks of grime all over their faces, and cosseted little Lord Fauntleroys of children all provided enthusiastic audiences for the very personal performance which she gave entirely for their benefit. This was her age group: the very young and wholly unself-conscious. With anything in between the age of innocence and the fully-matured creature her performance often misfired.'

No one, again, has better described the inner, loving, wholly private life of often-crowded Cliveden than Michael Astor. After telling of the childhood thrills of uncomprehended meetings with the world of Government and *The Round Table*, he goes on to say: 'There were, as well, quieter moods which were every bit as enjoyable and a good deal less precarious. When there were no visitors, which was not often, my father would read us an adventure story, or my mother would read us Uncle Remus; or else we would go into the boudoir, turn the lights out, and lie in front of the fire and listen to her "nigger" stories which she remembered from her own childhood. These stories were witty and humorous, with a touch of pathos which is inevitable in any Negro story. My mother acted every part with her voice, making her characters sound lazy and confiding, boastful or frightened. We were listening to the world of the coloured people at Mirador; a world of friendly, puzzled, grown-up children, interspersed with the high-spirited behaviour of her brothers, who in turn assumed the childish form of the Negroes when she introduced her father into the picture.'

Many actors and actresses, including some of the finest, are almost wholly dependent on a large audience and in private show none of their talents. Nancy, like her niece Joyce Grenfell, belonged to a different kind. An American friend, Mrs Ernesta Barlow, has this to say with reference to Nancy in the twenties: 'Many people have accused her of being a show-off. But a real show-off requires an audience. Nancy was just as funny, just as witty, just as ready to stage an hilarious performance for a ragamuffin she met in the streets as for a roomful of distinguished big-wigs. She played to amuse herself, played through pure animal spirits and never grew out of it.'

It will be remembered that Margot once accused Nancy of moving in too narrow a circle, especially in the political world. Whether there was ever any truth in the charge (and the writer believes there was none) the fault had been thoroughly remedied long before this time. She had close friends in all the parties. Mrs Snowden admired and loved her and when asked to oppose Nancy in Plymouth at the 1922 election indignantly and publicly refused. Philip Snowden, a supporter in principle, was nevertheless rather shocked at the horseplay in which she indulged at her dinner-parties in London. Ramsay MacDonald was made more shy than usual, though he liked her. J. H. Thomas and David Kirkwood were her special friends in the Labour Party.

She had sharp personal critics on the Left too. To quote Ernesta Barlow again:

'She either charmed or repelled. She left no one indifferent. "Lady Astor trades on her charm twenty-four hours a day!" an irate member of the first Labour Government said to me at one of her dinners. "Any serious talk is impossible in this house. We waste our time coming here." He watched her fan herself with a dinner plate, and push back her diamond tiara as if it had been an old hat.'

By 1922 the House of Commons which Nancy had entered in 1919 had changed drastically. Lloyd George was still a popular hero but his devoted following among experienced politicians was growing small in all parties, and the populace over whom he could still cast a spell now contained many critics. It was clear that a General Election would be held soon.

This is the sort of period when the practised member never acts without an eye on the constituents, when he listens to the advice of the local party agents with more than ordinary care, attends every division he possibly can, even at the expense of business, so as to anticipate his opponent's accusation of absenteeism;[2] above all, this is a period when

2. Parliamentarians may skip this explanatory note.

In Great Britain, when a candidate seeks re-election, his opponent makes great play with his 'division record'. Divisions or votings are taken on any measure put to the vote in the House after debate. These occur frequently in the course of parliamentary business. The names of the members who voted on both sides are printed in the official record, though the names of members who attended the debate are not. (Members often vote without attending the debate.) A member who *per impossibile* attended all debates and voted in all divisions would but very rarely see his constituents while Parliament was sitting, would grow ignorant of the world outside Westminster, and would rapidly become an idle and useless member of society. He would probably

the practised member avoids any public action of an unpopular kind. It is hardly needful to say that Nancy, unorthodox in most things, was unorthodox in this.

In the failing Parliament of the last half of 1922 Nancy took her usual, vigorous and unconventional stand. In feminist matters her stand was never a solitary one now. She persisted, with the able help of Mrs Wintringham, in pressing the claims of Women Police for survival and, again in collaboration with Mrs Wintringham, she supported the British Nationality (Married Women) Bill which sought to remedy the absurd anomaly whereby British women who married foreigners were automatically deprived of their British citizenship. Mrs Wintringham thus admirably described their dual parliamentary role: 'I felt she went about her task like a high-stepping pony, while I stumbled along like a country cart horse; but we both had our uses and worked in complete harmony together.'

None of the causes with which Nancy identified herself were generally unpopular, except one, and it was that one she embraced with the most ardour. In the House of Commons she never let an occasion go by on which she could find an excuse for pressing the cause of stringent, partial prohibition of intoxicating drinks, and she never refused, if she could help it, an invitation outside for a speech on the subject. She went farther and introduced a private member's Bill for further drink legislation.

The introduction took place on 3rd August 1922, the day before Parliament adjourned for the summer recess. Although it was thus allowed a first reading, the official text of the Bill was not issued till a month later. The details need not detain the reader, as the House of Commons into which Nancy's Bill had been brought never met again after the adjournment on the 4th August. The Bill, under these circumstances, needed to be introduced afresh, but in fact was abandoned and soon forgotten.

Of more interest to Nancy's biographer are the consequences of the endeavour. Her Bill was not prepared in hugger-mugger. Few things that she did were. Her intentions were known. They inevitably

---

also go mad. A conscientious member may well have a division record of under 25 per cent of the total. This is then represented as absenteeism by the opponent in the election campaign, and ignorant electors are often roused to indignation. No attempt seems to have been made at any time to correct the abuse.

angered many members of the Conservative Party, both in the country and the House. The Conservatives of Plymouth became split on the issue and a minority decided at the end of July to risk party defeat by proclaiming a rival Conservative candidate. He was to stand as the champion of an affiliated (or 'affiliable') party known as the 'Imperial Conservatives'. He was a gifted physician with a London practice, and his name was Dr Wansey Bayly.

Dr Bayly had no small following, and he was a man of tenacious character. If he had been as adroit or as well-advised as Nancy, he might have made a Conservative victory at the next election impossible. Mercifully for Nancy, he and his supporters overplayed their hand in ludicrous fashion.

From the moment that the Imperial Conservative Party was formed and Dr Bayly selected as its candidate, it was widely whispered that this was a conspiracy on the part of 'the Trade' to encompass the political ruin of the dangerous pussyfooting Viscountess. Dr Bayly, who was a capable speaker, poured scorn on this as a Titus Oates scare. Unfortunately for him, his backers in the trade had been so foolish as to proceed to extremes which proved that suspicions on this count were well founded. They went in for a policy of intimidation.

When such things became known in Plymouth they did Bayly much harm, and they counteracted some of the unpopularity which Nancy had incurred through her bill. Then Bayly made another false move. He wrote an article which was polite to Nancy personally but aimed to show her up as an old-fashioned and thus misguided sociologist. It was a thoughtful and well argued essay, and if he had published it in a widely read and respected paper it might have told against his opponent. But instead he chose to publish it in *John Bull*, where it appeared on the 16th September. As a Conservative candidate for a Plymouth constituency he could hardly have done anything sillier.

The General Election came with some suddenness in the last weeks of the year as the result of a revolt of the Conservative Party. Lloyd George's leadership became a matter for the utmost alarm in regard to his foreign policy in the Near East. The few facts that need to be remembered are the following. Bonar Law, the second man in Lloyd George's wartime coalition, had retired from politics in March 1921 owing to ill-health, but in the autumn of 1921 he returned, though not to office. He became the enigma of Westminster. A year later, when, on top of the failure of his Irish policy, Lloyd George's Turkish policy became not only dubious in itself but impractical, after the withdrawal from it of Britain's allies France and Italy, then Bonar Law was roused to protest. He did so by means of a letter to *The Times* published on the 6th October 1922. The Conservative revolt thereafter rapidly gained momentum. The decisive event was the famous party meeting at the Carlton Club on the 19th October. Though the Conservative ministers stood by Lloyd George, he offered his resignation to the King on the same day as the Carlton Club meeting. Polling day was fixed for the 15th November.

Philip Kerr's letters to Nancy of this time are of particular interest. He tells her of the advice he had given to Lloyd George with regard to the next General Election, namely that the Prime Minister should temporarily withdraw not only from office but from politics altogether; that he should not seek re-election, but instead spend a year or more in travel, and that, if he did this, he would then return greatly refreshed in mind and body and probably be called on to resume the premiership at no distant date. It is clear now that if Lloyd George had followed the advice he would, in all probability, have found himself enjoying great political influence by the mid-twenties.

The election of 1922 was as difficult as any that Nancy fought at any time. Her Conservative support had been gravely weakened by Dr Bayly's intervention, and further weakened by her own recent attempt to bring in drink legislation. The Labour candidate was Captain George Brennan, a popular man with none of Gay's handicaps: he could claim a fine fighting war record. She suffered another more subtle, but nonetheless important disadvantage compared with her first election. She had lost her hero and leader. The mutual affection of Lloyd George and Nancy had been a great asset in 1919. A vote for her then was a vote for the Pilot who weathered the Storm. Now she appeared before the electors as Lloyd George's opponent, and a vote for her was a vote for the less stirring figure of Bonar Law.

Nancy solved this 'hero-question' by a speech-making device which had served her well in 1919: she put forward her views with an unconventional challenge. She declared that she had no intention of attacking her former chief and his colleagues. 'If you want someone,' she said at her opening address, 'who is going to denounce Mr Lloyd George, Lord Balfour,[3] or Mr Austen Chamberlain – then don't waste your time with me.'

3. A. J. Balfour was made a peer in May 1922.

No Liberal candidate stood for the Sutton Division in 1922, so this was a three-cornered fight between a Conservative, a dissident Conservative, and a Labour candidate. Press reports of the time indicate that the main battle was between Nancy and Bayly, a circumstance which naturally raised Labour hopes. So far as the Nancy-Labour battle was concerned, it seems that she relied on a policy of stealing Labour thunder. She already had an impressive reformist record and Labour were frightening many electors with threats of a capital levy. The Nancy-Labour battle was fought with decent restraint, but the Nancy-Bayly battle was acrimonious.

At the beginning of the campaign Nancy's party made a serious mistake. Dr Bayly's wife had in 1919 written an article in a scientific journal on the subject of sexual morals. She had remarked that, regrettable as this was, sexual inconstancy in a husband carried less grave social consequences than the same weakness in a wife, as in the latter case paternity could be called in question. The Conservative Association issued a pamphlet, urging the constituents to vote for Nancy, and in the course of discrediting Dr Bayly's pretensions referred to this article, misrepresenting its widely accepted argument to the effect that a vote for Bayly was a vote for male sexual permissiveness. Bayly obtained a writ for libel against Nancy and Waldorf on the 30th October. The pamphlet was withdrawn and the matter was much later settled out of court, but it was good ammunition for the doctor. He referred to it throughout the campaign. 'I stand before you,' he would open a speech, 'an indignant man,' and then would dwell in more detail on the 'insolence, impertinence and wickedness' of his opponent's tactics. These certainly were open to criticism.

But here again Dr Bayly threw away his advantage. A writ served on the Astors for an admittedly unpleasant indiscretion by their party might have had a very damaging effect on Nancy's chances, but the indignant man forgot the 'law of parsimony' and proceeded to serve writs on a dozen or so other people including Mrs Foot (whose husband Isaac Foot was successfully standing as the Asquith-Liberal candidate at Bodmin), the respected feminist leader Maude Royden, and other prominent friends of Nancy, who may or may not have read and disseminated the libel. Maude Royden was interviewed by a reporter and expressed her amusement. The Press had a good laugh, and the idea began to spread that Dr Bayly was more than a little unbalanced.

But for all the element of farce introduced by Bayly's muffing tactics, this election was not the high-spirited merry-go-round affair of 1919. There was bitter feuding between the Trade and the suspected pussyfoot. Nancy did not miss the advantage given her by Bayly's recourse to *John Bull* and delivered some swingeing blows. With doubtful accuracy she declared in one speech: 'The Brewers paid Horatio Bottomley to destroy my reputation. But I've still got my reputation and Bottomley is in gaol.' Bayly sought to rouse anti-American feeling against Nancy, and he asked the electors whether it was right that an 'alien' should come to represent the city of Sir Francis Drake with the purpose of meddling (especially by means of drink laws) with our splendid old English way of life. The appellation 'alien' always galled this daughter of Virginia, and to such accusations she gave as good as she got. 'I *am* an Alien,' she defiantly answered in her next speech, 'alien to almost everything Dr Bayly stands for – in home life and in public life.'

Nancy got in with a reduced majority, and without an overall majority. The figures were:

Lady Astor	13,924	
Captain G. Brennan	10,831	
Dr W. Bayly	4,643	Conservative majority 3,093

It will be noticed that the votes for Nancy were only 571 less than in 1919, and it seems safe to say that without Bayly's intervention she would have increased the votes for herself by at least 2,000, possibly much more. Considering how she had courted unpopularity, the election result was undoubtedly a great personal triumph for her. Brennan had done valiantly in a General Election which for the first time saw the Labour Party as the second largest in Parliament. He had increased the Labour vote in Plymouth by over 1,500.

The general results showed a victory for the Conservative Party, giving them an overall majority of 87 in the House of Commons. Unfortunately for them they were wanting in leadership. Bonar Law had only consented to head the administration with reluctance. He was, and he knew that he was too broken in health to make an effective Prime Minister. Who should be his successor was a matter of much controversy and doubt.

From the feminist point of view the election was almost as great a disappointment as the Victory election of 1918. Nancy and Mrs

Wintringham (the latter with a slightly increased majority) were joined by no other women members, although women of uncommon distinction, some of them to make their mark in later parliaments, had stood as candidates for all parties. The reason for the feminist defeat of 1922, to follow informed opinion of the time, was not due to anti-feminist impetus in the country but rather to the reluctance of the party machines to risk a 'safe seat' by putting up a woman candidate. The women were thus doomed to stand for lost causes or marginal hopes, and so, except for the two very anomalous cases of Nancy and Mrs Wintringham, they were all defeated.

The election had its surprises, the greatest one, of course, being the extinction of the Coalition, the end of Lloyd George's authority and, from the stupid factionalism within it, of the Liberal Party as a dominant force. They had won 118 seats, a deceptively large number, as the suicidal division between the Asquithians and Lloyd George's followers precisely divided this figure in two. They abdicated to the Labour Party. There were of course personal surprises too. Some former members of the Government lost safe seats, and unexpected comics turned up like Jacks-in-Boxes to astound the public and the House of Commons. The first Communist member made his appearance. But of all these personal surprises the greatest occurred in Dundee. It was one which was of particular concern to Nancy.

The Coalition candidate in that city was Winston Churchill. He was the most unpopular member of the late Government. It was now, in the first post-war years, that he gained a wholly undeserved reputation of being a warmonger on account of his advocacy of the intervention policy in Russia, and his supposed primary responsibility for the disastrous policy pursued by the British Government in Greece and Turkey. To many minds among his political enemies, even to so discerning a one as that of E. M. Forster, Winston Churchill was a man who revelled in Othello's occupation and was seeking to relume the flames of the great and recent war. His fall not only from office but from Parliament was perhaps foreseeable, but hardly his fall at the hands of the Left Wing Independent antagonist who was the victor in this duel.

His name was Edwin Scrymgeour. He looked on himself as appointed by the Lord as a chosen vessel to accomplish His Heavenly Designs, especially as regards temperance. He made no secret of the fact that he intended to erect a monument to the Glory of God in the shape of absolute, total, uncompromising prohibition, exceeding in its severity the American model.

If there is one thing in political life more dangerous than a persistent and gifted foe, it is a ridiculous ally. Nancy had some protection from alliance with Scrymgeour through party divisions since, in so far as he went with a party, he inclined to Labour (who did not welcome the association). But what really saved Nancy from Scrymgeour was that his parliamentary performance exceeded all expectations in its absurdity and manifestly precluded alliance with anyone.

Having been defeated by events with her Liquor (Public Control) Bill she determined to try again in 1923. She had evidently been impressed by the adverse criticism which had met her earlier attempt and the new enterprise was modest in scope and was not concerned with local option or the unpopular Carlisle experiment. It was concentrated on one matter alone, the prevention of sales of intoxicating liquor to young persons.

It was such a mild measure compared to her proposal of the year before that to a hostile critic it might even have appeared as a pusillanimous surrender to opinion. It was certainly some surrender (for she never ceased to hope for prohibition), but it was not pusillanimous. It was more in the nature of a recognition of the first rule of the parliamentary game: that politics are the art of the possible. It was not a rule easily learned by the impetuous Nancy, but it was one thoroughly understood by Waldorf. Here one meets a remarkable paradox in the story.

The above suggests that Waldorf had a much more pliable and compromising character than Nancy, and that he was thus able to correct the obstinacy which was so strong in her. In fact, almost the opposite of this is true. Nancy was a woman of moods which she often obstinately followed, but she was rarely consistent. In this she was very unlike Waldorf. When he became a Christian Scientist he was much more rigid in his observance than she was, and he was far more inflexible than she in teetotalism. What appears as compromise in comparing the two bills introduced by Nancy in 1922 and 1923 indicates nothing more than Waldorf's mastery of parliamentary technique, a mastery which she never attained.

Waldorf was the architect of the Bill. The voluminous correspondence occupied with seeking support for it was undertaken by him. He took charge of organising the draft and obtaining legal advice on it.

He organised the deputations which gave Nancy much of her strength as the mover. Throughout he acted as her adviser, and throughout she followed his advice.

The Bill was first drafted (by whom is not mentioned) early in the new year, and the first item to be preserved of the ensuing correspondence is a letter of the 15th February 1923 from Arthur Sherwell in answer to one from Waldorf. Sherwell was one of the principals of the Temperance Legislation League. He had had a parliamentary career as a Liberal from 1906 to 1918.

His advice concentrated on the fact that the most dangerous criticism which could devitalise the measure, was likely to come not from diehards but from sensible people who would be in no way averse from a moderate degree of reform. He argued that they might make the reform so moderate as to be positively of no effectiveness.

On the 16th February 1923 the ballot was held for private members' bills. Nancy was lucky. Hers, officially entitled 'Intoxicating Liquor (Sale to Persons under Eighteen) Bill', obtained third place. But there was a snag. Mr Scrymgeour also had a private member's bill, for the introduction of total prohibition, and it obtained seventh place on the same day. This could not do other than cause Nancy's opponents to associate her, however vaguely and mistakenly, with the fanatic of Dundee.

She and Waldorf had to work hard. They had little time. The Second Reading was down for the 9th March, just under three weeks from the 17th February.

The state of British law then regarding the sale of drink to young people was simple and not very different in shape from what we have today. Nancy's Bill aimed to change the details. In 1923 it was illegal for an innkeeper to sell any sort of alcoholic beverage to any person under the age of fourteen. After that age he might without offence sell him or her beer or cider, but not wine or spirits. When his client had reached the age of sixteen the innkeeper might legally sell him or her anything on demand. Nancy's Bill aimed at a single reform, namely to raise the age qualification for the sale of all alcoholic beverages to eighteen.

One might have thought that so simple a measure would have occupied little parliamentary time. In fact, the Bill occupied a long debate on the Second Reading, four days in the Committee stage, and a further debate on the Third Reading after it had been delayed by the obstructive tactics of opponents. The records indicate that the major objection to the Bill, as Sherwell had foretold, was its failure to distinguish between beer-drinking, etc. and spirit-drinking. A majority of all parties in the House of Commons were agreed that sixteen was too early an age at which to allow indulgence in spirits, and it is arguable that if Waldorf, as the architect of the Bill, had given way over this discrimination, the Bill might have passed very quickly.

To return to the story. Sherwell referred the draft to an eminent lawyer, Robert Montgomery, K.C., who had written a classic work on licensing practice. Two new features, both negative, were recommended and accepted. One was not to make parents responsible for a breach of the proposed law because, to obtain a conviction, the young person concerned would have to testify in court against the parents. The other was to include no mention of 'treating' on the grounds that legislation on this matter could only take the form of elaborate and exasperating legal minutiae such as had given Dora her bad name. Later a new objection was accurately forecast by Sherwell, and by a Member of Parliament, Charles Roberts, who had been asked by Waldorf to pilot the Bill through the Committee stage.

The objection was that under the law as it stood, and under the proposed measure, the guilt or innocence of an innkeeper was difficult to establish because it is difficult to guess accurately any person's age. The existing law had got round this by defining the young person as 'apparently' fourteen or sixteen. It got to the ears of Sherwell, Montgomery and Roberts that moderate opponents were anxious to introduce the word 'knowingly' with reference to the offending innkeeper, and take out 'apparently'. Such an amendment they considered likely to make things all too easy for a dishonest innkeeper, and they even foretold that convictions would be impossible if this weakening adverb was agreed to. They convinced Waldorf and Nancy. Why they were so worried by the innovation has perplexed the present writer.

Within the three weeks before the Second Reading, Waldorf organised support by letters and articles in the Press (one in the *Manchester Guardian* by Nancy) and by representations from various public bodies, and a petition from 115,000 teachers and headmasters.[4]

Most Members of Parliament, including most old hands at the game, find the task of moving the Second Reading of a Bill, especially a

4. The figures are given as 115,000 in the memoranda presumably drafted by Sherwell. In the debates on the Bill it invariably appears as 116,000.

private member's bill, one of the most taxing of undertakings. The night before is spent in study followed by early retirement for what sleep anxiety allows. Arrangements made long before denied such a course to Nancy. She and Waldorf spent the evening of the 8th in giving an enormous and brilliant dinner-party attended by Bonar Law, Lloyd George, and other political leaders of all parties, the purpose of the entertainment being to allow the chief guests, the King and Queen, to meet Labour politicians. The party seems to have been entirely successful, a nice mixture of splendid formality and the boisterous gaiety that Nancy gave to her occasions. There were, of course, sneering comments by some journalists of the Left who affected to believe that Socialists should avoid meeting anyone else. This appears to have been the beginning of the friendship between J. H. Thomas and George V.

At eleven o'clock on the morning of Friday the 9th March, the House of Commons met. After 'private business', written answers, and some questions and oral answers, the House settled down to the Second Reading of Nancy's Bill. She started off with her usual unconventionality when she traced the history of the Bill. She assured the House in her opening words: 'This is not Lady Astor's Bill. Even what people were pleased to call Lady Astor's Bill was not Lady Astor's Bill: ... it was made an issue at my election as Lady Astor's Bill, but even then it was not Lady Astor's Bill.' She insisted that it expressed not merely her views but those of the most responsible elements in the population.

Reading Hansard's record one must be impressed by Nancy's performance. She had a large mass of evidence to put across to the House, and this she did effectively. She showed that she had the facts and figures at her fingers' ends. But if her opening speech in the debate was workmanlike in the main, it had certain weaknesses.

One was a prejudiced attitude which she could not disguise. At one point she said: 'Then it is said why not deal with spirits only and leave beer out. If alcohol is bad in its scientific effect it is obviously equally bad in whatever form you take it. People often feel that you can safely drink a good deal more beer than spirits because there is less alcohol, but the result is exactly the same. If there was not alcohol in beer it would be all right for adolescents. But there is alcohol in beer.'

One may be tempted to suppose at moments that the promoters of the Bill lacked one thing, the advice of a heavy drinker who could tell them about different causes and degrees of addiction. There was, in fact, a heavy drinker among the supporters, J. H. Thomas, but he does not seem to have given them the benefit of his experience.

The debate lasted about four and a half hours. Nancy's short opening speech was ably seconded by a fellow-Conservative, C. W. Cook. His endeavour was to allay fears. Both sides believed that they were faced by a conspiracy, the promoters by the dark designs of the Trade, the opponents by people desirous of introducing prohibition on the model of America and Russia which, under Lenin, was undergoing a brief and disastrous experiment influenced by the 19th Amendment.

Nothing memorable was said on either side, or rather nothing that is memorable now, about a matter that has been extensively argued, legislated for, and made the subject of experience since. Comic relief was consciously supplied by a breezy maiden speech by Rear-Admiral Sir Guy Gaunt, unconsciously by Mr Scrymgeour who rose repeatedly to catch the Speaker's eye, was not called but succeeded in entering a protest amid some derision, and half-consciously by the verbose reflections of Sir Frederick Banbury on the good old days when he was nourished on beer as a Winchester schoolboy. At one point he said after one of Nancy's interruptions: 'Do not be sure that I am not sufficiently able to stop this Bill, but we shall see.' The most effective speech for the Bill was possibly that of Nancy's old antagonist, Isaac Foot, who was one of the official backers and spoke late in the debate. Every speaker against the Bill declared that he had no connection with the Trade, except the last, Colonel John Gretton, the then chairman of Bass, Ratcliff and Gretton Ltd. He declared his interest and his opposition was cut short by the Speaker when, as the allotted time ran short, Nancy rose for the second time and 'claimed to move that the Question be now put'. Her claim was admitted and the Second Reading was passed in two divisions, the first by a majority of 265, the second by a majority of 272. The Bill now went into the Committee stage.

The Chairman of the meeting of Standing Committee C charged with dealing with amendments was J. H. Thomas. The Committee met on four occasions, on the 27th March, and on the 10th, 12th and 17th April. Charles Roberts, in keeping with his agreement with Waldorf, entered into somewhat reluctantly, was the main speaker for the Bill. He was an able parliamentarian, a former Under Secretary in the India Office, but had some disadvantage in a close association with teetotalism. He was a son-in-law of a fanatical and lately deceased prohibitionist, Lady Carlisle, whose extremism was still the subject of ridicule, gossip and alarm. His presence as a leading member of the committee could not but add to suspicions of conspiracy such as were voiced by a Conservative opponent, Sir Kingsley Wood, a political friend of Waldorf from his association with the Ministry of Health. The most strenuous of the younger opponents of the Bill was Lord Curzon[5] (not to be confounded with the Foreign Secretary of the same name), and the most strenuous of the younger supporters was Mr Oswald Mosley. From the official records, J. H. Thomas seems to have been an impartial and patient chairman. Nancy was called to order in the course of scenes not untypical of her.

After the Committee stage Nancy's Bill stood altered by only two important amendments: that an innkeeper, if he 'knowingly' gave intoxicants to a person under age, was an offender against the law, not otherwise, and that he might serve persons between the ages of sixteen and eighteen with beer or cider provided he did so in a part of his establishment separate from the bar. These two alterations appeared as bitter defeats to the promoters, but experience suggests that their fears were imaginary. With the Committee stage over, there remained the Report and Third Reading, while farther ahead loomed the awful possibilities of the House of Lords. Between the conclusion of the Committee stage and the agreed date for the next and last stage in the House of Commons there elapsed two and a half months, and in that interval there occurred on the 20th April the Second Reading of Mr Scrymgeour's Bill. It was an extraordinary occasion, no details of which need be recalled beyond the unusual fact that so inept was the drafting and so ludicrous Scrymgeour's speech of introduction that the seconder felt obliged to criticise the Bill severely.

Nancy wisely kept away from the Palace of Westminster on this day.

The Report and Third Reading of her own Bill were scheduled for the 29th June 1923. This was Sir Frederick Banbury's moment. He was in an embittered mood. In the same month a third woman had taken her seat as a member of the House of Commons, under circumstances analogous to those of Nancy and Mrs Wintringham: she had been elected by the constituency formerly represented by her husband.[6]

5. Francis Curzon, later 5th Earl Howe (1884–1964). He was M.P. for the South Division of Battersea, 1918–1929.

6. Captain Hilton Philipson was returned in the 1922 General Election as National

Was this a new form of corrupt family patronage? That when a
member died or retired from Parliament he automatically bequeathed
his seat to his wife! And there was new matter for disgust. To be forced
to accept an American Viscountess and a Liberal widow as colleagues
was bad enough, but now he was under obligation to accept a former
member of a disreputable profession as well, for in pre-war days Mrs
Hilton Philipson as Mabel Russell had been a leading London actress
of the musical comedy stage, appearing with great success in *The
Merry Widow* and *The Dollar Princess*. Could the degradation of the
House go farther?

If Sir Frederick had been 'the picture of misery' when Nancy first
walked into the House, he was even more woe-begone, if Press reports
are to be trusted, on the 6th June 1923 when the Dollar Princess came
in. Some Labour members chaffed him with cries of 'Cheer up,
Banbury!' as the little ceremony proceeded, but 'there was no answering smile'. He was out for the blood of parliamentary womanhood,
and now on the 29th June came his chance to thrust in the dagger deep.

On this day there were three Bills to be debated: the Agricultural
Credits Bill, the Honours (Prevention of Abuses) Bill, and Nancy's
Bill. The first two were Government Bills. All three had passed through
the Committee stage and were due for Report and Third Reading.

The Agricultural Credits Bill was controversial and the last stage
took longer than the Government had expected. During the day Nancy
grew increasingly anxious. By the rules of procedure, private members'
bills cannot occupy the time of the House after four o'clock on a
Friday, and as speech followed speech it became horribly apparent that
time might run out. Not the least prolific speaker on the agricultural
question was Sir Frederick Banbury. When the Third Reading of the
Bill did at length pass it was about a quarter to four, and there was still
the equally controversial Honours Bill to be considered. The Government signified that this Bill might be postponed. The way was clear
for Nancy's Bill, but the order paper for the day contained some new
amendments. They had been put down by Sir Frederick.

(Lloyd George) Liberal member for Berwick on Tweed but was disqualified when
corrupt practices by his agent were proved. His innocence was established but he was
not entitled to contest a parliamentary seat for seven years. His wife stood in the
ensuing election, but as a Conservative, against an Asquithian Liberal and a Labour
contestant. She obtained a majority of over 6,000.

With little more than ten minutes to go, and Nancy's only chance being that the Opposition would accept the amendments of the committee without debate, and that Sir Frederick would withdraw, the Speaker began proceedings on the Bill by saying that he 'did not propose to select the first Amendment standing in the name of the Right Hon gentleman the Member for the City of London'. This was to recommend the age of seventeen being substituted for eighteen throughout the Bill. Up leaped Sir Frederick to propose his second amendment which recommended that the conditions under which youths of sixteen to eighteen might be served with beer should be revised or suppressed. Time was getting very short.

What happened next is not easy to say for certain: it was widely reported in the Press but no two reports agree. Nancy herself gave two accounts of the scene. Hansard indicates a protest by Nancy but nothing more. She is said to have pulled at Sir Frederick's coat-tails to prevent him rising; she is said to have burst into tears and to have pommelled her elderly opponent in the ribs. She is reported to have caused the House to break into much laughter, which is probably true, before the Speaker called out the fatal word 'Order', to indicate that the hands of the clock now stood at four. What is certain is that Sir Frederick Banbury succeeded in talking out the Bill.

Nancy's own account is worthy of acceptance because it corresponds with a letter of protest which she wrote and with which Banbury agreed. According to her, she said to him before leaving the Chamber: 'Oh you old villain! I'll get you next time.' She shook her fist at him. There were no tears. She must have realised that Banbury's intervention made little difference. There was not time for the Report and Third Reading and Banbury had merely made assurance doubly sure.

Most of the ministers approved Nancy's Bill, and Bonar Law, a teetotaler himself though never a proselytizer, had given it encouragement. The new Prime Minister, Stanley Baldwin, continued this detail of his predecessor's policy, and time was set aside for the Report and Third Reading on Friday the 13th July.

On that day Nancy's Bill was the first item so that a talking-out manoeuvre would need uncommon staying power on the part of Banbury. In fact, he made no attempt of the kind. He had come in for more adverse criticism than Nancy, even from a fellow diehard Henry Craik who had written in disgust to *The Times*.

At eleven o'clock on the 13th the House of Commons met. After 'private business', written answers, and some questions and oral answers, the House settled down to the Report on and Third Reading of Nancy's Bill. The proceeding took about an hour and a half. The arguments heard in Committee were reiterated on both sides. The first main speaker was Sir Frederick Banbury who seems not to have been at the top of his form. He began with an apologia for his first amendment which had been set aside and believed that this had been his subject when he had talked out the Bill on the 13th. He was put right and withdrew. His voice seems to have been weak on this day, and Hansard has numerous entries of 'Hon. Members: Speak up!' He spoke at his usual great length, and when he noticed Nancy covering her ears with her hands he pointed to her saying that her action proved that she recognised the unbearable force of his arguments. Up leaped David Kirkwood. 'On a point of order,' he said, 'is it right for any honourable member to deliberately point to another honourable member? Is that a gentlemanly action? The right honourable Baronet claims to be a gentleman of the first water.' Kirkwood spoilt the effect of his intervention on behalf of order when a moment later he interrupted Banbury who was saying 'Will you tell me –' with a cry of 'Oh, you're just an old fule.'

The most remarkable episode in the debate was the intervention of Mr Scrymgeour who at last caught the Speaker's eye. He fulminated against the Bill with a violence even greater than that of Sir Frederick Banbury. He kept within the bounds of parliamentary propriety but he conveyed with strikingly mixed metaphor that Nancy was a traitress who, by compounding with 'the very forces that are the backbone of the liquor traffic, and the power that controls the Government', had done an irreparable disservice to the cause of prohibition, 'that great movement in America'. This declaration of faith was invaluable to Nancy, for the course of the debate showed that many members, by no means hostile to her Bill, were troubled by suspicions of her ultimate aim. Nancy had been asked several times to give a pledge that she would not support prohibition in Great Britain, but she would not agree to do so, and now here was Scrymgeour doing it for her.

The Third Reading was carried by 257 votes against 10.

Waldorf introduced the Second Reading to the House of Lords on the 19th July. This he did in a speech, summarising the alterations and declaring his interest. 'Those of your lordships,' he said, 'who have followed in the Press the events and procedure in another place will be aware of the fact that this Bill was piloted through that House by a relative of mine by marriage.'

Waldorf's speech was an able performance, marked by tact and good humour, and Scrymgeour's speech was of invaluable help to his task of persuasion. But the most remarkable speech on the subject in the succeeding debate was that by Lord Dawson of Penn. Hitherto the supporters of the Bill had dwelt upon the horrors of alcoholic indulgence. Lord Dawson took an opposite line. He extolled the virtues of beer, spirits and wine. He became lyrical about them. He waxed poetical. He spoke about them as Nancy's old companion Hilaire Belloc might have done. And this he did in passionate support of Nancy's Bill, his argument being that appreciation of wine and its pleasures depended on sobriety and moderation. He praised Nancy's Bill because by encouraging sobriety in formative years, it encouraged an intelligent interest in the delights of drinking.

It is a pity that there is no documentation or recorded memory to tell us what Nancy thought about these arguments. They were not hers. She would describe all fermented drink, from hooch gin to the noblest masterpiece of Burgundy, as 'that filthy stuff'. In fact, part of her strong prejudice against France was based on a conviction that too many French people spent too much of their time manufacturing intoxicants. She could hardly have approved Dawson's admirable apologia. But for her child, and a private member's bill is a private member's child, she would do much; for that pet lamb she would even accept sinful pleadings. One should not at this point forget her robust sense of humour.

The Bill, thanks to Waldorf's ability in presenting it to his fellow-peers for the Second Reading; thanks to Lord Dawson's support in a form which made it front page news; thanks, also, to the Bill's intrinsic merits, passed scatheless through the House of Lords. A monumental Nancy could now have claimed a monument, but, as noted earlier, this was not her character. She would probably have preferred to describe it as a fine 'hat-trick'. She had won an election and taken her seat as the first woman member; she had impressed the House by a maiden and then a later speech; she had got a private member's bill through Parliament. That was 'somethin''.

With this episode which marks the high point of Nancy's parliamentary career the curtain, it might be thought, should fittingly descend on Act 13 of the Drama. But biography being concerned with real life, the episodes are untidily arranged. The unpopularity of her Bill was greater outside Parliament than in it, and the belief that Nancy was engaged in a prohibitionist conspiracy died hard. If she had countless admirers she had countless enemies as well, and the hostility towards this 'interfering American' led to an unpleasant Press incident closely related to the one she had suffered from Horatio Bottomley.

What is extraordinary about this incident is the unlikelihood of the characters involved. To learn that Bottomley behaved in a mean and brutal way is to learn the expected, but on this occasion the people concerned were of highly educated and sensitive mind, acknowledged leaders of the intelligentsia. For that reason the incident cannot but come as a shock.

This is what happened. In the summer of 1923 a small book came out under Nancy's name. It was her only book and was called *My Two Countries*. Today we would describe it as an exercise in public relations. It consisted of a selection from her speeches in America during the 1922 tour, with an introductory article. In due course it was reviewed, politely and uncontroversially as befitted a minor work which made no pretensions to be anything else. To this mild reception there was one striking exception. This occurred in the *New Statesman* where the book was reviewed on the 14th July by the paper's most distinguished critic, Desmond MacCarthy.

One can only suppose that the editor, Clifford Sharp, and Desmond MacCarthy both entertained deep dislike of Nancy. In the case of MacCarthy this probably originated in a sense of outrage that this close friend of the Asquiths had not scrupled to exploit the unpopularity of the former Prime Minister for electoral reasons. For Asquith he had hero-worship and he passionately resented the misrepresentations to which his friend had been subjected. At all events Desmond Mac-Carthy seized the opportunity to hit Nancy hard. He described the contents of the book with sarcasm. 'Each speech,' he wrote, 'is a straight talk full of lofty sentiment.' He ended the article as follows: 'This is Lady Astor's theme. I doubt her postulates, and her eloquence is spoilt for me by remembering that having divorced her husband on the vaguest grounds she spoke as eloquently against relaxing the harshness of our divorce laws.' He signed the article by his pen-name, 'Affable Hawk'.

When the article came out the author, or the editor, or perhaps both, apparently felt uneasy. For whatever reason a letter to the editor appeared in the next issue on the 21st June.

'Sir, – On reading last week's "Current Literature" in print I noticed a phrase which went further in its implications than I intended, and was unfair to Lady Astor. The sentence, as it stood, suggested that she had not what would be generally considered good reasons for seeking divorce from her first husband. On such a point I had, of course, no right and no intention to express an opinion. My point was that, having taken advantage of the well-known facility of the American Divorce Courts herself, she had afterwards done her best to prevent men and women in this country having even approximate facilities, a proceeding which those who think our divorce law stands in need of reform find it impossible to forgive. – Yours, etc., Affable Hawk.'

The next part of the episode was more shameful. Waldorf consulted his solicitors who had originally drawn his attention to the article, urging him to take action. On the 23rd July they wrote to Clifford Sharp pointing out that MacCarthy had repeated a calumny first put into circulation by *John Bull*, and that Nancy had not obtained a divorce on grounds different from those allowed in England. The solicitor also pointed out that MacCarthy's withdrawal did not constitute an apology which they now formally requested.

Clifford Sharp, with a grossness which would be hardly credible in the roughest editor of the lowest newspaper, did not acknowledge the letter but published it in the next issue, with an editorial comment reasserting all Bottomley's calumny, though of course not mentioning Bottomley. Like the latter, Sharp seemed determined to force the Astors to sue. Nancy was determined not to sue. Showing remarkable patience, possibly too much patience in view of Sharp's revolting behaviour, the solicitors wrote again asserting that Nancy had never been guilty of seeking divorce on easier terms than those allowed in England. Sharp ran true to form. He published the letter in the next issue, adding a sneering comment.

'We are bound to draw attention to the fact that Messrs. Lewis and Lewis have quite abandoned the tone which they saw fit to adopt in their previous letter – printed here on July 28th. We have not, of course, and never had any objection whatever to publishing their client's version of the facts – leaving it to our readers to form their own opinions on the matter. – Ed. N.S.'

Against all probability, the story had a happy ending. The correspondence was followed by a lawyer, a certain Mr E. S. P. Haynes. He was only slightly acquainted with Waldorf whom he admired. He decided to undertake a thorough investigation of the case in America. He did so and proved beyond all doubt that the contention on Nancy's side was true in every detail. He wrote to the *New Statesman* to convey his information. His letter had all the more force because, unlike Nancy, he was in favour of divorce reform and said so. His letter was published on the 6th October 1923. This time there was no editorial comment. Neither Clifford Sharp nor Desmond MacCarthy apologised. It remains incredible that two such men could, under any circumstances, have gone into spiritual alliance with Horatio Bottomley. But they achieved a fortunate result. Their aim was to raise an evil spirit; they laid a ghost for ever.

In the first part of Chapter 13 the extracts from Walter Elliot, Victor Cunard and Mrs Ernesta Barlow are from the collection of essays made by Michael Astor. The same is true of the short quotation of Mrs Wintringham. The reference to E. M. Forster is based on his pamphlets written for the Labour Party in the early twenties. The record of the Intoxicating Liquors (Sales to Persons under 18) Bill is taken from the Press and Hansard as indicated. I remain indebted to *Women at Westminster*, by Pamela Brookes. The *New Statesman* episode is fully documented in the Astor archive.

The facts of Lady Astor's divorce from Robert Shaw in 1903, as they emerge from the *New York Herald* of February 1903, Lady Astor's speech in Plymouth in July 1920, and E. S. P. Haynes's letter in the *New Statesman* and his correspondence with Lord Astor, seem to have been as follows. By the law of Virginia divorce was allowed on grounds of desertion after an interval following separation. (There was and is no federal divorce law in the U.S.A.) The Shaw family, possibly in the interests of 'the other woman', wished to avoid grounds of adultery. The divorce proceedings in Charlottesville, according to the *New York Herald*, did begin as a desertion case, and when published, this fact was not challenged by the Langhornes or the Shaws. It will be recalled that Lady Astor left the whole conduct of the affair to her father. He may have agreed with the Shaws to a desertion plea by his daughter without her knowledge. For whatever reason the Langhornes abandoned this plea in favour of one on grounds of adultery, and it seems likely to me that this was through Lady Astor's protest when she knew what was happening. From her speech in Plymouth it would appear that Robert Shaw's lawyers attempted to drag out proceedings until the time-factor involved in desertion cases had been met. This 'filibustering' operation failed, still to follow the unclear statement in her speech. What is unquestionable is that in

January 1903 there was a meeting in New York of the Shaw and Langhorne lawyers, after which divorce from Robert Shaw was sought by Lady Astor on grounds of adultery. The *New York Herald*'s and Bottomley's suggestions of collusion are untenable in view of the fact that the case did not go by default, but was defended. Robert Shaw 'entered an answer and pleadings'. The secrecy of the first proceedings, which stung the *New York Herald* to attack, may have been organised by C. D. Langhorne whose dislike of the Press has been illustrated earlier. Whether or not his methods were open to criticism is not evidenced, but in either case do not affect the legal question.

Chapter 14

THE MIDDLE TWENTIES

THERE could be no resting on oars or laurels after the parliamentary triumph related in the preceding chapter. The Bill, after going through all the necessary stages in the House of Lords, was returned to the Commons without any amendments. It now only needed the official message from the Palace that *le roi le veult*, and in the first part of July 1923 the royal assent was given. The Act was now law, but this meant no diminution of the heated debate on the subject, conducted now in the newspapers and at public meetings.

The reason for this angry continuance of argument on what amounted to a small matter, for no one pretended that the absence of young persons under eighteen from bars constituted a grievous deprivation, was the persistence of suspicion on both sides. Both sides were mistaken.

Nancy was far too open, candid and honest a person to follow any conspiratorial line of conduct. With her frequent indiscretion she was the last person that any experienced conspirator would recruit into his ranks. For the same reason she made no secret (as a more agile politician would have done) of the fact that she approved of prohibition, and hoped that public opinion in Great Britain would in time cause the Government of the day to bring in an equivalent of the 19th Amendment. There was no contradiction in her attitude in this instance, but clever opponents could make it appear not only that there was, but with it horrible double dealing. Her popularity suffered. It was not a good time for her to face an election but this she was compelled to do at the end of 1923, only a year after her difficult success against Dr Bayly and Captain Brennan.

The 1922 General Election had resulted in Bonar Law's brief premiership. In May 1923 his ill-health was found to be due to cancer of the throat and he resigned. There followed the often-told episode of Lord Curzon's disappointment and Stanley Baldwin's succession. Nancy's biographer would like at this point to produce a poignant, or at any rate historic letter to her from her old friend Curzon. But unhappily there is no such document.

The Conservative Party had been successfully rallied by Bonar Law, but after his retirement in May disturbing signs of Party division began to appear again. Stanley Baldwin, though preferred as a leader by the great majority to Curzon, did not at this time command devotion such as Bonar Law had been able to count upon. He had many critics from the days when in January he had, as Chancellor of the Exchequer, made what was widely held to have been a weak agreement with the United States on war debts.

Aware that his position was deteriorating Baldwin decided to try to retrieve it by a bold stroke. The annual Party conference of 1923 was held in Plymouth. It was here that he announced his new political conviction that only in a partially protectionist economic policy was there any hope of mastering the unemployment problem. Such a policy had its admirers but also its detractors among Conservatives, and from this he came to the conclusion that he would only divide his party seriously if he attempted the policy without the sanction of a General Election. He had a remarkable understanding of the sense of the House of Commons, and in his calculation of a radical party-split he was probably right. He assumed that the enormous Conservative vote he had inherited from Bonar Law would remain with him for the most part, but in this he was entirely wrong. In mid-November he advised a dissolution. A General Election campaign opened with polling day fixed for the 7th December 1923, a little more than a year after the 1922 election. Nancy was again adopted as candidate for the Sutton Division of Plymouth.

As before there were rumours of every kind, notably that in the new election Nancy would stand as an Asquithian Liberal, and another that an Independent Conservative would again oppose her. The rumours were all false. Dr Wansey Bayly wrote to the *Western Morning News* urging his followers to vote for Lady Astor. In the end there were only two candidates in Sutton: herself representing Conservatism, and her former opponent, Captain Brennan, representing Labour.

It is to be guilty of a truism to say that the politician's art (especially at election time) is akin to the actor's. It may be said that there are two main kinds of successful actor: those who astound playgoers by their variety and range, who (like Sir John Gielgud) can perform with equal mastery as King Lear, as Oscar Wilde's 'Ernest', or as a character in one of Chekov's comedies, and those who never vary their performance except in minor detail, and yet never weary their audience. Supreme among these were Charlie Chaplin in his long first period, and the greatest clown of modern days, Grock. Nancy, as an electioneer (not as a private performer), belonged to the Grock class. Though the results in the seven elections she fought varied widely, her electioneering technique never did except in minor detail, and though its political success was sometimes disappointing to her (as on this occasion) she never lost her audience. The very sameness of the performance was part of its fascination, but because of that very sameness a detailed account of each one will not be found in this book.

In 1923 Nancy polled 16,114 votes but the contest had been close, though conducted with good humour. The Labour vote had risen and Nancy's majority was 2,676. In modified triumph she returned to a perplexed House of Commons.

Baldwin's appeal to the country had left the House in disarray. The Conservatives were still the largest party, with 258 seats. Labour followed with 191 seats, but the crucial element were the Liberals who, after patching up their differences and enjoying a revival, had 159 seats. Baldwin or Ramsay MacDonald could take on the Premiership with Liberal support, or Asquith could return to the premiership with Conservative or Labour support. Everything ultimately depended on Asquith. He himself had no doubt as to which was his right course: to give Liberal support to a Labour administration. The other two possible courses, he believed, would be not only unconvincing but would intensify class antagonism. On the 17th January 1924 a Labour vote of no confidence in the Government passed in the House of Commons with Liberal support. Baldwin resigned and recommended the King to send for Ramsay MacDonald. Thus began the first Labour government. The Conservatives were dejected. In a letter to Nancy of 7th December Mrs Baldwin wrote: 'Alas, most of the electors this time have been taken stupid', and this fairly represented Conservative feeling. It can account for Baldwin's immediate re-election as party leader.

Nancy was less dejected than most, because she was out of humour with her party. At the historic October Tory Conference of 1923 in Plymouth, Nancy, as a local member had inevitably taken a leading part. She had shown herself a loyal Conservative in her speech in support of the vote of confidence in Baldwin, and in her ferocious quelling of a Communist attempt to shout her down and break up one of the meetings. But her insistence that a radical reform of the hereditary

House of Lords should figure prominently in the Conservative programme was ill received. From this she suffered no wound, but she was angered at the inadequate interest shown by the party in social reform. Her main practical proposition in this respect was that the school-leaving age should be raised from fourteen to sixteen. Her argument in favour of such a measure was a cogent one: that as things stood multitudes of working class youths were seeking for employment at an age when they ought still to be learning; that their numbers increased the potential labour force at a time of widespread unemployment, and that a great number of these young people thus started life as poverty stricken unemployed persons. These ideas were treated as suspect and irresponsible.

When the election was over and the customary post-mortem discussion began in the Press, Nancy was swift to point out in a letter to *The Times* the likely connection of Conservative indifference to social reform with the astonishing reversal of Conservative fortunes. This did not endear her to the party and she was in the worst of tempers with her colleagues.

But there was another reason why Nancy was less dejected than her fellow-Conservatives by the great defeat. The election results showed that the feminist cause had made a modest but definite advance. The three women members of the House of Commons had all been re-elected, and there were now five others.

They were distributed as follows in the parties. The two Conservatives of the last Parliament were joined by the Duchess of Atholl; the Liberal Mrs Wintringham was joined by Lady Terrington, and for the first time women members were returned for the Labour Party. They were three in number, Miss Margaret Bondfield, Miss Susan Lawrence, and Miss Dorothea Jewson. Of the newcomers only the Duchess of Atholl succeeded to a family constituency, her husband, before succeeding his father as Duke of Atholl, having sat in the House of Commons.

From a personal point of view Nancy found some important changes in the new Parliament. She still had an affectionate and critical colleague in Lord Hugh Cecil, but she had lost her champion Lord Robert who had not stood for re-election and was now a member of the Upper House as Lord Cecil of Chelwood. She had also lost Walter Elliot who had been defeated, but was soon to return as the victor of a by-election in May, an election in which Nancy took a furious part. There was one parliamentary loss which was pure gain to her. Sir Frederick Banbury was no longer a member of the Commons. He had not stood for re-election, and, as a reward for his 'services', had been created a baron in the New Year Honours. He spent his last twelve years as a member of the House of Lords. He did not neglect his now lesser opportunities to harass progressive measures, and he found occasion to torment Waldorf as he had aforetime tormented Nancy.

The new Government made one innovation which caused much stir at the time; they appointed Miss Margaret Bondfield to be Parliamentary Secretary for the Ministry of Labour, the first appointment of a woman to a British Government post. Soon after the announcement, at the end of January, Nancy attended a conference of the National Union of Societies for Equal Citizenship held in Church House, Westminster. The meeting was to be addressed by four of the women members of Parliament, representing the three parties.

Nancy stole the show. Unorthodox in most of her political beliefs and action, she acted on this occasion in conformity with the accepted doctrine that 'it is the duty of an opposition to oppose'. It usually suited her temperament. So now Nancy, to the very great surprise of her audience who were expecting tributes to the imagination and sagacity of Mr MacDonald, rose to deliver an attack. She said: 'Each party has a special prejudice against women.' Miss Susan Lawrence shook her head and Nancy went on 'Oh yes – I must include the Labour Party (laughter) because I have carefully watched the members of that party in the House. I am not going to talk politics because I know we would have a fair and square free fight if I did (laughter) but I must say I am bitterly disappointed that the Labour Party has not given Cabinet rank to a woman. I had looked for the appointment of Miss Margaret Bondfield.' Lord Randolph is reputed to have said 'If you have to give a political concession – give it with a kick.' Nancy proved herself an apt pupil. Tory Democracy was dead by this time. Otherwise it would have supplied Nancy with a label. As it was she never found one.

The brief period of Ramsay MacDonald's first administration, about ten months, is not, from a political point of view, a very interesting part of Nancy's career. It shows no remarkable contrast to any other phase of her parliamentary life, and for a very simple reason, namely that since she was by temperament always in opposition, to be officially so did not add to the drama. Her most arresting moments now were when she unexpectedly praised the Government's social reform plans, to the occasional embarrassment of her own party and of some Labour members who only saw her as an undesirable social phenomenon, as a millionairess.

One of the Clerks of the House was Gilbert Campion (later Lord Campion) who officiated in the House of Commons throughout Nancy's parliamentary career. He hardly knew her in private life, and this gives his record the value of impersonal observation. He entitled the essay he wrote for Michael Astor 'Viewed Impartially'. Here is an extract describing Nancy's parliamentary conduct around the time of Ramsay MacDonald's first Administration.

'Lady Astor's recipe for speech-making combined the seemingly ill-assorted ingredients of jeering and exhortation, idealism and badinage – beaten up together with native good sense. Her speech in support of the Legitimacy Bill of 1924 contains an aphorism worthy of a political philosopher "Laws cannot make people moral, yet the more moral the people the higher their laws". When the Labour Government spokesman announced "no help from Government for the Temperance (Wales) Bill", a local option Bill, Lady Astor's indignation flared out in "My own party may be reactionary, but at least they are honest".

'Considering how readily she mastered the more difficult technique of parliamentary speaking, it was notable that Lady Astor picked up slowly, if never completely, the finer points of parliamentary etiquette. She would keep up a running and very audible commentary on a speech with which she disagreed or continue to interrupt when the Member speaking refused to give way. Her speeches were often so persistently provocative that they became dialogues with a series of interrupters. Her methods were, as she herself admitted, far from subtle.

'In one branch of practice, the drafting of questions to Ministers, I happened to have my closest personal relations with Lady Astor in her early days. It is the duty of the junior Clerk at the Table to "vet" questions to Ministers given in by Members and try to apply the rules on behalf of the Speaker (who has better things to do). This is a some-what delicate function (made more difficult in those days by having to be carried on at the Table of the House in whispers so as not to disturb Members speaking or listening) and it was under those conditions fruitful of misunderstandings. (It is now carried on outside the Chamber.) Lady Astor's questions were often, as might be expected, in the nature of propaganda – on behalf of temperance, etc. – which the rules particularly discouraged. These could however generally, with judicious trimmings, be squeezed through. But there was another type of question which was not so amenable. It would begin in some such way as this "Is it true that, as stated by the *Daily Blank*, the American Secretary for the Interior proposes . . ." This type of question would give any experienced Member a shudder and it is, indeed, like walking over the grave of Erskine May, three at least of whose fundamental rules it contravened. On the reappearance of this type of question I would try to get it through, while making the question innocuous, if given a free hand. But innocuousness was seldom what Lady Astor wanted. A whispered wrangle would ensue. On one of these occasions when my senior colleague, Sir Horace Dawkins, had been drawn in to my support, Lady Astor left the Table, registering frustration and rapping out not so very *sotto voce* "You two are the stickiest old men I ever came across".'

Nancy and Waldorf were involved in a very disagreeable episode during this Parliament. It had begun the year before and was not concluded till 1925. In May of 1923 Waldorf had proposed to the First Commissioner of Works a gift from himself to Parliament of a large-scale picture depicting the historic moment when the first woman member was introduced into the House by a past and a present Prime Minister. The First Commissioner sought ministerial opinion and reported back to Waldorf that the gift would be acceptable. Thereupon Waldorf arranged for the painting to be done by Charles Sims. Balfour, Lloyd George, and a few members, took the trouble to sit for the picture. Nancy sat often. Sims worked hard on the picture which was not finished till the summer of 1924. In July Waldorf presented the picture which was hung on the wall by the main staircase leading to the committee rooms lobby. There it hung for a week or so, long enough for the sillier sort of partisan spirit to get going.

If Nancy had cultivated 'the terribly pleasant' in her House of Commons manner, the picture would probably be there still. As things were it was resented. Protests came in from all sides. Here, it was said, was a dangerous precedent – a portrait, hung within the historic walls of the Palace of Westminster, of three living members of Parliament! Awful consequences were previsaged. The Government took fright. In early August Waldorf issued a statement relating the history of the picture and declairing that the Astors preferred that it should not remain in the Palace of Westminster if this was in any way disagreeable to members. An enquiry was instituted, and in the meanwhile the picture was covered with a dust sheet! At length during the Christmas recess, the picture was taken down and after being on exhibition for charity in Plymouth, it was stored by the Office of Works, to be hung later in the Bedford College for Women. At present it is on indefinite loan from the House of Commons to the University of Virginia in Charlottesville. It may find its way back to Westminster one day.

Nancy declared to Pressmen that the matter was one of complete indifference to her, but in fact she must have felt this ugly slight keenly. All the more, perhaps, because she knew that she had invited something of the kind by her sometimes utterly capricious conduct within the historic walls.

Nancy's Parliamentary work continued unchanged as regards subject: the betterment of the lot of women and children, the raising of the school-leaving age, the retention of women police, cheap supplies of healthy milk, etc. She took no part in the major political movements of the time, which led to yet another general election, the third in two years.

The Labour Government were running into serious trouble because the condition of their survival, the alliance with the Liberals, was endangered. The subject of their mutual disagreement was Russia. MacDonald and his chief colleagues had reasonable and enlightened views on the subject of Anglo-Russian relations. They believed that regardless of political differences, communication should be maintained between the two countries, and that in the economic area such communication was most easily initiated. These views were put forward with ineptitude by the Labour Party. It is an irony of modern British history that Asquith gave the weight of his support to MacDonald in the belief that thus he might educate the Labour Party out of their governmental inexperience, and that the partnership broke down through Liberal irritation with Labour inexperience.

MacDonald's administration came to grief through what Asquith described as 'two squalid crises, each of which could have been avoided with a modicum of either luck or skill'. In the first MacDonald culpably misled the House regarding trade negotiations with Russia. In the second the Government began the prosecution of a Communist journalist, Mr J. R. Campbell, for inciting to mutiny, and then in terror of their extremists dropped the case. In these circumstances, in the first week of October, the Government was heavily defeated. Ramsay MacDonald asked the King for a dissolution and there ensued the

General Election of 1924. Polling day was fixed for the 30th October.

In Sutton it was a repeat performance between Nancy and Captain Brennan, with the difference that this time Doctor Bayly's followers of the Imperial Conservative Association were advised to abstain from voting. It made no great difference to the result. Captain Brennan polled 343 fewer votes than in the year before, but the vote for Nancy increased by more than two thousand to 18,174, giving her a majority of 5,079.

Nancy's election campaign of 1924 had one surprising if negative feature. 1924 was the year of the Zinovieff letter, and this general election became famous as 'The Red Letter Election'. The famous letter (supposedly addressed to Communist Headquarters in Great Britain and urging preparations for a colossal revolutionary upheaval) was a forgery. A few Left Wing publicists at the time said it was, but they were interested parties and spoke truer than they knew. The forgery was ingenious, was known only to a very few, completely deceived the Foreign Office and their expert advisers, and remained an unsolved riddle for forty-two years. Coming on top of the Campbell affair (which may have inspired the forgers) its effect on the election is generally supposed to have been enormous. But here is a case where later history, informed by later fashions, may have taken some exaggerations on trust. The fact remains that in the election in the Sutton division of Plymouth, there is no reference recorded in the local or national press to Zinovieff or the Red Letter. The incident nearest to such a thing was an occasion when a man unfurled a red flag at one of Nancy's meetings, whereupon she gave him a severe and apparently triumphant talking-to about the Union Jack.

The Conservative victory was overwhelming and gained at the expense not only of Labour but of the Liberal party which, after its deceptive appearance of revival, sank to a minority status which gradually worsened with the years. Asquith himself was defeated at Paisley and his long career in the House of Commons came to an end. The state of the parties was now as follows:

Conservatives	414
Labour	150
Liberals	39

In one respect the general election results were again disappointing to Nancy. The increase of women members in 1923 was not maintained.

Their strength was reduced from eight to four. The three Conservatives were returned, Nancy, Mrs Hilton Philipson, and the Duchess of Atholl, but Mrs Wintringham was defeated and never sat in Parliament again, and none of the Socialist women members was successful, not even Margaret Bondfield. There was however one new socialist woman member, a clever, energetic, very pretty woman of diminutive size like Nancy, who now represented Middlesbrough. She was Ellen Wilkinson, often referred to as 'Red Ellen' or 'The Fiery Particle'.

She had things in common with Nancy: boundless vitality, an ebullient sense of comedy, a strong religious vein, a natural rebelliousness, a continual cheekiness which often masked inner doubt and anxiety. Unlike Nancy, however, she suffered from acute manic-depressive tendency, and the mask was a heavier disguise than ever it was with the other. Long after this time, Ellen Wilkinson's psychological weakness had fatal results.

Their political differences were great. None of Nancy's devotion to progress, none of her hostility to the extreme Right could ever make her Left Wing. Red Ellen was of the very essence of the Left. In 1920 she had joined the Communist Party, and in 1921 went on pilgrimage to Russia. But unlike her parliamentary predecessor, Susan Lawrence (who made her pilgrimage as an M.P. in the summer recess of 1924), she retained a 'bottom of sense' on this subject. She was deceived, as the whole English-speaking world was, by the Zinovieff conspiracy, but instead of adopting a contortionist attitude, as was the procedure of most of the extreme Left, she did the sensible thing and resigned from the Communist party. This showed loyalty to Labour for, as is sometimes overlooked, the supposed letter from Zinovieff provoked a protesting letter from the Foreign Secretary to the Russian Embassy, and the Foreign Secretary at the time was the Labour Prime Minister, Ramsay MacDonald.

Party differences meant much to Ellen Wilkinson and, less consistently, to Nancy. This did not prevent the two women not only becoming friends but devoted friends.

In the new Parliament Nancy found, among a great number of new acquaintances and new Conservative colleagues, an old friend, one of her oldest. Angus McDonnell had been elected member for Dartford. He was known in those days as Colonel McDonnell. He owed his rank to his service with the Canadian Army. This surely ought to have been a very happy occasion. It was not. In spite of all the claims of 'the consonancy of our youth' Nancy still could not forgive Angus's most pardonable breach of faith in marrying without her blessing. Angus did not stand up to her. Courageous and adventurous as was his spirit, ever youthful and joyous as was his character, Nancy had the power to make him quail. She knew she had this power and she used it, mercilessly.

On the 2nd April 1925 Angus McDonnell made his maiden speech. The occasion was a 'Committee of the whole House' on Supply. He chose a subject on which he could speak with authority. He seconded an amendment urging that the problem of mass-unemployment could be relieved and perhaps solved by large-scale emigration from Great Britain with the object of exploiting, in agreement with the Dominions and Colonies of the Empire, their large surplus of uncultivated territory. The speech was well received. His Labour follower, Sidney Webb, could show no fallacy in his arguments.

When it was all over, one of the first people he met outside the Chamber was Nancy. She had no affectionate word for him and only shook her head saying 'Angus I'm sorry. You really must do better than that'.

The cruelty of this blow struck deep. Angus said later that he could never again think of Nancy as a friend. But he was weak and could not keep away. Nancy's cruelty, so hard to reconcile with the sweetness in her nature, was to plague her happiness almost to the end of her days.

To return to the immediate post-election time.

Stanley Baldwin had no strong views on feminism, and was probably relieved rather than angry or glad that so few women had succeeded in the 1924 election. But he recognised that the appointment of Margaret Bondfield had set a precedent, and thus that if the Tory party was to avoid the accusation of reaction he would do well to appoint one of his three Conservative ladies to a Government post. The obvious choice was the Duchess of Atholl, a woman of remarkable ability and intellectual attainment, but hardly had her appointment as Parliamentary Secretary to the Board of Education been made public than there were some murmurs that this was grossly unfair; that the first Conservative appointment of the kind should have gone to the first woman member, and it was recalled that the Duchess had only ten months of parliamentary experience, exclusively in opposition, whereas Nancy had more than five times more and had piloted a Bill from First to Third

Reading. In some newspapers there were hints that the Trade was once again showing its malign influence on affairs.

Nancy took no part in this agitation (which was not widespread) and showed no sympathy with it. She vigorously expressed her approval of the Duchess of Atholl's appointment and showed not the smallest sign of resentment at being passed over. This was not a case of her assuming a part in order to cover hurt feelings: the little episode brings out a most unusual feature of Nancy's political career. In the ordinary meaning of the term, this politician was without political ambition. Though she agitated for the appointment of women ministers, though she strove to the utmost to influence legislation in accordance with her ideals, though she did all she could to drive ministers mad with her incessant bombardments, there is not the smallest evidence that she sought office at any time. At this period of her life, Nancy knew the extent of her abilities almost perfectly, and knew instinctively that she would never have made a good minister, or filled advantageously any Government post of any kind. She would have languished in a Government department. Apart from all else, as a member of the Government she would have had to forswear one of her major delights. Unless she resigned she would never be able to speak against the Government!

The new Parliament lasted from 1924 to the spring of 1929 and Nancy took a very vigorous part in it. She brought in two private member's Bills, one relative to the control of prostitution in July 1925, another for raising the school leaving age, but neither passed its second reading. These did not amount to setbacks, since failure was then an even more usual fate for private member's Bills than it is now. Her influence was not impaired.

As indicated, the reason for her continuing influence was that she kept her sights on those related targets whose movements she knew best and on which her aim was most certain. After the General Strike of 1926 she went with Mrs Wintringham on a visit of inspection to the poorest areas of South Wales to learn at first hand about the conditions in which the wives and children of miners lived. Her only frequent ventures into foreign affairs (and those were mostly outside Parliament) were concerned with the passionate belief in the merits and need of the League of Nations which she had learned from her friend Lord Robert Cecil.

For the reason that there is inevitably a certain sameness about

Nancy's parliamentary performance in the first fifteen post-war years, as there is with her electioneering tactics, the writer does not intend to give a close summary of her parliamentary career at that time, but instead to look again at her more personal life, though with Nancy at all times there was rarely a clear distinction between the personal and political. A good illustration of this is found in an emotional and very interesting friendship which had a strong influence on her political activity. The friendship was with Margaret McMillan and began in June or July 1926. Its origins are obscure. It may possibly have opened through a three-cornered friendship between Margaret McMillan, Bernard Shaw, and Nancy. It is probable that at this time there was some friendship between Nancy and Shaw, and between Shaw and Margaret McMillan, but slight and superficial in both cases.

It is known that when Nancy was first told about Margaret McMillan's work for nursery schools, she was sceptical. Party bias may have had something to do with that. In her pioneering work Margaret McMillan had become convinced that only through Socialism was there any hope of achieving her object: to allow the children of the poor to grow up with normal health. She became a member of the Independent Labour Party in 1893, and was mocked or saluted as 'the Labour prophetess of the North'. She and her sister Rachel toiled, first in Bradford and then in London, to establish official health supervision of schools. After setbacks they succeeded, before the First World War, in establishing clinics with subventions from the London County Council; also in the formation of camp schools for boys and girls and, perhaps most importantly, in founding a nursery school for little children. Their endeavour to establish an open-air nursery school (during the war) probably succeeded because of the official support given to it by H. A. L. Fisher. It may have been through Fisher that Nancy's friendship began.

Nancy and Margaret McMillan were both deeply religious, but in very different ways. Rachel McMillan had died in 1917, and for the rest of her life Margaret McMillan not only venerated her memory but held to a belief that the spirit of her sister was associated with her work and influenced it in some mysterious and vital manner. When Margaret McMillan became friends with Nancy, she assured her that her sister approved and was her friend too. Such ideas, and Margaret McMillan's belief in the mystical significance of dreams, were normally somewhat repellent to Nancy, and for that reason the intensity of their friendship is surprising. Nevertheless it was formed instantly, and any doubts that Nancy had felt vanished on meeting this mild and formidable woman. It was another affair of the Damascus Road, and as with most of Nancy's close relationships it was informed by her sense of humour. In a letter of 1926 Margaret McMillan wrote a postscript 'You haven't forgotten me? I was the poor thing you gave flowers to in the summer'. Nancy's answer begins 'Dearest Poor Thing, I am not so simple minded as you seem to think, and there are certain people that you can't forget even though you have never known them'.

For the five remaining years of Margaret McMillan's life, and for as long as Nancy was a member of Parliament, she gave all her influence and a great deal of her own and the Astor wealth to Margaret McMillan's cause. She brought that cause to the notice of the House of Commons. She saw that nursery schools could only expand if there were abundant training facilities for teachers and nurses. In 1926 these were on a modest scale. She interested Waldorf in the enterprise and took him down to the nursery school and training centre at Deptford. He immediately shared Nancy's enthusiasm and bought available land in the neighbourhood. Here the Rachel McMillan Training Centre was expanded into the Rachel McMillan College. Nancy herself raised £20,000, the major part of the funds. She gave the movement publicity, partly by obtaining Queen Mary's interest in it and helping to arrange royal visits. She laid the foundation stone of the college in November 1929, and did so in her own fashion.

'This is the best part of the ceremony', she said as she applied the mortar with her trowel. 'Making mud pies. I hope no union officials are here. I never saw a man laying bricks but I thought I could do it better and quicker.'

In the next year Queen Mary opened the college. On the 28th March of the next year 1931 Margaret McMillan died. Her last words were a message to Nancy. 'Tell her,' she said, 'I have no fear. I am happy.'

This is again to run ahead of the story. To return to Nancy in the twenties.

A very good letter written early in the decade gives a picture of her then, and as she remained for many years to come, never altered in any way by a mellowing process. The letter was written by Nancy's former secretary Miss Benningfield after a visit from Nancy's current secretary (also a Christian Scientist) who had formerly been in Philip Kerr's employment.

'Well – Miss X has been here with me this evening & we've had a lot of talk. She's very depressed and discouraged, &, as ever in such cases, the most amazingly futile molehills seem to her like the whole of the Rocky Mountains. She feels that you have no confidence in her, & that until you can trust her a little more she won't be able to give her best or to please you in any way. From what I know of your beloved, bewildering & exasperating character, I think she is right! . . . I know the one question with you is now "Will she do for me" or "is she the kind of employee I want". And to that question of course there are two sides. There is a good employer & one who is difficult to serve. Miss X is used to a very high standard where her employer is concerned. Mr Kerr must be a most considerate & just & thoughtful creature to work for . . . a very perfect gentle knight among employers. She's used to a certain amount of approval & satisfaction "for value received" & she's used to thinking of Mr Kerr and herself & – voilà tout. Now, suddenly, she's plunged into the whirlpool of St J Sq. where everything she does is in relation to what about a dozen other people are doing. She is faced with a mass of detail. She gets no sympathy, or encouragement, or patience, or consideration. Her chief faults are ignorance of your character & bewilderment. She's giving you her very best & is trying hard to learn your ways. *You'll have these difficulties with any secretary you take on.* . . . '

The above extract represents about a fifth of a long letter. How well Miss Benningfield wrote! Her insight into Nancy's aptitude to play the tyrant, is perfect. But before judging, one must allow that this interesting letter also shows Nancy's strength. Few people in the position she had attained would have accepted such severe strictures from a former employee without resentment, or at least self-defence. Of the latter there is no sign, of the former complete contradiction: 'Bunny' Benningfield continued to be a friend of the family for the rest of her life.

A main question about Nancy's character now rises and a search must be made for the answer. Was she essentially a bully prone to uncharacteristic impulses of good nature, or was she a good natured person prone to uncharacteristic impulses of cruelty?

People who stood up to her, as Miss Benningfield did, never fared badly. A striking example of this was in a friendship which was to continue for the rest of her life. It was with James Stuart who wrote of their relationship in his brief autobiography. After the war, in which he had fought as an officer of the Royal Scots, he served for a year and a half as aide de camp to the Duke of York (later King George VI), after which he went to seek his fortune in the oil business in the United States. He only succeeded, however, in becoming a driller. In June 1923 he came back to London on leave and when Nancy found that he knew rather few people, from having spent his young manhood in the army, in the closed society of the royal family, and in America, she became in some measure his protectress, asking him frequently to Cliveden, Sandwich and St James's Square. They both found in each other rewarding company, but the friendship which rapidly sprang up soon acquired a deeper foundation. All that can be said about that foundation here is that at the time of her meeting with Stuart Nancy was worried about one of her young women friends who seemed in danger of becoming involved in a scandal. She appealed to James Stuart to use his influence to prevent such a thing happening. He did so with success, and her affection was strengthened by gratitude.

At the 1923 General Election, shortly before he was due to return to Oklahoma, he was, to his great surprise, invited to stand as the Conservative candidate for Moray and Nairn. To his greater surprise he was elected to Parliament in that year of Conservative disaster, and his career in oil abruptly terminated. From then on until 1945 he and Nancy were not only friends but parliamentary colleagues. When Waldorf was unable to attend a dinner in St James's Square, occasionally being prevented by attacks of rheumatism, James Stuart would stand in as host. On one of these occasions the principal guests were Stuart's former chief, the Duke of York, and his wife, the present Queen Mother. Nancy was a little uneasy in her conscience because, while preaching the virtues of teetotalism, she served wine to her guests at her own parties. Sir Frederick Banbury had raised this very point against her. She decided to set an example by serving no alcoholic refreshment at this particular dinner. She informed James Stuart of her intention.

In his languid, low voice he replied in some such words as these: 'Well, if I'm to act as host, I only do so on condition that there's champagne for the Duchess – and me – at my end of the table, and I strongly advise you to have some at your end for the Duke. That is, if you ever want them to come here again. Have you ever thought of inviting the Prince of Wales? I wouldn't try giving him a pussyfoot dinner.' She yielded to his arguments.

They rarely agreed, but she never took offence at anything he said, and he never disguised how great was his disagreement with most of her ideas. At a later period, when James Stuart was closely concerned with Party management, he and Nancy had an argument concerning 'The Trade'. She said to him 'Why does the Party have to go to brewers for help all the time?'

'Why not?' answered Stuart. 'Brewers are no worse than other people, and some of them are very fine fellows.'

'Nonsense,' said Nancy, 'y'know very well that they live off vice – revoltin'.'

'Do they?' answered Stuart. 'Well, I see what you mean about them living off vice, but if it comes to that, so do you.'

'What d'you mean?'

'You make no fuss about living off the Astor rents in New York, and I can assure you that the Astor property contains a very large number of brothels.'

To this assault she merely replied, according to Lord Stuart's autobiography, that if he made any more remarks of the kind 'she would appeal to Mr Speaker for protection'. But he did continue to make remarks of the kind and no bones were broken at any time.

To answer the harsh question posed earlier.

An idea of her character may emerge as one who could only enjoy companionship with the strong, with people who had the force and courage to join battle with her and did not trouble too much about giving or receiving wounds; whereas with weaker people, with the touchy and vulnerable, with such a one as Angus, her self-assertion and desire to scare made her merely cruel, brought out the worst in her. There is an element of truth in this, but as with everything that can be said about her, this also must be drastically qualified. Here is an incident of this time, which is fully recorded in her papers.

She had a woman friend, somewhat younger than she was, who was married to a friend of the Astors. The couple were not very well off. This woman had the misfortune to be a compulsive gambler and on one occasion she lost a large sum. She did not dare tell her husband, confessed her plight to Nancy, and threw herself on her mercy. On condition that she stopped gambling Nancy paid the debt. The poor woman gave the promise but did not keep it and almost immediately lost the whole sum that Nancy had given her. Distracted, she confessed to Nancy what she had done, and Nancy instantly and without rebuke paid up again. That is all that is recorded of the incident in her letters but surely it is enough to keep one from too heavy a judgement on her occasional cruelty to the weak.

The fact is that she was literally importunate to help people in trouble, and people often get into trouble through their weaknesses. She often showed on their behalf a patience of which one might have thought her incapable. But people in trouble through their weaknesses were one thing, whereas people who were merely weak were another, and to them she was sometimes mercilessly impatient.

All this, it is safe to say, was the consequence of her possessiveness. Victor Cunard told how it made for difficult relationships with young people, who are in an inevitable state of weakness. Her predicament manifested itself with added force when it concerned her children, and all the more surprisingly because she proved by what she wrote in her autobiographical sketch that she was fully aware of the mischief that her father's possessiveness had wrought on her two elder brothers. A vivid picture of her merits and failures as a mother has been given with exemplary candour by Michael Astor in his book. There let it remain. What he wrote has been in general supported by the affectionate essay on Nancy written by John Buchan's widow, Lady Tweedsmuir. Here reference need only be made to the unfortunate consequences on a noble friendship of her domineering attempt to mould to her own liking her second son, Bill Astor.

In late 1927 Bill was at the beginning of his third year as a brilliant undergraduate at Oxford. He had gone from Eton to New College, as his father had done, and gained a first class in 'Moderations' after his first term. In Bill's second year, in 1926, his father's old tutor and the beloved friend of the family, H. A. L. Fisher, was elected Warden of New College. Not without regret for his political career, Fisher thereupon resigned his seat in the House of Commons and devoted his energies to his new post. In the winter of the next year Bill was taken seriously ill. Nancy had striven with all her energy to make Bill as dedicated a Christian Scientist as she was herself. To what extent he was a Christian Scientist at all at this time is not clear, but Fisher looked on with annoyance at Nancy's preventing her son receiving what he, Fisher, considered necessary medical attention. A letter of the 15th November 1927 from Philip Kerr to Nancy shows that Bill was given leave of absence from New College and went with Lionel Curtis and his wife to Honolulu to recuperate, and that at Nancy's request Kerr

Nancy as a candidate in 1919

Strobl's bust and the sitter

Left: The first woman M.P. about to take her seat accompanied by her son Bobbie Shaw. *Right:* Nancy on the terrace with the second woman to take her seat, Mrs Wintringham, in 1922

THE MIDDLE TWENTIES 289

had asked Curtis to see that Bill should have the attentions of a Christian Science practitioner. Curtis refused to be responsible, as he had no belief in Christian Science. He said that it was for Bill to decide; that if the latter wanted a doctor, he would see that he got one, but if Bill wanted a practitioner he would let Kerr know. As there is no further mention of the matter in the Kerr-Astor correspondence, it would appear that Bill was at this time in rebellion against his mother's religion. It is not possible to say with certainty.

Fisher was moved by this incident to enquire into the whole history, nature and purpose of Christian Science. He brought his massive power of analysis to the subject and reached the conclusion that Mary Baker Eddy was one of the most colossal religious frauds of all time, and that her whole enunciation of faith was a mixture of megalomania, self-delusion and conscious hoax. He wrote his famous book *Our New Religion*. Whether or not he was biased by his concern for Bill's well-being, this book remains one of the most remarkable pieces of destructive criticism in the English language. It is once referred to, contemptuously and without any attempt at refutation, as appears later, in Kerr's letters of 1929 when it was published.

By this time Bill had left Oxford. When the book came out, the friendship between H. A. L. Fisher and his parents instantly came to an end. It would have been impossible for it to have continued.

A terrible tragedy overcame the Astors' next-door neighbours in October of 1926. The third and only surviving son of Lord and Lady Desborough, Ivo Grenfell, was killed in a motor accident. It appears evident from the letters that passed from the Desboroughs to Nancy on this awful occasion that Nancy, who had till shortly before shown no diminution of her antagonism, did at last repent her misjudgement. Similar letters had passed after the deaths of Julian and Billy Grenfell more than ten years before, without conjuring away Nancy's fixed idea, but this time there was a difference in the result. There remains touching evidence that an absolute and complete change of heart was achieved. On the 19th October Lady Desborough sent a second letter, apparently after a visit by Nancy to Taplow Court. It runs: 'We'll never refer to "byegones", but I suppose the world has never taken so much trouble in its life to make mischief between two people as between you and me! and I do want to tell you, dear Nancy, that I am

N.

K

so glad we have got it all right, directly we got to know each other. I shall always be fond of you now.'

Nancy remained beautifully young-looking. It was what most people first remarked about her. A friend of her young days met her again in 1927, and she appears either to have made a new conquest or renewed an old one. The friend was Baron von Cramm. She tried to convert him to Christian Science and, when he returned to Germany, she sent him Mrs Eddy's book. He replied in October: 'If I was young I would certainly prefer a curl of yours to the book. But an old tree, which may not be transplanted, dare not say such things as that. So I don't do it.'

He ended the letter: 'Let me finish as a man not being "in desperate love" as you remarked, but with still stronger feelings for you, than is desired.

'Therefore it is better for you and me, if I do not go over to England again in November. . . . I must have time to set in order my feelings. . . . You kindly asked me for a ring – I bought one for you and hope, it will please you. You also spoke of fur for a shooting dress, but I am afraid not to choose the right kind. Au revoir, as soon as possible. I will write to you, when I am all right again.'

At the mention of the ring and the fur Nancy minuted the document 'I don't remember this. It sounds bad'.

Bad or not, she accepted a ring set with 'a rare *red sapphire*' not long after. This bizarre romance concluded as oddly as it began. Cramm had a son at Oxford and in December 1927 his wife travelled to England to see him, and also, it would appear, to report on the state of her husband's heart. 'My wife came back,' he wrote to Nancy on the 8th, 'was charmed to see you, your husband and your sons and very glad to have met you several times. She told me laughing, that you said you did not love me. I laughed also. I am all right again.'

It can be truthfully said of this period of her life, as of most others that it was full of alarums and excursions, a full account of which would occupy many pages. She 'continued hostess' and there was almost no resident or visiting celebrity who did not find himself or herself at some time or other at Cliveden or 4 St James's Square. As in the old days her lions were of many different breeds and included Charlie Chaplin and Lytton Strachey. In keeping with James Stuart's advice she very successfully entertained the Prince of Wales. Queen Marie of Rumania was the guest of the Astors at Cliveden and St James's Square on her visits to England and Nancy conducted the great lady round Plymouth. She took her three elder children to America in the autumn of 1926 and outraged opinion on both sides of the Atlantic when she declared to reporters in New York that she did not know who were the more horrible, English girls or American girls. She visited Palestine for the first time where, though often questioned by reporters, she was surprisingly discreet politically. She found her anti-Roman Catholic prejudices and her suspicion of all religious ceremonial fortified by what she saw of the Holy Places. She continued her religious correspondence with Philip Kerr whenever he was on one of his numerous journeys. When he was not she saw him frequently.

Let the chapter end with an interesting and typical episode which the writer has at first hand. The story was told to me by Doctor James Parkes, the leading English authority today on Jewish history, at that time working as the International Study Secretary of the Student Christian Movement. He represented the last named body on the executive of the National Union of Students which held a meeting at Bristol some time after the General Strike.

It was arranged that various prominent people, including spokesmen for the three main political parties, would address the students at various sessions. Nancy was invited to speak as the Conservative representative and she accepted. When the day came she addressed the students with characteristic forthrightness, verve, and absence of compromise. As James Parkes remembers the speech more than forty years after, it contained the proposition that Conservatism, having a broad programme, based on a broad patriotism which cared for general not sectional welfare, had something for everyone. It did not matter what your circumstances were, she said, whether you were a millionaire, a farmer, a business man, an artist, a shopkeeper, a miner – yes, even if you were unemployed – Conservatism would see you through! She was in spirited vein and was listened to with fascination rather than agreement. A great part of her audience were working class students achieving education at the cost of a bitter struggle against poverty at its bleakest.

At the end of the meeting James Parkes was introduced to her. He told her that he had something to ask her. She urged him to speak his mind freely. 'I put it to you like this, Lady Astor,' he said, 'if you were the wife of an unemployed man living on the dole, with several children to look after, and if your husband, through no fault of his own, was without any prospect of work – I ask you this: would you, under those circumstances, vote Conservative?'

Nancy answered with what James Parkes has described as a 'high-pitched scream'. 'What!' she cried, 'Me! Vote Conservative! In those circumstances! Why –' she went on, even louder, 'I'd vote Communist! I'd be a second Rosa Luxemburg! I'd –'

Suddenly she stopped and put a hand to her mouth. 'Oh my!' she said with a low moan, 'I oughtn't 'a said that, ought I?'

Several members of the local Conservative Association were standing by, and, of far greater menace, a number of reporters. But Nancy's luck held. There was no star reporter at this meeting, and the newspapers missed a headline story. Nancy and James Parkes were left to appreciate this comedy alone.

The main source of general information in the foregoing chapter is discussion with members of Lady Astor's family, notably Michael Astor, Mrs Nancy Lancaster and Mrs Alice Winn, and for details the contemporary Press. Maurice Collis's *Nancy Astor* has also provided continuous help. The references to the political situation caused by Bonar Law's sudden decline in health during 1923 follows Lord Blake's admirable biography, *The Unknown Prime Minister*, from which I have made (not, I hope, to his disgust) deductions of my own. In sketching the brief career of the first MacDonald administration and its succession by the second Baldwin administration I have been guided by the article on Ramsay MacDonald by Lord Elton, that on Asquith by J. A. Spender, and that on Baldwin by Thomas Jones in the *Dictionary of National Biography*. I am also indebted to the biography of Asquith by Roy Jenkins and to the present Lord Baldwin's study of his father. The story of Charles Sims's picture of Lady Astor's entry into the House of Commons follows Maurice Collis's book, Pamela Brookes's *Women at Westminster* (to which I continue to owe a debt for most of what I say about women Members of Parliament), but chiefly to the contemporary Press which reported the matter widely. The incident of Angus McDonnell's maiden speech was told to me by McDonnell's nephew, Lord Antrim. The account of Lady Astor's friendship with Margaret McMillan is drawn from their correspondence preserved in the Astor archive, and is also influenced by a correspondence between Dr Elizabeth Bradburn of the University of Liverpool and myself. Margaret McMillan's last words were reported by Miss Margaret MacColl to whom they were spoken. Miss MacColl wrote a full account to Lady Astor on the day Margaret McMillan died. The account of the origin of the friendship between Lady Astor and James Stuart, later Viscount Stuart of Findhorn, follows his autobiography, *Within the Fringe* (London, 1967), and personal discussion with the late Lord Stuart and Lady

Stuart. In the argument between Lord Stuart and Lady Astor regarding 'living off vice', I follow an account he gave me in conversation rather than the brief allusion in his book. I have deduced my account of H. A. L. Fisher's extreme hostility to Christian Science chiefly from what I have been told by friends of the 3rd Lord Astor. I am grateful to the Reverend Doctor James Parkes for his account of the incident at the students' meeting at Bristol. The date is uncertain.

Chapter 15

ENTER G.B.S.

WHEN Bernard Shaw died in 1950 Nancy said that she had known him for forty years. The statement may well have been accurate, but, if so, then the acquaintance was of a tenuous kind during its first seventeen years. Between 1910 and 1927 they exchanged no letters, nor is Shaw mentioned in any of Nancy's correspondence. It would seem that suddenly these slightly acquainted people took to each other, and after that became a major factor in each other's lives.

The first letter of the whole Shaw-Astor correspondence is one from G.B.S.'s wife, Charlotte Shaw, and is dated the 11th December 1927. It is strange to note that Charlotte Shaw's precise and neat handwriting is nearly identical with that of her husband. Here is the text:

'Dear Lady Astor,

'We've been thinking furiously about what you said.

'We have come to the conclusion that you asked us for Xmas in that delightful and friendly way in a fit of enthusiastic benevolence, & desire to be kind to two old crocks & brighten up their holiday for them.

'Now – on thinking it over – are you not appalled at the step you have taken? . . .

'If you can't face it now, in cold blood, (but your blood is never cold) one of the servants might have small-pox – or – that sort of thing.

'Yours really appreciatively C. F. Shaw.'

The omitted passage proposes that they should spend only the Christmas weekend at Cliveden, but the next letter, dated the 10th January 1928, shows that they made a long and happy stay. It is again from Charlotte Shaw, with a postscript from G.B.S., the first of his many writings to Nancy.

'Here we are, dear friend,' wrote Charlotte Shaw, 'safe & sound & we both agree that all that has occurred during the last 3 weeks is a wonderful & impossible dream, & that now we are awake again to the buffets & storms of life. But the lovely flower is alive & well to witness that we lie!

'My love to David.

'Ever C. F. Shaw

'All the same, I don t believe it ever happened. I ask you, is it likely? G.B.S.'

Nancy seems to have asked the Shaws to come for another visit to Cliveden a month or so later. This time he answered in a letter of the 27th January, which is the first of a hundred and forty-nine which he was to write to her in the course of the next twenty-two years.

'My dear N – I mean Lady Astor,

'Charlotte is in bed with a temperature. Nothing serious; but I have to answer her letters.

'Just at this moment, and until I get my book finally out I must have deadly quiet week-ends; for every Saturday finds me abominably tired; and to ask me to spend a Sunday with a volcano is not reasonable.

'Put it off until you get a copy of the book from me.

'Then if you are still of the same mind – !

'Ever G.B.S.'

Shaw thereafter addressed Nancy by her first name, occasionally diversifying this with 'Nan' and wilder inventions of the moment. Mrs Shaw and Nancy followed suit, but Shaw himself always remained 'G.B.S.' by address and signature. In its first phase most of the correspondence was between Charlotte Shaw and Nancy: in 1928 G.B.S. wrote her three letters, and Charlotte Shaw eight. They went to Sandwich to stay with the Astors again at Whitsuntide at the end of May.

On what did this deep and enduring friendship rest? At first sight nothing could seem more improbable than a close association of the intellectual Shaw and the emotional Nancy who never made the least pretension to be an intellectual. Again one might think that their differing attitudes to Parliament might have precluded close friendship. G.B.S.'s suspicion and contempt of Parliament was an obsession. It may be remembered that in an introduction he wrote to a cheap edition of Great Expectations he devoted a large part of his space to denunciation of House of Commons procedure, a subject nowhere mentioned in Dickens's masterpiece! For all her naughtiness in Westminster, Nancy had the reverence for Parliament of a Gladstone. Why should she love and revere a man who would like to see Parliament abolished in favour of some Socialist Ruling Committee composed on a recipe thought out by Sidney and Beatrice Webb?

Nancy did not only like people who resembled herself, or she would have had a very small circle of friends. There was very little resemblance between her and Philip Kerr and they might well not have been close friends without their common interest in Christian Science. There was no such common interest with Shaw. He looked on Christian Science as nonsense and made fun of it to this devout believer. About a year after the friendship began he wrote in a letter to Nancy: 'My Charlotte, I regret to say, is in bed with a swamping headful of sin and error, known to the mob as a bad cold.' No offence was taken. Perhaps one reason was that Shaw, like another hater of Parliament, Belloc, shared with her a deep if divergent concern with religion.

Yet when all is said, this great mutual affection was an improbable one, and G.B.S. himself was aware of the fact. Again referring to Charlotte Shaw in a letter, he wrote 'She is very fond of you. So am I. I don't know why.'

If one looks a little closer it is not impossibly difficult to 'know why'. Shaw always liked pretty women and Nancy, when she was nearing the age of fifty, looked twenty years younger than that. (It was at about this time that the writer first saw her and the first impression was of dazzling beauty.) Shaw's friendships with beautiful women sometimes broke down because the women concerned wanted to make a lover of him. According to St John Ervine he had special affection for Mrs Ervine and Nancy because they 'never made any attempt to flirt with him'. Like Nancy he was a Puritan, like her sometimes to an extent that was prudish. No one except an extreme prude could have written the masterly end of the first act of the first part of Back to Methuselah. Shaw ingeniously defended himself to St John Ervine against a charge of prudery here, but his apologia is not convincing.

Shaw at this time was at the height of his enormous fame and appeared to be at the very peak of his colossal strength and ability, though in fact his genius had just passed its zenith. He had in the last eight years produced the work by which he is likely to be most remembered: Back to Methuselah (first acted in 1922) and St Joan (1923). The book on which he was working when his friendship with Nancy became intimate was The Intelligent Woman's Guide to Socialism and Capitalism. Ahead of him lay the last of his great plays The Apple Cart. His fame extended far beyond Europe and America. Nancy was almost as famous within the English-speaking world. She also was at the height of her abilities. There is among famous people a freemasonry which is often resented by the obscure. The famous have troubles of their own, ceaseless publicity, though it is difficult to suppose that in the nineteen twenties Nancy or G.B.S. very much minded that part of the penalty of achievement. Another trial of fame is monotonous praise which can degenerate into flattery, and they both had their fill of that.

Few people admit to enjoying flattery, but few people have the strength of mind to be total abstainers. Max Beerbohm preserved a valuable story of his brother Herbert Beerbohm Tree when the latter's fame was at its height. 'Doesn't all this flattery disgust you?' asked a candid friend of the great actor. 'No, I like it very much,' replied Tree, 'provided it's fulsome.' The self-caricature probably applies with an uncomfortable degree of truth to most inhabitants of the Hall of Fame. Neither Nancy nor G.B.S. can be accused of encouraging the fulsome flattery that came their way, but both felt the need of the corrective. Nancy remained almost wholly uninfluenced by Shaw's ideas, and sometimes told him so. She never gave him a word of flattery, and at the same time she made it clear that she respected and admired him. As for G.B.S., it is hardly necessary to state that he never flattered Nancy. He never made any attempt to soften the harsh fact that his political ideas were in total contrast to her own, though, knowing her Rosa Luxemburg side, he endeavoured from time to time and in vain to convert her. Even when they agreed (long after this time) on the folly and cruelty of penal legislation on inheritance, they agreed in matters of detail, not of principle. Flattery from G.B.S. on her public work would have been literally impossible. She knew that, and for that reason his encouragement was precious.

Lastly they had a great thing in common. They were both actors, both specialising in comedy. With both of them it was a question of instinct. When their acquaintance turned into attachment some time in 1927, they became, in a way, theatrical partners, and as sometimes happens the partnership turned to love.

None of this must obscure the fact that G.B.S. had a serious regard for Nancy's judgement respecting his work. On finishing a play, it was his custom to hold at least one reading party, usually in his flat in London, and his audience most often included Granville Barker, Barry Jackson, a few of his leading players, notably Robert Loraine, and a few of his distinguished friends. During the severe winter of 1928–1929 he finished *The Apple Cart*, partly at Cliveden where again he and Mrs Shaw spent a long visit at Christmas. In February 1929 he appears to have held three reading parties, judging from a letter to Nancy which he wrote on the 11th, the main reading being in 4 St James's Square. Here is the text of the letter.

'Loveliest Nan. As to that list – what about Balfour? what about T.J.? (an authority on Cabinet procedure who needs cheering up)? what about Elliot (for dinner and the last act: he heard the first)? what about Mosley & his Cynthia? (to represent the Labor Party)? Griggs has suffered it all before: need we plague him again? Ward, dear lad, is only one of many journalists; but why not Geoffrey Dawson: wouldnt you like to see him wriggling on my skewer?

'Are you on visiting terms with Ellen Wilkinson? Dare she – if you asked her? I should rather like to know how my lampoon would strike her – whether she would detect portraits which dont exist. However, unless she would amuse *you*, disregard this suggestion, as I can easily get at her when I read for the Webbs and the Fabian lot.

'I shall have read the play professionally and privately to Sir Barry Jackson and the producer this week (it has come back from the printer); so there is no *need* to have him, though he might like to come and look at you under cover of the play.

'I can't think of anyone else for the moment; but I presume you dont want a mob.

'I hope you have not been devoured by wolves, though you would be if I were a wolf. Here it is blastingly, blightingly, blitheringly cold: 8 degrees of frost in the sun out of the wind at midday, and 1000° below zero *in* the wind.

'Probably Charlotte, who is up and about the house, is writing.

'In haste: the post goes at 4.30 in this village

Your G.B.S.

'P.S. Waldorf is bringing in a bill to get Lady Rhondda into the House of Lords to cheer him in your absence. What about *her*?[1]'

Underneath a pose of ruthless rejection of every form of sentimentality or even sentiment, Bernard Shaw was a kindly man, considerate to his friends. In this there was a distinct resemblance to Nancy, and this

1. Most of the names are familiar. 'T.J.' stands for Dr Thomas Jones, who appears later. 'Ward' is probably Robert Barrington-Ward (1891–1948), later editor of *The Times* in succession to Geoffrey Dawson. Lady Rhondda, a peeress in her own right, was the founder of the weekly magazine *Time and Tide*. For many years she campaigned for the admission of women to the House of Lords. Griggs may be Sir Edward Grigg later Lord Altrincham.

paradoxical part of his character comes out with much clarity in a letter
he wrote to her a week after the death of Charlotte Shaw's sister, Mary
Cholmondeley to whom he had dedicated *The Intelligent Woman's
Guide to Socialism and Capitalism*[2]. The letter is dated 13th April 1929.

'Dear blessedest Nancy, Charlotte is all right. I went down with her
to the funeral at the lovely little old village church of Eddastone on a
lovely day with a mountain of lovely flowers. I contributed enough
comic relief to wipe the black off without going so far as to turn the
afternoon into a wake. Still, I think we all enjoyed ourselves. The
Intelligent Woman had lived her life well out, and exhausted her health
so much through her struggle with asthma that it would really have
been terrible if she had recovered and had to die all over again. Those
who cared felt that all was well. Those who didn't had a pleasant
outing, and were relieved to find that long faces were not expected.

'If Charlotte ever has more distress than I can pull her through I will
send for you.'

This is to run ahead somewhat. The story must return to Nancy's
public life in the last year of the twenties.

As frequently happens to governments with large majorities
Baldwin's was growing lethargic, a hardly escapable predicament under
a Prime Minister who was prone that way personally. His indolence
was no state secret, and during the next three years the mood of the
nation became impatient. Baldwin did not believe this to be so. He was
confident that he had the country with him, and he may also have
believed that the Franchise Act of May 1928 which gave the vote to
women at 21 (a measure strongly supported by Nancy) would yield a
large grateful young vote. He asked the King for a dissolution in April
1929. Polling day was fixed for the 30th May. The Prime Minister led
the Conservative Party into battle, choosing as his war-cry 'Safety
First'. With this slogan he hoped to set all the youth of England on
fire.

Nancy was once more selected to represent the Conservative interest
in the Sutton Division. This time it was a three-cornered fight. Her
opponents were Mr William Westwood of Glasgow, representing
Labour, and a local man, Mr T. H. Aggett of Teignmouth, representing

2. Mrs Shaw and Mrs Cholmondeley were the daughters of Horace Payne-
Townshend of Derry, Co. Cork. Their husbands were remarkable for longevity.
Brigadier-General Hugh Cholmondeley was born before Bernard Shaw in 1852 and
died at the age of 89 in 1941.

the Liberal interest. It was to be a fierce contest. The protracted coal strike, persisting after the General Strike, had left an ugly feeling of hatred and frustration in many working class minds. Socialism seemed preferable to paternalism, and Nancy stood for the latter, no matter how advanced her notions of social reform. It was going to require all her energy, all her wiles, all her arts of canvassing, to win her seat again, for what Lloyd George had described as a 'torpid, sleepy, barren' administration. Lloyd George, vowing that he could solve the problem of unemployment given only power, was in the field again. This, if he had followed Philip Kerr's counsel, might well have been his moment. As it was he remained irrelevant.

Bernard Shaw, pondering these matters, was moved to write a letter of advice to Nancy. He was at the time in Jugoslavia, having been dragged abroad by Charlotte Shaw who loved foreign travel as much as he hated it. This incurable speechifyer disliked being in any place where the people could not understand what he said, and he was not a good linguist. He wrote a letter of electioneering guidance to Nancy on the 18th May 1929 from Dubrovnik.

'You are in a difficult situation: a violently Radical Conservative, a recklessly unladylike Lady, a Prohibitionist member of The Trade Party, and all sorts of contradictory things, including (on the authority of the late Speaker) the most turbulent member of the Party of Order. The only tune to which you can win in a seafaring constituency is Jack's Delight Is His Lovely Nan. In that sign you will probably conquer in spite of all the sober and virtuous publicans and brothel keepers who minister to the paid off mariners of our historic port. Knowing that you are on the side of the angels, they will give you a vote to set against their profits in the books of the recording angel, believing that you are too jonnick [sic] to cut any ice in parliament on your own account. Therefore be extreme on the Drink Question for if you compromise they will be afraid you might really hurt them, whereas if you go all out for a Dry England they will laugh at pretty Nancy's way and feel sure that you might as well try to dry England with blotting paper as with Prohibition. On the social question, just read chapters of my book at random and give them chunks of it: they will neither know nor care whether it is Socialism or Conservatism if you don't tell them. Give them what you like, and they'll probably like it too; and leave it to the others to "give em muck" (pêche Melba). Tell them you are making enemies all the time because you can't suffer fools gladly and are up against 600 of them every working night of your life, and that under God your refuge is Plymouth, and if Plymouth turns you down it will shut the gates of mercy on mankind. In short, dear Nancy, let yourself rip, and wear all your pearls: prudence is not your game; and if you ride hard enough for a fall you won't get it.'

The advice was sound, but also superfluous, as, omitting the proposed use of *The Intelligent Woman's Guide to Socialism*, the tactics outlined by G.B.S. were in accordance with her invariable procedure.

The campaign opened with the clang of battle. On nomination day, on the 20th May, Nancy and Mr Westwood arrived for the handing in of papers to the Mayor at the same time. The *Daily Herald* made strenuous efforts to work up the incidents which followed into a political and even national scandal. Nancy is reported to have said to him: 'The Liberals are going to give you the seat,' and he is reported to have clapped her on the back, saying: 'We'll win, Liberals or no Liberals, and don't lose your temper, although you're going to lose your seat.' Outside Nancy is said to have been booed by the crowd which cheered Westwood and began to sing *The Red Flag*. Thereupon Nancy began to sing *God Save the King* with a few supporters. When she saw a prominent Trades Unionist remaining with his hat on during the anthem she is said to have knocked it off. Waldorf issued a denial which the *Daily Herald* printed in full followed by comments to the effect that a misreport by their own correspondent was an impossibility. Both parties denied the remarks attributed to them, and the Trades Unionist said that Nancy had made as though to knock off his hat, without success. But the story did not catch on outside the *Daily Herald*. For all its exaggerations, the report indicated well enough the spirit of this contest.

In the later stages of the campaign, Nancy received support in a very surprising form. Margaret McMillan, a foundation member of the Labour Party, came down to Plymouth and spoke on her behalf. Even so, Nancy knew that the game might go against her. She was prepared for defeat. She decided that her only hope lay in a policy of *de l'audace et encore de l'audace*. Her boldest stroke was on the 27th May, three days before the poll. She went to what reporters described as a 'Red Stronghold'. She wisely took a reporter with her, a *Daily Express* man, so that the incident should become known. Here is an extract from the subsequent article in the *Express*:

' "So you are a pack of Bolshies eh?"'

'Lady Astor stood with her feet squarely planted, a large umbrella clasped by the ferrule in her right hand, like a club, and her smart cloche hat at a rakish tilt.

'She stood completely alone in the courtyard of the worst tenement of the worst street in Plymouth, a Communist stronghold, and glowered at balcony on balcony above her packed with more than a hundred shouting, shrieking, hostile women. "So you are a pack of Bolshies eh?" she challenged, waving the umbrella threateningly.

' "Better get away, Lady Astor," I warned, for a hefty woman with sacking over her head was reaching for a cabbage.

'She spun round fiercely. "Leave this to me." A man caught her roughly by the shoulder, and she raised the umbrella. He ran like a hare, and then she faced the crowd.

' "Too proud for the working woman, am I?" She laughed merrily, and struck an attitude, nose perked comically, and danced affectedly up and down outside the tenement.

' "They say I drink gin-and-bitters," she cried. "Hoy, you up there –" she pointed to a woman who had been shouting herself hoarse. "How many gin-and-bitters have I had with you, Pleasant?"

'A little dog flew snarling at the crowd. Somebody threw a brick at him. Like an avenging angel with her umbrella, Lady Astor dashed up, saved the little dog, and then, with arms akimbo, harangued the crowd. Her words burned like acid. With their own words and phrases she flayed and slashed at them.

' "Twenty years you have known me," she said. "Twenty years; and this Westwood man is brought against me. Who and what is he? He has only just come, and we do not even know what he looks like. I tell you, Cook[3] says this is the beginning of the revolution. They are out to smash the British Government. Believe me, don't believe darned idiots who come round touting fake promises."

3. Arthur James Cook (1883–1931). Socialist Trades Unionist, miners' leader and strike agitator. After the retirement from public affairs of Robert Smillie in 1924, Cook was the most prominent man on the extreme Left, and his stubborn insistence on the miners' claims was a major factor in bringing about the General Strike of 1926. He was supposed, as Lady Astor's remarks make plain, to be 'an extreme extremist', but, in fact, he had advised the miners' Union to accept defeat on the collapse of the General Strike and to reopen negotiations. History suggests that this was probably wise counsel which could have forced Baldwin out of his political and natural lethargy. As a conscientious democrat, however, he accepted the majority decision and in 1929 he could appear to be an uncompromising maniac. D.N.B.

'There was a moment's silence, and then they cheered her – cheered her like mad, and as her car left the place, roared and roared again: "Good old Nancy!" '

She only just made it. The results were:

Lady Astor	16,625	
W. Westwood	16,414	
T. H. Aggett	5,430	Majority 211

If there had not been a Liberal candidate she would probably have been defeated. It was the nearest to defeat that she came.

Bernard Shaw was, at the time, reluctantly enjoying an extension of the holiday enforced on him by Mrs Shaw. He was staying at the Hotel Danieli in Venice. He wrote to Nancy on the 4th June: 'The swing of the pendulum and the Unholy Alliance nearly got you; but a miss is as good as a mile. My secretary wired "Astor yes" the moment the figures were out, which rejoiced us. . . .'

By the Unholy Alliance, G.B.S. meant, of course, 'the Trade'.

The state of the parties in the House of Commons was now as follows:

Labour	287
Conservative	260
Liberal	59 (Others, including Independents, 9)

Ramsay MacDonald became Prime Minister for the second time, with the backing of the Liberal Party under Lloyd George. It was a similar position to that of 1924, with Labour far more dominant and the Liberal Party much weaker than then. It was thought that Labour and a socialist policy would now come into their own, but there was a difference between 1924 and 1929 which was little appreciated except by a few, and which was to be the cause of fatal Labour weakness. In 1927 Ramsay MacDonald had fallen seriously ill in America, and though he appeared to have made a complete recovery, and had performed with great brilliance in the General Election, he was never the same man again. His powers of leadership became shallow and theatrical. His deviousness and vanity increased and his will weakened.

Nancy was always as much interested in the feminist results as in the party results of an election. At the end of Baldwin's second administration the number of women members had risen from four to ten, the last to take her seat having been Miss Jennie Lee. After the election their numbers had risen to fourteen, three Conservatives, nine Labour, one Liberal and one Independent. The last two were Megan Lloyd George and Eleanor Rathbone. Mrs Wintringham had lost by a narrow margin and did not stand again. Mrs Hilton Philipson, not having stood, retired from politics and as Mabel Russell once again returned to the stage. She had a private member's bill concerning the registration of Nursing Homes to her credit. She was missed in the House as she had two unusual parliamentary merits: theatrical training had taught her to pitch her voice so that she was audible in every part of the Chamber, and she never spoke for more than five minutes.

Since Nancy's solemn undertaking not to be a 'sex-member' had proved unworkable years ago, she now had no hesitation in agitating for what might be called a 'Feminist Fourth Party'. There is an interesting personal account of how far she was prepared to go in that direction. It is written by Mary Agnes Hamilton, a Labour member. She called her essay, written for Michael Astor, *An Opponent's Viewpoint.*

'I was one of these new women M.P.s and I know we glowed, although probably, in the stolid British way, we did not show it, like crusaders. We believed in our mission. It was, therefore, in an almost solemn mood that a bunch of us proceeded to St Stephen's on the first day of swearing-in (which was also, as it turned out, a day of incessant photography), there bidden to lunch by Lady Astor. We recognised characteristic kindness in this gesture from the first woman to take her seat in the House. . . .

'At first, everything went well. Our hostess was gay, charming, delightfully easy and frank. She told us she fully realised how vexing it could have been to British women to have an American pioneer. But there had been certain advantages in her being the "ice-breaker" – her own phrase. The situation could have been alarming; she had not been alarmed. Familiar with many of the leading characters, introduced by Balfour and Lloyd George, she knew the ropes. Things were easier for one who functioned normally as a "popping gas jet" – again, her own phrase. This we fully accepted. To some extent we realised that the parliament she entered might easily have cowed a woman with less dash and aplomb. We knew that, while her bright repartee was amply publicised, much patient, strenuous and effective work got little or no notice.

'Although there was, therefore, nothing of resentment in our minds, the atmosphere changed when she moved on to what was, for her, obviously, the point and purpose of our being there. We were there to be told what we had to do. And what we had to do was to forget that we had been elected as representatives of the Labour Party, and its ideals and plans, and act, henceforth, as part of a Feminist phalanx. The nine Labour women among the 14 women M.P.s were to drop their Labour allegiance, and form the backbone of a Women's Party.

'This notion did not appeal to us. It would not, at any time, have appealed. Least of all did it appeal in 1929. We were "true believers". Sex equality, while an important item for long in the programme of our Party, was only one element in our creed. The timing of the proposal, further, seemed incredibly naive. In the new Government, Margaret Bondfield was a member of the Cabinet, and Susan Lawrence a junior minister. The Government had a tremendous task, in the social, the economic, and the international field; we were here to help in that task. Why, at this juncture, should we hive off and form a specifically female organisation?

'Thanks mainly to the gay charm of our hostess, the row that developed was a wholly good-natured one, but it was a row. She shouted at us; some of us (I fear I was one) shouted back at her. This she took in good part. She was disappointed in us, but she enjoyed a good row.

'Malice of any kind was wholly foreign to her. She could take, as well as give, hard knocks. That was that. Labour knocks she took in particularly good part. There was, indeed, in my time, a special friendliness in her relations with our backbenchers. Rough diamonds, like Ben Tillett, Jack Jones, David Kirkwood – to mention only a few – had a very warm spot in their hearts for her. Our intellectuals did not share it. They were apt to hear the somewhat strident tone and miss the eager human feeling behind it. They were "not amused", even by her pointed come-backs, her sharp thrusts all around the ring.

'A very gentle colleague remarked with a sigh as we came away from the lunch party I have described, "If only she did not have to boss us!" "Have to" was just; telling others what they ought to do was something she could not help.'

With only nine women members to choose from, the new Government could not make any dramatic advance in the appointment of women to the administration, but they did something. Margaret Bondfield was given the Ministry of Labour with a seat in the Cabinet.

George V was thus the first British sovereign whose hand was kissed by a female minister, an occasion, he said, on which he looked with especial pleasure. His words may say more for his politeness than his sincerity. Susan Lawrence became Parliamentary Secretary for the Ministry of Health, with Ellen Wilkinson as her Parliamentary Private Secretary. That was all, and this three-out-of-nine appointment was about as far as the Government could go in the distribution of 'the fruits of office'.

Whether or not the failure of her lunch-party in the House of Commons influenced Nancy, she made no comment on the appointments, not even on the first appointment of a woman to a place in the Cabinet. She probably shared the extreme irritation of Conservatives at a Labour victory which a more energetic Prime Minister would have avoided. There was a widespread Conservative desire that Baldwin should resign the party leadership, and so it might have fallen out, but that when in 1930 a party split seemed most probable Baldwin suddenly showed the spirit he seemed to have lost, in his famous counter-attacks against the Beaverbrook and Rothermere Press, and against the India diehards in his own party. The point to remember here is that Nancy was an orthodoxly angry member of the Opposition in this brief parliamentary period, even if, as Mrs Hamilton attests, there was some fellow-feeling between her and the rowdier members on the Labour back benches. Nancy would often make pointed allusions or audible asides on the condition of Jack Jones, the comic man of the House. On one occasion he went so far as to cry out: 'Jack Jones drunk is worth a lot more than Lady Astor sober,' a remark that Speaker Fitzroy[4] judged to be 'unparliamentary'.

She remained faithful to her causes, and the fact that G.B.S. supported them and admired her energy on their behalf, added to her crusading zeal. Women police, nursery schools, women prisoners and prisons, babies born in prison, allowances to widows, not one stop on that well-played feminist pipe was forgotten, and the ministries and the Whips' offices took note. Her influence persisted.

That Nancy used her suddenly inflamed friendship with G.B.S. for political ends is not to be denied. She was a politician. Why should she not? Anyway, she did. In July of 1929 an enormous garden-party for

4. The Hon. Edward Algernon Fitzroy (1869–1943) was a younger son of the 3rd Lord Southampton. He was Speaker from 1928 to 1943. He died suddenly while still in office. D.N.B.

Rhodes scholars was held at Cliveden. She persuaded G.B.S. to act as an extra host.

There were those who saw Nancy as a Circe, and G.B.S. as a foolish follower of Odysseus, to be debased by contact with the enchantress. They were wrong. Their error is due to the accident that the establishment of the great friendship coincided with the first manifest decline of Shaw's powers.

On the 15th October 1929 Shaw had agreed to open Astor Hall, a residential hostel for students of the University College of Exeter, and another of Waldorf's munificent gifts. As the central figure of the ceremony of opening, Shaw, with gold key in hand, decided to give his audience a real Shavian treat.

'The extraordinary devotion,' he began, 'of my friends Lord and Lady Astor to the City of Plymouth has always been a source of astonishment to me, because I have never been able to understand in what way the citizens of Plymouth have ever deserved it. . . .'

The speech was long and grew worse as it proceeded. Denunciation of universities in general was contradicted the next minute by praise of this particular one because it would be manned by the splendid population of Plymouth and the South West whom a moment before he had ridiculed for their incapacity to appreciate public spirit. Paradoxes of great silliness were mixed with flattery of equal silliness. 'I am very glad,' he said, 'that the name of the University will always be associated with Lord Astor, because I have a very large knowledge of what may be called the revolutionary world, not only in England but in Europe, and the most extreme Communist I have ever met is Lord Astor.' He finished by saying: 'I have done my best to make the sort of speech that is expected of me. That is, the sort of speech that is supposed to be scandalous. The joke is that I am saying the plainest common sense, and you all know it.'

In proposing a vote of thanks to G.B.S., Nancy said that there were few people who could speak as he did, and perhaps it was as well for the world that there were. Was this barbed? Probably not.

Shaw was news in those days, yet this speech was little noticed in the Press and only given a full report in the *Devon and Exeter Gazette*. It seems that even the editors of the sensational papers did not wish to waste their space on such embarrassing foolishness. Shaw's great days were over.

Nancy's friendship with Bernard and Charlotte Shaw intensified another friendship, that with T. E. Lawrence. It seems that she first met him through Lionel Curtis in the days of his first fame when he was living at All Souls College, Oxford, between 1919 and 1921. The Astor archive has one letter from her to him of 1924 in which she says 'I am one of the people who are very wealthy and would like a copy of your book, but I don't promise to read it. However, as that is your wish you won't mind.' On Lawrence's return from India where he had been stupidly posted by the R.A.F. at his own request, and where he had got into trouble through his indiscretions, he was posted to the R.A.F. station at Cattewater, Plymouth, in March 1929. He was now Nancy's neighbour.

When arranging for the reading of *The Apple Cart*, G.B.S. evidently asked Nancy to invite Lawrence and he replied from Cattewater on the 12th March: 'Dear Lady Astor, I'd immensely appreciate hearing that G.B.S. reading, and if I can possibly wangle leave for Saturday and Sunday I will attend (probably in uniform, but I shan't mind your being differently dressed!) on the 23rd.

'If I do not turn up, then please blame the R.A.F. rather than my expectant self. Yours sincerely T. E. Shaw.'

How like Lawrence to drag in the question of clothes! No one would have minded whether he appeared in uniform or a civilian suit, or in his Arabian robes, but to him clothes, especially if they caused him to be 'differently dressed', meant much. After this the letters are frequent, and the friendship became close, almost as close as that between him and Charlotte Shaw. Maurice Collis has given the opinion that in Nancy, as undoubtedly in Mrs Shaw, he sought a mother-substitute.

But the mutual relationship was chiefly but not only one of sentiment. In February 1931 there was a flying-boat accident which Lawrence believed was due to faulty regulations. He intrigued for reform through unofficial political pressure on the Air Ministry. He succeeded, and No. 434 of his published letters shows that Nancy was one of his clandestine helpers. Just how she helped is not known. But love of intrigue was not a bond between them. Unlike Lawrence, Nancy had little taste for it.

Many years after this time, when Nancy was old, her niece, Nancy Lancaster, asked her about her friendship with T. E. Lawrence, and what was its basis apart from her relish of famous people. Nancy Lancaster received the surprising answer: 'Oh he was a beau, and I've always liked beaux.' Augustus John's and Eric Kennington's portraits of him show that he had an essential handsomeness which his Arabian dress could enhance and his dreary uniform not extinguish. (He never seems to have been drawn or painted in ordinary clothes, and photographs of him in civilian dress are relatively uncommon.) He had bright blue eyes as brilliant and arresting as Nancy's own. In common with her and G.B.S. he was an actor, but in total contrast to them, his acting expressed both inner confusion and deep inner falsity. This Nancy never knew. G.B.S. and Charlotte Shaw discovered the painful truth much later, and there is no evidence that they disillusioned Nancy, or attempted to do so. They also loved T. E. Lawrence.

His letters to her are very typical of him, coy, mannered, boastful in a subdued, indirect way, self-pitying and playing 'hard to get'. Nancy had asked him to Cliveden and Elliot Terrace and, in a letter congratulating her on her 1929 election success, he refused her hospitality in these terms: 'Alas! I can't come to Cliveden. Nor will I use Elliot Terrace. Thank you all the same. The best way to be content in the service is to stick to it, taking only such reliefs as one's own pocket affords. The helplessness of money: that's a very often forgotten point.

'Some day, if you revisit Plymouth quietly, ring up 1634, and we'll brighten the life of the Exchange girls again.'

This letter represented an aspiration rather than a rule of conduct. Lawrence shared with Nancy a discriminating but strong taste for famous people and, in any case, if Nancy made up her mind that someone was going to be a friend and frequent visitor, the most reasonable course was to surrender. She was sure to have her way in the end. She did on this occasion. Lawrence became her friend. He became a frequent visitor, at Elliot Terrace more often than at Cliveden, Sandwich, or St James's Square, and he became also a friend of the family, of the younger generation equally with Nancy and Waldorf. To them all he seems to have shown his attractive qualities, the side of his character that made him beloved by many and very different sorts of people. With the Astors he could lay aside, if only temporarily and spasmodically, his emotional sickness. But the Astors were very famous and, in all innocence, they presented him with a temptation towards that exhibitionism against which he struggled, with varying success, during his whole life. Partly through his association with them he got into trouble before long. Or so it seems. It is impossible to be certain about what really happened as we know little of the incident except through Lawrence himself, and through David Garnett and Basil Liddell Hart, both of whom had their information from him. Neither Garnett nor Hart realised at the time they wrote that their friend, along with many virtues, was a pathological myth-maker, 'an infernal liar' as Charlotte Shaw described him when she at length found out the dreadful truth.

This is what is said to have happened. In September 1929 the air-race for the Schneider Trophy was held in Plymouth. Lawrence's commanding officer, Wing-Commander Sydney Smith, was a member of the organising committee, and Lawrence, acting as Smith's clerk, was much occupied in carrying out the arrangements. On the great day, so the story runs, Lawrence was much in evidence, taking responsibility, at the request of Italo Balbo who was leading the Italian team, to see that the slipways for the Italian machines were as clean as those used by the R.A.F. Balbo, Lawrence asserted, was an old friend, though how the friendship arose, if it did, remains very puzzling. The Minister for Air in MacDonald's Government was Lord Thomson (who was to die a year later in the airship R101 disaster), and he is said to have been angered at seeing Lawrence, or Aircraftman Shaw, hobnobbing not only with the world-famous aeronaut Balbo, but with Winston Churchill, Austen Chamberlain, Lord Birkenhead, Sir Philip Sassoon, and Nancy. Thereafter Lawrence was condemned to dismissal from the R.A.F., but (after influential intercession) allowed to remain on condition that he never left the country except with special permission, and ceased communication with the famous politicians above-named. To these cruel conditions he consented, and when Nancy invited him to Elliot Terrace some three months later he replied: 'Dear Lady Astor, What an undisciplined person you are! I was given positive orders to cease from meeting you, so far as that lay in my power: so I can't come and see you.' (403. Collected Letters.)

If there is any truth in this story of Lord Thomson's harsh treatment of Lawrence, then it is likely to be connected with the fact that, in India, Lawrence was widely credited with having conducted an immense secret movement on the North West Frontier resulting in the fall of King Amanullah of Afghanistan. This Kim-inspired Great Game nonsense contained no particle of fact, but it had led to awkward questions in the House of Commons (where Nancy rose up in Lawrence's defence), and was taken seriously by European statesmen and diplomats in plenty. It may have come to Lord Thomson's knowledge that Lawrence himself had been instrumental in spreading the rumours, and that he was addicted to intrigue. If so, his action, if ruthless, was understandable. On the other hand, the whole story may be just another of Lawrence's crazy inventions, like the yarn, which he endeavoured to impress on Nancy among others, that in 1925 he was offered the post of British High Commissioner in Egypt.

According to Lawrence's account, his senior officers conceded that he might continue his friendship with Bernard Shaw. Lawrence told Basil Liddell Hart that G.B.S. expressed some annoyance that he was not considered politically important enough to come within the ban. Whatever his faults, G.B.S. was a big man and petty vanity of this kind was quite out of character. This part of the story can be safely put on the rubbish heap.

At the end of 1929 Nancy was involved in a family crisis which has been the subject of much legend, indignation, and almost 'anything but to the purpose'. For that reason it needs to be told in detail.

In December 1929 her daughter Phyllis, or Wissie to give her her name, the beauteous daughter of a beauteous mother, and the adored of all the young men in London who knew her, was staying at Kelmarsh Hall in Northamptonshire with her cousin Nancy whose first husband, Ronald Tree, was a Joint-Master of the Pytchley Hunt. On the 18th she rode to hounds. The ground was dangerous for riding as is usually the case when a rapid thaw follows on a hard frost. In the afternoon, while the hounds were running through Guilsborough Park, Wissie rode her horse at a fence. The horse slid and could not get a grip to jump from the slippery ground. It crashed through the fence, fell on its forelegs, throwing Wissie, and then rolled on her, the pommel of the side-saddle striking into her back.

It so happened that Mr Henry Tiarks, who was also staying at Kelmarsh, was jumping the same fence at the same time, about a hundred yards away. He saw the fall, called to Ronald Tree who was a little ahead of him, and galloped over to Wissie. About six hunt followers heard his cry and came up to help Wissie who lay on the ground, conscious but unable to move. They unhinged a gate on which they carried her to Guilsborough House, where she was laid on a table. The local doctor and Doctor Whitling of Market Harborough came and examined her but found no sign of major injury. Numbed, she felt little pain, and this may have misled them. An ambulance was called to take her to Kelmarsh. In the meantime Ronald Tree rang up Wissie's mother in London and broke the news of the accident to her. She said that she and Waldorf would come immediately by car to Kelmarsh, bringing a Christian Science practitioner with her.

Henry Tiarks was standing by and he asked Ronald Tree to let him ring up a man he knew, the eminent radiologist Harold Graham Hodgson. Tiarks was the only person there who had seen the fall and he felt sure that the injury was serious. He knew that Hodgson was the only radiologist in London who had a large portable X-ray apparatus. Tiarks was also uneasy at the thought of this case being in the hands of Christian Science practitioners alone. He urged that in any case it could not be against any Christian Science principle to take a photograph to establish what the real or imagined injury might be. Ronald Tree agreed and Henry Tiarks rang up his friend, beseeching him to 'drop everything' and drive to Kelmarsh immediately, so as to arrive ahead of Lady Astor. When he heard why he was being sent for, Hodgson needed no persuading and started off with his technical assistant and the apparatus within minutes. He arrived at Kelmarsh at about nine in the evening. He undertook an immediate X-ray.

While the examination was still going forward and now in its last stages, Nancy and Waldorf arrived with the practitioner. Both were, of course, in a state of great agitation. It so happened that among the guests at Kelmarsh there was a woman who had been a friend of Nancy for many years. This friend had the impression, as Alice Longworth always had, that deep in Nancy's mind and feeling there was a certain fear of reality, a sleepless sense of insecurity, which she usually disguised, even to herself, but could not at this moment. It was her belief that Nancy's Christian Science was in some sort a shield against brute fact. However that was, Nancy clung with fierce optimism to the fact that at the first examination the doctors had only discovered superficial injuries.

When after a wait that seemed endless Graham Hodgson came into the room, she said: 'Well – it's nothing much, is it?' Graham Hodgson replied: 'I'm afraid you are mistaken. It's very serious indeed.' He then explained that the thrust of the saddle had caused structural injury to the spine in the area of the small of the back, and that had the area been higher in the spine it could have produced paralysis. As it was, instant medical action could and might prevent a lesser disaster. The doctors present had only been able to render first-aid; a thorough rearticulation needed to be done by an orthopaedic surgeon.

Nancy went white and her friend thought for a second that she was going to faint. The moment passed in a flash, and Nancy was her usual unflinching self. But she was at a terrible moment of crisis and choice. She and Waldorf had to make a crucial spiritual decision. Were they to follow the path of Christian Science or the conventional path of medical science? Were they to abandon the doctrine by which they lived to soothe their parental anxieties?

Their friends besought them to heed Graham Hodgson's advice. At length Nancy proposed a compromise. If a doctor must be called, which was against their faith, only one doctor was acceptable: Sir Crisp English who had successfully operated on herself and Philip Lothian. This was agreed. Nancy telephoned to him and he told her he would start immediately. He arrived at Kelmarsh late at night. He only knew that Wissie had been injured by a fall out hunting, but when he learned that this was a case of spinal injury, he flew into a rage. He pointed out that he was an abdominal surgeon and thus wholly unqualified to undertake any spinal case. Calling him in had only had the effect of delaying the right treatment. He expressed himself in terms of strong indignation.

At this Nancy's and Waldorf's resistance broke down. They agreed to follow English's advice. He thereupon telephoned to the leading orthopaedic surgeon in London, Thomas Fairbank, who arrived at Kelmarsh in the morning of the 19th. After examining Wissie, he also expressed himself with some anger. He insisted to Nancy and Waldorf that Wissie must be put in plaster of Paris immediately and that this ought to have been done twelve hours ago. Nancy raised objections. The argument was heated, and made more difficult by the fact that Fairbank was somewhat deaf. At length Nancy withdrew her objections and the task of rearticulation and applying plaster went ahead. Fairbank's ministrations were successful, though Wissie's return to a normal state of health was long and painful.

It is here that the legends begin. It was indignantly alleged, and is still alleged to the present day, that Wissie was forced to endure needless pain and was denied total recovery, by the fanaticism of her parents' Christian Science, the major blame being attributed to Nancy. As the above recital of the facts makes clear, Wissie was given the best medical

attention available, and the only blame that the Astors incur is in having
delayed orthopaedic treatment by twelve hours or so. It is impossible
now to know whether this made any difference. Wissie's recovery was
in fact complete, or else it would have hardly been possible for her to
bear children in the ordinary way, as she was to do a few years later.
The legends, in fact, are mere calumny.

What is most extraordinary about the whole episode is that the
legends were invented not by enemies but by Nancy herself. She came
to believe them and to describe Wissie's recovery as a proof of Mrs
Eddy's teaching. Fifteen years or so after this she was talking to Henry
Tiarks about Christian Science and insisting that doctors were unnecessary and a hindrance to the truth. (This was in 1944.) He asked her
if she remembered the facts concerning Wissie's accident, and if she
would go so far as to say that Wissie had then had no help from doctors.
Nancy replied emphatically that no doctor had attended Wissie at
that time. Henry Tiarks said: 'Not Graham Hodgson? Not Crisp
English? Not Fairbank?' She replied: 'Most certainly not.' In her
autobiographical sketch she stated much the same, though she did
introduce the name of English as an adviser.

No faith is fully understandable except to those who can share it.
Those who cannot must attempt sympathy nonetheless. Before condemning Nancy and Waldorf in this matter, one must remember that
at this moment their faith was under very strong challenge from H. A.
L. Fisher's book published shortly before. But if any faith except the
most vile deserves sympathy, the same is not true of distortion of fact,
of which Nancy was undoubtedly guilty. Yet, as so often in her life,
ordinary judgements do not apply. Let this be considered: where
there is deliberate distortion it is usually exculpatory in motive, but in
this instance something like the opposite is true. If Nancy had left the
facts alone, she would have been admired as a loving parent who acted
against inclination for the sake of her child; instead of being execrated
as an unfeeling fanatic, except by an extremist minority of her Church.
She courted the approbation of that minority in the spirit that might
have moved an early Christian. She stood for higher truth, but is there
in truth such a virtue as that of 'the noble lie'?

Almost nothing, oddly enough, of Nancy's and Waldorf's reaction
to this crisis is preserved in the letters of this time. The exceptions are
interesting. One concerns Philip Kerr. 'Just a line,' he wrote on the
24th December, 'to thank you again for what you did about Wissie.

It was, I think, a real step in advance; the right answer to the Fisher book & the new attacks on C.S. I welcome these, they are the tests and proofs of all true religion, & C.S. will be all the stronger if it is able to sustain them humbly & without fanaticism but with demonstration of power.' (Note the absence of any reference to Whitling, English, Fairbank, or Graham Hodgson.)

Charlotte Shaw wrote a letter of sympathy on the 31st December. It is very puzzling. It suggests that she held some form of faith-healing belief or healing by thought-transference, similar to if distinct from Nancy's. Here are her words: 'It was splendid to get your letter: the first real news I had of Wissie. Now I can work for her much better. Give her my truest love. I have always been so fond of her. I hate to think of her missing all the Christmas fun. But – well!' That is her first reference. A second one occurs in a letter of the 12th January. She wrote: 'Splendid news that Wissie is back at Cliveden. It seems extraordinarily different thinking of her there. The thoughts seem to go to her so much more willingly – to her own home – where I can picture her. I do long to have a talk straight – not letters – with you about her. It seems long to wait until the 31st, but I suppose it has to be. It is something I could say which *might possibly* help. But of course I know you are up to every possible thing that can be done, far more than I can be.' There is no further reference in Charlotte Shaw's letters to this episode.

A letter of T. E. Lawrence to Nancy written on the 19th January 1930 (the one already quoted in which he declares he is forbidden to visit her) contains these words which make it clear that Charlotte Shaw's proposition (whatever it was) had not been welcomed by Nancy: 'You are *distinctly unsatisfactory* about Wissie: please allow Mrs Shaw, who is as wise as 10,000 of you and me, to work for her and say the right word.' The phrases 'work for her' and 'the right word' certainly suggest something very like Christian Science. Were they both brought under Christian Science influence by Nancy? It is unlikely but just possible that Charlotte Shaw was. She occasionally accompanied Nancy to Christian Science services. As for T. E. Lawrence there is no other evidence in the great mass of evidence surrounding him, pointing in that direction. There is an enigma here, one which must fascinatingly and teasingly remain.

Some landmarks in her life vanished in the late twenties and early thirties. Asquith died in February 1928. Her and Waldorf's old sup-

porter, Lord Henry Cavendish Bentinck, was among the defeated
Tories in the 1929 election and he did not stand again. He died in 1931.
In March 1930 Arthur Balfour died at the age of 82. He had been unable to attend the reading of *The Apple Cart* at 4 St James's Square, and
his last correspondence with Nancy was to ask her to let him have a
copy of it, but he died before she could get one to him. In April of
the year of the election her old lover, Lord Revelstoke, died at the age
of 66. Her ambivalent attitude towards that ill-used man persisted to
the end, and Nancy remained for him the one and irreplaceable love
of his life.

Philip Kerr changed his name. In March 1930 he succeeded his
cousin as 11th Marquess of Lothian. From now on he will be referred to
by that name which he was to make famous. He wrote to Nancy
after his predecessor's death: 'The guillotine has fallen, or rather the
portcullis, & I am within the golden chamber, with my blood permanently changed in colour & my name forgotten. It is damnable, & as
Waldorf once said, the awful thing is that you begin to like it.'

A once large and ugly landmark, since removed, was now restored
for a short while but on a less imposing scale; in 1928 Horatio Bottomley came out of prison. *John Bull* had failed and passed to other ownership during his imprisonment, but Bottomley, resuming his pose as the
friend of the people, courageously started a new paper on the model
of the old and gave it the name *John Blunt*. He advertised it lavishly
and headlined his opening leading article 'I Have Paid But –'. As
before he devoted frequent paragraphs and articles to attacking the
Astors, Nancy in particular. Bottomley kept dupes to the end, but he
did not have enough of them now to float a newspaper. His attacks
were offensive and ineffectual. After a short career *John Blunt* came to
an end and Bottomley, supported by his valiantly loyal daughter,
lived the rest of his life, which ended in 1933, in poverty and obscur-
ity.

But as this dedicated foe went down, it appeared that another and
far more formidable one rose up in his stead. This was Professor
Harold Laski, the supreme intellectual, in many eyes, of the Left Wing,
and the most talented and persuasive of Socialist thinkers in Britain.
On the 19th April 1930 he published a scathing article against Nancy
in the *Daily Herald*. He called it 'Lady Astor. The Pollyanna of Politics'.
(Pollyanna is not a learned Greek term, but a reference to a character
in American fiction, famous for her unrelenting optimism.) The article

was among two or three of the most deadly attacks ever made on Nancy. Its aim was to show up this millionairess reformist, not as an evil person, but as an unimportant one who was utterly irrelevant to modern politics. The article was condescendingly good-humoured in tone and informed throughout by contempt.

It was one thing to be abused by Bottomley, by a coarse-grained and despised demagogue in coarse terms, another and infinitely worse thing to be dissected without anaesthetic by a respected man of keen mind. But there was something that the gross Bottomley understood better than the perceptive Laski, namely the art of propaganda. Bottomley knew that to succeed in a propaganda venture, one attack on your opponent makes no great difference. You have, in the words of Lord Beaverbrook, to 'go at him and at him'. These crudities were foreign to the mind of Laski, and with the self-satisfied myopia of his kind, he did not like to recognise their existence. He had written what he believed to be the truth about Nancy Astor. *'Quod scripsi scripsi'* – such was his spirit. Nancy, no doubt on Waldorf's advice, attempted no answer. The attack was forgotten. It was a lucky escape.

During these years at the turn of the decade Nancy had a private anxiety which was to increase and become the cause of great distress during the rest of her life. This was concerned with her beloved eldest son Bobbie Shaw. He was extraordinarily handsome, inheriting to the full the good looks of both his parents. Unfortunately he had also inherited his father's unbalance of mind. Many men of his age who had spent what would have been their university years in the trenches found themselves psychologically maimed. A frighteningly large proportion never wholly recovered. In the case of Bobbie Shaw the predicament was intensified by an ingrained emotional abnormality. His relations with his mother were painful and complex in a way that psychological science has made familiar. From early days he adored her, lavished on her a love that was abnormal in its extremity, and then, when he reached manhood, he came also to resent her, to react against her tyrannical possessiveness and openly accused her of wrecking his life; yet the mutual love persisted and this caused the relationship to be one of hardly bearable pain. Bobbie could play on Nancy's emotions as no one else could. He, and perhaps he alone, knew how to break her defences. He could reduce her to hysterical weeping, and in moments of ungovernable resentment he did not hesitate to do so.

It is easy to overdramatise this situation. One must not forget, for example, that Bobbie Shaw had inherited his mother's humour and there were occasions when he played pranks on her with a wit that must have delighted her. It will be remembered that one of the controversial scandals of 1928 was the publication of a novel about lesbianism, written by Miss Radclyffe Hall and called *The Well of Loneliness*. In August of 1928 there came a somewhat reproving letter from Messrs Hatchards reminding Lady Astor that the book had been suppressed at the instance of the Home Office, for which reason they could not legally supply the work to Mr R. G. Shaw at her request, as her ladyship had ordered. This is the kind of absurdity which must have made Nancy laugh.

But the main current of their unhappy relationship was nearly always a worsening one. Bobbie was a destructive rebel; destructive because he had so acute an insight into the psychological origins of his situation. When Nancy and his step-father took up teetotalism, Bobbie took up drink. Prohibitionist Cliveden was not lacking in 'speakeasies', as the children grew up, and in Bobbie's rooms on the top floor was the great speakeasy. It is difficult to know how aware or otherwise Nancy was about this: her passionate love of Bobbie made her liable to be self-blinded and, as mentioned already, she had, side by side with her intolerance, an unexpected broadmindedness. In June 1929, however, Nancy had to recognise the extent to which her son had grown irresponsible.

He had, in accordance with his step-father's wishes, chosen the army as his career. (Waldorf seems to have wanted all his own sons to go into the army, though none of them, except Jakie for a short time, became professional soldiers.) Bobbie Shaw at this time was a senior subaltern in the Royal Horse Guards, the 'Blues'. One evening in early June of 1929, when Bobbie was on duty, he was found drunk in the mess by the adjutant who ordered him to his room and appointed another officer in his place. The commanding officer found that he 'had no alternative' but to request Bobbie to 'send in his papers', to resign his commission in effect, so as to avoid a court-martial. This Bobbie did. It was a fatal moment. From then on Bobbie very gradually began to lose control over himself. In the society in which he lived, and where he was esteemed as a skilled horseman, and even in the family, little of his degeneration was noticed, but Nancy instinctively knew of it. She looked on in anguish as she saw what was happening to the being whom she loved above all others.

Nothing in Nancy's life testifies more to the essential nobility of her character than her conduct towards Bobbie Shaw. It is not hard to imagine her emotions being driven by exasperation from love to counter-love, and from disapproval to active dislike or even hate, as often happens in such cases. In this case nothing of the kind happened. She was driven to the utmost extremes of exasperation by Bobbie's perverse resentment, but she never withheld her love. If she can be accused of inordinate admiration of success, she cannot be accused of indulging any worldly scorn of Bobbie's failure. She knew his secret. She knew, as he possibly did not know, that he was not to be blamed for what he did. Only people who have been involved in such cases can understand how much generosity of mind is then needed to maintain justice of mind.

This scandal of June 1929 was only a portent of what was to come. What needs to be stressed at this point of the story is that, faced with the scandal, Nancy and Waldorf behaved with a moderation and an understanding that amazed even their admirers. It would have been natural for them to have had cold relations with Bobbie's commanding officer in the Blues. On the contrary, they went out of their way to show that they appreciated his difficult situation as a friend of the family. They invited him and his wife to Cliveden within the month.

As for Bobbie, they both made it abundantly clear that for all his misconduct he had a home, and a loving home at Cliveden. They avoided scrupulously any suggestion that he owed them great reparation for the great pain he had caused them. They showed themselves not only generous but enlightened. At this time Bobbie was still young but not very young, nearly thirty; he had reached that awkward age when the follies of youth still present a temptation and are not so easily forgiven as they were five years before. It has been said, notably by Nancy's friend Freya Stark in her masterly book *Perseus in the Wind*, that generosity is not the privilege of those who give; that, to put a gloss on a sublime utterance, however temerariously, it is blessed not only to give but to know how to receive. The unhappy Bobbie Shaw was too undisciplined, too incapable of discipline, too much under the influence of an accursed heredity, to be able to respond to the generosity of Nancy and Waldorf. He became a cynic and a secret debauchee. He

gloried in his ingratitude, at one moment, and the next he was overwhelmed with remorse and despair at what he had done to the human
being he most loved. He lost hope in himself. There are hundreds of
photographs of family groups, of weekend house-parties, of large or
small gatherings at Cliveden in which he figures, and in not one of them
is he ever shown smiling. When he lost hope in himself, he never
recovered it. To the very end Nancy hoped for her son.

As noted in the previous chapter, Nancy the born oppositionist was
never at her most dramatic when she was officially in opposition. It
follows that any account of her life between mid-1929 to late 1930 has
an untidy shape, one that would defy the skill of any dramatist. This
untidy shape was to be lost and a tidy one regained in the next and
very dramatic year of her life, 1931. Let the present chapter, therefore,
in keeping with its subject, end with something of a rag-bag quality;
with some oddments which may correct the generalisations to which
all biographies are prone.

Nancy had no musical education and no pretensions to any understanding or enjoyment, let alone criticism, of musical accomplishment.
It has been stated that there were no musical lions at Cliveden. Again a
qualification must be made. A sudden friendship between Nancy and
Ethel Smyth flared up in early 1929, when the composer and former
militant suffragette was seventy-one years old. ('My dear Lady Astor,'
she begins the correspondence on New Year's Day, 'May I call you
Nancy and, if I am not too old, will you call me Ethel.') They had
much in common, high spirits, burning feminist zeal, and a taste for
farce. They met, almost certainly, through Bernard Shaw who admired
Ethel Smyth's work and was shocked that, while it received abundant
recognition in Germany, it was neglected in her own country. The
friendship between her and Nancy was put to practical use: it seemed
to Ethel Smyth that women orchestral players suffered from prejudice
in the matter of appointments to orchestras, especially in what she
described as 'The Wireless Orchestra' then being formed by the BBC.
Nancy took up the cause, with some effect as appears from their
correspondence, though Ethel Smyth's compositions were probably
as meaningless to her as they had been to her patron King Edward VII

Electioneering in Plymouth

G.B.S. *Above:* the centre of attention on the terrace at Cliveden. *Below:* with Nancy and Waldorf in Soviet Russia

whose only recorded comment on her work was 'That's the second time I've been woken up by that damned *Rrrow*.'[5]

On the 6th March 1930 Mr Baldwin inaugurated the statue of Mrs Pankhurst in the Victoria Tower Gardens by the Palace of Westminster. As Prime Minister in the previous administration he had commissioned the statue. Nancy was accorded a prominent place. Robed as a Doctor of Music, Dame Ethel Smyth conducted the orchestra and choir and, judging by photographs of her at the ceremony, its comic aspect did not escape her.

In 1930 G.B.S. set about the republication with additions of a collected edition of his works. Nancy, with accustomed boldness, asked him to send her a set. He answered on 9th August:

'Harpy, Where do you think I can get a set for you? You would have to sell Cliveden to buy one.

'However, I'll give you mine. . . .'

In February of 1931 Nancy made a speech in the House of Commons which brought her into immense temporary unpopularity out of all proportion to the event. It was one of the most ludicrous episodes of her life. Edwin Scrymgeour still represented Dundee in the House of Commons and he still carried the standard of total prohibition on high, still convinced that it had been placed in his hands by the Creator of all things. Once again he introduced a private member's bill to establish total prohibition in Great Britain. On the 13th February it came up for the Second Reading. This time Nancy did not absent herself, unwisely, and spoke on the subject very unwisely. She entertained the House with characteristic indiscretions, recalling to the minds of members the enormous fortunes made out of intoxicants, so great, she said, and so wrongly honoured that the Peerage might well be renamed 'the Beerage'; whereat Speaker Fitzroy was moved to interpose: 'The noble lady must not say anything disrespectful of the other House,' and the laughter in the Commons redoubled. But then she suddenly lost the sympathy of her audience, and next day of the whole country. She uttered a blasphemy.

Great Britain was reeling from what was believed to be an immense national humiliation. A cricket team visiting Australia, under Mr Percy Chapman, had in the winter of 1928-9 won back the Ashes by

5. Sir Thomas Beecham in a BBC interview. He heard the story from one of the King's staff when Edward VII attended the first performance under Beecham of Ethel Smyth's opera *The Wreckers*.

a resounding victory of four matches to one. But when the Australians came to England in the summer of 1930 the Ashes were once again, by a narrow margin, lost. It was a tragedy (to a cricketer) of an utterly unspeakable kind. And Nancy had the effrontery to say 'that the reason England lost the Ashes was that the Australians did not drink'.

It would be fatiguing to a reader to recall in any detail the Press explosion that followed this remark which, in the House, was succeeded by 'interruptions'. Let it only be remembered that almost every paper in the country indulged in impressive denunciation of this 'hateful', 'cruel', 'foolish', 'brutal' slur upon our blameless cricketers. Lord Hawke, the Chairman of the Marylebone Cricket Club, was moved to inform the Press that he had hoped that 'our cricketers would be spared this insult'. Mr Chapman was understandably annoyed, but so, possibly to Nancy's great surprise, was the victorious Australian team. The idea that they were teetotalers did not please these men. Several of them, when interviewed by the Press, asserted that they had no sympathy with Lady Astor's analysis.

It was one of those spontaneous remarks that brought her into needless trouble, and (one must remember with regret) became more frequent from this time on when her self-confidence in Parliament often turned to over-confidence. Her best days as a parliamentarian were over by 1930, though she did not recognise this, any more than G.B.S. recognised that after *The Apple Cart* he had little more to teach the world, even though he remained a force. She remained a force, and a valuable one, to the end of her parliamentary life, but as a political force she began, even as early as this, her twelfth year in Parliament, to become a declining force. Such was her vitality, such was her intense sincerity, that few people recognised this until her last years as a member of the House, more than ten years from now.

Let the last paragraph be taken from Michael Astor's book *Tribal Feeling*. To the great names he mentions one may add that of Lytton Strachey who visited Cliveden frequently till shortly before his death in 1932. 'The prodigious talkers. Were there ever such talkers brought together in one place? Bernard Shaw commanded an audience and his talk demanded one. But J. L. Garvin, Walter Elliot, Lionel Curtis and Geoffrey Dawson had to compete. Garvin would go ten minutes, without eating when he was talking, otherwise he lost his place. Lionel Curtis on a Federated Europe evoked a sense of timelessness, of something inexorable which had to be stated and had to be heard, impervious to Bobbie's aside, voicing our unspoken thoughts, of "Can't anyone tell him to shut up?" which carried to his end of the table and roused my mother to ask Bobbie to shut up, and through the various requests of "shut up" Lionel boomed on, noble and unbowed. The food, which seemed incidental, was excellent though somewhat rich. The Christian Scientists, who were silent when talk was political, were the real enthusiasts at eating. It was their only vice. And drink – hock and claret and port and brandy, appeared when there was company. Teetotal principles were not obligatory for guests.'

Most of the material in the foregoing chapter has been drawn from the contemporary Press and the Astor archive, as indicated in the text. In his biography of Shaw, *George Bernard Shaw. His Life, Work and Friends* (London, 1956), St John Ervine has surprisingly little to say about the friendship of G.B.S. and Lady Astor, but what he has to say is valuable. He seems to have underestimated its prominence in his and her lives. His book is very stimulating and the reader is either in violent agreement or violent conflict with the author, almost throughout. The references to T. E. Lawrence, when not drawn from the T.E.L.–Lady Astor correspondence are taken from the Letters of *T. E. Lawrence*, edited by David Garnett (London, 1938), *T. E. Lawrence by his Friends*, edited by A. W. Lawrence (London, 1937), *Lawrence of Arabia*, by Richard Aldington (first published 1955, republished with an introduction by Christopher Sykes 1969), and the important biographical work by Colin Simpson and Philip Knightley, *The Secret Lives of Lawrence of Arabia*. The events surrounding the hunting accident to Lady Astor's daughter, now Lady Ancaster, follow Press reports of the time, and information given to the writer by Lady Ancaster herself and Mr Henry Tiarks. The political incidents as described owe much to the article originally written by Mary Agnes Hamilton for Michael Astor, and to the D.N.B. article on Ramsay MacDonald.

Chapter 16

1931

NANCY and Waldorf celebrated their silver wedding quietly with their family at Cliveden in March 1931. The City of Plymouth presented them later with a silver model of Drake's ship *The Golden Hind*. This tender commemoration was not reflected in any softening of Nancy's parliamentary style. A month later, on the 14th April, she delivered one of the most swingeing attacks she made at any time in the House, her victim being Arthur Greenwood, the Minister of Health.

This was not mere party warfare. She wrote to Charlotte Shaw: 'Never in your life have you seen anything worse than Arthur Greenwood and Susan Lawrence on Housing and Slum Clearance in the House of Commons yesterday. The most reactionary Conservatives in the world couldn't have done worse than that couple have at the Ministry of Health, and I happen to know from the inside that they are breaking the hearts of some of the go-aheads in the Ministry.'

Parliament, both on the Government and Opposition sides, was in a state of angry alarm. The Government was manifestly failing to deal with the difficulties which faced it. Yet, in spite of the evidence provided by her merciless assault on Greenwood, Nancy did not play and did not wish to play a great part in the political drama of that year. The reason was that the drama almost exclusively concerned economics, and this was an area in which she had little knowledge. She was certain only of one thing: that the Government must be changed because the economic crisis was proving far too much for the glowing crusaders of 1929, so well evoked by Mary Agnes Hamilton. Unemployment rose to terrifying percentages of the labour force everywhere in the civilised world. Something must be done, everyone said, but just what nobody knew.

Against this background of widespread perplexity one must appreciate the dramatic events, far more dramatic then than similar events would be now, in which Nancy and Waldorf were involved in the summer of 1931.

For many years, since long before the Revolution, Bernard Shaw had been known in Russia, though, as elsewhere, his merits and faults had been much misappreciated. He had been denigrated in Russia by the sort of people from whom he might have expected praise, and praised by people expected to dislike him. In 1931, however, his fame had grown very great in Russia and he was the only contemporary British writer whose name was known to the man in the street. As he always described himself as a Communist, it was assumed that he was one within the accepted meaning, and therefore Russia's most valuable ally in the outside world. Even if the contradictions in his character and principles had been known, it would probably have made little difference. Russians have a taste for sages. Tolstoy preached poverty and lived well; the fact was known to everyone and made no difference to the popular acclaim which surrounded him; he was a sage and that was that. G.B.S. was a sage too, and nothing else mattered.

His position as sage was greatly enhanced at this time by *The Apple Cart*. Though there was little Communism in his last major work, it contained telling and destructive criticism of government by parliamentary cabinet, and therefore of the parliamentary system. This made a great impression on Soviet authorities and party members, and it followed that G.B.S. did not only have an increased reputation with the Russian public at large, but also official approval. He was seen as a hero, for it was assumed that he must have shown considerable courage in producing and publishing such a play in a parliamentarily governed country, in defiance of the parliamentary police. Its royalist bias seems to have been completely and perhaps rightly overlooked: the moral of the play is not in favour of royalty but of dictatorship, which Russia was enjoying ever more openly under Josef Stalin.

In these circumstances G.B.S. was invited in late May or early June to visit Russia. The proposal probably originated with Madame Litvinoff, the English wife of the then Commissar for Foreign Affairs, Maxim Litvinoff. At all events Sokolnikoff, the Russian ambassador in London, suggested to Shaw that he should visit his country. What is odd about the whole venture is that the invitation was for midsummer when the heat in Moscow and the adjoining country is overpowering. G.B.S. knew that Charlotte Shaw had not the physical health for such a journey at such a time, so he replied that he was glad to accept the invitation if he could take some friends with him. He suggested Lord and Lady Astor. The ambassador welcomed the proposal. G.B.S. consulted the Astors who immediately fell in with the plan. They made up

a party consisting of themselves, David Astor, Philip Lothian, a
Christian Scientist friend Charles Tennant, and one of Nancy's oldest
American friends, Gertrude Ely.

After much discussion they decided to travel overland by Berlin
and Warsaw to Moscow, meeting David in Berlin. He was to join
them from Heidelberg where he was studying. They planned to leave
London on Saturday, July 18th. And then, ten days or so before they
were due to depart, Nancy and Waldorf suffered a shattering blow.

Bobbie Shaw was a homosexual, a fact not known either to his
mother or his step-father. (His father had died in 1930.) This brought
him into trouble through a familiar psychological process. As often
happens to a man, especially a man of unstable temperament such as
Bobbie, his response to disgrace was defiance, and after his virtual
expulsion from the Blues he pursued his homosexual tastes with
increasing recklessness. The law then was as severe as it had been in
Oscar Wilde's day; and though in practice it was more lenient, to be
caught by the police in homosexual offences was still almost as dangerous as in the 1890s. Inevitably Bobbie was caught, but the police tried
to avoid penal consequences. They informed Bobbie and also Waldorf
that a warrant for his arrest would be issued, though not for a few days.
It was a hint that if Bobbie immediately went abroad for a year or
possibly less, and gave the police no more cause to act, the matter
might be dropped. With that same suicidal determination that brought
Oscar Wilde to his ruin, Bobbie refused to leave the country. The
police had no alternative. The warrant was issued. He was now unable
to leave the country except secretly and permanently.

Philip Lothian wrote to Nancy on the 14th July:

'I've no doubt that the right thing is for Bobbie to face the music –
which I think means a period of gaol. It is really exactly what we have
all known he needs – a period when he will have to work & be kept
from idleness & false pleasures. It's just the charm of sensuality destroying itself. From the Science point of view it is a blessing for him & but
preparation for healing. Scientifically you can rejoice in it.

'From your point of view & Waldorf's we are all clear that there is
no reason why what mortal mind will claim to be grief, shame, outraged pride, the sympathy or censure of your friends or enemies,
should touch you or Waldorf at all. The tempest may roar but Jesus
saw that there was really calm & you & I can see & prove this also.
You can go through this wondering how it can touch you both so

little & how the whole experience is going to bless Bobbie & yourself
& Bill, Wiss, David & all.

'I don't see how you & Waldorf can go to Russia on Saturday whatever happens. So far as I am concerned I should like to be about in so
far as I can be any use to you or W. But Mind will adjust the situation
about G.B.S., Tennant, Gertrude Ely, David & myself. If you have
any news, tell W. to telephone & I will see G.B.S.

'Gosh. Mortal mind has planned a good one this time – But it can
only work out for the greater good of everybody, Bobbie, yourself,
W. & the family & Science itself. Best love from Philip.'

Lothian's optimism was falsified by the result. He had evidently little
idea of what imprisonment can do to men.

The immediate concern of the Astors was to shield Bobbie from
publicity. Waldorf as proprietor and chairman of *The Observer* and his
brother John Jacob Astor as proprietor and chairman of *The Times*
were in a strong position to appeal for goodwill, but they could not do
more than that. They succeeded in their aim through the efforts of
J. L. Garvin. He was close friends with Lord Beaverbrook to whom
he appealed for support. Beaverbrook gave it. No mention of the case
appeared in any newspaper. (There is a type of Fleet Street moralist
who may find this very shocking.) But there was one condition
attaching to this silence, not one imposed by editors but by the force of
circumstances. There could be no question of abandoning the journey
to Russia which had already been publicised in the Press and much
commented on: suddenly to cancel the plans would cause surprise
and speculation and then nothing could prevent the reason coming out
in public. So with a leaden heart Nancy went forward with the adventure which she had been looking forward to. Bobbie was sentenced
and was in prison for four months.

The movements of the party are easy to follow because Waldorf
kept a diary throughout the journey. It is very different from the diary
he kept during the Virginiad of 1922. The subject was grimmer and
this time he was travelling in a country that was utterly strange in
every detail. It follows that there is less in this record of his gentle and
infectious humour. It must be remembered that he was also, like Nancy,
carrying a secret load of sorrow.

On Saturday the 18th July Nancy and Waldorf motored to Dover
where they met the rest of the party except David. They met him in
Berlin, according to plan, the next morning. In the evening of the

19th they boarded the night train from Berlin to the Polish-Russian frontier, reaching Warsaw at seven in the morning of the 20th. On the station platforms at Berlin and Warsaw there were crowds and large numbers of photographers and reporters, a faint presage of the acclaim awaiting G.B.S. at the end of the journey.

At Warsaw they lost one of their number, Gertrude Ely. By an oversight her passport had not been visa'd for Poland. To obtain the visa would mean stopping a day in Warsaw so, to avoid embarrassment to the party, she returned to Berlin.

To make up for her loss they found two new travelling companions. One was the American author, Maurice Hindus, a man of Russian origin, a passionate admirer of his native country and a leading authority on the U.S.S.R. The other was Maxim Litvinoff who was travelling to Moscow for a holiday after a League meeting in Geneva. His presence on the same train as the distinguished travellers was put down to coincidence, and perhaps that is all it was. Maurice Hindus introduced them. In the evening of the 20th July they reached the Polish-Russian frontier. Here they had their first experience of Russian officialdom. Waldorf wrote as follows in his diary:

'The situation at the frontier is ridiculous and theatrical. There are two frontiers: a Polish and a Russian one with No Man's Land in between. Each frontier is guarded by armed sentries. There is heavy barbed wire to prevent anyone crossing. As one reaches the frontier (going either way) an armed guard mounts the train. At the U.S.S.R. frontier is an erection with mottoes under which the train passes. I believe it is to the effect that Communism abolishes all frontiers, which seems cynical as almost immediately after crossing the frontier a Communist demands passports, etc., and shows a very rigid frontier. The Custom house is full of posters and cartoons directed against capitalist countries.

'Whilst waiting at the customs we went and spoke to half a dozen girls, great strapping wenches, bare legs, each with a shovel. They were there because of technological unemployment – the introduction of machinery into their village. Nancy got an interpreter and began talking to them and soon hit on common (feminist) ground. A crowd of men gathered. Litvinoff joined in. To his amusement they asked him if he were also English. Stalin was the only leader whose name they knew.'

Knowing that living conditions in Russia were hard, they had brought a great many provisions, none of which they needed as the authorities provided sumptuous meals everywhere. They gave their provisions away before leaving Russia, and could hardly have guessed how heaven-sent these gifts must have seemed to those who got them. Waldorf's remark about the bare-legged young women workers is interesting: 'They were there because of technological unemployment: the introduction of machinery into their village.' One may note the long euphemistic words which probably echo the ideologically 'correct' statement of an interpreter. (He wrote the diary in Russia, and did some correction to it after, but this passage is identical in manuscript and typescript.) Nancy's 'feminist' talk with the young women (which one hopes did not cost them their lives) made her uneasy. Reflecting what she told him many years later, Maurice Collis wrote: '[The women] were in fact forced labour, farm workers conscripted as railway navvies. But she was assured they were volunteers, working happily for a good wage. The sight of them, however, gave her pause.'

On Tuesday the 21st July the visit began with a resounding opening chord. Waldorf's diary reads as follows:

'Breakfast on the train. The U.S.S.R. certainly have made everything most comfortable.

'The arrival at the [Moscow] station was unique.

'If one had told the late George Edwardes or the present Cochran to stage G.B.S.'s arrival in "Red" Moscow and his reception by the Proletariat they would have staged exactly what happened.'

This was one of the occasions when the Western Press reporters in Russia, always starved for news and liable therefore to invent, can be relied on. Here is one report from the *Daily Herald*:

'A brass band and a guard of honour of Soviet soldiers supplemented a crowd of several thousands of people who greeted Mr Bernard Shaw when he arrived at the Alexandrovsky station, Moscow, today.

'Among the people on the platform were M. Lunacharsky, former Commissar for Education, M. Khalatov, head of the State Publishing Trust, and M. Karl Radek, a leading journalist.

'When Mr Shaw appeared in the doorway of the special car in which he had travelled, the crowd broke into wild applause. Mr Shaw smiled and waved his hat.

'Then two lines of soldiers were formed to enable him to pass through the crowds.

'Lady Astor, who had travelled by the same train, received less attention. She patted a Russian baby on the head while Mr Shaw acknowledged cheer after cheer.

'Outside the station the streets were packed with thousands of people, above whom dozens of Red banners waved.

' "Hail Shaw!" roared the crowd.'

The party was lodged in the Metropole Hotel. They were taken to see Lenin's tomb and mummified corpse 'lying as if asleep with his hands exposed, his head on a red pillow and a reddish glow from above. Most impressive', so Waldorf recorded. They were taken to the Garden of Culture and Rest and other famous places of Moscow. Waldorf wrote: 'G.B.S. is presented to the Proletariat at the theatre, in the Park etc. I hear that the only two other people who had anything like a similar reception were Gorky and Fairbanks (with Mary Pickford).'

It was to be a brief visit, lasting only nine days. When asked by a reporter why he was staying for so short a time, G.B.S. replied: 'I would like to stay nine years, but we are busy people and I can only spare nine days.' Asked if he could really learn much in nine days, he said that he knew so much already that there was little for him to learn. 'I was a socialist,' he said, 'before Lenin was born. I only want to have a look at the people.' *Also sprach Zarathustra.*

They were taken to the Kremlin to be shown its ancient splendours. One very odd feature of the palace was that the spires, so late as 1931, were still surmounted by gigantic Imperial emblems in the form of double-headed eagles. They were not replaced by equally gigantic red stars till 1935.

They were taken to the theatre that night to see 'a Bolshevised version of *The Beggar's Opera*,' probably an adaptation of Berchtold Brecht's famous adaptation of the original, *Die Dreigroschen Oper*.

The next morning they were escorted round the Museum of the Revolution, a vast permanent propaganda exhibition arranged with the customary Russian skill in such things. Even Waldorf found it rather hard to resist this mass of organised persuasion. 'A huge building,' he wrote, 'most interesting and makes one realise what centuries of oppression and injustices lie behind this revolution. Serfs only abolished in 1861, poverty wages among the peasants with apparently flogging till recently. Executions and exiles by the hundred thousand. A letter from Rasputin showing the immoral corruption of his era, etc. etc. A certain amount of international propaganda. Ramsay caricatured in a top hat and, what tickled me most, a picture of an oppressed foreign worker and a bloated capitalist, portly, sleek, tail coat, cigar, top hat. . . I looked at it . . . sure enough they had a photo of old Shirley Benn!!'

G.B.S. felt that the time had come for some more Shavian wit. As they came out of the building reporters asked him for his views on the Museum, and in place of the conventional 'Very Impressive Indeed' type of comment, he said: 'I think your Government are mad to have a Museum of the Revolution. It is most dangerous from their point of view. All governments hate revolutions and will do everything they can to prevent them or crush them. The courage of the Russian Government seems to me foolhardy.' The remark did not pass the censor.

On the afternoon of Wednesday the 22nd the party was taken to a prison. Waldorf recorded the occasion:

'Then to a settlement for criminals, 18 to 26 years of age. It's for *real* criminals, not first offenders. They live without restraint in a colony and are taught trades and paid regular wages. We saw them making skis, skates, textiles, racquets, etc. About 12% escape. When there are vacancies the Committee of the Community themselves choose the worst criminals from the prisons to fill the gaps. The principles are "liberty", "work", "autonomy".

'Like so many strange things in this strange country it seems to be working.

'Litvinoff accompanied us.

'We dined at the colony.

'After the dinner at the Penal Colony a book was passed to G.B.S. for his signature and observations on what he had seen. He cleverly got out of it by writing "For what I have received may the Lord be thankful (written after an excellent meal) signed G.B.S."

'Then to a cinema to see a film dealing with the handling of criminals.'

On the next day the party (but not including Hindus) visited a factory in the morning. Needless to say everything seemed in order, and undoubtedly was on that day. Waldorf alone of the party knew how to look at a factory with a discerning eye, and in his non-committal account he said that he found the combined political and industrial control incomprehensible. G.B.S. seized the opportunity to sparkle. When the visitors' book was brought to him to sign, he wrote: 'My father drank too much. I have worked too much. I hope you may succeed with your Five Year Plan and then for God's sake take a rest.'

Nancy also had her moment. Before leaving the factory 'a party of young Communists', wrote Waldorf, 'wanted to greet G.B.S. One made a speech. G.B.S. answered. Nancy could not resist the temptation of speaking to the Bolshie crowd and telling them that they were in danger of becoming conceited – and without reason as capitalist countries also were making progress. She stood right up for capitalism. But made no converts.'

It is a pity that Waldorf did not give more details of what Nancy said on the occasion of her only public speech in Russia as the text never reached the public. She spoke, standing on the roof of a lorry, through an interpreter who seems to have translated her words into milk-and-water orthodoxy to the effect that her sympathies were all with the Soviet Union. Her alleged remarks caused more anger in England, oddly enough, than a truly detestable witticism of G.B.S. At one point in this final episode of the factory visit he was angrily asked why the English and capitalist Press told such disgraceful lies about forced labour in the U.S.S.R., to which he is reported to have replied, and in this case the report rings true: 'I wish we had forced labour in England, in which case we would not have 2,000,000 unemployed.'

That evening a reception for the party was given by the British Ambassador, Sir Esmond Ovey. It was marked by a dramatic incident. Here is Waldorf's account of it:

'As we were leaving a telegram was handed to Nancy, sent by a Russian professor (Krynin) at Yale asking her to get his wife out of Russia to go to America, addressed in not very complimentary terms about the Soviet. She dashed to Litvinoff; he said it had nothing to do with him and that she must see the G.P.U. By this time she was thoroughly roused and getting the third Secretary (Watson) who speaks Russian we started off for the G.P.U. headquarters she vowing to give them what for. However we had a consultation. It was agreed that the G.P.U. would already know the contents of the wire and so the woman's fate could not be worsened even if we intervened.[1] The appeal was also addressed to Shaw who ignored it.'

1. At this time Dimitri Krynin held a professorship at Yale University. He had formerly been Professor of Highway Transportation at the Technical University of Moscow. Contemporary Press.

Taken as a whole the incident was not untypical of Nancy and Waldorf. When they saw injustice, and especially when appealed to, they never passed by on the other side of the road. Typical too was Nancy's impulse to rush to the storm-centre, and Waldorf's restraining hand. This was not the end of the Krynin story which had a little way to go yet, but that belongs to a later passage.

They left on the *Red Arrow* night train for Leningrad, and in the old capital the bands and the cheering throngs and the photographers were out in force again. They drove to the Astoria Hotel, situated by the majestic Cathedral of St Isaac.

They were informed that an interesting programme had been arranged for them, but they asked that before setting out they might take a light meal as they were very hungry after their journey. Russians are the most hospitable of people and they show it in that reckless Slavonic manner which is endearing but often inconvenient to the recipient. 'We wanted,' recorded Waldorf, 'an omelette, and instead they gave us caviar, vodka, brandy, champagne, ice-cream, etc. After endless delays we got our omelette.'

The triumphal procession of G.B.S. continued through the beauties of the splendid city. Unfortunately these beauties bored him. He was as insensitive to the pleasures of the eye as he was discriminating about those of the ear. The first treat was a visit to the Winter Palace and the adjoining picture gallery, the Hermitage. The latter's collection, comparable only with the greatest in the world, was merely a fatiguing ordeal for the hero of the hour. Nancy told Maurice Collis that all he had to say about it after was 'We marched past acres of pictures but they all looked alike to me'. The next excursion was more to his taste. To quote Waldorf's diary again:

'We drove out to see some rest homes for workers. These are in fact old private houses and mansions in which workers go on full pay for a fortnight's holiday. We asked how they spent this fortnight and were told that they had lectures on sanitary and physical culture, that often a doctor went walking with them to show how to walk to the best advantage from the health point of view, that they had addresses on various matters calculated to develop their culture. All this they call a rest cure.

'In fact it is like the old German Kultur, only more so.

'Constant propaganda. In the press, in the factory, in the theatre, on the hoarding, and no counter propaganda allowed.

NANCY

'I believe that the standard of living of masses of the population has been improved and raised, but as someone remarked it hardly seems necessary to keep on informing the public of the fact if it is true.'

They were due to lunch with the editor of *Izvestia*, Karl Radek. At the moment he was a rising star in the Russian heavens, soon to be extinguished in Stalin's major purges in the mid-thirties. Unfortunately Waldorf made no mention of this meeting in his diary. It may be that at the last moment plans were changed and it never occurred.

The Astors had a special personal interest in the Leningrad part of their journey. In December 1925 Nancy, in the course of an anti-Socialist speech in Durham, had said that if any British worker was so foolish as to want to exchange life in Britain for life in the Soviet Union which he affected to admire so much, she would pay his passage and that of his family to Russia. A Communist working man of Liverpool, an ironmoulder called Jim Morton, accepted the offer, and in 1926 he and his wife and two children sailed to Leningrad at Nancy's expense. A year later Jim Morton was found to be ill with cancer, of which he died in 1927. His widow elected to stay on with the children. She was in Leningrad in 1931, and naturally the Astors wanted to see her, but this they were unable to do. Contact with her was confined to very unsatisfying limits: to a published and sarcastic letter from Mrs Morton to the editor of *Izvestia* in which she said that doubtless Lady Astor would like to know how she was living at present, and assured her that she and her children were living far better than they could possibly do in England, and had no intention of returning. She explained her absence from Leningrad by the fact that she was 'leaving for her holiday on the Soviet steamer *Smolny* on the 23rd'. Translated into English, the letter was republished by the *Daily Worker*, not without sneering comment against Nancy, and the paper's usual adulation of the U.S.S.R.

The Astors regarded the whole incident with puzzlement and suspicion, and their suspicion was deepened by their further efforts, which came to nothing, on behalf of Madame Krynin, and by the considerable difficulties that G.B.S. encountered when he wished to meet Lenin's widow. The affair of Mrs Morton had an interesting sequel which belongs to a later chapter.

To return to Friday the 24th July 1931. The day ended with the party being taken to see a film, and Waldorf well describes it and its impact on the audience:

'Propaganda – propaganda – nothing but propaganda. Jolly well done. When I saw the workers shot down by troops, trampled on by cossacks on the film I felt like waving the red flag. When I saw the ideals of the industrial development of Russia dramatically pictured, when I saw the factory government in the hands of myself (a worker) instead of a tyrannical boss, when I saw the horrors of war of young Russians and young Germans each intoxicated with ideas of patriotism disembowelling each other – then I too felt like becoming a Red Pacifist.'

On the next day, Saturday the 25th, they spent the morning at a Pioneer Camp, also known as a Home of Culture. This was a school for children who were suffering from some serious physical ailment such as tuberculosis. They came from the Communist elite. The visit passed off well enough. 'The children,' wrote Waldorf, 'were all very jolly and friendly, sang and danced. Nancy joined in the dance. The instructors were very proud of their work and installation. . . . But it is rot to talk of the actual work here being superior to what is done in England.'

It passed off well enough, but it was at this place that Waldorf had a further unpleasant experience of the degradation of what we now call brainwashing. 'At the Camp,' he wrote, 'I had several arguments and discussions. On one building was a protest against the lynching of negroes in the U.S.A. "What," said I, "would you think if we in England had an inscription on our schools that we did not shoot political prisoners but that the Russians did – would that be the way to increase international fraternity among the young?" "But," answer the Communists, "we have to shoot because of Counter Revolution, and we shoot because it is to protect the interests of the workers whereas you oppress and exploit and lynch for the selfish interests of the wealthy!!" It is hard to argue with fanatics.'

Later he expressed himself more forcibly and said that sometimes when he was subjected to the opinionated orthodoxy of Russia he 'saw red' of a different kind. He seems to have recognised reluctantly and slowly what happens to men who are governed by absolute power. Two days later, he and the rest of the party went to a convent near Moscow, now turned into a museum. There they met two old peasant women and asked them what they thought 'about an old painted picture showing a person being tried after death with saints or angels waiting on one side, and devils, ogres, boiling hell fires on the other side'. The old women said that the picture surely was a correct representation 'because God had painted it and put it in the Church'. Of course the interpreter may have cheated, but the reply is not incredible. The old peasants were victims of their former Little Father. The people at the Pioneer Camp were victims of their new Big Brother.

The last incident of the 25th was a visit to Peterhof, the magnificent rococo palace built by Peter the Great, and Bernard Shaw endured the boredom of its radiant beauty, though he may have been interested to watch parties of workers being escorted bewildered through the rooms by yelling propagandist guides, usually women with screeching voices. They left on the night train for Moscow where they arrived at eleven o'clock on Sunday the 26th July.

This was to be one of the oddest days of the whole of this odd enterprise. The 26th was G.B.S.'s seventy-fifth birthday. The authorities were aware of this fact, so they prepared celebrations for him. Knowing the British passion for sport, and assuming he shared Waldorf's interest in horses, they laid on a race-meeting in his honour and one event was named after him, the Bernard Shaw Handicap or something of that kind. When informed of the arrangements G.B.S. whispered to David Astor: 'And all for me who am the only Irishman who has never been to a race-meeting.'

After a morning occupied by Nancy in visiting welfare centres for children, and by Waldorf in organising representations on behalf of Madame Krynin, the party were taken to the Sports Stadium for a birthday lunch before G.B.S.'s first visit to a race-course. The lunch was a lengthy affair lasting from 2.30 to 4.30. Waldorf was placed between two officials of the Foreign Commissariat. They discussed the League of Nations which, Waldorf's neighbours assured him, was 'an instrument of the devil, forged to create war, full of tricks for Communists and a hopeless failure'. It is an intriguing entry in the diary. These officials were subordinates of Maxim Litvinoff. They could hardly have spoken in rebellious contradiction to their chief, and yet, at the time and later, Litvinoff was looked on as a sincere friend of the League and a guarantor of Russia's participation in its ideals. He is usually regarded so to this day.

There followed the race-meeting, with the Bernard Shaw Handicap as the main attraction.

This entertainment did not awaken any latent interest in racing on the part of G.B.S. Maurice Collis relates, on Nancy's and David

Astor's authority, that the sage, oppressed by the heat, fell into a deep sleep in the notables' box, while Nancy fanned him to keep the flies at bay. With a railway journey in stifling heat behind him, and another immediately before him, and seventy-five years now upon him, G.B.S. would have liked to go to bed, but that is the sort of need of which the Russian soul knows little. As a man in Leningrad once put it to the writer, 'Only bores go to bed', and the Moscow authorities had more birthday treats in store. A laconic entry in Waldorf's diary, recording as from about 11 p.m., tells the story: 'Late for dinner. Then to an official function to G.B.S. A huge ball. 2,000. Lots of speeches. G.B.S. replied. A bad effort. Then a good concert. Then a late visit to the British Embassy.'

Shaw's speech consisted chiefly of flattery of the Russia of the Five Year Plan, and an assertion that England should be thoroughly ashamed of herself for not having thought of this policy and initiated it first. It now remained, he said, for Russia to make a success of the Plan and England would then humbly follow. As for his companions, he said, pointing to the Astors and Lothian, they were immensely rich people, capitalists, landowners and exploiters. It was not their fault, he went on, and they were not in a position, by British political precedent, to alter the situation in which they found themselves. But let his hearers not lose hope, he urged, the British proletariat would indeed change the situation. That is as much of the speech as can be collected from contemporary Press reports, but reports were not free. 'So strict,' recorded Waldorf in his diary, 'is the censorship and propaganda that even G.B.S.'s speech, which we all thought too unqualified and unguarded, was doctored!'

Waldorf was right to describe this performance as a 'bad effort'. It was, even by the meagre reports allowed, the sort of utterance to arouse the most distrust in very untrusting people. Contrary to most liberal opinion then, Russians were and are nationalistic in outlook, in spite of much theoretic commitment to international ideas. These denigrations of Great Britain by G.B.S. must have seemed in shocking bad taste and his denunciations of his fellow-travellers must have deeply offended Russian notions of good manners, always very strict whether under Imperial or Soviet rule. It is, of course, possible that his hearers thought that, after so much feasting, he was suffering from drunkenness, a vice looked upon with compassion by Russians. His triumph continued.

One would expect the party to have spent most of the next morning in bed, but they were indefatigable. They went to the divorce courts and the marriage registry, and then paid that visit to the nearby convent which has been mentioned already. Early in the afternoon they set out by train, accompanied by officials of the Commissariat of Agriculture, and Maurice Hindus. Their destination was Krishnavo in the Tambov district, about four hundred miles south-east of Moscow. From here they were to visit the Communa Lenin, a very large collectivised farm which had been established eight years before. They arrived in Krishnavo early in the morning of the 28th.

The Communa Lenin was a model realisation of the Soviet ideal, a great showplace but something more than that as well. Descriptions of it and of other establishments like it show that the early ecstatic idealism of the Revolution survived long, and has perhaps never wholly perished.

They spent the whole day of the 28th in this place, the old and the young gazing on G.B.S. with the utmost amazement and admiration – just for what they might have been perplexed to say. Always old-fashioned in dress, he wore for this occasion a motoring cap of a style suited to the horseless carriages of the nineties, the sort of vehicle that Tolstoy occasionally drove in during his last years. Waldorf observed the agricultural effort here with his discerning eye and, while critical on technical grounds of much of what he saw, he was impressed by the spirit of the place.

They returned overnight to Moscow. 'A dusty night,' wrote Waldorf, 'but one had to choose between a shut window, no dust and oven-like heat, or an open window and a steady inpouring of dust which settles on one's bed, in one's eyes, ears, hair, nose etc.' They reached Moscow at 10.30 on the morning of July 29th. If the 26th was the oddest of their days, the 29th was the most historic. Stalin had signified his wish to see G.B.S. and that evening the dictator received him with the Astors and Philip Lothian. The only other people present were an interpreter from the Foreign Commissariat and Litvinoff. Their interview lasted for two hours and twenty-five minutes, and took place round a table in Stalin's study.

'He has a clear rather kindly eye,' wrote Waldorf, 'is a man of very few words, is supposed to owe his position to an iron will and to a close association with Lenin. He seemed shrewd rather than big mentally. He had quite a sense of humour and knew how to parry questions he did not wish to deal with. G.B.S. began the interview by explaining why he had brought us to it, said nice things about Nancy, Philip and myself.' They went on to an answer-and-question discussion about the Five Year Plan, and then Nancy broke in.

The best description of what now happened is to be found, not in Waldorf's diary, but in St John Ervine's biography. It may be taken as certain that at this point he is following an account given to him by Shaw: 'The honours of the occasion were won by Lady Astor who, having no veneration for dictators nor any awe of eminent persons, frightened the wits out of the interpreters during an interview with Stalin by asking that cunning Caucasian why he had slaughtered so many Russians. The interpreters were loth to translate it, nor did they do so until Stalin, observing their fearful embarrassment, demanded to be told what Lady Astor had said. He took it very quietly, replying that some slaughter is inevitable when the constitution of a country is fundamentally disrupted. The violent death of a large number of people was necessary before the Communist State could be firmly established.' Waldorf's account of Stalin's reply, written within two days of the interview, is a little different: 'Stalin evaded [the question] by quoting a case when some engineers had been convicted of inter-course with some foreign country with a view to sabotage, and assured her that he hoped the need for dealing with political prisoners drastically would *soon cease*.' (Author's italics.)

According to David Astor, who heard an account of the meeting immediately after it from his parents, Stalin also referred to the example of Oliver Cromwell. The point was not raised, not even by the Irish-man present, that the ill-effects of Cromwell's drastic policy in Ireland were painfully visible nearly three hundred years after.

There is yet another account which is of the highest interest as it gives a first-hand indication of the effect of Nancy's boldness on Stalin. It has to be taken with some reserve for obvious reasons: it was written more than ten years after the events it describes, and the author, H. G. Wells, disliked Nancy though he did not know her. He wrote: 'Lady Astor is represented as quelling Stalin by sheer unintelligent rudeness. . . . The account I had from Stalin varied widely from many of these versions. I think he tried to argue with her and lost his temper. She certainly annoyed him thoroughly and his memory of her rankled.'

No contemporary account hints that Stalin lost his temper. To return to the Kremlin in July 1931.

The conversation then turned to British politics and Stalin showed great eagerness to know about the position of Winston Churchill, especially what office he would hold if the Conservatives were returned to power. They assured him, correctly enough, that Churchill would be given no office in a new Conservative administration and added that, except by a negligible minority, his hostility to the new Russia was looked on as a foolish monomania. Stalin showed more perspicacity than his guests at this point, and insisted that a man of Churchill's enormous ability would be sure to reach a position of great political influence in the end. With a sharp fall in perspicacity he prophesied that in that event he was likely to rouse Europe to an anti-Soviet crusade and a second intervention. They assured him that Winston Churchill was a spent force. It would seem that Nancy took little part in this episode of the debate, but presently she found a card of entry and engaged Stalin's attention again. She touched on her favourite subject, child-care and welfare. She expressed herself rather paradoxically it would seem, from the Press reports of the time, though the reports are reliable here as they come from direct interviews with her, given only a little later in England. She said that she thought that the children she had seen in Russia were 'too clean', too perfectly drilled and managed, and that children ought to be allowed to run wild and get grubby and muddy as she had done in the old days of Richmond, Virginia. Stalin evaded this proposition with his customary skill. He replied that in England it was customary to whip children whereas in the Soviet Union if a parent so much as smote his or her child on the head, the child concerned not only could but would sue the parent in the courts. This reply deeply impressed G.B.S., as he told the I.L.P. Summer School shortly after.

The rest of the interview was concerned with discussion of a historical question, why Lenin's proposals for a peaceful settlement between the Allies and Russia had not received a fair hearing at the conference of Paris in 1919. Here Philip Lothian, as a former member of the British delegation, had much of interest to say, but whether Stalin believed a word of what he was told is to be doubted.[2]

They had given a promise to make no comment to the Press on the subject of their interview with Stalin, but this the Press did not know. When the party reached the Metropole Hotel, correspondents and

2. The details are given in full in *A Diary with Letters 1931–1950*, by Thomas Jones (London, 1954), p. 172.

camera men were there in force again. G.B.S. took charge. David Astor described the scene to Maurice Collis and much later to the writer. Here is Maurice Collis's account: 'Shaw brushed the newsmen aside and slowly mounted the staircase, a huge flight of marble steps. The reporters followed, begging him to tell them what happened in the Kremlin. Ignoring their pleas he continued his leisurely ascent. At the top he halted, turned round, folded his arms like a ham actor and said solemnly: "You want to know what happened? Well, I'll tell you. We discovered that Stalin has big black moustaches." '

The next day, Thursday the 30th July, was the last of their days in the Soviet Union. The immense skill of Russians in propaganda is apt to be immobilised occasionally by the social paralysis that goes with all autocracy. The party saw this happening on the morning of the 30th. The incident was described by Waldorf in his diary: 'At 11 we were due to go and see Krupskaya as Lenin's widow is called.[3] From the first day when we arrived, Nancy had expressed a desire to see her and talk with her about children. G.B.S. also had a book he wanted to give her. Always promises were made that we should see her. But it never came off. Nancy was getting more and more restless. . . . [She] Said that it had been obvious that the Government had never meant us to see her, that she was determined to see her even if she had to go alone and without a guide.' Latterly the party had been told that they could not see her as she was seriously ill.

After Nancy's latest protest permission was granted and Nancy and G.B.S. went to see her. The interview passed off agreeably enough, but nothing of interest came out of it. They found her in excellent health.

Litvinoff celebrated their last day by giving an enormous lunch, opening with Russian hors d'oeuvres or *zakuski* which formed a delectable and substantial meal in itself. There were farewell speeches.

Either on this day or the day before, Waldorf who had continued to strive valiantly on behalf of Madame Krynin, went with an American journalist to visit her. He reported as follows: 'She was a pathetic sight terrified lest her husband or son should be induced to return to Russia, evidently afraid of what might happen to them if they did come. It seems to me that he probably must have gone to America with a permit limited as to time and had not returned when he had been due to do so, but I didn't want to make too many enquiries on this point. I wrote to

3. She retained her maiden name, N. K. Krupskaya, throughout life.

Khalatov telling him that the lady had no complaints to make against the authorities about her treatment but was merely anxious to join her husband in America.'

At 10.30 in the evening of the 30th they left Moscow by train for the Polish frontier. For weeks after, Nancy and Waldorf continued their unavailing struggle to obtain permission for Madame Krynin to join her husband. Their only consolation was in the probability that after the publicity they had given the case, the Russian authorities were unlikely to contrive Madame Krynin's 'disappearance'.

Their train arrived in Warsaw in the afternoon of the 31st July. Once more there was a crowd on the platform to gaze at G.B.S. and reporters to interview him. He proclaimed his faith. 'Russia and the Five Year Plan is a great success;' he declared, 'to save themselves, England and the other European countries must follow the remarkable example in human effort taking place in Russia. There is no starvation in Russia and the workers live better than they do in other countries.'

At the Silesian Station in Berlin next morning he went further. 'It is torture,' he told the Press, 'to get back again after being in Soviet land. After you have seen Bolshevism on the spot, there can be no doubt but that capitalism is doomed.' Forgetful of the great quantities of caviar and other delicacies with which he had been stuffed, he said: 'Black bread and cabbage soup agree with me – and I have had plenty of both.' He continued to speak of Russia in this laudatory strain both in public and private for the rest of his days. 'Stalin is a giant,' he said, 'and beside him Western statesmen are but pigmies.' There was hardly any limit to his hero-worship and he gave it frequent and loud expression.

Nancy and Waldorf were, by comparison, almost silent on their adventures. Nancy said that she found Russia 'wonderful and remarkable' and never committed herself further than to say that she thought and hoped that the Five Year Plan would succeed. She did not throw herself into the disputes about the visit on their return. She did not make any speech on the subject. All this was unlike her, but the main reason is not far to seek. It is quite true that she and Waldorf had been given 'the treatment' in no small measure: everything had been done to persuade them that here in the Soviet system was the answer to the riddle of man's destiny on earth, and perhaps only those who have lived among Russians or been to Russia can easily appreciate how compelling such persuasion can be. Its effect on the Astors is easily appreciated from Waldorf's diary. Except for the account of the meeting with Stalin, some details of the Krynin affair, and a short terminal essay, Waldorf did not drastically edit or add to his original text, but it is clear from this text, and proved by the terminal essay, that he was kept informed of the horrors that were unfolding side by side with the uplift, progress, and true joy in endeavour which he and Nancy and their companions witnessed at the Communa Lenin. He owed his information chiefly to an American, George Barnes, at that time Russia correspondent of the *New York Herald Tribune*. Through Barnes he met other correspondents, and it was through him that he had his painful interview with Madame Krynin. Of course he shared all his information with Nancy. She was a good friend. Through loyalty to G.B.S. she did not expose him.

As on many other occasions in Nancy's life, Waldorf's part in this one went unnoticed because he was as naturally retiring as she was naturally forthcoming. Most people regarded this as a joint venture by G.B.S. and Nancy. The two of them disagreed about Russia from then on. The situation was very strange. Who was the more likely to discover the truth about the U.S.S.R.? The most famous intellectual of his age, or this back-chatting woman who made no pretensions to any kind of intellectual distinction? Manifestly the intellectual giant. But it was Bernard Shaw who was fooled, not Nancy.

The Astors arrived back at Cliveden on Sunday the 2nd August. All the family, except poor Bobbie, were there to welcome their parents and brother back, and to spend the Bank Holiday with them. Reporters called but Nancy and Waldorf only gave them disappointingly neutral answers, while simultaneously at Ayot St Lawrence G.B.S. continued his hymn of praise. He said that he only regretted that he was not a young man in which case he would migrate to Russia immediately, and he advised all young men to do so. At the same time the Press had begun a vigorous campaign on the subject of the visit. Some of the Left Wing Press had praise for G.B.S., but every article, Left or Right, had hard words for Nancy. The *Daily Worker* reprinted abusive articles which had appeared in the Russian papers, one by the former Commissar of Education, Anatoly Lunacharsky, who had shown the whole party much friendliness during the visit. He now related how the workers had scored over and over again in arguments with this capitalist ogress. To worship G.B.S. was one thing, but this did not mean that his friends were allowed to become popular and thus imperil the regime. The *Daily Worker* followed the party line. The paper gloated over Mrs Morton's sarcastic replies to Nancy, and taunted her silence. The Right sneered at Nancy as a poser, a traitress to civilisation.

Some big guns opened up. On Saturday the 1st August Chesterton devoted a hard-hitting leading article in *G.K.'s Weekly*. The article would have been telling but for one enormous flaw: Chesterton appears to have laboured under the delusion that Stalin was reviving Lenin's New Economic Policy. A fortnight after their return, they were subjected to a more massive, better calculated and cruel bombardment from heavy artillery. Winston Churchill came out, or rather crashed forth, in the *Sunday Pictorial* on the 16th August.

His article is well known as he republished it in 1937 after very little editing and some expansion. It appears in his masterly *Great Contemporaries*. For that reason it would be redundant to quote it at any length. The book continues to have many readers, and the main subject of Churchill's severe essay in this good-humoured book is not Nancy but G.B.S., his 'pet aversion'. It comes as a surprise to learn in the expanded text that G.B.S. sent Churchill a copy of *The Intelligent Woman's Guide to Socialism and Capitalism*, and that they enjoyed agreeable personal relations. For all that, the essay, originally entitled 'Lady Astor and G. Bernard Shaw', is one of the most devastatingly destructive criticisms of Shaw to appear during the sage's lifetime.

His criticism of Nancy was equally wounding, with the difference that here he wrote under a misapprehension. He believed like everyone that she shared G.B.S.'s indiscriminating admiration for the Soviet system, and his hero-worship of Stalin. Training his guns from the Shaw to the Astor target, Winston Churchill opened up against Nancy with a shattering barrage: 'Similar though different contradictions are to be observed in Lady Astor; and like Mr Bernard Shaw she successfully exploits the best of both worlds. She reigns in the Old World and the New, and on both sides of the Atlantic, at once as a leader of smart fashionable society and of advanced feminist democracy. She combines a kindly heart with a sharp and wagging tongue. She embodies the historical portent of the first woman member of the House of Commons. She applauds the policies of the Government from the benches of the Opposition. She denounces the vice of gambling and keeps an almost unrivalled racing stable. She accepts Communist hospitality and flattery, and remains the Conservative member for Plymouth. She does all these opposite things so well and so naturally that the public, tired of criticising, can only gape.'

As Winston Churchill was wont to say of Press attacks on himself: 'Not a very nishe article.' G.B.S. replied in the next issue of the *Sunday Pictorial*. His article was not the equal of Churchill's; he evaded the embarrassing points which had been raised regarding Soviet atrocity, but it is of interest because it gives details of Stalin's remarks about Churchill's likely return to office. Nancy maintained her silence until the 15th November when she interrupted a speech by the Duchess of Atholl in the House of Commons, pointing out that the Duchess was possibly overstating the anti-Russian case when she spoke of child-labour in the U.S.S.R. Nancy herself made no other speech or public comment on her visit, either in the House or outside. People continued to be perplexed by her silence. There may be another explanation, in addition to that given above: her continual nagging inner grief at the fate which had overtaken Bobbie. She was kept in contact with him, not only through the rare visits she could pay him, and the rare letters they could exchange, but through the reports of a prison visitor, a woman who signed herself 'Lilian B.', and was a relation of Stanley Baldwin. She and her relative did what they could to console Nancy, but she was not consolable. Grief of intense kind does often inhibit activity.

Shaw's reply to Churchill appeared on the 23rd August, and from that day onwards the nine-days-wonder of the Shaw-Astor visit to Russia was swept out of the newspapers to make way for the greatest economic and political crisis to have overtaken Great Britain since the war.

At the end of July 1931 a Government economic committee had reported that by 1932 the Budget deficit would reach £120,000,000. There followed a 'flight from the pound'. The Government instituted economies. These included a cut of £22,000,000 on allowances to the unemployed. The measure was resisted by the Trades Union Congress and in the Cabinet. The Prime Minister offered his resignation; the King urged delay, and after consultation between the party leaders a coalition was formed on the 25th August under Ramsay MacDonald. It was described as a National Government. A General Election seemed imminent but was not made certain until the Liberal Party joined the

demand for it in early October. Polling day was set for the 27th. A
National Government victory was expected, although the ministers
incurred a charge of broken promises. They had pledged themselves
to defend the gold standard, but on the 21st September the Chancellor
of the Exchequer, Philip Snowden, suspended it.

Nancy had her personal political worries, arising from her Russian
visit and from an episode which occurred just before the election on the
6th October, and brought her some unpopularity on the Conservative
side. On that day Philip Lothian introduced her to the Mahatma
Gandhi, then in London attending the Round Table Conference.
Being a person of as wide tastes as Nancy, Gandhi had easily made
friends with her, and Conservatives had noted the shocking event of
this 'half-naked fakir', as Churchill foolishly described him, sitting
cross-legged on the floor in No. 4 St James's Square, exchanging sharp
and sometimes witty conversations with its châtelaine.

But she had a deeper worry than her unpopularity in some political
circles. She seems to have recognised that she had passed her zenith
as an effective Member of Parliament, and had suggested that possibly
she should not stand in the forthcoming election but let Bill Astor
stand instead. Waldorf thought that by now (the 6th October) it was
too late to change, but she remained in doubt.

A great friend of Nancy and Waldorf was Dr Thomas Jones, always
known as 'T.J.' He had first met Waldorf as a member of Lloyd
George's secretariat and was now a Deputy Secretary to the Cabinet.
He had been asked to give advice, and on the 7th October he called
to hear Nancy's decision, as he related in his diary.

'11.15 a.m. To 4 St James's Square. Shown upstairs. Lady A. propped
up with pillows, issuing instructions to a private secretary at lightning
speed. The p.s. withdrew. Bed sprinkled with Bibles, large and small;
daily papers on a side table; letters all over the place. My business was
to try and persuade her to let Bill fight Plymouth in her place. She
began at once on a high religious note – what did the Lord want her
to do? She had for days been trying to discover this. Nothing else
mattered. Waldorf had phoned from Plymouth to say it was not too
late to propose Bill. I knew it was useless to tell her that the fight would
be a hellish one for her – I did say so, with the expected result. Did I
think that she could be killed or broken by anything outside her? It
was the duty of all to help the country, to fight class consciousness and
bitterness. The new House might need her for though she could not

make speeches she would weaken the forces of hate. Only Waldorf on the spot could judge. I argued for half an hour, secretly admiring her more and more as she swept aside my appeals to prudence, health, the work needing to be done outside the House. I felt humble and ashamed in her presence. Flippancy was far away from her speech this morning. I sat at the foot of the bed looking straight into the eyes of the most remarkable woman it has been my fortune to know intimately. I kept thinking of Joan of Arc, precisely as when I saw Sybil Thorndike play the heroine in Shaw's play. I could not get Nancy Astor out of my mind.'

She decided to stand.

In October, as the General Election approached, a book on Russia came out in England. It was by Mrs Cecil Chesterton, G.K.C.'s sister-in-law, and was called *My Russian Venture*. At about the same time as the Shaw-Astor venture she had travelled, without any of their privileged treatment, to White Russia and the Ukraine. By a remarkable coincidence she had been helped on her way by Maurice Hindus whom she met in Minsk. Though devoted to the religious and social ideas of her husband (who had been killed in the war) and her brother-in-law, she emerged from her ordeal, which had been as hard and bug-ridden as the other had been officially softened, with much the same starry-eyed belief in the ultimate beneficence of the Soviet system as literally stupefied G.B.S. No greater evidence could be produced to show the power of Russian persuasion and the excitement and capti-vating delight of Russian life. In only one respect was Mrs Chesterton's venture similar to that of G.B.S. and the Astors. Though she had seen something of the horrors of enforced collectivisation, she had also witnessed the impressive selflessness of a model *communa*, the one visited by Mrs Chesterton in the Ukraine bearing the forbidding title of 'Sparta'. The last words of her book are: 'A new and terrific chapter in the history of mankind, Soviet Russia, is the writing on Europe's capitalist wall.'

G.B.S. was interested in the book and he sent a copy to Nancy.

By the time she received it she was in the thick of her sixth election-eering campaign. Even so she found time to read the book. Here is her reply to Shaw written from Plymouth on the 13th.

'Dearest G.B.S. . . . It is very disturbing this about Russia, and I am afraid I believe that most of it is true. The more one thinks of it, the more natural it is with community farming even with the Russians.

So far it hasn't come up in the election. If you could come down here and hear the Socialists' twaddle, you would vote for me gladly, and no doubt you would come out and help me. The first two or three days I was not feeling my usual lively self, but am quite all right now. . . .'

She flung herself into the electoral fight with all the old abandon. In spite of the criticism she had incurred, her victory was never in much doubt. Her opponent was Mr George Ward, not to be confused with the Conservative minister of the same name and of a later date. The *Daily Herald* screamed that 'Lady Astor May Lose', but it was abundantly clear that the MacDonald coalition candidates would carry all before them except in Socialist strongholds. Mr Ward appears to have been an able candidate and he maintained some 70 per cent of the Labour vote in Plymouth.

Nancy's success was even greater than expected. The results for the Sutton Division on the 27th October were:

| Lady Astor | 24,277 | |
| Mr G. Ward | 14,073 | Majority 10,204 |

The overall returns showed that this spectacular victory reflected the mood of the country, resulting in an enormous Conservative landslide. 471 of the party's candidates obtained seats in Parliament. 35 National Liberals followed Sir John Simon, and 33 Asquithian Liberals followed Sir Herbert Samuel into the coalition with 13 Labour members. This gave the new Government 552 seats over 56 oppositionists. So enormous and unprecedented a majority depended on so disparate a coalition that it could not last, but it persisted for a year and in essence ruled the country for the next eight and a half years. It left its influence on subsequent administrations for the next fourteen years.

The new Government made one appointment of considerable interest to this story. Anxious to recruit a Liberal spokesman for the National Government in the House of Lords, MacDonald had in August persuaded Lord Lothian to accept the Chancellorship of the Duchy of Lancaster. Lothian accepted in the belief that the coalition was necessary. He had grave doubts, however, about the need or justification for a General Election. The divided counsels of the Liberal Party were reflected in him, and he became more Hamletish than usual. On the 7th October he wrote in a letter to a friend, 'An election at this moment is criminal folly,' but then went on to say, later in the same paragraph, 'I don't see how we could [have] adopted any other course

than that the National Government should go to the country for a
doctor's mandate. . . .'

In public he spoke and acted more in accord with the second of
these remarks which evidently represented the deeper of his feelings.
He had aided Nancy's electoral triumph in Plymouth by coming
down and speaking for her. With the reconstitution of the Government
in November, Lothian was offered and accepted the Undersecretary-
ship of State for India, and since this meant demotion, technically
speaking, he was given the right of access to the Prime Minister. In
this post he again proved his statesmanlike qualities which always
showed at their best as an executive with advisory powers. Unfortunately, owing to a disagreement on a matter of principle (to be
mentioned later) his tenure was very short, less than a year.

From the feminist point of view this General Election, as with most
returning Conservative majorities, was disappointing. On the dissolution there were fifteen women members; the new Parliament
contained the same number. All the women Labour candidates had
been defeated, though a few were soon to return to the House from
bye-elections. The numbers were made up to fifteen by the re-election
of Nancy, Lady Iveagh, and the Duchess of Atholl; the election of ten
new Conservative members; one Independent, Eleanor Rathbone;
and one Liberal, Megan Lloyd George. There had been great innovation in two constituencies: at East Islington and at Wallsend the
electoral struggle had been between women only. Margaret Bondfield
had been defeated at Wallsend and was never to return to Parliament
again. As before, Nancy, as the undisputed doyenne of the women
members, showed the newcomers round the Palace of Westminster.
She lamented that there were still so few and that Ellen Wilkinson had
lost her election.

In November Bobbie Shaw came out of prison. He went to Sandwich
to be alone with his mother. T. E. Lawrence wrote to her on the 12th:
'I hope the Sandwich stay is successful, for both sakes. Coming out
will be very hard.' Philip Lothian wrote to Bobbie at the same time.
'Delighted to get your letter. Yes! A rest won't do your "mommer"
any harm. She's had a lot of strain lately, though, as usual, she comes
up smiling. Why our mothers are so fond of their children, I do not
know. And the worse we treat them the more they love us. True

mother love is the best revelation to man of what the Love of God is, & all the experts on religion say that even the purest mother love is only 30 cents on that! So go on giving her a helping hand. She needs it & nothing will make more difference to her life than to realise that you have found a way of life which will bring happiness to both others & to yourself. Everybody is going to leave you alone together for a bit longer. But after that I shall come down & beat you at golf!'

At this emotional crisis in Nancy's life, Bernard Shaw showed the depth and sincerity of his friendship. As has been often remarked, his apparent callousness was largely an act, an act which is pardonable if one remembers how large was the element not only of kindliness but of sentimentality which it was designed to smother or hide. He succeeded in hiding it most of the time, but it is to be noted that very few if any actresses have coped with success and authority with the climax of the trial scene in *St Joan* because of the manifest sentimentality in the writing.

He wrote to Nancy on the 28th November to tell her that he and Mrs Shaw were sailing for South Africa on Christmas Eve. 'Charlotte wants sunshine;' he wrote, 'and I, who have been working like fifty plantations of niggers since our return from Russia, will be the better for a break in my routine.' He refers to his real purpose in oblique fashion: 'You ought to see the Empire you govern. The parliamentary Whip will be quite independent of you for five years to come. Why not come to the Cape with the whole Astor-Shaw tribe, Charles Tennant, Phil [Lothian], old Uncle Tom Cobley and all. Phil could leave the Lords to an understudy: he is wasting his time as completely as Gandhi; for while they are playacting at the Round Table the real conflict of competitive murder is going on in India.'

He must have known that Philip Lothian could not possibly take leave from his governmental appointment almost immediately on receiving it! That his real purpose was to take Bobbie out of himself by foreign travel is made quite clear by a letter that Charlotte Shaw wrote to Nancy the next day.

In the event Nancy and Bobbie did not accompany the Shaws on this journey during which, in a period of convalescence following a motor accident, G.B.S. wrote his remarkable and absurd pamphlet *The Adventures of The Black Girl in Her Search for God*.

It will be seen from the foregoing that there were friends of the Astors (and other names could be added) who befriended Bobbie Shaw in his troubles, and the conduct of Waldorf towards his stepson was throughout generous and tactful, in keeping with all that was best in his fine character. Nevertheless, Bobbie was ruined. Not only was he lacking in mental resources but, being essentially unbalanced in temperament, he could not overcome the blow to his self-respect. The blow fell hard. He had always been a very popular man in fashionable society, in spite of the fact that his homosexuality was widely known. Once it was officially condemned, however, his fashionable acquaintance took a disapproving view. He was dropped, utterly and completely, by all except those relatively few friends who were above the claims of vulgar respectability, and those who shared his debauchery. He could go nowhere without the fear of a humiliating snub, and he lacked the firmness which would have enabled him to be indifferent to the disdain of the hollow creatures who had once sought him. His drinking became worse and in time he developed suicidal tendencies. He had no religion to give him inner strength. But it must not be thought that he gave in without a struggle. Nancy's papers prove the opposite. He tried hard, again and again, to make his life anew, and he failed, again and again. He became an increasingly helpless being.

As indicated in the text, most of the material on which the foregoing chapter is based comes from the Astor archive and the contemporary Press. St John Ervine's biography of Bernard Shaw has again proved a valuable source of information. The details of the distressing episode concerning the late Bobbie Shaw have been told to me by various of his friends, notably the late Sir Malcolm Bullock who remained faithful to him in his adversity. The account given of the Astor-Shaw visit to Russia follows chronologically that given in Lord Astor's diary mentioned in the text. The episode of Bernard Shaw's visit to the Revolution Museum follows an account given to me by David Astor. Some slight personal experience of life in the U.S.S.R. four years later has also been of help. (I was in Moscow when the double-headed eagles of the Kremlin were being replaced in 1935.) The account of Lord Lothian's political attitudes in 1931 is drawn from Sir James Butler's biography. As before a debt is owed to Pamela Brookes's *Women in Westminster* and to Maurice Collis's biography of Lady Astor. A new debt begins with mention of *Diary with Letters 1931–1950*, by the late Doctor Thomas Jones, C.H. (London, 1954).

Chapter 17

INTERMEZZO

BETWEEN 1931 and 1935 there was no dominating feature in Nancy's life to be compared with the visit to Russia. For that reason, although great conditioning events occurred in the world at this time, the record may be brief. During these years Nancy's life was not a quiet one, it was never that, but it was without great innovation.

Here is a convenient place to introduce a character who played a considerable part in Nancy's life. This was Rose Harrison who became Nancy's lady's maid shortly before the trip to Russia in 1931.

She had originally been Wissie's maid, while Nancy maintained French maids in accordance with the prevailing custom of fashionable English ladies. The fashion did not suit Nancy: with her intense dislike and distrust of the Latin nations, she did not get on agreeable terms with these hand-maidens, and in the course of one year, around 1930-1931, three of them left, two literally running away. Then Nancy called Rose Harrison to her service and obtained an untried novice for Wissie. The novice proved dishonest and was removed. Nancy then urged Rose to go back to Wissie, but Rose replied: 'No. Having got so far I don't take second place in this house.' And that was that.

Nancy attempted to rule the other with a rod of iron, and Rose returned the treatment with greater success. Nancy found Rose deficient in some of the niceties of her French predecessors, and was once moved to exclaim 'You and your Yorkshire accent!' According to a tape-recording which Rose made for Mr Kenneth Harris, she replied: 'Well m'lady, what would I sound like if I was affected? Isn't it better to be natural and to be me. I am me and me I'm stopping.' When Nancy once made a disparaging remark about housemaids, Rose gave her a severe scolding. 'Now, m'lady,' she said, 'I'm going to talk to you woman to woman. I have a sister who is a housemaid and so don't you ever talk to me about housemaids like that again. Who do you think housemaids are? The scum of the earth? Just you remember they are women like yourself.'

Rose was Nancy's persistent and merciless critic, but she had not only a blunt incapacity to be intimidated but a blunt and robust sense of humour which made her delight in Nancy's fun. In her account of herself she tells of how she warned the other servants not to be alarmed if they heard her screaming in her room, it was only her laughing at the things Lady Astor said that day. With her love for Nancy, she had a profound understanding of her mistress's character.

In December 1931 G.B.S. invited Nancy to a reading of his play *Too True to be Good*. She was unable to go, though the play had a particular interest for her. The second act introduces a character called Private Meek, manifestly based on their friend T. E. Lawrence. The production in 1932 in America and Britain marked a melancholy turning point. For the first time in forty years a new Shaw play was received with neither acclaim nor anger but merely disappointment.

In February 1932 he and Mrs Shaw went to South Africa as already mentioned. On their return he wrote Nancy a long letter (of very great biographical interest for students of his life), the main purpose of which was to discourage her from seeking a solution for Bobbie's troubles in her religion. He wrote: 'Mrs Eddy, bless her, is no use; the Bible, with its rubbish about Lot's wife, is positively dangerous'. He also warned her not to discuss the matter with her son. There is no further evidence of Shaw's intervention in the case, but the fact that Bobbie put himself under psychological care several times may be due to the influence of this letter which seems to have been addressed to him rather than to his mother. If this appreciation is correct, it is ironical, as *The Black Girl* contains mockery of Freud and his school. Whatever the truth the episode shows a very attractive side of G.B.S.'s character.

From January to April 1932 Lord Lothian was away from England in India as the Chairman of one of the three Committees of Enquiry sent by the Government to recommend legislation regarding India policy. The Government's official aim since October 1929 was the attainment by India of Dominion status. Left to herself, Nancy, with her paternalist Virginian ideas, would probably have joined Winston Churchill in opposition to the policy. As it was she became a supporter, probably under the influence of Waldorf, of her friend the Viceroy Lord Irwin,[1] and most certainly of Philip Lothian who wrote to her frequently during this time. Her unexpected attitude worsened her relations with Winston Churchill. Lothian's Committee dealt with the most controversial of all the subjects of enquiry, the reform of the

1. Formerly Edward Wood, M.P., later Lord Halifax.

franchise. He showed great skill. He was an ideal public servant but unfortunately his Under Secretaryship ended in September 1932 when the Liberals, headed by Sir Herbert Samuel, and including Lothian, resigned from the Government because of differences about Free Trade and Protection. After this the Government, though still so described, was no longer a true national coalition. Philip Lothian did not hold an official post again for seven years. Instead he devoted his political talents to activity in fields where they were not adaptable. That belongs to the next chapter.

In the summer before he resigned, his and Nancy's friend Dr Thomas Jones gave this description of Lothian to Stanley Baldwin:

'He is apt to be the victim of his most recent experience. I remember him coming back from the U.S.A. full of American mass-production; then before going to Russia he was so convinced of property as the root of all evil that he was hardly distinguishable from a Communist; then last Sunday . . . he was certain that the world could not get on without capitalists and captains of industry. India had showed him the need for leadership.' Baldwin described him as 'a queer bird' and 'a rum cove'.

It was in this same year, 1932, that Bill opened his public career. In February he went to the Far East on the staff of Lord Lytton who had been put in charge of the League of Nations Committee of Enquiry into the Japanese aggression in Manchuria. Nancy took small interest in Far Eastern affairs, so this crisis of fate need not detain the reader. Bill was away until the autumn.

Nancy's life went forward much as before; she defended her favourite causes in Parliament, rallied her supporters in Plymouth, and frequently entertained weekend parties at Cliveden and numerous guests in St James's Square. At one of her London dances there was to be a cabaret, but the artists were held up in Paris by bad flying weather. Nancy and her friend Lady Islington proved equal to the emergency, and after a brief consultation with the band leader they did a caricature *pas de deux* in masks. They scored a hilarious success. In the autumn of 1932 Nancy and Waldorf visited America for the first time for four years. Considering that a Presidential election was in progress and that Nancy had strong views on the folly of Hoover's economic policy, she was (relatively) discreet in her numerous public statements.

On the 30th January 1933 Adolf Hitler became Chancellor of the Reich. The Press of the time shows that the attainment of power by the Nazis did not disturb public opinion in Great Britain as it should have done. There was a general feeling that Germany had been hardly used in the treaty of 1919 and Hitler was given the benefit of most doubts. Among the more informed, who had studied and met him, the notion grew that he was an idealist not to be confused with the atrocities committed in his name. Many of the Astors' friends, especially those of the Kindergarten, and most notably Philip Lothian, fell into this guilt-haunted and wish-fulfilling belief. Nancy went along with them, but not altogether easily: she felt the promptings of a Virginian enmity to tyranny from the beginning. Early on in the new era she made two public pronouncements, in May and June of 1933, about the Nazi regime. That of May was made at a Foyles lunch at which Nancy was asked to respond to the toast of literature. She wandered from her subject to denounce tyranny in general, making it clear that she indicated Nazi rule. The June occasion was at a meeting, in the Palace of Westminster, of the National Council for Equal Citizenship, from which she conveyed to the German Embassy an unanimous motion, proposed by herself, protesting at the illiberal treatment of professionally employed women in the Third Reich.

The most interesting episode of this time, from the point of view of Nancy's biographer, belongs to early May. It may have been a non-event. On the other hand, Nancy's caustic and public anti-Nazism in late May and June may just possibly have been a reaction from what had happened a little earlier.

The known facts are as follows. *The Times* correspondent in Berlin in 1933 was Norman Ebbutt. He had long experience of Germany and knew far more than the Nazis liked him to know, especially about themselves. They began an intrigue against him. The scholar of the party was Alfred Rosenberg, and this author of unreadable books was sent to England in the first part of May 1933 to help forward pro-Nazi sentiment in the country. He laid a wreath at the Cenotaph, a gesture which somehow failed of effect. His major object was less benevolent: to get Ebbutt removed from Berlin. The Nazis knew that direct protestation to the chairman or editor was only likely to cause irritation, so Rosenberg chose an indirect approach which shows a wonderful mixture of ingenuity and ignorance. He and his friends decided to represent Ebbutt to Nancy as a person who was despised in Berlin as a drunkard. Ebbutt was not a teetotaler and enjoyed a drink, but that was as far as the libel could be taken. He was among the best Press reporters of his century, comparable to the greatest, an impossible feat for an alcoholic. It was hoped, nevertheless, that Nancy's extreme views might mislead her into intervening with her brother-in-law against Ebbutt. Rosenberg was evidently unaware of the fact that Nancy never attempted to interfere with the running or the policy of *The Times*. She only discussed such matters with the editor, Geoffrey Dawson, when his views coincided with hers. Rosenberg was also unaware that the chairman, J. J. Astor, and Nancy were on difficult and sometimes rather hostile terms. He overlooked that underneath her contradictions and eccentricities she had a common sense which usually (alas not always) warned her off the undiscovered country, as it was mostly to her, of foreign affairs.

What happened is uncertain. That there was this intrigue is undeniable. That it was put into action seems questionable and unlikely. The name of Rosenberg occurs nowhere in Nancy's correspondence, or in the many remarks to the Press about Nazis which she made before, during, and after the war. It has seemed to the writer that if Nancy met Rosenberg, the latter's nerve failed him when he found himself confronted by her fierce blue eyes. Whatever the truth, Norman Ebbutt remained in Berlin as *Times* correspondent for four more years.

As happened with most people, the old life went on into the new age with little alteration on the surface. The lion-hunting persisted but Nancy's resistance to one likely lion is interesting. The claims of H. G. Wells were pressed on her by many friends that they had in common, but she refused to meet him because she was shocked by what she had been told about his private life. Analogously, she had let her friendship with Lloyd George lapse after she learned about *his* private life, but she maintained her political hero-worship of him undismayed. To the end of his life she would like to have seen him reinstated as Prime Minister. This impersonal admiration was very untypical of her.

The most surprising new lion of these years was the Communist Irish playwright Sean O'Casey. He never abated his ferocious preferences in their correspondence. 'Up with the neck and clap the wing, red cock, and crow' is a typical sentence in his numerous letters to Nancy. As is not always the case with the fiercely irreconcilable, there was no inferiority complex struggling for disguise in his defiant attitude. His pride was natural and not assumed, and he could accept kindness and hospitality from the Astors without feeling a perverse duty to sneer. When his play *Within the Gates* was produced in early 1934, he and his wife Eileen stayed at 4 St James's Square throughout the rehearsal period, and after the first night Nancy gave a party for the cast and the author. The friendship continued till Nancy's last years.

The great friendship remained that with G.B.S. In 1933 he persuaded Nancy to sit for a bust to the distinguished Hungarian sculptor Kisfalud de Strobl, who seems not to have enjoyed the commission in its early stages. G.B.S. wrote to her on the 12th May 1933:

'My dear Nancy,

You must go to de Strobl's studio and give him one real sitting: that is, you must behave exactly like a professional model with her livelihood (half a crown an hour) at stake. The bust is a beautiful work: you will never get anything like it brought into existence again in point of beauty and refinement; but it lacks the final touch which will completely identify it with you. Charlotte made him do something to the eyes which brought it nearer; but it will only be a "Bust of a Lady" unless you do your clear duty as a civilized woman (as distinguished from a Virginian savage) and take the work quite seriously for an hour or two.

He says the conditions under which he has worked have been frightfully distracting, difficult, and distressing, as you are incapable of stillness and silence. I suggested chloroform; but I now appeal to one of your several better selves. He is a very fine workman and should be treated with genuine respect. And he is too amiable to resort to the poker or the broomstick, which is what you deserve. Unless you enable him to superfinish that bust angels won't never love you. Nor will G.B.S.'

These scoldings were effective.

The original intention was that Waldorf and G.B.S. should buy the bust from Strobl and present it to the Palace of Westminster, but mindful of the picture fiasco, the plan was abandoned and G.B.S. bought the bust privately. It turns up later in the story.

Almost alone among the prominent figures on the Left, G.B.S. conceived an admiration of Hitler. He never worshipped him as he did Stalin, but he saw in him, as he did in Mussolini, a personification of that Socialist strong-man-rule which he came more and more to admire. He made occasional attempts to convert Nancy to his preferences. She remained convinced that he 'knew nothing about politics'.

The great family event of 1933 was the first marriage in its younger generation. On the 27th July Wissie married Lord Willoughby de Eresby, the heir of the Earl of Ancaster. Nancy could hardly be other than gratified at her daughter's choice of this popular and admirable man, but when the engagement was announced she gave way to that odd American delusion, previously mentioned, that it is somehow reprehensible for a woman of American origin to marry into the British peerage. She confided her misgivings to an American woman friend who asked her candidly whether her scruples were not something of an act, and whether, given her position, they made sense. Not without giggling, Nancy was brought to agree with her friend.

An extraordinarily acute description of Nancy as she was a little before and a little after this time was written by Mr William Douglas Home. He first met her as an Eton boy in a party of nature-ramblers allowed to explore the grounds of Cliveden. 'She was talking,' he relates, 'to the master in charge of our party.

'He, like most schoolmasters, when confronted by a woman, and, like all schoolmasters, and indeed most men, when confronted by Lady Astor, was giving a fairly creditable imitation of a rabbit waiting at some woodland cross-rides for a passing stoat.

'As I looked up from the clatter of the tea which was laid out on a long trestle-table on the terrace, Lady Astor, having abandoned her strictures on schoolmasters in general and on that one in particular, and having reloaded her verbal guns with lighter shot, then turned her broadside on the crowd of chattering small boys and raked the tea-table from end to end. She told us collectively first and then individually later, that we were the stupidest, ugliest, dirtiest boys she had ever seen. As most of us were of the opinion that we were some of the cleverest, prettiest, and best-groomed adolescents in our age-group, this initial broadside had nothing but a salutary effect. To those of us whose parents she knew she vouchsafed the information that she had warned them against having children which were bound to be morons and now she saw how right she had been. On the whole, as she worked her way down the table, she shot well. Only occasionally did a missile which had been launched from the mother ship as a laughing gas shell, burst on impact with all the destructive force of a high explosive, leaving the unhappy target purple in the face and fighting back an angry and embarrassed tear.

'While she was thus engaged, I looked shyly up into a pair of kindly sapphire-blue, compelling eyes, which sometimes danced and sometimes filled with tears, as though in her dynamic little person, comedy and tragedy walked step by step and hand in hand. And suddenly, I was not shy at all.

'When we returned to Eton that evening in the bus, we most definitely knew that something had hit us – something that was beneficial to the health, provided one could swallow the initial dose. Some could and others couldn't. I discovered, when I met her again, ten years later, at the age of twenty-five, that I was one of those who could.

'To her dynamic personality, all humbug was a wicked waste of time. Invariably she put her own cards on the table in order to facilitate and hurry up the game. She expected other people to do likewise. If they didn't, she devised a simple remedy. She merely looked over their shoulders and then broadcast to the world what cards they held.

'She wanted no misunderstandings, no secrets She preferred open covenants, openly arrived at.

'For the truth is that Lady Astor could not help speaking the truth. Of course, she had no tact, but very honest people seldom have. They look on tact, with some justification, as a form of intellectual dishonesty, a smothering of fact, a clipping of the buds of spontaneity, a compromise with fraud. She would have none of it. She was a seeker after truth, a debunker of hypocrisy, a scourge of sinners, so long as they exposed their sin as readily as she exposed her own.

'If she had a fault it was that since she applied this treatment indiscriminately she sometimes failed to bomb only military targets.'

In that last sentence, William Douglas Home points to an important truth about Nancy. She was often cruel, but not often with intent.

During the years 1931 to 1935, Nancy's parliamentary performance began to grow very uneven. The stand she took on most questions of the time is such as is easily approved today: with Captain Harry Crookshank and Harold Macmillan among others, she fought the Government in 1934 on their policy towards the unemployed, urging a full restitution of the cuts to allowances imposed in 1931. In the same year, in February 1934, she made a speech of offensive indiscretion which angered the whole House. Somewhat in the spirit of Belloc's maddest ideas, she alleged that brewers bribed members and ministers to back their interests. Asked to produce evidence she floundered. It was a ridiculous and disastrous episode. Yet within four months she made what many good judges believed was the best speech of her whole career.

This occurred in the course of a debate on education in early June. Nancy's subject was Nursery Schools. Read today, this speech emerges through the dry prose of official reporting as a masterly performance. She used the rhetorical technique most acceptable to the House of Commons: she proved by citing facts and figures that she had a firm grasp of her subject. She used the emotional appeal sparingly, but when she did, as in an evocation of Margaret McMillan's character and career, it was effective. Her main proposition was that the number of poor children in need formed so small a minority that the most generous treatment by the Government could not conceivably involve an economic risk.

What effect this speech had on policy is hard to say. Such is always the case with the exertion of influence. It is safe to say that Margaret McMillan had made the success of her cause certain. It seems equally safe to say that without Nancy's work for the cause inside and outside Parliament that success would have been much more gradual.

On the 13th May 1935 T. E. Lawrence was killed by a fall from his motor bicycle. The injury to his brain was so severe that he could only have survived into a state of imbecility. Mercifully he died six days later. On the 19th May Nancy, who seems to have been kept in ignorance of the gravity of the accident, was presiding at an animated lunch-party at Cliveden. Mr Lee, the butler, brought a message to her. She turned pale, was unable to speak, handed the message to her next-door neighbour and hurried from the room.

On the 21st she was at the Dorset village of Moreton for the funeral of Lawrence of Arabia. By his request there were to be no wreaths nor other signs of mourning, but the men wore black ties, the women dark clothes, and an unidentified small girl ran forward at the last moment and threw a bunch of flowers on his coffin. Winston Churchill was present and had difficulty in restraining his emotion during the service. After the burial the chief mourners were given refreshment in Moreton House. Winston Churchill left early, but before he reached his car Nancy rushed out after him and cried, 'Winnie! Winnie!' She took his hands in hers and they stood together in silence and in tears.

Both of them were to see Lawrence's name held up to contempt before the end of their lives. How Winston Churchill reacted to the exposure of the man he had venerated is not known at the time of writing. We know how Nancy reacted. She simply refused to accept the hateful facts. He had been her friend and she rarely abandoned a friend, in this life or hereafter. For her he remained to the end one of the greatest of men. Another of the chief mourners was Basil Liddell Hart. No man more than he had been responsible for forming a reputation which at the time was seriously compared to that of Napoleon. When Liddell Hart died in 1970 he received much and deserved praise as a great military authority, but the name of T. E. Lawrence appeared nowhere in the obituaries. When the world has been fooled, the world usually prefers to forget the incident and to put the name of the deceiver out of mind. Not Nancy, however. She was made of different stuff, worldly as she was.

In June 1935 Stanley Baldwin took over the premiership from Ramsay MacDonald, and in the autumn he called a General Election. It was possibly the last British General Election to be conditioned by Foreign Affairs. Fascism and Nazism were getting into their stride; the public was alarmed, and the great issue was British rearmament. The issue was confused by the simultaneous rise of pacifism as a popular philosophy. It was widely reflected in the Press and promoted by honoured thinkers such as Bertrand Russell and Aldous Huxley. It found expression in June 1935 in a privately organised referendum called the Peace Ballot whereby loaded questions resulted in about eleven million voting for pacifism with more radical disarmament. The opposition Liberal and Labour parties hoped to capture the electorate by standing for a policy based on this Peace Ballot: resistance to the dictators and no rearmament, with lots of Collective Security which, without rearmament, would not have been secure. They blundered by following lunacy with logic. Baldwin was scared by the national state of mind, but instead of trying to change it, he endeavoured to compromise with it. 'There will be no great armaments,' he declared, all too truthfully.

Nancy, like most of her party, followed Baldwin's popular and escapist lead, but with an important and great difference. Some years later, in the war, she publicly declared that she had been utterly mistaken.

Polling day was set for the 14th November. In Plymouth Nancy was once more opposed by George Ward. Her son Bill stood for the East Fulham constituency in one of the most interesting contests of the election. In a by-election in 1933, a National Government candidate had been defeated by a Socialist who obtained a majority of 4,840. The victor's main proposition had been intensified disarmament.

Nancy scored a great electoral success again. The results were:

Lady Astor	21,491	
Mr George Ward	15,394	Majority 6,097

She would have been astonished and distressed to know that this was the last election she was to fight.

All her family and connections who stood were successful in the General Election, and Bill brilliantly opened his political career by wresting back East Fulham with a majority of 1,054. Had the future of the young men of Europe been different, he might well have enjoyed a distinguished political career. The general victory for Stanley Baldwin was enormous; he had a reduced but still overwhelming majority of 247. It was composed of 387 Conservatives, 33 Liberals under Sir John Simon, and a melancholy rump of only 8 members of the National Labour Party. The Opposition was composed of 154 members of the Labour Party now under Clement Attlee, 21 Liberals now under Sir Archibald Sinclair, and 4 members of the Independent Labour Party, under no one in particular except occasionally that melodramatic waver of Red Flags, James Maxton.

The National Labour Party suffered grievously from the electoral defeat of the former Prime Minister Ramsay MacDonald, and of his son Malcolm MacDonald who before the election had been Under Secretary for Dominion Affairs. The diminution of the party and the loss of its two foremost members made it now really impossible for the National Government to continue to appear national, though they kept the name. Safe seats in by-elections were found for the Mac-Donalds within the year, but the effect of their defeat was lasting.

There was one striking addition, however, to the thinning ranks of their party. Harold Nicolson was elected by a small majority to represent West Leicester in the National Labour interest. He plays some part in Nancy's story. She never liked him and he never really liked her. It was another case of mutual antipathy tempered by mutual attraction.

As with the 1931 election, Nancy's delight at the result was mixed with disappointment at seeing another setback to the feminist cause. Only nine women members were elected in 1935: they included six Conservatives, among whom were the Duchess of Atholl and Nancy's particular friend Mavis Tate who had boldly advocated large-scale rearmament in her election campaign; one Independent, Eleanor

Rathbone; one Independent Liberal, Megan Lloyd George; and one Labour member, Ellen Wilkinson, whom Nancy rejoiced to see back at Westminster.

The letters quoted in the preceding chapter are taken from the Astor archive and, except where indicated, contemporary events are described from the contemporary Press. The references to Bernard Shaw continue to owe their substance to St John Ervine's biography and Lady Astor's correspondence. The reference to the late Bobbie Shaw depends on Bernard Shaw's letter and Lady Astor's correspondence with members of her family. The account of Lord Lothian at this time is drawn from Sir James Butler's biography, Lord Brand's article in the D.N.B., and Dr Thomas Jones's book *A Diary with Letters 1931-1950* (London, 1954). The worsening relations between Lady Astor and Winston Churchill as a result of her attitude to the India question was told to me by the late Lord ('Bill') Astor. The account of Lady Astor dancing a *pas de deux* with Lady Islington is taken from a personal memory. My attention was drawn to the odd Rosenberg incident by Mr Robert Cecil, at present Reader in Modern German History at Reading University. The story of Lady Astor's aversion to meeting H. G. Wells was told to me by Bernard Shaw's cousin, Mrs John Musters. The account of Lady Astor by Mr William Douglas Home is taken from an essay which he wrote for Michael Astor. The incident of Lady Astor receiving news of T. E. Lawrence's death was told to me by Mr Alastair Buchan who was present. The rest of this passage follows *The Secret Lives of T. E. Lawrence*, by Colin Simpson and Philip Knightley (London, 1969). My opinion of Harold Nicolson's relations with Lady Astor are chiefly drawn from his published diaries. I remain generally indebted as before to Mrs Nancy Lancaster, Mrs Alice Winn, Mr Michael Astor and to Maurice Collis's biography. As before, I follow Pamela Brookes's *Women at Westminster* for details of women members.

Chapter 18

THE CLIVEDEN SET

THERE is only one important question to be asked or answered about the subject of this chapter: did the Cliveden Set exist or not? Was there a conspiracy which conducted its intrigues and machinations under the roof of Lord and Lady Astor's Buckinghamshire country house; or was this one of those mass delusions that suddenly, and especially in times of stress, haunt and at the same time soothe the minds of men? Should it be counted among fooleries such as the Popish plot supposedly revealed by Titus Oates; the recurrent belief that Jews use the blood of Christian infants in their religious observances; the once enormously widespread terror of witches; or the mild but nonetheless passionate faith that the works of William Shakespeare could only have been written by a member or a Committee of the House of Lords? Or was there something in it?

In this chapter I will endeavour, while tracing the course of Nancy's life, to reply to this question: was there a Cliveden Set or not?

The first thing is to state how belief in a Cliveden Set came about. It was first given currency by one of the most brilliant journalists of the 1930s, Mr Claud Cockburn. He had been correspondent for *The Times* in New York and Washington from 1929 to 1932. He had also served in Berlin under Norman Ebbutt. In 1933 he abandoned this promising career and published *The Week*, which is still remembered as one of the most extraordinary and successful enterprises in modern British journalism. Claud Cockburn had learned one important lesson from *The Times*: that in the forming of public opinion by the Press, circulation must not be mistaken for influence. The thirties illustrated this perfectly. The influence, despite manifest absurdities, of the *New Statesman* under Kingsley Martin's editorship, especially on a younger generation, has become one of the journalistic wonders of that age, while Lord Beaverbrook's championship of Empire Free Trade in the much more widely read *Daily Express* is largely forgotten. *The Week* took the example further than had been tried hitherto in England. It was a yellow-tinted micrographed bulletin of a few pages only, published on Wednesdays, the least fashionable day then. The cheap process of home-made publication made large circulation impossible and denied large profits to the dedicated men who ran it.

The bulletin was an instant success. It is not going too far to describe it as a raving success, for the fashionable philosopher of the thirties and forties, Cyril Joad, was moved to rush round the Café Royal screaming the praises of the new publication amid general applause. The success depended on a journalist technique usually called 'inside information'. Claud Cockburn never seemed to lack it. *The Week* became important. It was read by all the embassies in London, by members of the British and foreign governments, and by as many of the home and foreign intellectual public as could procure copies. Month by month the little bulletin became harder to obtain, as its influence spread.

There comes a fatal moment in all success, best illustrated by the example of the successful spiritualist medium. As her clients accumulate the temptation grows to fake the prophetic ecstasy in order to keep business going. Concealed banjoes and stuffed gloves manipulated in the dark have to do service for 'gods ascending out of the earth'.

The Week became an oracle of the frustrated Left, and thanks to Claud Cockburn's astounding journalistic flair, the oracle seemed never to fail. The inside information seemed ever to come from deeper and deeper recesses of the ministries and the services at home and abroad, but in the light of published State documents and later knowledge, relatively few of *The Week*'s revelations have turned out to be accurate.

The first move in the Cliveden Set business was made on the 27th October 1937. The only principal mentioned was the British Ambassador to Germany, Sir Nevile Henderson. He was as yet little known in England. That he was an admirer of Hitler could be guessed by pessimists, however, from his attendance at the Nazi Party rally of 1937, soon after he had been accredited. *The Week* seems to have been unaware of Henderson's character in other respects. It credited him with great if sinister imagination and a forceful will, to neither of which the poor man could lay any claim. The article of the 27th October reported that Henderson was planning a conference to be attended by Germany, Italy, Austria and Hungary. To this conference Jugoslavia would be artfully lured, thus detaching her from the

central European 'Little Entente'. With Germany thus greatly strengthened France would be seriously weakened. How did they know all this?
Henderson, it seems, had told his Danish colleague who had passed it
on to his government with which *The Week* had valuable contacts.

No more was heard of this story, but it had made *The Week's*
readership Henderson-conscious'. Three weeks later on the 17th
November *The Week* produced, with its customary assurance, a story
allied to that of the 27th October. This one had the advantage of close
particularisation and topicality. The same day as the number came out,
on the 17th, Lord Halifax arrived in Berlin. As a Joint-Master of the
Middleton Hounds, a position to which he attached an extravagant
importance, Halifax had been invited by Hermann Goering to a
hunting expedition in Berlin. He had accepted and it was known that
he would also meet Hitler. In the same month as Halifax paid his visit,
the Foreign Secretary, Anthony Eden, was intermittently absent from
England, attending the Nine Power Conference of November 1937 in
Brussels.[1] This was all that the public knew from the newspapers. *The
Week* made haste to help them to a clearer understanding.

Claud Cockburn's article on the 17th November 1937 may be described as the launching of the great ship *Cliveden Set*, though the name
was not set on its prow till a month later. The subject was the Halifax
visit to Germany. Sensation followed sensation. *The Week* claimed
perfect knowledge of Halifax's instructions which it described as
follows: he was under orders to propose to the Führer (whom he was
to meet on the 19th) that in exchange for an Anglo-German truce,
Great Britain would in no way interfere with German expansion to the
East. This Grand Design had no German origin, *The Week* insisted,
but a strictly British one. Halifax would convey it to Hitler as if it
came from the British Government, but in fact it was the invention
of a hidden cabal which directed the Government in secret. The plan,
The Week now revealed, had been concocted on the 23rd and 24th
October, under the aegis of the Astors. The article went on: 'Sub-
scribers to *The Week* are familiar with pro-Nazi intrigues centring on
Cliveden and in Printing House Square [*The Times* office] on the eve
of the outbreak of the Spanish War. The expulsion of *The Times*

1. The conference was composed of the signatories to the Nine Power Pact of 1922:
Britain, U.S.A., Belgium, China, France, Italy, Japan, Netherlands and Portugal.
This conference followed China's appeal to the League after the Japanese aggression
in Manchuria.

correspondent from Berlin[2] put a spoke . . . in the wheel of certain Germanophile plans. The intrigue however continued with Lord Lothian, the Astors, Mr Barrington Ward of *The Times* and its editor Mr Geoffrey Dawson (né Robinson) at the heart of it.' The Halifax plan was described as an attempt 'to satisfy the appetite of German Imperialism by the offer of an alternative' – namely aggression in the East instead of the West.

This was the meatiest fare that *The Week* had supplied to its customers at any time, but it proved too much for their digestive powers. As Claud Cockburn relates in an autobiographical volume: 'When I published the story, absolutely nothing happened. It made about as large a bang as a crumpet falling on a carpet. A few weeks later, I ran the whole thing again, in slightly different words, and with a similar result.'

Mr Cockburn's memory played him false here. The next article appeared in the next issue on Wednesday the 24th November. He had to rectify quickly a cardinal error in the previous article. It was quite true that on the 23rd and 24th October there had been a weekend party at Cliveden of a political character, and that Nevile Henderson, Philip Lothian and Geoffrey Dawson had been among the guests. What *The Week* had overlooked was that the principal guests were not Lord and Lady Halifax, as the story required, but Anthony and Beatrice Eden. The guests had also included the Deputy Under-Secretary of State in the Foreign Office, Sir Alexander Cadogan. Eden and the Foreign Office were supposed to be the intended victims of this great Germanophile conspiracy, and there they were fully represented at the plotting session. Worst of all the Halifaxes were not there. Something had to be done about all this, and was.

With a journalistic skill which can only arouse the admiration of anyone who has worked in Fleet Street, Claud Cockburn turned his disadvantage to advantage by presenting his correction not as something requiring apology but as a new and unexpectedly spicy piece of information. 'Among those present,' said *The Week* of the 24th November, 'at the fateful meeting at Cliveden, where the plans were laid, was Mr Eden himself. He was asked there for a purpose which, it seems, he himself did not understand. He was asked in order to "associate" him with the intrigue. He expressed his immediate and profound opposition to the whole perilous business.' This the Astors

2. Norman Ebbutt was expelled from Berlin on the 21st August, 1937.

might have anticipated. Then why did they ask him? The answer was simple. If Anthony Eden was there when the conspiracy was hatched he would be compromised: the arch-fiend of Great Britain, the Prime Minister Neville Chamberlain, could then claim, if the plot misfired, that his Foreign Secretary knew about these dealings before he himself did. The chief plotters were named afresh, this time with the addition of Lord Londonderry and the Aga Khan. Lord Lothian was described as the liaison agent between Cliveden and *The Times*. Why Lord Astor needed a liaison between his brother or his friend Dawson was not explained. The absence of Lord Halifax and the presence of Sir Alexander Cadogan were conveniently ignored.

By the time this issue appeared rumours and information about Halifax's meeting with Hitler had appeared in the Press. Halifax had returned to London on the 22nd November. It was clear that his conversation with the Führer had had no positive result. *The Week* put this down to the fact that Ribbentrop, at the time German Ambassador in London, had not been consulted and so, in a mood of injured vanity, he had contrived to wreck this tremendous machination. The comment shows admirable understanding of Ribbentrop's character, if not of his activity in October and November of 1937.

The argument was too involved, sophisticated and improbable, even for the intellectuals of the day. Once more the crumpet fell on the carpet. Once more Claud Cockburn followed his uncanny skill in journalism. He waited and then four weeks later, on the 22nd December, he returned to his prey. This time he attached a label to it, and as every journalist knows, that is half the game.

The main article on the 22nd was entitled 'The Cliveden Set'. Its subject was acceptable. In contrast with the two preceding attacks on the Astors, with their prophecies of doom, this one told of a defeat of the powers of darkness and a blow struck for freedom by the good knight Anthony Eden. The article opened: 'Following the resounding defeat of "The Cliveden Set" and Printing House Square after the return of Lord Halifax to London and the visit of the French ministers,[3] it was correctly assumed that a new putsch from the same "friends of the Third Reich" was to be expected.'

The Week recalled that the invitation for Lord Halifax to attend Goering's hunting exhibition and his subsequent visit to Hitler at

3. Camille Chautemps, French Premier, and Yvon Delbos, French Foreign Minister visited London shortly after Lord Halifax's return from Germany.

Berchtesgaden had prompted a great many people to write to *The Times* proposing the return of former colonies to the Reich. This was not, as it seemed, an explosion of English sentimental Germanophilism (often to be found in other papers), but was a putsch organised by the Astors. But the putsch, *The Week* maintained, had been halted and flung back. The letters, the article went on, were 'of the same character as those which preceded and prepared the Halifax coup. However, instead of being followed up by other letters and developing into another campaign similar to that of October and early November, the letters abruptly ceased. It turns out that they ceased as a result of the intervention of the Foreign Office with the Prime Minister. What with the presence of Mr Eden, whose absence in Brussels on the earlier occasion [the letters in early November] had left Mr Chamberlain immediately exposed to the demands of the Astor family presented through the intermediary of Sir Samuel Hoare – and what with the somewhat grisly impression made on the Prime Minister by Lord Halifax's final report of his trip, Mr Chamberlain was in no mood to have the whole shindy start over again. . . . Mr Eden received permission to intervene directly with a member of the Astor family, and the correspondence ceased as abruptly as it had reopened.

'The financial power of the Anglo-American set is as extensive as their social ramifications and is greater than their direct political influence. . . . It is regarded as certain that sooner or later Britain's "other Foreign Office" at Cliveden will be brought very powerfully to bear on the Prime Minister.' (The picture of Eden having 'received permission' was little to the credit of their hero, but no one seems to have noticed this.)

The 'Halifax coup' was regarded as the proof positive of the power enjoyed by the other Foreign Office. *The Week* correctly pointed out that there had been no Foreign Office interpreter at the meeting of Hitler and Halifax on the 19th November. A simple and thrilling explanation was offered: 'A Foreign Office interpreter could not be sent because the trip had been arranged behind Mr Eden's back. Lord Halifax was going as the representative rather of Cliveden and Printing House Square than of more official quarters.'

Lord Halifax was reported as perturbed by the confrontation and especially by evidence of Hitler's anti-Christianity and persecution of the Churches. 'It caused him to brood no little on the discrepancy between the Third Reich as it looks from Cliveden and as it is seen in

the flesh of the roaring champion of totalitarian Teutonism at Berchtesgaden; his brooding affected no little his report in Whitehall.'

There were six items on the Cliveden Set in *The Week* during 1938,
five of them appearing between January and April, the last on the 9th
November. The Astors and their friends were often referred to as *les
Cagoulards*, the 'hooded ones', the name by which French fascists were
known in France, and *The Times* became the *Clivedener Neueste
Nachrichten*; but apart from a long article on the Cliveden Set on the
30th March 1938, Claud Cockburn at no time added substantially to
his article of the 22nd December 1937. Even in the 30th March article
there is relatively little fresh material. One great surprise is that
Anthony Eden's resignation on the 20th February 1938 was not
ascribed to the machinations of the Cliveden Set. Claud Cockburn
seems to have got tired of his toy for it hardly appears in *The Week*
at all during 1939.

Since the results of the article of 22nd December 1937 were enormous, it seems proper to look first at the major allegations and find
what if any truth they contained. It has already been noticed that it is
not easy to reconcile the supposed mission of Lord Halifax to Hitler
behind Anthony Eden's back, with Anthony Eden as the principal
guest at Cliveden when this evil plan was hatched. In fact, the clandestine character of Halifax's mission was wholly fanciful. Apart from
anything else, as anyone in the least conversant with official life will
quickly recognise, such a secret mission by a minister to a foreign head
of state would be impossible of contrivance. As is now known, Halifax
consulted Neville Chamberlain and Anthony Eden officially, and
Winston Churchill unofficially in the presence of Eden, before accepting. *The Week*'s story faintly resembled the fact at one point. While
Anthony Eden was in Brussels on the 11th November, news of the
invitation found its way into the *Evening Standard*. Chamberlain and
Halifax both wanted a Prime Ministerial statement on the subject
without delay in the House of Commons. This irritated Anthony Eden
who had never been enthusiastic for the visit. He demanded twenty-
four hours' delay – which he obtained. This is as near as one gets to
the notion of Halifax acting behind Eden's back, and it is not near
enough to matter.

Considering that Claud Cockburn was as skilful as a journalist can be
in the plying of his craft, he seems to have paid small attention to
ascertaining the basic facts on which his whole case rested. To believe

in the dishonestly secret mission of Halifax, the proof of Cliveden's power, was to believe that Anthony Eden had been absent during most of November and during the period of the mission. In fact, during the whole of November he had been absent in Brussels for only eight days: from the 2nd to the 5th, and the 9th to the 14th. His visits to the Nine Power Conference were not kept secret. He was not out of contact with the Foreign Office at any time. *The Times*, in common with the *Daily Telegraph*, caused uneasiness in the Foreign Office by exaggerating, after the leak on the 11th, the scope and importance of the Halifax visit. It is a thing papers sometimes do with their news. This is the only evidence, and not strong evidence, of any extreme interest taken by any of the Astors in the visit.

The major newspoint was missed and probably unobtainable by Claud Cockburn in his ingenious record. It was to be found in the determined efforts by Nevile Henderson to make of Halifax a messenger of surrender to German claims far exceeding anything tolerable to the Foreign Office or the Cabinet. With characteristic and opinionated intransigence he insisted (independently of his instructions) that Halifax should play soft and say nothing, even on a matter of principle, to excite Hitler's easily aroused anger. (This was in accord with Cockburn's story but wholly unconnected with the Astors.) Henderson's strenuously urged advice seems to have had some unfortunate effect on Halifax's conduct of the conversation with Hitler. He seems to have erred on the side of politeness and so caused uneasiness to Eden who feared that Hitler might later claim from his visitor's sympathetic and liberal remarks that he had been given the go-ahead for aggression in eastern Europe. This is exactly what Hitler did do, and this fitted in with *The Week*'s report. But its accuracy was manifestly coincidental. No such go-ahead was proposed from Cliveden. In so far as it had an English origin it came from the muddle-headed weakness of the wishful-thinking man whom, in an evil hour, Eden and Sir Robert Vansittart had chosen for the Embassy in Berlin. Nevile Henderson was no more a close friend of the Astors than were Lord and Lady Londonderry, or the Aga Khan.

The absence of a British interpreter at Halifax's meeting with Hitler was an extraordinary piece of incompetence which made it doubly easy for Hitler to misrepresent the interview. It is odd that there is no mention of this in the diaries of Lord Harvey. The duty of supplying such an interpreter would normally fall on the Embassy. One may be

tempted to suspect Nevile Henderson of culpably not supplying the
translator, but it is to be noted that no such suggestion appears in
contemporary documentation. One need not go further into the allegation that the absence of a British interpreter was because the Cliveden
Set had not got one handy.

There can be no serious doubt today that this article was a piece of
successful sensationalism and no more; to be treated, as a source of
information, with no greater seriousness than is accorded to Lord
Northcliffe's early *Daily Mail* report that the entire British Legation
in Peking had been massacred. But sensationalism can pay.

Claud Cockburn tells how, after the flop of his attacks on the Astors
of the 17th and 24th November, his third article blazed into life.

'I think it was *Reynolds News*, three days later, which first picked up
the phrase from *The Week*, but within a couple of weeks it had been
printed in dozens of newspapers, and within six had been used in
almost every leading newspaper of the Western world. Up and down
the British Isles, across and across the United States, anti-Nazi orators
shouted it from hundreds of platforms. No anti-Fascist rally in Madison
Square Garden or Trafalgar Square was complete without a denunciation of the Cliveden Set.

'In those days, if you saw cameramen patrolling St James's Square at
lunchtime or dusk, you could be nearly sure they were there to get a
picture of the Cliveden Set going in or out of the Astors' London
house. Geoffrey Dawson, then editor of *The Times*, and a prominent
member of the "Set", comments petulantly on this nuisance in his
diary. If you talked to American special correspondents, what they
wanted to know all about was the Cliveden Set. Senators made speeches
about it, and in those London cabarets where libel didn't matter,
songsters made songs about it. People who wanted to explain everything by something, and were ashamed to say "sunspots", said
"Cliveden Set".'

Claud Cockburn even underestimates the speed with which the
success of his story was attained. The *Daily Worker* and the *Manchester
Guardian* were ahead of *Reynolds News* in giving the story publicity,
and at the same time it had been commented on in the French and
German Press. In England the story, with editorial belief in it, persisted
for something like eighteen months, *Reynolds News* and the *Daily
Worker* maintaining their lead but closely challenged by the *News
Chronicle* and the *Tribune*. David Low was inspired to draw some

wonderful cartoons, and to rename the Cliveden Set 'The Shiver Sisters' whose motto was 'Any Sort of Peace at any Sort of Price'. Low, however, introduced a note of total farce into the excitement, notably in a drawing showing Nancy in a *Cagoulard's* hood prowling about the cellars of Westminster, which may have helped to introduce some semblance of reason into the affair. Unexpectedly *Time and Tide*, edited by Nancy's friend Lady Rhondda, published an article called 'Clivedenism' on the 2nd April 1938. It was by the most eminent of its regular contributors, Sir Norman Angell. He also had swallowed the story whole. Letters exchanged between Waldorf and Lady Rhondda suggest that she herself was not in complete agreement with Sir Norman. But the article appeared all the same, and Lady Rhondda's language is guarded. She evidently thought that there was something in it.

All sorts of strange interpretations were put on the supposedly revealed conspiracy. One very interesting theory, for the light it throws on the theorist, was that this aristocratic clique was working, not in Chamberlain's interest, as was usually supposed, but against him, seeking to rectify the weakening of the peerage occasioned by the choice of the middle-class Baldwin in preference to the nobly born Curzon in 1923! The theory indicates the strong element of class-antagonism which was behind this agitation. To the general acceptance of the story by the newspapers, especially on the Left, there was one honourable exception. The *Daily Herald* gave Clivedenism no publicity.

One blaze of wrath against the Cliveden Set was of definite advantage to the Astors. The British Fascist paper *Action* heaped scorn on the 'powers of money and the Press' as represented by Cliveden, and described them as exercising a brutal dictatorship over Great Britain. But *Action* strenuously denied that the members of the Cliveden Set could possibly be friendly to Germany, as Nazis were much too nice to make friends with such nasty beings. *Action* had little circulation and little influence, so this testimony was barely noticed. In the forming of opinion the Left remained in possession of the field, and outside the Astor-owned *Times* and *Observer* very few papers rejected or showed total scepticism towards the Cliveden tale. The *Spectator*, edited by Wilson Harris, was another honourable exception to the general trend.

Enough has been said by now, in the writer's opinion, to show conclusively that the story of the Cliveden Set rested on a false premiss:

the 'Halifax coup' was no attempted *coup d'état* by an extra-govern-
mental body but a very ordinary political transaction. All the same . . .
Was there something in the story after all? Propaganda concocted with
little respect for the truth does sometimes point the right way. For
example, it is now known that *The Brown Book of the Hitler Terror* was
compiled in 1933 largely from rumours conveyed by unreliable and
even mendacious people with little attempt to get at the real facts. But
it remains true that *The Brown Book*, for all its inventions and disregard
of research, was a much surer guide to the character of Nazism than
the carefully documented criticism of fair-minded and learned ex-
plorers. Was something of this kind true in this case? Was the Cliveden
Set a myth which portrayed in crude and picturesque terms a reality?
Innocent as the Astors and their friends may have been of the impossible
feat of sending Lord Halifax to Hitler behind Anthony Eden's back,
did they nevertheless exert an unwholesome influence on the British
Government in the age of Hitler?

An outline of Nancy's life, and a look at the Astor papers dating
from the middle thirties till the outbreak of war, should indicate a
firm answer to this question.

The idea of a Cliveden Set, not necessarily a sinister group, was
probably first suggested to journalists by the state of Parliament immediately before and after the General Election of 1935. Rarely in
modern times have so many members of a single family enjoyed the
privilege of membership. Nancy, her son Bill, her brother-in-law J. J.
Astor, her son-in-law James Willoughby, and her nephew-in-law
Ronald Tree, made a family group of five, in the same party, in the
House of Commons. To this could be added in the House of Lords,
Waldorf and James Willoughby's father, Lord Ancaster. The latter
was not a person who claimed to be a force in the political world,
but the man in the street did not know this, and when Lord Ancaster
became a hereditary Lord Great Chamberlain a little later, he was
easily represented to the ignorant as a person wielding great powers.
A family group of seven was without doubt an unusual phenomenon.
It seems to have first been the subject of a newspaper article in June
1936 in the *New York Times*. This was a well-planned little essay which
pointed out that the Astor family grouping could give rise to false ideas,
as it did not involve political grouping. There was no reason to suppose

that Ronald Tree's views and voting necessarily followed those of his aunt by marriage, or that Major J. J. Astor took political cues from Lord Ancaster. All this was not only sensible but could be easily illustrated: in fact, Nancy had interrupted a speech by her son in order to express disagreement! But to say such things did not lead to what Fleet Street calls a 'strong' story. Something more exciting was to the public taste, and to the commercial interest of editors. The real wonder is that the different story was so long in coming.

Cliveden and the Astors were not much in the news during 1936, and (by her own exacting standards) Nancy played little part in public affairs during this year. The national interest was centred on the death of the venerable King, George V, and then on the new reign and 'the King's matter': whether or not Edward VIII could marry the woman he loved and remain King. The first great international success of Hitler in his military movement into the Rhineland, and the beginning of the Spanish Civil War during the summer, caused surprisingly small reactions in Great Britain. Concern with the royal problem posed by Edward VIII made the country more insular than usual. The problem affected the Astors personally. Nancy had liked the King as Prince of Wales, had often entertained him, had charmed him as he had charmed her. She had done valuable work in introducing him to Labour members whom he might otherwise not have met. In 1933 Nancy and the Prince had come into the public eye together when he only just won from her in the Parliamentary Golf Handicap.[4] They were friends, but she and Waldorf were never of the Prince of Wales's intimate circle. Nancy's royal devotion, which was considerable and, as one might expect, very emotional, was most fixed on the Duke and Duchess of York, and the dowager Queen Mary.[5] She knew Edward VIII well enough, however, to speak her mind to him on the subject of his possible marriage. This she did in June 1936, some time during the Ascot meeting. She gave two accounts in letters. According to one, 'I went to see him myself and begged him not to do as he was doing'.

4. From a letter to the writer from her son David Astor: 'My mother was really quite a good golfer – she won the Parliamentary handicap tournament one year. She played most methodically and she never ever took a risk – it was really quite boring to play golf with her. The odd thing is that she played golf in the opposite style from the way she behaved in real life, which was with little method and lots of risks. I can offer no explanation for this paradox.'

5. According to Edwin Lee, Queen Mary was the only person of whom Lady Astor stood in manifest awe.

According to the other she 'spoke hotly and loudly'. The circumstances of the encounter are not recorded. It is evident that she believed that she had succeeded in dissuading him from his intention of marrying Mrs Simpson. She was away in America when the Abdication crisis occurred.

On her return she was asked to broadcast to America, when it was over. She was at pains to assert that the abdication had been exclusively caused by the fact that the King wished to marry a divorced woman, and not, as some journalists had said, by the fact that Mrs Simpson was American. She spoke with great difficulty and nearly broke down.

One might suppose from Press reports of the time that 1936 was a year from which nothing regarding Cliveden Set allegations can be learned. This is not so. A later publication, *Diary with Letters 1931–1950*, by Thomas Jones – T.J. – provides interesting evidence. In 1936 Joachim von Ribbentrop held the odd position of being Hitler's ambassador at large. He was head of an office in Berlin which could be correctly described, as Cliveden was to be fallaciously described, as a supplementary Foreign Office. This office had to its credit the Anglo-German Naval Treaty of June 1935. In 1936 (before his appointment as German Ambassador to London in the early autumn) Ribbentrop was frequently in England. It is odd that Claud Cockburn did not make more of his impact on the Astor circle. One can only assume that he did not know about it.

Ribbentrop was a person of such manifest evil that the present-day reader has to be reminded that he reached political heights largely through exerting a very effective social charm. As a wine salesman he showed a mastery of flattering and winning demeanour, but when he had found favour with Hitler and saw power beckoning to his puny soul, he changed his manners which he now closely modelled on those of the former Crown Prince. He would stride into a room with a military stamp and come to an abrupt halt before his host or hostess. He would then shoot out his right arm and announce his name as though it was a declaration of war before shaking hands. Many people found in this behaviour a ridiculous exhibition, but it did not alienate him from Hitler. The reason is not far to seek. Among people who impressed Ribbentrop either by their influence, power, or social status (and he was a pathetic snob as his dubious 'von' alone illustrates), he could at will revert to the insinuating exercise of charm, which had not only deceived fools. He was a clever man and he would have quickly seen that his pseudo-Potsdam performance was unlikely to succeed with the Astors or Tom Jones.

The date of Nancy's first meeting with Ribbentrop was early in this period of special missions to London. She invited him to lunch at 4 St James's Square. As a political hostess this was a normal courtesy. From a memory of her son David Astor who was present, she was not in diplomatic mood. She rallied her guest on the absurdity of many of Hitler's public performances, and with such quick-firing jesting that the other soon found himself bewildered. She made fun of Hitler's appearance and asked Ribbentrop how people could take him seriously while he persisted in wearing Charlie Chaplin's moustache, with other remarks of the same sort.

Ribbentrop may have been offended but if so he hid his feelings. He often met the Astors in the social life of London though he never became intimate with them. He was the Astors' guest on only one other occasion, through the instrumentality of T.J.

In mid-May of 1936 T.J. was asked to spend a long weekend with Ribbentrop at his house in Berlin-Dahlem. He accepted. He had been asked as the confidant of the Prime Minister. Ribbentrop had a proposition: that Baldwin and the Führer should meet, and to win T.J.'s approval of the scheme Ribbentrop assured his guest that Hitler resembled Baldwin in character, surely one of the major mis-statements of the time. He represented such a meeting as the key to European peace. T.J. fell in with the proposition completely. On the 17th May he flew with Ribbentrop to Munich for an interview with the Führer who enlarged on his overriding desires for peace and his hopes of meeting Baldwin. T.J., on returning, endeavoured to bring the meeting about, but, as the reader need not be reminded, it never took place.

It is a very curious thing that so astute, decent and experienced a man as T.J. should have been deceived by the face of innocence assumed by Ribbentrop and Hitler, whose criminality was fully evidenced by 1936. He was clearly guilty of believing what he wanted to believe. He wished the Astors and their friends to share in his good opinion of Ribbentrop and so help on the Hitler-Baldwin meeting. He took his friend to Rest Harrow in the summer of 1936. Here is his account:

'June 2. Lunch alone with von Ribbentrop at the Carlton. Reported what had transpired since my visit to Berlin with special reference to the proposed secret meeting of Hitler and S.B. Said S.B. has never flown and does not much like the sea. I assumed one could not expect

Hitler to land in England any more than our P.M. in Germany. Von R. said he could arrange for Hitler to come quite close to our coast, two or three miles from Dover or Folkestone. I said that would help, and that S.B. would almost certainly want Eden with him, to balance von R. He agreed that to postpone the meeting until S.B. went on his holiday to Aix was undesirable, and if the attempt to secure S.B. failed the sooner Halifax met the Führer the better.

'I proposed that von Ribbentrop should come with me that afternoon to Sandwich where, particularly, he would meet a Cabinet Minister in the shape of Inskip, now Minister for the Co-ordination of Defence, as well as Lothian and the Astors. He agreed. I phoned to Sandwich and announced our visit. At 5.10 p.m. von R. picked me up at Tufton Court. He had with him von Wussow and a valet. At 7.30 we were at Rest Harrow and dressed for dinner at once. Waldorf had gone to Geneva to preside over his Nutrition Committee. On the way down I had warned von R. that Inskip was an evangelical churchman. The dinner had not been going many minutes before he brought up the Nazi persecution of the Church in Germany. Von R. tactfully prefaced his defence by saying he knew the Archbishop of Canterbury and George Bell [Bishop] of Chichester, and went on to explain that a new Reformation was proceeding in Germany in the interests of religion. The orthodox Lutheran Church was petrified and had no message. Out of the present confusion a new and better Christian Church would emerge. It was absurd to imagine that there was not enough vitality in Christianity to surmount the present troubles. Which of its many heterodox variants now clashing with one another would triumph no one could prophesy. Nancy broke in with "The Roman Catholics make God material and the Communists make man material".

'After dinner we plunged, and von R. got properly going and put with conviction the arguments he had used to me in Berlin. Inskip questioned him freely and admitted to me that he was impressed. I underlined the strength of the pro-League party in this country, which Lothian was inclined to pooh-pooh as having been knocked out by the fall of Abyssinia. Nancy supported me and said "I've never known Philip wrong on foreign politics in twenty years, and never right on home politics". Von R. stressed the importance of a collaborating England and Germany forming a new centre of crystallization for the smaller powers in Europe and hinted that Germany was at this moment receiving advances from some of them secretly. He told us that a number of English trade unionists were paying a private visit to Germany just now. We talked till nearly midnight and when the others had retired Lothian and I talked on till 12.45 with von R. in Waldorf's study. There Lothian impressed upon von R. that in any agreement with us it must be made plain that it contemplated the peaceful revision of the Treaties as they affected Austria, Memel and the rest. We must not get into a position of a breach of faith should Austria fall to Germany. Von R., of course, agreed.

'*June 3*. At breakfast Nancy chaffed von R. about the "bad company" he kept when in England – Lady Londonderry and Lady Cunard. Von R. pleaded that they had both always been extremely kind to him and his friends.

'We left soon after 9.30. . . . Nearly two o'clock before they dropped me at Tufton Court.

'Later in the afternoon, von Wussow came to the Pilgrim Trust office and we arranged a short secret code, for communication between us when he returned to Berlin. I rang up Geoffrey Dawson and arranged with Wussow that he should see von R. this evening between 6.30 and 7.30.'

The reader has been given this extract at such length because, so far as the writer knows, this is one of only three detailed and informed records of the Cliveden Set in action to have been published. There is no reason to question its accuracy. T.J. was the most candid of men and, though his reader may be shocked at the badness of the counsel he sometimes gave to Baldwin, and at his culpable ignorance of the European affairs and tensions on which he presumed to advise, he must admire the absence of any attempt to conceal wrong opinions when he published these papers at a time when Chamberlainite appeasers were the subject of unreflecting censure. There is another Cliveden Set record by T.J., shortly to be quoted, and a third one, of German origin, which belongs to three years later and is of very doubtful accuracy. It will be discussed later in the story.

What does this, the most interesting record of the Cliveden Set, amount to? Precious little, would seem the right answer. This was the only time when Ribbentrop was Nancy or Waldorf's house-guest. He was never asked for a Cliveden weekend. His name is not to be found in the visitors' book. (Nancy did not take to him and, though frequently urged to do so, positively refused to invite him.) The facts concerning the visit to Rest Harrow should be quickly scrutinised. A friend of the family asks a famous political hostess whether he may bring a German engaged on a special diplomatic mission to stay for the night. She says yes. To have done otherwise could have been interpreted as a gratuitous affront. So she says yes. Her husband is away. Hitler's ambassador at large arrives to be received by the Cliveden Set in force – for it should not be forgotten that Nancy was always represented as the central figure. When he arrives does he find a wholehearted Naziphile greeting awaiting him? On the contrary, he finds that 'the dinner had not been going many minutes before' he is being challenged on the persecutions practised by his Government. Ribbentrop 'tactfully' counters the charges. In the subsequent conversations indiscretions are certainly made from the British side. It was certainly not wise to discuss treaty revisions outside the Foreign Office with this man, but the main point insisted on, that Great Britain could only enter an agreement with a Germany which ruled out the use of force, and to which 'von R. of course agreed', was in complete harmony with Governmental policy. It was extremely foolish to make any suggestion to any Nazi that British loyalty to the League was wilting, but it may be remarked that it was Nancy, the queen of the set, who checked Philip Lothian's exposure of weak knees.

The reference to Lord Halifax in the earlier part of the extract is interesting. It suggests strongly that the idea of inviting him to Germany originated not with Goering, as is usually believed, but with Ribbentrop. The reference to a code between Wussow and T.J. may look sinister to anyone who has not read T.J.'s book and does not therefore appreciate his loyalty to Baldwin and other political leaders who made use of his services. Codes and suchlike were necessary in the German police state, as even this optimist knew.

Referring to *Diary with Letters* in an unpublished essay written for Michael Astor, Harold Nicolson said this:

'Clandestine meetings between Herr von Ribbentrop, some Cabinet ministers and others were certainly arranged at St James's Square or at Lady Astor's sea-side residence at Sandwich; from these meetings the German Ambassador did acquire the idea that there existed an influential minority in England prepared, if only the British Empire were left undisturbed, to accord Nazi Germany a free hand against Russia, and the resultant mastery of Europe. This was a disastrous impression to have conveyed to so ill-judging a man as Herr von Ribbentrop, and Lady Astor must certainly bear her part of the blame.'

It seems a harsh judgement on only one meeting (at which Russia was not mentioned), a meeting moreover arranged at the last moment, and not on Nancy's initiative. In his later years Harold Nicolson contracted the reviewer's weakness of pronouncing judgement without a serious effort to master the facts.[6]

The *Diary with Letters* of Tom Jones continues throughout the next eighteen months or so to furnish as complete a picture as can be found of the attitude on which Neville Chamberlain, after becoming Prime Minister on the 28th May 1937, based the policy of Appeasement. Many of the leading personalities of the thirties appear in this fascinating and distressing document, but when it comes to pertinent evidence of Appeasement policy and action, the Astors never seem to be there, and the relevant events never seem to happen at Cliveden or St James's Square. Until the famous weekend of the 23rd and 24th October 1937, it might seem that yet another year flowed by from which nothing about the Cliveden Set can be learned. In the Press of the time, however, there is one item which might have provided material for mischief. As often before and later Nancy was guilty of an indiscretion.

At the beginning of May 1937 she again made one of her rare speeches on foreign affairs. The occasion was a Conservative meeting in her constituency. She urged the need of an 'Anglo-German pact'. The speech was of a conventional well-worn kind and was not pro-Nazi. She stressed that mankind 'did not live in a world of angels' and that one must manage to live at peace with people of whom one might not wholly approve, rather than inflict a world war on mankind. The speech reflected Philip Lothian's ideas. It expressed familiar sentiments and did not cause much stir. There the matter would normally have rested.

She was appointed a Companion of Honour by the new King and attended his coronation (not as a member of the House of Commons but as a peeress) later in the month. Then, braving the hot weather, she sailed for the United States early in June, where she stayed for over three weeks, returning on the 30th. The reason for this visit was to see her brother Buck Langhorne who had fallen gravely ill and had little more time to live. At the end of the visit, on the day of her departure from New York, she was interviewed by reporters. Again she made one

6. In the same essay he invokes *The Memoirs* of Ribbentrop (English version, London, 1953) as an authority for the 'clandestine meetings'. The Astors are not mentioned in the book, nor are any clandestine meetings with anybody in England.

of her rare pronouncements on foreign affairs. To follow the account given by the *New York Times*:

'Lady Astor voiced a warning that the backers of anti-German feeling were over-playing their hands, and declared that "if the Jews are behind it they are going too far, and they need to take heed.

' "I am a pro-Jew and have always been a Zionist," Lady Astor declared, "but anyone who reads the papers can see what is coming; it will react against them. And I tell all my Jewish friends the same thing. I am against Communism which may also be partly responsible for this sentiment. Communism is the most horrible thing in the world today. I hate all dictators and it is appalling to see this propaganda playing into their hands." '

She pointed out that the agitators against Germany, 'and mind you I'm not at all pro-German', were forgetting completely the 'atrocities going on in other nations, in Russia, in Spain, and in Ethiopia'.

The editor was moved to write a not friendly though polite note after the report.

What Nancy said may have been clumsily reported, or she herself may have spoken impromptu and thus confusedly on a difficult subject, but her main points seem to have been reasonable enough: that hatred of Nazism should not be allowed to degenerate into anti-Germanism, and that Jews ought to be particularly careful not to allow their anti-Nazism to associate them with Communism. These are not disgraceful opinions, but when Nancy's remarks reached the British Press in July they were represented as such. It was, in the emotional excitement of the time, almost inevitable. She was widely reported as saying that the violent anti-German feeling in America was due to Jewish and Communist propaganda, rather than to Nazi crimes. Unfortunately Nancy did not defend herself with great skill. She changed her ground and declared that her object had been a 'plea for an atmosphere of constructive goodwill' – with Hitler. She did not come out of the affair victoriously and those who remembered her speech in May could carelessly imagine her to be friendly to the Nazis.

Nancy was fully aware of her tendency to indiscretion, but she never learned to master it. Earlier in this same year she made an appallingly indiscreet remark to David's friend Adam von Trott whom she had not met before. She told this young German that she was '*prodeutsch*', giving as her reason that she thought the Germans were quite right to rearm as they were surrounded by hostile Roman Catholic powers!

Happily Trott was a devoted anti-Nazi and was amused rather than outraged by this very unexpected appraisal, but there is no reason to suppose that she did not make equally thoughtless remarks to people who were not well-intentioned. If the Cliveden Set had an origin in fact, it was most likely to be found in Nancy's sometimes grotesque 'ad-libbing'.

To return to more material fact: the famous weekend of the 23rd – 24th October 1937. This, like the Ribbentrop visit to Sandwich, was described at first hand by T.J. For believers in the Cliveden Set his record may come as something of a disappointment.

'*October 24*. Cliveden, Taplow. Here the house is pretty full. Thirty to lunch today but this included three boys from Eton. The Edens are the highest lights and Nevile Henderson the newest. Sir Alex Cadogan and his brother, the Speaker and his Lady, Curzon's two daughters, Lady Alex Metcalfe and Lady Ravensdale,[7] Geoffrey Dawson, Lothian, Brand and Curtis, Nichols of the F.O., married to Spender-Clay's daughter, Bernays M.P. and so forth. Politics all day and all night. Eden has aged since I saw him six months ago and is dog-tired at the start of the Session. I sat between him and Henderson after the ladies left last night and found they differed widely in policy. Henderson struck me as sensible and informed without distinction. He has lived in the countries we talked about and Eden has not and this was apparent.

Eden himself thinks the Cabinet very weak and the armament programme far in arrears. On the other hand, he seems to argue that we can't do business with Germany until we are armed – say in 1940. This assumes that we can catch up with Germany – which we cannot, and that Hitler takes no dramatic step in the meantime, which is unlike Hitler. We have spurned his repeated offers. They will not be kept open indefinitely. His price will mount and he will want the naval agreement revised in his favour. It is believed that Mussolini has sold Austria to him at the recent meeting, in return for what, I don't know. All this the P.M. sees and says, but I think it goes no further and that

---

7. Lady Alexandra Metcalfe and Lady Ravensdale, daughters of Lord Curzon by his first marriage. Through their sister, Lady Cynthia Mosley, who died in 1933, they had been sisters-in-law of Sir Oswald Mosley, a fact commented upon in *The Week*. In October 1934 Lady Astor had had a correspondence with Lady Ravensdale in which the latter, in a friendly manner, protested against what she took to be Lady Astor's intemperate criticisms of the British Fascist movement. Lady Astor stood her ground while regretting having caused her friend pain.

meanwhile Vansittart is trying hard to bring N.C. round to the secular F.O. view'

The above extract is all that can be learned from T.J. about the Cliveden Set and Germany on that date. This is another point in which the principals appear to miss their cue and not make their eagerly expected appearance on stage. Even at Cliveden, where are the Astors? For that matter, where is Sir Nevile Henderson? As it stands the entry in the diary appears to record the views of Anthony Eden, which history shows to have been sound, and those of T.J. which have proved to be wrong. It is possible that what appear as T.J.'s ideas are in fact Henderson's, though the assumption certainly strains the text. Independent evidence in great quantity and of high quality does make it abundantly clear, however, that the extreme Appeasement-attitude adopted by T.J. regarding this question was more or less exactly the same as that of Henderson. It would seem reasonable to suppose that implicitly T.J. is recording his agreement. But the question which has often confronted the writer in the course of research remains unanswered: where were the Astors? One thing may be taken as certain. They were not in a magnificent backroom of Cliveden plotting the Halifax mission.

The story has now reached again that point, at the end of 1937 and the beginning of 1938, when the revelation of *The Week* burst upon a world anxious for explanations. The question remains whether or not there was 'something in it'.

The biographer of Nancy naturally turns at this point to the Astor archive, and his first choice is, inevitably, the Bernard Shaw correspondence. Here he may have hopes of finding a solution.

Shaw, after all, was the only one of Nancy's friends to admit warm approval and admiration of Hitler openly. The Shaw-Astor correspondence is witty, amusing, teasing, but entirely personal until late 1938. He sent Nancy a Press photograph of himself with the beautiful Lady Mary Lygon at Malvern. Underneath he wrote: 'We are not, as you might suppose, getting married; but it very nearly came to that. Ain't she lovely? G.B.S.' But of Hitler, Nazism or Germany there is no word until the Cliveden Set business had been going for more than a year.

The Lothian correspondence is the next obvious choice. Most of its contents, as with the G.B.S. letters, are concerned with private subjects, in this case with the pursuit of Christian Science; frequent advice, similar to that often given by T.J., on her handling of her children, with appeals to her to let them go their own ways and not to be too easily alarmed by their vagaries; but a sizeable proportion is occupied by political matter. Lothian saw Hitler twice in this period, in February 1935 and in May 1937. There is nothing in the Astor correspondence about the second of these occasions, but he wrote to Nancy about the first. He came back from his meeting full of optimism. He wrote: 'I hope the British Government will go and have a real talk in Germany as to how Europe is to be pacified. Hitler is a prophet – not a politician or an intriguer. Quite straight, full of queer ideas, but quite honestly wanting no war.'

He maintained this consoling belief for more than three years, but a letter written to Nancy in August 1936 after a brief visit to a German Labour Camp, shows some trace of uneasiness. He wrote: 'The trouble is that it is all done by compulsion from outside. They are not taught to think for themselves. . . . As you know, I don't think Hitler means war. I think he means the recovery of Germany's position in the world without it. But if Hitler goes, or through the follies of others there is another war, Germany will go into it better prepared, better disciplined, and more formidable than ever.'

The publicisers of the Cliveden Set were without information on, and so made no use of Philip Lothian's second visit to Hitler on 4th May 1937. It was not a happy move politically. An alert ambassador, alive to German mental habits, would have protested and prevented the meeting, or would at least have insisted on being there himself. For some reason the British constitution easily baffles German minds. Hitler, in common with many Germans, never shook himself free of the idea that a British lord, because he belonged to an assembly called the Upper House, exerted by right greater political authority than an untitled person. However much Lothian or Halifax or Lord Redesdale might protest that their visits were unofficial, they were not believed.

At Lothian's interview with Hitler in May 1937 he was accompanied by Mr T. P. Conwell Evans, a former Member of Parliament who specialised in Anglo-German relations, and who at this time was an admirer of Hitler and the Nazis, though a year later he was to be wholly disillusioned. Hitler ranted to his visitor about the terrible sufferings of the Nazis in Austria at the hands of what he described as a 'papal government', and asserted that the enormous majority of

Austrians wished to join the Reich. To follow Lothian's own record: 'Lord Lothian replied that England at any rate was not the obstacle here but Mussolini and the Pope. The Pope certainly, said the Chancellor smiling. Lothian said that neither England nor Germany liked the political activities of the Pope very much, and jokingly reminded Hitler that one of Franco's chief supporters was the Pope. Well, said the Chancellor with a laugh, it's the lesser of two evils; he had forbidden his ambassador to interfere with Franco's military operations or to talk about National Socialism. After this diversion the atmosphere became considerably lighter and there were smiles all round.'

The rest of the conversation was occupied with tirades against Czechoslovakia and Lithuania, praise of Poland, and protestations of Germany's desire for peace. Cecil Rhodes's plan for a union of Germany and the whole Anglo-Saxon world was raised by Philip Lothian, but Hitler doubted if American isolationism would allow such a scheme. He said he wanted an Anglo-German union. In conclusion, Mr Conwell Evans assured Hitler that British public opinion was becoming more and more pro-German and he regretted such lapses of taste as British reports in the Press alleging that German planes had taken part in the bombardment of Guernica.[8] So ended the interview which must have given Hitler an agreeable impression that Great Britain would not seriously resist him. Lothian wrote nothing about the meeting to Nancy.

On the 26th September Nancy received a letter from a German woman who seems to have been a slight acquaintance, through friends in common of herself and Philip Lothian. Nancy's June indiscretion in New York bore unwelcome fruit. The letter ran as follows:

'Dear Lady Astor. Ever since reading your courageous words, uncovering the anti-German propaganda in the United States, when leaving New York some time ago, I have wanted to write & say, how happy it made me feel. It is a joy to me to realise how much clearer the good our Führer is doing, is becoming to all those who are honestly *labouring* for the salvation of mankind. . . . With all good wishes, sincerely yours, Retha Susan Speiser. Please remember me to Lord Lothian.'

To this Nancy answered as follows on the 1st October:

'Dear Mrs Speiser, Thank you so much for your nice letter. I am afraid I don't share your enthusiasm for your Führer, but I do feel

8. Guernica had been dive-bombed on a market day eight days before on the 26th April by the German Condor Legion of airmen.

that there is a strong right thought in Germany which should not be downed by false propaganda.'

On the 27th November 1937 Nancy wrote to Philip Lothian, who was in India at the time, to tell him of Lord Halifax's news from Germany. To believers in the Cliveden Set this should be a critical document, for to them it records Halifax reporting back to the chieftainess who sent him. The letter certainly shows her agreement with the Appeasement policy, but throws no light on the object of search, namely her directing hand. She wrote: 'Edward Halifax came to luncheon the day after he returned from Germany. He liked everyone he met in Berlin and particularly Goebbels. What struck him most was the attitude towards the League of Nations and anything like Collective Security. He said he felt that he was speaking a completely different mental language, but he realized that it was absolutely necessary for us to get on with them. However, by the time this reaches you, you will know more about it all than I can tell you. Tom Inskip says that those against it are working violently and subtly, for Vansittart has changed his tone, and people are beginning to realize that France is no use either in munitions or men. Apparently Neville sees the situation very clearly and is very firm about it. He does not use T.J. but Horace Wilson.

'Your girl friend is still here. Kindly as she is, never have I met anyone like her. Matrimony with her would bring you back on your knees to me, so I ought to encourage it, as I want to keep your wavering affection.'

The last paragraph requires some explanation. On one of his journeys to and from America Lothian had met an attractive young woman who was a fellow Christian Scientist. They were drawn to each other and he seems to have contemplated marriage, how seriously it is impossible to know. Judging from a letter which the lady wrote after a telephone conversation with her, Nancy took a less detached view of the situation than the paragraph may suggest.

In a letter, written to Lothian on the 12th December 1937, Nancy comments for the first time on the Cliveden Set and *The Week*. She does not sound unduly perturbed: 'Neville Chamberlain is lunching with me on Thursday, and I hope Edward Halifax and Tom Inskip. A letter from Rebecca West will be coming to you from Waldorf. Apparently the Communist rag has been full of the Halifax-Lothian-Astor plot at Cliveden, and then *Time and Tide* has taken it up; people really seem to believe it. Musso leaving the League, and Goebbels

taking the line – "we will have our Colonies" – certainly makes thing,
very difficult for the Prime Minister. I will write you after seeing him
on Thursday.' This promised letter and the reply to it are unfortunately
lost, if they existed.

In the meantime, before receiving the last quoted letter, Philip
Lothian wrote to Nancy on the 17th December, and the letter is of
interest because it contains *his* first preserved remark on the Cliveden
Set. 'I saw in the papers,' he wrote, 'that you & the Londonderrys have
been regarded as the heart of the pro-German movement. But I'm
glad to think that it has got well entrenched in the Government long
ago, & does not depend on so feeble a support as Londonderry House.'

While in America, in February 1938, Waldorf received a letter from
the still unconverted Conwell Evans who evidently confided to him
that Anthony Eden was the major obstacle to Anglo-German accord.
Waldorf sent the letter to Nancy with this comment: 'Anthony's
manner always gets Hitler and Musso on the raw – It's no good
lecturing people or talking down to them if you want to improve
relations or avoid a war. His letter is marked private but you can show
it to Philip or even Neville.' This is the only evidence in the Astor
archive of an attempt from Cliveden to influence policy. Whether it
was effective or not is most doubtful. It may have confirmed Chamberlain in a course on which he was already set with determination. He was
very rarely influenced by people who disagreed with him.

By March 1938 Anthony Eden had been manoeuvred by Chamberlain into resigning, to be replaced by Lord Halifax; Hitler had taken
over supreme command of the army, and Ribbentrop had been promoted to Foreign Minister the month before, though he stayed till
mid-March in London. On Friday the 11th March, according to a letter
from T.J. to Abraham Flexner of Princeton University, Waldorf,
Inskip, T.J. himself and 'Dr Woermann who is R's right hand man in
London' breakfasted with Ribbentrop at his Embassy. Waldorf had
to travel to Plymouth and left early. They discussed Austria. Ribbentrop gave a soothing picture of German-Austrian negotiations, describing Hitler's interview with Schuschnigg as 'friendly and unforced'.
He assured them that the *Anschluss* 'was to be reached by gradual
stages'. He may genuinely not have known that Hitler had signed the
order for the movement of the German army the night before.
(According to his memoirs he never knew anything discreditable to
the Nazi regime.) He had, however, been present at the ferocious

bullying of Schuschnigg by Hitler. As his guests went away they felt that 'R. had not been frank'. The next day they could be sure. By Sunday the central land of the former Empire was a province of Nazi Germany. The incorporation of Austria was the most defensible of Hitler's aggressions, in theory. In practice it was otherwise. In Vienna alone the S.S. arrested 76,000 people. The episode caused distress to the followers of the Appeasement policy, but judging from the tone of T.J.'s letter, which was written on the 20th from Blickling, Philip Lothian's country house in Norfolk, it did not suggest that they should abandon the policy, and they still clung to many illusions. T.J. wrote to Flexner: 'I don't think "scoundrel" describes Hitler; it applies more accurately to some of those around him.'

A common complaint about the Astors and their political friends, and one not only made by believers in the Cliveden Set story, is that they entered into political discussions with German leaders and representatives, without reference to the Foreign Office, and thus, it is held, they did confuse policy by acting not as a second Foreign Office but as a second and independent diplomatic service. The accusation has obviously a great measure of truth regarding Jones and Lothian; little if any regarding Waldorf whose breakfast with Ribbentrop (in company with a minister) is the only recorded occasion when he could conceivably incur such criticism. But Nancy was distinctly guilty on one known occasion of by-passing official channels in order to make her views known to Ribbentrop's successor, Herbert von Dirksen.

The circumstances were these: Felix Frankfurter, the eminent American politician and judge, had an uncle who was among the thousands of Viennese Jews rounded up and imprisoned by the invading Nazis. Felix Frankfurter sent a telegram to Nancy asking for help. He was probably thinking of a question in Parliament. Nancy knew the heart-breaking time-lags between question and action even with a sympathetic Government. She knew enough about foreign affairs to know that in small matters Foreign Offices tend 'duly to weigh and consider', etc. till the purpose is lost. So she simply darted into the midst of the fray in the spirit of 'To Hell with Protocol'. Her undated answer to Felix Frankfurter's telegram shows this.

'Dear Friend, The minute I received your wire I spoke to the German Ambassador in London, and gave him, in no uncertain terms, our views on arresting aged scholars. He promised to do what he could. Three days afterwards, having heard no more, I talked to him again and warned him that unless I received good news of Herr Frankfurter, I should go myself to Vienna! He assured me that it would be alright. As you know, your Uncle was released on the 28th March. The Ambassador tells me that he was only imprisoned a few days as a result of some unguarded remarks.'

That the supreme figure of the Cliveden Set acted in disregard of correct procedure on this occasion is undeniable.

The darkening of the European scene was due to many causes, some of them obvious, some obscure, a few of them still a matter of dispute. The Left and Liberal Press continued to find a single simple cause for their readers: the Cliveden Set. With disarming candour Claud Cockburn has given his own opinion of his invention's subsequent development: 'The fact was that, however it started, it presently became a myth.' The problem of the Astors was to know what to do with the myth. For nearly half a year they had borne it in silence, treating it as beneath notice. Of course Nancy chatted about it, and when confronted by reporters would laughingly tell them it was 'nothin' but a lot of nonsense', but there was no serious rebuttal of the charges. Being the subject of a myth poses rare problems. One has entered an unreal world where fact, reason, and normal laws of probability cease to apply. All this the Astors were finding to their cost as the rumours multiplied and spread beyond Great Britain to America and France and, of course, Germany. A young Frenchman who had stayed at Cliveden to help the young men of the family with their French wrote a lurid account of life in the great house, of its ceaseless political intrigue and of the multitude of Lord Astor's horses 'most of which had run in the Derby' and all of which were at the disposal of guests who enjoyed a gallop. This act of treachery gave Waldorf a contemptuous view of French horsemanship and did not lessen Nancy's suspicion of 'Roman Catholic Latins'. Yet such absurdities in no way impeded belief. The legend only grew.

Towards the end of April 1938 Waldorf discussed with the Conservative Central Office what might be done to stop the rot. He drafted an apologia which, he suggested, should be issued as a pamphlet to serve as a 'counter-blast' to a Communist Party pamphlet entitled *The Cliveden Set*. This had been published earlier, in March.[9] The Chairman

9. An unexpected detail appears in the Astor archive. Queen Mary told Sir Gerald Chichester that she wished to read the Communist pamphlet, so Lady Astor sent her a copy.

of the Central Office, Douglas Hacking, was against Waldorf's proposal on the grounds that defensive propaganda was usually ineffectual,
and that such a pamphlet would only draw additional attention to
ridiculous rumours. He suggested that the simpler procedure of a letter
to *The Times*, containing a condensation of the main arguments of the
apologia, would achieve better results. Waldorf accepted the advice.
He duly sent a letter to *The Times* which was published on the 5th
May. On the same day the *Daily Herald* published a similar letter from
Nancy. Both letters contained the obvious defence that a house in
which men and women prominent in public life met and discussed
politics did not mean that the house in question was a clandestine
Government. Both letters also produced what to a rational mind might
have seemed the ace of trumps. The Communist pamphlet asserted as
a fact that towards the end of January 1938 a more than usually sinister
meeting had taken place at Cliveden with the Astors and Philip Lothian
in the leading roles. It was not difficult to scotch this story as at the
time the Astors were in America, Philip Lothian was in India, and
Cliveden was shut. One might have supposed that the exposure of so
enormous a mistake would have annihilated the whole legend. It did
nothing of the sort. Legends are toys. It is no use telling a child that
his golliwog is only a piece of stuffed cloth. He loves his golly, and
that is all he knows, and if anyone tries to take it away and throw it
in the dustbin he screams. Reflecting the mood of the day, the Press
with few exceptions only screamed louder after the 5th May.

Then towards the end of the month the believers enjoyed what
looked like a little windfall of evidence that Golly was alive. There
were further indiscretions, this time not only by Nancy but by Neville
Chamberlain who outran her. On the 10th May Nancy gave a lunch-
party in 4 St James's Square at which the Prime Minister was the
principal guest. The purpose was for him to meet thirteen American
and Canadian journalists. He was unused to meeting journalists and
seems to have handled the encounter with a truly remarkable lack of
skill. He was unguarded. He told them, according to their reports,
that the resignation of Eden was not only due to differences over
Anglo-Italian relations but also Anglo-American ones. This was quite
true, and it was fortunate for the Prime Minister that none of the
journalists picked up the scent: none of them found out about Roosevelt's offer of intervention to Eden which, in Eden's absence, Chamberlain had calamitously turned down. It was madly rash of Chamberlain

to have referred to such a thing. He seems to have spoken with gratification of the recently concluded Anglo-Italian Agreement and they felt from what he said that he intended to follow it up with a similar Anglo-German one. Some of them asked him about Czechoslovakia and the Sudeten German business. From his answer they got the impression that he thought the Czechs should reach agreement with the Nazis. When they asked about an Anglo-Russian Agreement he seemed unfavourable to the idea.

As a result of this lunch articles appeared in the *Montreal Daily Star* and the *New York Herald Tribune* to the effect that British foreign policy, according to the highest authority, aimed at a Franco-British-Italian-German Four Power Pact, with concessions to the totalitarian states, and directed against the U.S.S.R.

On the 21st May in Parliament the Opposition demanded to know why the Prime Minister had disclosed policies to journalists before telling the House of them. A storm arose which Chamberlain failed to ride. He lost his temper and was badly battered by the Labour and Liberal parties, while he was half-heartedly defended by his own. He made the mistake of dismissing the whole business as 'foolish rumours'. In the excitement Nancy rose and said that 'there's not a word of truth in it'. Like the Prime Minister she gave the impression of denying that the lunch-party had taken place. Everyone knew it had. When the subject was resumed next day she made a personal statement to the effect that, not having read the articles in question at the time, she was confused. What she had meant was that the Prime Minister had not given an official interview in her house but had taken part in an informal conversation. She said she had nothing to say against the accuracy of the articles. The statement was ill-received by the Opposition and not applauded on the Government benches.

Nancy's lunch-party, intended as a contribution to forming goodwill between Britain and America, had proved a distinct failure, resulting in as much American as English anger. But believers in the legend saw Chamberlain's indiscretions in much more exciting terms than this. They saw Nancy at the head of her table as a female Svengali, and Chamberlain, with his wild talk of an anti-Russian Four Power Pact, as her helpless little Trilby.[10]

10. In the articles themselves and the numerous Press attacks which followed their publication, there is no mention of Lord Astor. This suggests that he was regrettably

In August 1938 Philip Lothian was appointed ambassador-designate to Washington in succession to Sir Ronald Lindsay. Lord Halifax who had suggested the appointment wanted Lothian to take up his duties in January 1939, but the King requested that Lindsay should stay on till after the royal visit to the United States, scheduled for 1939, so the appointment was deferred for a year. In the later part of 1938 Lothian went on another of his journeys round the world in pursuit of his life-long purpose: the unity of the British Empire and the English-speaking world. When the Czechoslovak crisis broke in September 1938 he was in Australia. He wrote frequently to Nancy during those days. His reactions to events were at first what one would expect: 'I'm sure that the last thing Hitler wants is a general war' he wrote.

Then suddenly in a letter dated the 16th September and sent from Sydney he shows a different mind altogether. It is as though all his misconceptions fell from him suddenly at the approach of war. 'I confess I feel rather alarmed at Neville's visit to Hitler. Heroic and courageous, but terribly liable to lead to another Hoare-Laval plan. Hitler, I fancy, holds all the military cards unless we are prepared for a World War to stop Nazi expansion. He won't budge & therefore N will be forced to offer a compromise. That, if it is to suffice, will let down the Czechs & split the united country & world he now has behind him, or if it does not suffice to bring Hitler to abandon his designs on the Sudeten Germans in Czechoslovakia, will still leave us confronted with the necessity of world war if we are to stop him, in effect, breaking up C-Slovakia & bring all Eastern Europe not into a sphere of influence but under his control.

'It's a horrible dilemma. But having got so far as we have I'm inclined to think that rather than split the country and the democratic world by immoderate concessions we ought to say that if Hitler invades Czechoslovakia it means war.'

He was in some doubt as to whether he should return to England and sent a telegram to Waldorf asking for advice. Waldorf urged him to come home, but before he had time to make arrangements the news of the Munich conference reached him, so he continued his journey. His mood rapidly began to change. His praise of Neville Chamberlain was unstinted but he had not yet resumed his illusions. 'Your faith in

---

absent and that otherwise, as an experienced newspaper man, he would have saved Neville Chamberlain from his indiscretion by guiding the conversation.

him,' he wrote, '& I should think in Halifax, has been entirely justified. If he hadn't had his treaty[11] with Musso could he have got him in at this last moment? However I'm afraid there will be some nasty moments as the Germans march into the Sudeten territory & the wretched Czechs & Social Democrats flee before them – but no worse than the Greeks & the Turks.'[12]

This compassionate attitude was soon to give way to another one. On the 4th October he wrote to Nancy from New Zealand: 'I'm not very sorry for the Czechs. Benes has been the Quai d'Orsay's principal tool in Europe since 1920 & if Czechoslovakia is saved it is not because of Benes. His policy led inevitably to world war. . . .' Of Chamberlain he said: 'He is the only person who steadfastly refused to accept the view that Hitler and the Nazis were incorrigible & would understand nothing but the big stick – the Quai d'Orsay's view & Bob Cecil's – the real war-minds in Europe today.' Elsewhere in the letter he summarised the outcome thus: 'My own impression is that Europe including the Nazis have now turned their back on world war because a general war means letting Russia loose in Europe & [I] trust a final settlement including disarmament may be possible if Neville's lead is followed up.' Neville's lead was not followed up, as the world knows. It is a pity that no one told Philip Lothian of the angry remark about the British Prime Minister which the Führer made to his S.S. guard in Berlin on his return from Munich. 'That fellow spoiled my entry into Prague.'

Chamberlain was received in London on 30th September with delirious joy, and those who deplored the Munich agreement were looked on angrily as fools and knaves by the overwhelming majority of the people. Nancy felt this popular wave of gratitude and admiration more keenly than most. She loved Neville Chamberlain with a devotion she had given to no political chief since Lloyd George. The unhappy lunch-party fiasco of May had made no difference to their deep mutual affection, for he in turn gave her ardent friendship. Due to his historical unpopularity and his snarling lack of generosity or even honesty towards his political opponents, especially those in his party, it is easily forgotten that in his private character Chamberlain was a man of considerable charm, by no means lacking in humour and wit. His few

11. The reference is to the Anglo-Italian Agreement of April 1938.

12. This refers to the defeat of the Greeks by the Turks under Mustapha Kemal Pasha in the summer of 1922, and the later exchange of Greek and Turkish populations in Asia Minor amid appalling suffering.

letters to Nancy indicate a very pleasing relationship. She felt that those who opposed Chamberlain at this hour were guilty almost of treason. The political battle following Munich engaged her emotions and she departed from her usual wise custom not to speak or even interrupt in a foreign affairs debate. The battle also involved her family indirectly.

On the 3rd October Alfred Duff Cooper, the First Lord of the Admiralty, resigned. He maintained that the Prime Minister had surrendered far more than he needed to. The speech was one of the most remarkable that Duff Cooper made in the House at any time. It moved his hearers but outraged opinion nevertheless.

The Times correspondent who reported it was Anthony Winn, the younger brother of Reginald Winn who had married Alice Perkins and was thus Nancy's nephew by marriage. Anthony Winn, who was twenty-nine and a young man of brilliant promise, felt as deeply as Duff Cooper about Munich. Geoffrey Dawson felt otherwise, and it seemed to Winn that he allowed his preference to interfere excessively with his editing. So Anthony Winn resigned from *The Times*. He was not the first to do so in these years. The precedent of Claud Cockburn will be remembered.

Anthony Winn's bold gesture was condemned by those not in sympathy because he had looked to his defences by securing a contract with the *Daily Telegraph*. He had arranged not to suffer too painful a martyrdom. 'I hear,' wrote Dawson to Nancy on the 6th October, 'that our young friend A.W. had secured a job on the "DT" before his convictions were allowed to ruin his career on "the Times"!' 'When I get back to the House of Commons,' wrote Nancy in reply, 'I will deal with the situation of this fellow who, after having committed an indiscretion for the "Times" was taken on by the "Daily Telegraph". Your loyal and obedient slave Nancy.' In fact, Nancy seems not to have done anything further in the case.

Less than four years later, to remember what G. K. Chesterton once wrote of a friend whose early death makes him forgotten now, Anthony Winn's promise was cancelled by his fulfilment of another promise when he was killed in battle as an officer of the Eighth Army in 1942.

This departure of Anthony Winn from *The Times* was a small thing compared to the other episode in Nancy's political career of the same time.

After Duff Cooper had made his resignation speech, Neville Chamberlain presented the case for the Munich Agreement to the House of Commons. The ensuing debate occupied four days and was not concluded till the 6th October. At ten minutes past five on Wednesday the 5th, Winston Churchill was called by the Speaker and delivered what was one of the greatest speeches of his life. From now on, though excluded from office for another eleven months, and although the speech was resented by many people and not gladly received by the House, he became an increasing influence on Parliament and the nation while his mistakes over India and the Abdication came to be forgotten.

'If I do not begin this afternoon,' he opened ominously, 'by paying the almost invariable tributes to the Prime Minister for his handling of this crisis it is certainly not from any lack of personal regard.' The first passages of the speech were occupied with telling the House of his admiration for the indifference to popularity which had been shown by Duff Cooper's resignation, adding that the Prime Minister had also showed the same virtue. He then moved to the attack. 'Having thus fortified myself,' he went on, 'by the example of others, I will proceed to emulate them. I will therefore begin by saying the most unpopular and the most unwelcome thing. I will begin by saying what everybody would like to ignore or forget but which must nevertheless be stated, namely that we have sustained a total and unmitigated defeat, and that France has suffered even more than we have.'

At this point Nancy could contain herself no longer and shouted 'Nonsense!'

The effect of this interruption, and the one that shortly followed it, was that the first climax of this great speech took on an appearance of being directed at Nancy and the extreme Chamberlainites who had to take the full weight of Churchill's eloquence at its greatest. Though the words of this climax have become very famous some of them should be remembered here.

Churchill said: 'When the noble lady cries "Nonsense" she could not have heard the Chancellor of the Exchequer [Sir John Simon] admit in his illuminating and comprehensive speech just now that Herr Hitler had gained, in this particular leap forward, in substance all he set out to gain. The utmost my Right Honourable friend the Prime

Minister has been able to secure by all his immense exertions, by all the great efforts and mobilisation which took place in this country, and by all the anguish and strain through which we have passed in this country – the utmost he has been able to gain – '

Here Churchill was momentarily silenced by members, including Nancy, who shouted 'Is peace!'

Master of the House as he was, he let the noise die down and then continued his remorseless castigation with no sign of discomfort.

'I thought,' he said, 'that I might be able to make that point in its due place and I propose to deal with it. The utmost that [the Prime Minister] has been able to gain for Czechoslovakia, and in the matters which were in dispute, has been that the German dictator instead of snatching his victuals from the table has been content to have them served to him course by course.'

It was in the next passage that Churchill made his most famous comment on Chamberlain's three visits to Hitler, at Berchtesgaden, Godesberg and Munich. The transactions, said Churchill, 'can be very simply epitomised. £1 was demanded at the pistol's point. When it was given £2 were demanded at the pistol's point. Finally the dictator consented to take £1.17.6d and the rest in promises of good will for the future.' Even the most extreme supporters of Chamberlain were shaken when a few minutes later, with a sudden change of mood, and with a display of emotion such as the House only tolerates in a chosen few, he declaimed 'All is over. Silent, mournful, abandoned, broken Czechoslovakia recedes into the darkness. She has suffered in every respect by her association with the Western democracies and the League of Nations of which she has always been an obedient servant.'

Churchill was once more interrupted in the speech, this time by Nancy alone. Towards the end he said: 'We are in the presence of a disaster of the first magnitude,' and pointed out that this was the end of the French alliances in Eastern Europe. He recalled a tactless remark made in a broadcast speech by Chamberlain in which he described Czechoslovakia as a far country 'of which we know nothing'.[13] 'We are talking,' said Churchill, 'of countries which are a long way off and of which, as the Prime Minister might say, we know nothing – '

Nancy shouted: 'Don't be rude about the Prime Minister!'

13. By 'we' he meant the British public not the Government. The remark was later often quoted as if he meant the Government.

'Mr Churchill: The noble lady says that that very harmless allusion is –

'Viscountess Astor: Rude.'

Once again (though Churchill was always punctilious about addressing the chair) the next remarks in the speech had the appearance of being directed at his unequally matched opponent. He went on:

'She must very recently have been receiving her finishing course in manners. What will be the position, I want to know, of France and England next year and the year afterwards? If the Nazi dictator should choose to look Westward, as he may, bitterly will France and England regret the loss of that fine army of ancient Bohemia which was estimated last week to require not fewer than thirty German divisions for its destruction.'

This was the last passage in which Nancy was involved.

So great was the impression which this speech made that, with the exception of Harold Nicolson's speech in the same sense, it is what is chiefly remembered of the great debate of 3rd–6th October 1938. In these circumstances Nancy's ill-judged interruptions are little remembered, but they made much impression at the time. Among Chamberlainites they were praised as much as they were deplored on the (everdisarming) Left.

The Munich crisis saw great invigoration of the Cliveden Set myth, but this was chiefly due to an unfortunate coincidence. Rather unexpectedly, blame for the unfavourable terms of the agreement was not much laid at the door of Cliveden except by *Daily Worker* contributors who were too extreme to be taken seriously; the new stimulus came not from Nancy's clash with Churchill, but from a Press misreport. There was (and still is) a club which at that time met weekly in Westminster, and which was called the Romney Street Group. It was mainly political in character, and several Members of Parliament, of all parties, belonged to it. It was considered a place where speech was privileged, but one of the members played the traitor when, soon after the crisis, T.J. introduced as his luncheon guest Colonel Charles Lindbergh. In the summer of 1938 Colonel Lindbergh had gone as an invited guest to Germany and Russia where both Governments had directed propaganda at him. He saw through the Russian propaganda but not the German. He was invited to tell the club of his conclusions. He gave as his opinion that the Nazi air force was vastly the superior of the Russian. As an authority on aviation technique he was not impressed by the expansion of the R.A.F. nor by the general state of French armament in the air. He gave the impression that in his opinion no European combination could stand against a German air attack. His remarks were repeated to the Press who gave them publicity and distortion.

Harold Nicolson's diaries establish that Lindbergh was prone to be favourably impressed by life under the Nazis, that he saw the merits and ignored the horrors, and that at this time he greatly overestimated Nazi power. His views were known and to many people made him suspect. It was also known that he was acquainted with the Astors. His wrong-headed ideas made him an ideal member of the Cliveden Set. The problem was how to elect him, but the Press solved this by the simple device of reporting his remarks to the Romney Street Group as having been spoken in 4 St James's Square to politicians and journalists convened for the purpose by Nancy. There was a Cliveden Set revival in the British Press, and this was taken up on a large scale in the United States. Abraham Flexner's daughter wrote to his friend's daughter Miss Eirene Jones on the 10th October: 'The Cliveden "Set" has come in for much reviling, and Lady Astor is not much cherished in her native land these days. Tonight she and Lindbergh are being fantastically united to the whole Hitler-Chamberlain combination.'

At this time of extreme emotional tension Nancy seems to have almost gone out of her way to make herself disliked. On the 9th November at question time in the House, Mr Harold Macmillan asked assurance that refugees from the ceded Sudetenland of Czechoslovakia, especially the Social Democrat Germans, were receiving generous treatment.

Before Mr R. A. Butler could reply up leaped Nancy who was called. She said: 'Supposing these Sudeten German refugees are Communists, would it not be safer to send them to Russia?' There was an indignant cry of 'Insult!'

Mr Butler replied to Harold Macmillan's question and ignored the other. Up leaped Nancy again. 'May I have an answer to my question? Communists should be sent to a Communist country. I do not see any insult. The Communist countries would not take Capitalist refugees from this country.'

Mr Butler said he would not trespass further on the ground of the Home Office and evaded the issue which Nancy had raised.

Four days later Harold Macmillan wrote to her.

'Amidst the necessarily divergent views & opinions at the present, there is no need for any confusion about facts.

'You said in the House of Commons last week that the Sudeten German refugees were Communists & shd. be sent to Russia. I do not of course know the views of all the 350 for whom the British Govt. has granted visas & of which I think less than half have (I think) yet arrived.

'But we have about twelve of them here. Dorothy has just motored 6 of them to East Grinstead to the Roman Catholic Church; I have taken 1 to the English parish Church; the rest I think are cooking & cleaning.

'These are mostly of the middle-classes and intelligentsia. One was mayor of Aussig until a few weeks ago. One is the leading advocate of the Sudeten district.

'All seem quiet & cultivated people – dazed and overwhelmed by their plight, but hard-working, courteous, & grateful. With all that they have to suffer, I do not see why they should be insulted in our Parliament in addition.'

Such an incident as that of the 9th made it easy for doubters to believe in the reality of pro-Nazism at Cliveden.

In America the revived and redecorated myth reached a climax in an article by Frederick L. Collins published in the widely read magazine *Liberty*. The article was supposedly about Colonel Lindbergh, and discussed with thoughtful grief how he had come to accept an official decoration presented to him by Hitler. In fact, most of the article was about the Cliveden Set to which Charles Lindbergh had by now been formally accredited by reporters. Nancy evidently sent the article to Bernard Shaw and sought his advice as to what she and Waldorf should do. Ought they to answer this latest attack or treat it with the contemptuous silence which a year earlier had served them so ill? Shaw's reply on New Year's Day 1939 shows him again as the best of friends.

'My dear Nancy, I agree that the Liberty article should be contradicted; and since you authorise me to blab about Cliveden I am by this post sending to Liberty a full dress article (gratuitous) about you and Waldorf and Garvin and Geoffrey which will, I hope, explode the Collins story. Possibly it may infuriate you; but I think it will do the trick. And you will like the bits about the two editors.'

Shaw's covering note to the editor (which was published) included the following:

'The Astors have become the representatives of America in England; and any attack on them is in effect an attack on America. As they have gained that position solely by being a transparently good couple underneath the irrepressible vitality of Lady Astor, which explodes in all decent directions, it is important to genuine good relations between the two countries (now very important politically) that the American Press should stand by the Virginian lady.

'That is what makes me think that the last word should not be with Mr Collins.'

The article appeared in January. It was furnished with a photograph of Waldorf and Nancy dressed in conspiratorial black, unsmiling and so somewhat grim, and thus possibly sinister. The solemnity of their clothes and expressions was less sinister if one knew that the picture was taken as they were going to the memorial service in honour of their friend Rudyard Kipling in 1936.

Here is an extract from the article.

'Cliveden is like no other country house on earth. Mr Collins' list of noble conspirators is authentic; but you meet these aristocrats at Cliveden because you meet everybody worth meeting, rich or poor, at Cliveden. You meet the Duchess of Atholl; but then you meet also Ellen Wilkinson, the Leftest member of the Labor Party in Parliament. You meet Colonel Lindbergh, the friend of Herr Hitler's chief of staff; but you meet also Mr Charles Chaplin, whose dislike of the Nazi rule is outspoken to a degree which must seriously threaten his interests in Germany. You meet the Marquess of Londonderry, descendant of Castlereagh and so far to the Right that he was too much for even the existing "Nationalist" Cabinet, with his famous majestically beautiful wife; but then you meet also ME, an implacable and vociferous Marxist Communist of nearly sixty years' standing, with MY beautiful wife. By simply suppressing Mr Collins' list and extending my own, I could prove that Cliveden is a nest of Bolshevism, or indeed of any other bee in the world's bonnet. . . .'

G.B.S., as Hitler's only important apologist in the West (a fact which gave the article much of its strength), could not end without some salute to the socialist Führer. He claimed that he had disposed of 'the silly notion that big historic changes can be effected by the country-house clique of a wicked British aristocracy, and that Herr Hitler, who has earned the devotion of what the said aristocracy calls the lower middle classes by a socialization of property unparalleled anywhere except in Russia, is the type of ruler whom it is conspiring to establish in England.'

He ended with the words: 'Never has a more senseless fable got into the headlines.' The article was widely reprinted in Great Britain.

There remains the question as to whether Shaw 'did the trick'. In a sense he did, for after this time the Cliveden Set story, judging by Press-cuttings, began to lose its thrill and immediacy, began gradually to become 'old hat'. But so deep had it gone, so great was the credence given to it, that at the time of writing, thirty-five years after it was launched on the world, it is still gladly believed in England, and yet more in the United States. What gave Claud Cockburn's story long life was that, unlike most mare's nests, it was accepted as fact not only by thoughtless readers of sensational stuff but by educated and intelligent people, by the sort of people who read Hansard week by week. It is certain that the legend nearly cost Philip Lothian his mission to America.

Early in January 1939 he visited Washington in the course of the last stages of his world tour. He was received by the President and according to his own account to Nancy, written on the 5th, he enjoyed a gratifying reception. 'I had an hour with the President,' he wrote, 'whose views are entirely sound & means to do everything he can to block or defeat the dictators. Indeed it is quite clear that the real struggle is going to be between the U.S.A. & Hitler.' The last sentence indicates faintly a turn in the conversation which may have been weakly conducted by Philip Lothian. At all events the conversation did not have the same reassuring effect on the President as it had on his visitor.

Oliver Harvey's diaries contain the following entry for the 3rd March 1939:

'One amusing thing. Lothian, whose appointment as Ambassador to Washington when Lindsay goes has been approved but is actually held in abeyance, recently passed through America and went to see Roosevelt. George Trevelyan wrote to H.[alifax] the other day and sent him a copy of a letter he had received from Merriman of Harvard, enclosing a copy of a letter he had had from Roosevelt himself. In this the President described the conversation with Lothian, who had taken the completely defeatist line that we could not possibly stand up to Germany and Italy, that our day was done and it was now for America to step forward and take up the torch of civilisation from our drooping fingers. Roosevelt was furious with Lothian and went for him: as R. told Merriman, if Great Britain took that line and not one of robust self-help, American opinion would never consent to help. This is, of course, just typical of the line that conceited ass (and the whole Cliveden set) takes. If any man had his hands dripping with guilt for the Versailles settlement it was Lothian, who was then Lloyd George's Private Secretary. Yet, according to himself, he knows America well and expects "to swing public opinion there!" However, I hope and pray this fortunate letter will kill the appointment. H. has sent it across to the P.M. who is much concerned at it. Alec Cadogan does not think L. can possibly be sent there now.'

Halifax persisted in his support of Lothian's appointment, and he would seem to have been helped by Lothian's unawareness of having incurred the President's contempt. For the moment what is interesting in the episode is to find a man such as Harvey referring to the Cliveden Set not as a hypothesis but as a fact. It seems to the writer that Roosevelt, more pardonably since he had no first-hand knowledge of English ways, had fallen into the same error, and in retrospect took a less friendly view of Lothian than he had at the meeting.

The policy of Appeasement and Munich came to an end when on the 15th March 1939 German troops marched to Prague and Czechoslovakia ceased to exist as an independent state. In the House of Commons two days later Nancy rose at question time to ask: 'Will the Prime Minister lose no time in letting the German Government know with what horror this country regards Germany's action?'; whereat a fellow-Conservative Vyvyan Adams interjected: 'You caused it yourself!' The myth did not die. Upton Sinclair answered Shaw in *Liberty*, proclaiming the myth anew as fact, but his article could not compare in force with that of G.B.S. *The Week* had abandoned the Cliveden Set by now, but *Reynolds News*, *Tribune*, *Time and Tide*, the *News Chronicle*, and the great cartoonist David Low, cherished it almost till September. Sir Stafford Cripps, who had taunted Nancy in the House of Commons as 'the honourable member for Berlin', published a rousing condemnation of the Set in *Tribune* in May. The announcement of Philip Lothian's appointment to Washington in April had given the Press a fresh card of entry. Not till the outbreak of war did the legend fade, but not into invisibility.

To the last phase of the supposed malpractices of Cliveden belongs the third picture of the Cliveden Set in action drawn from the inside. It is contained in a German document written by David Astor's friend Adam von Trott zu Solz, and published after the war. It need not detain the reader for more than a paragraph because, as mentioned already, its truthfulness is highly suspect, though for reasons honourable to its author.

Adam von Trott, a Rhodes Scholar, was an anti-Nazi who was working in the German Foreign Ministry in an unofficial capacity. His report was intended for the eyes of Hitler and Ribbentrop, for which reason it was artfully disguised as a pro-Nazi document. Trott was a believer in the Appeasement policy. With invincible optimism he was convinced that concessions would give confidence to the moderate elements in Germany, which he overestimated, and result in the fall of Hitler. His visit to England in June was connected with an intrigue of obscure origin. It probably began in the German Foreign Office, certain of whose members apparently hoped to persuade Hitler into a withdrawal of direct German rule from Czechoslovakia. They believed (it seems) that after such a withdrawal international negotiations would find a promising ground. Trott believed that, if denied war, Hitler's fall was inevitable. He went to Cliveden with David Astor on the 3rd June 1939 and spent an evening and a day there. The leaders of the Cliveden Set were present in force, notably Sir Thomas Inskip, Lord Lothian, and the most distinguished of the 'honorary members' Lord Halifax.[14] Lothian knew the young German already through Rhodes House at Oxford. Trott's first aim was to get the withdrawal plan to the ears of Halifax through Lothian, but as he had a long conversation with Halifax at Cliveden he may have put forward the plan to the Foreign Secretary himself. In the report the plan is attributed to Lothian, an impossible coincidence in view of later information, but the report may here indicate Lothian's agreement. Otherwise what Trott has to say about this, and about his own conduct at Cliveden, may be dismissed as necessary fiction contrived for Hitler's benefit. But there is no reason to suspect his account of Lord Astor's, Lord Lothian's and Lord Halifax's comments on Anglo-German relations in general. Indeed, to have reported these wrongly could only have resulted in endangering most seriously what Trott and his unknown supporters

14. The contemporary Press rarely associated Halifax with the Cliveden Set. An exception was David Low who depicted him (in female attire) reading *Mein Kampf* in a corner. It is doubtful whether Lord Halifax ever took this wise step.

hoped to achieve. Through Lord Astor he later met Neville Chamberlain, and from him he had the same impression as he had received at Cliveden, of a great desire for Anglo-German accord, and a conviction that this had been made virtually impossible by the immorality and cruelty of Hitler's seizure of Czechoslovakia. He recorded no dissent from this view among those he met at Cliveden. That is all that needs to be remembered of this strange episode for the purpose of Nancy's biography, but perhaps another purpose demands that something else should be remembered here too, namely that Trott persisted in his anti-Nazism till the end of his life. In 1944 he was arrested after the July Conspiracy. He had many associates and he gave not one away. He was executed in August 1944 at the age of thirty-eight. Today he is honoured by his countrymen.

There is one very obvious question about the Cliveden Set which has not been asked or answered. How deeply did Nancy mind this constant campaign of libel and calumny? She herself gave no indication of suffering, but plenty of her impatient annoyance. Her appeal to G.B.S., which has not survived, may have been an exception. Her normal reaction, as one would expect, was to laugh at so much rubbish. But beneath the surface she may have suffered greatly. Indeed this is probable. The Cliveden Set myth arose at a period of great grief in her private life. Early in 1937 her beloved sister Phyllis Brand died. The circumstances of her death were particularly tragic. Six months before, her son by her first marriage died by a fall from a window in New York. Suicide was suspected, but it may have been an accident. He was on his honeymoon at the time. The blow to his mother was fatal. With the tenacity of her family she tried hard to rally, but she could not. Unlike Nancy, she had remained a keen horsewoman, and in escapist mood she took to hunting again in the winter. She went out on a rainy day and caught cold which turned to pneumonia. Within a few days she died, in January 1937. Nancy was with her.

This was the greatest and most painful bereavement that Nancy suffered since the death of her mother. So appalling was the shock at the moment of death that for a while she was almost out of her reason. Rose Harrison was with her and gave this account: 'Lady Astor screamed and prayed. The butler came to me and said: "For God's sake, Miss Harrison, go to her ladyship." I went and I said: "Now

m'lady, it's no use screaming and crying. Nothing that you and I can
do can bring her back." And then she put her face next to mine and I
put my arm round her. I knew then that she had the affection but
couldn't give it, but that then she gave it to me. I knew it.' In her sister
Nancy had lost one of the very few to whom she could give all the
love that she felt.

In the summer of 1938, Buck Langhorne, her last surviving brother,
died. Her conduct in this emotional crisis was typical of her at her best.
The two great Cliveden parties of the year were for Christmas and the
Royal Ascot meeting in June. The news of Buck's death reached her a
few days before the Ascot party. No offence could have been taken if
she had cancelled it, but she considered that to do so would impose an
unfair disappointment on the younger members of the family who had
not known their uncle well. So she went through with it, apparently
as gaily as ever. Her letters show that under the surface she was
desolated. The immediate pre-war years were ones in which she was
emotionally vulnerable to a special degree.

She never showed it in her manner. Least of all when another family
tragedy threatened. Her youngest son Jakie was involved in a serious
motor accident in 1939. No one in the party of young Oxford men
(which included Peter Wood, Halifax's second son) was permanently
or badly injured. But it was a very alarming accident. Jakie, however,
was not cast for the role of tragedian and even in the worst of disasters
brought a different spirit to bear. He was knocked unconscious. When
he came to, one of his first coherent remarks was: 'I've lost my
memory. Has anyone got it?'

This chapter on the Cliveden Set may now draw to a conclusion. It
would have been shorter if belief in the Set at the time of writing were
less.

The writer feels confident that the tale of 'the Second Foreign Office'
on the Thames by Taplow needs no further discussion, and that the
only question of interest remaining is whether, for all the manifest
absurdity of the Cliveden Set legend, the people who most often met
there formed a bad influence on the Government. Geoffrey Dawson
and J. L. Garvin were very often there, and *The Times* and the *Observer*
were influential papers, though one distinction, carefully blurred by
The Week, needs to be asserted: the influence of the Astors of Cliveden

on *The Times* was very small. John Jacob Astor was not a frequent visitor to Cliveden. Though Nancy often corresponded with Garvin and Dawson their letters have almost no political content, and none of interest. The influence of *The Times* and the *Observer* was exerted independently.

Influence usually involves innovation. To agree with an orthodox classical scholar that Homer is a great poet is not to influence him. But to persuade the same scholar that the Odyssey was written by a woman is to exert great influence. Those who were believed to compose the Cliveden Set showed little originality of idea. The most wrong-headed of them was Philip Lothian, yet his was not the wrong-headedness of an original mind. Most of his political ideas at that time were the commonplaces of the thirties in England. The opinions publicly expressed by Dawson and Garvin were likewise, for all their learned manner of expression, the opinions of the average man. On the subject of Europe they were all to be found in the Beaverbrook Press. It is even arguable that neither the Astor-owned Press nor the Beaverbrook Press exerted much influence on British public opinion in those years. They agreed with an opinion that was already there. Though many people prefer not to admit the fact now, Chamberlain's Appeasement policy was very welcome to the overwhelming majority, and *The Times* and the *Observer* were among its faithful proclaimers. These facts remain as awkward memories. Even more awkward to some is the fact that Nancy was only one of the very few politicians or members of the public, openly associated with the Appeasement and disarmament policies, who in the war years frankly admitted, in public, that she had been gravely mistaken. To return to the pre-war time.

The mood of the country was pacifist: what might be called more precisely a mood of national repentance for the follies of war-hysteria and for its emotional misjudgement of the Germans twenty years before. All this fitted in with the Appeasement policy and was especially congenial to some of the Astors' closest friends. Philip Lothian regretted the harshness of the Versailles Treaty which he had helped to frame. Lord Halifax had indulged hatred of the Germans in the war years to an extraordinary degree. Waldorf had been criticised for a hate-propaganda speech in 1917. These had all become memories from which they recoiled, and they shared a sense of shame with millions of their fellow-countrymen. In the world of feeling this was a confused time, longing for peace was mixed with simultaneous suspicion of the means of defence against the warlike predators of Germany and Italy. Wishful thinking became common. The idea that armament was the cause of war was widely shared, and moreover, people said, intense rearmament was needless because surely the dictators would prefer to be appeased rather than to enter a world war. Let them be given the chance, people said, by friendly approaches without threat. This was the view that was frequently to be met in *The Times* and the *Observer* and in the popular Press. Most people on the Left and on the Right agreed with it. It was not the invention of any particular person or group or party.

British history had a traditional and honourable record of successful appeasement, and to many minds this was most strikingly evidenced by fairly recent events. Lord Halifax's conduct as Viceroy seemed to have brought peace to the Indian Empire by means of appeasement, and the settlement in South Africa seemed to all the members of the Kindergarten to have achieved the same there. Baldwin's 1936 agreement with Egypt seemed another shining triumph for this fine British form of international negotiation. Why, then, when a group of people, some of whom, such as Dawson and Lothian and Halifax, had been personally concerned in the past success of political appeasement – why, when they were credited with a far greater share than they really had in the carrying out of Chamberlainite Appeasement – were they vilified?

The answer, as with all matters involving mass psychology, can only be guess work. Here is my guess. By late 1937 an uneasy suspicion began to spread that there was something wrong with the modern British policy. It never seemed to produce results; it never seemed to make Fascism or Nazism less aggressive or more reasonable. The thought slowly grew that Churchill was right and Chamberlain wrong, yet the great majority, in spite of such suspicions, continued to believe in Chamberlain's policy because it was dedicated to absolute avoidance of war, and this seemed the overriding interest. There was a wish for the best of both worlds. Chamberlain remained very popular, unlike the members of the Cliveden Set. In the willingness to believe fantastic yarns about the Set, and the indignation that these yarns provoked, there may have been some element of the laying of the sins of the people on the scapegoat, and also some element of the rage of Caliban seeing his own face in the glass. This can help to explain why the legend lived on after March 1939, and after Appeasement had been abandoned by the Astors and their friends, as by the nation in general and Chamberlain himself.

In more rational terms public opinion was in a desperate and angry mood when the bright hopes of Appeasement began to fade and were finally quenched. Following a common and repulsive habit, men sought to find the traitors within, and they believed they had identified them in this largely haphazard group of friends who often met at Cliveden. These friends were not traitors; they were not Nazis; they were not admirers of Fascism; they were not, except for Halifax, influential on foreign policy, but until mid-March 1939 they were believers in, and ardent publicists for Chamberlain's Appeasement policy. That is the only faint shadow of reality in the myth, and the reality, pursued to its logical end, means that most of Great Britain belonged to the Cliveden Set. The attempt to appease Hitler, as practised in its later stages especially, is open to criticism and has been generally and perhaps justly condemned, but for all that it has not yet been proved to have been utterly vain. In three sentences Thomas Jones described why he himself believed in it. He wrote the sentences in the course of a letter to Abraham Flexner: 'I do not regret Chamberlain's reversal of Eden's policy, even if it proved too late. We have to convince the world that for the sake of peace we are prepared to go to absurd lengths. Our people will not fight unless they are satisfied that fair treatment of the potential enemy has been tried.' Winston Churchill spoke in somewhat the same sense as that of the last quoted sentence in the first speech he made as a Minister in the Second World War.

A large proportion of the foregoing chapter is based on study of the contemporary Press, notably of *The Week* for 1937, 1938 and 1939, preserved in the Newspaper Department of the British Museum at Colindale. Books consulted are *Failure of a Mission*, by Sir Nevile Henderson (London, 1940), *The Chamberlain Cabinet*, by Ian Colvin (London, 1971), *Crossing the Line*, by Claud Cockburn (London, 1958), *The Diplomatic Diaries of Oliver Harvey*, edited by John Harvey (London, 1970), *Diary with Letters*, by Thomas Jones (London, 1954), *Hitler: a Study in Tyranny*, by Alan Bullock (revised edition, London, 1962), *Europe of the Dictators*, by Elizabeth Wiskemann (London, 1966), *In the Chair*, a biography of Robert Barrington-Ward by the late Donald MacLachlan (London, 1971), *Troubled Loyalty*, a biography of Adam von Trott by Christopher Sykes (London, 1969), *Tribal Feeling*, by Michael Astor (London, 1963), *Nancy Astor*, by Maurice Collis (London, 1960), and *Halifax*, by Lord Birkenhead (London, 1965). The last named book contains an interesting account of the conflicting advice given to Lord Halifax by the Foreign Secretary and Sir Nevile

Henderson in November 1937. The description of Ribbentrop's change of manner after obtaining political preferment was given to me in 1934 by Mr Tim Breen, at that time Press Officer in the British Embassy in Berlin. I met Ribbentrop in Berlin before his Nazi days, and after in London, but I only saw the insinuating manner. Of Lady Astor's refusal to invite Ribbentrop to Cliveden I was told by her son the late Lord Astor. Lady Beit (formerly Miss Clementine Mitford) who met Hitler with her cousin Unity Mitford, told me of his absurd misunderstanding of the British peerage, which he expressed to her. The account of the mutual relations of Lady Astor and Neville Chamberlain is deduced from a letter from her husband to her, written some years after the war. The account of Winston Churchill's speech on 5.10.38 follows Hansard except for Lady Astor's last interruption which was more fully reported in the Press. The account is also influenced by memory of a description of the scene in the House of Commons given to me many years ago by Sir Harold Nicolson. The story of Jakie Astor's remark about his lost memory is from a letter written by Lady Astor to Lady Moyra Cavendish. In my book *Troubled Loyalty*, I wrote of the intrigue (for a German partial withdrawal from Czechoslovakia), in which Trott was involved, as having an origin in Ernst von Weizsacker, or rather I wrote with a strong assumption to that effect. Later discussions in Germany have persuaded me that such an origin is most unlikely. The riddle remains unsolved. For the general modern history of Appeasement I am indebted, as all his readers must be, to Martin Gilbert's brief and masterly book, *The Roots of Appeasement* (London, 1966). The account of Lady Astor's grief at the death of her sister is taken from a recorded interview with Miss Harrison made by Kenneth Harris.

Chapter 19

THE SECOND WORLD WAR
1939-1940

ON the 23rd August 1939 Philip Lothian left for the United States on board the *Aquitania*. Before sailing he wrote a short letter to Nancy. 'I feel a beast,' he told her, 'leaving England just as the new crisis is beginning & as you may all be approaching a war – though I still think not. But it's the right time to go to U.S.A.' Most of the letter is concerned with Christian Science, but at the end he mentions political matters again: 'I saw the P.M. & Halifax this morning. All firm but not over-confident that H. doesn't mean trouble.

'Thank you again for all your unfailing help & support. If I need any in Washington, I'll wire.'

Two days later he wrote to her again after hearing of the Molotov-Ribbentrop agreement. 'We land tomorrow morning early. The news, as we get it by radio, seems worse & worse. At least everybody is clearly preparing for war. But I still hope that at the last moment the clouds will clear as they did last year. But you never can tell. The Bible certainly seems to prove that there will seem to be some pretty livid happenings before the dawn. But we can know that none of this is going on in the One Mind & that [if] in preparation we can purify ourselves sufficiently to reflect that Mind, "this world" will lose its power to influence & control us. Anyhow I am sure that Scientists are working far more intelligently about world affairs than they ever have before & that whatever the commotion may be through which we have to go, in reality good is coming through. We may get Union Now in a new & better form.[1]

'Love to everybody. I'm sorry I am not with you to share your risks and perplexities.'

In striking contrast are the letters Nancy received at the same time from G.B.S. His admiration for Hitler had weakened but his devotion

1. In 1939 a movement for promoting European Federal Union made some stir in Great Britain. One of its main scriptures was *Union Now* (1939) by the American author Clarence K. Streit.

to Stalin had if possible increased since 1931. When news came that
the Russo-German pact had been signed by Ribbentrop and Molotov
in the dictator's presence on the 23rd August his optimism knew no
bounds. He publicly declared in a letter published in *The Times* that
the danger of war had been removed, and he repeated the message to
Nancy in a letter of the 27th: 'I wrote to The Times about the absurd
jitter when Stalin took the Führer by the scruff of the neck, but the
letter was meant to give Geoffrey a jolt: I did not expect it to be
inserted. We should have celebrated the news with illuminations.

'Stalin's grin was immense.'

When the history of modern Europe developed in unshavian ways
nonetheless, G.B.S. was moved to appeal to Nancy to help to put it
back on the right lines. After the defeat of Poland he wrote to her on
the 28th September, urging her to agitate for immediate peace and to
put her faith in Stalin. He summed up his views thus at the end of this
long letter:

'What we have to do now is at once to give the order Cease firing
and light up the streets: in short, call off the war and urge on Hitler
that Poland will be a greater trouble to him than half a dozen Irelands
if he oppresses it unbearably. But we must remember that as far as
Poland's business is anybody's business but Poland's, it is more Russia's
business and Germany's than ours. Also that we cannot fight Germany
à l'outrance without ruining both ourselves and Germany, and that we
cannot fight Russia at all (neither can Hitler). The diehards who are still
dreaming of a restoration of the Romanoffs and Bourbons and even
the Stuarts, to say nothing of the Habsburgs, must be booted out of
politics.

'We should, I think, at once announce our intention of lodging a
complaint with the International court against Hitler as being unfitted
for State control, as he is obsessed by a Jewish complex: that of the
Chosen Race, which has led him into wholesale persecution and
robbery. Nothing should be said about concentration camps, because
it was we who invented them.'

Nancy's reply has not survived but G.B.S.'s next letter to her makes
it clear that she expressed her disagreement and spoke her mind about
Stalin. He wrote another long letter to her on the 5th October which
contained the following: 'As you are the only living person known to
have bullied Stalin with complete success; and as he is by countless
chalks the greatest statesman you ever met, and the pleasantest man

except myself, you must stop blackguarding him like an Evening Standard article writer. To our shame we have betrayed and ruined Poland out of sheer thoughtlessness; but it is to our credit, and to that of France and Germany, that when it came to the point of starting a European bombing match we funked it and left Poland to her fate.

'Stalin rescued her. Do you remember that journey through Poland with the harvest still standing and the long wheel spokes of golden strip cultivation turning round us. It looked lovely; but did you know, as I knew, that strip cultivation means poverty and ignorance, savagery, dirt, and vermin? Not to mention landlordism. Well, Stalin will turn that into collective farming; and the Pole will no longer be a savage. The Pole will keep his language, his laws, his character as a citizen of a Federation of Republics like the United States, only much more highly civilized. And with such an object lesson staring his part of the booty in the face, Hitler will have to make his National Socialism emulate Russian Communism or else find Poland worse for him than ten Irelands. So be comforted; and join me in three cheers for the Red Flag (*young* Glory) the Hammer and the Sickle.'

This is to take the story forward to a month after the declaration of war. The family situation, as it had formed in the meantime, should be briefly outlined. Bobbie Shaw had hurried to Edinburgh to enlist as a trooper in the Scots Greys, believing that the regiment was to keep its horses. The report was untrue, so he returned. (He could not have passed the medical examination, having suffered a trepanning operation following a steeplechase accident.) He went back to Wrotham in Kent, where he had lived since 1931, and there he took service in the end with the balloon barrage squadrons. Bill Astor had qualified as a Royal Naval Volunteer Reserve officer more than two years before and in March 1939 he had been posted as an Intelligence Officer to the Middle East Command. He remained for the next eighteen months in Palestine and the Canal Zone, later to be transferred to Syria. (The writer often saw him in this period.) He did not return to England till 1942. David (who was to be commissioned in the Royal Marines in 1940) was, in the first months of the war, a member of an unofficial political committee whose purpose was 'to study the desired shape of things to come in Europe', a peace-planning group whose members included his father, Lionel Curtis, Sir Arthur Salter, Sir Norman Angell, Warden Adams of All Souls College Oxford, and Tom Jones. Until the fall of

France such committees were frequently formed, and discussion of the future of Germany and post-war Europe almost became a national habit until events imposed more immediate preoccupations. Later in 1939, when his friend Adam von Trott was in the United States, David conveyed an invitation to him from himself, his father and T.J., to defect from Nazi Germany and join the committee in England, an invitation that was refused because acceptance would have dangerously reflected on his family and friends. It is interesting to note that in the correspondence with Trott, David, contrary to much political fashion of the time, said that he expected a long destructive war and that the committee's deliberations would be without result. Michael was an officer in the Berkshire Yeomanry and began his war service with them. Of his subsequent adventures he has given a hilarious and misleadingly self-denigratory account in *Tribal Feeling*. Jakie was already an officer in his uncle's old regiment, the Life Guards. He made an interesting remark to his mother on the first day of the war. 'Everything looks the same,' he said, 'but feels different.' James Willoughby was an officer in the Leicestershire Yeomanry.

'I still cannot believe that it has happened,' wrote Nancy to Charlotte Shaw on the second day of the war, and in that cry one can recognise how deeply the influence of Philip Lothian's optimism in the face of facts had penetrated. But like him she could flash from mood to mood, and it is a reasonable guess that the day was not done before her war-like spirit was roused and other thoughts forgotten.

As in the First World War, Nancy and Waldorf offered the use of Cliveden as a hospital. This time the offer, made on the 13th September, was a direct one to the Canadian Government. The offer was accepted in principle, and negotiations concluded a month later. As before the main house was considered unsuited to hospital requirements, but in contrast to 1914 it was put to immediate war use. It will be remembered that, in expectation of instant air attack, there was large-scale evacuation of children from major cities. Eighty-three infants arrived from London in the first week of the war, many with their mothers. But the design of Cliveden with its large rooms and relatively few small ones was soon found impractical as a refuge, and gradually the children with their mothers were settled in houses on the estate. Throughout the war they were given the freedom of the park and grounds. Eventually the great house was used, as it had been from 1914 to 1918, to accommodate doctors and nurses, a few convalescents, and visiting politicians and journalists from allied countries, especially America. Nancy and Waldorf did much Government entertaining at their own expense. The difficulty was to find domestic staff, and requests for some governmental help in the matter were invariably turned down. For security reasons Rest Harrow was shut and uninhabited till 1945.

The offer of the hospital, to be erected on the same site as the Duchess of Connaught hospital in the First World War, was officially accepted by the Canadian Government on behalf of the Canadian Red Cross Society on the 17th October. The land was leased to the Society for a nominal rent by Waldorf, and work, to which the Astors generously contributed funds, was started immediately. The first plan was to build a 300-bed hospital, but by the time it was officially opened towards the end of July 1940 it contained 480 beds and a research centre. It had taken many patients long before the opening and was to grow greatly after. Nancy played a large part in the activity of the hospital, but a less direct one than formerly. The reason was that she and Waldorf were far less often at Cliveden. Their main centre of activity was Plymouth throughout.

As soon as war was declared, Mr Dunstan, the chairman of the Conservative Party Association and a prominent member of the City Council, a man who was admired, resented and sometimes mocked as Plymouth's uncrowned king, moved that in the abnormal circumstances the Council should choose as their next Lord Mayor not one of themselves but Lord Astor. The election was due in November. It was a far-seeing proposition on Dunstan's part, and with his formidable personality and influence he swayed the Council. In November 1939 Waldorf was elected without opposition. He was to fill the post for five years, submitting to annual re-election.

It has been noted already that Nancy's public and emotional identification of herself with her constituency was far more typical of American than British politics. This was entirely to the benefit of her constituency. In the same way Waldorf's conduct of the mayoralty was far more in keeping with his American origins than with his father's anglophilism. Nancy was never the mayor-consort according to accepted usage; she was the co-mayor, and since, later in the war, she often deputised for Waldorf when his ill-health incapacitated him, she sometimes caused the impression that Plymouth had two mayors. American and Canadian newspapermen often referred to her as the Lord Mayor.

Considering how much time she spent in Plymouth it is remarkable how frequent was her attendance in the House of Commons. Through-out the war she would often travel up to London from Devon by the night train and after attending a debate go back to Plymouth the next night. From the opening days of the war she found much to speak about in the House of Commons, mostly matters of feminine interest. Delays in the payment of allowances to soldiers' wives, futile discrimin-ation by which smaller allowances were paid to women than to men who suffered war injuries, denial through suspicion of the right of British women married to aliens to regain their nationality in wartime, the plight, ignored by the Home Office, of some 1,500 British women married to Germans and separated by the chance of war – these were among injustices which she fought from September 1939 onwards, using her well-tried weapon of incessant and awkward questioning. As hardly needs saying, she again and frequently voiced the need of en-larging the force of women police.

On the 17th December 1939, Britain enjoyed her first victory of the war in the Battle of the River Plate. Three cruisers, the *Exeter*, the *Achilles* and the *Ajax*, fought the German pocket battleship *Graf Spee*, compelling her to seek refuge in the harbour of Montevideo. Here the German captain, on orders from Hitler, scuttled the battleship rather than resume the fight or submit the ship to internment. (The captain then committed suicide.) Six weeks later the *Ajax* returned to Plymouth and to a civic welcome led by the mayor and mayoress. Later in the month of February the *Exeter* also returned to Plymouth and the crew were likewise feasted. In a letter to Philip Lothian Nancy described the occasion: 'We lunched at Admiralty House with Winston and Sir John Simon. The latter put his arm round the captain's wife and spoke with tears in his eyes and voice, so that it almost made you sick. She, poor soul, didn't understand the politicians, but even she was a bit suspicious.' The grim events which were soon to follow have dimmed the memory of the victory of the River Plate.

This was still the period of the 'phoney war', in which, while every-thing threatened, the armies stood still; in which life went on much as before though everything 'felt different'. There were optimists who insisted that victory was near because the British naval blockade would cause a rapid economic collapse in Germany, but most people lived under a sense of unease and, as usually happens, unease aroused dis-satisfaction. This was strong in the House of Commons, and had some origin in feelings of guilt at the fact that while Poland was annihilated Britain and France had made no warlike move on land. The feeling was almost as strong on the Government side as in the Opposition, but on the Government side members felt inhibited from speaking their minds. Neville Chamberlain continued to command admiration and loyalty, but doubt as to whether he was the man for the hour, whether by any stretch of imagination this model Health Minister could prove another Chatham or Lloyd George, increased among his followers. Most surprisingly Nancy was among the first Conservative members to give expression to these hushed feelings.

It was not a matter of a sudden change of mind. Although her allegiance to Neville Chamberlain was emotional, it was, except at moments such as Munich-time, somewhat critical. As early as January 1939 she had written to Philip Lothian regretting Chamberlain's refusal to broaden his Government. Not till the outbreak of war did he do this, and then the inclusion of Chamberlain's former opponents, Winston Churchill and Anthony Eden (inclusions impossible to resist), had not been reflected in junior Government appointments, nor even in the humble world of temporary civil service. The mediocrity of his appointments was causing indignation and anxiety.

Nancy first expressed this dissatisfaction in a small intervention in Parliament on the 21st February 1940 over a coal shortage. She said: 'May I ask the Prime Minister, in fairness to himself, the House, and the country, whether he does not think he really ought to get Ministers who will save us from this muddle?' Chamberlain replied: 'I thank the noble lady for her care for me – (laughter) – but I have every confidence in my Ministers.'

It was a small incident, and Chamberlain may be said to have scored, but Nancy's intervention received wide publicity.

On the 9th April 1940 the phoney war came to an end. The period of *Blitzkrieg* opened with the German invasion of Denmark and Norway. The event was at first misinterpreted in England as a German blunder inevitably leading to defeat, as the value of the British naval successes over the Germans was exaggerated. Then optimism was followed by pessimism and in the House of Commons Chamberlain's weak appointments once more came in for criticism voiced again by Nancy, among others. She concluded her speech by saying: 'Many people who do not distrust the Prime Minister feel that he is not a wise selector of men. Duds must be got rid of even if they are one's dearest friends, and when there is a sweep it must be a clean sweep and not musical chairs.' She was supported by Eleanor Rathbone.

As with the incident of 21st February Nancy's speech, with that of Eleanor Rathbone, received much notice in the Press. 'Two women,' wrote J. L. Garvin in the *Observer*, 'had the pluck in Thursday's debate to express the smothered conviction of the House.' Rebellion was latent and growing in Chamberlain's own party. It needed another crisis for it to break out. The crisis came a month later on the 8th May.

The House debated the Norway fiasco on the 7th and 8th May and the division took the form of a vote of confidence. One should remember that Chamberlain's administration was still known as a National Government. The need for such was beyond question and the House was asked in effect if it was satisfied that the Government deserved its name. The Government won the vote by 281 against 200, but it was no parliamentary victory. Winston Churchill's defence of his chief was vehement but weak. Many Government supporters abstained but, far more ominously, forty supporters, led by L. S. Amery who displayed an eloquence which has become part of British political history, voted with the Labour opposition against the Government. Nancy was one of these forty. She did not speak in the debate. Two letters to Philip Lothian contain some account of her feelings which were not those of enthusiasm. 'The new Government,' she wrote on the 21st May, 'on the whole is a distinct improvement, though personally I don't believe it will ever do much until Lloyd George is taken in.' (Lloyd George was at this time aged seventy-seven.) In a letter of the 28th May she wrote:

'It has been very trying lately getting the Government out but thank God they have gone and in time. The whole country is relieved about it. I don't think we shall have any trouble from anyone except a few die-hard Tories whom, like the extreme Left, nothing will change. However, nobody's thinking about politics but about production.

'It is sad about Ironside, but I had always heard that Dill was the better man and certainly the General fought a good deal too recklessly.[2] We are all relieved to have Oliver Stanley away from the War Office. You never saw such surprised people as Simon, Neville, and Sam

2. On 27th May, 1940, General Sir John Dill replaced General Sir Edmund Ironside as Chief of the Imperial General Staff.

Hoare. I don't believe that any of them had the slightest idea of how the country had lost faith in them. I'm not saying that of Neville because I think most people admire him enormously and feel that no man did better for peace but feel that he was hopeless for war.'

In the coalition Government formed on Chamberlain's resignation on the 10th May, Winston Churchill offered Waldorf the post of Parliamentary Under-Secretary to the Ministry of Agriculture, but Waldorf found himself in disagreement with the policy of the Minister, Robert Hudson, so he refused reluctantly. His health would, in any case, have hardly allowed him to fill a Government appointment and concurrently discharge his duties in Plymouth, which were shortly to become very heavy.

The late Prime Minister joined the new Government as Lord President of the Council. He remained in this post till the increasing pains of cancer, following an unsuccessful operation, forced him to resign on the 1st October. He died on the 9th November. In later years Leopold Amery, the immediate instrument of his fall, compared the conduct of Neville Chamberlain with that of Asquith, at similar crises in their lives. He considered that Neville Chamberlain behaved with far finer judgement and public spirit. In the hurry, danger and tragedy of that summer this dignified episode was hardly noticed. There is little to be learned about it in the war-time correspondence between Nancy and Philip Lothian. There was discreet silence on his part, but on Nancy's some severe comment which one may regret, remembering the former and emotional allegiance. Not till a few years later did she remember her old and deep affection worthily. There was cruelty in her nature and political life brings out cruelty.

The Lothian-Astor correspondence was full in 1940 when, except for Lothian's visit to England from mid-October to mid-November, the two friends were separated. They wrote to each other at least once a week, and sometimes as often as twice on the same day when there was some specially interesting piece of late news. On Nancy's side the letters are of much interest today, for they reflect the variety of moods and the dedicated sense of purpose which affected everyone in England then, all with the vividness of her unquenchable spirit and courage. The letters on his side are mostly of very small interest, not because he lacked material or insight – far from it – but because he was now a public servant, and no man had a keener sense of the need, in that circumstance, of discretion in private communication.

In his last phase Lothian not only redeemed a mass of past mis-apprehension and misguided initiative, he added in positive measure to the undoing of the ill that he had served. Once he faltered, it is true, after the fall of France, but his recovery was immediate and his stumble had no effect on his achievement. His task was of much difficulty. American opinion was confused to the point of distraction between a desire to help the cause of the Western Allies and the isolationist faith which encouraged the United States citizenry to have done with 'decadent old Europe'. The second of these preferences was the more tempting. In one letter to Nancy Lothian impatiently (and forgetfully of his past) described the America of 1939–40 as 'the very home of the Munich spirit'. The President openly desired the first alternative, and it was the task of Lothian to make as certain as he could that he was followed by an adequately large majority. In a sense his task was negative: he could initiate nothing, but it was vital to stop the isolation-ist rot.

He succeeded in his task because he enjoyed two great advantages. First he had wide experience of America and Americans: he had the sixth sense which allowed him to play boldly without loss of tact, to go to the limit of what was acceptable to American audiences. His second major asset was that he believed in the cause which he pro-pounded with all the dedicated enthusiasm of a convert. His mission was largely accomplished by visiting as many of the States as he could and giving public addresses, many of them broadcast. It needs no great imagination to picture the increase of his difficulties when the war news from France was only of mounting defeat, and the successfully con-ducted retreat of the British army from the Continent was the only success out of which propaganda appeals could be made. And yet there is no evidence that any speech by Lothian throughout his ambassador-ship was badly received.

In Europe there was a fearful pause between the final collapse of the French army on the 17th June and the beginning in earnest of the Battle of Britain on the 10th July. The first raids on Plymouth occurred at the end of this pause on the 6th, 7th and 8th of July, but although the city was to suffer twenty-five raids during 1940, most of these were very minor (though nearly all involved loss of life) and the most severe would have been counted as minor in the terrible days of 1941. Ply-mouth was not a Luftwaffe target in Goering's strategy for 1940. This relative immunity came as a great surprise and relief, but it had to be paid for: pre-war planning had left Plymouth with utterly inadequate civil defences, and without the challenge of bombardment little was done to build them up. In June the Commander of the Canadian First Division, General McNaughton, stayed with the Astors in Plymouth[3] and was shocked at the deficiencies he noted. He was also disturbed at the fact that the great naval base was not commanded by the most energetic and gifted of the service leaders. Nancy decided that she must take action, but made the mistake of approaching Lord Halifax who was not only inclined to correctitude but, as Foreign Secretary, was in a weak position to intervene. He seems to have been annoyed by her visit to the Foreign Office, judging by a letter from Nancy to Philip Lothian written on the 2nd July: 'As I was leaving, I told him about General McNaughton, and all he said was "Well, if he wants my job he is welcome to it". Personally, I think when people get to that place about a job, they should give it up.'

She wrote at the end of the same letter:

'I expect all the friends of Britain in France and Italy will be bumped off. You know what you said about Grandi? Well, Mrs George Keppel arrived in Plymouth looking like a disturbed blancmange, having been evacuated from Italy, and she says that Grandi is more hostile to England than anyone out there. You always said it. I am beginning to doubt my own judgement. Ironside has been a failure, and when I saw X waiting outside his car, and realized that out of all the world he had chosen him as his A.D.C., my heart sank. Then there is Neville, my blue-eyed boy, and Tom Inskip. I hope and pray that I have not been wrong about you!'

Two weeks later Philip Lothian momentarily faltered. Nancy was not involved but the episode should be briefly indicated.

On July 19th Hitler addressed the Reichstag, declaring that 'at this hour, I feel it to be my duty before my own conscience to appeal once more to reason and common sense in Great Britain as much as elsewhere.' He appealed for an end to the war, hinted at a forthcoming offer of favourable peace terms to Britain but gave no details. In London the Prime Minister consulted his colleagues as to what was the best way to reject the offer. They decided that this would be most effectively done by a broadcast by the Foreign Secretary. From his own record of the incident it would seem that Winston Churchill was

3. His division sailed from Plymouth to France just before the French surrender and returned immediately.

alive to the possibility that the offer might conceivably be tempting to Lothian. The German Chargé d'Affaires in Washington had approached him through neutrals. Churchill requested the Foreign Office to tell Lothian 'on no account to make any reply to the German Chargé d'Affaires' message'.

If the Prime Minister's mind has been rightly interpreted here, then his anxieties were not groundless, judging from Harold Nicolson's diary for July 1940. Nicolson was at this time Parliamentary Under-Secretary to the Ministry of Information under Duff Cooper, and for the 22nd the diary has the following intriguing entry:

'Philip Lothian telephones wildly from Washington in the evening begging Halifax not to say anything in his broadcast tonight which might close the door to peace. Lothian claims that he knows the German peace-terms and that they are most satisfactory. I am glad to say that Halifax pays no attention to this and makes an extremely bad broadcast but one which is perfectly firm as far as it goes.'

The sequel to the story shows how perfectly T.J. had described Lothian to Baldwin. On the same day as Halifax made his broadcast Lothian was due to give an interview to be broadcast throughout the United States. To appreciate what happened one must remember the six-hour difference between the East and West Atlantic. When the ambassador telephoned 'wildly' to London in the evening, it was morning in Washington. This gave Lothian six hours at the very least to meditate before evening on the resolve he had encountered in London, and to reappraise his reversion to Chamberlainite Appeasement. Reconversion was swift.

The most critical single item in the Anglo-American diplomatic dialogue of those days was the British desire to obtain destroyers from the United States for the escort of convoys. The discussion, of which the American Press and public knew nothing, had been held up by the Party Conventions in June and July during which time the President had felt reluctant either to approach Congress or act independently. The story is very complex. What needs to be noticed is the broadcast interview of the 22nd July. Philip Lothian publicly discussed the question and 'proclaimed from the housetops,' to quote his biographer, 'in language which the American public would not resent, the same doctrine which, at the Prime Minister's behest, he was speaking in the ear of the President'. He was asked about the British need for armaments, and he answered 'most urgently we need destroyers and armed motor boats; 100 of these now might make the difference between success and failure'. It was obviously very dangerous to bring this into public discussion, yet so masterly was his touch that the interview was successful politically as well as from the propaganda point of view. The broadcast marked a turning-point. The difference between the morning and evening Lothian could hardly have been greater.

To return to London.

The Battle of Britain slowly moved towards the climax of its first phase, the fight for the mastery of the air, which the Luftwaffe was to lose by a narrow margin in the second half of September. No one could see the shape of the German strategy and an immediate attempt at the invasion of Britain seemed likely to most people. 'We have been expecting Mr Hitler hourly' wrote Nancy to Philip Lothian on the 20th August.

Her two youngest sons, Michael and Jakie, had joined a unit (which they both seemed to regard as a colossal lark) whose purpose was to form small armed motorised groups to provide liaison between different headquarters and between headquarters and the troops under them during the land battle in Britain. Since (as the reader may remember) Britain was not invaded by the German army, the organisation took other forms in the course of the years. Bill was still at Ismailia, David was in a defence-building unit of the Marines on the South Coast. Later, in the middle of October, Bobbie Shaw was severely wounded. Nancy told Charlotte Shaw in a letter that a bomb had fallen near his barrage squadron and that he and one other man only had survived. In fact, at the time Bobbie was in a public house at Wrotham, and the bomb fell on it, killing everyone there except him and a few others. When in Maidstone hospital afterwards, as David Astor has told the writer, 'he was keen' that an edited version of the incident should reach his mother. On the same night that Bobbie was thus injured a bomb hit 4 St James's Square, destroying several rooms. This was the first of four direct hits on the house during the war. At this time Waldorf was in much pain from his recurrent rheumatism and Nancy decided that he must have a rest in Jura.

They left for Jura on the 17th September. This was the day when Hitler decided to call off 'Operation Sea Lion', the invasion of England. No one in the country could possibly guess this. The battle only seemed to be growing fiercer. G.B.S. wrote to Nancy a few days later from Ayot St Lawrence: 'We can see the flashes over London and hear the distant thunder of the guns. Casual raiders occasionally drop a bomb near enough to shake the house and alarm the shelterless village; there is a dump about a mile off where they make me jump by banging off all the delayed action bombs that fall into the county; and we have a little pip-squeak of a siren that gives us all the London alarms quite unnecessarily; but we sleep in our beds regardless.' When the Astors returned towards the end of the month the next phase in the battle was slowly approaching climax: the Battle of London.

In America, the Presidential election was to take place on the 4th November 1940 and Lothian considered he would be wise to be absent from America at this time. He also needed rest. He had injured his health by overwork and this showed in periods of lassitude. He became prone to drop off into sleep, and once or twice he did so on a public occasion. In fact his condition was much more serious than anyone knew. He was suffering from the disease of the kidneys known as uraemia. What he needed was a complete holiday for at least a month, but what he did was to take a short leave most of which he spent in London, then enduring the German bombing at its very height. He gave himself almost no rest and occupied the greater part of his time in consultation with his chief, Lord Halifax, with other Ministers, and with heads of Foreign Office departments. In the stress and hurry of wartime life he even saw relatively little of the Astors. Nancy was in Plymouth when he arrived in London on the 23rd October, but he found a message from her awaiting him at the Ritz Hotel: 'Welcome to the Blitzkrieg.' Not long after, his bedroom furniture was up-turned by a nearby blast.

She arranged a weekend at Cliveden and collected as many as she could of the Kindergarten: Bob Brand, Geoffrey Dawson, the Prophet and Dynamo Lionel Curtis. It was the last meeting of most of them with Lothian.

As in the preceding weeks Lothian's condition was changeable so that while some who met him described him as vigorous and well, others found him 'dreadfully ill', and Lord Halifax noted his odd tendency to fall asleep. But in the most important meeting of this visit he was manifestly enjoying a moment of physical contentment and mental alertness. It occurred while he was staying at Ditchley, the Oxfordshire home of Nancy's nephew-in-law and niece, Ronald and Nancy Tree. Ditchley, the most beautiful of all English country houses, was frequently used by Winston Churchill, thanks to the hospitality

Golfing with Philip Lothian

Cliveden,
from the South Lawn

Visiting Devonport in the Blitz

of the Trees, and to Ditchley Lothian went for a weekend in the first part of November to meet the Prime Minister.

As may be easily imagined, Winston Churchill who knew Lothian personally but not well, was not much predisposed in his favour. The two men were not made for each other. We have no record of Lothian's personal reactions to this meeting, but let Churchill's own words be used to recall his: 'Ditchley is only four or five miles away from Blenheim. In these agreeable surroundings I received the Ambassador. Lothian seemed to me a changed man. In all the years I had known him he had given me the impression of high intellectual and aristocratic detachment from vulgar affairs. Airy, viewy, aloof, dignified, censorious, yet in a light and gay manner, he had always been good company. Now, under the same hammer that smote upon us all, I found an earnest, deeply stirred man. He was primed with every aspect and detail of the American attitude. He had won nothing but goodwill and confidence in Washington by his handling of the Destroyers-cum-Bases negotiations. He was fresh from intimate contact with the President, with whom he had established a warm personal friendship. His mind was now set upon the Dollar Problem; this was grim indeed.'

Lothian left England on the 14th November, sending a farewell message to Nancy and the family by telegram. His first stop was at Lisbon where he was held up for nearly a week while awaiting a passage to New York by the newly organised Clipper service.[4] On the 16th he wrote to Nancy: 'I had a very good trip here – without incident. There were four American air officers on board – you had seen them at Cliveden a week before – all of whom had been much impressed by what they had seen. I don't know when I get to New York. They promise a clipper on Monday (18th) but only seeing is believing. I shall not mind a week's holiday anywhere. I shall [have] been three days here anyway.

'Sam & Maude are here.[5] They are evidently having an awful life in Madrid. The Germans are dominant everywhere & the town is half in

4. At this time Pan American Airways were operating transatlantic services by Boeing 314 flying boat, with intermediate stops. The Lisbon service flew from Lisbon to New York with one intermediate stop at Horta in the Azores. The term 'Clipper' was short for 'Flying Clipper Ship', the trade name then used by P.A.A. for all types of aircraft in their services.

5. Sir Samuel and Lady Maude Hoare. He was British Ambassador to Spain, May 1940 to December 1944. Later he was created Viscount Templewood.

ruins & the British Embassy uninhabitable. But he seems to be doing a good job in difficult circumstances.

'I am sorry to leave England. It is an inspiring place. But I know I have a job to do in U.S.A. this next year. Stick to your Science & it will see you through – with perfection as reality in the background of your thinking.

'Thank you for all your help. I greatly value it.'

This was Philip Lothian's last letter to her.

Before she had received it she wrote to him on the 21st November: 'I hope and pray you have safely landed, but no word yet.

'No news since you left, except that Bobbie [Shaw] is still a-bed and really far from well. Apparently this is the case with many people who have been bombed. It has a devastating effect upon them. I have not felt able to leave him to go to Plymouth yet, but hope to go on Sunday night.

'The news here is only a good deal of discontent about the people around our boss. They feel he must get stronger and better men, particularly Trenchard. . . .

'Your visit seems like a dream, and I can't believe that you have been here. I am longing to hear what success you have had in Washington. Poor Joe Kennedy seems to have spilled the beans, but no one here is surprised as they say he talked that way to many people.

'Please send me some molasses candy – old-fashioned molasses candy – anyone in Washington will tell you what it is. The children eat it like hungry hounds, and sugar is getting scarcer and scarcer. You might remind any of my loving friends to send me some too.

'Miss Irvine, I regret to say, was elected Second Reader at the Meeting on Saturday, so after seventeen years she is leaving me for the Lord. We have another C.S. in view already, who seems really nice and whom we both hope will come.'[6]

On the 23rd November he sent her a telegram from Washington

6. Miss Irvine had been Lady Astor's private secretary. 'Joe Kennedy' is the United States Ambassador to the Court of St James 1937–1941 Joseph P. Kennedy, the father of President John F. Kennedy. He had become very unpopular in Great Britain since from acting as a spokesman of anti-Nazism in the last years of peace he had become an advocate of American isolationism and expressed defeatist opinions about the country to which he was accredited after the outbreak of war. During the bombing of London he appeared to lose his nerve. At this time he had returned to the United States and given Press interviews. He did not return. He was succeeded in 1941 by John G. Winant. 'Our boss' in the second paragraph is Winston Churchill.

'Arrived safely best love Lothian.' No later communication between them has survived. The 23rd was long remembered in the United States. In his official capacity Philip Lothian played more boldly on that day than at any time before. Winston Churchill's last quoted words should be recalled: 'His mind was now set upon the Dollar Problem; this was grim indeed.' Lothian held to his conviction not only that public opinion was the decisive factor, but that it must be taken into confidence, so far as conceivably possible, throughout negotiations. He followed the League of Nations ideal of 'open covenants openly arrived at' in the most literal sense, and in July he had acted on his principles with audacity and success in the 'Destroyers-cum-Bases negotiations'. He acted with audacity again now. He had a short time on the 23rd November in New York between leaving the Clipper and flying on to Washington. The Press were there in force and asked him amid much flashing of bulbs for his impressions of beleaguered Britain. He replied: 'Well, boys, Britain's broke. It's your money we want.' There was a gasp, a rush for the telephones, and the newspaper and radio headlines were assured for that night and next day.

After his calculated indiscretion on the 22nd July, Philip Lothian had correctly reported to a friend on the 23rd 'Today not a murmur'. On the 24th November 1940 there were many murmurs, from the White House, from Congress, and from London. According to his biographer, Lothian himself is said to have felt some temporary regret for his words, but in the end 'came to recognise that his remarks had served a useful purpose: they had brought this delicate matter to a head and put our need squarely before the American people'. As with the destroyers deal, apparent clumsiness seems in fact to have eased the negotiation.

Lothian arrived to find a great mass of work, official and semi-official, the latter largely occupied with reassuring, consoling and informing British people separated from their families or interests. He took on personally all that he could, so much so that, as his biographer remarked, 'even breakfast was apt to become a conference'.

He lived long enough to see the fruition of some of his work. By the late autumn of 1940 the American Service chiefs were asking the President for secret talks with the British, a matter which caused more embarrassment to the President than the ambassador who had never ventured so far. Further difficult problems arose, notably food-provision for Great Britain, a little later to be handled magisterially by Bob Brand, and there were a hundred urgent but smaller matters.

Lothian was gravely ill and his few days in Portugal had been quite inadequate to his need for rest. But as in the far days when Lionel Curtis had 'yearned' for him, he could not resist the temptation of overwork. He overworked to the end.

It was nearly five months now since he had given an address and he decided to take the first opportunity to do so again. An opportunity had presented itself when he was invited to address a meeting in Baltimore of the American Farm Bureau Federation on the 11th December. He had accepted from London, and on his return took great pains with the composition of the speech. As before, he would be over-come by drowsiness, and more frequently. He was well enough, how-ever, to play nine holes of golf on Saturday the 7th December. He worked through the next Sunday but in the evening he was suddenly taken seriously ill. He rallied on the Monday and Tuesday but had to abandon his appointment in Baltimore where his speech was read for him by his second-in-command, the Minister Nevile Butler, on the Wednesday.

It was perhaps the best of all Lothian's speeches. Its last words became famous at the time and are still remembered by a few. 'Since May there is no challenge we have evaded, no challenge we have refused. If you back us you won't be backing a quitter. The issue now depends largely on what you decide to do. Nobody can share that responsibility with you. It is the great strength of a democracy that it brings responsibility down squarely on every citizen and every nation. And before the judgement seat of God each must answer for his own actions.'

The newspapers of Thursday the 12th December carried full reports of this address. They also carried the news of Lothian's death. It had happened suddenly in the night. Faithful to his beliefs he had refused ordinary medical attention and was ministered to at the last by a Christian Scientist male nurse, and a Boston friend of many years who was a Christian Science practitioner.

On Nancy, the death of Philip Lothian inflicted a loss which was never repaired. The news came with all the shock of the unexpected. The two great friendships with men which she enjoyed were with Lothian and Bernard Shaw, and there can be no doubt that the first of these meant most to her. Lothian was among the very few, perhaps the only man apart from Waldorf, who influenced her ideas and conduct. Shaw did not belong to this small category, and though she loved him, indeed seemed to cling to his friendship with all the more intensity after Lothian's death, he never replaced him. He appealed to a less serious part of her being than had the other. The mutual love, friendship and esteem of Nancy and Philip Lothian was a unique thing in her life.

Letters of condolence came to her in great numbers both from English and American friends. It was an extraordinary tribute to a modern instance of sacred as opposed to profane love, an extraordinary relationship, such as few enjoy.

One of the English letters to Nancy came from Stanley Baldwin. 'My dear Lady Nancy,' he wrote, 'This needs no acknowledgement but I think I know what this means to you and I just want to grasp your hand for a moment. With affection and regard S.B.' At this time Baldwin was suffering one of the swiftest and completest eclipses of political reputation in our history. An immense volume of abuse and blame for the misfortunes of the country fell on him from the multitudes of his former worshippers. In the past he had put on the airs of coarse indifference to attack, but in his later years the pretence broke down and he showed himself to the few who saw him as a sensitive man forced to suffer in silence. No man in the afflicted Britain of 1940 was more unhappy, and in his grief he wrote this short note to Nancy in her grief.

Most of the foregoing chapter is drawn from the Astor archive and the contemporary Press. The wartime dispersal of the Astor family has been traced from *Tribal Feeling*, *Who's Who*, correspondence between myself and J. J. Astor, and Lady Astor's correspondence with Lord Lothian. The circumstances of Lord Astor's election to the Lord Mayoralty of Plymouth were given to me on a visit to the city by Mr John Paton Watson. The account of the invitation to Adam von Trott and his refusal are taken from my book, *Troubled Loyalty*, based at this point on Trott papers. L. S. Amery's views on the changes in government of 1916 and 1940 are taken from memories of a conversation with him in 1956. The offer of a junior post to Lord Astor by Winston Churchill is recorded in a letter from Lady Astor to Lord Lothian. Except where stated otherwise, the account of Lord Lothian's last year of life follows Sir James Butler's biography. The general account of his character in this and in preceding chapters is influenced by Kingsley Martin's obituary article on him which appeared in *The New Statesman* in 1940. It remains the best brief account of him. It may seem to some readers that I have omitted one incident in Lady Astor's life at this time. In September 1940 she incurred great unpopularity (which I well remember) among the Middle East forces. This was on account of an alleged open letter from her to the

Daily Mirror comparing the easy life of the army in Egypt to the ordeals being endured by the civilian population of Britain at the time. The matter was reported in detail by three Canadian newspapers. A search of the *Daily Mirror* file in the British Museum Press Library in Colindale reveals no such letter or any news item which could conceivably be interpreted in the sense of the reports. It appears to have been one of the numerous rumours of that gossipy time; the myth of the Angels of Mons, as it were, in reverse. I am grateful to B.O.A.C. for information on the Clipper Service.

Chapter 20

THE SECOND WORLD WAR
1941–1945

WITH the new year the Battle of Britain could be accounted precariously won in the air, though this meant no lessening of the *Blitzkrieg*. There were triumphs in Egypt and North Africa, but they could not be decisive while Britain's only allies were the distant Dominions. Though the spirit of the country remained defiant and exalted, there entered into it also the impatience, depression and irritation of the siege mentality. In these circumstances Nancy did not mellow.

Early in 1941 she took the unpopular side in a dispute which caused much indignation. A certain Colonel Bingham, who was commandant of an officer cadet training unit, took the highly irregular course of writing to *The Times* to complain about the quality of his pupils. He asserted that those of them who came from the working classes had 'largely fallen down' during training. 'These classes,' he wrote, 'unlike the old aristocratic feudal classes, have never had "their people" to consider. They have never had anyone to think of but themselves.' He cited Winston Churchill as an example of the more agreeable categories.

Not only the Left Wing was roused by this reactionary opinion, and for a few days it was the main topic of the newspapers. On the 21st January a Labour member, Malcolm Macmillan, raised the matter in a parliamentary question. The Secretary of State for War, David Margesson, assured him that explanations had been called for, but Mr Macmillan was stirred to ask further: 'Will the Minister make sure that more discretion is exercised over the publication of a letter of this kind?' to which the Prime Minister, to the surprise of the House, cried: 'Hear! hear!' Margesson replied: 'I regret profoundly that the letter was published, but Mr Macmillan will realise that I have no powers over the Press.'

Up jumped Nancy who was called. 'Will the Minister bear in mind,' she said, 'that a great many of the ordinary soldiers think that there is a great deal of substance in this matter, and everybody knows it?' There were bellows of 'Nonsense' from every side of the House; there was no reply from Margesson, and Nancy got a bad Press in the morning.

This experience did not deter her from courting further unpopularity in the House only a week later; if anything it encouraged her. The occasion was again question time, in this instance the topic being initiated by Nancy herself. Sir Robert Vansittart had just published his famous anti-German book *Black Record*, and the dispute raised by that touched Nancy on a matter of principle. The book had an origin in talks given by Vansittart on the BBC. Nancy had been moved to write to the Foreign Secretary, Anthony Eden, on the 3rd February as follows: 'One of the reasons I felt that Sir Robert Vansittart's broadcast was so lamentable was because of the German anti-Nazis in America. It is bound to have had a lamentable effect on them and as you and I realise it is not Europe we are going to get support from, but America, and it is a pity that anyone in the position of Sir Robert should have been so blind as not to have realised that.'[1] Anthony Eden returned a non-committal reply.

On the 28th January she had a parliamentary question down for the Prime Minister about this book and about the propriety of a civil servant publishing such a thing. During question and answer the House grew restive. A Labour member, Mr Ellis Smith, rose to ask: 'Has not Sir Robert Vansittart proved himself more British than *other people*?' A Conservative, Mr Henry Strauss, rose to put the matter with more precision: 'On the subject of Germany have not the views of Sir Robert Vansittart been proved to be generally right while the views of the noble lady have been almost invariably wrong?' At this there were cheers and derisive laughter. The scene was widely reported next day, and most of the comments were hostile to Nancy. The Cliveden Set was not forgotten.

On the 3rd March 1941 Nancy said in a speech in bombed Birmingham: 'Hate is a deadly poison. Kill the Germans, don't hate them.' She never surrendered to mass-hate throughout the war. For her it was a matter of principle, one that was to be put to the severest test soon.

By the 20th March 1941 Plymouth had had 37 raids and hundreds of alerts. Most of the raids had been indirect: German aircraft returning from Bristol or Liverpool had unloaded their bombs on the way home. There had been a few raids with Plymouth as the target but no massive

1. Lady Astor probably knew more than most about the anti-Nazi interest in the U.S.A. from her son David's correspondence with Adam von Trott in October and November 1939, when Trott was in America.

attack to compare with those on London or Coventry. This apparent and illogical immunity of Plymouth continued to lull the harassed authorities of Whitehall into complacency. It had been originally assumed in 1939 that despite the importance of its naval base, Plymouth lay so far to the west that it would not be the object of heavy air attack. There was some revision of these calculations after the fall of France, but not nearly so drastic as it should have been. By the spring of 1941 there were still no plans for the removal of old people and children to country areas, and the fire-fighting services were still such as suited relatively small-scale bombing. General McNaughton's criticisms have been noted already, and Nancy's fruitless efforts to act on them. She and Waldorf continued such efforts but with little success. Neither of them could raise the matter in Parliament without giving information to the enemy. They had to work behind the scenes and so far their efforts had been unavailing. Then in March the authorities found themselves forced into action by terrible events.

On the morning of the 20th of that month the King and Queen arrived for an official visit. They were met at the Central Railway Station by the Lord Mayor and Lady Mayoress, by the City Council, the Service chiefs and members of their staffs, and by the Australian Prime Minister, Robert Menzies, who was spending a few days in Plymouth as a guest of the Astors. The King and Queen went for a long tour of the city, noted the damage caused by the raids, inspected the defences and shelters, visited the various Service Headquarters, and spoke with the citizenry who received them with much applause. It was a well-organised and successful visit, Nancy's respectful chaff keeping the King in the best of humours. The visit ended with tea for the King and Queen with the Astors and a few guests at 3 Elliot Terrace. After tea, the royal visitors, escorted by the mayor and mayoress, drove through streets full of cheering crowds to the station. From here the royal train was scheduled to leave at 6 p.m. At the end of the drive to the station, and while the King and Queen were saying goodbye to the Astors, the alert was sounded. No one paid special attention. In Plymouth alerts were frequent, and only about one in ten had been followed by action so far. The train moved off. Two and a half hours later Plymouth was subjected to an air-raid which was one of the most terrible on an English city in the course of the war.

The raid struck at the city centre and nearly obliterated it. On the succeeding night the raid was repeated in detail, with Germanic precision, and after that there was little of the ancient centre left. These two raids were the beginning of a sustained *Blitzkrieg* on Plymouth. Once begun it was maintained until the end of 1941. Then there was a respite.

There are two first-hand descriptions of Nancy in her first experience of a major air-raid. One is from the American writer and journalist Ben Robertson who was staying with the Astors in Elliot Terrace on the 20th March. He gave an account of the raid in his book *I Saw England*. He tells how after the departure of the King and Queen, 'at 8.30 p.m. we had eaten some chicken and stewed rhubarb and the cakes left over from the royal tea-party, when the . . . guns began to thunder. From the very start there was something about the intensity of the whole which made us think that this was it. We had all the tubs in the house filled with water and saw that spades were handy. The maid Rose said: "Lady Astor, I must tell you, I have a sailor visiting me." "Tell him to stay," said Lady Astor. . . . We heard a stick of bombs coming nearer and nearer and fell flat on our faces by the hall door.'

A bomb exploded near the house and smashed all the glass on the Hoe side of Elliot Terrace. An air-raid warden came down the street and ordered the inhabitants of the houses to go down to the basements. The Astor party obeyed, and Ben Robertson recalled how Nancy 'talked about Virginia and her childhood and the tobacco fields and about Rose Harrison, her maid, saying that Rose and she had worked together for thirty years'. Rose gave her own account of the night to Maurice Collis: 'Someone told us we must go into the shelter. An American journalist, Mr Ben Robertson, was with us. In the shelter I spent the time picking bits of glass out of her ladyship's hair. Mr Robertson was taking down notes for his book . . . [Lady Astor said:] "Nobody would keep Rose but me, and nobody would stay with me but Rose."'

The house was struck by one of the thousands of little incendiaries which the Germans scattered over the city. To follow Ben Robertson again: 'Someone came in to say that an incendiary was on the roof. "Come on everybody," called Lady Astor, "get the sand-bags. Where in hell are the buckets?" From this we were up and down the stairs. Once she stopped by a blasted window to look at Plymouth which for miles was a blazing fire. Her eyes filled with tears, and pushing back her steel hat she said: "There goes thirty years of our lives, but we'll build it again." '

The next morning there were many newspaper reporters in Plymouth from the provincial and metropolitan Press, and inevitably they sought to extract a story from the Lady Mayoress. They got the usual sort of thing, until one of them looked up to ask her what was the strangest sight she saw. She had seen very little as she had been in the basement most of the time, but there had been that moment at the window, and she did remember something strange that she had seen. She said: 'At the height of the raid I saw a man who walked along calmly exercising two dogs.'

On the evening of the 21st March Nancy and Waldorf went to the hostel they had founded in the centre of Plymouth and which they had named Virginia House. They had invited Mr Menzies to address a meeting there. Hardly had he begun to speak than the sirens wailed. Mr Menzies wondered whether to go on, and Nancy hastily assured him that a stirring oration was the best way to take the minds of the people off their danger. He agreed and gallantly went through his speech. Shortly after the conclusion of the meeting Virginia House was struck. By this time the Astors were escorting Mr Menzies back to Elliot Terrace. She was worried about the safety of her staff, and when she saw Rose Harrison she burst into tears and said she would never leave them again. Nevertheless, when she had seen them to the shelter, Waldorf and she decided that as mayor and mayoress their duty lay in going round the main city shelters to give what help they could. She had been in most of the shelters already during raids, and had done much to make them less uncomfortable and more practical.

There was little practical help that she could give now as the scream and crash of bombs could be dimly heard above, but she could raise spirits. She chaffed, backchatted, used all those arts that had served her so well in her seven elections. She nursed babies, comically rebuked anyone she saw fortifying himself with a drink – 'That man will drink a couple of bottles while another is looking for the corkscrew' – but above all she and Waldorf rallied the people by their courage, by the absolute indifference to fear that they showed. They did not wait for a lull in the storm before walking out in the streets to visit another shelter. They walked through the streets by the light of the burning city as though unconcerned, and had cheerful words for the few people they met.

Such conduct became routine through the terrible nights of April and till the attacks died down in the last quarter of 1941. As in her election campaigns she always dressed well on these occasions, even wearing jewellery sometimes. On one occasion, when she was accompanied by her niece Alice Winn, she went into a shelter where the morale seemed to her rather low. She looked around, said nothing, then made a tour of the room, not walking but turning cartwheels and somersaults till she came back to the staircase. 'Are we downhearted?' she cried amid roars of admiration, and walked up, back into the streets. She wrote in a letter to a friend: 'Only I and the P.M. enjoy the war, but only I say so.' This was not entirely facetious. A Plymouth woman was later reported as saying: 'The bombing was cruel but Lady Astor made it all right.'

From the 20th March onwards there was an exodus of many homeless people from Plymouth, and since the city was not an evacuation area, the flight was spontaneous and unorganised. The fugitives wandered into the countryside with what provisions they could gather, taking rugs and blankets for protection from the cold weather. They were lucky if they could find a barn or disused cowshed for a makeshift dwelling. For the main part the exodus was a flight from fire. Whole blocks of houses were destroyed by incendiaries and by the conflagrations following explosions, before any kind of help could get through. The cause of this inefficiency was that fire-fighting remained a strictly local responsibility and depended, to quote a witty leader in the *Daily Mirror*, on 'local patriotism in control of the village pump aided by the vicar's garden hose'. In vain Waldorf and Nancy had drawn attention privately to these wrongs. In April 1941, after the first great raids, they decided to ignore the old and valid argument that public exposure of deficiencies helped the enemy; the enemy was doing his damnedest and without public outcry against incompetence he was likely to do still more. So on the 4th April there appeared a letter in *The Times* on fire-fighting needs which caused much stir. It was signed by Nancy under the address of the House of Commons.

She did not, surprisingly, urge the formation of a national service (the solution reached in May) but 'entirely new local organisations'. The letter was applauded in the Press but was also to be adversely criticised later. As for the evacuation question, Nancy made her views very plain at the end of the month. Among numerous remarks of the same kind she told newspapermen that 'It is a great scandal that Plymouth, which is a fortress, should not have been made an evacuation area long ago', and she described the Government's failure in this respect as 'the biggest flop of the war'. Stirred on by the mayor and mayoress, the City Council made a request to the Ministry of Health for Plymouth to be registered as an evacuation area, and the Ministry acceded on the 29th April. 10,000 school children were removed to country areas.

While the memory of the second of these disputes with the Government was still fresh, and the fire-fighting problem was still to be resolved, the Prime Minister visited Plymouth on the 2nd May. It was a solemn and moving occasion, but behind the scenes there was some tension and some comedy in which Nancy played a leading part. Waldorf had fallen ill and was away, so Nancy deputised for him.

The Prime Minister was accompanied by Mrs Churchill and Mr Averill Harriman, the American President's personal envoy to Mr Churchill. Mr Harriman had not met the Astors and, having heard all the rumours of the Cliveden Set and of Winston Churchill's supposed enmity towards its members, had not sought to do so. Certainly Winston Churchill was not in his most affectionate mood towards Nancy at the moment; he was a despotic democrat, easily irritated by 'interference with the Government with which I am entrusted', and always disapproving of 'indiscretions' such as Nancy's Press interviews and her letter to *The Times*. Nancy likewise was not in her most affectionate mood towards the Government of which Winston Churchill was the head.

An element of political rivalry arose to sharpen the situation. Nancy and Winston Churchill were both politicians and both had therefore a professional interest in popularity. (Let those be shocked who may.) Nancy saw a chance of making some political capital out of the visit, and she had arranged that the programme should include visits by Mrs Churchill, not accompanied by her husband but escorted by the Lady Mayoress, to various places where women would be the majority in the audience. By appearing on the same platform as the beautiful and popular wife of the great Prime Minister, so she seems to have argued to herself, Nancy would augment her own very considerable popularity. Similar ideas had entered the mind of Winston Churchill. If there was some dissatisfaction with his Government in this great city, what better way in which to soothe it, especially among its women voters, than to appear in it with his beautiful and popular wife?

The difference came into the open about an hour after Winston Churchill's arrival from London by the night train. As a former First Lord of the Admiralty it had been agreed that he and his party should immediately be taken from the train to naval headquarters for a bath, breakfast, and a short preliminary conference on the programme at Admiralty House. Nancy joined the party there. It was a fine day and most of the post-breakfast conference took place on the lawn. Mr Harriman was an interested if occasionally embarrassed spectator.

Winston Churchill expressed dissatisfaction with the programme. He said that he wished his wife to accompany him to all the public meetings. Nancy replied that the programme could not be altered so late as now. The Prime Minister was in no mood to be contradicted. A clash threatened. Time was short. At length he strode away by himself, stood alone looking at the sea, then with long steps strode back to the group. Assuming his gravest manner he made an announcement: 'In time of war,' he declaimed, 'the supreme decisions must rest with the Prime Minister, and with him alone. . . . Mrs Churchill will come with me.' It was a clear victory for Winston Churchill, and as he made his way out to the waiting cars he dropped his solemn expression to wink at Averill Harriman, and then resumed it before facing the cameras.

(Later, when looking at photographs of the occasion with David Astor, Nancy pointed to one which showed the Churchills entering the car with her, he in the plain naval uniform of an Elder Brother of Trinity House and wearing looks even gruffer and more bulldoggish than usual. She said: 'Isn't he an old repertory actor?' But perhaps the very gruff looks indicated lingering anger at meeting this sudden and unexpected opposition.)

They drove round the city which Churchill knew well, and at the sight of the cheering crowds along the streets of ruined houses, he could not restrain his tears. Nancy was in a hard indignant mood. At one point she said in the hearing of others: 'It's all very well to cry, Winston, but you got to do somethin'.'

Nancy summed up her own impressions of the visit a fortnight later in the course of a letter to Lady Halifax whose husband had gone to Washington as Lord Lothian's successor. Nancy wrote: 'Winston and Clemmie came and Waldorf got a chill and I had to meet them. He was almost lyrical and talked about Virginian courage and so forth. He drove round the city with tears running down his cheeks, taking his hat off, and saying "God bless you". It was a moving sight, but why it has not moved him to action I cannot understand.'

On the 19th May, three days after writing this letter, Nancy went into action in the House of Commons. The occasion was the Second Reading of the Fire Services (Emergency Provisions) Bill, introduced by the Home Secretary Herbert Morrison. In effect this Bill established a national fire-fighting service and achieved everything that she and Waldorf had been striving for. Nancy supported the Bill but in no conciliatory spirit. 'The very fact,' she said, 'that the Government are bringing in a Bill like this after we have had six months of fire blitz and bomb blitz shows that there is something fundamentally wrong with the Home Front. I welcome the Bill but it horrifies me to think we have waited six months to bring it in.' Herbert Morrison was much respected as a strong man of the Labour Party and thus as a vital element in holding the coalition together. In consequence he was treated with almost more respect by the Right than by his own Left Wing, and thus when Nancy came to personal criticism of him she was heard by the House in general, and especially by her own party, with alarm. 'I put this to the House,' she said, 'Supposing you had a general who had lost twelve battles, would you not begin to wonder whether you ought to get rid of him. The Home Secretary has lost twelve battles because there have been twelve towns blitzed, bombed and burnt. I do not blame him entirely. I blame the whole Government.' She urged that Lord Trenchard should be put 'at the head of this Battle of Britain'.

The House had been impressed by the delicacy and tact which Herbert Morrison had shown towards the susceptibilities of local government authority. Nancy crashed into these without a thought for anyone's feelings. 'I know that when the battle came to Plymouth I had no respect for the feelings of local authorities. I was not thinking of them; I was thinking of the people, and I believe that if we had not written to *The Times* we should not even have had this Bill. . . . Everyone knows in the country, and in these blitzed towns, and in the House of Commons – I don't know whether the Government knows it – that the first thing a local authority wants to do when a town is blitzed is to cover up its mistakes. I was not going to have mistakes covered up in Plymouth.' She wandered from the subject and the Deputy Speaker called her to order. She ended: 'I appeal to the Home Secretary: let him make his speeches, let him rouse the country, but for Heaven's sake get Trenchard to do the job.'

She had succeeded in irritating most of her hearers, and her Trenchard proposal was regarded as ridiculous. Lady Rhondda was very shocked and *Time and Tide* raked up memories of the Cliveden Set: the Trenchard proposal was regarded as a characteristic attempt at Fascism! Several other papers joined in with similar denunciations. The *Daily Mirror*, however, was on Nancy's side. She herself later claimed that the institution of the national fire service was largely due to her, and the claim may be exaggerated but is not baseless. Certainly after this time, as a result of Morrison's Bill, fire-fighting improved rapidly. As before, a Home Secretary may have been influenced by the thought that any failure might unbridle the tongue of 'that intolerable woman'. It is also possible that Nancy's indiscreet letter to *The Times* had had its influence on the Bill being brought into Parliament in the first place.

Unfortunately Nancy spoiled the effect of her public-spirited action by taking her protestations in Parliament to indefensible extremes. The part of her mind and character which had led her to disapprove *Black Record* again lay dormant, and she fancied that she had discovered a new collective enemy. Local government officials joined Catholics, Latins and other evil tribes as objects of her impassioned prejudice.

Her phobia was mercifully short-lived. What is very odd about it is that, for all its intemperance, it seems not to have adversely affected her position as the Lady Mayoress of Plymouth. One reason for this is that the contradictoriness of Nancy's character was perhaps never stronger or more in evidence than now. Her positive courting of unpopularity was obviously the outcome of frayed nerves, such as afflicted many people during the four years of siege and when claustrophobia became a common malady. But these flashes of ill-humour and ill-temper affected a restricted area of her life. If a newspaperman came her way, she could hardly resist saying to him what had been better left unsaid, and in the House of Commons she rarely missed an opportunity to make an interjection which would either anger or hurt; but away from the Press and outside Parliament there was nothing of this in the way she lived her life or carried out her duties. She was in love with Plymouth and in her conduct there she showed everything of her generosity and imagination. She and Waldorf added codicils to their wills to the effect that in the event of their being killed in an air-raid they were to be buried in the common grave with the other victims. (This was not known till Waldorf disclosed it in 1946.) She knew instinctively that the greatest danger to the city was a failure of

Nancy in retirement: a study by Cecil Beaton

Nancy on her 80th birthday: a study by Jane Bown

morale. There was no sign of such a thing happening but she knew that it could happen. In June 1941 she persuaded the City Council to institute music and dancing on the Hoe. Every night, while the weather and light allowed, a band played. The first dance was held on the 10th, the Lord Mayor and Lady Mayoress opening the festivities and waltzing round together. The experiment was instantly successful and these Hoe dances continued till the end of the war during the fine weather. Whenever a famous visitor was in Plymouth, and Nancy saw to it that plenty of them came down, they danced on the Hoe perforce.

She was near enough herself to old age to recognise the special misery of war to old people, and she seems to have heard about the wretchedness of one with whom she had had a now long broken friendship, Hilaire Belloc. He was seventy-one, but seemed more. The fall of France had come to him as a personal blow, and to this there was added in 1941 a further, crushing sorrow. On the 2nd April 1941 his son Peter who was serving in Scotland, died of pneumonia. Towards the end of June Nancy wrote to invite him to Cliveden. He replied to her on the 24th.

'How nice of you to have written to me, who live alone in the shadow! I value your kindness; indeed I do!

'No, as to Heavens, you will go to the right one. Mine requires a long preliminary sleep, from which I hope to rise up yawning, but refreshed.

'When I arrive in your heaven you will know me by my long white Beard. I have been shaving it off lately, because after the usual 3 days, it gets unsightly, and I cant be bothered to wait weeks and weeks for a great beard to grow.

'Yes: let us meet, for the love of mike: I particularly desire it. But there are 2 crabs [crossed out sketch] (I cant draw crabs!) Crab (1) is that I cant go to a big house. I am not suited for it, since I became crabbed. I have no clothes – or rather such as I have, are unworthy of High Society. (2) is that I am away for some few days – wandering among the rich, as usual.

'But I *must* see you again & when I return from my tour in the West I will instantly write to you: nay, before that!

'I take it that Cliveden is your permanent address so I write there. No I don't! I write to Plymouth Hove [sic], c/o dear old Drake the mythical (Plymouth Hoe of which the Anti Catholic Hero Drake is said to be dreaming – which I doubt for he thought of nothing but

money). I am very fond of money too, but I wouldn't sink so low as
Drake did to get it. But he was a very brave murderer & a good seaman.
Give him my respects.

'And all that's balderdash & Persiflage – not to say Badinage – The
point is when can I see you? In town when I return, by God's grace,
from the deadly furies of the West Circuit. My humble messages &
accept my unchanging, my fixed, my rooted devotion: which indeed
you deserve! H.B.'[2]

The first sentence of his next (and last) letter suggests that he had
tried to telephone to her.

'I have piped to you & you have not danced. I want to see you again
very much indeed – but where can I meet you & when? Any day
you give me in London after next Tuesday June 8th I would run up
to London from here or from Oxford.

'I live in a dazed condition & forget nearly everything – but I
will not forget any time & place you give me. Tonight I'm going to
have another shot at getting through to Cliveden. But I doubt my
success.

'Blessings upon you still & always. H.B.

'Send me a line here. Belloc Cookham. As I told you, I can't go to
rich houses. I havent the clothes nor the manner. But I *do* want to see
you again.'

To this Nancy dictated a reply directly to a typewriting secretary
who (happily for the biographer) was very economical, so that for
the carbon copy she used the same under-paper twice. Nancy had
been irritated by Belloc's postscript and she began to answer as
follows:

'I don't believe you realise what the life of a Lady Mayoress, Member
of Parliament and mother of six is. If you did you would not
think about clothes or the houses of the rich. But there are no rich
peop . . .'

Evidently she thought that this was sententious, stopped, started
again, and the letter in its final form went to him as follows:

'I am afraid this week is not possible for I am busy with Michael and
his unit Thursday when I go to London to look after some American

2. 'The West Circuit' probably refers to Pixton Park and the Manor House, Mells,
both in Somerset, the first being the house of Mrs Herbert, the widow of Aubrey
Herbert (1880–1923), and the second being the house of Mrs Asquith, the widow of
Raymond Asquith. Both these ladies gave Belloc hospitality till his last years.

Red Cross Nurses, then I take the 4.0 train to Plymouth. I will be back
here by Monday, so will you come here on Tuesday 15th and spend
the night. You won't find any rich people because 6d in the £1 does
not give people much to play with – so stop that nonsense and come
on.'

Full quotation from the two texts can be defended on grounds better
than those of pedantry. They perfectly illustrate the contradictory
character of Nancy in this crucial year of her life: the easily aroused
irritation and the equally impulsive generosity. Belloc did go to
Cliveden for two or perhaps three visits in 1941. In the next year he
suffered a severe stroke. His memory was badly affected, so much so
that he often failed to recognise people whom he had known well.
His mind grew dim. Nevertheless he lived on till 1953, but after 1941
he never seems to have met Nancy again.

In the same summer of 1941 she went to the help of another friend
stricken in years, Bernard Shaw. She invited him and Charlotte Shaw
to come to Cliveden in the second part of August. Her letter has not
survived but its contents are very evident from Shaw's answer dated
the 19th July.

'Dearest Nancy, Dont bother about eggs: I loathe eggs and never
eat them when I can get anything else. People are always trying to
stuff me with them in the belief that I must die if I dont eat something
that is not vegetarian.

'As to your Canadian soldier I dare not give him a book or an
autograph. I should have the whole lot of them down on me clamoring
for autographs. As it is, they stop me in the streets. What I will do is to
inscribe a copy of St Joan to you. You can then inscribe it to the
Canadian, who will have the autograph of a Viscountess to shew as
well as mine. But tell him that it is a unique treasure, as I am absolutely
unapproachable by autograph hunters. . . .

'We shall be a horrid imposition. Ten years ago I could still earn my
keep by entertaining your guests by my celebrated performances as
G.B.S. Now if I attempt to talk my teeth fall out. I am a decrepit old
bore; and you must hide me in a corner of your house as best you can
or your friends will begin to shun Cliveden. You have not the faintest
notion of what it is to be 85 and three quarters dead. Charlotte is still
a bit of an invalid, and cannot walk. She cannot even ride one of
Waldorf's horses, though she could perhaps manage an elephant (if you
have such a thing) with a very comfortable howdah.

'This is the explanation of my hesitation to accept invitations which I should once have jumped at. By the end of August you may be saying Never Again.

your quondam G.B.S.'

The Press got wind of the visit and there were photographs of Nancy and G.B.S. on the terrace. So far from her saying 'Never Again' she was in the not distant future to make strenuous efforts to set up G.B.S. as a permanent resident of Cliveden.

During this summer there had occurred a distressing event which was to remain a secret known only to a very few, perhaps only to herself, Waldorf, her sons Bill and David, and her maid Rose Harrison. In Nancy's letter to Lady Halifax, already quoted, she had told her friend that Waldorf had been away from Plymouth on the occasion of Winston Churchill's visit because he had a 'chill'. In fact, he had had a heart attack which may have led to a minor stroke. The immediate occasion was unworthy of its consequences: the attack was brought on by a dispute about chocolates. Nancy had a passion for chocolates and sweets of any kind. Her correspondence with Lord Lothian, who shared the taste, contains a surprising number of references to chocolate shops. One day in the later part of April the Astors had a lunch-party at 3 Elliot Terrace at which various of the city dignitaries were present. Waldorf and Nancy had arranged to go for a couple of days' rest to the house of a friend in the little village of Rock, across the water from Padstow in Cornwall, starting that afternoon. It so happened that on the same day a large consignment of chocolates and sweets had arrived from America addressed to the Lord Mayor, as a gift to the people of Plymouth. Towards the end of lunch Nancy said that she wanted some of these. Waldorf said no, they were not intended for her or him but for people in greater need. Nancy flew into a temper and in the presence of her guests was extremely rude to her husband and told him she was not coming to Rock with him. Waldorf left the room and went upstairs to his office. Seething with wrath she told the maid who was waiting at table to tell Rose Harrison to unpack her things. It was a most unpleasant and embarrassing scene. When she was beginning to unpack, Rose received a message from Waldorf to come to him.

As soon as she entered his office Rose saw from his unnaturally high colouring and his breathing that he had had a heart attack. He said to her: 'Rose, whatever happens Lady Astor must go to Rock with me and I wish you to come into the drawing-room at the same time as I do.'

Rose Harrison has given the writer an account of her conduct in this crisis. It was bold. She waited for Waldorf to go into the drawing-room after the guests had left. Then, to follow her account: 'Out I came and went in. I said to Lady Astor "I hear from Florrie, my lady, you are not going to Rock." "No I am not" says she and flew out of the room. I was as quick and got her on the stairs going up to her room, and I was so mad I got hold of her and shook her and told her it was very plain to see Lord Astor had had a heart attack, and I said "If anything happens to him I shall tell all the children it was your fault as you kicked up such a row at the lunch table over a few old sweets." Believe it or not she turned to me and said: "All right, Rose, I'll go" and we did.'

Nancy went with Waldorf to Rock. She returned to Plymouth the next day, but he remained there for six weeks, nursed by Rose. He recovered. As to whether or not he had suffered a slight stroke it is impossible to know, for he kept strictly to his Christian Science.

What is certain is that if Rose had not been there when Waldorf suffered his attack the consequences might have been very grave; he might have been obliged through illness to resign the mayoralty and abandon the great work on which he and Nancy were intent, and on which they were already working in 1941: the rebuilding of Plymouth.

It is the opinion of many of the citizens, including some of those who worked with the Astors in local government at that time, that the determination to plan the rebuilding of Plymouth in detail and so soon as after the first heavy raids, had its origin in Nancy. When she said 'We'll build it again' to Ben Robertson, she meant it. As with other of her enterprises she was an influence, not more than that, for the major executive role was Waldorf's and in this he showed that toughness in his nature with which his quiet and modest demeanour contrasted. After some argument he and the council selected as the planning consultant Professor Patrick Abercrombie. Waldorf knew that this was a time for initiative and that to await the signal for action from an overburdened Government was to wait a very long time. Contrary to his usual (but not invariable) correctitude he facilitated the task by taking advantage of friends in office. From late 1940 to 1942 Sir John Reith was Minister of Works and Building (later described as

Works and Planning). Waldorf, usually accompanied by Mr James Paton Watson, would visit Reith privately and make it plain to him that the city of Plymouth intended to rebuild itself, preferably in harmony with the Government, but that, whatever happened, it would rebuild itself. He won Reith round. Abercrombie began work on Plymouth reconstruction in 1941.

The family situation remained little changed in the last part of 1941 and into the next year. Bill was still in the Near East, Michael and Jakie were still, in Nancy's words, 'careering round the country in their little tanks', and David was still with the Marines, shortly to be transferred to the recently established Combined Operations Command. In the summer of 1941 Bob Brand had left for Washington as head of the British Food Mission. He was to remain in the United States till 1946. Bobbie found service in the balloon barrage tedious and he sought a more active career in the ambulance service in London. He was popular in his unit which was largely composed of taxi-drivers.

1941 is an interesting year in Nancy's life because it was one of great challenge and change. The subsequent war years, though full of incident, follow the currents whose flow and direction were determined at this time, and they do not need so much detailed treatment. Before leaving 1941, however, two matters may be mentioned.

The first is an interesting trifle. Following in the footsteps of many of her feminist predecessors Nancy addressed a crowd in Trafalgar Square from the pedestal of Nelson's column. This was on the 21st September. The purpose of the meeting was to protest against the continuing injustice whereby women injured in air-raids received less compensation than men. One might expect Nancy to have been a frequent orator on that venerable platform which has been used by rebels from the age of the Chartists onwards. In fact, this was the only time in her life that she made a Trafalgar Square appearance.

As has been noted already, Lord Halifax went to Washington as Lord Lothian's successor. His biographer has shown that he undertook what Winston Churchill described as 'this high and perilous charge' with much misgiving. Nor was his reluctance unwarranted: his knowledge of America was as scanty as that of Lord Lothian had been thorough. It looked for a while as though Halifax's mission might end in failure.

It ended in a triumph only to be compared with that of Lothian. The tide turned before America was an ally. One happy appointment to his staff changed Halifax's prospects in a remarkably short time. It was that of his cousin and Nancy's old friend and lover, Angus McDonnell. His knowledge of America could rival that of Lothian and in other ways he was a complementary influence. 'They were a strange pair,' writes Lord Birkenhead, 'Edward's formal courtesy was offset by his cousin's ribald joviality. He seemed to have friends who welcomed him with open arms in every corner of the United States and the whole atmosphere of the tours was to be transformed by his Rabelaisian presence.'

Nancy as always was critical of Angus. 'I hear,' she wrote to a friend, 'that Angus, in his effort to sell him to the Americans, tries to make him too matey, which I think is a mistake.'

Angus used occasionally to spend a weekend with the Halifaxes at Mirador which was now owned by Ronald and Nancy Tree who had lent it to the Embassy as a holiday place. From there Angus wrote her nostalgic sentimental letters recalling the days of Chillie and his old love for her. 'I certainly was deadly in love with you then,' he wrote in one letter. The friendship had a little revival, but it did not enjoy a second spring.

1941 was the year when Hitler's genius deserted him. Certain of a swift victory, the Führer invaded Russia on the 22nd June, 'Napoleon's day'. He was not as superstitious as was believed at the time. If he had been, he might have thought again. In December he solved Halifax's main problem in simple and drastic fashion. Within a week of the Japanese aggression on Pearl Harbour (on the 7th), Hitler, seconded by his battered ally Mussolini, declared war on the United States. To quote Elizabeth Wiskemann: 'Thus Hitler had deliberately created an alliance between the British Empire, the U.S.S.R. and the United States. But for the series of staggering blows dealt by the Japanese at the Americans and British in the Far East it would have been clear from now on that Hitler's megalomania would destroy him. Yet for another year he seemed to be completely victorious.'

From the moment of Hitler's invasion of Russia British public opinion passed through a phase of total transformation. The brutality of Stalin's regime and his treacherous and soulless alliance with Nazism were forgotten, and the Soviet Union became almost an object of worship. G.B.S. found himself in a rare position for him as the spokesman of popular passion. He did not, however, find a willing audience in Nancy. She remembered the evil of which she had had a glimpse in 1931. She kept her thoughts to herself for a long time, but she was, of course, incapable of keeping them hidden for ever. She made some appropriate gestures, such as joining in a message of comradeship to Russian women, but in spite of Shaw's exhortations she could show no enthusiasm for our great ally. It so happened that Bill Astor incurred some unpopularity at the same time in the Middle East for expressing the opinion that now the anti-Nazi side would lose its idealism.

It is a remarkable irony of their story that Waldorf and Nancy had a special reason for gratitude to the Russians. Luftwaffe priorities in Russia resulted in a slackening of the German raids on Britain, in the later part of 1941. In 1942 Plymouth was not once raided.

Nancy first came into parliamentary prominence in 1942 in a manner that shocked and estranged many people. The occasion was a Supply Committee of the House of Commons in which broadcasting was debated. Nancy took the opportunity to warn the House of the dangers of Roman Catholic influence. The subject may seem remote from the conflicts in Russia, North Africa and the Far East, or from broadcasting policy in the Second World War, but it was always close to Nancy from the time she had come under Philip Lothian's influence.

She had for long been distressed by the fact that the personnel of the Foreign Office contained many Catholics, and she was horrified to discover what she took to be a sinister preponderance of Catholics in the organisations responsible for communication with isolated and Nazi-dominated Europe. The Director of the Psychological Warfare Executive was the well-known author Mr Robert Bruce Lockhart, a Roman Catholic and a former official of the Foreign Office. Working in close collaboration with him was Ivone Kirkpatrick as Controller of the European radio services of the BBC. He also was a Roman Catholic, and was a member of the Foreign Office. His second-in-command was a member of the BBC staff, Mr Harman Grisewood, also a Roman Catholic. To Nancy all this looked as dangerous as could be and she decided to rally the House.

When Nancy had a subject which invited large generalisations she could easily get lost, and usually did so. If syntax and form appear in the Hansard report nonetheless they were supplied, according to her son and colleague Bill, by the reporters. But these same reporters, who had affection for her, could do nothing with her speech of the 17th February 1942 and it reads incoherently. She spoke wanderingly to a restless House till the Minister of Information Brendan Bracken interposed. 'Would the noble lady,' he said, 'tell the House exactly what she means.'

'I think,' went on Nancy, 'the Right Honourable gentleman knows perfectly well what I mean.' But she failed to be precise. Her speech rambled on with shaky history and abuse of the Foreign Office and hints at its interpenetration by papal agents.

At the conclusion of the debate, when Bracken summed up, he had harsh words for Nancy.

It was a sad incident. The attempt to denigrate three loyal public servants such as Lockhart, Kirkpatrick and Grisewood, was utterly unworthy of Nancy even at her most impetuous and unthinking. Her endeavour to start a conspiracy scare came particularly badly from one who had recently suffered cruelly from the Oatesish myth of the Cliveden Set. That is perhaps the darkest aspect of what in the main was a ludicrous episode: how ill it contrasts with her generous protests against Vansittart! But there is a third and quite different reason why this is to be accounted a sad incident. Never before had Nancy given a speech of such length which was so wholly incompetent. After this performance she began by hardly perceptible stages manifestly to lose her whole parliamentary position. Within the closer circles of party organisation she had begun to lose it some time before the war. After February 1942 her declining status in Parliament was obvious.

A large event in Astor family history occurred in this same month, but Nancy herself seems to have played only a peripheral part in it. For a long time Waldorf and J. L. Garvin had been in a tense relationship. Waldorf wished for some reorganisation, including the appointment of a joint editor since Garvin no longer came to London but edited the paper by telephone from Beaconsfield. But the ageing Garvin resisted Waldorf's wishes and clung tenaciously to his rights and authority. Then in February 1942 the two men came into open conflict. Winston Churchill reshuffled his Government but retained, as before, the post of Minister of Defence. Of the changes the most remarkable was the departure of Lord Beaverbrook for health reasons from the Ministry of Supply. Waldorf, in common with Nancy, was suspicious of Churchill's judgement and had for some time regretted that he should continue to combine the Premiership with the Ministry of Defence. He had expressed this opinion publicly. Like Nancy he distrusted Beaverbrook and was thankful that he was no longer in the Government. Garvin took an exactly opposite view on both questions. Regarding his position of editor as unassailable, he published a leading article under his own signature on the 22nd February expressing the extremest satisfaction at Churchill's continued amassment of power, and fervent hopes that Beaverbrook would soon return to the Government. Such opposition to the known views of his chairman was against both the letter and spirit of his contract. Waldorf had recourse to the provisions of the *Observer* constitution whereby unreconciled differences were submitted to arbitration by an agreed tribunal.

The tribunal found against Garvin and he resigned, thus terminating an editorship which he had held for thirty years. He found employment with the *Sunday Express* and was succeeded as editor of the *Observer* by Mr Ivor Brown. This reshuffle in Tudor Street, following on the reshuffle in Whitehall, had family repercussions. Before the war David Astor had worked in the north of England on the *Yorkshire Post*. He was the only member of the family who had professional training in journalism, and so he was an obvious choice as Waldorf's successor. Waldorf decided, however, more on political grounds, that he wished David to edit the paper. Bill would not succeed Waldorf as chairman, but would be on the board of directors, over which the editor would preside. For the moment, David, as a serving officer, took no part in *Observer* affairs beyond helping Ivor Brown to recruit a number of distinguished émigré writers as contributors. Nancy was glad at the changes in the *Observer* but later she became much concerned with the consequences and sighed for the days of Garvin.

In the spring of 1942 Bill was transferred from the Middle East to Naval Intelligence in London. He came home after more than three years' service overseas. He was overjoyed to be back; overjoyed to see his family again; glad to be able to resume his parliamentary duties and to work in his constituency; most glad to see his home and country again. But when the raptures of return were over he found some cause for dismay. He was distressed at what he felt was the way he had been in some measure passed over in the *Observer* reorganisation and the alienation of the paper from the central family property. Nevertheless, after the war, he served loyally as a director.

He found graver matter for disquiet in the emotional field. When he had left for the Middle East in 1939 he had found his parents in complete accord: he had found their deep mutual affection reflected in their agreement on the public matters in which they shared interest, above all in their concern for social reform. Neither of them had lost this concern in any way, but they had lost their former close agreement on how it should be translated into action. Since the beginning of the war there had been a great deal of discussion in the Press and on radio, occasionally in Parliament, of the sort of society which should be established after the achievement of victory. It was represented as a war aim (quite sincerely it seems), and the presence of Labour men in the Government and among the backbench supporters of the coalition gave this impetus a socialist character. In 1942, at the end of which Sir William Beveridge produced his famous report, the movement for intense socialism in Britain grew apace. Waldorf was not antipathetic to it; Nancy was. He saw its fulfilment, not as popular imagination did as the reason why we went to war, but as a natural development of British history. He saw that the kind of paternalist social reform which he and Nancy had pursued with such devotion was becoming an anachronism. Nancy, always influenced by Virginian memories, saw nothing wrong in paternalism and had no use for the word anachronism whose precise meaning was perhaps unknown to her. All this represented a considerable division of opinion which affected their private relationship. The point must not be overstressed, but it must be recorded that a change in their relationship was noticed by their eldest son and came to him as a shock.

Many years after this, Bill Astor suggested a further explanation. He suggested (he did not assert) that Waldorf's illness in 1941, which he believed was a stroke, had had a commonly observed effect on his emotional responses so that his relationships with, and his feelings for, other people became liable to alteration. Waldorf had always been a critic of Nancy, sometimes a severe one as her early letters to him show, but his criticism had been thoroughly subordinate to his loving admiration. Now it seemed to be otherwise as a result of his illness; he tended to see Nancy's faults more clearly than he did her merits. Whether this is a valid explanation or not, only one thoroughly acquainted with psychological science can say, and then probably only one familiar with the details of this case. Certainly there was a new and marked difference in Waldorf's outlook.

One must never forget the irritations of 1942 which were immense, and affected everyone on the Western side personally. They also affected public life in Britain. The cup of victory had been handed to the Allies and then snatched away. The Germans had met defeat in Russia but so had the Russians. In the Far East Singapore had fallen in February and thereafter the Japanese pursued a triumphant career up to the frontiers of Assam. Nearer home in the same month the German battle-cruisers *Gneisenau* and *Scharnhorst* with the cruiser *Prinz Eugen* escaped destruction in the British Channel as they sailed, sometimes close to our shores, from Brest to German ports. In the summer Rommel began his successful offensive against the 8th Army and the first battle of El Alamein appeared (wrongly) to be a yet further defeat.

There was a revolt in the House of Commons against the direction of the war and a motion for a Vote of Censure. This was debated on the 1st and 2nd July. Though the Government won, they did so awkwardly.

Nancy did not take any part in the debate, but she attended. Once again she courted unpopularity though her purpose was more than this. Whatever her differences with Waldorf she agreed with him that Winston Churchill had been entrusted with excessive powers, and she felt this strongly. The published diaries of Sir Henry ('Chips') Channon, a fervent Chamberlainite and anti-Churchillian, give the atmosphere in the House on the 2nd July very neatly: 'The argument against voting against the Government is strong and, on balance, I decided I hadn't "the guts", so slowly walked into the very crowded Aye lobby to the derision of the few abstainers, perhaps 20 in all. I saw Winterton and Archie Southby muttering to one another. They had abstained, as had Lady Astor, Megan Lloyd George and others who sat silent on the benches.'[3]

This seems the only reference, in memoirs or newspaper articles of her time, to Nancy's silence.

A month later she found unpopularity again, though once more she did so in pursuit of a right cause. Prompted by generous admiration of the courage of the Red Army, the Russophile emotion in Britain had grown into hysteria, so far indeed that a political party which took

3. Lord Winterton (1883–1962) was at this time the 'Father of the House'. Sir Archibald Southby had enjoyed a distinguished naval and then parliamentary career. Before World War II he had served in the Conservative Whip's Office.

the name of 'Common Wealth' (from Cromwell rather than the British Empire), and which announced that its aim was to remodel the British state largely in the style of the Soviet Union (including its prison camps), was founded with so much acclaim that it even succeeded in getting some members into the House of Commons through by-elections. There was almost no limit to the uncritical adulation and admiration offered to the Soviet Union. There was a general sharing of joyous credulity. Nancy was irritated by all this, and it may be that she was helped into common sense by her large naval acquaintance in Plymouth. The sailors did not join in the hysteria, having a grievance against the Soviet authorities on account of the abominable treatment they often received after reaching Murmansk on convoy duty.

Nancy received an invitation to speak at two successive meetings: at Southport and Altrincham in August. Judging by reports she was at the top of her form, bantering, provocative, comic and very irreverent. She was not unpopular with her immediate audience.

The first occasion was a United Nations Rally, but Nancy seems to have noted it down wrongly in her engagement book and was surprised to find herself escorted to a platform placarded with the names of all the Allies and decorated with their flags.

She opened in the gayest manner: 'I have been got here under false pretences. I was told that this was going to be an Anglo-American rally. I did not know that all the other nations of the Allies were going to be present, so I prepared my oration to be about Anglo-American relationships.' She turned from gaiety to gravity and spoke about the shared Christianity of the two nations. She turned to gaiety again in describing the House of Commons, and then led to her major theme. She recalled the vital help which the United States had afforded the country at the time of the Battle of Britain. 'I am grateful to the Russians,' she said, 'but they are not fighting for us. They are fighting for themselves. In the Battle of Britain it was America who came to our aid. The Russians were allies of Germany. It is only now that they are facing German invasion that they have come into the fight. To hear people talk, you would think they came to us in our own dire need. Nothing of the kind. It was the United States of America, and don't you forget it!'

Lord Strabolgi was so shocked that he not only made a speech of denunciation at Warrington next day, but followed it up by an article in the Press entitled 'Cliveden and Stalingrad'. Yet, as though to make certain of causing yet more uproar against herself, Nancy repeated the offence at her meeting at Altrincham. Here she expressed the temerarious opinion that though the warlike valiance of the Russia of Stalin and the China of Chiang Kai-Shek was worthy of admiration, she doubted whether either of those countries equalled Britain or the United States in terms of sound modern civilisation. At this there were cries of dissent and Nancy turned to the dissenters. 'When you are grown up,' she said, 'you will know as well as I do that I am telling you the truth. Don't worry meantime. I'll give you time to grow up.' This rejoinder got her audience back where she wanted them.

It did not get the Press where she wanted them, unless she wanted to drive home her message by means of scandal. 'Storm over Lady Astor's Speech' correctly reported the *Southport Guardian*. The storm roared for some days, then still continued to blow, though with diminishing force, till the end of the year. To get some notion of the extent of the delusion against which Nancy was arguing, one may refer to the description by H. G. Wells (which has been quoted) of Nancy's encounter with Stalin in 1931. This was written in an article of literary criticism published in November 1942. The reader of today may see in it praise of Nancy, but the contemporary reader saw in it the opposite, as did Wells himself.

However the storm this time did not have a totally prevailing wind to add to its force. Worship of Stalin and Stalinism had gone to extremes that had provoked some reaction, and this time, in contrast to the affair of Colonel Bingham, Nancy had numerous defenders in the Press. They were not only diehards. She would have had more defenders if the Press had reported her fully. The *Southport Guardian* seems to have been the only paper that did so.

Nancy's life continued as before, in Plymouth, Westminster and Cliveden, in speechmaking in many parts of the country, in striving for Anglo-American accord especially in the easily quarrelsome forces. Yet for all the energy with which she pursued these varied and usually self-imposed duties, her life became monotonous, as did the lives of most people in those days. What remained of her private life is of more interest.

1942 was a very full year in her correspondence with Bernard Shaw. At the end of March he had acted as peace-maker between Nancy had Lord Berners. This gifted man, best remembered as a composer, and a

strong appetite for practical jokes which usually made him the aggressor in the numerous estrangements between himself and his friends.[4] On this occasion, however, he, not Nancy, had taken offence. The whole affair seems to have been due to a misunderstanding. His health was bad and he had grown angrily sensitive towards people who thrust advice on him. (Let it be remembered again that this was the age of irritation.) He seems to have written rudely to Nancy and she told Shaw about the quarrel. G.B.S. wrote to her on the 30th March.

'We have known B. for years and years. He is no ordinary peer: he writes, paints, and composes music quite outstandingly, and is enough of a good fellow to be friends with us.

'It would be a misfortune to have him at feud with you merely because some C.S. zealot has sent him a book which he supposed came from you. I am (rashly) sending him a line to say that this must not be, as you two are to my knowledge deserving persons in spite of your unfortunate rank.

'Charlotte is much better, and horrified at the notion of your trying to keep her alive superfluously when Waldorf needs all your care with half his career still before him.

'You exaggerate the value of the Christlike. There are lots of them about, mostly even more futile than I. You yourself have quite as much Christ in you as is good for you. In great haste – G.B.S.'

As there is no further reference to Berners in the Shaw-Astor correspondence it may be assumed that the quarrel was composed.

The reference to Charlotte Shaw covers by its light tone the fact that she was entering the last stage of her life. She was developing the very painful disease of the bones known as *osteitis deformans* which is (or was then) incurable. Shaw knew that she must die soon, yet he maintained the gay tone in his letters, partly through natural bravado, partly because he rejoiced to see the world developing on lines he approved. In the course of a long, wildly erratic letter which he wrote to Nancy on the 25th May, he said:

'The times are changing with a vengeance. Cripps, the Leader of the House, makes speeches which might be made by Stalin; and The Times leaders on them next day approve of every word of them. The Arch-

4. Of his many pranks one of the most famous was when, knowing her taste for eminent people, he invited Lady Colefax to luncheon 'because I've got the P. of W. coming'. On arrival at his house, dressed for royalty, she was introduced to the Provost of Worcester College, Oxford.

bishop of Canterbury comes out with a Penguin volume advocating a full Socialist program. Nobody expresses the least surprise. . . .'

Nancy invited the Shaws to come to Cliveden to rest. The visit was arranged for the 21st July to the 17th August, and she made arrangements for a nurse to look after Charlotte and remain with her after the visit. Charlotte wrote to her on the 16th July, the day before they left London.

'Nancy – dear darling I do love you. No one but you could possibly have done all this so beautifully & *happily* – I am so looking forward to getting to Cliveden and you!

'The nurse will give me courage as I am rather anxious – it will be in London I shall really want her – after Cliveden – to trot about with me & it will be good to get to know her first at Cliveden.

'Remember Whitehall Court is there all the time if you want to get rid of us. Ever Charlotte.'

That was the last letter Charlotte Shaw wrote to her friend. The visit to Cliveden did her good but, as with every recovery of which there were several, the subsequent relapse was more serious than the one before. Her pain gradually ceased to be intermittent and became part of her normal condition. And yet old Shaw continued to treat the matter with lightness. He began towards the end of 1942 to treat the war with lightness too and recovered some of his old admiration of Adolf Hitler with his contempt for democratic leaders. Here is an extract from another long letter of the 22nd October:

'I have been reading Hitler's Mein Kampf really attentively instead of dipping into it. He is the greatest living Tory, and a wonderful preacher of everything that is right and best in Toryism. Your Party should capture him and keep him as a teacher and leader whilst checkmating his phobias. On the need for religion, on the sham democracy of votes for everybody, on unemployment and casual labor, he is superb. The book is really one of the world's bibles, like Calvin's Institutes (written when Calvin was 23), Adam Smith's Wealth of Nations, Marx's Capital: it has changed the mind of the reading world. . . .

'*Do* tell Churchill and Ll.G. that the House of Commons way of speechifying is pitiably ridiculous through the mike. Stopping for ten seconds between every word to wonder what the devil you can say next ("thinking on one's legs") is not made good by uttering the word when it comes as if it were an oracle, especially when it is only a preposition or conjunction.'

It may be that the irrepressible old non-conformist was becoming weary of his new popular position, but it is as well that no believer in the Cliveden Set saw the letter at the time.

In justice to the memory of G.B.S., however, it should be remembered that not all his political judgements at this time were as foolish as these. A letter of three months later may be remembered here. Referring to the policy of 'Unconditional Surrender', first agreed by Winston Churchill and President Roosevelt at the Casablanca conference of January 1943, he wrote to Nancy: 'Tell Winston to stop talking alarming nonsense about unconditional surrender. Make him explain that the surrender cannot be unconditional, but that we shall dictate the conditions. As to whether "we" includes Uncle Jo, the less said just now the better.'

In December 1942 two important events occurred in the Astor family. Michael was married to Miss Barbara McNeil, and Waldorf with the agreement of Nancy and Bill made over Cliveden to the National Trust with an endowment sufficient for its upkeep. The Astors continued to live there by arrangement with the new owners, opening the house and grounds as often as had been agreed with the Trust at the time of transfer. The arrangement helped to preserve a beautiful part of the Thames and avoided the destruction of the Cliveden estate through death duties. The Astors remained at Cliveden till the death of Bill as his father's successor in 1966. Till then, Cliveden remained outwardly as before.

The gloom of 1942 was dissipating. A happier time seemed to arrive at the turn of the year. In the East the Red Army had opened their counter-offensive in November, and the Battle of Stalingrad was moving to its climax and a gigantic German defeat. In North Africa Rommel had been defeated by the 8th Army in the second battle of El Alamein. British and American forces had landed in French North Africa. There was wide expectation that the Second Front in Europe would be successfully opened in 1943 with victory before its end. Optimism was once more the national mood for the first time since Munich. The ordeals in store were not reckoned with. Again to quote Elizabeth Wiskemann: 'The Battle of Stalingrad, and with it the Second World

War, had been lost by Hitler. This was the turning-point, though the greatest sacrifices had yet to be made.'

On the 26th January 1943 the sirens wailed again in Plymouth. It proved a false alarm. Plymouth was not the target but the lovely little village of Aveton Gifford, not very far off. This aimless daylight raid resulted in the almost total destruction of the village and the death of a child. There was no further alert till nearly three weeks later, on the 14th February. On that night Plymouth suffered its first heavy raid for nearly eighteen months. It lasted for an hour and twenty minutes. Then there were no raids till the 14th June, and then again not till the 12th August when the city was subjected to one of the worst attacks of the whole war. After this there was a respite once more till the 16th November.

People who lived through these raids say that in some ways, and in spite of the fact that they were so widely separated, they were harder to bear than those of 1941. The immunity of 1942 had lulled people into a sense of false security which they knew to be false but which made them feel secure all the same. To arouse themselves anew, to return to the hideous front line, was a great ordeal. It is always a test of troops whether they can go into battle more than once. The people of Plymouth could, and they owed something to good leadership, including that of Nancy and Waldorf.

Their life in Plymouth was rather different in 1943 to what it had been in 1941. 3 Elliot Terrace had been put to some new uses since the entry of the United States into the war. Nancy billeted a certain number of American officers in the house and rightly looked upon herself as a person uniquely placed to act as an unofficial Anglo-American liaison officer. She showed much imagination. One of the problems of the new situation was that a large number of Negro troops were billeted in Plymouth and this gave rise to latent antagonisms, between the Negroes and the American white troops, and between the Negroes and the civilian population. It was Nancy's belief that if one gave way to any segregation impulse, even of the most excusable kind, these antagonisms would break out. For example, when black troops were a novelty, a proposal came from one of their units for a concert to be given by them. It was suggested that this would be unwise, but Nancy emphatically approved the idea, and took two white American soldiers as her own guests. There was no trouble. She set an example as a non-racist from the very first, and gave it all the force of her character. The senior Negro conductor-officer (whose duties combined those of billeting and welfare) was one of her lodgers in Elliot Terrace. If he was treated any differently to the other officers it was in this way only: that whereas, when she had many guests, she would occasionally ask some of the others to be out for dinner, she never asked this man to go out. Her admirable example was all the more remarkable, and all the more to her credit, because she was not a person with modern views to whom this attitude came easily.

Sometimes she went beyond her unofficial liaison activity and took command. Only a few of the American troops in Plymouth had had battle experience. The great majority had come there straight from the United States in 1942 during the raid-free period. No amount of tough training can act as a substitute for the experience of being under fire. When the first heavy raid of 1943 came on Plymouth, Nancy's first thought was for American troops billeted in a house nearby. She put on her tin helmet and marched out into the storm of exploding bombs, whizzing shrapnel, fireworkish flak, and the bellowing of the AA guns. She never lost her American accent but it had become much modified in the course of her long residence in England, but when she talked to American troops she reverted, part consciously, to strong Virginian. 'What's goin' on here,' she said as she entered the billet, 'the city's watchin' you and wonderin'.' She marched into every room. 'Come on, men,' she said. 'Get out of it an' do somethin'. Come on you there, get out from under that table. Get out and make yourself useful.' She had enough experience of air-raids by now to tell them just how they could be useful. She seemed impervious to fear as she pushed them around. Between the immediate threat of this American woman in the heart of bombarded Plymouth, and the remoter threat of the bombarders, the men swiftly recovered their morale and obeyed her. Such was not an isolated incident. Like her visits to the shelters in 1941, it became routine in 1943, though as the troops became hardened her manner softened. But there were always new raw troops to be bullied – and consoled.

Several people who saw her at that time believe that she had to pay in heavy psychological coinage for her self-mastery in the face of danger. She took it to heroic excess. This may in part explain her parliamentary decline, in which another deplorable episode occurred early in the year.

On the 18th March 1943 there was a debate in the House of Commons on the proposed Foreign Office reforms the chief of which was to fuse the diplomatic and consular services. Nancy addressed the House in a spirit of protest against the failure of the reformers to include women in the service, but she took occasion again to attack the Foreign Office spirit. It was an incoherent speech similar to her scare-speech on Lockhart, Kirkpatrick and Grisewood. Like that one it was anti-Catholic in spirit and intention but, remembering the ill-reception of her former remarks, she made no direct reference to religion but instead appealed to the history which she had not read.[5] 'The Foreign Office,' she said at one point, 'has been dominated by the Latin point of view. That is why the policy is dominated by France. Since the last war France has been a shell-shocked nation and everyone knows it but the Foreign Office. The Latin point of view is dangerous. What is wanted is the British point of view.'

She was followed by Harold Nicolson. He opened by saying that he agreed with the last speaker that there were many occasions when it would be in the public interest to appoint to the service well-known women of intelligence, ability – and balance. At this there was laughter. He wrote an interesting account of the debate on the same day in a letter to his two sons.

'The debate went wrong as usual. The women Members felt that their rights were being trampled on, and staged a full-dress attack on the exclusion of women from the Service. Nancy Astor, as the senior woman Member, insisted on voicing their complaint. She has one of those minds that work from association to association, and therefore spreads sideways with extreme rapidity. Further and further did she diverge from the point while Mrs Tate beside her kept on saying,

---

5. It should be remembered that at the time the Pope, by his clumsy diplomacy, had antagonised the anti-Nazi allies and strained Catholic loyalties. A year before, in March 1942, Pius XII agreed to receive a Japanese ambassador, the first ever to be accredited to the Holy See. The Apostolic Delegation in Tokyo was thereupon given official diplomatic status. The arrangement took effect in May. No explanation was given by the Vatican in answer to American and British protests. Later, Vatican spokesmen asserted that the Pope had strengthened mutual representation with Tokyo in view of the fact that there would now be many Christian prisoners of war whom the Vatican wished to help. Subsequent events gave some substance to this claim, but inevitably other explanations were favoured at the time, and still are by some.

"Get back to the point, Nancy. You were talking about the 1934 Committee." "Well, I come from Virginia," said Lady Astor, "and that reminds me, when I was in Washington . . ." I was annoyed by this, as I knew that I was to be called after her. It was like playing squash with a dish of scrambled eggs. Anyhow I made my speech and it went well enough. Lady Astor had said that women had never been given any chance to show their capacity in foreign politics. I said that they might not have been *given* chances, but . . . they had *taken* chances. . . . "You mean mistresses," shouted Lady Astor. I said No, I was thinking of women's virtues and not their frailties. Intuition and sympathy were the two main feminine virtues, and each of these was of little value in diplomacy.' He did not mention the dangers of sympathy without intuition as exemplified by Sir Nevile Henderson, Sir Basil Newton, the British diplomatic admirers of Mussolini, and several other male officials of his time. His speech is easily criticised today as superficial, but Nancy's had never a hope of acceptance.

1943 was not a year of repeated gloom, but it did not live up to expectations. It was a year of victory in North Africa and the Mediterranean, while the Russian counter-offensive of Kursk-Oryol made the ultimate doom of the German army in the East irrevocable. Mussolini was deposed. But in spite of these things, and although the Battle of the Atlantic was all but won, though the air supremacy of the Allies over the Germans was becoming not only an irrefutable calculation but an observable fact, Great Britain, for all the vast easement of its communications with the outside world, was still a besieged island so far as the ordinary citizen was concerned. There was hardly any easement of the claustrophobia. The Second Front in Europe, which to almost everybody meant a second front in France, was not attempted. It was a year of continually deferred hopes. As often happens in times of frustration myths began to spread widely, and a commonly heard legend of the time was that the Second Front was being postponed as a deliberate attempt by the reactionary chiefs of the British and American Services and the Tory Prime Minister, in order to damage the Soviet Union. The Russians supported their champions abroad in the next year by a revival in the Soviet Press of the myth of the Cliveden Set. This time, however, the myth did not make much impression. G.B.S. wrote to Nancy on the 17th June encouraging her to believe in further

NANCY

legends based on his antique theories and, in spite of his denials, endeavouring to influence her views in accordance with the ministrations of the Russian Ambassador Ivan Maisky. Here are two extracts:

'The war will end when the interest on gilt edged rises again to five per cent, just as it began in 1898 and 1914 when the rate fell to two and a half. All the rest is hot air, guff, and bugaboo.

'. . . I know what it is possible to know here about Russia because I get it from the horse's mouth. . . .'

One should not be too disapproving of legends and belief in them in war-time. They are part of the madness of conflict and there are few people who have lived at such times and have not believed them. Stories about Nancy went the rounds in Plymouth. Most of them sound like caricature of fact. One which was widely told at the time, and was said to have been repeated by Nancy against herself, concerned the unfortunate fact that, contrary to popular belief, a certain amount of ill-feeling arose between the townsmen of Plymouth and the Royal Navy. One obvious reason was that the navy alone made Plymouth a target for German bombers. This ill-feeling distressed Nancy greatly. The story runs that she put it to the naval commander-in-chief that he should apply himself more energetically to cultivating good relations between the Fleet and the people. She suggested that he should go round some of the poor districts which had suffered most in the bombing. She suggested further that he should follow her example, put on his best and avoid any appearance of slumming. He was won over and they set out together, he in his impressive uniform, she as smartly dressed as in London in the season. So far the story in no way strains belief. Then, it is said, they came to one of the most melancholy of poor houses, with boarded windows and paper in some panes where there was still a window to let in light, yet, for all its wretchedness, evidently still a human abode. The commander-in-chief was not the first sailor to have called here. After knocking two or three times, a little boy opened the door. They asked him if his mother or father was in. He answered: 'Muvver's ote but 's'll be a'roight if y' leave foive shillin' on th' mantelpiece.'

In July of this victorious and yet unhappy year, Nancy was involved in a genuine and undeniable scandal, and one which shows that in spite of her ceaseless patronage of unpopular causes – notably, severe drink legislation which she urged on the House throughout the war – she retained a general feeling of affection in the country. This event of July was never taken up by the Press in a way to harm Nancy, although it was just the sort of scandal to kindle Puritan indignation.

One of the main exasperations of life in besieged Britain was the rationing of every sort of commodity and necessity from food to clothes. Everyone in the country, rarely or often, was at some shift to escape the rationing net, legally or otherwise. The regulations were so numerous and sometimes so complicated that it was often difficult to know just what the law was. Nancy broke the law as regards clothes. She wrote to a friend, Mr Yandell, in the American Red Cross asking him to bring her, on his next flight to England from America, silk stockings, gloves, evening shoes, two dresses, some shirts and a fur jacket. The letter was opened by the censor, Nancy was informed on and told to appear before the magistrate in the Bow Street Court on the 30th July.

She went to her doom with a pleasing wit. That morning the House was debating the educational reforms originated by Mr R. A. Butler. She spoke briefly in their support. She then swept up her papers and began to leave the Chamber as the leader of the Common Wealth Party, Sir Richard Acland, was called by the Speaker. Sir Richard began by saying he was sorry to see the noble lady leaving as he wished to refer to her speech. She stopped on her way out and turned to the Chair (for once). 'If,' she said, 'the honourable Baronet is going to attack me, will he please do so now before I leave? I have to go to Bow Street.' The House roared with laughter. Sir Richard said he did not plan an attack so she left.

She pleaded guilty. Her defending Counsel read out a statement by her: 'I realised duty would have to be paid. I had no idea I was doing anything wrong, and certainly nothing to impede the war effort. I knew Mr Yandell would be returning by air, and that therefore no shipping space was involved.' She expressed her regret.

The magistrate fined her £50 with £10 costs. He accepted her apologies and expression of regret but in so grudging a manner that he might as well have called her a liar and perjuress. He dwelt on her unusual opportunities for knowing the law and concluded by saying that her conduct showed 'a depth of ignorance and degree of careless-ness which is startling'.

His unnecessary harshness may have helped Nancy. Some of the

Press did publish rude remarks about her, but there was much more sympathetic indignation at her ill-treatment at the hands of a jack-in-office. The American Press, in Canada and the United States, also took the matter up and marvelled at the equity of British justice. The youth of Henry V was remembered. Nancy herself seems to have regarded the incident with indifference, but Bernard Shaw, probably having read an account of the proceedings in an evening paper, seems to have assumed Nancy's resentment and sent her a letter of consolation the day after.

'. . . That afternoon after seeing Waldorf I met your youngest in civvies in Bond St and asked him anxiously what had happened. He knew nothing of the case. I explained the gravity of the situation. His view was that you are working much too hard and that a year in the clink would do you a world of good. He may be right; so go slow for a bit.

'Be very careful not to use the Red Cross car for private visits. By an odd accident I have just learned that Y's use of it was being watched. And that is in fact why I indite this note; for you must not put your head in the lion's mouth again.

'And speak well of Russia. Ask the new ambassador to tea; and convince him that you are Stalin's first and dearest friend in England. That will not cost you a single vote; but a word to the contrary may cost you your seat.

'sagely your G.B.S.'[6]

Shaw's remark about meeting Jakie in Bond Street is of interest. Nancy and Waldorf shared one strong characteristic in their very different temperaments, a passionate taste for overwork. Until his heart-attack and possible stroke in 1941, Waldorf had indulged the taste to the full, but he was now rather more careful. Nancy had received no such terrifying signal and she continued as recklessly as before. She rarely stayed away from Plymouth for more than a week and she continued her frequent to-and-fro night journeys. She worked till her capacity for overwork was strained, and then started again. Many unreadable pages could be filled with details of her strenuous work at the Canadian Hospital at Cliveden. It is sufficient to say that

6. The new Russian Ambassador to Great Britain was Feodor Tarasovich Gousev who remained in his post till 1946. He was entirely without his predecessor's skill in making contact with people in England, a fact which may explain his appointment by Stalin. 'Y' may refer to Mr Yandell.

it was a repeat performance of the one she had given from 1914 to 1918, especially as regards the rallying of men who had lost hope of recovery. Like everyone in England then, she was continually worried about transport.

In 1940 she had bought a motor-bicycle for her journeys between London and Cliveden. This motor-bike solution of her transport problems seems to have lasted a short time. Probably Waldorf stopped it. He would like to have prevented her driving at all. She learned the art too late in life to let her acquire sound road judgement, and everyone who was driven by her testifies that to do so was a most perilous and anxious experience. Rose Harrison has a war-time memory of driving with her from Cliveden to London during one of the severer winters of that time and her car skidding on the icy surface of Constitution Hill, and so dispersing in shameful disorder a body of troops preceded by a band.

Till the very end of the war she remained a popular figure in Plymouth as Lady Mayoress and as the Member for the Sutton Division. But in the later stages, as the bold reconstruction took shape, she made the mistake of mixing in local politics, without adequate study and far beyond her rights as the wife of the Lord Mayor. The plans of Professor Abercrombie and James Paton Watson for the new Plymouth were not only brilliant but radical in their forward-looking character. They were naturally resented. All radical plans are, sometimes rightly, but in this case wrongly. One of the most interesting features of the plan was the construction of a market-place which would house not only the great stores but the little shops which had been obliterated or damaged beyond repair, and those which were situated in streets scheduled to be completely redesigned. Economically this was all to the advantage of the small shopkeepers, but many of them disliked the innovation, and Nancy encouraged their resistance. She mistakenly and Virginianly saw herself as defending the little man against the big, rich, crushing combines, a frequent feature of economic development but not present in this instance. Her interference was naturally much resented by the planners. It came to nothing and again the influence of Waldorf may be deduced.

On one public question she showed sound and generous judgement, with all her familiar courage and indifference to popularity. In the most perilous days of 1940 the British Fascist leader Sir Oswald Mosley had been imprisoned with his wife, and with the principal members of his party. In November 1943 the Home Secretary, Herbert Morrison, decided that this imprisonment without trial had become indefensible and the fascists were freed though under stringent conditions. There immediately arose a nationwide and ignoble agitation for the return to prison of these defeated people. Nancy, who had once been a close friend of Sir Oswald, refused to have anything to do with the nonsense, and as a result she had the unusual experience of being booed by members of the public in the Palace of Westminster. Many deputations went to the Houses of Parliament to demand Mosley's reincarceration, and on the 7th December one which was about thirty strong, and largely Communist in membership, came to Westminster as part of a delegation from Lancashire. They claimed that they represented nearly two million workers. While they were waiting in the lobby Nancy bustled by on her way to the Chamber. One of them stopped her and asked her to hear their petition. She thereupon stamped over to where they were standing and said in her harshest manner: 'I don't want to hear what you've got to say. I want you to know what I think of you. You're the same bunch as stabbed us in the back in 1939.' To this accurate statement they replied with boos and jeers.

Press reports of the scene prompted Sean O'Casey to write a letter of rebuke to her. She replied: 'As you know, I hate dictators – whether they are from the Right or Left. Like St Paul I was born free. All I know is that that outcry about Mosley was an organised affair. When I see you I will explain exactly what I mean. Anyhow, it's not the British way to keep people in prison if they are uncondemned. I am sure you would be the last to do it, for in spite of all you say – no one has a tenderer heart.' O'Casey was not converted and replied with a letter on the wrongs of Ireland.

In the course of that autumn Charlotte Shaw's life drew to its agonising close. 'The difficulty with which she crawls about is heartbreaking,' Shaw had written to Nancy as early as June. Terrified of any accusation of giving preferential treatment to rich people, the Ministry of Labour refused to exempt her from the regulations governing employmen int, spite of the advocacy of Shaw, Waldorf, Nancy and others. It followed that for lack of attendance her last days were harder than they need have been. She died at the age of eighty-six at their flat in London on the 12th September 1943.

Of Shaw at that time St John Ervine wrote: 'The loss of his wife was more profoundly felt than he had ever imagined any loss could be: for he prided himself on a stoical fortitude in all loss and misfortune.' Elsewhere Ervine wrote: 'As was customary with him, he moved from one form of emotion to another with such rapidity that those of his friends who did not fully perceive how he strove to keep his deeper feelings dark, imagined that he was hysterical or callous when, after shedding tears, an act of which he was supposed to be incapable, he would begin to sing almost hilariously. This was the grief which is abandoned.'

There is no documentation in the Astor archive to cover this terrible moment in the life of G.B.S. The reason is that he saw Nancy all the time. She was in Plymouth and he telegraphed to her to come quickly as Charlotte looked so young and beautiful in death. She rushed to him and gave him what comfort she could. She was with him when Charlotte Shaw's remains were cremated at Golders Green. She went with him, his secretary Blanche Patch and his cousin Mrs Musters to the chapel. He was his old witty self and seemed wholly unaffected by the tragedy that had come upon him, but when he saw the look of anxious surprise on Nancy's face he said: 'You mustn't think I don't mind, but I have done my mourning and now it is over.'[7]

He tried henceforth and with all his strong will to live up to his ideal of stoical fortitude. He may have succeeded. He certainly tried to persuade Nancy that he had. He wrote in his light vein to her at the end of September: 'The letters have stopped at last; and correspondence, though copious, is normal and Patchable.' A month later he ended a letter to her: 'When I come across some intimate thing of Charlotte's I still quite automatically say an affectionate word or two and am moved just for a moment.'

In November Waldorf was elected Lord Mayor of Plymouth for his fifth and last year of office. On the 16th the Germans attacked Plymouth in the last of their 1943 raids on the city. By this time the defences were efficient and the casualties correspondingly low, if ghastly enough, 18 killed and 60 injured, all civilians.

There is a story told by Nancy's niece and namesake, Nancy Lancaster, of an undated occasion in London during a raid when Nancy was seeking to reach the lodgings she and Waldorf had taken in

7. Cf a similar remark made by Shaw about his mother's death to Desmond MacCarthy. It is recorded in the preface to MacCarthy's collection of essays, *Experience* (London, 1935).

Babmaes Street behind St James's Square. In Jermyn Street she came on a drunken American soldier. She was not the only woman interested in him, but when she insisted on her priority in the matter, the bomb-happy prostitutes yielded to a greater force of personality than their own. The soldier was beyond expressing himself coherently, only muttering 'I wanna woman – I wanna woman . . .' 'Well you gotta woman' barked back Nancy and dragged him off to Babmaes Street. She applied restoratives (notwithstanding her faith) and got him into a somnolent state not remote from sobriety. She tucked him into Waldorf's bed. He awoke to a soul-shaking lecture on the evils of drink. A similar story is told of Nancy's adventures in Plymouth and can be true of 1943. The similarity of the stories need not indicate confusion, for as Rose Harrison has said: Nancy's two main pleasures lay in 'meeting people and telling off drunks'.

A last view of Nancy in 1943. It is taken from the observation of Harold Nicolson, an unfriendly critic, and one whom she liked to goad outside Parliament in his capacity as a BBC governor, even as she had goaded him within Parliament when he was the Parliamentary Under-Secretary for the Ministry of Information. They agreed on very little.

In late 1943, Harold Nicolson's wife, the poet Victoria Sackville-West, had published a book about Saint Teresa of Avila and her name-sake St Teresa of Lisieux. This had given Nancy the idea that Victoria Sackville-West was about to become a Roman Catholic (a 'candlestick' in private Nicolson parlance).

'I went to the House all afternoon. We had a reception for the Chinese mission. They grinned and bowed under the arc-lights. Then that foul man John Simon made a speech. How dare he? – since he is the main betrayer of China. We walked out. Nancy Astor (who has guts about these things) walked out snorting loudly. She thinks you are going to become a candlestick. I said I did not believe in God at all. She gasped like a fish. But you know, tiresome as she is, there is some-thing in her. A flame somewhere.'

On the 30th April 1944 the sirens wailed again in Plymouth, this time at 3.15 in the morning. There was another heavy raid on the city. Once again the defences proved efficient. The anti-aircraft guns and rockets defended the port and the fighters of the R.A.F. brought down four of the attacking craft. But the raid was a much heavier one than that of November 1943. The casualties which included 27 people killed were worse, and the destruction, though not to be compared with that of 1941, was appalling. Afterwards the 30th April was long remembered in the city. This was the fifty-ninth and last German raid on Plymouth.

Nancy's work in the war was now completed as to its shape and scope. This may sound an odd thing to say of the beginning of the *annus mirabilis* of 1944, with D-Day ahead, and after that the first phase of the final victory over the Nazi Reich. With all her zest she continued her work but she added nothing to it: she maintained in all its vigour the completed achievement. She knew remarkably little about Europe and this was the year of Europe, of its attempted salvation and restoration. She made several speeches in the first half of the year to audiences composed of troops who knew that they were soon to take part in the invasion. At Cliveden she addressed American troops stationed in the neighbourhood, speaking from the Church pulpit on 'Mother's Day' Sunday in May. Her address was an exhortation to them to carry the Anglo-Saxon Biblical spirit to benighted Europe which, for lack of Biblical knowledge, had fallen under Hitler's tyranny. It showed an embarrassing degree of ignorance. It was mercifully not reported outside the local Press. This was not her moment, as the years of siege had been.

But as before she could be trenchantly to the point when she spoke (not so much in the House as at public meetings) on subjects which could be described as belonging to the Home Front. Most of these have become familiar to the reader in the course of this book and need not be enumerated again here, but one of them is more of a rarity. The Younger Generation Movement was getting under way again in 1944 and her debunking of the nonsense perennially associated with it was valuable, enjoyable and fittingly exasperating to fashionable thinkers.

But with the great events of that year Nancy had (strictly speaking) no particular relationship: she shared with thousands of others the anxieties of one who has sons in the field and many friends. She escaped loss in her immediate family, but her son-in-law James Willoughby was seriously wounded in the second campaign of France, losing a leg. At this crossroads of history her private rather than her public life is of the greater biographical interest.

It was Nancy's belief that Charlotte Shaw had exacted a promise from her that, if Mrs Shaw died before her husband, Nancy would look after the widower. G.B.S. did not share this belief, nor did Waldorf. They both regarded it as a wish-fulfilling hallucination which it probably was, for it is certain that Charlotte Shaw had said nothing about this to G.B.S. Early in 1944 Nancy began to worry about his servant problem. On the 10th January he assured her that with one maid he was well provided for. 'I am on velvet,' he assured her, 'so don't worry about me.' But she returned to the attack, to the possessive operation, rather, of making G.B.S. comfortable in her own way. He answered her on the 24th January, assuring her: 'I'm all right bodily.'

Nancy seems to have made no more efforts to take up her supposed obligations for another four months. On the 6th April he wrote her an interesting and, for a change, a commonsensical political letter. There had been something of a scandal in the House of Commons. A clause in the new Education Bill dissatisfied many members on both sides because it perpetuated what they held to be an unjust difference in pay between men and women teachers. As a result, in Committee the Government was defeated on an amendment by one vote. It is hardly necessary to state that Nancy voted for the amendment. Many of Winston Churchill's friends advised him to bow to the storm and accept the amendment, but he demanded a vote of confidence. 'You have knocked me off my perch,' he said to Harold Nicolson, 'and I won't sing until you put me back.' Reluctantly the dissident members of his party (including Nancy) withdrew their opposition. Surprisingly enough G.B.S. was not in sympathy with the dissidents. He wrote on a postcard:

'To old hands like me Equal Pay is a masculine Trade Union dodge to keep women out of industry, the calculation being that if employers have to pay a woman as much as a man they will always choose a man!! So the Unions admitted women on condition that they earned the Union wage: that is, on the same terms as men. Artful, wasn't it?'

At the age of eighty-eight G.B.S. could still see the funny side of war, as appears in his account to Nancy of the following episode:

'We had a parachute mine dropped here in one of the recent raids. It stuck in a tree and not only blew the tree to bits but killed all the pheasants. The whole countryside rushed for them. Local feeling towards Jerry is friendlier in consequence.'

In May 1944 Nancy returned to her mission. Gregarious herself she found it hard, indeed impossible, to imagine the feelings of a man who cherished his 'blessed solitude'. He liked being visited by Nancy, by a few friends, by his cousin Mrs Musters, by old business acquaintances and actors and actresses who wanted his advice about parts in his plays, but if he wanted to see people he wanted to see them as visitors to his solitude. When Nancy asked him to come to Cliveden for an extended visit he replied in decisive terms on the 8th May.

'Why should I come to Cliveden? I am quite well and contented here, where the spring is delightful and I can bore nobody with my old stories and general obsolescence. At Cliveden I should see Waldorf occasionally for five minutes at breakfast and you precariously for a few words later in the day when you were not away in London or Plymouth. All the rest of the time I should be either trying to get through my work and business out of reach of my papers and books of reference, or trying to entertain the fearfully miscellaneous crowd of nobodies whom your reckless Virginian hospitality tolerates. Now that the old Round Table South African group of Curtis, Dawson, Elliot and Phil is gone, I have to act as the Cliveden Set. Do you want to kill me?

'But perhaps that would be the kindest thing.'

There the matter remained for the time being.

A most distressing matter for family difference arose in the later part of 1944. Nancy's youngest son Jakie became engaged to be married to Ana Inez Carcano, always known as Chiquita. She was the daughter of the Ambassador of the Argentine Republic. Nancy was highly displeased. To quote from an essay which Chiquita wrote for Michael Astor: 'After all I, a Latin and a Roman Catholic, was the embodiment of everything she disapproved of, and, added to that, a daughter-in-law.' At a later time, when Nancy had four daughters-in-law, she confessed to several of her friends that the relationship aroused feelings of jealousy in her which were beyond her control.

Chiquita has told of her first meeting with Nancy: 'When I went down to Cliveden to meet Lady Astor, I filled a small bottle with sherry and took it with me ready to gulp down as soon as I got there.' She has also left an admirable impression of Nancy as she was then in 1944, at the age of sixty-five.

'What struck me first was her voice and way of speaking. Not only did her accent seem old-fashioned and quaint, but the tone of her voice cracked and ginny! I was astonished at how small she was, but her size was hardly noticeable so strong was the impact of her personality. She emerged as a woman of stature, the sort of stature that goes with an unbowed head. Her figure almost gave me a shock; she was amazing, not only in her agility and energy but also her shape. That strongly built little body tends slightly to thrust itself forward. The shape of her torso shows that it is closely acquainted with the stays of the nineteen hundreds. This impression is accentuated by the walk, which possibly wasn't noticeable with the bustle and long skirts of the Gibson Girl, but now, with shorter ones, makes her look sometimes like the imitations she is so fond of doing.'

It was to be a stormy relationship as her relationships with all those close to her were, though it was to end happily. The upheavals usually left little if any damage behind, but in this case the first clash had lasting effects. When Jakie and Chiquita were married on the 23rd October at the Catholic Church in Cadogan Street, Nancy was not there and, it is sad to have to relate, neither was Waldorf. Jakie's father was without the physical strength that is usually needful for the exercise of moral strength, and here was one of Nancy's fixed ideas with which he was not in disagreement. Jakie understood his father's position, but not his mother's. Many years later he told Kenneth Harris that though he never lost affection for Nancy, it was some time before he could forgive this merciless slight in his heart, and he even went so far as to say that his relations with his mother, though always abounding with the old love, were to some extent never quite the same again.

At the age of sixty-five Nancy and Waldorf were both nearing the age when people retire from their professions. As November 1944 approached Waldorf found himself under pressure not to stand for re-election as Lord Mayor of Plymouth. It had been his hope that he would be mayor in the year of final victory and would thus have the honour of proclaiming it; he was also loth to withdraw from the great work of reconstruction. The municipal king-maker, Mr Dunstan, was deter-mined, however, that Waldorf should retire, partly on the grounds of his ill-health, and still more because he believed that, with the end of the war in sight, the city council should return to its normal ways and elect a mayor from among themselves. These arguments were most unwelcome to Waldorf, but when he learned that they represented a majority opinion he reluctantly accepted them and did not seek re-election. It is difficult to think of any other mayor in Great Britain during this century whose record of public service can compare with his.

But a far more painful retirement threatened Nancy. The Government had announced that as soon as the fighting in Europe was over, the coalition would disband and there would be a General Election. Nancy looked forward to it. She had no notion that her position within her party was one of weakness. In her local Conservative Association she had more critics than supporters, and the chairman and other members confidentially advised Bill to dissuade his mother from standing again. The Conservative Whips' office had for long regarded her with apprehension as a party liability. Waldorf knew that her precarious situation made it probable that she would not be adopted as a candidate. Furthermore he reluctantly recognised that Nancy's critics were in the right, and so he determined that she should not be humiliated by attempting to stand. He fully recognised how much her parliamentary performance had deteriorated. He told his son Michael that, listening to her from the Peers' Gallery, he had felt unbearable indignation at seeing her mocked by unworthy people who had not the right even to criticise her. He found his family in complete agreement with him. In November he told Nancy of his and the family's wish in the matter, saying that if she refused their advice and stood for Parliament nevertheless, he would give her no support.

The blow to Nancy was appalling. It is by no means an exaggeration to say that, as with the death of her mother and sister, it was one from which she never recovered. In her agony of mind she wrote to Bernard Shaw for advice. He wrote to her on the 19th November. It is a curious letter which shows that he, like Nancy, knew nothing about the circumstances. Here are the relevant passages:

'I really don't know what to say, because I don't know why you are being pressed to retire.

'Sometimes people who are first rate for starting a movement upset it if they don't withdraw at the right moment and start something else.

'Sometimes M.P.s stick to their seats too long, having worn out their authority, novelty and patience with the futility of the House under the Party system. . . .

'How am I to know what is in the mind of W. and your serpent Brood if they really want to hound you out of public life? They may have a dozen other reasons that I know nothing about. Obviously you have 20 years work left in you yet, and are getting deeper instead of being merely quick-witted and inconsecutive.'

The rest of the letter is devoted to an outline of the political future of Great Britain which bears no resemblance to anything which has since occurred.

On the 1st December 1944 Nancy and Waldorf announced in the Press that she would not contest her seat again. A euphemism was employed: that since Waldorf's health did not allow him to undertake the exertions of an election, she was standing down out of consideration for him. On the same day she spoke about the announcement at a large women's dinner held, ironically enough, in order to celebrate her twenty-five years as a Member of Parliament. With her strong aversion to sentimentality, Nancy did not make the graceful farewell speech that was expected. 'Today,' she said in her speech, 'Today I have done a thing that has been terrible for me – one of the hardest things I have ever done in my life, but a thing that every man in the world will approve of. I have said that I will not fight the next election because my husband does not want me to. I have had twenty-five years in the House of Commons, and I am bound to obey. Isn't that a triumph for the men? But whether in or out of the House, I shall always stand for what women stand for.' Before sitting down she recalled Henry James's remark about the dauntless decency which, she said, she had found abundantly in Parliament.

Reporters who were there said that as she spoke her eyes filled with tears. If their report was true, she was likely to be irritated by the very weakness she was at harsh pains to avoid. When the function was over, an *Evening News* reporter asked her what her plans for the future were. 'Oh go away!' she said to him, 'I haven't any idea. Of course I shall be interested in lots of things.'

Although the announcement had been made in the Press and in her speech, no official action had been taken, and as a result Nancy allowed herself to have second thoughts about the whole proposition. This is implied strongly in a letter written to her by G.B.S. on the 14th January 1945.

'Heaven forbid that I should interfere between man and wife! Both of you must, however, bear in mind that the question of your contesting Plymouth again is not a domestic one. It goes far beyond that. No man has a right to make his wife give up a public career to look after his grown-up and married family. No woman has a right to throw over her public work merely to make things comfortable for herself at home. So you twain must fight it out on other lines.'

Soon after this Nancy returned to her mission as protectress of

G.B.S. Again she invited him for an extended visit to Cliveden and again he emphatically refused. His reply, dated the 20th January, was sterner in tone than the previous one on this subject.

'These excursions are wildly impossible for me at my age, even if I were not loaded with business that I cannot deal with apart from my papers. Miss P., losing her sanity by living in a shopless theatreless village with one very old man of whom she must be very tired, has braved the bombs and returned to London, which makes my presence here still more compulsory. . . .

'You must get a younger understudy for Phil. My next journey will probably be to Golders Green; and you should in common prudence replace me betimes, however inferior the substitute.'

Again Nancy did not persist in the mission – for the moment. But she did continue to have second thoughts about her decision to retire from politics. She wrote to G.B.S. who answered on the 24th January: 'I cannot write to W. I could not broach the subject with him unless he opened it. It is beyond all question that the decision rests with you.' He wrote to her again on the 13th February.

'With regard to Sutton I am really quite in the dark as to what you are going to do: for though your wish is to contest the seat your intention seems to be to succumb to family pressure, the real grounds of which I cannot make out, as all their interests point to your being settled in Westminster.

'I must not interfere: all I can say is that your right to the seat if you want it is beyond all question, and the family opposition therefore inexplicable.

'But as the constituencies are announcing their candidates in all directions the question is pressing. If a Conservative candidate is chosen in Sutton, or a Labor candidate with Waldorf's support, you will be checkmated; for the situation created would be intolerable if you then resolved, too late, to split the vote against Waldorf and your own party.

'If you are going to contest the seat you must announce your change of mind at once, and thus make a split practically impossible. It all depends on who gets in first. Your claim must be jumped, and jumped quickly, or it will be equally impossible.

'Keep this to yourself, or the other side will take the hint and jump first. It is now or never.

'I cannot advise you: I can only warn you of the situation.'

Later G.B.S. had a constructive idea which he put to her in a letter of the 6th April. By this time Nancy's retirement from the forthcoming election was definite and official, and a fresh Conservative candidate, Colonel Grand, had been selected. G.B.S. remembered that there are two Houses of Parliament and the thought prompted him to write as follows:

'Winston's mother was an American. England grossly insulted the United States by actually dethroning her king for marrying an American. To soften the smart of that, Winston should make you a peeress in your own right. Ask him flatly to do it. Keep at him until he does. Then join Lady Rhondda in an agitation beginning with the opening of the House of Lords to peeresses in their own right (consort peeresses are impossible) and carry the movement on for a constitutional amendment making all elected authorities consist of men and women in equal numbers, each voter having two votes, one for a man and the other for a woman.

'This is program enough for the rest of your life. Consider it seriously; and do not let your Conservative riffraff persuade you that I am a society clown and write letters to amuse you. I am deadly serious. What alternative program have you if you are not game for it?'

Nancy took this proposition very seriously although she could not but know that her chances of success were slight. The coalition was manifestly foundering into party division, and was in fact to be dissolved, in favour of a 'caretaker government' in the next month, the month of victory in Europe, May 1945. Any government which carried over from the coalition to the ultimate party government was in no position to introduce highly controversial legislation such as the admission of women to the House of Lords. In these circumstances, nonetheless, Nancy approached the Chief Whip of the Conservative Party, her old and faithful friend James Stuart. She wanted him to ask the Prime Minister to enact the main G.B.S. proposition. He advised against her proposal, as he was quite certain that it would be refused. She asked him why.

'Well,' he replied in his characteristic drawl, 'if you make a habit of being as beastly to Winston as you can both in public and in private, I fail to see why he should risk his political future by conferring a peerage on you.'

This answer did not satisfy Nancy. She insisted that the proposition should be put to Winston Churchill. With reluctance the Chief Whip agreed to the request. The writer once asked James Stuart what happened and he replied in some such words as these: 'I put it to Winston as convincingly as I could, though I knew it would be no use. It wasn't, of course, and just as I expected, there was no answer.' 'But,' I protested, 'there must have been an answer of some sort.' 'Oh well,' said James Stuart, 'if you call an embarrassingly long silence followed by an angry grunt an answer, there was.'

If Winston Churchill had known that the proposal originated in his 'pet aversion' G.B.S., the answer might have been much more ferociously negative.

Nancy made one more attempt to achieve her new ambition. She raised the matter in public, ineffectively. The melancholy occasion was recorded by Harold Nicolson in a diary entry of the 23rd April 1945, and though Nicolson may have drawn the picture with a hostile touch, his record does dispose of any doubts as to whether Waldorf and the Astor family were right to insist that Nancy should terminate her political career. On this day a Press luncheon was held in the House of Commons. Winston Churchill made the main speech, Nancy the secondary one. Churchill, according to Nicolson, spoke very well, Nancy more incoherently than usual. She wandered from Virginia to the Elizabethans to Lord de L'Isle V.C. to the Conservative Party to the Prime Minister to the Merchant Navy to Plymouth when 'at this stage,' wrote Nicolson, 'Waldorf, who was sitting beside her, gave a slight tug at her dress. "Now, where was I?" she said, looking at her notes. "Oh yes . . ." and then she started again. This was perhaps the last speech she would make in the House of Commons and she had a favour to ask Winston, would he please make her a peer, as she would wake up the House of Lords as she had woken up the House of Commons, and Philip Lothian always used to say . . . At which came another tug from Waldorf so strong that Nancy sat down suddenly with an expression of pained surprise. I suppose her rambling is amusing, but it rather saddens me, as I like her, and I wish that she would not make quite such an idiot of herself in public.'

No more was heard about this plan, and so incoherent had been Nancy's speech that the point (which was 'newsy' to say the least) appears to have been completely missed by the Press.

On the 8th May 1945 the war against Nazism came to an end. Three months later the Japanese Emperor and Government surrendered. The Second World War was over.

On the 11th June Nancy rose in the House of Commons to ask a question concerning the teaching of religion in schools. She wandered from her point and was called to order from the Chair, for the last time. At question time on Thursday the 14th, the last day but one of the wartime Parliament, a Labour member, Mr Leach, asked the Minister of Agriculture 'if his attention had been drawn to the expressed intention of certain hunting interests to secure the importation of foxes from Belgium'. The Joint Parliamentary Secretary gave a suitable reply when up leaped Nancy who was called. She said: 'Could my honourable friend ask the hon member where he got his story, because it sounds to me like so many other Socialist stories.' Those were her last words in Parliament.

Polling Day was fixed for the 5th July but, owing to the delay imposed by servicemen's votes from abroad, the results were not declared till the 26th. 396 Labour members were returned against an opposition of 189 Conservatives and 25 Liberals. For the first time the Sutton Division of Plymouth returned a Socialist member, but continued, and was to continue for the next six years, to be represented by a woman. The new member was Lucy Middleton.

The fall of Churchill, one of the most unexpected events in modern political history, probably caused Nancy little disquiet, but she did not like the way his fall was brought about. She hated Socialism and its point of view and she was exasperated at the Leftist tendency in the *Observer* which she believed, with many others, had contributed to the Leftist victory. But above all she minded being out of the battle, and she had no illusions about what that meant. On her last day in Westminster a fellow-member told her she would be missed. 'I'll miss the House;' she replied, 'the House won't miss me. It never misses anybody. I've seen 'em all go – Lloyd George, Asquith, Baldwin, Snowden, MacDonald – and not one of 'em was missed. The House is like a sea. M.P.s are like little ships that sail across it and disappear over the horizon. Some of 'em carry a light. Others don't. That's the only difference.'

Completely wrongly and completely understandably Nancy felt that Waldorf had injured her. They entered a period of difficult mutual relations. But if Nancy incurs some blame for not reconciling herself to the inevitable, it must not be thought that she did not make any attempt to do so. On the 3rd September 1945 she wrote as follows in a letter to Bernard Shaw:

'No, I won't go to the House of Lords. I am very much occupied.
I started out to make myself a Christian. So far I have utterly failed.
Now at long last I will start afresh. It's a big job and a very narrow way.
Yet it seems to me it's the only way left to poor mortals. You can't
make Christians of others, but we know some have succeeded with
themselves. . . . [Had Waldorf] taken your advice – well at least I
could have gone on my wicked way. Now I am forced to face up to
my new short (oh so short) chances to go another way.'

The Press and Hansard have afforded me a reliable guide to Lady Astor's public and
political career in the period dealt with in the foregoing chapter. With regard to her
activity in Plymouth I have relied most on the local Press, and I am also much indebted to Mr James Paton Watson, Mr Leslie Paul, Mr Harold Pattinson, Mr and Mrs
Stephen Dalston, and Mr Randolph Henri Baker, all of whom worked as official
colleagues of Lord Astor in the municipality of Plymouth during the war years. Mr
Dalston was as well the Warden of Virginia House. For a general account of the
bombing of Plymouth during the war I am indebted to Mr Baker who gave me
access to the contemporary official maps of bomb-damage in the city and its surroundings. He also brought to my attention Mr H. P. Twyford's detailed record, *It Came to
Our Door*, published in Plymouth in 1946. It was in the introduction to this book that
Lord Astor disclosed his and Lady Astor's wish to be buried in the common grave
in the event of their being victims of the raids. I am also indebted to Miss Felicia
Seymour Taylor for an amusing account of Lady Astor's methods of maintaining
morale among American troops in Plymouth, and for an illuminating assessment of
the likely psychological effect of her reckless courage in the face of danger. During
the war Miss Seymour Taylor worked in the United States Red Cross Clubs in
Plymouth. On the subject of Lady Astor's position, conduct and impact as the Lady
Mayoress, I am also indebted to Miss Harrison's account, recorded by Kenneth Harris,
and also to a letter from her to myself; to Mr Ben Robertson's *I Saw England* (London,
1943), and Maurice Collis's *Nancy Astor*. I have been given additional information
by Mrs Alice Winn. The episode of Lady Astor's difference with Winston Churchill
over Mrs Churchill's role on the occasion of his visit to Plymouth in May 1941 was
told to me in detail by Mr Averill Harriman when I met him in Washington in 1969.
The detail of Lady Astor's harsh remark to the Prime Minister when he broke down
was told to me by Mr Paton Watson. The question as to whether Lord Astor suffered
a stroke in 1941 remains controversial. If he did suffer a stroke it must have been very
slight. As mentioned in the text, no definite assertion can be made as he was never
examined by a qualified person in the accepted meaning. The details of the arrangement whereby Lord Astor conferred the ownership of Cliveden on the National Trust
were given to me by the Chairman at the time of writing, Lord Antrim. For some
further details beyond their letters, regarding Lady Astor's revival of her friendship
with Hilaire Belloc in 1941, I am in debt to Belloc's daughter, Mrs Jebb. The contribution of Angus McDonnell to Lord Halifax's ambassadorship in the United States is

vividly recorded in Lord Birkenhead's *Halifax*. The break of Lord Astor with his
editor J. L. Garvin is related in considerable detail in Lord Astor's papers, but dealt
with only briefly in this book since I find no evidence that Lady Astor took any part
in the affair beyond supporting her husband. The account given here of the last days
of Mrs Shaw and Lady Astor's relations with Bernard Shaw after her death follows
material in the Astor archive and in St John Ervine's biography. The last quoted
letter from Lady Astor to Bernard Shaw, however, is not in the Astor archive but in
the Shaw papers in the British Museum. Descriptions of Lady Astor's political position
at the end of her parliamentary career follow discussions with the late Lord Stuart
and Mr Ronald Tree. I am indebted to Mrs Nancy Lancaster for the story of the
American soldier in Jermyn Street. As appears in the text, I have drawn on an unpublished essay by Mrs J. J. Astor. I have also drawn on the published diaries of Sir
Harold Nicolson and Sir Henry Channon. The remark of Winston Churchill concerning the one-vote Governmental defeat, was told to me the day after the incident
by Harold Nicolson.

Chapter 21

NO PEACE IN RETIREMENT

In September 1945 an intriguing official order was discovered among the captured documents of the German Secret Police. It had been written in 1940 and contained the names of over 2,300 people resident in Great Britain who were to be arrested as soon as possible after the successful invasion of the country by the Wehrmacht. Among the names were those of Nancy and her brother-in-law John Jacob Astor. By some oversight Waldorf was not included. Nancy declared this discovery to be a proof that the accusations about a Cliveden Set were nonsensical, and the Press did not contradict her, except, of course, for the *Daily Worker*. That paper ingeniously contrived to see in the discovery final and conclusive evidence of Astor pro-Nazi activity.

Later in the year, in November, the Cliveden Set came into the news once more. The Nuremberg trials were proceeding and Ribbentrop's defence counsel asked for the attendance of Lord and Lady Astor, Lord Londonderry and Winston Churchill as witnesses for his client. The prosecution resisted the request which was not pursued. Of course there were then a few to say that the Astors did not dare face legal examination for fear of the treason that would be exposed, but, apart from some natural curiosity about so bizarre an incident, it passed without much comment.

In June of 1945, Bill was married and in the following August David also. The whole of Nancy's family was married now. As mentioned earlier, she was never an ideal mother-in-law because that position in life challenged her possessiveness, and she reacted against it sometimes with cruelty. But it must never be forgotten that she owned to this fault with astonishing candour, and she was often at pains to make amends. But the fault was there, ineradicable, and was to add to the difficulties of her later life.

On the 11th December she attended a sad and memorable function: the ashes of Lord Lothian were returned by the United States Government to his native land, and interred in Jedburgh Abbey.

The war was over, even if it had not been succeeded by peace. The

N.   Q blessings were negative but real. There was no more Hitler, Goering, Goebbels or Himmler. There was no Final Solution, in Western Europe at least; no more Wehrmacht, Luftwaffe or Swastika. Through the habits of power and in economic panic, British Governments, and others, for long tried to maintain the isolation of the people, but the attempt, though never totally abandoned, was a failure: there was no more claustrophobia. As had happened 130 years before, every British person who could do so went abroad to see the world outside. Nancy and Waldorf were taken with this impulse of the time, and on the 7th January 1946 they sailed for New York.

Transatlantic shipping was still in much confusion as a result of the war and the Astors found that the only way to avoid a long wait was to take berths on a small freighter of 6,000 tons, the *Eros*. The season was stormy and the crossing, scheduled to take eight days, took two weeks. Nancy and Rose Harrison spent most of the first days in bed, but Waldorf, for the sake of whose health this journey was undertaken in large part, was a good sailor. When the weather became a little calmer Rose recovered and began to go around the boat on errands for her mistress. The crew had heard that Nancy was aboard and were not prejudiced in her favour for, among her last deeds as a Member of Parliament, she had put forward a suggestion at question time urging the termination or at least restriction of the naval right to duty-free grog. 'She's the one,' they said to Rose, 'who got our rum ration stopped during the war.' Rose did not tolerate criticism of Nancy from other people. 'Oh no she didn't,' she said (and this was true but not by Nancy's wish), 'and I'll get her down here to tell you about it.' 'Oh no,' they said, 'don't you bring her down here.' But she did bring Nancy down, and Nancy won them over, just as she had won over crew-members of a great liner in her young days. When the *Eros* berthed in New York on the 21st January the crew were all watching her on the icy decks, and when she walked down the gang-way to the shore they broke into a ragged chorus of 'She's a jolly good fellow'. She stopped halfway down and looked up to the deck. She shouted at the men: 'Don't let them put anything over on you – keep the flag flying!' 'Them' in this context meant the nationalising Labour Government.

As was to be expected there was a great crowd of reporters and cameramen waiting at the foot of the gangway. She was immediately asked for a statement. 'I am an extinct volcano,' she replied in ringing tones, and then, having been escorted from the icy cold of the pier to the chill of a waiting-room, she proceeded to erupt with her accustomed violence. Why had they travelled on a small freighter? Because, she said, the British Labour Government had not given them priority passages on the *Queen Mary* or the *Queen Elizabeth* but, she added, 'Laski gets a priority, by gum.' When asked what her plans were, she threatened to run for Congress. Was it true that she hoped to be the first woman member of the House of Lords? There had been a report – She replied sharply: 'Winston might have done it for me, but I've no hope since this Labour Government got in.' This led to mention of the fact that Winston Churchill had shortly before arrived in the United States. Did she intend to meet him? 'No,' she said, 'it would be a busman's holiday for both of us. He hasn't come to America to meet me.' This led to questions about the change of Government in Britain, and the impending revolution. She scoffed at the notion of revolution. England, she said, was 'still full of lords and ladies, and anyhow the English are a very unified people and even if they don't like the captain, they won't sink the ship.' Shortly before, the former Vice-President Henry Wallace had said that this is 'the century of the Common Man'. Nancy said she wished to comment on that: 'It isn't the common man at all who is important, it is the uncommon man. You Americans like to quote Abraham Lincoln as a great common man, but you've had only one Lincoln.' She was questioned about the Cliveden Set and treated the myth with ridicule, while, regarding the unmythical and awkward matter of the £50 fine, she deftly replied: 'That's all right because I hope to get a fur jacket on this trip, if I still have any gentleman friends.' She was asked to make a considered statement on international relations. For this she had a prepared statement, full of the expected clichés, which she read out. The cinema cameras whirred and the photographers flashed. She damped the effect of the statement by saying as she put down the paper: 'That's the worst speech I've ever heard.' As she left she said with a winning smile to the Pressmen: 'Goodbye, you horrors!'

This opening Press conference set the tone for her numerous public appearances during the visit. The tone went down well with most of her audience, but she had a mixed Press. Her high-spirited fooling was not wholly to the taste of new and more sombre generations. The *New York Herald Tribune* struck a warning note next morning. 'Perhaps,' said the leader, 'she demonstrated, in spite of the coruscations, that her initial statement was valid, and that she, like so much else of the '20s and '30s, is "extinct".' Her disparagement of the common man seems to have offended many people, as similar remarks by her had already done in Great Britain. But she did not meet real opposition until later when she was in Washington.

Lord Halifax was still ambassador, due to retire in the spring. The moment was one of great tension in Anglo-American relations. The British Government were negotiating with the American administration for a loan. Hostility was in the air. It was a moment for tact or boldness. Nancy preferred boldness.

Having stopped at Baltimore, she arrived in Washington to stay with the Halifaxes on Friday the 31st January. The Press had asked the ambassador to arrange for an interview with her, and this he did. Waldorf had arranged to join her later in the day from New York, so she was without his restraining influence. 'Now look here,' she began, 'I want to interview you for a change.' The assembled Pressmen gazed at her in silence, and she quickly continued before they could recover from the shock: 'Tell me what is Britain's crime? Why all this criticism? What has Britain done that is so wicked? You should get down on your knees and thank God for Britain. Who's been making all this criticism? It's not the people of America who try to make trouble? Is it the politicians? Certainly no English politician has ever used hatred of America to get votes, because he knows he wouldn't get 'em. Who started this country anyway?'

In the stunned silence following this fling a reporter put in the first question from the Press. Was she serious about standing for Congress? 'No I'm not,' she replied, and hastened to the great indiscretion of the afternoon, 'I was only pulling the reporters' legs, but there's nothing I would like better right now. I would like to be up there in Congress just until this Lease-Lend business is through.' (She meant the loan.)

The interview drew forth three days later a bellow of Anglophobe, anti-expatriate, isolationist and almost incoherent rage from the *Chicago Tribune*, and also some injured growls from the *New York News*. But she had her defenders and the State of Virginia invited her to address a joint session of the House and Senate in Richmond, as did also the State of South Carolina.[1]

One of the objects of the visit was to attend the 94th birthday cele-

---

1. The Virginia House and Senate meeting had to be abandoned owing to a technical error in the motion which caused a delay.

brations at Lynchburgh of Nancy's aunt Mrs Lewis. She flew there from Washington on the day after her Press conference, accompanied by her sister Irene, her niece Alice Winn, and younger relations. As on her former visits to her family shrines in South Virginia an enormous quantity of relatives appeared on the scene and at the reception Nancy and her party had to shake hands with 400 of them, the fatigue of the occasion being greatly increased because each relative liked to explain in detail his precise degree of kinship, adding an outline autobiography. The festivity was not an unqualified success. Aunt Lewis was too frail to appear in person and two days later she died.

The main ostensible object of the 1946 visit to America was to allow Waldorf to enjoy some sun. He was suffering from his long-endured rheumatism, and also asthma, for which reason he had been spared the birthday celebrations, and was to be spared most of Nancy's future engagements. On the 3rd February he and Nancy left Washington by train for Miami which they reached the next evening, and where they spent a little over two weeks on the yacht of a friend, Clarence Dillon. Nancy went ashore, more often than her husband, to address meetings specially convened to hear her, to visit friends and to play golf. Then on the 19th February they left Miami by air for Charleston. On the way, as a result of bad weather, they were diverted to Savannah where they had to wait for two hours before going on by rail. Nancy seems to have been much put out by the enforced delay. They had two hours to fill in and, to quote Waldorf's diary, 'We hired a taxi and visited that ancient and at one time most important city with its old-fashioned houses, its numerous squares, its azaleas and camellias in bloom.'

By the time they reached the railroad station the news of the presence of these notables had spread to the Press. 'Wherever we land,' runs a weary note in Waldorf's diary, 'expected or unexpected, the local photographer and reporter.' What did Lady Astor think of Savannah? She replied in harsh terms: 'The city is very beautiful, as everybody knows it is. It's one of the most beautiful cities of America. But the way y'keep it. It's revoltin'. Never seen anythin' so revoltin' in m'life. Litter. Wherever y'go, there's litter. I'll tell you what I think of Savannah. I think it's a beautiful woman with a dirty face. One of the loveliest women in th'world who's forgotten to wash.'

This denunciation of the city might have been deemed tactless in any circumstances, but to the agony of Waldorf, and perhaps of Nancy's own subsequent second thoughts, it was especially tactless in Savannah, as she was scheduled to appear as the guest of honour at a Rotarian luncheon to be held in the city in about three weeks' time, on the 12th March.

They continued by rail to Charleston and there they stayed in a house lent to them by a friend, till Nancy's lunch engagement in Savannah. Waldorf was still in need of rest, and Nancy worked off her tireless energy independently by motoring round South Carolina and playing golf. Waldorf's diary tells that she found the Charleston course first-rate but had some complaint that most of the members of the Golf Club were too old to play her round the full 18 holes. On the 11th March, possibly in some trepidation, she returned to Savannah for her Rotarian lunch.

Her remarks about Savannah being an unwashed beauty had been the topic of the town since the 19th February and a journalist who wrote to her in Charleston told her she had been 'more cussed, discussed and applauded than anyone here in a long time'. On this occasion she had nothing to fear, however. She had voiced the discontent of many citizens and the civic authorities found themselves forced by opinion to undertake cleaning operations. When Nancy arrived she found the city swept and garnished, and herself the darling of Georgia. On the 21st March she went to Columbia and addressed the House and Senate of South Carolina assembled in special session to hear her.

At the end of March Waldorf went north to stay with friends in Connecticut intending a little later to go to Montreal, his reason for the Canadian visit being not only a desire to maintain the special Cliveden-Canada connection, but also that unless he broke his sojourn in the United States by a visit to British territory he would be liable to penal taxation. Nancy did not join him because she had an appointment which was to be the climax of the visit, an extended tour during April through Virginia with speech-making visits to Washington. On the 2nd she arrived in Danville and spent two days crammed with informal and civic receptions. The occasion was again attended by multitudes of relations, and Danville gave herself over once more, as in 1922, to celebration of her most famous daughter. Nancy quipped and backchatted. It all followed expected lines. She had nothing new to say, except for one surprising item in her Press interviews. For the first time since January she made some public comments about Winston Churchill. They were not flattering.

It will be remembered that Winston Churchill had arrived in

America shortly before the Astors. In February he had made his great and controversial speech at Fulton in which for the first time he used the expression 'the iron curtain' with reference to Russian-Western relations. Nancy approved the speech thoroughly, and in Press interviews, both before and after it, had made in her own fashion similar points as those unforgettably made by Churchill. But this did not mean that she was now totally reconciled to him. She described him as having been 'admirable to win the war with' but no peace-time Minister.

From Danville she went to her beloved Mirador, and she made speeches in Charlottesville, and later in Richmond. Ironically she was asked, as a former Member of Parliament, to represent Winston Churchill at a ceremony held in the old State capital, Williamsburg. The citizens had subscribed to present the great man with a 'Bell of Freedom', a replica of an old-fashioned watchman's bell wrought in silver and suitably inscribed. She received the bell and expressed the thanks of Great Britain and Churchill with becoming dignity, but having spoken, she could not resist turning to the mayor and saying to him in a low voice: 'It's very nice, but why did you give the bell to Winston? You ought to have given it to me.' The mayor's reply is not remembered.

She made one speech in Washington towards the end of April, which was much criticised. She was invited to address the Dunbar High School in Washington for coloured pupils. She told them how, like many Southerners, she had learned to understand and admire the coloured people through her 'black mammy', Aunt Liza, and reminisced about a Negro porter in the family employ. She denounced the night club life and immorality of Harlem because, as she asserted, 'no race can develop beyond its moral character'. She did add that the same perils threatened the white people. She urged a return to the simple faith of the 'Aunts' and the 'Uncles' of old. All this might have gone down well twenty or thirty years before, but it was strongly resented by many of the pupils of 1946, and the resentment was duly exaggerated by contributors to the Press, some of them coloured people.

Both in Charleston and during her stay in Virginia Nancy saw a great deal of her youngest sister Nora, now married to her second husband, a former athletic star called 'Lefty' Flynn. Little has been said about her in this book. She was the madcap of the Langhorne family and to relate her adventures in any detail would be either to write a book about her alone, or to write a digressive one of excessive length.

During her life she became involved in many scandals and ran up many debts, from both of which she was rescued regularly by the Astors, on conditions which were regularly broken. She shared three principal things with Nancy, comic acting ability, an extraordinary power to attract affection so that everyone who knew her, including her numerous and often infuriated critics, loved her, and an ardent faith in Christian Science. She and her husband were with Nancy during most of this time.

Having spent a few days in Canada, Waldorf travelled south and rejoined Nancy in Richmond. In May they both went to New York where they joined Bill and his wife. Bill soon after left them for a journey of political exploration in South America, and on the 14th May Waldorf and his daughter-in-law sailed for England on the *Queen Mary*. Among their fellow-passengers were Lord and Lady Halifax who were leaving the United States for the last time. Angus McDonnell had left already. (He never received any official recognition for his remarkable services to his cousin.) Nancy stayed on in America for another month. She had received invitations to speak at various meetings, receptions and luncheons and had accepted them. In her last weeks she travelled widely again, back to Virginia and North Carolina, then north to Canada and back to New York via Boston. Those expecting further indiscretions were not disappointed. In Boston she adversely criticised the local government, and in New York she spoke scathingly of Winston Churchill's war-leadership. At a Press-interview she dwelt on the undemocratic character of Congress, as compared to the British Parliament. On the 20th June she sailed for England on the *Queen Mary*. Her five months' visit was over.

The visit cannot be described as a success or a failure. As the *New York Herald Tribune* had so cruelly remarked at the beginning of the journey there was some truth in her self-description as 'an extinct volcano'. She was not taken seriously. Her object, as before, had been to act as an ambassadress of good will. Her particular purpose, politically, had been to laugh the Americans out of an Anglophobe mood, and impress on them the need and the moral obligation of a generously conceded loan. But in the event she had been more attacked than defended on what the majority felt to be her unwarranted interference. One has only to remember the good impression she made in America twenty-four years before when she championed the equally unpopular cause of American participation in the League of Nations, to realise

how less sure her touch had become. But some remoteness from the
spirit of the time did not preclude success. Americans like a show and
a shake to complacency and she gave them both. In the Southern
States these were very much to the taste of her audience. The Dunbar
Hill School incident seems to have been the only occasion when her
instinct played her false, and the reaction there, it should be remembered, was not unanimous. She would perhaps have been wiser to
confine her visit to the South, but she stayed on, mostly in the North,
till late June. If a guess may be allowed, she stayed because she dreaded
going home. To explain why the story must go back a little in time.

It will have been noticed how often Waldorf and Nancy were not
together during this American visit. The given explanation was that
while Nancy was there to fulfil numerous public engagements,
Waldorf was there for the sake of his health and thus had to go carefully, avoiding crowds, ceremonies and fatigue. This was in no way a
fiction, but it disguised other and darker facts. Since the autumn of
1944 when Waldorf had first insisted that Nancy must retire from
Parliament, her sense of injury against him had grown rapidly and
terribly, and was far more intense and bitter than anyone outside the
family guessed. Conceivably, Bernard Shaw might have reconciled
her to a necessary retirement, but it is doubtful. Her mind was closed
on this subject. T.J. had been temporarily exiled from her friendship
because he agreed with Waldorf. She only listened to those of her
friends who strenuously urged her to stand for Parliament again.

It is allowable to see in the conflict a clash between the Langhorne
and the Astor temperaments; the one fiery, unreflecting, intuitive, uninhibited, irrational, at the mercy of moods; the other calm, consistent,
cool, reasonable, long-seeing. Yet to see it thus is to see it only partially.
It was not only a struggle between emotion and logic, but also between
emotions. Not for one second did Waldorf lose his passionate love
for Nancy, and for this reason the conflict was agonising to him. On
her side she was thrust on by an anger she could not control.
Waldorf became another of her prejudices, and in her conduct towards
him, it must be said, she showed a terrible degree of her cruelty.

By September 1945 G.B.S. had guessed their situation, though he
remained unaware that he had been instrumental in causing it. He
wrote to her: 'You are very puzzling about W. Have you separated?
You write as if you have no latchkey of Cliveden nor he of Rest
Harrow. I hope not. You will neither of you do better. But of course

you should both have Sunday spouses to keep you young.' And in the following December he wrote: 'Why don't you and Waldorf, now that you have done your job of repeopling the world, get married seriously and settle down to the real thing? "The best is yet to come." '
She had followed his advice when it was bad. She paid no attention to it now that it was good. She seems to have entirely forgotten the high-minded renunciation of ambition that she had expressed to him in the same month.

Added to the main conflict, there were subsidiary ones of almost equal intensity. The policies of the *Observer* and the refusal of Waldorf to check its left-wing attitudes in general and that of David in particular, exasperated her, and since the family agreed with their father's views, she appeared to herself to be surrounded by deserters from her cause. There was at this moment no positive point of agreement between her and her husband, only the weak support of a negative one, their shared hatred of what they referred to in their letters as 'R.C.', and 'R.C.' was at this moment quite irrelevant to their lives.

The sheer violence of the storm caused it to blow itself out – for a while. So they went to America together in 1946. When Waldorf was away from Nancy during those journeys, he often wrote to her. The letters read like those of ten years before. There are no appeals, no protestations, only the normally affectionate tone of a loving husband writing on neutral matters to the beloved wife to whom he has been long married. But this emotional tranquillity represented no more than a truce. She knew that when she went back the conflict would blaze up anew. So she dreaded her return.

In 1946 Waldorf sold 4 St James's Square to the Government. It had been requisitioned for the last three years of the war, and badly damaged by bombs. He sold it on the understanding that the Government would make the house available to the Arts Council, and as this was an institution in which he had much belief he did not ask for the full market price. He and Bill subscribed together to buy a house in London which would be chiefly Nancy's, 35 Hill Street. He gave up their wartime lodgings in Babmaes Street. As appears from G.B.S.'s letter of September 1945, the house at Sandwich, Rest Harrow, had been reopened after the wartime disuse, already noted, which befell many seaside houses. At Cliveden the Canadian hospital had been formally made over to the Ministry of Health in May. The greatest of these family changes in 1946 was undoubtedly the end of

4 St James's Square as the Astor town house. That noble piece of old London architecture held all Nancy's memories of herself as a famous hostess, and she felt, as she told Bob Brand, that she had lost her London home. A tragic picture must not be attempted. With the children married, 4 St James's Square had lost its purpose, and she had more houses than most people have, but no matter how many houses one may have, the loss of a home is always grievous. To her credit she did not repine, and accepted the loss without complaint.

But the mutual situation of Waldorf and Nancy remained as anomalous as it was unhappy. He tended to live most of the time at Cliveden, she at Rest Harrow. She would go to Cliveden whenever their joint presence was necessary, but rarely otherwise. He would sometimes go to Sandwich. At 35 Hill Street they did not meet as often as a married couple, even one with different interests, usually do, as their correspondence testifies. Their meetings were often very painful. Waldorf's main interest in London was the Royal Institute of International Affairs, Chatham House, of which he was a foundation member, and chairman since 1935. Nancy had never taken the least interest in Chatham House and would hurt Waldorf at this time by treating it with ridicule. David was now Foreign Editor of the *Observer*, and this was a cause of angry argument. But the main conflict still raged over her parliamentary retirement. In 1946 she had still not abandoned the idea of attempting a re-entry into the House of Commons.

G.B.S.'s remarks in 1945 about 'Sunday spouses' were more serious than they may appear. He knew that she needed a counsellor from whom she would take unwelcome advice, and needed such a one now more than ever. The later phases of her life might have been very different and happier if she could have had the advice of Philip Lothian who had always shown sound judgement in personal matters affecting her, especially regarding her relations with her children. G.B.S. knew that he himself could not fill the role and that Nancy wanted him to. He seems to have lost some, if not all of the Bergsonian faith he expressed in *Back to Methuselah*. He had no faith, at all events, in the value of his own senescence. He had written to her in 1945: 'I want you to forget and drop me because I am an old and dying man (actually I am dead and considerably decomposed) and you must find a Sunday husband young enough to last your time.' He conveyed the same warning in yet harsher terms on the 4th April 1947.

'Nothing to write about.
'Under such circumstances it is my point of honor not to write.
'Duty letters and duty visits are intolerable curses.
'I care for nobody, no not I; and nobody cares for me.
'Waste no care on the old: make young friends – young enough to outlast you. I only waste your time. Activities are what you need, not the society of dotards. Be warned: I am a dotard; and I know. G.B.S.'

It so happened that shortly after moving into Hill Street there had appeared on Nancy's horizon the most perfect of counsellors: her brother-in-law Bob Brand. His mission to the United States had come to an end after the conclusion of the loan negotiations. He had been away for more than five years, and on his returning to England to his normal occupation as a director of Lazard's Bank, he had nowhere to live in London. He was glad to accept Nancy's offer of a room in 35 Hill Street.

She had always loved Bob Brand, and he, though extremely critical of her, always loved Nancy. Both she and Waldorf had frequently turned to him for advice in the course of the years. Unlike most business men he had extraordinarily good political judgement. He was about the same age as Nancy, and he was doubly bound to her by the tender memory of Phyllis. He had recently suffered greatly, and this made him sympathetic to the unhappiness of others. In March 1945 his only son had been killed in action. Surely this loving and wise man could have filled the role of the counsellor she so sorely needed. That he did not is probably due to the fact that, unlike Philip Lothian, he did not share any of her deeper impulses or beliefs. He saw nothing sinister, or hateful, or alarming in 'R.C.', in Jewish people, or in the Latin nations, and he regarded Nancy's prejudices on those subjects as deplorable. On her side she misunderstood his tolerance, and disliked his rejection of her religion. When she called him 'Antichrist' there was a little core of seriousness in the jest. He not only had no belief in Christian Science but he continued to regard it as a grotesque delusion. He used to chaff her about it, as G.B.S. and Alice Longworth and other of her close friends did, and she took no offence. He recalled himself 'asking her, for instance, whether, since she used cold cream daily, the outside of her skin "existed" but not the inside'. He added this illuminating note: 'Since our views on religious subjects had been formed by entirely different processes, controversy between us would have been useless. I told her that the "scenery" I saw was different from what she saw; that I used to see her scenery, but in the course of the years I had been through a long tunnel and had come out amid scenery quite different from hers.' All this appealed to her curiosity, and his chaffing to her sense of fun, but it did preclude Bob Brand from taking on the task once successfully discharged by Philip Lothian.

She fulfilled many public engagements during the winter of 1946/47, but these occasions were inadequate outlets for her abounding vitality. They may even have aggravated her embitterment. They all belonged to the 'little career', and but a short while since she had shone in the Great Career, in the only career worth pursuing as it seems to those who have experienced its victories and defeats.[2] To appease her restlessness she decided to go back to the United States in May 1947. She went alone.

On the morning of the 23rd, the reporters and cameramen of New York were drawn up in battle formation on the quays as the *Queen Elizabeth* swung into her berth with Nancy aboard. As soon as the gangways were down they charged up to the sundeck where she was awaiting the attack. She opened the engagement by correcting the first sally of the last campaign. 'The last time I saw you disreputable fellows,' she said, 'I called myself an extinct volcano. That's not right. I'm not an extinct volcano, I'm a politically suppressed one.'

This time she did not reverse the roles of reporter and victim but allowed the Press to open the assault. What did she think of the Labour Government? This attack was swiftly routed with a counter-manoeuvre. She replied: 'I'm not a member of the Labour Government and I don't think it wise to criticise any British government when I'm abroad. I am not Henry Wallace.' In England Henry Wallace had been very critical of Mr Truman's administration.

She spent most of her visit at Mirador where her nephew-in-law John Polk (who had married Bob Brand's daughter Virginia) lay mortally ill. Here she had her last meeting with Archdeacon Neve who was to die in 1948. Her public engagements were all in Virginia; at Charlottesville, Williamsburg, Christiansburg and Richmond. In the first week of August she returned North before sailing home in the *Queen Mary* on the 8th. The Press were waiting for her in New York, but most of her remarks were unexceptionable. She praised the Marshall Plan, as well she might. But when she was on board the great

2. When the young Lamartine asked Talleyrand whether the latter advised him to follow a political career, the aged statesman replied, 'Is there another?'

liner she showed the old bellicose spirit that the reporters were after.

'You'll have to write out your questions,' she said to the assembled reporters, 'if you want to interview me. I wouldn't trust a reporter farther than I can throw a cat. Now don't print that.' They did. They got her on to the Palestine troubles. She praised the patience of the British soldiery. 'Do you think,' she asked, 'that if one American soldier had been shot in the back we Americans would have been so patient?' She went on to thinner ice. 'It's alarming,' she said, 'when you consider the fact that the Presidency depends on the New York vote which is a Jewish and foreign vote. There are too many people in New York that don't belong anywhere – they have no roots.' She courted further peril. 'American money is keeping the Jewish underground in Palestine going. It's a racket. The Palestine movement is not a spiritual movement. It's purely political. Do you know of any American or British Jews who want to live in Palestine?' To this the Pressmen were silent.

Later she was reported to have said: 'I don't mind how many Jews are killed in Palestine. My only interest is in the number of innocent British who are slaughtered.' Emanuel Celler, a Democrat and Congressional representative of New York, was so enraged by this remark that he urged the State Department to instruct all American Consulates to refuse Nancy a visa in future. 'She is a vicious anti-Semite,' he said. 'There's only one way to stop this harridan.' Nancy denied having made the particular remark in question. It is possible that it is a contortion of something similar which she did say about the followers of Menachem Beigin in Palestine, in which case it would have been acceptable to many minds; but it is to be noted that in the fullest report of the interview, that in the *New York Herald Tribune*, there is no mention of any remark bearing any resemblance to the words which so disturbed Emanuel Celler. After a little the whole matter was forgotten.

Later in 1947, in November, Nancy went on a journey to Germany. Oddly enough, she went as a reporter for the *Observer* and turned in a good article, possibly with help. She saw Berlin. Used as she was to scenes of devastation in London and Plymouth, she was greatly appalled by what she saw here. She owned in a letter (dictated to an unidentified friend) that 'it really frightened me. The people looked grim and nobody smiled except the children.'

There were two interesting consequences of this *Forschungsreise*. Nancy received a letter while in Germany from Baroness von Neurath,

the wife of the former Foreign Minister and Gauleiter of Czechoslovakia, complaining of the cruel conditions under which her husband
had to endure the prison sentence inflicted on him at Nuremberg. She
took this up vigorously with the British Minister in the Government
charged with German affairs. He was a friend of long standing, Lord
Packenham, better known now as Lord Longford. He wrote to her in
February and March of 1948 to tell her that he had enquired into the
matter and that he was satisfied that Neurath was receiving no more
odious treatment than others of the condemned survivors of Hitler.
He added a characteristic and indiscreet note in manuscript to indicate
that he was on her side. Years before Nancy had implored Frank
Pakenham not to become a convert to Roman Catholicism. She had
acted in the spirit of a guardian angel addressing a lost soul. He had
erred from her counsel nonetheless, and typically this made no difference to her affection.

The other consequence of this journey into post-war Germany was
that Nancy received a letter from a German who lived in London
and had a distinguished name. He had a questionable claim to being an
anti-Nazi. He suggested to her that she should organise a movement
in the United States with the object of making Hanover and then all
Germany a constituent part of the British Empire. She does not seem
to have answered him. Oddly enough the proposal to incorporate
Hanover in the Empire was widely expected in that province then,
and even hoped for.

In 1947 Nancy suffered two painful losses of friends through death.
In February Ellen Wilkinson had died at the height of her career as
Minister of Education. In June, while Nancy was in America, Mavis
Tate died. She had contracted some infection while on an official
parliamentary visit to the Nazi concentration camps immediately
after the war, and her health had never recovered. She became subject
to harrowing depression. Both women had a tendency to neurasthenia,
and both died by suicide. Nancy was intensely shocked by these
tragedies, but in her deranged state she contrived to see a grievance
even here. She wrote to Waldorf accusing him of callousness because
he had not telephoned to Mirador to tell her of Mavis Tate's death so
that she had read the news in the papers before his cable arrived. Then
she repented her injustice and asked him in a later letter to come out
and join her, but this he was unable to do at short notice. At the end
of 1947 the situation between Nancy and Waldorf remained what it

had been before she set out for America: painful, undefinable, yet all this under a cover of normal relations which was false but effective.

It would be as fruitless as it would be melancholy to record in detail the long estrangement, its varying phases, and what appeared, until near the end, to be the impossibility of a reconciliation. In 1948 there was again a truce when they both went with Michael Astor and his wife to the United States, to Arizona. Away from Cliveden, London and Sandwich they could easily be happy together. They were in America for three months from late January till the beginning of May. They returned by way of New Mexico and Texas, and in the latter state they had an interesting encounter with the Press at Houston. The train drew in at 7.15 in the morning; the reporters were ready for her and knocked at the door of her sleeper for an interview. 'Go away!' she shouted to them. 'It's scandalous! Woken at dawn! I'm an old woman. I don't look pretty. Go away and read your Bible. Read Proverbs. Read what it says about virtuous women.' Since they did not take her advice she poked her head out of the door to say: 'Can't understand all the tins lying about in Houston and all over the prairies. Filth and tin cans. What are they going to do about them?' A reporter said: 'Send them to England.' 'Well fill 'em up first,' she replied, and slammed the compartment door.

This was Waldorf's last visit to the United States. On their return their relationship became calmer. She came more often and for longer to Cliveden. There was less of Nancy's fierce, merciless, accusing antagonism: the persistence of Waldorf's love blunted her aggression, even if it did not disarm her. She was still a long way from what Waldorf wanted: a complete revival of their partnership and life together. Her bitterness remained unappeased. She never mellowed.

Her need remained the same. She lacked a counsellor. She in no way lacked for sympathetic critics, Bob Brand notably, and above all her husband. 'Think of the historian,' Waldorf wrote to her on one occasion. 'Whatever you may feel about it you cannot avoid being a historic personage and having played a historic part. The historian is now and in the future to write about you. Please please do nothing – say nothing – which may mar the historian's account.' She was criticised in homely fashion, and perhaps more effectively than by anyone, by Rose Harrison. The latter has an interesting story about an occasion when Nancy made a most preposterous suggestion. 'I'm going to invite all my sons to lunch,' she said, 'but they can't bring their wives.'

Rose was instantly up in arms. 'Look, m'lady,' she said, 'you can't do a thing like that.' And when Nancy began to reply Rose went on: 'The child leaves his mother and cleaves to the wife, and you get that into your head. Suppose they'd done that to you when you married Lord Astor – "Lord Astor may come but he's not to bring you" – what would *you* have said?' Either the wives were subsequently invited or the enterprise was abandoned.

Of the considerable 'Astor-connection' in Parliament little now remained. In the 1945 election Bill and Nancy's brother-in-law John had been defeated, but, somewhat to his own surprise Michael, who had stood for the first time, was elected for the Eastern Division of Surrey, a seat he held till 1951 when he did not seek re-election. Of the pre-war and war-time Astor connection only James Willoughby continued in the House of Commons. By 1949 Bill had been adopted as Conservative candidate for the Wycombe Division of Buckinghamshire, and Jakie for the Sutton Division of Plymouth. Nancy spoke in all the constituencies where her family were interested, but her sons did not encourage her. They wanted to make their political ways by their own efforts, and they all saw something ludicrous in the position of a candidate or member appearing as the protégé of his mother. Unfortunately Nancy's possessive character made it impossible for her to act in a way to diminish such an impression. It is unjust to say that she was impervious to reason. She always recognised reason unless there was one of her insurmountable prejudices standing in the way, but she found it harder than most people do to be guided by reason against inclination. She said to her friend Ernesta Barlow: 'Bill wants to get into Parliament on his own, and I understand.' But later she told Mrs Barlow that she was deeply hurt at his reluctance to ask her to speak for him.

She was restless. She was without employment. Her reconciliation with Waldorf was still only partial. In these circumstances Nancy again sought to carry out Charlotte Shaw's supposed wish that she should take the august widower under her care. She reopened the question with G.B.S. and suggested a meeting to discuss it in May 1949. G.B.S. replied on the 8th.

'My dear Nancy, You must positively not come on the 13th. If you will not let me manage my work and my household in my own way you must not come at all. I have arranged with Mrs Laden that there are to be no visits for the next three weeks; and no visits there shall be.

'All this nonsense about my having to be looked after, and the job bequeathed to you by Charlotte, is a worn-out joke which you are beginning to believe in yourself. Let me hear no more of it. You need looking after far more than I do; and nobody knew this better than Charlotte, except perhaps your unfortunate secretaries. You must upset your own household, not mine.

'I write in great haste, and am rather angry with you for forcing me to put my old foot down and make you understand that in this house what I say, goes.

'As a keeper of a mental patient you are DISCHARGED.

'Quite unchanged nevertheless G.B.S.'

That was the last time that Nancy tried to obtain the agreement of the old man to her protection.

A comedy arose between them which is worth remembering. At the end of June 1949 G.B.S., who had moved from his flat in Whitehall Court to a smaller furnished one in the same building, sent his own London furniture and his 'superfluous belongings' to be sold by Sotheby's. He wrote to Nancy on the 27th after finding a mistake in the catalogue, namely ' "a Terra Cotta bust of Mrs Sidney Webb" . . . without any sculptor's name. As I possessed no such object I realized at the last moment what it was, and hastily warned Sothebys and Auctioneer A that as a bust of Beatrice, and fictitious at that, it would fetch a few shillings; but as a bust of you by Strobl it might fetch billions.

'Auctioneer A instantly wrote to you for a bid. You (or your secretary) telephoned Loewenstein, my domestic German Jew, Doctor of Philosophy. He came to me and asked what he should say – what I was going to do about it. I, being busy, shouted "Oh, let them go ahead and sell it; I want money, money, money." Dr L., deeply shocked, said I could not possibly do such a thing. I reminded him that I am practically on the point of death; and what, I asked, will become of the bust then. But he stuck to his point, and at last wakened my sense of decency. I have written Auctioneer A to withdraw the bust from the sale, and keep it until I have ascertained your wishes.

'There are three courses open to me. I can present the bust to the House of Commons as a memorial of its first woman member. I can present it to the Plymouth Municipality. Or you can have it back and be damned.'

In the end 'the Bust question' was settled after consultation with the

Speaker and Clerk of the House of Commons. G.B.S. made a presentation of the bust to the Palace of Westminster where it was placed in the Speaker's official residence.

In February 1950 Nancy met Mrs Morton whom she and Waldorf had vainly searched for in Leningrad in 1931, and who had been the supposed author of the deriding letter in the Russian Press. She had been among the liberated foreign workers in Germany at the end of the war. After much trouble she had regained the British passport that she had relinquished on becoming a Soviet citizen. She made her way to England, wrote to Nancy, and was invited to visit her at Cliveden. When she arrived Nancy asked her how she had managed 'to get out of that double-dyed hell', to which Mrs Morton answered: 'Yes, it was Hell. Real Hell.' Needless to say she had never written the letter, but she had signed it, so as to avoid trouble with the police and for the sake of her two children. She told how her life as a suspected foreigner was just bearable till 1934 when, as the purges slowly began, suspicion increased. With forged evacuation papers she escaped from Leningrad in the war with her daughter and her grandson. Her own son was by then dead. He had been killed in action. The mother and daughter and child had made their way to the Caucasus. There they had been captured by the Germans and conscripted into the labour force. At the end of the war they had made their way to the British zone. After long delays she had been granted her passport. Her daughter and grandson had remained in Germany. That was the story.

In the same month Nancy became involved in preparations for the forthcoming General Election. In spite of her embitterment at what she believed to be an enforced resignation, she had taken a vigorous part in Colonel Grand's election campaign in 1945, a thing greatly to her credit, and she was determined to take part in this election. She intended to speak on behalf of her three sons who were standing, Bill, Michael and Jakie, and also for several friends who were standing in the Conservative interest.

Nancy conceived the highly original but highly questionable manoeuvre of asking G.B.S. to speak for her sons Bill and Michael whose constituencies were not distant from Cliveden. He declined.

Of her family only Michael was successful in this closely run election in which the 1945 Labour majority of over 200 was reduced to 17, and without the Liberals to 8. James Willoughby had succeeded to his father's post as Lord Great Chamberlain and thus was ineligible for the House of Commons. Nancy had shown a vigorous revival of her back-chatting powers with hecklers in Paddington.

In June 1950 Mirador was sold. Nancy Tree had retained her exclusively American citizenship till 1944 when she became a British subject. In view of her anomalous position as property-owner in America she had been allowed exemption from certain currency restrictions, and this allowed her to keep Mirador. Since then her marriage with Ronald Tree had been dissolved and they had both re-married. The Labour Government did not look kindly on proprietors and were under some anti-American influence. With no sense of gratitude for the free use of Mirador by the British Embassy in Washington throughout the war, the Treasury revoked the exemptions. The sale of the Langhorne family house became unavoidable. Nancy, always straining for some way to appease her restlessness, crossed the Atlantic once more, to help with the arrangements for the sale: 'to see about it', as she wrote in her autobiographical draft.

She told in that fragment how she went to Mirador but could not bear to enter the house. She added this remarkable passage: 'Going there made me think of a day in my own childhood when Phyllis and I went with mother to Danville to see her old home. The war had swept through Virginia leaving desolation everywhere. The house was in ruins, the once beautiful garden overgrown. Mother hunted for the graves of the children who had been buried there and she could not find them. She sat on the steps and cried, and Phyllis and I who were running about enjoying ourselves, could not imagine why she was crying. But now I know. She had been a young girl there. She re-membered the Yankees coming down the river, and she and her mother hastily burying the silver and what valuables they could. No one had looted Mirador. It looked peaceful and beautiful as ever – but I too could have cried.'

Towards the end of September 1950 G.B.S., who was now over ninety-four, fell down in his garden while pruning trees. He broke his leg at the thigh. He was taken to the hospital at Luton where the limb was reset, and to the great surprise of the surgeon and doctors he began to recover. Then it was found that a kidney and the bladder were damaged and there could be no doubt now that the end of his life was near. He knew it. He had no regrets but asked that he should be taken back to his home, 'Shaw's Corner', at Ayot St Lawrence, to die there. As soon as she heard the news Nancy rang up the hospital and, according to her own account, took charge of the case so far as she could. She told the hospital authorities to allow him no visitors, and was vexed to hear that an actress (for whom he had a great liking) had been allowed to see him for a few moments. Nancy told them to let him know that she had rung up and that she would come to see him, but only when he asked for her. A few days later he said: 'Let her come if she wants.' On the 15th October she wrote the following record:

'I've seen G.B.S. three times since his accident – first in hospital where he seemed very glad I had come. I had kept away purposely and I asked him if he wanted anything and he said, "Yes, I want to die". I replied, "I often did too". Then he said, "Don't let them bother me", and I said, "Who bothers you", and he replied: "I don't want to see anyone". I said, "No one at all", and he said, "Just Laden, Judy, Patch, and you". (The housekeeper, Mrs Musters, Miss Patch, and me, and I realised he wanted not to have to play up. None of us, the above-mentioned, ever made him do so.)

'A week later I went to Ayot and found him looking lovely and gazing over his small garden. Again he said all he wanted was to die "But, Nancy, this confounded vitality won't let me". I said "Yes, I know – I've got it too". He grunted and said, "So you have". I was anxious he should not talk, so offered to rub his head. He asked, "Have you got healing hands?" I said, "Yes, the children say so". I had started him off to sleep. He woke after about fifteen minutes; he always pronounced minutes "min*u*tes", and said "You can go on all night if you like". I thought he might like his head scratched and asked him if it ever itched. He replied, "Only before it rains I have an itching scalp. So has Patch. It's the one thing we have in common". I said "The one thing" and he smiled and said "Yes".

'His mind is as clear as crystal, and he could put on a show at any moment, but naturally I never encouraged him to. I told him a story of an old negro woman who was asked about herself on arriving at a hospital. Was she married? How many children, etc.? She replied: "I've been married two times; I've got six children – two by my first husband Jim, two by my second husband, then I has two by myself". He laughed really heartily and I left him.

'Four days ago I went again. . . . He has two nurses – the day nurse a charming woman who was with Mrs Shaw. Yesterday Mrs Laden and nurse both said he was changing daily. The night before he had had a dream and shouted out "Charlotte". It woke Mrs Laden, whose room is upstairs. I found him asleep, but waited till he awoke. He said he had been very depressed all the day before, so that is why they had telephoned to me. He seemed pleased to see me. I say this for very often before he has not seemed pleased to see me when I visited him, but that never stopped me, as Charlotte made me promise to look after him.

'He spoke a lot of Charlotte and I asked if he dreamed, and he said "Yes" and the best thing about dreams was that he was always young, and so were those he dreamt of. . . .

'He told me his night nurse was a scream; was fifty and dressed like a young lady of fifteen. She told him she had nursed Adelina Patti's last husband – a foreigner who took a large house in Wales. He gave a grand gala party with all the best of the neighbourhood there, when, in the midst of a dance, he rushed into the ballroom screaming "Stop the music". The music stopped and he said, "Please all go home. I have found my wife upstairs in bed with a man". He rushed out and the guests began to depart, when he came rushing back and said, "Stop, don't go. The gentleman has apologised". G.B.S. laughed and chuckled over that. He then spoke of Ellen Terry and said she had had five husbands and two children who were illegitimate, and she told him what had always sustained her in trouble was the knowledge that she had never done anything she knew to be wrong. I must some day write what he told me about Ann Besant wanting to marry him. . . .

'I said yesterday, "I don't believe you've much heart". He said: "A soothsayer once said I had no heart but great imagination".'

She went to see him again a few days after writing the above, and then paid him her last visit on the 1st November, his last day of life. She told a reporter: 'He gave me such a lovely smile, but he is very, very tired. I bent down and spoke to him. He said "Oh Nancy, I want to sleep, sleep". I sat beside him just gently rubbing his head to help him to sleep.' She succeeded, as she often did with her marvellous touch. He does not seem to have spoken again. He died a little before five in the morning on the 2nd November 1950.

There was much public hope that his ashes would be interred in Westminster Abbey. Nancy wrote to the Prime Minister about this. Mr Attlee was sympathetic and consulted the Dean before answering. It was concluded that, apart from sectarian objections, Shaw's will showed a clear preference that his and his wife's ashes should be scattered in the garden of 'Shaw's Corner'. This was carried out with Nancy present as one of the few privileged mourners.

Nancy was now seventy-one and she had few older friends left. T.J. had been taken into favour again and in October she had spoken at the dinner given in the Palace of Westminster to celebrate his eightieth birthday. On the 15th November she did what she had never done before: she attended the State opening of Parliament, at which she had been present many times as a member, as the consort of Lord Astor, as a peeress. She was not much seen again in public that year. It can be said with some certainty that despite all her frequent merriment and laughter, and the continuous flow and overflow of her high spirits, the five years between the end of the war and 1950 were the unhappiest of her whole life.

The incidents first related in the foregoing chapter, the Gestapo list, Ribbentrop's request, the family marriages, the second funeral of Lord Lothian, are taken from contemporary Press cuttings. This is also the case with most of the account of the 1946 visit of Lord and Lady Astor to the United States. There are five exceptions. The description of Lady Astor's success with the crew of the S.S. *Eros* follows an account given by Miss Rose Harrison to Mr Kenneth Harris on the tape recording already referred to. The account of the birthday party for Lady Astor's aunt, Mrs Lewis, is based, with much else, on what is described in the text as Lord Astor's diary. In fact, this diary was a letter, written in diary form, addressed to all his children. As is evident from the text I have used this letter-diary and Lord Astor's contemporary letters to Lady Astor as a basic document for the description of the whole of this visit, and dating is often based on it. The story of Lady Astor's conduct when she received the 'Freedom Bell' on behalf of Sir Winston Churchill in Williamsburg was told to me in 1969 by Mr Virginius Dabney who was present on the occasion and heard the remarks exchanged. The unrecognition of Angus McDonnell's services in Washington can be verified in *Burke's Peerage* and a contemporary *Who's Who*. The account of Lady Astor's 1947 visit is taken almost wholly from the Press, but with frequent reference, as appears, to her correspondence with her husband. The distressing subject of Lady Astor's relations with Lord Astor immediately before and during the five years after her retirement from the House of Commons depends on private information except (as indicated) on an essay written for Michael Astor by Lord Brand, on Lady Astor's correspondence with Bernard Shaw, and on the correspondence between Lord and Lady Astor at this time. The account of Lady Astor's visit to Germany in 1947 is taken from contemporary Press cuttings and letters in the Astor archive. The account of her meeting with Mrs Morton is based on a record to be found in *Reynolds News* who engaged a reporter to be present at their meeting. I owe knowledge of the facts relating to the sale of Mirador to the Astor archive and to Mrs Nancy Lancaster. As before, I remain indebted to Mrs Lancaster for general views on Lady Astor's character and career. An old friend in source matter is found again in Lady Astor's description of her last visit to Mirador. It occurs in her autobiographical draft.

The account of Lady Astor's 1948 visit to the United States with Lord Astor and the Michael Astors is largely taken from the Press and from Maurice Collis's *Nancy Astor*. He gives the story about Lady Astor and the reporters at Houston. The account of her relations with Bernard Shaw during his last years depends, apart from some quoted Press references, on the correspondence preserved in the Astor archive. Details concerning his last illness are taken from the Press and St John Ervine's biography. One detail of Shaw's cremation may be mentioned here. On Lady Astor's first visit to him at Ayot St Lawrence after he had left Luton hospital in 1950, he confided to her what music he wanted to be played at the funeral service: Verdi's *Libera Me Domine* from his Requiem, and Elgar's *We are the Masters*. When she conveyed Shaw's wishes to the representative of the Public Trustee in charge of arrangements some confusion followed, since no work under the title *We are the Masters* is to be found among Elgar's compositions. Fortunately Lady Astor had told of Shaw's choice of music to a *News Chronicle* reporter, and these details were published in the paper. The Public Trustee's office had, on advice, chosen Elgar's *We are the Music-Makers* as the correct title which Shaw had misquoted or Lady Astor misheard. But the singer, Miss Irene Jacob, having read the paragraph in the Press, rang up the *News Chronicle* to suggest that the far more appropriate *We are the Ministers* from Elgar's *The Apostles* was the intended item. Mr De Winton Wigley passed on this information to Lady Astor and the Public Trustee's office. Both agreed with the correction and the arrangements were accordingly changed.

Chapter 22

THE LAST CHAPTER

DURING the late autumn of 1950 Waldorf had suffered a stroke. It had not impaired his mental faculties but had affected him physically. His asthma and high blood pressure increased and he had to live very quietly. For a while he stayed with David at Sutton Courtenay in Berkshire. Later he returned to Cliveden where he had ground-floor rooms in the East Wing. The rest of the family situation in 1951 was as follows. David was now editor of the *Observer*. Waldorf had made over most of the Astor estate in Britain and America to Bill who took over the management. Michael remained a Member of Parliament but had made up his mind not to stand at the next election because he wished to pursue his painting professionally. Jakie, like Bill, was a defeated Conservative candidate determined to win at the next election. It was his present mission to reconquer the Sutton Division for the honour of the family, though he did not have the dedicated political interest of either of his parents or of Bill. He positively forbade his mother to speak in his constituency at the next election.

Nancy spent more time at Cliveden and Waldorf tried gently to persuade her to settle there permanently, but her restlessness prevented her falling in with his wishes. She was probably right to indulge her impulse. During 1951 and 1952 her relations with Waldorf, though never fully restored to what they had been ten years before, were easy and harmonious, and it was of help, maybe, that they were not strained by impatience. She sought an outlet for her energy in travel to America and Canada, in accepting many invitations to speak, in going out in society in London, but nothing could disguise the fact that she had not got enough to do. Then, early in 1951, there appeared the possibility of a solution of this major problem of her life.

It was now that an approach was made to Waldorf from friends who were publishers in America that Nancy should write her autobiography. The later adventures of the proposition have been related in the first chapter of this book. It was the cause of much family debate at Cliveden, conducted in the furious fashion instituted by Nancy. 'You can't describe yourself as you really are, Mum,' Jakie is remembered saying, 'the results would be too horrifying.' 'What d'you mean horrifyin'?' she would answer. 'How dare you make such a suggest'n?' 'Because you are so possessive,' replied Jakie. 'That's why we are all cases of arrested development. Though I admit,' he added, as an after-thought, 'that Bobbie is the only one of us actually to have been arrested.' On another occasion Nancy said: 'If I did write the thing I wouldn't know what to call it.' 'That's easy,' said Jakie. 'Call it "Guilty but Insane".'

Nancy failed in the undertaking because she was not given what she needed: a good stenographer and a good editor, both prepared to give the whole of their time to a gigantic task. It would have been worth it for she was a wonderfully good self-portraitist, and though she showed a lack of self-knowledge on her retirement, she never lost a capacity for self-criticism. Once she was asked her opinion on some burning question of the day. 'How do I know what I think about it?' she said. 'I haven't had a chance to talk about it yet.' In the same perceptive spirit, when a friend checked her for making a rash and wounding remark, she defended herself by saying, 'Well, you don't suppose I'd have said it if I'd thought.'

Though the plan never got beyond the draft which has been used in this book, and though Nancy emphatically refused to attempt autobiography again, suggestions for a life written with her collabor-ation continued to be made, to be toyed with, and to be rejected by her, for several years. In 1956 William Douglas Home put forward an interesting proposal as follows:

'My dear girl,

'What about your biography? I want to write it. I don't much care whether you want it written. Somebody will do it anyway.

'I hear rumours that you may allow yourself to be seduced into giving the rights to some distinguished man of letters. Ridiculous. It's like Trevelyan writing the life of Groucho Marx.

'You must have it written by a volatile and sensitive buffoon who loves you and understands your approach to life. I fulfil both those qualifications. While appreciating the importance of your career I also appreciate your own importance as a glorious and rather beautiful girl. Michael agrees and he's always wise when he agrees with me. Love William.'[1]

1. A biography, based on published (chiefly newspaper) material, was attempt-ed, in spite of Lady Astor's strong discouragement, by Mr Geoffrey Bocca. It

In the end the biography by Maurice Collis was written with Nancy's collaboration and published in 1960. Michael Astor's memorable portrait came out three years later.

But in 1951 Nancy's failure in autobiography, though she laughed about it, was a serious thing. It forced her back onto herself and onto her unhappiness. Her continual sense of injury, deprivation and loss was added to by the increasing and inherited unbalance of her eldest son Bobbie. Few people saw her unhappiness, but one who did, her friend Ernesta Barlow, has left a poignant description of her at this time: 'Nancy was such a triumphant creature that it was sad, in the later years of her life, to see her meet frustration. She had retired; her children were grown up and gone; none of them sought the help she was so eager to give. . . . Nancy drove golf balls down the long greenway above the river at Cliveden, took the chef's little boy out rowing, swam the river against the current while husky youngsters panted and puffed. But her still furious energy had no channel through which to race. . . .

'Her husband, an ill man, was unable any longer to face the flame of her vitality. He moved alone into a wing of Cliveden. On a Monday morning after a weekend at Cliveden I saw for the first time the spring of her gaiety run dry. Her eyes were red and troubled when she said goodbye to me. She put her strong fingers over them to keep me from seeing that she had been crying. "Bobbie and I have been sayin' what we think of each other," she said. "I don't think it did either of us much good. And I'm not goin' to drive up to town with you after all. Waldorf may ask to see me. Sometimes he likes to have me read to him. I never know."

'I left her standing in the front door, waving her hand; after a crowded, tempestuous life, a lonely woman.'

The expected General Election came in October 1951. Bill and Jakie were both successful. The state of the two main parties was almost precisely reversed but, with a further Liberal decline, decisively to the Conservative advantage. Winston Churchill was once again Prime Minister with a small but working majority. Nancy often visited the Palace of Westminster and asked for Jakie or Bill. She could not keep away from the place.

It was clear that Waldorf was reaching the end of his life. In 1952

was serialised in the *Sunday Express* in January 1956, but not published as a book.

his heart-condition made it dangerous for him to walk more than a few steps and he had to use a wheel-chair. His mental alertness still remained unimpaired and his final state of mind was serene. His son Michael has recorded: 'The sternness which as a child I had found disconcerting had evaporated. Instead, his innate gentleness and his consideration for other people made him a delightful man to meet. He enjoyed a short Indian summer in the evening of his life.' Elsewhere Michael Astor has written in his book: 'He no longer felt compelled to act as the leader of his family. He came to see that his family could have no leader. It was no longer a pack. In this mood he showed a sympathy with those of his children who, at some point, had challenged his decrees. He responded to what I believe to be the natural law: that the son must at some point challenge the father on level terms if he is to assert his manhood.' He never complained though his suffering was sometimes acute. When he recognised the approach of death he met it with fortitude and resignation. Only one thought vexed his calm: how would Nancy face life alone? His love for her was un-dimmed to the end. His last words to Bill were: 'Look after Mother', which he repeated urgently several times. He died in the evening of the 30th September 1952. He was buried at Cliveden.

Three weeks later Nancy wrote to T.J.:

'Thank you for your letter. You need not tell me how fond you were of Waldorf. I know that, and he was devoted to you. My only regret is that he was ever influenced by you!!

'I am down here by myself, trying to get over the shock, and am simply inundated with hundreds of letters, or I would write you more, only there's so little to say. We had 40 happy years together. No two people ever worked happier than we did. – These last 7 years have been heart breaking – but thank God he was like his old self the last ten days and oh how it makes me grieve of the years wasted! I think you know what I mean. I wish I had never saved *The Observer*. You can see why it has caused me more misery than I would have thought possible. But I don't want to look back but forward and thank God I had such a long happy life and that Waldorf is now safe. Oh T.J. your wife would understand.'[2]

At length Nancy had found a counsellor, and if the last phase of her life was less tormented than the penultimate one, it was in large measure

2. Lady Astor's meaning in the sentence: 'I wish I had never saved the *Observer*', is

due to this friend. She was G.B.S.'s cousin, Mrs Judy Musters. They had first met in the war when Mrs Musters used to help G.B.S. both at Ayot St Lawrence and at Whitehall Court. Their correspondence began immediately after Shaw's death, by which time their mutual affection had become close. Unlike Bob Brand she entered to some extent into Nancy's beliefs. She was a strong opponent of Roman Catholicism, and though she never came near conversion she was impressed by Christian Science and respected its doctrine. They had a great thing in common: they shared a passionate interest in G.B.S., and both inclined to be critical of the interest of other people in the great man. Both were very shocked by the published memoir of Blanche Patch and Mrs Musters expressed dismay at St John Ervine's biography when it appeared in 1956, yet neither of them were un-critical of Shaw. They were not thoughtless hero-worshippers. In a most strange and unmistakable way Nancy's friendship with Mrs Musters took on the character of a continuation of the former's friend-ship with G.B.S. His cousin had much of his literary talent and her letters to Nancy (over 300 in number) are often as witty and vivacious as those of Shaw himself. Most of them are on the subject of G.B.S. and contain a great accumulation of information about him and Charlotte Shaw and many of their friends. Nancy felt that Mrs Musters should have been G.B.S.'s heiress and urged her friend to contest the will. When she would not do so Nancy herself intervened, without her friend's knowledge, in 1954. She admitted to her action: 'Yes: I was responsible for the Public Trustee because I think it nothing short of a scandal that you whom G.B.S. loved so much should not be living in splendour and luxury on his ill-gotten gains.' But she could not move her. Later Nancy tried in vain to persuade her friend to accept a sum of money or a jointure on her estate to allow her to live in easier circumstances. All this is very reminiscent of Nancy's obstinate, generous and unsuccessful efforts to install G.B.S. in the luxury of Cliveden. Mrs Musters loved Nancy as the great man had done, and like him was aware of the danger of her possessiveness.

After the death of Waldorf she wrote to Nancy: 'You have been

explained as follows by David Astor in a letter to the writer: in her husband's early parliamentary days, she 'discovered that her father-in-law was going to sell the *Observer* without consulting my father and persuaded him to pass it on to my father instead. She often spoke of this.'

constantly in my thoughts and I dreamt of you last night – in which dream you were following G.B.S.'s advice to me and facing the world with courage and hope – the two best words in the language!' In the shock of her expected widowhood Nancy found in Mrs Musters one whose wisdom could have enabled her to find her way. Her friend put it to Nancy that the roles of the girl, the wife and the widow were not only of different quality but could be rewarding. She told her that she herself, as a widow of some years who had accepted her state, would not now wish to go back to the role of wife, any more than as a wife she had wished to go back to the role of the young unmarried woman. Slowly, not without set-backs, and never reaching a state of absolute acceptance, Nancy at a later date yet found it easier to live with her difficulties and her temperament, thanks in a high degree to the wisdom of her friend. Characteristically she once expressed her agreement in a broad jest. On a hot summer day at Rest Harrow, Nancy and Mrs Musters were lying on a bank in the sun when Nancy said: 'If what they say about the after-life is true, then our two husbands could be lookin' down at us now from that blue sky – did you ever hear of anythin' so ghastly!'

Bill, as the new head of the family, told his mother that if she wished she could continue to live at Cliveden. Wisely she did not accept his offer. With Bill she had more difficult relations than with any of her Astor children. She foresaw and avoided an intolerable situation but (it has to be said) not without distressing incident on the way. She left Cliveden in December 1952. Her headquarters were now 35 Hill Street. She went to Rest Harrow in the summer and throughout the year she paid frequent visits to her beloved Plymouth. Rooms were kept for her use at Cliveden where she would sometimes go for weekends.

Although she no longer needed to trouble herself with the expenses of the great house, she was, in money terms, less rich as a widow than she had been as the wife of Waldorf, and from this time she began to have occasional moments of panic when she fancied that she was in danger of poverty. Bob Brand would as regularly reassure her.

For the moment, before the influence of Mrs Musters had had time to work, England had grown unbearable to her. She still had all her abundant energy, that 'infernal vitality' which she had shared with G.B.S., and no real means of outlet. Once more she sought the anodyne of travel and in 1953 she travelled more and longer than she had done in any year before.

She began with a wide-ranging visit from early March to late April in the United States. Her main purpose was to see her two sisters Irene and Nora, the eldest of them being now an old woman. It was during this visit that she met Senator Joe McCarthy, then approaching the height of his atrocious career. He may have thought that in this dedicated enemy of Communism he was to find an admirer. If so, disillusion was rapid. When she was introduced to him he was, as usual, holding a glass in his hand. 'What's that you're drinkin'?' she asked him. 'Whisky,' he answered. 'I wish it was poison,' she said, and the banter was not good-humoured. Nancy's remark was reported widely, and one editor demanded her arrest.

While still in the United States she made plans by telegraph with her friend Lady Kennedy, the wife of the Governor of Southern Rhodesia, for an African tour in June. The family became alarmed, and when she returned to London they urged her to abandon this new project. She refused to do so though she did consent to confine it to Northern and Southern Rhodesia. She set out at the beginning of June.

An unknown country, new problems, contact with people engaged in tasks which had never come into her experience – all this was freshening and had its good effect on her. With the Kennedys she was old friends, but she had never met her second host, the Governor of Northern Rhodesia, Sir Stewart Gore-Browne. It was a moment of surprise for him when on Nancy's arrival by air she answered to his expression of welcome: 'Welcome to you, as one slave-owner to another!' Sir Stewart has recorded: 'It was unexpected but it put us on good terms with one another at once.' She had meetings, she indulged in back-chat in Northern Rhodesia, but she did not meet the people of Africa there. She met the whites only. But when she went back to Southern Rhodesia she encountered the great modern challenge.

The story is best told in a letter written to Lady Kennedy in 1964 by Sir Robert Tredgold. In the following passage a few words are omitted or queried because of illegibility: 'The incident I remember most clearly was the visit to – [?] – to meet the African intellectuals. They began at their most difficult and prickly, but at the end they were roaring with laughter and eating out of her hand. In fact I could not help thinking that, with a change of decor, the final scene might have come straight from the old plantations of Virginia. They plunged in all the most difficult and controversial [?] subjects to receive devastating replies. One asked her if her daughter had to choose between marrying an Indian with a very Eastern background and a Rhodesian African with an English culture, which she would choose? "The Rhodesian African, of course, and God forbid she should marry either." She then took them off their stand in this by explaining, very sympathetically, that marriage was a very intimate thing and that it was unwise for people to marry when their backgrounds were totally dissimilar. Another asked her, rather truculently, if she thought her son better than his. She replied, "Which are you talking of? I have five sons. One I would trust to rule [?] the Empire. Another I wouldn't trust to take me across Berkeley Square." She never forgot her Rhodesian friends and kept in touch to the end. . . . It would have paid the country to employ her as a permanent public relations officer to the Africans.'

Sir Robert did not know that she had in no way become converted to modern notions of race-relationships. Her ideas on this remained unchanged – and paternalist.

Her journey in Africa had interesting results which show this. She was back in England in the middle of July and was soon making plans to return to the United States at the end of the year. She went in order to spend Christmas with her sister Irene, and of course she was soon back in Virginia. She stayed with her friend Mrs Gordon Smith. During this visit she was asked to preach, this time from the pulpit of Emmanuel Church which her family had rebuilt to the memory of their parents. Most of the congregation were coloured people, and to them she addressed most of her remarks. She is remembered as having said something of this kind: 'You have had a good deal. I have recently been in Africa and I have seen something of the poverty, misery and wretchedness of Africans in Africa – your cousins. You, through being brought here, have found Christianity. You, unlike them, have been emancipated from slavery, and you've moved forward socially. You have moved much farther towards prosperity than the peasants of Europe – except in England. Those peasants, unlike you, are still where they were two hundred years ago, and you can thank God for your luck.' The minister had turned pale and looked as if he would have gladly sunk through the floor until he heard the murmurs of the coloured people present. A few had begun to say something and it was taken up by the others until they were all murmuring: 'Amen. But that is true.'

It is possible that the Africa journey of 1953 had brought another influence on Nancy, tending to (if not accomplishing) that reconciliation with the world that was her deep spiritual need. Her companion on these travels was Margaret Leeke, a devout Anglo-Catholic who later became a nun. They had been friends for a long time and it is possible that Margaret Leeke softened (even if she did not obliterate) Nancy's furious antagonism to Catholicism. A contrast can make this possibility clear. In 1948 Lady Hartington, the sister of J. F. Kennedy, was killed in an air accident. Nancy believed and vehemently insisted that the accident had been engineered by Vatican agents because Lady Hartington, a Roman Catholic, had married in a register office without the Church's blessing. About ten years later Nancy met a French Roman Catholic priest, John Charles-Roux, through her niece Nancy Lancaster. He had been warned of her prejudices and was prepared for the worst. He found no sign whatsoever of any anti-Catholic bias. They became friends. He was left with the impression that he had been completely misinformed.

In 1954 Nancy suffered a blow which came on her like a new bereavement, and which was shared by many friends. In Paris Richard Aldington's biography of T. E. Lawrence was published in a French translation. Its publication was held up in Britain, largely through the strenuous efforts of Lawrence's admirers to prevent it. Nancy was very active in the attempt, and she and Basil Liddell Hart had hopes of succeeding. They rested their hopes on the fact that Aldington, harshly ignoring that Lawrence's mother was still alive, had based much of his character-analysis on Lawrence's illegitimacy, and that consequently in Great Britain, if nowhere else, the publishers would be open to legal proceedings. It turned out, however, that a statement of Lawrence's illegitimacy had been published in England already – in T.J.'s *Diary with Letters*! T.J. had not known that old Mrs Lawrence was still alive. Mrs Musters took a regretful view but calmer than Nancy's. 'I'm sorry to read in today's Times,' she wrote to her on the 27th November, 'that Richard Aldington's book on Lawrence is to be published after all: the delay made me hope it wouldn't be. I see it's already out in France under the title *Lawrence l'Imposteur*. Another instance of this age's love of debunking, against which there is of course nothing to be said so long as the protagonists thereof know bunk when they see it, and don't empty away the baby with the bath water.'

When the book came out in 1955 Nancy was in the United States and Mrs Musters wrote to console her with an account of its bad reception by the critics. At the end of February she wrote again: 'Well, the Lawrence hullaballoo seems to have died down & Sydney Cockerell thinks the Aldington book won't do his memory any harm.' In fact, it destroyed the myth of Lawrence of Arabia for ever.

In the meantime, while battling for Lawrence's reputation, Nancy had again opened the question of Mrs Musters's inheritance from her cousin. It must be explained that this was not mere busybody interfering but part of something bigger. Nancy was trying hard to organise a movement for the invalidation of Shaw's will which she, with much good opinion on her side, regarded as ridiculous. The movement wholly failed. Mrs Musters was only concerned in a personal way.

In early January she had written on her major theme to Nancy: 'Of course you have had a wonderful life and have lived it to the full. All I say is that now is the time to start another, which may be just as wonderful though different; and it struck me that a Crusade of some kind is indicated. . . .' Three days later, after Nancy had sailed for the United States, Mrs Musters wrote to her again: 'When I suggested that you should start a Crusade, I did not – repeat NOT – rerepeat NOT suggest that the crusade should be The abolition of Judy's poverty or the Liberation of Judy from Indigence: I DONT WANT to be liberated. To begin with, my poverty is not so bad as all that, and to end with, I – queer as it may sound – am content. All of which sounds very incongruous coming from me after accepting your very generous bounty last April; but I accepted because I didn't know how to say "no"! Think of the fate of many just because they couldn't say NO – "worse than death", the Victorians called it. . . .'

She ended the letter: 'My dear, your friendship has been the greatest help to me; I wish mine could do a little for you.'

The wish expressed earlier that Nancy would not worry about Mrs Musters's money affairs was acted on in the end, but not immediately. The last letter of the correspondence in which the matter was mentioned belongs to June 1957.

Her memory had been weakening since the middle period of the war, and in the later fifties this began to become serious. It was for long the only sign she gave of old age. Her very erect carriage, her clear blue eyes, and her fresh complexion all made her look younger than she was. Photographs of this time do not do her justice: after her young days she was not photogenic. Her defective memory, as often happens with the old, was hardly noticeable when she spoke of the distant past, and, as the letters to Mrs Musters show, was not much in evidence when she was talking or writing to an intimate friend. The first long conversation the writer had with her (some time in the middle fifties) was confined to the past. I may recall my impressions.

I had often met her in St James's Square as a young man, through my friendship with Bill and Wissie. I was frankly terrified of her then and in her presence felt rather like one of the little Eton boys so alarmingly evoked by William Douglas Home. Many people I knew had been mauled by her, but I had escaped unscarred. In those days she was probably on the lookout for bigger game. I did not see her during the war and when I first did so a year or so after, I was shocked to see how much she had aged. She looked harder and fiercer than I remembered. On the occasion of the long conversation, about 1956 or '57, she seemed to me to have recovered something of her younger looks, and was as I have described in the preceding paragraph. It was a very pleasant occasion. I may have been fortunate in that my hostess was one of her younger friends who, like William Douglas Home, was allowed every licence of disrespect, and also that the presence of the Queen Mother ruled out mauling. It should also be mentioned that though Nancy was incapable of showing servile deference to 'the great', as Belloc called them, she had a romantic veneration for royalty. Their presence was pleasing to her. She was in a good humour.

I was explained to her. 'Oh yes,' she said as she motioned me to sit next to her, 'I remember about you. I knew your disreputable father, and your disreputable grandmother, and there was a disreputable uncle of yours with your name, but I was spared him. And I suppose you're disreputable too.' She was at the top of her form. I asked her about my grandmother of whom I only had a childish memory, and she gave me a fascinating picture of her and the Edwardian world in which she had known her. I did not know then that I was one day to write Nancy's biography, so I made no note of the conversation. I remember little of its content, but I do remember that what most impressed me in her conversation was the extraordinary and flashing acuteness of her observation. I also remember that when she said goodnight to the Queen Mother she curtsied with a grace that a dancer might have envied, her back remaining perfectly straight.

Among her family she was closest in her last years to her daughter Wissie, now Lady Ancaster since the death of her father-in-law in 1951.

She had once been hard on Wissie. Her daughter had rebelled, then had relented, and Nancy now found in her one to whom she could give the love that she had so abundantly within her and yet found so difficult to show to those near her. She wrote of Wissie to Mrs Musters: 'I love being with her and she is so good to me.' It is one among many expressions of her love for her daughter.

In 1956 there was a brief revival in the Press of the Cliveden Set myth. This occurred as a result of an official publication by the British Government: *Documents on German Foreign Policy 1918–1945 Series D. (1937–1945) Volume VI.* This far from catchy title proved a boon to editors. On page 674 of the volume there was printed Adam von Trott's report on his visit to Cliveden in June 1939. The origin and purpose of the report have been discussed already in the chapter on the Cliveden Set. The public could not be expected to know the intricate deception which had been practised by Trott as an anti-Nazi, but even a reader who was convinced that in spite of his execution by Nazis Trott was, in fact, Hitler's agent, even such a reader, if he bothered to read the words of the document, would have found proof that the Astors were severe critics of Nazi policy. But such a reader was a rare one, and the vast majority had neither time nor inclination to go to so much trouble, so the calumny was re-established. *The Spy at Cliveden* was a typical headline. The weakening credit of the myth shot up, and this in part accounts for its persistence to this day. The little episode needs to be mentioned in this book, but there is no sign in her letters that it worried Nancy. She might be described as having grown blasé about calumny.

She continued her journeys. Twice she accompanied Wissie and James Ancaster and their family, once to the south of France, and once to Marrakesh. Until 1958 she continued her yearly journeys to America. The impulse was gradually lost after 1956, by which time both her sisters had died. She was now the last of her generation of Langhornes. One detail of her later American journeys should be remembered. It shows how she remained the same forthright, unreflective though self-critical being from youth to age. In Virginia she had a young woman relative who had an unhappy tendency to run into debt from which she was sometimes rescued by Nancy. On this visit Nancy asked her outright whether she was in need of money 'as usual'. She admitted that she was. Nancy immediately sat down, pulled out her cheque-book and pen and said: 'Will 25,000 dollars help you?' This was beyond all dreams of avarice and the answer was a gasped and grateful yes. 'Very well,' said Nancy, 'I'll make out the cheque on two conditions.' The first one was something innocuous, now forgotten, to which the young woman readily agreed. What was the second condition? Her conversion to Christian Science. The young woman told Nancy that she had not the faith and could not agree to this. 'Very well,' said Nancy, putting away the cheque-book, 'you get nothin'.' 'But, Cousin Nannie,' said the other, 'if I accepted, and became outwardly a Christian Scientist without any belief, and for the sake of money, what in the world would you think of me? Could you have any respect for me again ever?' 'Oh!' said Nancy, as though brought up to a sudden halt. 'Yes. I hadn't thought o' that.' And out came the cheque-book again.

In 1958 Nancy sold 35 Hill Street, and leased a large flat at 100 Eaton Square. Bob Brand agreed to take some of the rooms. While the redecorations and removals were going forward she went to stay with her niece Nancy Lancaster at her house, Haseley Court, in Oxfordshire. Though she visited Cliveden fairly often after this time she gave up her rooms there and Haseley Court became more and more her country home, while Rest Harrow, which she often lent for seaside holidays, became, like Cliveden, a place she visited. Nancy Lancaster was apprehensive of having her formidable aunt for an extended visit, because, not surprisingly, Nancy had an evil reputation as a guest. Bob Brand tells of how she would take command of his house when she came to stay, and he was led to agree with Max Beerbohm's theory that a capable host is usually an intolerable guest. But to her great surprise and relief, Nancy Lancaster found that as her long-term and frequent guest her aunt, with whom she had had many clashes in the past, was a model guest, and a delightful companion. Haseley is an eighteenth-century house of the utmost beauty, and under Nancy Lancaster's ownership became as beautiful within as without surrounded by a garden worthy of its noble architecture. It may be that the magic of Haseley worked some transformation on Nancy and that here, belatedly, there was a little mellowing of character.

She showed it in one unexpected way. She became more tolerant about drink-prohibition. The occasional tots of brandy she consumed when these were thrust on her by American soldiers at the height of the bombing in Plymouth may be regarded as exceptional, but not so an occasion at Cliveden, very shortly after the war, when she burst into her daughter-in-law's bathroom where she had heard voices. In fact, she had unknowingly raided a speakeasy. Her daughter-in-law stood by the lavatory with her hands behind her back. They talked together when suddenly there was a crash of glass. 'What's that noise?' asked Nancy. Almost in tears her daughter-in-law said: 'It's a whole bottle of gin which I've dropped and now it's gone down the loo.' Nancy only said: 'Silly child, why did you have to hide it? I wouldn't have taken it from you.' At Haseley she continued to disapprove of the cocktail-tray, but one day she asked her niece 'What that thing' was. 'It's Dubonnet,' said Nancy Lancaster. 'Is it intoxicatin'?' asked Nancy. 'Not really,' said the other, and poured her out a glass. Nancy thought it good and had another. She thereafter often took a glass of Dubonnet. Once when she was suffering sleeplessness, Nancy Lancaster offered to mix her an egg-nog. She had no moral objection to eggs so drank it with relish. Thereafter she quite often asked for one. Whether she knew or suspected the truth about Dubonnet and egg-nogs is a question that no one has answered.[3]

Bob Brand did not stay long at 100 Eaton Square. He found the noise in that area deprived him of sleep, and he left to live with his daughter and son-in-law, Virginia and Edward Ford, in the tranquillity of Stable Yard, St James's Palace. Nancy was not pleased at this show of independence. Later she sub-let part of the flat to Diana Campbell-Gray (now Lady Gage) who gave her joyous companionship for the rest of her life. The faithful Rose Harrison was with her, as she had been with her everywhere, including Rhodesia. She had a butler, Charles Dean, who was later to show himself a friend in need and of much resource.

If there was some mellowing, it was spasmodic. Her visits to Cliveden were sometimes agreeable, often not. She should have remembered her father-in-law's vow never to return there after giving it to Waldorf. She should have remembered how when he broke that vow she fled in panic to her bed. Bill must have been often tempted to do the same. He took great pride in the house and made some needed alterations in the rooms of the top storey. By her refusal to comment on his innovations she hurt him, as she intended. This was not an isolated occurrence.

It must be remembered, if one is tempted to judge, that during all

3. Mr Handasyde Buchanan, a close friend of Lady Astor and from whose place of business, Heywood Hill, she bought most of her books, tells an identical story concerning Dubonnet which occurred in his presence.

this time the deterioration of her memory was proceeding rapidly, and that without a fairly normally working memory all mental activity tends to be impaired.

I remember the last time I saw her. It was at 100 Eaton Square, some time in 1959. Diana is an old friend and one day I was to have lunch with her in her part of the flat. There were other guests and Diana had asked me to come early to help her to lay the table. I rang the bell and, as on a previous visit, the door was immediately opened, not by Mr Dean but by Lady Astor.

'Oh!' she exclaimed, 'it's you again. Why are you always hangin' around this flat? I never asked you to lunch.'

I said: 'But Diana did. I'm lunching with her.'

'Oh that woman. Why do you lunch with Diana instead of me?'

'Because you never asked me, Lady Astor.'

'No, I didn't. And I'm not going to now.'

By this time Diana had appeared and Nancy went off to her rooms. While we were laying the table she came in and said something of this kind: 'Why you come and have lunch with that woman – if you knew what I know about that woman – the things I could tell you about her –' and so on. This, of course, was a comedy put on for my benefit. 'If you can do anything about that woman – but o' course you can't, nobody can –' she said as she walked out of the room. It may not strike a reader as funny when written down, which is true of many comedian's scripts, even some written by Shakespeare, but the effect was extremely comic – until she returned and said it all over again. It was obvious that she had forgotten what had happened within the last few minutes. Suddenly what had been funny became sad.

On the 19th May 1959 she celebrated her eightieth birthday. 'I thought it would be fun to be 80,' she wrote to Mrs Musters a few days later, 'until I got my post. However your letters are always delightful to get.' Plymouth celebrated the occasion in the summer when she was made a Freeman of the City. 'I am very proud,' she wrote to Mrs Musters in July, 'of getting the Freedom of Plymouth, but I think it is almost too late to accept it! I am not speaking personally, but they should have given it years ago and, had I been a man, they would have done so.' If this sounds ungracious, then one should remember that she had earned the honour as few Freemen of few cities have done, and that it would have been a consoling gesture if made shortly after Waldorf's death. The delay, though inexcusable, was in

part Nancy's own fault. She had done nothing since 1945 to diminish
party antagonism in Plymouth and much to augment it. This had had
its effect on the city council. Administration is rarely conducted by
large-minded men, and it has to be recorded that when the decision to
confer the City Freedom on Nancy was taken, the Labour Party in
Plymouth decided that councillors belonging to the party should not
attend the festivities. To the honour of the party, two Labour members
of the council did attend nonetheless. At the banquet which followed
the ceremony on the 16th July Nancy presented the Lady Mayoress
with a diamond necklace to be worn by her and by succeeding mayor-
esses while in office. The Freedom of Plymouth was the last public
honour paid to her in her lifetime.

Jakie did not stand for Parliament in the General Election of the
autumn of 1959. After that she rarely went to Plymouth. When she
did, the visits were in the nature of a return to the past in which she
could feel at home. Her preoccupation with the past led to a new
acquaintance, with Sir Alec Guinness. In October 1960 she went to see
his performance as T. E. Lawrence in Terence Rattigan's play Ross,
and was so impressed by it that she invited him and Lady Guinness
to lunch. The play, with its sympathetic portrayal of Lawrence, soothed
the bitter hurt she had received from Aldington's book. In 1961 she
exchanged letters with Angus McDonnell for the last time. His letters
were full of the old days and they planned to meet again, though
whether they did so is not evidenced. In October 1962 she was able to
give a spirited television performance on the BBC, being interviewed
by Kenneth Harris. Her subject was the past. The accuracy of her
reminiscences was inevitably much at fault, but she still showed her
abundant vitality. She wrote to Mrs Musters: 'I am glad your friends
liked my television interview. You have no idea how difficult it is to
speak to an unseen audience – even if you are being interviewed – as
you have no means of telling whether people are bored or not. I hope
I will never have to speak on the "tele" again.'

In 1963, when she was eighty-four, and her memory was diminishing
day by day, Bill was involved in the Profumo scandal. If the worst
possible construction is placed upon his conduct (and nothing whatsoever against him was proved), his part in this affair was peripheral.
But the British public was passing through one of its 'fits of morality'
and, perhaps urged on by a folk-memory of the Cliveden Set, the
Press held him up to execration. The family were determined that

somehow or other knowledge of the affair must be kept from Nancy. For a time it was, thanks to the ingenuity of Charles Dean. He scrutinised the newspapers as soon as they arrived and cut out all references to John Profumo, to Ivanoff, Ward and Bill. Furthermore, he arranged, with the help of Mrs Gordon Smith who was in London at the time, that at a minute to one o'clock and to six o'clock every day a friend should ring her up and keep her in conversation until the Profumo items had passed on the BBC news. The ruse was successful until Nancy went away in June to stay with David at Sutton Courtenay. There the same routine was followed. The newspapers were censored daily and the radio was never available at one or six o'clock. Then the scheme broke down.

One morning she got up early, before anyone else, and took in the papers herself. She read them and learned all. Her reaction was instant and typical of all that was finest in her. She told David that they must drive to Cliveden that morning, to rally round Bill, and in order that she would be seen at Cliveden by the side of her son. So it was arranged. A telephone message was sent and Nancy went off with David and Rose Harrison. On the way she turned to David and said: 'Why are we going to Cliveden?' 'To see Bill,' he answered cautiously. 'Why am I going to see Bill today?' she asked. She had forgotten.

Lunch at Cliveden passed pleasantly and before returning to London she drove round some of the estate with Bill and saw a few people. There is no reference anywhere in her letters to the Profumo scare. It seems that she was, thanks to her lapsed memory, spared all suffering from it. One wishes that Bill had been spared too.

In the same month of June 1963 she wrote her last letter to Mrs Musters. It was on their usual subject in common. 'I have just returned from the country,' she wrote, 'and have your letter. As soon as I have "Mrs G.B.S.",[4] which I hope to do soon, I will tell you what I think of it.'

A curious thing about Nancy's last letters is that the handwriting, which in earlier ones often defied the recipients and herself, becomes quite clear and easy to read after 1960.

In the summer of 1963 Bob Brand died. With him went her last link with Philip Lothian and her friends of the Kindergarten; with him too went the last close contemporary link with her beloved sister. After this she wrote few letters to any of her friends. Her life was over,

4. A biography of Charlotte Shaw which had been recently published.

so she seems to have felt, yet her abundant vitality was not to be quenched for a little, and it was like her that she could take even this shattering blow with a jest. After the memorial service, as she walked down the aisle of St Margaret's, Westminster, with Virginia Ford, she murmured to her niece: 'Y'know, I c'd kill your father for dyin'.'

In March 1964 Nancy was staying with Wissie in the south of France. At the end of the month Bobbie Shaw attempted suicide by taking an overdose of sleeping tablets. He lay unconscious for three days in St Stephen's Hospital in the Fulham Road, and the doctors believed that he would not recover. Bill was in America and on being told the news came back to England. When Wissie was told she wanted to keep the matter from her mother, but her brothers insisted that she must be told. In the end Wissie told Nancy that Bobbie had had a stroke, and they returned to England. Nancy went to see her son with David. Wissie was staying in Nancy's flat in Eaton Square and was shocked by her mother's appearance when she came back from the hospital. Nancy Lancaster saw her too that day, and told afterwards that she seemed to discern an indefinable change in Nancy's appearance, as though something physical had happened to her. It seems likely that Nancy had guessed what had really happened. But as always, even at this moment of great shock which she was ill-equipped to withstand, Nancy was lively and changeable.

That evening Michael went to see her, taking his two little girls. He recorded in a diary he kept at the time:

'She was dressed in mauve, a stylish, rather old-fashioned dress trimmed with mink. She looked quite well and particularly beautiful and she was sweet to the girls. She was quite lively. When I told her she was the only well-dressed woman I ever saw these days, and asked her if she still bought new clothes, she replied: "I like your cheek. What do you think I do: buy old ones?"'

At the end of the week she went to Lincolnshire to stay with Wissie and James Ancaster at his family house, Grimsthorpe. It was her last journey. On the same day as she arrived she suffered a stroke of which Nancy Lancaster may have witnessed a preliminary sign. She was carried up to her bedroom. Though the stroke was mild no one doubted that this was the end.

The stroke came on her on Saturday the 18th April. For the first two days after that she was able to leave her bed for an hour every day to sit in a chair. She could speak slowly and understand what was said to her. At first she often had difficulty in breathing and seemed to be putting up a fight for life, but this phase passed. Michael noted in his diary on the 21st: 'I could see her quietly, gently, uncertainly dying: going at no particular pace, but dying in the same way as she (particularly as a young woman) must have done most of her living, unevenly, at different paces. Dying, gliding, reviving, trying, submitting. What a relief to see her not struggling.' Her old jesting spirit did not leave her. She told the doctor that, considering that she was dying, she was very well. Michael noted in his diary: 'Sons, servants, nieces, nephews, and the odd grandchild made the pilgrimage to Grimsthorpe, by car and train, to pay their respects.' She was most at her ease with Nancy Lancaster because she alone could talk to her about Mirador and tell her stories in the accent of the 'Uncles' and 'Aunts'. Of all those around her the most unhappy was Bobbie Shaw. He was almost out of his mind with grief. In his house in London his housekeeper found a bottle of fifty sleeping pills which he had bought on an old prescription before leaving for Grimsthorpe.

She was soon beyond speaking except for the occasional phrase. She liked being read to. On one occasion, Michael records, he found her trying to read Mrs Eddy's *Science and Health*. He tried to read it to her but found he could not do so with sincerity, so he turned to Lord Wavell's anthology *Other Men's Flowers*. He tells: 'After a bit Mother went to sleep. She dozed. I'd been reading to her in rather a slow, firm tone of voice. After a few minutes she stirred in her sleep. Then she cried "Waldorf, Waldorf – wake me up. Please!" '

On the 30th April he read her the 23rd Psalm, 'The Lord is my Shepherd', and the 91st, 'He that dwelleth in the secret place of the Most High', and she enjoyed the 23rd Psalm so much that he read it to her several times.

Here is Michael's last picture of her:

'Mother seemed to be living already on another plane, and the practical and mundane observations of her nurse seemed out of place in the room. I had the feeling that she was free of relationships. At last. That it was of no significance if someone was her son, her husband, or her father: if someone was young, or old, or no relation. At that age, family relationships do not count for a pin. She seemed to be searching for an essence, not a person. Or was this my imagination? She gave me the feeling of someone who was moving or attuned to very simple values and to a belief in a spiritual existence. She was no longer concerned with the innuendoes, shades of concealment, shades of meaning revealed in ordinary conversation.

'I forgot to mention a curious detail. At one moment yesterday, in between when I was reading to Mother, she raised her hands in front of her, like a pope giving a blessing. The gesture did not imply that she was full of holiness. It wasn't a benediction. It was more like a supplication or a gesture of surrender.

'Mother with her nurse. Typical. The nurse brought in from a nearby hospital. Mother, dying though she is, manages to take the solemnity out of the occasion. The nurse bent down to pick up something that had fallen off the bedside table. Mother extended a frail arm and gave the posterior a little slap.

'Once or twice Mama has taken me for one of her brothers. A lot of the time she is back in Virginia.'

She had the reward of many whose lot it has been to face the ordeal of old age, a slow, painless end. One of the last audible things she said when her last hour was near was to Jakie. She asked: 'Am I dying or is this my birthday?' Jakie answered: 'A bit of both.'

Late in the afternoon of the 1st May, when Rose Harrison was with her, she raised her hands, looked straight before her, and cried 'Waldorf!' Thereafter she slowly relapsed into a coma. Early in the morning of Saturday the 2nd of May 1964 she died.

She was buried at Cliveden in the same grave as her husband. At the service the casket containing her ashes was covered by the Confederate flag according to a wish she had expressed long before. The flag, which was one that had been carried in the War between the States, had been given to her in 1922 in Danville by an old family friend, Mrs Lewis E. Harvie. On the 13th May a memorial service in her honour was held in Westminster Abbey before a great congregation. The Royal Family was represented, as was also the Speaker of the House of Commons. The Prime Minister, Sir Alec Douglas Home, and his predecessor Harold Macmillan attended. The lesson was read by the American ambassador. In the great church there was a host of people drawn from all walks in life, who were moved to remember her. Not long before her death she had heard from a widow of the First World War whom she had consoled. She may have been the woman mentioned in Nancy's autobiographical draft, in her description of her

first attendance at a military funeral. She may have been among the
unrecorded mass of mourners.

It is customary to say of any person of great age and fame that with
the individual death an age passed away. Of Nancy this venerable
cliché cannot be used with any meaning. She belonged far less than
most people, especially most famous people, to any age or place, and
in so far as she did so belong it was most to the nineteenth-century
Virginia which was already swiftly vanishing in her first years of
womanhood. This certainly does not mean that she can be described
or explained as a survival of something archaic. Nor was she a portent,
as she sometimes believed, of coming times. Bernard Shaw seized her
character well when he sent her his letter of advice on how to win
Plymouth in 1929. She fitted into no party, no category of British
history or of the history of the United States. She was 'from without',
a phenomenon that cannot be repeated, and for that reason one that
astonished her own time as much as it can our own.

By a rightly accepted convention a biography ends with an assessment of its subject. In Nancy's case there can be no summing-up with
any definitive or satisfying results. This suggests a mysterious character,
though there was little mystery about her. Throughout her long life
she was open, but because she was also perplexingly contradictory, it
follows that if an attempt at assessment is made, almost any generalisation about her needs to be qualified, and then qualified again, and then
qualified just once more to make sure that the verdict is just, until all
definition is lost.

There are a few salient features of her being that were persistent and
little modified. Of these her ever-present religious sense was the
strongest. She faltered in her pursuit of Christian Science far less than
most religious people do in the sincere pursuit of more easily accepted
beliefs and moral systems. In her last years she had a tooth extracted,
and a small wart on her face, which was (wrongly) suspected of being
malignant, was removed by an operation. Otherwise she was as faithful
to her practice as it is humanly possible to be. When her family became
anxious about her health in her last years, and wanted a professional
medical opinion, they invariably needed to resort to subterfuge and
benevolent deceptions. She was attended in her last days by a doctor
when her mind was wandering, and when no doctor could be of help

to her. She was never faintly tempted to lose her belief in God. She
had the cardinal virtue of faith.

Her possessiveness never left her. She manifestly inherited it from
her father. In his case it literally destroyed the lives of his two eldest
sons. In her case it came near to estranging all her children in turn.
It was the cause of unthinking cruelty, even after death. She had left
instructions that each one of her sons was to receive a packet of letters
selected by her from the individual correspondences. They contained
touching affectionate letters, and also letters which brought back
terrible memories of agonising differences. It must be remembered
that this design may well belong to the embittered years after 1945
when she felt betrayed by all her family, and that in her last years she
forgot all about it. It was nonetheless a terrible expression of her most
persistent fault, and the possessiveness which made her discontented at
all marriages of her friends may seem to have been a defect above which
she could never rise. But remarkable exceptions have been mentioned
in this book, notably one of positive character when she acted as the
go-between when Lionel Curtis wished to get married. The friendship
remained a strong one, and if it has not been much noticed in later
chapters it is only because the later letters between them were of
ephemeral interest.

One of the strongest features of her character was her constancy in
friendship. If she was inhibited, probably from some psychological
cause now undiscoverable, from giving her love, she experienced no
impediment to friendship. In a revealing remark, Bill once said that
in order to enjoy affection with her as a mother one 'had first to kill
one's love'. It was for friendship not love that she had a genius. (Again
one must qualify by remembering the case of Philip Lothian with
whom her relations were those of ardent platonic love.) Her friendships
were of the most varied kind, and they were never influenced by fair
or adverse circumstances. As her nephew-in-law Reggie Winn once
said of her to the writer: 'If you were in Wormwood Scrubs and guilty,
who'd be the first person to come to see you?' She would go to all
lengths that she could to help those who had fallen on evil days,
whether through their own fault or not, to recover self-respect. A
revealing little incident may be remembered, even if it digresses from
the theme of friendship. A reformed ex-convict who had become a
successful member of a well-known dance orchestra wrote to ask for
her patronage. His past had been inadvertently disclosed in a book by

a fellow-convict about life in prison. He had been forced to leave the band, and was now starting his own, but under obvious handicap. He wanted to play for one of her dances in St James's Square. He had written to her because, while he was serving his sentence in Dartmoor, Nancy had stopped to talk to him in the course of a visit. Nancy's reaction was typical. Having established the man's identity and *bona fides* through the Prison Governor, she immediately wrote back to him telling him that he could count on an engagement for a St James's Square ball in the next year, her present engagements being filled. Unhappily all this occurred in the summer of 1939 so the story was deprived of its end.

It has been noted that she rarely broke a friendship. There are few examples to the contrary. Her abandonment of her personal friendship with Lloyd George was untypical, not only on her side: the scale of the provocation by him to a puritan mind was abnormal. The fading of the once very close friendship with the Asquiths shows a more remarkable exception. This may be a very rare example in her life of a friendship foundering on political antagonism, but Margot's waspish-ness and Asquith's drinking may have had more to do with it. The friendship with Belloc was broken by him, not her, and it was revived by her. She remained faithful to her friendship with J. H. Thomas after his ruin and disgrace.

She had enemies among those who did not know her, but few indeed among those who did.

She left a legacy of valuable public work, of controversy, and the curiosity that must attach to a personality so extraordinary that it must always puzzle even the closest scrutiny; but among those who had her friendship, she left above these an abiding and precious affection.

The final chapter is drawn from family letters of the time, Mrs Ernesta Barlow's essay, written for Michael Astor, a three-cornered correspondence between Lord and Lady Astor and Lady Astor's prospective publishers, and Michael Astor's *Tribal Feeling*. With one exception the letters quoted are from the Astor archive in which the correspondence between Lady Astor and Mrs Musters is preserved almost in its entirety. In addition, Mrs Musters made her collection of letters from Lady Astor available to me. A few of them were in MS and are thus not represented in the archive. I am also grateful to Mrs Musters for having spent so much time in discussing her friendship with Lady Astor with me. Regarding the archive, the exception noted above is the letter from Sir Robert Tredgold to Lady Kennedy which was lent to me by Lady Ancaster. Lady Astor's encounter with Senator Jo MacCarthy is described in a letter of congratulation to her on the incident from Mr Stewart Perowne. Mrs Gordon Smith told me of the occasion, at which she was present, when Lady Astor preached in her family church at Greenwood, Virginia. The later Virginian episode, concerning a gift of $25,000, was told to me by the lady concerned in 1969. The extraordinary belief of Lady Astor concerning the tragic death of Kathleen, Lady Hartington, was confided by her to my brother and sister-in-law at the time. Her friendship with the Rev. John Charles-Roux was described to me by Mrs Nancy Lancaster and later discussed by Father Charles-Roux in a letter to me. Details of the Trott report on a visit to Cliveden can be found in the H.M.S.O. publication mentioned in the text, and the circumstances surrounding it are described and discussed in my biography of Trott, *Troubled Loyalty*. Most of what I have said regarding Lady Astor's relations with her son the late Lord Astor is taken from his candid radio-interview with Kenneth Harris (not broadcast). I am also influenced by memories of conversations with him, before I was invited to write this book, and by conversations, of which I took notes, with Mrs Vincent Astor when I was researching in the United States. What I have written about the conferring of the Freedom of Plymouth on Lady Astor in 1959 is based on conversations with those authorities whom I mentioned in connection with Chapters 19 and 20. With regard to Lady Astor's conduct in the Profumo Affair, I follow discussions with Mr Charles Dean and Mrs Gordon Smith; a telephone conversation (in which I took a minor part) between Mr J. J. Astor and Miss Rose Harrison, and memories of a conversation with Mr David Astor while these events were proceeding. In the final episode I have followed a discussion with Mrs Nancy Lancaster and the diary, mentioned in the text, kept by Michael Astor at the time. The detail about the Confederate flag used at Lady Astor's funeral is taken from a letter to me from Mr S. Rutherfoord Harvie of Danville.

INDEX

compiled by the Rev. S. B. R. Poole

538

INDEX

Rosenburg, Alfred, 355–6
Round Table, 123, 124, 127, 249
Royden, Maude, 254
Rumania, 'Carmen Sylva' (Marie of Wied) Queen of, 84
Rumania, Carol I, King of, 84
Rumania, Ferdinand I, King of, 84, 170
Rumania, Marie (of Edinburgh), Queen of, relations with N.A., 84–6, 105–6, 148–9, 170–1, 183, 245, 291
Rumania, Prince Mircea of, death of, 170
Russell, Bertrand, 361
Russia, N.A.'s visit to (1931), 325–43

Sackville-West, Victoria, 468
St James's Square (Astors' London house), 91, 104, 112, 133, 146, 147–8, 149, 179, 204, 215, 233, 244, 286, 290, 291, 298, 309, 316, 346, 354, 356, 372, 377, 380, 381, 391, 399, 423, 490–1, 515, 527
Salisbury, Alice, Marchioness of, 197
Salisbury, James, 4th Marquess of, 196–7, 201
Salisbury, Robert, 3rd Marquess of, 120 and note 6
Salter, Sir Arthur (later 1st Baron), 413
Sam (servant), 39, 50
Samuel, Rt Hon. Sir Herbert (late 1st Viscount), 181, 348, 354
Sandwich (Rest Harrow), Astor's house at, 91, 125, 138, 142, 143, 147, 177, 244, 286, 295, 309, 349, 377, 378–9, 380, 383, 489, 490, 491, 496, 510, 517
Sargent, Sir John, 89, 91, 99–100
Sassoon family, 134, 141, 146; Sir Philip, 310; Siegfried, 170
Saturday Review, The, 209, 222
Saunders, Private, 162
Schuschnigg, Kurt von, Austrian Chancellor, 388–9
Scott, Sir Leslie, 116
Scott, Miss (later Mrs Lionel Curtis), 183, 184
Scrymgeour, Edwin (Prohibitionist M.P.), 256–7, 258, 261, 262, 265, 266, 321
Seely, Major-General J. E. B. (later 1st Baron Mottistone), 205
Selborne, Beatrix Maud, Countess of, 201
Shakespeare, William, 364, 519
Sharp, Clifford, editor of New Statesman, 267, 268, 269
Shaw, George Bernard (G.B.S.), beginnings of his friendship with N.A., 283, and its nature, 294–9; his view of N.A.'s political position, 300–1, and his personal support for, 306–7; his feelings towards T. E. Lawrence, 308–9, 311; his works collected by N.A., 321; visits Russia with Astors, 324–6, 327–343; enters into controversy with the Chestertons and Churchill over Russia, 343–5, 347–8; his concern for N.A. in her troubles with Bobbie Shaw, writes Adventures of the Black Girl and visits South Africa, 350; renewed concern over Bobbie Shaw, 353; persuades N.A. to have bust made by

de Strobl, and declares his admiration for Hitler, 357; his attitude to Cliveden Set, 384, 400–2, 403, and to Stalin, 411–12; writes to N.A. about London blitz, 423–4; invited to Cliveden but does not go, 443–4; continued enthusiasm for Russia, 448; effects a reconciliation between N.A. and Berners, 454–5; goes to Cliveden and sets out his ideas on the war, 455–7; advises N.A. on her personal and political position, 464; death of his wife, 466–7; N.A.'s concern for, 469–71; his advice about N.A.'s proposed retirement from Parliament, 473–7, and her reaction to, 478–9; his attitude to N.A.'s differences with W.A., 489–90, and with her children, 491–2; declines to have N.A. organise his domestic life, 497–8; presents Strobl bust to Palace of Westminster, 499; his accident and death, 500–2. Mentioned 132, 141, 245, 322, 428, 509, 510, 525
Shaw, Mrs G. B. (Charlotte Payne-Townshend), her friendship with N.A., 294–5, 298, 299 and note 2, 300, 303, 307; view of Lawrence, 309, and of Wissie's accident, 315; unable to go to Russia, 325; accompanies G.B.S. to South Africa, 350, 353; her interest in de Strobl's bust of N.A., 357; her ill-health, 443, 455–6, and death, 466–7. Mentioned 423, 469–70
Shaw, Robert Gould I (N.A.'s father-in-law), 57, 59, 60
Shaw, Robert Gould II (N.A.'s first husband), 56–60, 61, 62, 89, 209, 221, 222, 224, 326
Shaw, Robert Gould III ('Bobbie') (N.A.'s son), birth of, 59; accompanies N.A. to England, 68; grandfather's affection for, 94; education of, 147; serves in World War I, 179; his instability and end of his army career, 317–20; involved in homosexual scandal and sent to prison, 326–7, 343, 345; released, 349; concern of Shaws for, 350; his steady deterioration, 351; serves in World War II, 413 (wounded 423, 426), 446; N.A. worried about, 507; his attempted suicide, 507; his grief at N.A.'s death, 123. Mentioned 323, 353, 506
Sheridan, Richard Brinsley, 208
Sherwell, Arthur (temperance supporter), 258 259
Sibthorp, Charles, 229
Simpson, Mrs Wallis (later Duchess of Windsor), 376
Sims, Charles (painter), 277
Sinclair, Rt Hon. Sir Archibald (later 1st Viscount Thurso), 362
Sinclair, Upton B., 403
Smith, Adam, 456
Smith, Sir Allen (Conservative M.P.), 203, 213
Smith, Ellis (Labour M.P.), 432
Smith, F. E., 116, 119, 135, 153; thereafter see Birkenhead, Earl of

НЭ